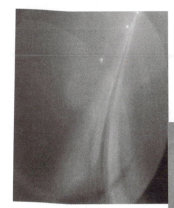

Healthcare Management

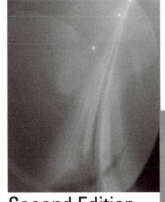

Second Edition

Healthcare Management

Edited by Kieran Walshe and Judith Smith

 Open University Press

Open University Press
McGraw-Hill Education
McGraw-Hill House
Shoppenhangers Road
Maidenhead
Berkshire
England
SL6 2QL

email: enquiries@openup.co.uk
world wide web: www.openup.co.uk

and Two Penn Plaza, New York, NY 10121-2289, USA

Open University Press 2011

A catalogue record of this book is available from the British Library

ISBN10: 0-33-52438-19 (pb)
ISBN13: 978-0-33-52438-15 (pb)
eISBN: 978-0-33-52438-22

Library of Congress Cataloging-in-Publication Data
CIP data has been applied for

Typeset by Aptara Inc., India
Printed in the UK by Bell & Bain Ltd, Glasgow

The **McGraw·Hill** Companies

This book is dedicated to our children – from Kieran to Siobhan, Ruth, Michael and Daniel and from Judith to Richard and Kathryn.

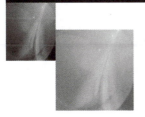

Contents

Part 3   Healthcare organizations

Part 4   Healthcare management and leadership

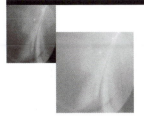

Figures

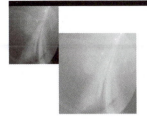

Tables

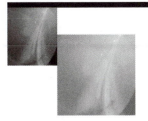

Boxes

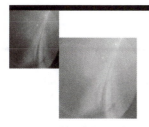

Contributors

Vidhya Alakeson is the Director of Research at the Resolution Foundation in the UK. She was previously a Senior Fellow in Health Policy at the Nuffield Trust where she was responsible for developing the Trust's comparative international health policy work. Prior to joining the Trust, Vidhya worked as a policy analyst for the Assistant Secretary for Planning and Evaluation at the US Department of Health and Human Services, having first moved to the USA in 2006 as a Harkness Fellow in Healthcare Policy. Prior to moving to the USA, Vidhya worked in the UK Government and in several public policy think tanks. Alongside international health policy, Vidhya's principal areas of interest are individual commissioning and patient health budgets, mental health, social care financing and integrated care.

Ruth Boaden is Professor of Service Operations Management at Manchester Business School and Deputy Director of the National Institute for Health Research Collaboration for Leadership in Applied Health Research and Care (CLAHRC) for Greater Manchester, which seeks to carry out applied health research, put it into practice and build capacity in the NHS to continue to implement research. Her research interests cover a wide range of areas in health services management and now focus on quality and improvement and the use of 'industrial' methods within the NHS, as well as the implementation of new approaches. Ruth's area of interest focuses on knowledge transfer arising from high quality research, to ensure that the findings are accessible and applicable to practice.

Jeffrey Braithwaite is Professor and Foundation Director of the Australian Institute of Health Innovation and Professor and Director of the Centre for Clinical Governance Research at University of New South Wales, Sydney, Australia. His research examines the changing nature of health systems, particularly patient safety, leadership and management, the structure and culture of organizations and their network characteristics. His most recent book is *Culture and Climate in Healthcare Organizations*, edited with Paula Hyde and Cathy Pope (Palgrave Macmillan, 2010).

Iain Buchan is Professor of Public Health Informatics and Director of the Northwest Institute for Bio-Health Informatics, at the University of Manchester, and an honorary Consultant in Public Health in the English National Health Service. He has backgrounds in clinical medicine, public health and computational statistics, and runs a multidisciplinary team bridging health sciences, computer science, statistics, social science, and management science. His work centres on building realistically complex models of health to support the planning of health systems and informatics innovation in early and preventive healthcare.

Mirella Cacace is an analyst with the RAND Europe Health and Healthcare team in Cambridge, UK. She holds a PhD in Economics from the University of Bremen, TranState Reseach Centre (SFB 597), in Germany. In her former position as a research fellow she compared the changing role of the state in OECD healthcare systems. Her PhD thesis applies New Institutional Economics to the changing governance structures in the American healthcare system. In 2008/09, Mirella was a Harkness Fellow in International Health Policy and Practice, sponsored by the Commonwealth Fund and hosted by Columbia University in New York. Mirella's main areas of research concern institutional economics and international healthcare systems, especially in the USA.

Naomi Chambers is Professor of Health Policy and Management at Manchester Business School in the University of Manchester, and Head of the Health Management Group there. Her teaching, advisory and research interests include international comparisons of health systems, leadership, board governance, primary care, and commissioning. Naomi has been a non-executive director on a health authority, and subsequently a mental healthcare trust and two primary care trusts from 1996. She was also president of the European Health Management Association from 2007–10.

Elaine Clark is a Fellow in Action Learning and Healthcare Management at Manchester Business School. Her particular interests build on her previous roles as an actress and as a manager in health and social care and include Action Learning (particularly critical Action Learning), patient and public involvement, narrative inquiry and social movements.

Helen Dickinson is a Senior Lecturer in healthcare policy and management and head of the health and social care partnerships programme at the Health Services Management Centre, University of Birmingham. Her research is centred on collaboration between health and social care organizations, and her interests include critical theories of leadership, priority setting and decision-making and the role of the third sector in health and social care services.

Jennifer Dixon is the director of the Nuffield Trust, Visiting Professor at LSE, Imperial College and the London School of Hygiene and Tropical Medicine, and Board member of the Audit Commission. Her recent research focuses on the development and application of risk adjustment techniques in healthcare. Her main interests are in macro system reform of healthcare.

Barrie Dowdeswell is Director of Research of the European Centre for Health Assets and Architecture, Utrecht, the Netherlands. He was formerly the Chief Executive of an NHS Teaching Hospital Trust prior to moving into the field of health service research, which included a period as visiting Research Associate, University of New South Wales, Australia. His personal research interest centres on the application of Public–Private Partnerships for the delivery of healthcare. He was co-author and co-editor of *Investing* *in Hospitals of the Future* and *Capital Investment for Health: Case Studies from Europe*, published as part of the European Observatory on Health Systems study series.

Jon Glasby is Director of the Health Services Management Centre at the University of Birmingham and Professor of Health and Social Care. His research interests include health and social care partnerships, personalization and community care. He is also a Non-Executive Director of the Birmingham Children's Hospital.

Scott L. Greer is Associate Professor of Health Management and Policy at the University of Michigan School of Public Health, and Senior Research Fellow at LSE Health, London School of Economics. He is the author or editor of seven books including *The Politics of European Union Health Policies, Devolution and Social Citizenship in the UK*, and *Federalism and Decentralisation in European Health and Social Care* (with Joan Costa i Font). He currently leads the team evaluating partially elected health boards and alternative models of public participation in Scotland.

Anthony Harrison is a research associate at the King's Fund where he has worked since the early 1990s after a career in the government Economic Service. He has published several articles and a book (*Acute Futures*) on hospitals and the organization of health-care services and is currently analysing the evidence base for hospital reconfiguration. He was one of the King's Fund team that worked with Sir Derek Wanless on the updating of his 2002 report on the future financing of the NHS.

Paula Hyde is a Senior Lecturer in Organization Studies at Manchester Business School and co-convenor of the healthcare workforce research network at University of Manchester. Her research concerns workforce modernization and her interests include managerial roles and behaviours and organizational dynamics of healthcare work.

Valerie Iles is an independent academic consultant in the field of health management. She is currently Director of the RCGP leadership programme and honorary senior lecturer at the London School of Hygiene and Tropical Medicine. Her publications include the books: *Why Reforming the NHS Doesn't Work: The Importance of Understanding How Good People Offer Bad Care* (2011); *Really Managing Healthcare* (1997 and 2006); *Developing Change Management Skills* (2004); and *Managing Change in the NHS: A Review of the Evidence* (2001).

Ann Mahon is a Senior Fellow at Manchester Business School and Associate Head of Teaching in the Strategy Division. After training as a medical sociologist, she worked in health services research specializing in primary care. Her research interests include evaluating models of healthcare commissioning and international comparisons.

Russell Mannion is Professor of Health Systems in the Health Services Management Centre, University of Birmingham. He also holds visiting professorships at the Australian Institute of Health Innovation, University of New South Wales, Sydney, and the Faculty of Medicine, University of Oslo. His research interests are in health system reform, health system organization and management, especially healthcare quality, clinical governance and patient safety.

Anne McBride is a Senior Lecturer in Employment Studies at Manchester Business School and co-convenor of the healthcare workforce research network at the University of Manchester. Her main research interests are workforce modernization in the NHS and gender relations at work, with a particular focus on workforce development and the management of skill mix change.

Andrew McCulloch is CEO of the Mental Health Foundation, a UK charity focusing on research and development in mental health and learning disabilities. Andrew's research and publications have been in the areas of mental health policy and life span developmental psychology. He has been involved in mental health services for many years both as a non-executive director and in providing consultancy on planning, quality and risk management issues.

Shirley McIver is a sociologist by background who has worked in the field of health services research and development for over twenty years. She joined the Health Services Management Centre (HSMC), Birmingham University, in 1993, and is engaged in teaching and research, mainly in the areas of quality management and public and user involvement. She is Co-Director for the MSc in Healthcare Policy and Management.

Matt Muijen is Regional Adviser for Mental Health for the World Health Organization's Regional Office for Europe. Previously he spent more than a decade as Chief Executive of the Sainsbury Centre for Mental Health as a researcher, analyst and campaigner for improved mental health services. He is a psychiatrist and epidemiologist by training.

Ellen Nolte directs the Health & Healthcare Policy programme at RAND Europe, and before that was Senior Lecturer at the London School of Hygiene and Tropical Medicine (LSHTM) where she held a prestigious Career Scientist Award from the National Institute for Health Research, England. Her research interests are in comparative health policy and health systems research, including health system performance assessment and international healthcare comparisons.

James Raftery is Professor of Health Technology Assessment at the University of Southampton and Chair of the NIHR Evaluation Trials and Studies Cooodinating Centre. His group provides health economics input mainly to clinical trials. Research themes include the costs and benefits of clinical trials, overdiagnosis/overtreatment and the political economy of healthcare. He has written widely on health economic matters particularly relating to NICE, including a NICE blog on the *BMJ* website.

Suzanne Robinson is a Lecturer in Health Economics and Health Policy at the University of Birmingham. Her research is focused on health economics, financing and resource allocation, and priority setting in health and social care.

Rebecca Rosen is a Senior Fellow at the Nuffield Trust and a General Practitioner in a 23,000-patient multi-site practice in South East London. In the practice, Rebecca has led work to improve continuity and quality of care for people with chronic complex ill health and to apply principles of the chronic care model in a practice setting. Until April 2008, Rebecca was Medical Director of Humana Europe, a subsidiary of the US Health Benefits Organisation, Humana Inc., with an emphasis on the use of data integration and analysis to guide and improve service provision. Prior to joining Humana, Rebecca was Senior Fellow in Health Policy at the King's Fund where she worked on long-term conditions, primary care policy, patient choice and other areas of health services research.

Judith Smith is Head of Policy at the Nuffield Trust in London, and before that was a Senior Lecturer and Director of Research at the Health Services Management Centre, University of Birmingham. From 2007–9 she was visiting senior research fellow at the Health Services Research Centre, Victoria University of Wellington, New Zealand, and adviser on primary healthcare reform to the New Zealand Ministry of Health. Her research is focused on health commissioning, physician organizations, health management and leadership, and primary care.

Helen Sullivan is Professor of Government and Society at the University of Birmingham. Her research and writing explore the changing nature of local governance with a particular focus on the role of collaboration. She has undertaken numerous studies for government agencies in England, Scotland and Wales, and she has published widely on different aspects of collaboration in both academic and practitioner media.

Anne Tofts is Managing Director and a founder of Healthskills. She is primarily involved in working with the boards and senior teams of healthcare organizations on strategy and leadership development. With over 35 years experience of the NHS, including in a hospital-based operational role and six years at the Department of Health, Anne brings an in-depth understanding of management and leadership issues. Anne has a current interest in working with clinicians on leadership and commissioning issues, identifying the benefits that will engage them to achieve real and lasting change in service provision and organizations.

Kieran Walshe is Professor of Health Policy and Management at Manchester Business School, Director of the Institute of Health Sciences at the University of Manchester, and director of the National Institute for Health Research's service delivery and organization research programme. His research is centred on quality and performance in healthcare organizations, and his interests include the effective use of evidence by managers and policy-makers.

Iestyn Williams is a Lecturer in Health Policy and Management at the Health Services Management Centre, University of Birmingham, having previously worked in management and service development in healthcare and the third sector. His research is focused on decision-making and priority setting, public value and the spread of innovation.

Juliet Woodin's career combined both academic and managerial experience. She was initially a lecturer and researcher in political science and public policy, and gained her PhD for research into urban policy. She then spent 20 years in NHS management, and was Chief Executive of Nottingham Health Authority from 1995 to 2002. Subsequently she joined the Health Services Management Centre at the University of Birmingham as a Senior Fellow, undertaking teaching, research and consultancy in the fields of public policy, health service commissioning, and leadership development.

Steve Wright is Director of the European Center for Health Assets and Architecture (ECHAA), on secondment from the European Investment Bank. ECHAA is a research centre and strategic advisory group looking at the interface between the estate in the widest sense and the delivery of healthcare services. He is an Honorary Research Fellow at the London School of Hygiene and Tropical Medicine. He was an editor and chapter author on two analytical books published in 2009 and 2010: *Investing in Hospitals of the Future* and *Capital Investment for Health*, from the European Observatory. His research interests are in services/capital translation, PPP, healthcare in countries in transition, quality and safety of the estate, and substainability.

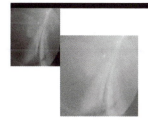

Preface

These are challenging times for healthcare organizations and health systems the world over. While the first edition of this book was published at the crest of a sustained international economic boom, this second edition emerges just after a worldwide economic crisis which resulted in a recession in almost all developed countries, from which most are only slowly emerging. The economic recovery has been faltering and fragile, and some countries have such difficult economic problems that it may be years before the good times return.

At this time of unparalleled austerity in government and public services, healthcare systems in many countries now face severe financial constraints as spending is cut but healthcare demand continues to grow. More than ever, we need effective evidence-based management, visionary leadership, and exceptionally robust and rigorous governance.

We hope this book makes a contribution to that need, by helping managers and healthcare professionals to learn and develop, both experientially in the workplace and in more formal settings such as training courses and postgraduate programmes. Our aim has been to provide a book that is practically useful but which also encourages managers and healthcare professionals to look beyond their own job and organization, to think critically about how things are done, and to bring evidence to bear in their decision-making.

Any edited book like this – with 27 chapters and over 30 contributing authors – is a team effort and we owe a great deal to the many people who worked to produce this second edition, especially the contributors who wrote and revised their chapters to a demanding deadline, and the staff at the Open University Press who turned the text we provided into this finished article. But it simply would not have happened without the help and support of Jane Mann at the Institute of Health Sciences, University of Manchester, who kept track of draft chapters, amendments, copyright permissions, proofs and the like and kept the process on track with unflappable efficiency.

Kieran Walshe and Judith Smith

CHAPTER 1

Introduction: the current and future challenges of healthcare management

Judith Smith and Kieran Walshe

Introduction

The aim of this second edition of our textbook is to support the learning and development of practising managers in healthcare organizations and health systems, and those undertaking postgraduate study on programmes concerned with health policy, health management and related areas. Increasingly, these two groups overlap – more and more managers are undertaking a master's degree as part of their intellectual and career development, and we are firm believers in the power of the interaction between academic and experiential learning that this brings. No one learns to be a manager in a classroom, or from a book. Management is learnt by doing, by experiencing the challenges and opportunities of leadership (Mintzberg 2004). But the best and most successful managers are reflective practitioners – profoundly aware of their own behaviours, attitudes and actions and their impact on others and on the organization, and able to analyse and review critically their own practice and set it in a wider context, framed by appropriate theories, models and concepts (Peck 2004). The future leaders of our healthcare systems need to be able to integrate theory and practice, and to have the adaptability and flexibility that come from really understanding the nature of management and leadership.

This chapter sets the context for the book, by first describing the challenges of the political and social environment in which healthcare systems and organizations exist, and how that environment is changing. It then describes some of the particular challenges of those organizations – some of the characteristics and dynamics which make healthcare organizations so interesting and yet so difficult to lead. Then the chapter sets out the structure of the rest of the book and explains how we anticipate that it might be used, both in support of formal programmes of study and by managers who want simply to develop and expand their own understanding and awareness.

Healthcare systems, politics and society

In most developed countries, the healthcare sector encompasses anything from 8 per cent to over 15 per cent of the economy, making it one of the largest industries in any state – bigger generally than education, agriculture, IT, tourism or telecommunications, and a crucial component of wider economic performance. In most countries, around one worker in ten is employed in the healthcare sector – as doctors, nurses, scientists, therapists, cleaners, cooks, engineers, administrators, clerks, finance controllers – and, of course, as managers. This means that almost everyone has a relative or knows someone who works in healthcare, and the healthcare workforce can be a politically powerful group with considerable influence over public opinion. Almost everyone uses health services, or has members of their family or friends who are significant healthcare users, and everyone has a view to express about their local healthcare system.

In many countries, the history of the healthcare system is intertwined with the development of communities and social structures. Religious groups, charities, voluntary organizations, trade unions and local municipalities have all played important roles in building the healthcare organizations and systems we have today, and people in those communities often feel connected in a visceral manner to 'their' hospitals, community clinics, ambulance service, and other parts of the healthcare system. They raise funds to support new facilities or equipment, and volunteer to work in a wide range of roles which augment or support the employed healthcare workforce. That connection with the community also comes to the fore when anyone – especially government – suggests changing or reconfiguring healthcare provision. Proposals to close much loved community hospitals, reorganize district hospital services, or change maternity services, are often professionally driven – by a laudable policy imperative to make health services more effective, safe and efficient. But when evidence of clinical effectiveness and technocratic appraisals of service options collide with popular sentiment and public opinion, what matters is usually not 'what works' but what people want.

For many local and national politicians, health policy and the healthcare system offer not only opportunities to shine in the eyes of the electorate when things are going well, but also threats to future electoral success when there are problems with healthcare funding or service provision and people look for someone to hold to account. Constituents bring to politicians in their local offices concerns about healthcare services, and politicians are keenly aware of the attitudes and beliefs of the public about their local health service. While they will happily gain political benefit from the opening of a new facility, or the expansion of clinical services, they will equally happily secure benefit by criticizing the plans of 'faceless bureaucrats' in the local healthcare organization for unpopular changes in healthcare services, and argue that there are too many managers and pen-pushers.

Finally, for the press, TV, radio and on-line media, both locally and nationally, the healthcare system is an endless source of news stories, debates and current affairs topics. From patient safety to MRSA and pandemic flu, from dangerous doctors to hospital closures, from waiting lists to celebrity illnesses, the healthcare system is news. Big healthcare stories can command pages of news coverage in national dailies and repeated presentation on TV news bulletins, while at a local level it would be rare to find a newspaper which did not have some content about hospitals, clinics or other healthcare services in every issue. Healthcare organizations can use the level of media interest to their advantage, to raise public awareness of health issues and communicate with the community, but they can also find themselves on the receiving end of intense and hostile media scrutiny when things go wrong.

In other words, healthcare organizations exist in a turbulent political and social environment, in which their actions and behaviour are highly visible and much scrutinized. Leadership and management take place in this 'goldfish bowl', where their performance and process can be just as important as their outcomes. But as if that were not enough, in every developed country the healthcare system is subject to four inexorable and challenging social trends:

- the demographic shift;
- the pace of technological innovation;
- changing user and consumer expectations; and
- rising costs within a context of global economic recession.

The only certainty is that if it is difficult to make the sums add up for the healthcare system today, these pressures mean it will be even harder to do so tomorrow.

The demographic challenge is that because people are living longer, the numbers of elderly and very elderly people are rising fast – and those people make much heavier use of the healthcare system. People may live longer, but they cost more to keep alive, they are more likely to have complex, chronic health conditions, and their last few months of life tend to be more expensive. A further dimension to this demographic challenge is the rising incidence of chronic disease in the wider population of developed countries. The World Health Organization suggests that this is a direct result of risk factors such as tobacco use, physical inactivity and unhealthy diets (WHO 2005).

The second challenge is related to the first in that it reflects an increasing ability to control chronic disease and thus extend life – the pace of technological innovation. Most obviously in pharmaceuticals, but also in surgery, diagnostics, telehealth and other areas, we keep finding new ways to cure or manage disease. Sometimes that means new treatments which are more effective (and usually more expensive) than the existing ones. But it also means new therapies for diseases or problems which we simply could not treat before. Previously fatal conditions become treatable, and interventions to monitor and slow the progress of disease or manage its impact become more available.

This in turn connects with and feeds the third challenge – changing user and consumer expectations. People want more from the health service than their parents did. They are not content to be passive recipients of healthcare, prescribed and dispensed by providers at their convenience. Accustomed to ever-widening choice and sovereignty in decisions in other areas of life – banking, shopping, housing, education – they expect to be consulted, informed and involved by healthcare providers in any decisions that affect their health. They are better informed, more articulate and more likely to know about and demand new and expensive treatments.

The first three challenges are in large measure responsible for the fourth – rising costs. Each of them contributes to the constant pressure for more healthcare funding, a pressure which for many countries is currently more acute as a result of the global economic recession. However much governments or others increase their spending, it never seems to be enough. In almost every other area of the economy, productivity is rising and costs are falling through competition and innovation. We have better, faster, cheaper computers, cars, consumer goods, food, banking, and so on, yet, in healthcare, costs are stubbornly high and continue to rise, along with demand for services. In a time of economic recession, this challenge is made more acute by real-term reductions in the resource available for healthcare in many countries, and hence a focus on setting priorities or rationing availability of services.

In short, the social, political and economic context in which healthcare organizations have to exist is often a hostile, fast-changing and pressured environment. Managers and leaders strive to balance competing, shifting and irreconcilable demands from a wide range of stakeholders – and do so while under close public scrutiny. The task of leadership in healthcare organizations – defining the mission of the organization, setting out a clear and consistent vision, guiding and incentivizing the organization towards its objectives, and ensuring safe and high quality care – is made much more challenging by the social, economic and political context in which they work.

Healthcare organizations and healthcare management

Organizations are the product of their environment and context, and many of the distinctive characteristics and behaviours of healthcare organizations result from some of the social, political and economic factors outlined above. However, some also result from the nature of the enterprise – healthcare itself. The uniquely personal nature of health services, the special vulnerability and need for support and advocacy of patients, the complexity of the care process, and the advanced nature of the technologies used, all contribute to the special challenges of management in healthcare organizations.

Of course, we should be cautious that this does not lead us to be parochial or narrow-minded in our understanding of what we do, or of what we can learn from other sectors and settings. We are all prone to exceptionalism, believing that our job, organization, profession or community is in some ways uniquely different. It can give us an excuse for why we perform less well. We may claim that our patients are sicker, facilities less modern, community disadvantaged, and clinicians more difficult or disengaged. It also provides the perfect reason for not adopting new ideas from elsewhere – it would not work here, because our organization or health system is different. Healthcare systems and organizations have a strong tendency to exceptionalism, something that needs to be challenged on a regular basis. Healthcare organizations are large, complex, professionally dominated entities providing a wide range of highly tailored and personalized services to large numbers of often vulnerable users. But those characteristics are shared in various degrees by local authorities, police and emergency services, universities, schools, advertising agencies, management consultancies, travel agencies, law firms and other organizations. Healthcare is nevertheless distinctive, and three important areas of difference deserve some further consideration: the place of professions; the role of patients; and the nature of the healthcare process.

For managers entering healthcare organizations from other sectors – whether from other public services, commercial for-profit companies or the voluntary sector – one of the first striking differences they notice is the absence of clear, hierarchical structures for command and control, and the powerful nature of professional status, knowledge and control. Sir Roy Griffiths, who in the 1980s led a management review of the NHS in the UK, famously wrote in his report about walking through a hospital looking vainly for 'the person in charge' (Griffiths 1983). But to do so would be to miss the point, which is that healthcare organizations are professional bureaucracies in which more or less all the intellectual, creative and social capital exists in the frontline workers – clinicians of all professions, but particularly doctors. Like law firms and universities, it makes no sense to try to manage these talented, highly intelligent individuals in ways that are reductionist, or which run counter to their highly professionalized self-image and culture. This does not mean that they should not be managed – just that the processes and content of management and leadership need to take account of and indeed embrace the professional culture. Things get done not through instruction or direction, but by negotiation, persuasion, peer influence and agreement. Leaders need to make skilful use of the values, language and apparatus of the profession to achieve their objectives, and learn to lead without needing to be 'in charge'.

The people who use healthcare services, whether you call them patients, users, consumers or whatever, are ordinary people, but they are not like the consumers of many other public or commercial services. First, there is a huge asymmetry of power and information in the relationship between a patient and a healthcare provider. Even the most highly educated, confident, internet-surfing patient cannot acquire the detailed knowledge and expertise which comes with clinical practice. Very few patients are prepared to go against the explicit advice of senior clinicians, and many patients actively seek to transfer responsibility for decision-making to these professionals. At some level, patients have to be able to trust that healthcare providers are competent, and take their advice on important decisions about their health. No amount of performance measurement, league tables, audit or regulation can substitute for this trust.

Second, when people become patients and use healthcare services, they are often at their most vulnerable and are much less able to act independently and assertively than would normally be the case. They may be emotionally fragile following an un-welcome diagnosis of disease, and weakened by the experience of illness or the effects of treatment. When lying flat on a wheeled trolley, nauseous and in pain, surrounded by the unfamiliar noise and clatter of an emergency department and frightened by sud-den intimations of mortality, we are at our most dependent. We are not well placed to exercise choice, or to assert our right to self-determination. We want and need to be cared for – a somewhat unfashionable and paternalistic notion which does not sit comfortably with concepts of the patient as a sovereign consumer of health services. This all means that healthcare organizations, and those who lead them, have a special responsibility to compensate for the unavoidable asymmetry of power and information in their relationships with patients, by providing mechanisms and systems to protect and advocate for patients, seek their views, understand their concerns, and make services patient-centred.

Despite all the high technology medicine, complicated equipment and advanced pharmaceuticals available today, the healthcare process itself is still organized very much as it was a hundred years ago. It is a craft model of production in which indi-vidual health professionals ply their trade, providing their distinctive contribution to any patient's treatment when called upon. This is not mass production. Healthcare organizations such as hospitals are much more like marketplaces than they are like factories, with the patients moving from stall to stall to get what they want, not being whisked smoothly along on a conveyor belt from start to finish. Fundamentally, it is an unmanaged and undocumented process. Usually, there is no written timetable or plan showing how the patient should move through the system, and no one person acts as 'process manager', steering and coordinating the care that the patient receives and assuring quality and efficiency. This model has endured because of its flexibility. The patient care process can be adapted endlessly or tailored to the needs of individual patients, the circumstances of their disease, and their response to treatment. But the complexity of modern healthcare processes, with multiple handovers of patients from one professional to another, the ever-accelerating pace of care as lengths of stay get shorter and shorter, and the risks and toxicity of many new healthcare interventions (the flip side of their much greater effectiveness) all mean that the traditional model is increasingly seen as unreliable, unsafe, and prone to error and unexplained variation (Walshe and Boaden 2005). More and more, healthcare organizations use care pathways, treatment plans and clinical guidelines to bring some structure and explicitness to the healthcare process. Techniques for process mapping and design, commonplace in other sectors, are increasingly used not just to describe the healthcare process but in so doing to identify ways in which it can be improved (McNulty and Ferlie 2004). Like any area where custom, practice and precedent have long reigned supreme, healthcare processes are often ripe for challenge. Why does a patient need to come to hospital three times to see different people and have tests before they get a diagnosis? Can't we organize the process so that all the interactions take place in a single visit? Why are certain tasks only undertaken by doctors or nurses? Could they be done just as well by other healthcare practitioners? Gradually, the healthcare process is being made more explicit, exposed for discussion debate and challenge, and standardized or routinized in ways that make the delivery of healthcare more consistent, efficient and safer.

In conclusion, there is one other important feature of healthcare organizations. Whether they are government-owned, independent not-for-profits, or commercial healthcare providers, they all share to some degree a sense of social mission or purpose concerned with the public good (Drucker 2006). The professional values and culture of healthcare are deeply embedded, and most people working in healthcare organizations have both an altruistic belief in the social value of the work they do and a set of more self-interested motivations to do with reward, recognition and advancement. Similarly, healthcare organizations – even commercial, for-profit entities – do some things which do not make sense in business terms, but which reflect their social mission, while at the same time they respond to financial incentives and behave entrepreneurially. When exposed to strong competitive pressures, not-for-profit and commercial for-profit healthcare providers behave fairly similarly, and their social mission may take second place to organizational survival and growth. The challenge, at both the individual and organizational level, is to make proper use of both sets of motivations, and not lose sight of the powerful and pervasive beneficial effects that can result from understanding and playing to the social mission.

About this second edition and how to use the book

The first edition of this book received very positive and encouraging feedback from the outset, particularly in relation to the balance between academic rigour and practical application of concepts and ideas. When given the opportunity to prepare a second edition, there were a number of key areas where we wished to focus our attention, these being:

- making the book more international in its content and outlook;
- being more critical and reflective in tone and content; and
- addressing more explicitly those areas which had become more significant over time, such as the globalization of healthcare, the rising prevalence of chronic disease, priority setting within resource allocation, and the role of social and home care.

We have therefore made significant revisions for this second edition. First of all, in relation to the structure of the book, this time we organize our material within: systems; services; organizations; and management and leadership. Thus we move from macro topics such as politics, funding, resource allocation, through an examination of the issues concerned with the management of specific services such as primary, secondary, mental health and social care, to an examination of organizational concerns such as user involvement, health purchasing, and the use of IT, and focus finally on the specifics of leadership and management in a more practical context, such as finance, human resources, and the use of research.

In addressing the need for the book to be more international in its focus, we have drawn this time on a more international group of authors, including from the USA, Australia and Germany, and have included a new chapter on the internationalization of health systems and policies. All chapter authors were encouraged to draw on a wider range of international material, and this they have done, with many examples of research and practice from across the world.

In terms of adopting a more reflective and critical approach, we asked authors to draw on a wider base of evidence when exploring their topic, and, in the context of taking a more international approach, to avoid any undue focus on their own health system, and instead to question their own experience using international and critical research material. We have also added a chapter to this second edition with explores the management of knowledge within healthcare – this in itself provides the context for a more critical and reflective approach to healthcare management and leadership.

Finally, in respect of topics we felt needed to be addressed in this second edition, the new entrants are:

- Allocating resources for healthcare – setting and managing priorities (Chapter 4)
- The internationalization of health policies and systems (Chapter 7)
- Healthcare services: strategy, direction and delivery (Chapter 8)
- Chronic disease and integrated care (Chapter 10)

- Social care (Chapter 13)
- Managing knowledge (Chapter 27).

All other chapters have been rewritten and edited to a significant degree, reflecting both the pace of change within the world of healthcare, but also our desire to ensure that the book is constantly improved in the manner that we exhort within a number of the chapters. We hope that you will appreciate the changes that we have made, and find the book to be as useful and thoughtful as ever, but with a much stronger international flavor, and a deeper base of evidence from research and practice.

The 26 chapters of the book which follow this introduction and overview are split into three main parts as follows.

Part 1: Health systems

Chapters 2–7 aim to set out the wider political, social and economic context in which healthcare organizations exist, namely 'health systems'. These chapters provide the 'big picture' which helps to explain how health systems are shaped, and the way in which their constituent healthcare organizations behave, remembering that, as observed earlier, organizations are very much a product of their environment and context. This part covers health policy and the political process (Chapter 2); healthcare financing and funding (Chapter 3); allocating resources, and setting and managing priorities (Chapter 4); healthcare technologies, research and innovation (Chapter 5); health and well-being and the wider health agenda (Chapter 6); and the internationalization of health systems and policies (Chapter 7).

Part 2: Healthcare services

Part 2 aims to covers the issues and topics which are particular to the services which make up the business of healthcare itself. In other words, it explores the different care sectors of a health system, examining the management and other issues associated with each sector. It starts with a chapter on the overall strategy, direction and delivery of health services (Chapter 8). There are then five chapters about managing in different care sectors: primary care (Chapter 9); chronic disease and what is increasingly referred to as 'integrated care' (Chapter 10); acute care including secondary and tertiary services (Chapter 11); mental health (Chapter 12); and social care (known as disability services in some countries) (Chapter 13).

Part 3: Healthcare organizations

Part 3 focuses on the underlying architecture of health systems and organizations – the human resources, management mechanisms, and policy levers which are at the disposal of managers as they seek to organize, coordinate, and enact the delivery of services within different care sectors. It concludes with an examination of the role of the most important stakeholders within healthcare: users and patients. The first chapter in this section is concerned with how healthcare is purchased or commissioned

(Chapter 14) – the way in which managers in a health system allocate resources to providers in a way that ensures that people's health needs are met. This is followed by a consideration of the issues associated with buildings, facilities and equipment in healthcare (Chapter 15) and another chapter which explores the ways in which information technology and information systems are used in healthcare, and the challenges and opportunities presented by their increasing capability and complexity (Chapter 16). The array of issues associated with the healthcare workforce is explored in Chapter 17, and then the final chapter of this part (Chapter 18) considers the role and experience of patients, users and the public within health systems and organizations.

Part 4: Healthcare management and leadership

In this final section of the book, the focus shifts to the day-to-day business of healthcare management – what managers and leaders do, how they do it, and what the research evidence has to offer such practice. Part 4 opens with a chapter on leadership and governance (Chapter 19), exploring how organizations can ensure that they operate in a manner that is transparent, efficient, and accountable, and in so doing, develop a culture that is open, healthy and supportive of the provision of high quality healthcare. Chapter 20 homes in on the individual manager or leader, examining personal and organizational development, and the ways in which managers can adopt reflective practice for themselves and the teams and organizations they lead. The management of change is a constant challenge for healthcare managers, and this is considered in detail in Chapter 21. In Chapter 22, the management of resources in healthcare is explored, including issues such as budgeting, business planning, paying for activity, and the use of incentives such as pay-for-performance. The most important and costly healthcare resource – people – is the subject of Chapter 23 which explores in a very practical and direct manner what is required for effective management of people.

The final four chapters conclude the book with an exploration of generic issues that preoccupy and bedevil healthcare management throughout the world: quality and service improvement (Chapter 24); the management of performance (Chapter 25); managing across organizations in networks and partnerships (Chapter 26); and managing knowledge – research, evidence, and decision-making (Chapter 27).

While the content of each chapter has led its design, we asked our authors to follow a broadly consistent format in order to make the materials in the book as useful and readable as possible. You will therefore find each chapter is structured into around five or six sections, and we make liberal use of figures, tables, charts and diagrams to illustrate the content. Each chapter concludes with the following:

- **Summary box** containing key points drawing together the main messages from the chapter.
- **Self-test exercises** designed to help you to apply the content of the chapter and your learning to your own organizations. The exercises generally consist of a number of questions which we suggest you use as the basis either for personal reflection or for discussion with colleagues.

- **References and further reading** with details of books, reports, journal articles and other materials referenced in the chapter or intended to provide background reading for you on the topic.
- **Websites and resources** where you might seek further information. We have done our best to ensure these are as up to date as possible, but bear in mind that content on the internet does change rapidly and so some links could no longer be current.

Finally, we would welcome comments on and ideas for improvement of this book. Whether you use it casually for your own development or more intensively as part of a postgraduate programme of study, we would like your feedback. Please email either one of us at kieran.walshe@mbs.ac.uk or judith.smith@nuffieldtrust.org.uk.

References and further reading

Drucker, P. (2006) *Managing the Nonprofit Organisation*. London: HarperCollins.

Griffiths, R. (1983) *Report of the NHS Management Inquiry*. London: Department of Health and Social Security.

McNulty, T. and Ferlie, E. (2004) *Reengineering Healthcare: The Complexities of Organisational Transformation*. Oxford: Oxford University Press.

Mintzberg, H. (2004) *Managers Not MBAs*. London: Prentice Hall.

Peck, E. (2004) *Organisational Development in Healthcare: Approaches, Innovations, Achievements*. Oxford: Radcliffe Medical Press.

Walshe, K. and Boaden, R. (eds) (2005) *Patient Safety: Research into Practice*. Maidenhead: Open University Press.

World Health Organization (2005) *Preventing Chronic Diseases: A Vital Investment*. Geneva: WHO.

PART

1

Health systems

The politics of healthcare and the health policy process: implications for healthcare management

Jennifer Dixon

Introduction

All governments in the developed world have a firm interest in shaping healthcare. There are several reasons for this. Healthcare expenditures of a variety of payers, not least government, are significantly large and pressures on these expenditures are high. Since governments are major payers, they are accountable in a highly visible way for expenditure, not least at the ballot box: every voter is a potential user of healthcare. Care and supplies are purchased from powerful corporate bodies or professional groups. There is a large difference in knowledge between providers (and their suppliers) and users (and often payers) of care, which may result in excessive care and avoidable costs.

The healthcare sector employs a large number of people: for example, in the National Health Service (NHS) in England, it employs 1.3 million people out of a population of 51.5 million. The nature of healthcare is such that it is highly emotive and features frequently in the media, for there are distinct ideological and moral issues on which political parties are likely to disagree, for example, who pays for care (such as the individual, the employer, the government) and the factors which improve performance in health systems (for example, direct or indirect government intervention or market incentives). For these reasons, healthcare is rarely out of the sights of politicians.

It is no surprise then that governments and other payers regularly try to reform the healthcare sector. Managers working in provider or commissioning bodies are often at the receiving end of what might seem to be arbitrary and burdensome change. In doing their job it is important for them to understand, and therefore possibly predict, the pattern of reform that impinges on their work, partly to be able to plan better for change and, where appropriate, to attempt to modify the type and level of specific interventions.

This chapter focuses on reform that is the direct result of government action. It starts by examining how healthcare reforms come about and the main factors which shape them. It goes on to examine briefly the broad pattern of reforms in the healthcare sector across Europe. Then, using the example of the NHS in England, it outlines the menu of policies now being developed and implemented, and tries to weave a narrative around these changes in order to predict future change, thus attempting to assess the power of managers to shape reforms in future.

The dynamics of reform in the health sector

Why change occurs

In a lucid and sophisticated account of health sector reform in the 1980s and 1990s in the USA, Canada and Britain, Carolyn Tuohy (1999), a Canadian political scientist, reflected on why change occurred. She observed that 'particular windows of opportunity for change occur at certain times and not others, a pattern of timing that derived from factors in the broader political system not in the health care arena itself'. She argued that significant features of health systems arising from major reform were in fact accidents – byproducts of ideas in wider circulation at the time that a window of opportunity opened – and that decisions taken between the episodes of major reform were heavily influenced by the parameters or 'logic' that such major reforms put in place. These parameters were influenced by history, or the reforms that had gone before, the sequencing of reforms and rational (evidence-based) choice, as well as two other characteristics which she termed 'institutional mix' and 'structural balance'. By institutional mix, she meant the balance of power between three main forms of social control: state hierarchy ('authority-based' control); professional collegiate institutions ('skill-based' control); and the market ('wealth-based' control). By structural balance, she meant the balance of power between three main stakeholders: the state, healthcare professionals and private financial interests. Tuohy's argument was that reform of healthcare in different countries would most likely be incremental, and heavily bounded by the particular political system, social values, past history (including of major reforms) and the power of institutions and key groups. The resulting pathway of reform would thus be different across countries.

Tuohy also noted that there were few instances of significant changes in power between these stakeholders necessary to achieve episodes of very major reform in healthcare. Evans (2005) described the period when these episodes occur as 'punctuated equilibrium' and also noted that the 'punctuation marks may be wholly external to the system, even random – war or economic crisis . . . and their effects are unpredictable' as well as 'decidedly unpleasant'. However, between episodes of major reform Tuohy thought that the success of change would depend upon 'the "goodness of fit" between the strategy of change proposed and the internal logic of the system to which it is addressed', itself influenced by the structural balance and institutional mix. In turn, she argued that these last two factors, in particular, the role of the state, are heavily influenced by the ability of the prevailing political system in a country to exert authority over health systems, either directly (where the state was the payer for and possibly also the provider of care) – which is most effective – or less directly through regulation or through mobilization of other key stakeholders – which is likely to be less effective, since it relies upon achieving consensus between different and powerful parties.

The dynamics of healthcare reform and the theory underpinning it, described by analysis of reform in three countries by Tuohy (1999), have also been identified and developed by many other writers, often political scientists (Hacker 2002; Hall and Taylor 1996). At present, three theories appear to be mainly in play: historical institutionalism; rational choice institutionalism; and sociological institutionalism. Historical institutionalists believe that the power and mix of institutions are the main factors influencing the outcome of reform (Tuohy's institutional mix), and that 'institutions push policy along particular paths, where early choices and events play a crucial role in determining the subsequent development of institutions or policies', otherwise known as 'path dependency' (Oliver and Mossialos 2005). Rational choice institutionalists seek a further explanation as to the basis for the choices made by institutions, which is often rooted in welfare economics where institutions act to maximize benefits along the range of options they make available to key actors. Sociological institutionalists believe that the actions of institutions are not just informed by a welfare-maximizing logic, but also by culture or identity within institutions and that 'policy and institutional reforms will occur only if they are socially legitimate' (Oliver and Mossialos 2005) or chime in with a nation's culture.

In truth, as theorists grope towards better conceptual models which explain the dynamics of healthcare reform with more accuracy, in a subject as complex as health reform, any single theory is likely to be inadequate. As Oliver and Mossialos (2005) put it with respect to healthcare reform in Europe, the answer to the question asked by Hollis (1994) 'does structure determine action, or action define structure?' is probably a bit of both.

Healthcare reforms across Europe

Regardless of the preferred theories of change, Evans (2005) suggested that the three most important questions driving health sector reform were:

- Who pays for care (and how much)?
- Who gets care (what kind, when, from whom)?
- Who gets paid how much, for doing what?

Evans suggested that conflict between major stakeholders revolves mainly around differences in viewpoints as to how these questions should be answered.

The extent to which government (or 'politics' as termed in the title of this chapter) is involved in healthcare depends heavily not just upon the extent to which political systems can consolidate authority, or upon the appearance of a window of opportunity for change, but on the extent to which government (national or local) is motivated to act. A primary factor to induce motivation must be the extent to which government pays for healthcare and thus seeks to control expenditure. Figure 2.1 shows that across OECD countries the government is a major payer, even in countries such as the USA, and thus is constantly seeking to reform healthcare. In middle- and low-income countries, as much as 80 per cent of spending on healthcare comes from private incomes and impoverishment as a result of healthcare expenses is all too common. In recent years,

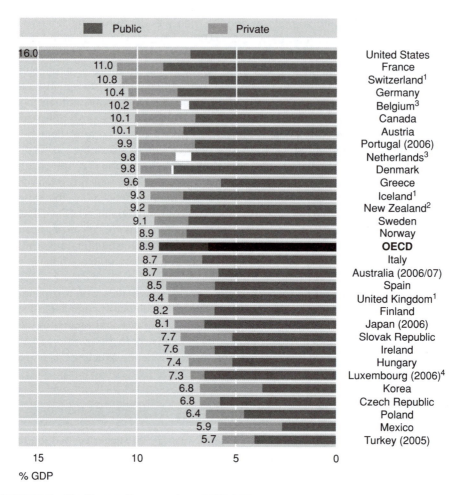

FIGURE 2.1 Total health expenditure as a share of GDP, 2007
Note: 1. Total expenditure on health in both figures. 2. Current expenditure on health in both figures. 3. Public and private expenditures are current expenditures (excluding investments). 4. Health expenditure is for the insured population rather than resident population.
Source: Health at a glance, 2009: OECD indicators.

some countries have moved towards an expanded role for government, for example, both Mexico and Columbia have put in place publicly funded insurance systems (Frenk et al. 2006; Guererro 2007). In general, however, reform is concentrated at the provider, individual and community, levels with little observable at national level.

In the face of rising health expenditures and pressures to spend more from providers, users and other supply-side stakeholders, all governments in Europe have been constantly active in attempting to reform healthcare. Analysing recent reforms across 11 European countries described in a special edition of the *Journal of Health Policy Politics and Law*, Evans (2005) notes a surprisingly similar story over the past 50 years –

different reforms but 'parallel development' – in contrast to what might have been expected given the unique set of conditions (such as institutional mix as highlighted by Tuohy) in each country. He describes two distinct phases to reform. The first was the establishment of near universal and comprehensive systems of collective payment for healthcare (through taxation and/or compulsory social insurance) – major reform which in many European countries was prompted by significant political events in the case of northern and central Europe linked to the Second World War, and in southern European states such as Greece, Spain and Portugal linked to the later overthrow of right-wing authoritarian regimes. The second phase (from the mid-1970s onwards) was essentially one of containing costs, which has been difficult since governments have been faced 'by highly intelligent and highly motivated opponents who are trying to drive them up' (Evans 2005: 287), such as the pharmaceutical industry and doctors. Modifying physicians' behaviour, Evans warns, has led to 'head-on conflict over professional organization and autonomy' where the public are unsurprisingly likely to side with the professionals arguing for more funding rather than governments demanding parsimony. He also notes that while each country has a unique history and institutional mix, surprisingly reforms since the 1970s across European countries have focused on similar objectives and the pathway of reform has not been dissimilar.

Closer inspection of ongoing attempts at reform across Europe in the past two decades reveals some broad patterns, at least across central and northern European countries (e.g. Anell 2005; *Journal of Health Policy, Politics and Law* 2005). First, the main goals of reform have been similar: to control costs, improve cost effectiveness and access to care while protecting key social or collective objectives such as equity of access to care and public satisfaction. Second, incremental rather than radical change has generally been the norm – change bounded in part by the institutional mix and power both within the political and healthcare arena. Progress has been limited in particular by, as Tuohy (1999) described, governments in some countries needing to achieve consensus with other political parties or key corporate bodies, such as in Germany and the Netherlands. Third, there has been an emphasis in some countries of devolution of health reforms to regions or other geographical areas and central frustration (and resulting central intervention) with lack of progress. Fourth, there has been an emphasis in many countries, such as Germany (Wörtz and Busse 2005), Holland (Schut and Van de Ven 2005), Austria (Stephan and Sommersguter-Reichmann 2005), and England (Oliver 2005), on reviewing the incentives operating on providers, with the tentative development of market-style incentives, such as competition and greater consumer choice underpinned by new methods of paying hospitals using case-mix based tariffs derived using diagnostic-related groups.

Maynard (2005) observed that the weak evidence base of many of the reforms in Europe had resulted in 'a lack of clarity in defining public policy goals, establishing trade-offs and aligning incentives with those objectives'. He also observed that many governments, such as in France and the USA, had taken the 'wrongheaded' step of introducing reforms to curb the demand for care by increasing co-payments for users, a policy which tended to penalize those least well off and the needy as well as the worried well, rather than the more important priority of tackling providers over the more significant problem of supplier-induced demand. For example, he noted a failure across Europe by governments to act or be effective in addressing specific problems of: variations in use of care arising from variations in medical practice; the lack of evidence on the cost effectiveness of treatments; and specifically the management of people with chronic medical conditions. This observation is perhaps is understandable. It is far easier for governments to introduce co-payments than it is to tackle powerful suppliers – especially doctors – about their behaviour.

The overall result in Europe over the past decade, argues Evans (2005), has been mixed and tentative – a drop in inpatient utilization, a continued rise in the expenditure on pharmaceuticals, and the costs of physicians' services somewhere in the middle. He concludes by reflecting that 'effective coping depends both upon the resources of the state and upon the degree of democratic responsiveness of the state itself to broader public values' (Evans 2005: 291), but warns that the obvious political difficulty of the Phase two agenda may strengthen the hand of those who seek to erode the Phase one reforms in Europe. An additional warning might be that attempts to increase efficiency and quality of care using sharper market incentives might also lead to the undermining of social objectives, unless there is effective monitoring and regulation to counter it.

To a manager, the discussion so far may not make comfortable reading. If, on the one hand, major reforms are influenced heavily by factors in the wider political and institutional arena and are heavily bounded by history, then what hope is there to influence the shape of reform? On the other hand, if episodes between major reforms are influenced by the shifts in power between and probably within major stakeholders, among whom are the professionals running institutions, then there may be hope. Such high-level analysis might help those managing healthcare to understand and predict the pathway of reform and identify the features that may or may not be modifiable nationally or locally. In the next section the influence of politics on healthcare in the UK National Health Service (NHS) is focused upon. The objective is to help promote understanding of the pathway of reform in a specific system and predict what might happen in the short to medium term.

Reform in the UK NHS

The main objectives driving healthcare reform in Europe are also in play in the UK NHS. But, considering England as a case example, there are particular features about the political system, and the healthcare system and the ideology of the government in power over the past decade, which are distinctive and help to explain the pathway of reform, compared to Europe. These features are discussed briefly below.

The political system in the UK

A distinctive feature of the UK political system is a parliamentary system of government with a 'first past the post' method of electing Members of the UK Parliament at Westminster (since the late 1990s, Scotland, Wales and Northern Ireland have had devolved government – intermittently in the case of Northern Ireland – in which there are separate elections for members, not discussed here). On occasion, this has allowed governments to be elected with sufficiently large majorities to create an 'elected autocracy', with little need to achieve consensus over policy with either other political parties or indeed key corporate and professional stakeholders. This allows significant reform, for better or worse, in healthcare to be made relative to other European states.

The healthcare system in the UK

A distinctive feature in the UK is the extent to which government pays the costs (compared to other countries in Europe) and the extent to which health services are state-owned and state-run. In 2005–6, 8.3 per cent of gross domestic product (GDP) was spent on healthcare in the UK, and 7.1 per cent of the GDP was spent on the NHS, funded largely through general taxation. Unlike the case across most of Europe, in the UK the state not only funds most healthcare but also owns all of the commissioners of state-funded care. For example, in England, the state contracts almost exclusively with independent providers of primary care, general practitioners (GPs) and semi-autonomous NHS bodies – NHS Foundation Trusts – as well as all NHS Trusts and community health services. In addition, the state funds all strategic health authorities, primary care trusts and in future will fund clinical commissioning groups (DH 2010a).

The NHS across the UK has some unusual features compared to other enterprises; for example, its budget is cash-limited and NHS organizations must either break even each year or not breach an annual funding limit; it provides comprehensive services which are (largely) free at the point of use; individuals cannot buy NHS care directly but have care bought on their behalf by commissioners (for example, primary care trusts in England); there are enormous information discrepancies between individuals and service providers, which means that individuals rely heavily on informed agents (for example, GPs) to help direct them to the most appropriate care; and service providers are formally accountable directly to the Secretary of State rather than to the patients treated or populations served (with the exception of Foundation Trusts in England, and GPs).

Historically, the government largely left it to the professionals to provide a good quality service. As Rudolf Klein has noted, there was an implicit pact between the government and the profession whereby the former set the overall budget for the NHS and the latter largely spent it, provided each did not challenge the other (Klein 2000). By the 1980s, this had changed and the government, through the Department of Health and local NHS bodies, took an increasingly direct role to improve the performance of NHS institutions, particularly providers of care. This was done through primary and secondary legislation, directives from the centre, and performance management locally, regionally, or sometimes nationally. Where the government was not able to act directly through operational directives and performance management, in particular with respect to GPs as independent contractors, it has attempted to shape the activities of GPs through legislation and the financial incentives of the national GP contract. The bulk of these efforts has been largely to improve the performance of institutions with respect to politically determined priorities, rather than the quality of care provided by professionals, which has more often been the preserve of the professional regulatory bodies such as the General Medical Council and the Royal Colleges.

FIGURE 2.2 A simple model to understand healthcare reform

In Scotland, Wales and Northern Ireland, the devolved governments and assemblies have autonomy to shape healthcare. As a result, there has been a divergence of approaches to reforming the NHS, the main one being to abolish the separation between purchaser and providers, and in Wales and Scotland to discourage the use of competition and the private sector (Connolly et al. 2010). But the prevailing environment across the UK is one in which government has a very strong role in reforming the health system, mainly because of the extent to which the NHS is funded from the public purse.

Some organizing principles to help understand reform

However, there are a limited number of levers at the command of government to reform care to improve performance. Figure 2.2 suggests some of the main levers available, either to improve quality, efficiency or control costs, and the area in which they have influence. Figure 2.2 is divided into a 'system reform' area (outer), an 'intra-organizational' area (middle) and an 'individual' area (inner).

System reform

The 'system reform' area represents policies that are crafted by government to influence providers, or commissioners/funders of care. These levers are designed to exert external challenge on an organization to do better. As shown, these include:

National directives, with national targets and performance management and guidance. These can be reinforced by active management and sanctions for non-achievement. In England over the past decade, this lever has been the most effective in making relatively rapid targeted improvements in the NHS, for example, in reducing waiting for care (Propper et al. 2010). But too many national targets, many argue, can cramp local initiative, distort local priorities, and lead to perverse outcomes. Others argue that targets work to reduce poor performance but do not increase excellence. Hence the number of targets has dropped, and the current UK Coalition Government elected in May 2010 has pledged to reduce them.

Major payers, such as government (in the UK) or statutory sickness funds (in Germany, The Netherlands and France), can also issue a wealth of mandatory or non-mandatory guidance to providers, effected through direct performance management or via contracting. Examples include guidance issued to PCTs and NHS trusts by the UK Department of Health on a range of subjects such as care pathways for common clinical conditions, or by the National Institute for Health and Clinical Excellence (NICE) on which new treatments will and will not be funded by the NHS on grounds of cost effectiveness.

In many countries, there have been attempts by government to control more fully the healthcare benefits paid for from the public purse, thus limiting supply of and demand for these services. For example, in 2010, the Danish government announced that it would no longer pay for assisted reproductive treatments. Denmark used to offer three cycles of publicly funded in vitro fertilization to all citizens but the economic downturn has led to treatment only being offered to those with special needs.

The government can also issue a wealth of mandatory or non-mandatory guidance to providers, effected through direct performance management or via contracting, for example, as issued to PCTs and NHS Trusts by the Department of Health on a range of subjects such as care pathways for common clinical conditions (DH 2004a, 2004b), or by the National Institute for Health and Clinical Excellence (NICE) on which new treatments must be funded by the NHS on grounds of cost-effectiveness (www.nice.org.uk).

Institutional regulation

Public organizations, at arm's length from government, charged with assessing and improving the quality of care in providers are part of the landscape in a few countries. In most countries, they simply accredit providers against a basic standard of care rather than aim to improve care. In England, the Care Quality Commission and Monitor were created to assess and improve various aspects of performance in primary care trusts, NHS trusts and foundation trusts, to publicly report the findings and to provide external challenge. The main rationale for doing so was to enable ministers and the Department of Health to loosen their grip on assessing and managing performance in the NHS. It is clear that regulated bodies have shown year-on-year improvement in the areas of care assessed (Healthcare Commission 2009a). But as recent high profile scandals in the quality of care in several hospitals have shown (Healthcare Commission 2009b), it is not possible for regulators to spot every problem: regulation has limits.

Financial incentives

Significant efforts have been made across the OECD countries to craft greater financial incentives on providers to encourage better performance. Prospective DRG-based payment for hospitals has been introduced in many countries, initially in the USA and then in Europe, Australia, and Asia (Igekami 2009), to reduce over-supply of care associated with fee for service payment. In England, prospective payment (*Payment by Results*; DH 2002a) has been associated with modest reductions in length of stay and unit costs (Farrar et al. 2009). More contentious has been the encouragement of competition between providers (for example, in Sweden (Harrison and Calltorp 2000), Switzerland (Zweifel 2000), England, China (Wen 2009) and between statutory health insurers – for example, in The Netherlands (Schut and Van de Ven, 2005), and Germany.

Competition between providers for patients remains contentious in part because of the threat it poses for key interest groups, the potential to reduce equity of access and necessary clinical collaboration in care, ideological opposition, and the absence of hard evidence on impact (although early signs in England are promising; Cooper et al. 2010; Gaynor et al. 2010).

Other financial incentives crafted by national policy-makers, or large insurers, have included 'pay for performance' schemes, of which one of the largest in the world is the increased payments for general practices in England to improve chronic disease management (the so-called Quality and Outcomes Framework) which has had an impact (Dolan et al. 2006). Current initiatives in England to pay hospitals extra for higher quality (the Commissioning for Quality and Innovation (CQUIN) initiative) are currently being evaluated (NHS Institute for Improvement and Innovation 2010b). Medicare, the public insurance programme for older adults in the USA, stopped paying for 'never' events in 2008.

Local accountability

Attempts have been made in several countries to increase the external challenge on particularly providers by giving the populations they serve more influence in shaping local services, for example, in New Zealand (Barnett et al. 2009) and Scotland where, in the latter case, there have just been direct elections of 22 members of the public on two regional Health Boards (Redding 2010). In England, the Coalition Government initially proposed similar direct elections to the boards of primary care trusts (The Coalition Government 2010), and subsequently to abolish primary care trusts (DH 2010a). Whether such requirements will fall on the new clinical commissioning groups is presently unclear. NHS foundation trusts must in part be governed by members drawn from staff and the local community, and local health services are required to be publicly and formally scrutinized by locally elected councils. The impact of both of these mechanisms in England has not yet been sufficiently evaluated.

Intra-organizational levers

To many staff working in healthcare, 'system reform' is a completely alien concept. The reality for them is the institution in which they work, and how to improve the care within it – represented by the middle in Figure 2.2. External challenges, coming from regulators, competing providers, direct financial incentives or national targets are at best external distractions from the real work at hand – to improve services, or the care for individual patients.

Across more developed health systems, for example, in Europe and North America, there has been growing engagement of clinical professionals in improving whole services within, and increasingly across, provider organizations. For example, by taking management and leadership responsibility, using a range of 'improvement' techniques borrowed from industry to improve quality and efficiency (NHS Institute for Improvement and Innovation 2010a), in developing clinical governance and patient safety, using information to assess and peer review the quality of care provided, crafting better and evidence-based and coordinated pathways of care, and developing incentives to help motivate their peers. This is in part a response to developments within medicine, constraints on resources, information technology and the growing challenge of managing older populations with more chronic disease which requires multidisciplinary working and coordinated care. In the USA, activities by the Institute for Health Improvement, and in England, by the NHS Institute for Improvement and Innovation, the National Patient Safety Agency, and NICE, have helped to develop clinicians and managers in this way.

But what kind of 'intra-organizational' environment can help motivate this virtuous professional behaviour? There have been many studies, including those that examine high performing integrated care organizations in the USA. The ingredients of suggested success typically include:

- good information systems providing transparent patient-level information on use cost and outcomes;
- effective clinical leadership and peer review of performance against a desired set of goals;
- a set of financial and non-financial incentives that are aligned to improve performance; and
- the governance of an organization that heavily involves clinicians (Minott et al. 2010; Dixon et al. 2004).

Evidence on collaboration and integration is examined in more detail in Chapters 10 (chronic disease and integrated care) and 26 (managing strategic collaboration).

Individual motivation and behaviour

Probably the most potent force to improve care is the intrinsic motivation of clinical professionals to do what they think is a good job, and the intrinsic motivation of patients to improve their own health and reduce avoidable demand on formal healthcare – the inner part of Figure 2.2.

Professional bodies in place in most countries primarily try to improve standards of care that professionals give, but often do not address the fundamental issue of intrinsic motivation. Similarly in England, clinical governance and audit as noted above are also intended to encourage reflection by professionals and improvement of care, as are initiatives to improve the analysis by professionals of data on use costs and outcomes. With relatively little focus and understanding of intrinsic motivation, reforms have tended to focus on institutional competition for resources, or direct financial incentives to shape the performance for clinicians (Thaler and Sunstein 2008) – a largely economic paradigm.

Encouraging patients to take a more active role in prevention of ill health and their care has been a feature of policy in England as elsewhere, albeit secondary to the initiatives outlined above. There is a huge emphasis on providing more information about self-management, choice of care options and supporting individuals to make decisions. Rather than a secondary focus, health education is a critical strategy for health improvement in low-income countries. In contrast to wealthier nations, health education in low-income countries tends to be more integrated into community development and is seen as an integral part of developing economic self-sufficiency (Peters et al. 2009).

To help individuals be more in control of their healthcare, pilots in which individuals are given personal budgets to pay for healthcare are in place in several countries, for example, England, the USA and the Netherlands with encouraging results (Alakeson 2008, 2010). As with clinicians, direct financial incentives have been tried to encourage healthy behaviours with some effect (Wilkinson 2008). This is one area where global exchange has been particularly significant, with Mayor Bloomberg's use of micro-incentives to encourage a range of positive health and social outcomes among low-income populations in New York borrowing directly from Mexico's successful Opportunidades programme (Riccio et al. 2010).

The bluntest tool to reduce demand and contain costs (albeit with possible adverse impacts on health), is to require patients to share the costs of care. Governments unwilling or unable to curb provider incomes directly have often chosen this route for reform because it is easier. Other experiments have been tried to reduce the problem of 'moral hazard' in healthcare – where individuals who do not face the full cost of care at the point of use may demand more care than they need. Medical or health savings accounts have been tried in several countries such as China, Singapore, South Africa and the USA with to date modest impact on use or costs (EuroObserver 2008).

Applying this framework to the UK NHS

The simple conceptual framework outlined above can help to understand the broad pathway to reform of healthcare taken in England in the past two decades. For a policymaker, deciding on the most appropriate blend of levers is highly complex, and more a function of opportunity, values and ideology rather than an evidence base: evaluating reforms is difficult methodologically and takes time.

The reform pathway in England

The broad thrust of the 1991 NHS reforms, which introduced the 'internal market' was to introduce competition between NHS trusts to try to improve performance. Since 1997, three broad phases to NHS reform in England have been described: Phase 1, central direction (national standards and directives); Phase 2, financial investment and support (for example, the work of the then Modernisation Agency); and, the most significant, Phase 3, 'constructive discomfort' (Stevens 2004) or 'edgy instability' – the introduction since 2000 of market-style incentives to improve the quality and efficiency of care. This was underpinned by policies such as patient choice (DH 2005a), encouraging private providers (secondary, community and primary) to compete for NHS business through the letting of contracts (nationally by government as well as locally by commissioners) to non-NHS providers (DH 2006a), introducing a new system of prospective payment to hospitals, *Payment by Results* (DH 2002a,b), allowing NHS trusts to achieve foundation status with much greater freedom to operate independently of the state (for example, NHS foundation trusts are not subject to directives by the Secretary of State or performance management by the centre) (DH 2006b), and attempting to develop commissioning by primary care trusts (DH 2005b).

A review of the impact of these reforms was commissioned by the Department of Health from a range of independent researchers. In brief, the analysis shows that:

- choice is being offered to patients but providers were generally marketing their services to GPs rather than patients (Dixon et al. 2010);
- there had been an increase in the number of providers competing for elective care, and performance (as mainly measured by mortality rates for acute myocardial infarction) had increased in more highly competitive locations relative to locations with less competition (Cooper et al. 2010; Gaynor et al. 2010);
- there was little difference in patient experience of care in NHS versus independent treatment centres (Healthcare Commission 2008);
- commissioning remains under-developed and weak (Smith et al. 2010);
- the introduction of Payment by Results was associated with reductions in length of inpatient stay, an increase in the proportion of day cases and falls in inpatient mortality (Farrar et al. 2009);
- setting standards and targets had worked, for example, in reducing waiting times for elective care (Propper et al. 2010);
- regulation has helped to increase performance on measured indices (Healthcare Commission 2009a).

Other work shows the obvious impact of direct financial incentives on behaviour, such as the impact of the Quality and Outcomes framework (pay for performance) in general practice introduced in 2004 (Dolan et al. 2006). Much less is known about the impact of the fourth 'lever' – that of increased local democratic challenge.

The picture so far is that, in the 'system reform' arena of Figure 2.2, all the levers pulled have had effect, some strong (central control) and others weaker than expected (competition) perhaps because of slow implementation rather than latent effects. In the 'intra-organizational' area of Figure 2.2, the NHS Institute for Innovation and Improvement has tried to quantify the impact of some improvement factors (such as leadership) and techniques (such as introducing 'lean' methods) (Ham 2009), but to do this to assess the impact on a national scale relative to 'system reform' would be a very complex task and so far has not been attempted. Similarly the impact of initiatives to improve motivation of staff has not been evaluated in this way.

The UK Coalition Government, elected in May 2010, is continuing along the reform path begun in 1991 – using greater financial incentives such as competition and choice to influence the behaviour of NHS trusts to greater quality and efficiency. The White Paper *Equity and Excellence: Liberating the NHS* (DH 2010a) also proposes to cut back the influence of the central lever – central directive – by not enforcing targets, by abolishing primary care trusts and strategic health authorities and setting up new GP commissioning consortia (subsequently remodelled as clinical commissioning groups), and a quasi-independent NHS Commissioning Board to support and challenge them (DH 2010b). Instead there is faith that local democracy – local people – will force improvements (DH 2010c) through informed patient choice (through better information on outcomes) and competition between providers. Regulation is also likely to be scaled back, but still relied upon, since the Care Quality Commission will remain, and the regulator for foundation trusts (Monitor) is to be expanded into an economic regulator (DH 2010d). There has also been a view, evidenced by speeches by the Secretary of State to 'give the NHS back to the professionals' – a *cri de cœur* which appeals to the innermost circle in Figure 2.2, that is how to improve the motivation and professionalism of staff such that external challenge is less necessary. But so far the proposed policies address this indirectly, rather than directly.

Reform in Scotland, Wales and Northern Ireland

In the UK, the Labour government in 1997 committed to greater devolution of political power. The immediate result was the creation in 1998 of an elected Parliament in Scotland, an elected Assembly in Wales and, until it was suspended in 2002, an elected Assembly in Northern Ireland (NI). While the specific powers of each political body are different, each has significant freedoms with respect to public policy including healthcare. The speed of public sector reform has been different across the UK, partly dependent upon the need to achieve a consensus among political parties in the devolved political bodies in different countries, the shape of the reform programme and the tools designed by governments to implement it.

The period following devolution in 1999 was followed by large increases in funding for the NHS across the UK. Only in England was this funding contingent upon the NHS meeting Public Service Agreement targets set by the UK Treasury. Funding for the NHS in the devolved countries is determined by their governments from a global sum for 'devolved services' that is based on the Barnett formula and bilateral negotiations with HM Treasury.

In Scotland and Wales, the so-called purchaser–provider split was abolished, and organizations recreated to meet population needs and run services within defined geographical areas (NHS health boards in Scotland, and since October 2008, local health boards in Wales). While there have been targets in each of the devolved nations, for example, to reduce waiting and healthcare acquired infections, they were not backed up, as in England, with tough performance management. In addition there have been other differences that are more obvious to patients. In Scotland, there is free personal care for older people, while in Wales the Assembly Government abolished prescription charges. In Scotland and Wales, there have been policies to reduce the use of private providers of care, and discourage competition between NHS providers. In Northern

Ireland, devolution was suspended between 2002 and 2007 and reform there has been much slower.

There have been two complementary and comprehensive reviews of performance of the NHS across the four home nations over the past 10 years. The first assessed quality of care and broadly found no systematic differences in quality across the four nations (Sutherland and Coyle 2009). The second assessed the productivity of care, and found lower productivity and higher costs in Scotland, Wales and Northern Ireland relative to England, but in particular relative to regions in England that were more comparable on a range of health indices (Connolly et al. 2010).

Health reform across Europe

Across Europe, as in England, there is increasing recognition that a blend of levers to reform healthcare is needed, and that blend will appropriately include market-style incentives (such as competition between institutions, patient choice and pay for performance). As has been demonstrated across Europe in the past two decades, how prominent these incentives will be in that blend will depend on a number of factors, including the ideological complexion of governments, the relative political power of other key stakeholders (such as the professions) and the extent to which there is convincing evidence that these incentives are helping to solve key local problems.

Again, as demonstrated across Europe, the pathway of reform is unlikely to be linear and likely to be stalled by cautious implementation. For example, in The Netherlands in the late 1980s, the Dekker Plan promoted radical reform – regulated competition to give more incentives to providers and insurers to improve performance (Schut and Van de Ven 2005). While the theory of how this would work appeared convincing, in practice implementation was very difficult, not so much because of political conflict in this case but because a number of technical aspects of the reforms had not been worked out or implemented to allow regulated competition to occur. In particular, the following had not been determined (Schut and Van de Ven 2005): risk adjustment to reduce adverse selection by insurers; pricing and product classification for providers to reduce the temptation to skimp on care provided; a better system of outcome and quality measurement so that contract negotiations between insurer and provider would focus on these areas not just price; better information to promote choice among consumers; and an effective regulatory framework. While progress has been made on these in the intervening years, implementation is still in a very early stage.

In Sweden, the process of reform towards market-style reforms has proceeded crabwise, delayed perhaps less by technical problems as experienced in The Netherlands but more by the political process (Anell 2005). In Sweden, healthcare is mostly funded and provided by the county councils, whereas overall goals and policies are set by national government. The county councils and national government may be of a different political complexion and the lack of political stability between central and local government has contributed to difficulties in developing and implementing policies, resulting in delay.

Box 2.1: *UK bodies with influence on the pathway of healthcare reform*

- professional bodies (e.g. General Medical Council, Royal Colleges)
- other trade representative groups (e.g. the NHS Confederation and the Foundation Trust Network, the British Medical Association, the Royal College of Nursing, the NHS Alliance, the National Association of Primary Care)
- trade unions
- regulatory bodies (e.g. the Care Quality Commission, Monitor, the Audit Commission)
- the NHS Ombudsman
- research organizations (e.g. universities, think tanks)
- private consultancy organizations
- private industry (private providers and suppliers of goods and services, e.g. pharmaceutical industry, private hospitals) and private payers e.g. private insurance companies
- the legal system
- media

Influencing the dynamics of reform

In the discussion above, readers can be forgiven for concluding that in the UK, at least in England, government alone is responsible for influencing the path of healthcare reform. But as noted earlier by Tuohy, clearly other bodies can have significant influence on healthcare reform. In the UK these include bodies shown in Box 2.1. Across Europe, the bodies having biggest effect in stalling reform have included professional groups and trade unions. But in the UK both groups in the past two decades have been weakened by a combination of external events, suboptimal leadership and erosion of their powers by Parliament. The power of the medical profession in the UK was severely assaulted by public outrage over two significant events in the 1990s – the poor quality of heart surgery in a children's unit in Bristol Royal Infirmary (2001) and the case of Dr Harold Shipman, a GP convicted of murdering dozens of his patients (Shipman Inquiry 2005). Each case in its own way demonstrated the weakness of the medical profession in regulating itself, and an arrogance towards responding to public concern about the quality of care. The General Medical Council and to an extent the Royal Colleges have been preoccupied since then with improving the quality of care and regulation rather than developing a national stance over the shape of healthcare reform. In the case of the unions, their powers had been eroded in the 1980s by successive Conservative governments and they have faced declining membership. Together with some of the trade bodies (such as the British Medical Association), they have been active in lobbying for, or more often against, recent reforms.

In general, research institutions have not mounted a comprehensive critique of policy based on evidence and followed it through with effective lobbying. Evaluations take time to complete, and many research groups do not cover the development of reform more widely. And arguably lobbying is not their role. In the past decade a number of new independent regulators have been created by the UK government, and their influence on the NHS is a prominent feature. But while having an 'arm's length' relationship with government and exerting a strong 'behind the scenes' influence on policy, the regulators must choose very carefully the issues on which to criticise policy makers. The pharmaceutical industry is highly influential, not least because of the strong relationship it has with the Department of Health (DH) which is chief government negotiator with the industry about the prices the industry can charge for supplies to the NHS under the pharmaceutical price regulation scheme (DH 2005c). The media have had a strong role, but more in criticizing policy and identifying perverse consequences locally rather than developing a constructive alternative vision.

The institutional mix and structural balance in the UK have thus been skewed heavily in the government's favour in the past two decades and have resulted in a greater number of more radical healthcare reforms than have been possible elsewhere in Europe. With greater plurality of providers, particularly with new private suppliers entering the healthcare market in England at least, corporate interests may be more influential in future. But as long as the government remains the major payer of healthcare in the UK, there is a workable majority in Parliament, and the professional bodies and trade unions remain on the back foot, further major reforms are likely. The door to greater market forces is likely to remain open, given the apparent political consensus that these incentives have some role in improving system performance. The conflicts in the UK and Europe will revolve around how strong these incentives should be, ideologically and in the light of evidence of their impact. The far greater looming issue in the UK will be, given the economic and political climate, the extent to which social objectives can be traded off against the universally desired objective of improving efficiency.

Conclusion

This chapter has outlined a few of the theories that might underpin the dynamics of change in the health sector internationally. It has examined briefly the broad pattern of reforms in the healthcare sector across Europe and in more depth in the UK NHS, showing that reforms have been designed with similar objectives, that reform has been incremental, and much focused on altering the behaviour of patients rather than the suppliers of care. More radical reform has been stalled chiefly though conflicts over fundamental questions relating to who pays, who gets care, and who gets paid; conflicts which have been played out mainly between government, powerful professional and private interests and unions. Then, using the example of the National Health Service in England, it has described the direction of travel of policies now being developed and how and why government has been able to design and begin to implement radical reform relative to many other European countries. It suggests that the institutional mix in England at least has broadly favoured the government's agenda, and suggests that the power of managers to shape national reforms in the short- to medium-term future will be limited, but there may be increasing power to shape reforms locally. In other countries, that power may be greater given the different structural balance and institutional mix, the political processes in play and the more unpredictable windows of opportunity often created by events external to the health arena.

Summary box

- Governments across the developed world are constantly active in reforming health-care, chiefly because of the extent to which governments pay healthcare costs, and the proportion of GDP that healthcare consumes.

- Although incremental reform has been the norm, radical change is usually influenced by external political or economic events unrelated to healthcare. Reform is highly influenced by the balance of power of key professional and corporate institutions present in each country and the system of government.

- Conflicts between key stakeholders tend to revolve around who pays, who gets care, who gets paid, and how much.

- In Europe over the past two decades, reforms have typically been designed with similar objectives, but much has focused on 'demand-side' rather than 'supply-side' issues.

- In the English NHS, radical reform appears to have been more possible because of the Westminster system of Parliament, the significant democratic mandates usually given to governments in power, and the relative weakness of other professional, trade and corporate stakeholders.

- The reforms in England, as in many other countries in Europe, have introduced market-style incentives into healthcare. This is likely to continue and a prevailing conflict will be the extent to which social objectives such as equity of access to care are traded off with efforts to improve efficiency using these incentives.

Self-test exercises

1 What has been the broad thrust of healthcare reform in your country over the past decade?

2 What are, and are intended to be, the main levers to improve performance in the health sector in your country? For example:

- control from central government, regional or local government
- market-style incentives (such as competition between providers, insurers/commissioners, consumer choice)

- the local democratic voice of the population (such as through local councils, citizens' juries)
- patients
- third-party regulation
- other.

3 How has the broad approach to health sector reform affected your organization?

4 How much intra-organizational reform has there been to improve performance, and to what extent was this driven by external challenge?

5 What attempts have there been to improve the motivation of staff to do better? Or to encourage patients to stay well?

6 How could barriers to progress be best overcome locally?

7 How influential have you been in helping to shape health sector reforms at local or a national level?

8 How might you be more influential in future?

Acknowledgements

Vidhya Alakeson helped to provide some international examples and references, for which many thanks.

References and further reading

Alakeson, V. (2008) Let patients control the purse strings. *British Medical Journal*, 336: 807–9.

Alakeson, V. (2010) *International Developments in Self-Directed Care*. New York: Commonwealth Fund.

Alvarez-Rosete, A., Bevan, G., Mays, N. and Dixon, J. (2005) Effect of diverging policy across the NHS. *British Medical Journal*, 331: 946–50.

Anell, A. (2005) Swedish healthcare under pressure. *Health Economics*, 14: 237–54.

Barnett, P., Tenbensel, T., Cumming, J., Clayden, C., Ashton, T., Pledger, M. and Burnette, M. (2009) Implementing new modes of governance in the NZ health system: an empirical study. *Health Policy*, 93: 118–27.

Bristol Royal Infirmary (2001) *The Bristol Royal Infirmary Inquiry: Final Report July 2001*. Available at: http://www.bristol-inquiry.org.uk/.nal_report/ (accessed 1 January 2006).

Connolly, S., Bevan, G. and Mays, N. (2010) *Funding and Performance of Health Systems in the Four Countries of the UK before and after Devolution*. London: The Nuffield Trust.

Cooper, Z., Gibbons, S., Jones, S. and McGuire, A. (2010) Does competition save lives? Evidence from the English NHS Patient Choice Reforms. LSE Health Working Paper No 16. LSE Health. Available at: http://www2.lse.ac.uk/

LSEHealthAndSocialCare/LSEHealth/whosWho/profiles/zcooper@lseacuk.aspx (accessed 24 June 2010).

Department of Health (2002a) *Reforming NHS Financial Flows. Introducing Payment by Results*. London: Department of Health. Available at: http://www.dh .gov.uk/assetRoot/04/06/04/76/04060476.pdf (accessed 1 November 2005).

Department of Health (2002b) *Introducing Payment by Results: The NHS Financial Reforms*. Available at: http://www.dh.gov.uk/en/Publicationsandstatistics/ Publications/PublicationsPolicyAndGuidance/DH_4003104 (accessed 24 June 2010).

Department of Health (2004a) *Information on the National Service Framework for diabetes*. Available at: http://collections.europarchive.org/tna/20100509080731/ http://dh.gov.uk/en/Healthcare/Longtermconditions/Vascular/Diabetes/DH_4015717 (accessed 24 June 2010).

Department of Health (2004b) *Information on the National Service Framework for Coronary Heart Disease*. Available at: http://collections.europarchive.org/tna/ 20100509080731/http://dh.gov.uk/en/Healthcare/Longtermconditions/Vascular/ Coronaryheartdisease/Nationalserviceframework/index.htm (accessed 24 June 2010).

Department of Health (2005a) *Patient Choice*. Available at: http://www.dh.gov .uk/PolicyAndGuidance/PatientChoice/fs/en (accessed 1 November 2005).

Department of Health (2005b) *Commissioning a Patient-led NHS*. Available at: http://www.dh.gov.uk/PublicationsAndStatistics/Publications/PublicationsPolicy And-Guidance/PublicationsPolicyAndGuidanceArticle/fs/en?CONTENT_ID= 4116716&chk=/%2Bb2QD (accessed 10 November 2005).

Department of Health (2005c) *The 2005 Pharmaceutical Price and Regulation Scheme*. Available at: http://www.dh.gov.uk/PolicyAndGuidance/MedicinesPharmacy AndIndustry/PharmaceuticalPriceRegulationScheme/ThePPRSScheme/fs/en (accessed 1 January 2006).

Department of Health (2006a) *DH Commercial Directorate. Aims and Objectives*. Available at: http://www.dh.gov.uk/AboutUs/HowDHWorks/DHOrganisation-Structure/DHStructureArticle/fs/en?CONTENT_ID=4110133&ampchk=yF4Vft (accessed 1 January 2006).

Department of Health (2006b) *NHS Foundation Trusts*. Available at: http://www.dh .gov.uk/PolicyAndGuidance/OrganisationPolicy/SecondaryCare/NHSFoundation Trust/fs/en (accessed 1 January 2006).

Department of Health (2010a) *Equity and Excellence: Liberating the NHS*. Available at: http://www.dh.gov.uk/en/Publicationsandstatistics/Publications/PublicationsPolicy AndGuidance/DH_117353 (accessed 4 August 2010).

Department of Health (2010b) *Liberating the NHS: Commissioning for Patients*. Available at: http://www.dh.gov.uk/en/Consultations/Liveconsultations/DH_ 117587 (accessed 4 August 2010).

Department of Health (2010c) Liberating the NHS: Increasing Democratic Legitimacy in Health. Available at: http://www.dh.gov.uk/en/Consultations/Liveconsultations/ DH_117586 (accessed 17 August 2010).

Department of Health (2010d) *Liberating the NHS: Regulating Healthcare Providers*. Available at: http://www.dh.gov.uk/en/Consultations/Liveconsultations/DH_117782 (accessed 17 August 2010).

Dixon, A., Robertson, R. and Appleby, J. (2010) *Patient Choice: How Patients Choose and How Providers Respond*. London: King's Fund.

Dixon, J., Lewis, R.Q., Rosen, R., Finlayson, B. and Gray, D. (2004) Can the NHS learn from US managed care organisations? *British Medical Journal*, 328: 223–6.

Dolan, T., Fullwood, C., Gravelle, H., Reeves, D., Kontopantelis, E., Hiroeh, U. and Roland, M. (2006) Pay-for-performance programs in family practices in the United Kingdom. *New England Journal of Medicine*, 355: 375–84.

Euro Observer (2008) Edition on medical and health savings accounts. *Winter*, 10(4).

Evans, R.G. (2005) Fellow travellers on a contested path: power, purpose and the evolution of European health care systems. *Journal of Health Policy Politics, and Law. Special Issue: Legacies and Latitude in European Health Policy*, 30(1–2): 277–93.

Farrar, S., Yi, D., Sutton, M., Chalkley, M., Sussex, J. and Scott, A. (2009) Has payment by results affected the way that English hospitals provide care? Difference-in-differences analysis. *British Medical Journal*, 339: 3047–51.

Frenk, J., Gonzalez-Pier, E., Gomez-Dantes, O., Lezana, M.A. and Knaul, F.M. (2006) Comprehensive reform to improve health system performance in Mexico. *Lancet*, 368: 1524–34.

Gaynor, M.S., Moreno-Serra, R. and Propper, C. (2010) *Death by market power: reform, competition and patient outcomes in the National Health Service*. Working paper No 16164. National Bureau of Economic Research, 2010.

Guererro, R. (2007) The road to universality: lessons from the Columbian healthcare reform. Available at: http://www.ciss.org.mx/cams/pdf/en/2007/ramiro_guerrero.pdf (accessed 2 July 2010).

Hacker, J.S. (2002) *The Divided Welfare State*. Cambridge: Cambridge University Press.

Hall, P.A. and Taylor, R.C.R. (1996) Political science and the three new institutionalisms. *Political Studies*, 44: 936–57.

Ham, C. (2009) *Health in a Cold Climate: Developing an intelligent Response to the Financial Challenges Facing the NHS*. London: Nuffield Trust.

Harrison, M. and Calltorp, J. (2000) The reorientation of market-oriented reforms in Swedish health care. *Health Policy*, 50(3): 219–40.

Healthcare Commission (2008) *Independent Treatment Centres: The Evidence So Far*. Available at: http://www.cqc.org.uk/_db/_documents/Independent_sector_treatment_centres_The_evidence_so_far.pdf (accessed 30 November 2010).

Healthcare Commission (2009a) *The Annual Health Check 2007/08: A National Overview of the Performance of NHS Trusts in England*. Available at: http://www.cqc.org.uk/_db/_documents/0708_annual_health_check_overview_document.pdf (accessed 29 November 2010).

Healthcare Commission (2009b) *Investigation into Mid Staffordshire NHS Foundation Trust*. Available at: http://www.cqc.org.uk/_db/_documents/Investigation_into_Mid_Staffordshire_NHS_Foundation_Trust.pdf (accessed 24 June 2010).

Hollis, M. (1994) *The Philosophy of Social Science: An Introduction*. Cambridge: Cambridge University Press.

Igekami, N. (2009) Games policymakers and providers play: introducing case-mix based payment to hospital chronic care units in Japan. *Journal of Health Politics, Policy and Law*, 34(3): 361–80.

Journal of Health Policy, Politics and Law (2005) *Special Issue: Legacies and Latitude in European Health Policy*, 30(1–2): 1–309.

Klein, R. (2000) *The New Politics of the NHS*. London: Prentice Hall.

Maynard, A. (2005) European health policy challenges. *Health Economics*, 14: 255–63.

Minott, J., Helms, D., Luft, H., Guterman, S. and Weil, H. (2010) *The Group Employed Model and a Foundation for Health Care Delivery Reform*. The Commonwealth Fund, Issue brief 10. Available at: http://www.researchgate.net/publication/43297318_The_group_employed_model_as_a_foundation_for_health_care_delivery_reform (accessed 24 June 2010).

National Audit Office, Audit Commission (2004) *Financial Management in the NHS. NHS (England) Summarised Accounts 2003–4*. London: The Stationery Office.

NHS Confederation http://www.nhsconfed.org/ (accessed 1 January 2005).

NHS Institute for Improvement and Innovation (2010a) *Releasing Time to Care: The Productive ward*. Available at: http://programmeforgovernment.hmg.gov.uk/files/2010/05/coalition-programme.pdf (accessed 29 November 2010).

NHS Institute for Improvement and Innovation (2010b) *Commissioning for Quality and Innovation (CQUIN) Payment Framework*. Available at: http://www.institute.nhs.uk/world_class_commissioning/pct_portal/cquin.html (accessed 24 June 2010).

OECD (2009). *Health at a Glance 2009 – OECD Indicators*. Paris: OECD.

Oliver, A. (2005) The English National Health Service, 1979–2005. *Health Economics*, 14: S75–S99.

Oliver, A. and Mossialos, E. (2005) European health systems reforms: looking backward to see forward? *Journal of Health Policy, Politics and Law. Special Issue: Legacies and Latitude in European Health Policy*, 30(1–2): 7–28.

Peters, D., El-Saharty, S., Siadat, B., Janovsky, K. and Vujicic, M. (eds) (2009) *Improving Health Service Delivery in Developing Countries: From Evidence to Action. Directions in development*. Washington, DC: The World Bank.

Propper, C., Sutton, M., Whitnall, P. and Windmeijer, F. (2010) Incentives and targets in hospital care: evidence from a natural experiment. *Journal of Public Economics*, 94: 318–35.

Redding, D. (2010) Scottish health boards tap into public spirit. *Health Service Journal*, 17 June. http://www.hsj.co.uk/news/policy/scottish-health-boards-tap-into-public-spirit/5015984.article (accessed 24 June 2010).

Riccio, J., Dechausay, N., Greenberg, D., Miller, C., Rucks, Z. and Verma, N. (2010) *Toward Reduced Poverty across Generations: Early Findings from New York City's Conditional Cash Transfer Programme*. New York: MDRC.

Schut, F.T. and Van de Ven, W.P.M.M. (2005) Rationing and competition in the Dutch health-care system. *Health Economics*, 14: S59–S74.

Shipman Inquiry (2005) *The Shipman Inquiry: Final Report January 2005*. Available at: http://www.the-shipman-inquiry.org.uk/home.asp (accessed 1 January 2006).

Smith, J.A., Curry, N., Mays, N. and Dixon, J. (2010) *Where Next for Commissioning in the English NHS?* London: The Nuffield Trust and the King's Fund.

Stephan, A. and Sommersguter-Reichmann, M. (2005) Monitoring political decision-making and its impact in Austria. *Health Economics*, 14: S7–S23.

Stevens, S. (2004) Reform strategies for the English NHS. *Health Affairs*, 23: 37–44.

Sutherland, K. and Coyle, N. (2009) *Quality in Healthcare in England, Wales, Scotland, Northern Ireland: An Intra-UK Chartbook*. London: Health Foundation.

Thaler, R.H. and Sunstein, C. (2008) *Nudge: Improving Decisions about Health, Wealth, and Happiness*. New Haven, CT: Yale University Press.

The Coalition Government (2010) *The Coalition: Our programme for Government*. London: Cabinet Office. Available at: http://programmeforgovernment.hmg .gov.uk/files/2010/05/coalition-programme.pdf (accessed 24 June 2010).

Tuohy, C. H. (1999) *Accidental Logics: The Dynamics of Change in the Health Care Arena in the United States, Britain and Canada*. Oxford: Oxford University Press.

Wen, M. (2009) *Averting Crisis: A Path forward for China's Healthcare System*. Carnegie Endowment for International Peace. Issue brief from Beijing, March 2009. Available at: http://www.carnegieendowment.org/files/China_Healthcare_ System_Full_Text.pdf (accessed 16 May 2011).

Wilkinson, E. (2008) Can you pay people to be healthy? *Lancet*; 371(9621): 1325–6.

Wörz, M., and Busse, R. (2005) Analysing the impact of health-care system change in the EU member states – Germany. *Health Economics*, 14: S133–S149.

Zweifel, P. (2000) Reconsidering the role of competition in health care markets in Switzerland. *Journal of Health Politics, Policy and Law* 25(5): 937–44.

Websites and resources

Commonwealth Fund. Contains an up-to-date analysis of the state of healthcare and reform in the USA and some international issues: http://www.cmwf.org/.

Department of Health. Contains a full description of policies in the English NHS and useful sources of data: http://www.dh.gov.uk/Home/fs/en.

European Observatory on Health Systems and Policies. For up-to-date description and analysis of health sector reform in Europe:
http://www.lse.ac.uk/collections/LSEHealthAndSocialCare/europeanObservatoryOn HealthCareSystems.htm.

Health Affairs. A journal covering health sector reform in the USA but also some European countries: http://www.healthaffairs.org/.

Journal of Health Policy, Politics and Law. A journal covering the political science aspects of health reform in the Americas and Europe: http://jhppl.yale.edu/.

King's Fund. Contains analysis of health sector reform in England:
www.kingsfund.org.uk.

National Assembly for Wales. Contains information about healthcare policies and relevant data for Wales: http://www.wales.gov.uk/subihealth/index.htm.

Northern Ireland Executive. Contains information about health policy in Northern Ireland: http://www.northernireland.gov.uk/az2.htm.

Nuffield Trust. Contains analysis of health sector reform in England and the UK: www.nuffieldtrust.org.uk.

Organisation for Economic Co-operation and Development (OECD). Contains an analysis of international health policies, and also key data on health and healthcare for all OECD countries:

http://www.oecd.org/home/0,2987,en_2649_201185_1_1_1_1_1,00.html.

Scottish Office. Contains a description of policies in the Scottish NHS and useful sources of data: http://www.scotland.gov.uk/Home.

World Health Organization Regional Office for Europe. Contains information about a range of health issues and health policies across Europe:

http://www.euro.who.int/programmesprojects.

CHAPTER 3

Financing healthcare: funding systems and healthcare costs

Suzanne Robinson

Introduction

Healthcare funding in developed countries accounts for a large percentage of gross domestic product (GDP) and is usually the largest single industry. Increased demand and technological advances mean that healthcare expenditure continues to grow, while on the supply side there is a constant pressure because resources are scarce. Policy-makers face tough decisions in this regard. Do they increase funding, contain costs, or both? Policy-makers and managers alike need to balance the books and thus find enough revenue to meet healthcare expenditure. The recent economic downturn and increasing financial pressures make public sector borrowing a less attractive economic policy option in developed countries, thus policy-makers are increasingly looking towards the structure and organization of healthcare systems – including revenue collection (the demand side) and organization of service provision (the supply side) – as a means of managing ever-increasing pressures on health expenditure. 'As resources become scarce, providing more efficient public services with less spending has become an absolute necessity' (Vraniali 2010: 2). Redesigning budget processes and allocation of funds between services has become a key element across the developed world (Vraniali 2010). At the time of writing, a number of systems are currently going through radical reform, and these include the United States, Germany, Australia and France. This chapter explores four areas relevant to financing of healthcare in developed countries:

- The first section draws on the work of Mossialos et al. (2002) and Murray and Frenk (2000) to provide a framework by which to facilitate understanding and analysis of healthcare funding.
- The second section draws on data from the Organization for Economic Co-operation and Development (OECD).
- The third section looks at examples of how money is distributed through healthcare systems.
- Finally, the fourth section identifies some of the pressures on healthcare costs and expenditure.

Healthcare funding: an analytical framework

Financing and provision of healthcare represent a transaction between providers who transfer resources to patients, and patients or third parties who transfer resources to providers. This has been described as the healthcare triangle, see Figure 3.1 (Mossialos et al. 2002).

While different countries have different funding systems in operation, the underlying logic is the same. The simplest transaction occurs when direct payments are made between patients and providers of healthcare services. Uncertainty surrounding ill health and the need for expensive healthcare means that most healthcare systems have a third party element, that is, a body that collects the resource from individuals and makes decisions as to how to allocate that resource to providers, this third party being either public or private. This third party element offers financial protection against the risk of becoming ill and allows that risk to be shared among the protected population. Third party provision may cover part or all of a country's population, for once revenue has been collected, it can then be used to reimburse either patients or providers of services. The healthcare funding system is therefore a way in which funds are collected, either via primary (patient) or secondary (third party) sources, and hence distributed to providers.

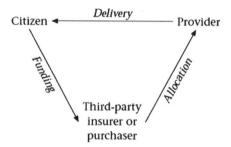

FIGURE 3.1 The healthcare triangle
Source: Mossialos et al. (2002).

Functional components of healthcare financing

The functional components of healthcare financing can be subdivided into three categories: revenue collection; fund-pooling; and purchasing (Murray and Frenk 2000). The combination of these functions varies between countries. Figure 3.2 illustrates various funding sources, mechanisms and collection agents that operate in healthcare systems.

Revenue collection

Revenue collection refers to the way money is moved around the system and is concerned with: sources of funding (examples include individuals or employers);

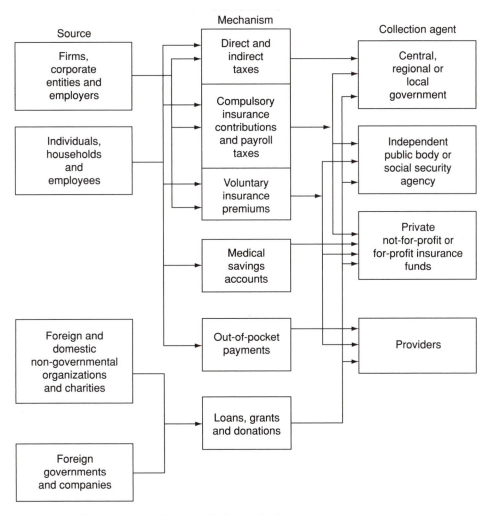

FIGURE 3.2 Funding sources, contribution mechanisms and collection agents
Source: Mossialos et al. (2002).

mechanisms of funding (examples include direct or indirect taxes and voluntary in-surance); and collection agents (examples include central or regional government). The main mechanisms of revenue collection are through taxation, social insurance contributions, voluntary insurance premiums and out-of-pocket payments.

Taxes can be levied on individuals, households and businesses through direct taxes, and they can also be applied to transactions and commodities in the form of indirect taxes, such as taxes on fuel and alcohol. Direct and indirect taxes can be collected nationally, regionally and locally, with variation occurring between countries. Social insurance contributions are income-related and generally shared between employees and employers, with contributions usually collected by an independent public body. Private insurance contributions are paid independently by individuals, as part of an employment package, with employers paying all or part of the insurance. Patients may incur out-of-pocket payments for some or all of their healthcare. The strategic design of revenue collection can affect the performance of a health system (Murray and Frenk 2000).

Fund-pooling

Fund-pooling (or risk-pooling as it is sometimes called) is when a population's healthcare revenues are accumulated, with financial risk being shared between the population, rather than by each individual contributor. Fund-pooling incorporates both equity and efficiency considerations: equity in so far as risk is shared among the pool or group, rather than it being assumed by individuals; and efficiency as pooling can lead to increases in population health and reduce uncertainty around healthcare expenditure. (Smith and Witter 2004: iii).

Fund-pooling is distinct from revenue collection, for not all mechanisms of collection, such as medical savings accounts (which currently operate in the USA and are a tax-free savings account for medical expenses), and out-of-pocket payments enable risk-pooling. Factors associated with this approach that may affect performance include: separation of fund pools for different population groups; and subsidization across different risk groups (Murray and Frenk 2000).

Purchasing is the allocation of fund-pools to healthcare providers. There is a wide range of purchasing activities in operation, some involve governments acting as both collection agent (raising revenue through general or local taxation), and purchaser of services from providers. Such countries include the UK, Finland and Denmark (Ervik 1998; Hurst and Siciliani 2003). Strategic issues include decisions on what is to be purchased, including the selection criteria for interventions. Other aspects include how to make a choice of providers and which mechanisms to use for purchasing. A large number of purchasers can lead to competition between purchasers and increased demands on providers (Murray and Frenk 2000).

There are policy issues which relate to all of these categories. The main policy decisions tend to focus on the equity and efficiency of healthcare systems. Equity of financing will depend on both the level and distribution of contributions, for example, how much money is needed and who should contribute. Equity of access relates to accessibility of services and to issues around informal payments and user charges (Wagstaff and van Doorslaer 2000; Dixon et al. 2004). Efficiency is largely concerned with management and distribution of resources and can be influenced by pooling and purchasing mechanisms (see Dixon et al. 2004 for a more detailed discussion). Policymakers are faced with ensuring resources are spent efficiently, in order to maximize the health benefits of the population, while also making sure that they safeguard ethical principles over access and distribution of resource.

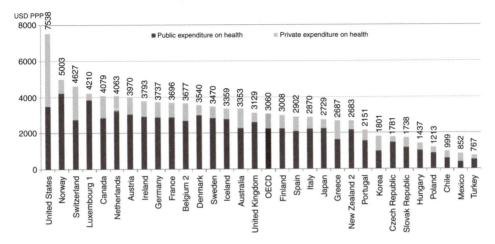

FIGURE 3.3 Total health expenditure per capita (US$ PPP, 2008)
Source: OECD Health Data (2010b), copyright OECD (2010).

Funding healthcare

Figure 3.3 presents figures on the total health spending on healthcare in 2008 across OECD countries. The OECD median total health spend was US$3060. The USA had the highest healthcare spend per capita ($7538) of all the countries assessed, and is well over the average OECD spend. The next biggest spenders are Norway and Switzerland, who, while they spent less than the USA, still spend around 50 per cent more than the OECD average. Turkey had the lowest spend per head at $767.

The economic downturn in 2008–09 saw GDP falling across countries and healthcare costs rising, leading to a sharp increase in the ratio of health spending to GDP. In Ireland, the percentage of GDP increased from 7.5 per cent to 8.7 per cent and in Spain it rose from 8.4 per cent to 9 per cent (OECD 2010a, 2010b).

Table 3.1 presents the share of expenditure as a proportion of GDP for a selection of OECD countries. Figures show a rise in healthcare expenditure in all countries over the last 40 years. The highest expenditure was in the USA, France, Germany, Belgium and Canada. Even in the UK, where increases in healthcare spending have tended to be less than most other OECD countries, there has been an increase in healthcare expenditure. Allowing for inflation, the UK National Health Service (NHS) in 2002 cost seven times more than in 1949, with the average cost per person rising nearly six times above the 1949 level (OHE 2004).

Rises in healthcare expenditure across OECD countries are due to a number of factors including: increased pay and price inflation; population growth; expansion of services and increase in technological advances. The fact that healthcare sectors are one of the major employers in almost all economies means that the pay bill is the single largest component of many healthcare budgets. It is suggested that on average

TABLE 3.1 Total expenditure on health as a percentage of GDP in selected OECD countries, 1960–2006

	1960	1970	1980	1990	2000	2001	2002	2003	2004	2005	2006
Australia	3.8	4.3	6.3	6.9	8.3	8.4	8.6	8.5	8.8	8.7	8.7
Austria	4.3	5.2	7.4	8.3 b	9.9	10.1	10.1	10.3	10.4	10.4	10.2
Belgium	3.4	3.9	6.3	7.2	8.6	8.7	9.0	10.2 b	10.5 e	10.3 b	10.0 e
Canada	5.4	6.9	7.0	8.9	8.8	9.3	9.6	9.8	9.8	9.9	10.0
Denmark	3.6	5.9	8.9	8.3	8.3	8.6	8.8	9.3 b	9.5	9.5	9.6
Finland	3.8	5.5	6.3	7.7	7.2	7.4	7.8	8.1	8.2	8.5	8.3
France	3.8	5.4	7.0	8.4	10.1	10.2	10.5	10.9	11.0	11.1	11.0
Germany	4.7	6.2	8.4	8.3	10.3	10.4	10.6	10.8	10.6	10.7	10.5
Greece	3.6	5.4	5.9	6.6	7.9 b	8.8	9.1	9.0	8.7	9.4	9.5
Iceland	3.0	4.7	6.3	7.8	9.5	9.3	10.2	10.4 b	9.9	9.4	9.1
Ireland	3.7	5.1	8.3	6.1 b	6.3	6.9	7.1	7.3	7.5	7.3	7.1
Italy	3.6	5.1	7.0	7.7	8.1	8.2	8.3	8.3	8.7	8.9	9.0
Japan	3.0	4.6	6.5	6.0	7.7	7.9	8.0	8.1	8.0	8.2	8.1
Netherlands		5.7	7.4	8.0	8.0	8.3	8.9	9.8 b	10.0 e	9.8 e	9.7 e
New Zealand		5.2	5.9	6.9	7.7	7.8	8.2	8.0	8.5	9.1	9.4
Norway	2.9	4.4	7.0	7.6	8.4	8.8	9.8	10.0	9.7	9.1	8.6
Spain	1.5	3.5	5.3	6.5	7.2	7.2	7.3	8.1 b	8.2	8.3	8.4
Sweden	4.4	6.8	8.9	8.2	8.2	9.0 b	9.3	9.4	9.2	9.2	9.1
Switzerland	4.9	5.4	7.3	8.2	10.2	10.6	10.9	11.3	11.3	11.2	10.8
United Kingdom	3.9	4.5	5.6	5.9	7.0	7.3	7.6	7.8	8.1	8.2	8.5
United States	5.2	7.1	9.0	12.2	13.6	14.3	15.1	15.6	15.6	15.7	15.8

Key: b: break in series; e: estimate; d: differences in methodology
Source: OECD Health Data (2010a), copyright OECD (2010).

between 40–50 per cent of total expenditure goes on wages and salaries (Hernandez et al. 2006). Ginsburg and Nichols (2003) suggest that prices are crucial drivers in cross-national differences in health spending. For example, in the USA where health expenditure is high, salaries, medical equipment, pharmaceutical and other supplies tend to be more costly than other OECD countries (OECD 2010a). The fact that markets, including labour markets, do not satisfy conditions necessary in the perfect competitive market leads to varying degrees of monopoly power on the supply side of the market and varying degrees of monopsony power (that is when the product or service of a number of sellers is only demanded by one buyer) on the demand side (Ginsburg and Nichols 2003; Donaldson and Gerard 2005). Thus, functional components of healthcare financing do have an effect on healthcare expenditure, with bargaining power of both providers and payers of services differing between countries.

Figure 3.4 presents the public and private healthcare expenditure as a percentage of total healthcare expenditure for a selection of OECD countries. All countries have a mix of both public and private health expenditure with Denmark, Japan, Luxembourg, Sweden and the UK all having over 80 per cent health expenditure incurred through public funds. Public funds include state, regional and local government bodies and social security schemes. Even in the USA, which has the largest private expenditure on healthcare (55 per cent), public healthcare expenditure still accounts for 45 per cent of total health expenditure.

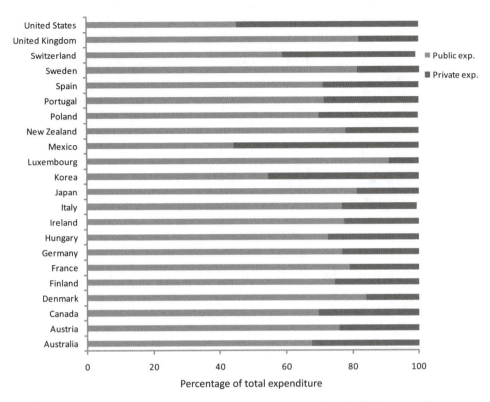

FIGURE 3.4 Public and private spending on healthcare as a percentage of total healthcare expenditure selection of OECD countries, 2007
Source: OECD Health Data (2010a) copyright OECD (2010).

Revenue generation

This section outlines the different methods of revenue generation and their associated effects on healthcare costs. Insurance-based methods – private or public, compulsory or voluntary – are in operation across all healthcare systems in OECD countries. In addition, all countries have some form of direct payments by citizens made up of charges and/or co-payments. The different types of revenue generation methods include:

1 private insurance
2 taxation
   1 different sources – direct or indirect
   2 different types – general or hypothecated
   3 different levels – national/local
3 social health insurance
4 charges and co-payments.

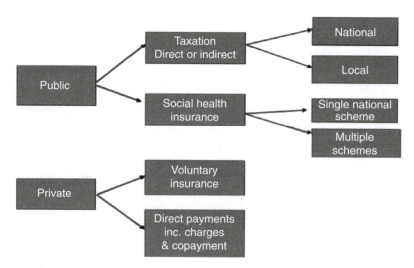

FIGURE 3.5 Different forms of revenue generation methods

Figure 3.5 highlights the public and private revenue sources. Methods which fall within the public sphere (with the exception of indirect tax) use financial mechanisms to achieve a set of social objectives, such as redistributing resources across the population. In contrast, private sources such as voluntary insurance focus on an individual's need and self-interest, rather than that of the wider population (Saltman et al. 2004).

Choice of revenue generation methods is strongly influenced by the underlying norms and values of a society. For some societies, healthcare is seen as a social and collective good, while for others it is perceived as a commodity that can be bought and sold (Saltman 1997). However, even in countries that subscribe to the latter, there are usually funding mechanisms that allow for redistribution of funds to those who are unable to pay for healthcare.

Direct taxation is often seen as a progressive means of raising revenue, while indirect taxes such as value added tax (VAT) are more regressive in nature (O'Donoghue et al. 2004; Glennerster 2006). Studies have shown that poorer households pay a higher percentage of gross income in indirect taxes (O'Donoghue et al. 2004; Manning et al. 1989). From a health perspective, it could be argued that indirect taxes on things like cigarettes and alcohol are justifiable as they can lead to a reduction in consumption of these harmful products (see Manning et al. 1989, for further discussion). Nonetheless, '[i]ndirect taxes have had a growing part to play in counteracting the equalizing effect of direct taxation since they fall most heavily on the poor' (Glennerster 2006: 28). All OECD countries have some form of indirect taxation on certain goods and services. However, it is difficult to ascertain how much of this revenue is used to fund healthcare.

General taxation

The UK is an example of a healthcare system that is funded predominantly through general (direct) taxation. The UK Treasury sets out what budget will be spent on healthcare, and once that is set, resources are distributed to the purchasers of care, with the majority of services being free to users at the point of provision. Other countries that primarily use a universal tax-based funding mechanism include Denmark, Finland, New Zealand, Australia, Canada and Spain.

Funding healthcare through general taxation is seen as a progressive way of raising revenue. In most countries, tax is proportional to income, with those on higher incomes paying more tax than those on lower incomes, thus allowing for redistribution of resources from wealthy to the poor, from healthy to sick, and from those of working age to the young and old. In addition, the financing of services is divorced from provision of services, which is important for equitable access, with resource being based on clinical need rather than ability to pay (Savedoff 2004).

However, there is evidence to suggest that access to care is also affected by age, gender, education, wealth and race (for further discussion, see Pickett and Wilkinson 2010). Further, while tax-based models are progressive, the degree to which the whole system of funding is progressive depends on what other funding mechanisms are being utilized. For example, even though general taxation is used to fund healthcare in Portugal, the high share of out-of-pocket payments make the overall system regressive (Wagstaff and van Doorslaer 2000; Ping Yu et al. 2008) and similar concerns have influenced recent health policy developments in New Zealand, where co-payments for primary care have traditionally been high.

An additional advantage of tax-based revenue collection systems is that they are relatively efficient to administer. This is due to the collection of funds being through the existing taxation system, and thus not incurring additional administration costs for the health sector. The fact that government is the main payer for and purchaser of healthcare allows general taxation to act as a mechanism to control costs, with providers not easily being able to increase revenue by raising prices or premiums, as in private insurance and social insurance (Baggott 2004; van der Zee and Kroneman 2007).

The major disadvantages of a system based on general taxation include the fact that health services are closely tied to the economy and government taxation policies. In times of economic recession, reductions in tax revenues can have major effects on the health budget. The recent global economic downturn has meant that all countries have had less to spend on public sector services and tough choices around public sector healthcare spending are having to be made. This is particularly evident in countries like Spain, Greece and Ireland who have seen the largest rises in the ratio of health spending to GDP. Such pressures impact on all insurance-based systems (public and private) that rely on employer and employee-based contributions. Lavarreda et al. (2010: 1) suggest that in 2008 around two million Californians lost their private insurance due to the economic crisis, meaning that individuals had to rely on public programmes, or were simply not covered.

In general taxation systems, all public services need to compete for limited revenues which means there will always be winners and losers. Health budgets may suffer if government gives high priority to public services other than health and/or to low taxation rather than public services. It can be difficult to raise revenue because an increase in the health budget means that the budget to other services (such as education and defence) may need to be cut, or tax increased, both of which can prove unpopular with electorates. It is suggested that tax raises might be more popular if the government were explicit about their spending intentions, with, for example, taxes earmarked for health. Commentators suggest that the population are often more comfortable with rises in taxation to pay for healthcare in comparison to other non-health demands (Normand 1992; Mossialos et al. 2002). The fact that taxes are not hypothecated in many countries means that the population is unable to judge the fiscal viability (i.e. affordability) of health services.

Local taxation

Denmark's healthcare is predominantly funded through general taxation, but unlike the UK, its main source of funding is from local (county and municipal) taxation. Analysis has shown that local taxes are generally less progressive than national taxes (i.e. local taxes often take a larger proportion of tax from people whose income is low), as is demonstrated by the experience of Denmark and other countries such as Finland, Sweden and Switzerland, who also have a high proportion of revenue generated by local taxation (McDaid 2003; Health Policy Consensus Group 2005; Ping Yu et al. 2008).

In the absence of a national system of redistribution, local taxation could therefore create regional inequity. For example, if local tax rates vary by region, this could lead to horizontal inequities (i.e. compromising equal treatment for equal need, irrespective of any other characteristic such as income, sex, race, etc., see Mossialos et al. 2002). Variations in local tax rates for both Denmark and Sweden suggest that horizontal inequities are evident when such mechanisms of revenue collection are used (Mossialos et al. 2002). There are suggestions that local taxation could lead to inefficient resource allocation and priority setting (Mossialos et al. 2002). In an attempt to curtail costs and fragmentation, increase efficiency and sustainability of financing across the system, the Australian government has increased central government control over financing and governance of healthcare at the local level (Smith 2010).

The decentralization of local tax funding is seen as a major advantage over national taxation as the clear link between revenue raised and local spending allows potentially much greater transparency. There is also greater direct political accountability for healthcare funding and expenditure, as local politicians are likely to be closer to the electorate than their national counterparts. A further advantage is that healthcare is separated from national priorities with this mechanism of decentralization, allowing local needs to be met more easily.

Social insurance

Social health insurance tends to be hypothecated tax, that is funds are specifically earmarked for health. Like general taxation, the system of social health insurance is redistributive and allows for universal entitlement to healthcare services and is based on need rather than ability to pay (Glaser 1991). There are large variations in the features of social health insurance systems across countries. Box 3.1 sets out some of the typical features of social health insurance systems.

> ## Box 3.1: *Typical features of social health insurance systems*
>
> - Insurance is compulsory for the majority of or the whole population.
> - Insured individuals pay a regular, usually wage-based contribution, which may be flat rate or variable.
> - Employers may also pay a contribution.
> - There may be one or more independent 'sickness funds' or social insurers.
> - Individuals may or may not be able to choose which sickness fund they join.
> - Transfers are made from general taxation to cover premiums of the unemployed, retired and other disadvantaged and vulnerable groups.
> - All allow the pooling of revenue and typically, insurance is not risk-related.
>
> Adapted from McDaid (2003: 167).

Countries which operate a predominantly social health insurance system include Germany, France, Austria, Switzerland, Belgium, Holland, the Netherlands, Luxembourg and Japan. In addition, a number of central and eastern European countries have also adapted such models, including Hungary, Lithuania, the Czech Republic, Estonia, Latvia, Slovakia and Poland (Saltman et al. 2004). A number of countries such as the Netherlands, Germany and France have made substantial changes to their funding systems. These changes are due to the ever increasing financial pressures which have been further exacerbated by the recent economic downturn.

Under social health insurance schemes, premiums tend to be collected directly by sickness funds (Austria, France, Switzerland) or distributed from a central state-run fund (Israel, Luxembourg) with Belgium using both methods. With the exception of France and Switzerland, sickness funds are private not-for-profit organizations that are governed by an elected board. The rules under which sickness funds operate are usually governed by national legislation (Saltman et al. 2004). The funds use revenues raised to fund contracts with providers who vary in terms of private not-for-profit, private for-profit and publicly operated. The number, size and structure of sickness funds vary between countries. Busse and Riesberg (2004) noted that Luxembourg had nine sickness funds while Germany had 1000 funds in the early 1990s which was reduced to 355 in 2002 (see Saltman et al. 2004 for further discussion of the organization and structure of social insurance schemes). Recent healthcare policy in Germany means that by 2011 employee and employer contributions will flow directly to the healthcare fund (*Gesundheitsfonds*). In France, almost all residents are covered by one of the three social insurance schemes: general; agricultural; or self-employed non-agricultural. Under this system, resources are levied (as a social insurance contribution) from employees and employers and, as with general taxation, these contributions are generally set as a proportion of income, regardless of health need.

Funding using social health insurance tends to be more transparent than tax-based methods and traditionally this meant that health services were distanced from the political arena, with concerns tending to be around contribution rates rather than political or health service matters. However, recent economic pressures mean that governments are looking at funding mechanisms including social health insurance in an attempt to curb public spending. In Germany, recent reforms meant that compulsory insurance, either statutory (through one of the 170 not-for-profit organizations) or private, can be provided by authorized German health insurers only, and this legislation came into effect in January 2009.

The majority of social health insurance systems do require some level of subsidies from general and/or local taxation. For example, a large part of hospital care is paid for by general taxation in Austria and Switzerland. Recent reforms in Germany mean that for the first time taxes will contribute to health insurance funds – this supplement is being introduced to finance growing healthcare costs. Van der Zee and Kroneman (2007) compared social insurance systems with general taxation-based approaches and found that the latter seemed better at cost containment, while the former demonstrated greater population satisfaction with the system.

In 2006, the health insurance system in the Netherlands underwent fundamental market reforms. The 'private' social health insurance system in the Netherlands is compulsory, with all health insurers offering standardized level of services. The aim of the reforms was to increase market forces through the expansion of the private insurance sector, allowing individual choice (in terms of insurer and packages available). This in turn (it was hoped) would increase efficiency and quality of care. Further, regulation of private insurers would allow more equitable coverage. Research suggests that the system has provided more transparency and opened up consumer choice, with dramatic consumer mobility at the onset of the reform, but relatively little shift after that (Greβ et al. 2007; van de Ven and Schut 2008). A recent study by Davis et al. (2010) suggests that the Netherlands as a health system ranks third after the UK (1st) and Germany (2nd) for efficiency and first for equity. However, other studies suggest that the Dutch model does not meet policy-makers' expectations in terms of achieving cost containment, with insurance premiums rising and insurance companies reporting large losses (Rosenua and Lako 2008).

Private insurance

Private insurance can be classified into the following categories: substitutive; supplementary; or complementary (Mossialos et al. 2002). Private healthcare insurance markets often develop around publicly funded systems and in many countries private insurance plays a residual role in terms of healthcare funding. For example, in systems such as the UK where private insurance provides supplementary cover to the public system and can enable faster access to certain services such as elective hospital care or, as in the case of France, it can 'provide reimbursement for copayments required by the public system' (Buchmueller and Couffinhal 2004: 4).

In Germany, individuals earning higher incomes or those who are self-employed can opt out of the public health insurance system. This form of substitutive insurance undermines the redistribution effect of taxation or social insurance and leads to a regressive system of funding. Furthermore, as income is related to risk of ill health (the poorer you are, the more likely you are to fall ill), substitutive insurance means that those with the poorest health or at greatest risk are left in the public system, which reduces the overall pooling and risk-sharing mechanism in the health system, and those with the lowest income could potentially end up paying the higher premiums.

Systems that rely heavily on private insurance are often criticized due to their inequitable nature; that is, these systems are based on a person's ability to pay for care rather than on clinical need (Wilper et al. 2009). Around 16 per cent of Americans had no health insurance coverage in 2008, with the majority of the uninsured being those on the lowest incomes (Wilper et al. 2009; the Commonwealth Fund 2010). Van Doorslaer et al. demonstrate that 'unequal distribution of private health insurance coverage by income contributes to the phenomenon that the better-off and the less well-off do not receive the same mix of services' (2008: 97).

Recent healthcare reforms introduced in the USA by the Obama administration in 2010 aim to reduce the inequities inherent in the American system. The Patient Protection and Affordable Care Act (PPACA) is intended to provide affordable health insurance coverage for the majority of American citizens, improve access to primary care and reduce overall healthcare costs (Doherty 2010).

At the time of writing, the legislation has only recently been signed in law and while the bill is more than 2000 pages long, there still remain a number of areas to be decided (Aaron and Reischauer 2010). Thus, it is too early to tell what effect these complex polices will have on the financing and delivery of healthcare in America. Critics of the reforms suggest that they still do not provide universal coverage which is an 'affront to the notion that healthcare is a fundamental human right' (Yamey 2010: 1674). Others suggest that while the reforms address one of the major barriers to care (insurance), the lack of primary care physicians could limit access to primary care (Bristol 2010). Himmelstein and Woolhandler (2010: 1778) suggest that the 'new law will pump additional funds into the currently dysfunctional, market driven system, pushing up costs that are already twice those of most other wealthy nations'. They also claim that the reform does little to address inadequate coverage and that many Americans could still end up bankrupt if they had a serious illness (Himmelstein and Woolhandler 2010). In contrast, the work of the Commonwealth Fund suggests that the reforms *could* improve efficiency and equity (Commonwealth Fund, 2010).

In countries such as Australia, the UK, New Zealand, Germany and Spain, private health insurance plays a supplementary role, with this being an additional option to add to public insurance for those who desire and can afford it. In Australia, individuals are eligible for a government rebate on private health insurance, and this policy is aimed at encouraging take-up and retention of private health insurance.

An advantage of supplementary insurance is that it allows quicker access to services for people holding private insurance, especially in systems such as the UK and New Zealand which have traditionally experienced significant waiting times for diagnostic tests or elective treatments (Hussey and Anderson 2003). Complementary insurance has the ability to free up capacity in the public system by allowing those who can afford to pay to receive treatment in the private sector. Those who oppose a system of supplementary private insurance claim that it encourages a two-tier system that allows quicker access to services for those who can afford to pay and thus should not be allowed on overall equity grounds.

Private insurance systems tend to incur higher administrative costs per insured person than public health coverage systems (Litow 2006). The higher administrative costs of private insurers tend to be ascribed to marketing, underwriting and other costs such as billing, provision of care and product innovation (Colombo and Tapay 2004). Countries like the United States, which has a relatively high percentage of private insurance, have the greatest difficulty in controlling healthcare costs and tend to have the biggest healthcare spend per head of population.

Moral hazard and supplier-induced demand

Insurance reduces the cost of treatment at the point of consumption and makes 'illness' a less unwanted state. This is often termed the moral hazard associated with insurance i.e. the fact of being insured leads to over-provision of services to these insured people. Moral hazard can also occur on the supply side with medical staff not having to bear the full cost of the decision over supplying treatment. This is termed a supplier-induced demand (see Donaldson and Gerard 2005).

There is some evidence to suggest that supplier-induced demand does take place in countries with private health insurance. For example, Savage and Wright (2003) suggest that moral hazard is evident in the Australian private health insurance system, with evidence of an increase in the expected length of hospital stay for people who are privately insured. In Germany, demand for physicians was higher among privately insured patients (Jurges 2007). However, moral hazard and supplier-induced demand are problems of insurance *per se* and can be a feature of both public and private insurance systems. A study by Birch (1988) showed that supplier-induced demand was evident in NHS UK dental surgery.

Out-of-pocket payments and charges for healthcare

Out-of-pocket payments and charges make up a proportion of healthcare spending in all health systems. This is the main mechanism that allows for price consciousness, that is, for patients to have a true notion of the costs of service and thus be able to make judgments on the price and (possibly) value for money of care received. Charges are often seen as a way of raising additional revenue. Even in a publicly funded system such as the English NHS, charges have been levied on things like prescriptions since the early days of the NHS.

As patients demand better quality services, including non-clinical services such as bedside computers, phones, televisions and car parking, the question arises as to where charges should stop. Nutritious food and pleasant surroundings are commonly considered to be essential components of good quality care, but each system has to make a judgement as to the point at which services are deemed to require an additional payment from users, and if this payment is to be levied on all or just some people according to their ability to pay. Charges and co-payments are criticized for being a regressive means of raising revenue, limiting access to services and discriminating against those on low incomes (Tamblyn et al. 2001).

Patient fee-for-service payments are used in a number of countries including New Zealand, Australia, France, Germany and the USA. There are a number of different schemes in operation across countries such as charges to visit family doctors and charges or co-payments for treatment or services (e.g. hospital stays or dental care) (Thomson et al. 2010). There is evidence to suggest that fees can deter patients from accessing services and that access problems have tended to be less in the UK and Canada where services tend to be free at the point of use (Thomson et al. 2010).

Recent policy reforms in New Zealand have tried to alleviate this problem by moving from fee-for-service payments to GPs, towards capitation funding of primary health organizations, although this mainly acts as a subsidy, and fee-for-service activity still forms part of the payment mechanism for many patients (Ashton 2005; McAvoy and Coster 2005; Cumming et al. 2008; Cumming and Mays, 2009). France and Germany have also adopted policies that are aimed at improving efficiencies, such as 'value-based' user charges. This involves reducing or waiving charges if individuals visit a physician or general practitioner and obtain referrals to specialist care rather than go directly, and if they have adhered to a coordinated care pathway. This is similar to the UK system where the general practitioner acts as the 'gatekeeper' in relation to accessing specialist and hospital services (Thomson et al. 2010).

While patient charges are often seen as a means of curtailing costs, there is a suggestion that they actually provide incentives to increase healthcare activity (Carrin and Hanvoravongchai 2003; Rosenthal 2005; Shomaker 2010). That is, they reward providers for productivity regardless of need, effectiveness or quality (Shomaker 2010).

A further inefficiency relating to fee-for-service is that patients are often reluctant to pay for elements of their care at the point of delivery, and appropriate systems have to be developed to collect charges. However, such systems can often be costly to administer and are not always cost-effective, especially when charges are small (Carrin and Hanvoravongchai 2003).

Funding distribution methods

Distribution of funding

Countries vary in terms of the methods used to distribute funds around the system, with a mix of systems in operation within and across countries. The three main methods are: cost-based reimbursement; global-based funding; and activity-based funding. This section will briefly outline and explore the different methods of distribution.

Cost-based reimbursement

Cost-based reimbursement involves making payments based on the cost incurred by patients. This involves detailing all costs for each item and provides no incentive to reduce costs and/or limit activity. This method assumes no financial risk, hence the more procedures performed, the more money that is reimbursed; and this could incentivize over-production (i.e. encourage supplier-induced demand) (Rice and Smith 2002; Street et al. 2007). Over the past 20 years there has been a shift away from this method of funding especially in public and private not-for-profit organizations (Crainich 2006).

Global-based funding

Global-based funding (sometimes referred to as block funding) involves placing a limit on the amount of money spent on healthcare. A fixed level of payment is agreed in advance of the treatment activity taking place, with a block of money going to healthcare providers. The amount of funding is often based on historical patterns and demographic data. This method of funding has tended to be seen more in social democratic countries as opposed to more private insurance-based health systems (Dredge 2004). One of the advantages of this method is that costs can be controlled, with a cap being placed on spending. Other advantages cited include: the certainty of funding (once the amount is agreed); it is usually easy and cheap to administer; and it can help improve the planning and co-ordination of services (Dredge 2004). This method provides the opportunity for healthcare priority setters to decide which services are needed (based on the population at risk) and then healthcare expenditure can be set prospectively against that plan (Rice and Smith 2002). The main criticisms of this approach are: that there is no incentive or reward for being productive or efficient; it is not sensitive to the volume and nature of the activity; it lacks transparency and fairness; and it limits the notions of the actual cost associated with treatment (Collier 2008).

Activity-based funding

This model of funding is called a variety of names including: episode funding; activity-funding; pay for performance; payment by results; case-mix; or diagnosis-related group funding. The escalating costs of healthcare have meant that there is increased pressure to make efficiency savings. One of the policy directives on funding has been the shift towards activity-based funding in a number of countries, and this focus tends to be around hospital services. Crainich et al. (2010: 1) note that 'In the last few years most of the OECD countries joined the US who had initiated an activity-based payment for both public and private hospitals as early as in 1983 for the Medicare program.'

This approach involves providers being paid for the activity they undertake. The activity-based system works on a flat amount per admission which is based on the patient diagnosis. In some countries such as England, price is fixed using regional tariffs, but in other countries such as the USA prices may vary between providers (hence under the former system competition on price is excluded). This approach provides incentives to improve efficiency, and the opportunity to increase transparency with regard to how the money is being spent in the system (Dixon 2005). Critics suggest that the incentive is to reward volume, not quality, of service, and that there is a real possibility of hospitals developing cost-cutting strategies that could compromise the quality of services. However, recent studies suggest that activity-based funding has made little real difference to the quality of care (Anderson 2009; Farrar et al. 2009).

A recent study comparing waiting times found that they are less of a problem in countries which rely mainly on activity-based funding than those that have mainly fixed budgets. Results from these countries suggest a rise in activity leads to shorter waiting times and shorter lengths of stay in hospital (Hurst and Siciliani 2003; Kjerstad 2003; Farrar et al. 2008; Farrar et al. 2009). However, in England, reduction in waiting times may be due to the impact of other government policies (Farrar et al. 2009). Norway and Sweden have also seen efficiency savings in relation to productivity, although these have declined over time (Street et al. 2007). In the USA, while length of stay decreased, so did the rise in acute illness after discharge and the need for nursing home or home healthcare (Anderson 2009).

While activity-based funding may help to improve efficiency, it could impact on equity and needs-based funding. With the focus being on productivity and throughput rather than on meeting population need, providers may 'cherry pick' patients and procedures which provide greater financial reward rather than providing services that meet the population's need. Further, there is no incentive to redirect patients to other services, e.g. from hospital to community-based services.

Pressures on healthcare costs/spending

The following is a government health warning: just when you thought your health spending was under control, the cost pressures are likely to start rising again (OECD 2003).

A common feature of all healthcare systems is the scarcity of resources necessary to meet the continually growing demand. Health expenditure continues to rise year on year in all OECD countries, with total spending on healthcare rising faster than economic growth (OHE 2004). The major factors which impact on increases in expenditure are the rise of new technology, the ageing population, and increasing population expectations. The cost of new technology is an issue for all countries. OECD data (2010a) show that there has been a major increase in the use of expensive new technology. For example, on average across OECD countries the use of Magnetic Resonance Imaging (MRI) units per capita has more than doubled since 2003 (6 machines per million population in 2000 to 13 in 2008). There is also a big difference in usage across countries with the usage in the USA being highest (OECD 2010a). The rise in expensive technology means that policy-makers are under increasing pressure to make efficient use of resources, while ensuring equitable access and provision (see Chapter 4 for further discussion on allocation of resources).

Other factors which impact on healthcare spending include: the increase in incidence of chronic illness (including cardiovascular disease, cancer and diabetes); rising levels of obesity; and the growth in consumerism.

The proportion of the world's people classified as older (defined as those over 65 years of age) is expected to rise from around 6.9 per cent of the total population to 15.6 per cent over the next 50 years (Mahal and Berman 2001). This demographic change is the result of a combination of increased life expectancy, a decline in mortality rates and subsequent declines in fertility rates. Projecting over the next decade, Cotis (2005: 1) suggests that

> [The] implications of these demographic developments mean that the number of elderly will rise significantly relative to the number of working age. By the mid-century there will be only two people of working age to support one person of 65 or more.

As the population age increases, so does the prevalence of certain diseases: 'Dementia presents a significant and urgent challenge to health and social care in terms of both numbers of people affected and cost' (Audit Commission, 2007: 11). It is estimated that in developed countries the number of people affected will be around 81.1 million by 2040, with even greater numbers predicted in the developing world (Ferri et al. 2005). The ageing population and the rise of chronic diseases such as dementia have implications for the cost and provision of healthcare and are a continual challenge for policy-makers and the wider healthcare system.

A further issue for healthcare funding and planning more widely is what Taleb (2007) terms 'Black Swan Events', i.e. rare events that are high impact and hard to predict, such as terrorist attacks, natural disasters, and outbreaks of disease. Such events can and do have a significant impact on the funding and planning of healthcare. Examples include the SARS outbreak in South-East Asia in 2003, the Swine flu pandemic of 2009, and 1918 flu pandemic (which killed over 50 million people). The cost and impact of such events on health systems are difficult to estimate and mean that additional healthcare resources above those estimated may be needed.

Conclusion

This chapter has explored the systems of funding used in the field of healthcare. All healthcare systems have some mixture of public and private financing. While the funding sources, mechanisms and collection agents vary between countries, all countries are feeling the pressure of increasing expenditure, scarce resources and the need to provide both an efficient and equitable healthcare service.

The past decade has seen the expanding use of expensive new technology such as cardiovascular equipment, dialysis machines and telemedicine. These advances, along with ongoing and more sophisticated developments in pharmaceuticals, have all had an impact on the range and quality of care provided to patients, yet are very costly to administer and place increasing pressure on overall healthcare spending (OECD 2003). The past 20 years have seen a rise in consumerism as societies gain greater access to health information, extending across regional and country borders, and users of healthcare systems increasingly see themselves as 'consumers'. Patients demand the latest technology that can assist in their care and expect to receive high quality services that offer good access and a degree of choice (Cotis 2005).

The increase in demands and the limitation of resources mean that governments are forced to look at the way in which funding systems operate. This can lead to changes in the way resources are collected and distributed around the health system (Kutzin 2008). As part of wider health system reform, a number of countries are currently adopting activity-based financing. The idea is that this more market-based approach will allow for greater transparency in terms of funding and activity and provide more market-like incentives (i.e. money follows activity), which in turn will lead to the provision of more efficient and high quality services.

The recent economic downturn means that even greater pressures are being placed on governments who are struggling with growing financial deficits and limited public resources. This is forcing countries to look at both funding mechanisms and distribution methods in an attempt to provide efficient and equitable healthcare. Furthermore, politicians and healthcare planners need to make tough decisions on the allocation of scarce resources and the setting of healthcare priorities.

Summary box

- Healthcare funding in developed countries accounts for a significant percentage of gross domestic product (GDP).
- Country variations exist between the amounts of healthcare expenditure both in terms of total healthcare spending and healthcare expenditure as a percentage of GDP.
- The United States has the largest percentage of private health activity and the highest healthcare expenditure in the world.
- All healthcare systems have some mix of public and private financing, and usually are based on some element of taxation.
- All countries have both private and public insurance systems in operation.
- The funding source, mechanism and collection agent vary greatly between countries.

- Growing demands for healthcare place increasing pressures on expenditure, with these increases being due to: technological advances; an ageing population; an expansion in the incidence of chronic disease; and rises in consumerism and patients' expectations.

- Increased demands and limited resources are leading policy-makers to look at the funding of healthcare structures as a mechanism to improve efficiency and quality of services.

Self-test exercises

1 What are the main factors that have influenced the rise in healthcare expenditure over the past 20 years? To what extent is this having an impact on your own country's healthcare system, and how is that impact visible?

2 The recent economic downturn is placing immense pressure on the available funding for healthcare. Drawing on examples from OECD countries, explore why and how governments may look to funding mechanisms and distributional methods to help them reduce the financial pressures. What impact could such changes have on the efficiency and equity of healthcare systems?

3 Thinking of your own country's funding contribution mechanisms, what are the major disadvantages evident in your system? How do these compare with other OECD countries?

4 Again thinking of your own country's funding contribution mechanisms of healthcare funding, what are the major advantages evident in your system? How do these relate to the experience of other OECD countries?

References and further reading

Aaron, H. J. and Reischauer, R. D. (2010) The war isn't over. *New England Journal of Medicine*, 362(14): 1259–61.

Anderson, G. (2009) The effects of payment by results. *BMJ*, 339: b3081.

Ashton, T. (2005) Recent developments in the funding and organisation of health services in New Zealand. *Australia and New Zealand Health Policy*, 2(9), 1–8.

Audit Commission (2008) *The Right Result? Payment by Results, 2003–07*. London: Audit Commission.

Baggott, R. (2004) *Health and Health Care in Britain*, 3rd edn. Basingstoke: Macmillan.

Birch, S. (1988) The identification of supplier-inducement in a fixed price system of health care provision: the case of dentistry in the United Kingdom. *Journal of Health Economics*, 7(1): 129–50.

Bristol, N. (2010) US passes landmark health-care bill. *Lancet*, 375: 1149–50.

Buchmueller, T. C. and Couffinhal, A. (2004) Private Health Insurance in France. OECD Working Paper 12. Paris: Organisation for Economic Co-operation and Development.

Busse, R. and Riesberg, A. (2004) Health Care Systems in Transition: Germany World Health Organization Regional Office Europe.

Carrin, G. and Hanvoravongchai, P. (2003) Provider payments and patient charges as policy tools for cost-containment: how successful are they in high-income countries? *Human Resources for Health*, 1(1): 6.

Collier, R. (2008) Activity-based hospital funding: boon or boondoggle? *CMAJ*, 178(11): 1407–1408.

Colombo, F. and Tapay, N. (2004) Private health insurance in OECD countries: the benefits and costs for individuals and health systems. OECD Working Paper 15. Paris: Organisation for Economic Co-operation and Development.

Commonwealth Fund (2010) Affordable Health Insurance, Commonwealth Fund. Available at: http://www.commonwealthfund.org/Content/Program-Areas/Health-Reform-Policy/Affordable-Health-Insurance.aspx (accessed 12 September 2010).

Commonwealth of Australia (2010) *A National Health and Hospitals Network for Australia's Future: Delivering the Reforms*. Canberra: Commonwealth of Australia.

Cotis, J. (2005) *Challenges of Demographics*. Paris: Organisation for Economic Co-operation and Development.

Crainich, D., Leleu, H. and Mauleon, A. (2006) Hospitals' activity-based financing system and manager–physician interaction. Discussion paper available at: xxchttp://lem.cnrs.fr/Portals/2/actus/DP_200605.pdf (accessed 14 July 2011).

Crainich, D., Leleu, H. and Mauleon, A. (2010) Hospitals' activity-based financing system and manager–physician interaction *The European Journal of Health Economics*. Available at: http://www.springerlink.com/content/gk8615336l0q6662/fulltext.pdf.

Cumming, J. and Mays, N. (2009) New Zealand's Primary Health Care Strategy: early effects of the new financing and payment system for general practice and future challenges. *Health Econ Policy Law*, 6(1): 1–21.

Cumming, J., Mays, N. and Gribben, B. (2008) Reforming primary health care: is New Zealand's primary health care strategy achieving its early goals? *Aust New Zealand Health Policy*, 5: 24.

Davis, K., Schoen, C. and Stremikis, K. (2010) *Mirror, Mirror on the Wall: How the Performance of the U.S. Health Care System Compares Internationally, 2010 Update*. New York: The Commonwealth Fund.

Dixon, J. (2005) Payment by results – new financial flows in the NHS. *British Medical Journal*, 328: 967–8.

Dixon, A., Langenbrunner, L. and Mossialos, E. (2004) Facing the challenges of health care financing. In J. Figueras, M. McKee, J. Cain and S. Lessof (eds) *Health Systems in Transition: Learning from Experience*. Geneva: World Health Organization, European Observatory on Health Systems and Policies.

Doherty, R. B. (2010) The certitudes and uncertainties of health care reform. *Ann Intern Med*, 152: 679–82.

Donaldson, C. and Gerard, K. (2005) *Economics of Health Care Financing: The Invisible Hand*. London: Palgrave Macmillan.

Dredge, R. (2004) Hospital global budgeting, HNP Discussion Paper. Washington: the International Bank for Reconstruction and Development, and the World Bank.

Duncan, A. and Jones, A. (2003) Economic incentives and tax hypothecation. CPE Working Paper 2/04, York: CPE.

Ervik, R. (1998) *The Redistribution Aim of Social Policy: A Comparative Analysis of Taxes, Tax Expenditure Transfers and Direct Transfers in Eight Countries.* New York: Syracuse University Press.

Farrar, S., Sussex, J., Yi, D., Sutton, M. et al. (2008) *National Evaluation of Payment by Results.* York: HERU.

Farrar, S., Yi, D., Sutton, M., Chalkley, M., Sussex, J. and Scott, A. (2009) Has payment by results affected the way that English hospitals provide care? Difference in differences analysis, *BMJ*, 339: b3047.

Ferri, C. P., Prince, M., Brayne, C., Brodaty, H., Fratiglioni, L., Ganguli, M. et al., for Alzheimer's Disease International (2005) Global prevalence of dementia: a Delphi consensus study. *The Lancet*, (366 9503): 2112–17.

Ginsburg, P. B. and Nichols, L. M. (2003) *The Health Care Cost-Coverage Conundrum Annual Essay.* Washington, DC: Centre for Studying Health System Change.

Glaser, W. A. (1991) *Health Insurance in Practice.* San Francisco, CA: Jossey-Bass.

Glennerster, H. (2006) *Tibor Barna: The Redistributive Impact of Taxes and Social Policies in the UK, 1937–2005.* London: London School of Economics.

Greβ, S., Manouguian, M. and Wasem, J. (2007) Health insurance reforms in the Netherlands, *CESIFO DICE Report*, 5(1): 63–7. Available at: www.cesifo.de/DocCIDL/CESifoDICEreport107.pdf (accessed 14 July 2011).

Health Policy Consensus Group (2005) *Options for Healthcare Funding.* London: Institute for the Study of Civil Society.

Hernandez, P., Dräger, S., Evans, D.B., et al. (2006) *Measuring Expenditure for the Health Workforce: Evidence and Challenges, Evidence and Information for Policy.* Geneva: World Health Organization.

Himmelstein, D.U. and Woolhandler, S. (2010) Observations on US health reform: Obama's reform: no cure for what ails us. *British Medical Journal*, 340: c1778.

Hurst, J. and Siciliani, L. (2003) Tackling excessive waiting times for elective surgery: a comparison of policies in twelve OECD countries. OECD Working Papers. Paris: Organisation for Economic Co-operation and Development.

Hussey, P. and Anderson, G.F. (2003) A comparison of single and multi-payer health insurance systems and options for reform. *Health Policy*, 66: 215–28.

Jurges, H. (2007) Health insurance status and physician-induced demand for medical services in Germany: new evidence from combined district and individual level data. Socio-Economic Panel Study Paper No. 8. Mannheim: Mannheim Research Institute for Economics of Aging.

Kjerstad, E.M. (2003) Prospective funding of general hospitals in Norway: incentives for higher production? *International Journal of Health Care Finance and Economics*, 3: 231–51.

Kutzin, J. (2008) *Health Financing Policy: A Guide for Decision Makers.* Geneva: WHO.

Lavarreda, S.A., Brown, R., Cabezas, L. and Roby, D.H. (2010) Number of uninsured jumped to more than eight million from 2007 to 2009. *Health Policy Research Brief,* (March) Los Angeles: UCLA Center for Health Policy Research.

Litow, M. E. (2006) *Medicare versus Private Health Insurance: The Cost of Administration.* Health Watch Newsletter, May 2006, Issue 52, Society of Actuaries.

McAvoy, B.R. and Coster, G.D. (2005) General practice and the New Zealand health reforms – lessons for Australia? *Australia and New Zealand Health Policy,* 2: 26.

McDaid, D. (2003) Who pays? Approaches to funding health care in Europe. *Consumer Policy Review,* 13(5): 166–72.

Mahal, A. and Berman, P. (2001) *Health Expenditure and the Elderly: A Survey of Issues in Forecasting, Methods Used and Relevance for Developing Countries.* Cambridge, MA: Burden of Disease Unit.

Manning, W.G., Keeler, E.B., Newhouse, J.P., Sloss, E.M. and Wasserman, J. (1989) The taxes of sin: do smokers and drinkers pay their way? *Journal of the American Medical Association,* 261(11): 1604–9.

Mossialos, E., Dixon, A., Figueras, J. and Kutzin, J. (eds) (2002) *Funding Healthcare: Options for Europe.* Maidenhead: Open University Press.

Murray, J.L. and Frenk, J. (2000) A framework for assessing the performance of health systems. *Bulletin of the World Health Organisation,* 78(6): 717–31.

Normand, C. (1992) Funding health care in the United Kingdom, *Br Med J,* 304: 768–70.

O'Donoghue, C., Baldini, M. and Mantovani, D. (2004) Modelling the redistributive impact of indirect taxes in Europe: an application of EUROMOD. EUROMOD Working Paper No. EM7/01

OECD (2003) Making health systems fitter. *OECD Observer,* 238(4). Available at: www .oecdobserver.org/news/fullstory.php/aid/1021/Making_health_systems_tter.html (accessed 12 September 2010).

OECD (2009) *OECD Health Data 2009: Statistics and Indicators for 30 Countries.* Paris: Organisation for Economic Co-operation and Development.

OECD (2010a) *OECD Health Data 2010: Statistics and Indicators for 30 Countries.* Paris: Organisation for Economic Co-operation and Development.

OECD (2010b) *Growing Health Spending Puts Pressure on Government Budgets According to OECD Health Data 2010.* Available at: www.oecd.org (accessed 12 September 2010).

OHE (Office of Health Economics) (2004) *Compendium of Health Statistics 2003–2004.* London: Office of Health Economics.

Pickett, K. and Wilkinson, R. (2010) *The Spirit Level: Why More Equal Societies Almost Always Do Better.* London: Penguin.

Ping Yu, C., Whynes D.K. and Sach T.H. (2008) Equity in health care financing: the case of Malaysia. *International Journal for Equity in Health,* 7: 15.

Reinhardt, U.E. (1990) *OECD Health Care Systems in Transition: The Search for Efficiency*. Paris: Organisation for Economic Co-operation and Development.

Rice, N. and Smith, P.C. (2002) Strategic allocation and funding decisions. In E. Mossialos, A. Dixon, J. Figueras, and J. Kutzin (eds) *Funding Healthcare: Options for Europe*. Maidenhead: Open University Press.

Rosenau, P.V. and Lako, C.J. (2008) An experiment with regulated competition and individual mandates for universal health care: The new Dutch health insurance system, *Journal of Health Politics, Policy and Law*, 33(6): 1031–55.

Rosenthal, M.B., Frank, R.G., Li, Z. and Epstein, A.M. (2005) Early experience with pay-for-performance: from concept to practice. *JAMA*, 294: 1788–93.

Saltman, R.B. (1997) Convergence versus social embeddedness: debating the future direction of health care systems. *European Journal of Public Health*, 7: 449–53.

Saltman, R.B. and Dubois, H.F.W. (2004) Individual incentive schemes in social health insurance systems. *Eurohealth*, 10(2): 21–5.

Saltman, R.B. and Dubois, H.F.W. (2005) Current reform proposals in social health insurance countries. *Eurohealth*, 11(1): 10–14.

Saltman, R.B., Reinhard B. and Figueras, J. (eds) (2004) *Social Health Insurance Systems in Western Europe. European Observatory on Health Systems and Policies Series*. Oxford: Oxford University Press.

Savage, E. and Wright, D. (2003) Moral hazard and adverse selection in Australian private hospitals, 1989–1990. *Journal of Health Economics*, 22(3): 331–59.

Savedoff, W. (2004) *Tax-Based Financing for Health Systems: Options and Experiences*. Discussion Paper No. 4. Geneva: WHO.

Shomaker, S.T. (2010) Health care payment reform and academic medicine: threat or opportunity? *Acad Med*. 85: 756–8.

Smith, P.C. and Witter, S.N. (2004) *Risk Pooling in Health Care Financing: The Implications for Health System Performance*. HNP Discussion Paper. Washington, DC: World Bank Organization.

Smith, S. (2010) *Health Reform*. NSW Parliamentary Library briefing paper 1/2010.

Stone, D.A. (1993) The struggle for the soul of health insurance. *Journal of Health Politics Policy and Law*, 18(2): 287–318.

Street, A., Vitikainen, K., Bjorvatn, A. and Hvenegaard, A. (2007) Introducing activity-based financing: a review of experience in Australia, Denmark, Norway and Sweden. Research Paper No. 30. York: CHE.

Taleb, N.N. (2007) *The Black Swan: The Impact of the Highly Improbable*. New York: Random House.

Tamblyn, R.R., Laprise, R., Hanley, J.A. et al. (2001) Adverse events associated with prescription drug cost sharing among poor and elderly persons. *Journal of the American Medical Association*, 285(4): 421–9.

Thomson, S., Foubister, T. and Mossialos, E. (2010) Can user charges make health care more efficient? *BMJ*, 341: c3759.

Timmins, N. (2005) Use of private sector health care in the NHS. *British Medical Journal*, 331: 1141–2.

Van Doorslaer, E., Savage, E. and Hall, J. (2008) Horizontal inequities in Australia's mixed public/private health care system, *Health Policy*, 86: 97–108.

Van de Ven, W.P.M.M., Beck, K., Buchner, F. et al. (2003) Risk adjustment and risk selection on the sickness fund market in five European countries. *Health Policy*, 65(1): 75–98.

Van de Ven, W.P.M.M. and Schut, F.T. (2008) Universal mandatory health insurance in the Netherlands: a model for the United States? *Health Affairs*, 27(3): 771–81.

Van der Zee, J. and Kroneman, M.N. (2007) Bismarck or Beveridge: a beauty contest between dinosaurs. *BMC Health Services Research*, 7: 94.

Vraniali, E. (2010) *Rethinking Public Financial Management and Budgeting in Greece: Time to Reboot?* Greece Paper No. 37, Hellenic Observatory Papers on Greece and Southeast Europe. London: LSE.

Wagstaff, A. and van Doorslaer, E. (2000) Equity in healthcare finance and delivery. In A. J. Culyer and J. P. Newhouse (eds) *Handbook of Health Economics*, Part One. Oxford: Elsevier.

Wagstaff, A., van Doorslaer, E., van der Burg, H. et al. (1999) Equity in the finance of health care: some further international comparisons. *Journal of Health Economics*, 18: 283–90.

Wilkinson, M. (1994) Paying for public spending: is there a role for earmarked taxes? *Fiscal Studies*, 15: 119–35.

Wilper, A.P., Woolhandler, S., Lasser, K.E. et al. (2009) Health insurance and mortality in US adults. *American Journal of Public Health*, 99(12): 1–7.

Yamey, G. (2010) Obama's giant step towards universal health insurance. *British Medical Journal*, 340: c1674.

Websites and resources

Australian Institute of Health and Welfare (AIHW): http://www.aihw.gov.au/

Commonwealth Fund http://www.commonwealthfund.org/.

Department of Health, England. Contains full description of policies and useful data sources: http://www.dh.gov.uk/Home/fs/en.

Department of Health and Social Services Northern Ireland: http://www.dhsspsni.gov.uk/.

European Observatory on Health Systems and Policies. Provides details of funding and healthcare system information: http://www.euro.who.int/observatory.

Health of Wales: http://www.wales.nhs.uk/.

Ministry of Health Welfare and Sport. Provides details of the recent changes to the Dutch funding system: www.denieuwezorgverzekering.nl.

New Zealand Ministry of Health: www.moh.govt.nz/moh.nsf.

NHS Scotland: http://www.show.scot.nhs.uk/.

Office of Health Economics. Provides detail on economic issues including information and data on healthcare funding: http://www.ohe.org/.

Organisation for Economic Co-operation and Development (OECD). Key source for healthcare funding data and relevant publication from 30 OECD countries: http://www.oecd.org/about/0,2337,en_2649_201185_1_1_1_ 1_1,00.html.

World Health Organization (WHO). Provides international information on healthcare expenditure, including country data and publications: http://www.who.int/en/.

National and local government websites also provide information relating to health funding and expenditure.

CHAPTER 4

Allocating resources for healthcare: setting and managing priorities

Iestyn Williams

Introduction

Those allocating resources for healthcare have long had to contend with the problems posed by resource scarcity, and this has been exacerbated by the recent economic downturn. As governments seek to constrain rising healthcare expenditure, the invidious role of resource distribution is invariably assigned to healthcare managers. However, the traditional cost-containing 'safety valves' of waiting lists and bedside rationing are becoming increasingly outdated, and therefore new solutions are being sought. Research and practice have consistently demonstrated the limitations of any one prescription for successful priority setting and it has become increasingly clear that the 'golden bullet' may never be found. Those involved have therefore been forced to say 'goodbye to the simple solutions' (Holm 1998: 1000) and to rethink and rebuild strategies for managing scarce healthcare resources. So just as the need for effective priority setting has become most pronounced, the mechanisms for its attainment appear ever more elusive. This chapter looks at the implications of these developments for the management function within healthcare. The discussion draws on consideration of the differences in resource allocation systems before concentrating on the main dimensions of priority setting such as ethics, evidence, process and politics, and considers these from the point of view of the strategic manager and decision-maker. Finally, a series of suggestions and recommendations are put forward for managers seeking to allocate scarce healthcare resources.

Rationing and priority setting

The terms 'rationing' and 'priority setting' are increasingly used interchangeably (see for example, Ham and Coulter 2000; Martin and Singer 2003) despite some subtle differences of emphasis. Common to each is the assumption that limits need to be placed on the provision of healthcare as a result of scarcity of resources (including physical resources such as transplantable organs). Whether as a result of ad hoc and implicit rationing, or planned and explicit priority setting, the implications are the same: some patients will be denied interventions that may be of benefit to them. In this context, *resource allocation* – the distribution of resources among competing programmes or patients – is the process by which these decisions and denials are enacted (Singer and Mapa 1998). This chapter is therefore intended to build on the preceding discussion of revenue *generation* in healthcare.

The factors driving the demand–supply gap in healthcare are commonly considered to include:

- **Changing demographics.** The reduction in size of the economically active as a percentage of the population creates cost pressures as the overall contributions pool decreases relative to healthcare need/demand.

- **Developments in medicine.** The rate at which new, expensive healthcare interventions come to market has accelerated and this creates pressures on healthcare systems operating with fixed budgets.

- **Patient expectations.** Expectations of what public services can and should provide have changed in line with the broader 'consumerization' of Western societies. The argument goes that as patients become more expert in understanding their healthcare needs and more empowered to make demands of healthcare providers, they are prepared to tolerate fewer of the discomforts and inconveniences of previous generations (Florin and Dixon 2004).

These factors, allied to the recent global economic crisis, have reinforced the view that rationing in healthcare is inevitable and therefore there is a need to establish fair and rigorous methods for doing this. However, the way that such resource allocation takes place varies significantly according to setting. There are a number of obvious reasons for this. The previous chapter outlined the range of approaches to revenue generation in healthcare. Although the link between method of funding and resource allocation is not mechanistic, certain patterns can be observed. For example, tax-funded systems create a stronger hand for government to influence distribution of resources whereas independent payers have a more substantial role to play in systems funded through social or private insurance. Approaches to priority setting also reflect broader civic cultures and societal expectations about the role of government in relation to individuals and communities (Blank and Burau 2008).

As with all healthcare policy decision-making, there is a tension between the role of local and national bodies in the field of priority setting. Resource allocation decisions can be made at various levels, including the national (through government departments and national organizations), local (for example, through health authorities and other purchasers) and at the level of the individual patient and clinician. Historically, governments have often sought the 'path of least resistance', preferring to devolve responsibility for unpopular decisions, for example, by setting budget ceilings on provider organizations or by delegating responsibility for resource allocation.

More recently, however, a number of attempts to take a national approach to priority setting have been implemented. Sabik and Lie (2008) divide these into two categories: those focusing on *outlining principles*; and those focusing on *defining practices*. The first approach involves collective discussion among specially convened panels of stakeholders and experts to identify key principles and criteria for priority setting. However, these commissions – particularly prevalent in Scandinavian countries in the

1990s – have generally been shown to have minimal impact on actual resource allocation which remained driven largely by considerations of political and institutional expediency (Calltorp 1999; Ham and Robert 2003). The second approach (in countries such as the UK, Israel and New Zealand) seeks to prioritize between healthcare interventions and is characterized by decision processes dominated by experts and analysis. Although these have been shown to have had more of an impact on decisions in practice, they have created tensions and difficulties for those operating at local levels (Shani et al. 2000; Ham and Robert 2003; Birch and Gafni 2006).

Priority setting as a management challenge

Despite these differences in national approaches, those charged with public resource allocation at local levels face a series of common challenges. These are mapped here using Mark Moore's (1995) 'strategic triangle' which depicts the strategic decision-maker as sitting at the intersection between three imperatives (Figure 4.1).

The first point of the triangle in Figure 4.1 is the 'value circle'. This relates to the substantive aims of (in this case) priority setting by which impact and performance should be measured, and underlines the normative importance of pursuing aims that will bring measurable benefit to the population served. Negotiating and articulating these aims requires ongoing deliberation with the public. The second point of the triangle relates to operational capability; that is 'how the enterprise will have to be organized and operated to achieve the declared objectives' (Moore 1995: 71) and the resources that can be mobilized in pursuit of these. This acknowledges that substantive aims must be

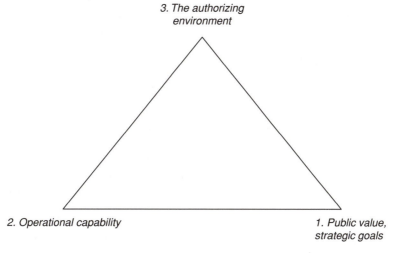

FIGURE 4.1 The strategic triangle
Source: Moore (1995).
Key, Point one of triangle – value circle (aims of priority setting).
     Point two of triangle – operational capability (organizing to achieve aims).
     Point three of triangle – authorizing environment (context within which priority setters operate).

practically achievable given that resources – finance, personnel, skills and technology – are limited. The third point of the triangle relates to the 'authorizing environment' within which priority setters operate. Decision-making requires the support of key external stakeholders including government, interest groups, and donors (primarily tax-paying citizens). Priority setters must be accountable upwardly and outwardly to these groups as priority setting can only be pursued with prior authorization from government and ongoing support from the public that fund the enterprise. Priority setters must therefore use the strategies available to them to create this platform of legitimacy.

The challenge for priority setters is to engage the public over the fundamental aims of healthcare by which their investment and disinvestment decisions will be judged and to use the levers and resources available to ensure value is delivered. To secure legitimacy for these endeavours, they must also develop strong relationships with their authorizing environment – government, citizens and powerful opinion formers such as the medical profession and the media – so that the 'bitter pill' of priority setting is more easily swallowed.

Ethical considerations

In systems funded primarily out of public money it is logical to assume that our priorities should be those that meet public duties and deliver demonstrable benefits in terms of the 'public good' (Newdick and Derrett 2006). Deciding what we mean by public duty and public good requires us to engage, at least in the first instance, with questions of social values and ethics. As Tauber (2002: 18) asserts, the dilemma of which 'ends we wish to secure . . . is fundamentally a moral question, not one of economics or organization'. Furthermore, in a context of resource scarcity, it is not enough for priority setters to show that their decisions bring about some benefits to the public: they must also be able to argue that more benefit could not be achieved by using resources in a different way (opportunity cost).

Although these propositions may seem uncontentious, establishing precisely what we mean by the 'public good' in healthcare priority setting remains a considerable challenge. Health economists such as Alan Williams have argued that: 'in health care, 'doing good' means improving people's life expectancy and the quality of their life' (1998: 29). From this perspective, successful resource allocation will generate the greatest increase in overall population health. This maximizing principle is based on a utilitarian commitment to the greatest benefit to the greatest number of people. Health Technology Assessment (HTA), informed by cost effectiveness analysis, has emerged as the primary vehicle for choosing between investment options on such grounds (Sorenson et al. 2007).

However, few if any contemporary commentators would advocate utilitarianism, or HTA, as the single driver of priority setting. The primary ethical objection stems from the need to demonstrate *distributive justice* in the allocation of public resources and therefore the belief that considerations of fairness and equity should not be entirely overridden by the health maximization principle. For example, an egalitarian perspective might hold that we should all be entitled to an equal proportion of healthcare resources regardless of our capacity to benefit, or, more commonly, that we should all be given equal opportunity to enjoy good health (Austin 2001). From this perspective, resource distribution should be linked to levels of need with the 'worse off' receiving greater priority than the relatively healthy.

A number of models have been developed to help identify who the 'worse off' might be and how we might weigh benefits more highly in these groups. For example, Eric Nord (2005) proposes a disease severity approach in which severe conditions are granted higher importance, and Alan Williams advocates a 'fair innings' model in which resources are allocated so as to distribute the number of healthy years most equitably throughout a population (Williams 1997). However, both of these approaches are controversial, subject to critique (see, for example, Holm 1998; Rivlin 2000), and far from being universally accepted.

The rise of individualism in attitudes to healthcare has destabilized these and other principles of collective distributive justice. For example, modern political liberalism would hold that the rights and choices of the patient-consumer outweigh considerations of equity and fairness in the allocation of scarce resources. However, this poses acute challenges for the priority setters as they seek to balance the interests of individuals against those of broader population groups.

A focus on the individual also brings into play a number of other ethical considerations. For example, commentators have argued that the 'rule of rescue' – the imperative to save the lives of individuals where these are endangered – should be a key ethical tenet of priority setting (Jonsen 1986). Others have explored the principle of 'desert' whereby individuals are required to take responsibility for maintaining their own health and forego prioritization if they engage in personal behaviour that increases the risk of poor health (Dolan and Tsuchiya 2009). As with the collectivist principles of equity and justice, notions of choice, rescue and desert have been heavily criticized and it is to the priority setter that the unenviable task of negotiation between these competing ethical stances falls. It should not surprise us therefore that healthcare resource allocation often appears to reflect a confusion of ethical considerations, or that there is often controversy and contestation over underlying principles.

Decision-making processes

These dilemmas reflect the absence of consensus over the desired ends of resource allocation and this in turn creates a powerful argument for investigation of the values of the public in order to resolve these long-standing ethical debates (Richardson 2002). Furthermore, it is frequently argued that in an explicit priority setting process, public engagement can help to provide the informed deliberation required for the unpalatable realities of rationing to be understood and accepted (Mooney 1998). This argument is often associated with communitarianism in its commitment to a process of citizen dialogue over the means and ends of public services. Communitarian citizen engagement requires those involved to take on the 'veil of ignorance' (Rawls 1972), thereby shedding all considerations of personal interest when deliberating on priorities and trade-offs (Hope 2001). Although meaningful engagement of this kind remains relatively rare and presents considerable challenges, it is increasingly accepted as essential to priority setting decisions.

Box 4.1: *Deliberative involvement methods*

Citizens' juries	12–24 citizens deliberate over a decision over a period of several days.
Citizens' panels	A similar number of citizens meet over a longer period to reach decisions.
Consensus conferences	Citizens meet in small groups to discuss scientific or technical issues. A second meeting assembles experts, media and the public to draw together observations and conclusions.
Deliberative polling	Deliberative processes are incorporated into opinion polling through follow-up discussions with respondents.

Source: Adapted from Abelson et al. (2003).

Although public involvement promises to offer much to the rationing enterprise – helping to resolve disputes over substantive aims, increasing democratic accountability, and raising awareness of the difficulties faced by decision-makers – caution is required. The evidence base on deliberative methods in priority setting remains under-developed (Mitton et al. 2009). Furthermore, commentators have cautioned against the assertion that deliberative engagement can or should be viewed as a panacea for the difficulties of priority setting (Abelson et al. 2003; Sabik and Lie 2008).

Citizen engagement is invariably costly and complex and deliberative approaches (see Box 4.1) tend to be small-scale and therefore do not equate to a democratic mandate for action. It is also important that the consensus-seeking facilitated by deliberative engagement is not pursued at the cost of respect for diversity and recognition of genuine differences where these exist. Finally, the logic of involvement requires that decisions are genuinely open to be shaped by public preferences. This would suggest that plans need to be in place to integrate these with other decision inputs, and that engagement should be avoided when decisions are subject to strong government direction.

The communitarian commitment to procedural (as opposed to substantive) justice is behind Daniels and Sabin's framework 'Accountability for Reasonableness' (A4R) (Daniels and Sabin 1998, 2008). They argue that social value pluralism is irreducible and therefore priority setters should set their sights on achieving decision-making processes that stakeholders will consider to be fair. This fairness, they claim, can be measured by performance against four conditions (see Box 4.2).

Through the development of a consistent approach to resource allocation decision-making, Daniels and Sabin argue that it becomes possible for a body of case law to emerge which both constrains and informs future decisions and protects decision-makers against unreasonable challenge. In this way, A4R seeks to address the legitimacy deficits of rationing as well as the challenges posed by ethical pluralism and poorly developed decision processes. Although A4R is not without its critics, it has proven useful to decision-makers operating in a variety of settings (Kapiriri et al. 2009). Ultimately, however, A4R cannot entirely substitute for engagement (and public engagement in

Box 4.2: *The four conditions of Accountability for Reasonableness*

- **Publicity**   Decisions taken over the allocation of healthcare resources should be made accessible to the public.
- **Relevance**   Decisions should be influenced by evidence that fair-minded people would consider relevant.
- **Appeals**   There should be mechanisms for challenge and review of decisions reached and for resolving any resulting disputes.
- **Enforcement**   There should be effective mechanisms for ensuring the other three conditions are implemented.

particular) on the ethical trade-offs involved in rationing as the notion of 'relevance' remains inherently subjective and therefore contested (Friedman 2008).

Decision analysis and deliberation

Health Technology Assessment (HTA)

In recent years, the pursuit of explicit priority setting has been accompanied by the development of decision support tools and methodologies. HTAs typically incorporate information relating to the efficacy, safety, ethics and costs of an intervention and help bodies making resource allocation decisions deal with the uncertainties they face. For example, this may be in determining what the benefits and risks of a new technology are and what the financial implications of coverage might be. In many countries, HTA agencies have been set up as advisors to government although variation exists in both their legal standing and their relationship to reimbursement and pricing (Sorenson et al. 2007). For example, whereas adherence to guidance produced by the Institute for Quality and Economic Efficiency in Health Care (IQWiG) in Germany and the French National Authority for Health is discretionary, much of the guidance of the National Institute for Health and Clinical Excellence (in the UK) has until recently been legally binding on the health service in England (Schmidt and Kreis 2009).

Inclusion of cost-effectiveness analysis (CEA) within HTAs has become increasingly routine and prospective economic evaluation of technologies is now also a regular accompaniment to clinical trials. CEA can be defined as information on the inputs or costs and the outputs or consequences associated with alternative healthcare interventions and procedures. HTA and CEA results are increasingly reported in generic, summary outcome measures which facilitate comparison across intervention areas (Gold et al. 1996; Drummond et al. 1997). Summary measures of results include: the incremental cost-effectiveness ratio (ICER), which is the ratio of additional costs to additional health effects associated with a new intervention (e.g. cost per quality-adjusted life year gained (QALYs)); and the net-benefit statistic, which expresses the additional health effects in monetary units by using an estimate of the 'maximum willingness to pay' per unit of health gain, where available. These techniques are designed to inform resource allocation decisions. Typically, they enable interventions to be ranked according to their cost effectiveness (the league table approach) or to be measured against a 'critical threshold value' (Lord et al. 2004) in order to determine cost effectiveness. By contrast, a profile, or cost consequence, approach to reporting results sets out the impact of the intervention on resource use and costs (including specific healthcare service use and costs, and productivity losses) and health outcomes (including disease symptoms, life expectancy and quality of life) in a tabular form, without any attempt to summarize or aggregate them.

The international evidence confirms, however, that use of HTA and economic evaluation remains far more prevalent among national, guidance-producing organizations than it is among local decision-makers operating with fixed healthcare budgets (Williams et al. 2008). This disjuncture reflects a number of factors which include a lack of the requisite resources and expertise within healthcare organizations. Perhaps more significant, however, is the failure of decision analytic models to capture the range of factors which influence priority setting decisions at local levels such as: budgets; service structures and arrangements; organizational practices and norms, and social and political considerations. The aims of priority setting (as we have seen) are likely to be multiple, and in order to be appropriate, decisions will need to reflect local population characteristics and trends, as well as being compatible with local systems and structures.

Programme budgeting and marginal analysis

Evidence that is more relevant to the local context of resource allocation can be generated through long-established methods such as needs assessment (Stevens and Gillam 1998) and newer applications such as predictive modelling based on local data. Programme budgeting and marginal analysis (PBMA) is an approach based on economics which offers a set of practical steps to enable decision-makers to maximize use of resources (Gibson et al. 2006) (see Box 4.3). The benefits of such processes are invariably cited by decision-makers that adopt them. However, the costs of taking such evidence-based approaches to decision-making are considerable when measured in terms of the time, resources and expertise involved. Furthermore, the optimal division of responsibility for evidence generation and analysis – for example, between internal and external, national and local bodies – will vary from context to context. The challenge for local planning is to achieve the ideal trade-off between local specificity and appropriate economies of scale.

Box 4.3: *Understanding PBMA*

'Programme budgeting' enables decision-makers to analyse current expenditure and 'marginal analysis' enables comparison of the costs and outcomes of programmes (Mitton and Donaldson 2004). The emphasis is on identification of areas where more impact could be achieved from within a finite resource to inform future allocation decisions. Typically, PBMA involves an expert panel which draws upon local knowledge and evidence, and operates according to economic principles of maximization and opportunity cost.

Deliberation

Even with full access to decision analysis and information support, decision-making processes will also incorporate elements of deliberation and this aspect of priority setting processes remains largely non-codified and implicit. Opening up the 'black box' of deliberation is not straightforward. Priority setting bodies at the local level usually operate according to formally adopted decision criteria. However, such frameworks can either be incidental to deliberation or else take the form of a 'litany', stifling full engagement. For example, in a case study of a priority setting committee, Russell and Greenhalgh (2009: 61) note the tendency to shut down discussion of complex ethical trade-offs when considering whether or not to fund new treatments. In this setting, 'predefined principles' were employed as 'rules that minimise rather than open up space for deliberation and judgement'.

Achieving an appropriate balance between adherence to decision rules and encouraging informed deliberation is a constant challenge to those leading priority setting at local levels. The approach adopted stands a greater chance of success (i.e. through consistency and coherence) if participants fully understand and support the model adopted and the implications for them and their contribution.

Legitimacy and external interests

Priority setting tends to be characterized by ambiguity over ends and means as well as conflict over decision outcomes. Unsurprisingly therefore, the best laid rationing plans – from the Oregon experiment of the 1980s to the UK National Institute for Health and Clinical Exercise (NICE) technology appraisal programme – have been damaged by lack of support from government, the public, key stakeholders, or a combination of all of these (Jacobs et al. 1998; Syrett 2003; Klein 2006). In the case of the US state of Oregon, the legislature sought to develop a list of core services to be funded through Medicaid but saw ongoing political revisions to the plan to the extent that the original objective of rationalizing the process of technology coverage became largely lost (Jacobs et al. 1998).

The role of government

It is not easy to determine what the role of external parties in priority setting ought to be. For example, it is often said that the NHS (both in England and the broader UK) lacks democratic legitimacy and therefore that upward accountability to government provides an essential check on the power of local bureaucrats. However, the same local decision-makers are also urged to exercise leadership and dynamism on behalf of their local communities (Department of Health 2007). The extent to which such local leadership is possible and desirable will inevitably vary according to broader political structures and the relative responsibility afforded to elected and non-elected public sector functions. However, the international experience suggests that governments will not hesitate to intervene where they feel the actions of subordinates threaten their own interests (Rhodes and Wanna 2008). For example, Yeo et al. (1999) found that the attempts of a Canadian provincial health board to adopt a principled approach to priority setting were undermined by political instability and government intrusion. This was a clear example of how the democratic authority of governments can be exercised in ways run counter to locally-determined processes and priorities.

Interest groups

As well as responding to government, priority setters must also contend with a plethora of sectional and cause-based interest groups. High profile rationing decisions are in-variably accompanied by media coverage and objections from patient organizations, the clinical community, industry, and so on. As we have seen, the response of Daniels and Sabin is to attempt to tie such stakeholders into formalized processes so that the 'fall-out' from tough decisions can be minimized. However, this assumes that the fun-damental premise of priority setting – i.e. that resources are scarce and must therefore be allocated between valid claims for investment – is commonly accepted. In practice, stakeholder contributions often reflect a rejection of the entire foundation of rationing. Therefore while A4R can help us choose between investment options and can reduce undue influence from interest groups, it does not, in itself, rescue the overall enterprise from the threat of backlash and disengagement.

Implications for managers and leaders

It is arguable whether the local priority setter should carry the responsibility to raise awareness of resource scarcity and lead deliberations with stakeholders over its im-plications for healthcare services. It is difficult to see how explicit decision-making can progress until this nettle is grasped. It could be argued, for example, that raising awareness of the need for fair distribution of scarce resources and building a coalition of support for the priority setting enterprise carries greater long-term importance than does getting individual decisions 'right' according to decision criteria that few stakeholders understand or support. What is clear is that the local decision-maker needs skills that embrace multiple accountabilities and a potentially hostile external environment. High profile public engagement and a strong media and communications strategy would seem to be prerequisites of a process in which leadership, political acumen and change management expertise are also likely to be beneficial.

This terrain is rarely trodden by commentators on the topic of priority setting but much can be applied from the study and practice of leadership and management more broadly (Reeleder et al. 2006). Characterized by ever-changing political and social tensions, the challenges of rationing are 'adaptive' and therefore require skills in areas of profile and relationship management as well as decision analysis and policy implementation (Heifetz and Laurie 2001). More controversially, it could be argued that 'pragmatism' should be added to 'principles' and 'processes' in prescriptions for effective priority setting inasmuch as this denotes the flexibility and judgement required to assess, respond to, and shape, the prevailing authorizing environment in pursuit of longer-term public sector goals.

Implementation

Until now this chapter has depicted priority setting as a series of decisions and/or decision processes. In practice, formal coverage decisions are a necessary but not sufficient element of priority setting and equal focus is required to the subsequent enactment of these decisions within healthcare delivery systems. Much of the priority setting literature concentrates on decisions and fails to draw insights from disciplines such as implementation science, organizational studies and diffusion of innovation. However, such research as there is suggests some key areas of considerations for those implementing priority setting systems at local levels of healthcare.

The first of these is the need to connect priority setting activities to actual resource allocation processes (including budget setting and finance). Where these links are weak – i.e. priority setters make recommendations which may or may not be actioned by organizations – the priority setting enterprise runs the risk of losing 'clout' and being circumvented by other drivers and pressures (Williams and Bryan 2007). Where ties are stronger (for example, decision-makers have veto over entry onto a formulary list), the priority setting function is likely to be subject to greater levels of internal and external scrutiny, requiring processes that are highly robust to challenge. A second area of importance is the relationship between priority setting and other aspects of strategic planning, performance measurement, and so on. Arguably, priority setting should suffuse each of these activities. However, embedding decision-making in this way requires greater clarity over roles, responsibilities and relationships than is often evident in local healthcare systems (Williams and Bryan 2007).

A third issue area of concern is the lack of attention paid to the implementation of priority setting decisions, with decision-making often considered a satisfactory endpoint in itself. A wealth of literature developed in other arenas supports the claim that healthcare systems tend to be 'complex' – involving multiple interactions between groups across boundaries – and it therefore appears naïve to assume that the introduction and withdrawal of healthcare interventions can proceed in a simple, mechanistic fashion. Sophisticated implementation and improvement strategies are required if priority setting decisions are to be fully adopted and adapted into practice.

Implementation barriers take on even greater significance when the priority setting enterprise turns to 'disinvestment' (or 'decommissioning') of obsolete practices. This is an area on which little published evidence or good practice exists (Elshaug et al. 2007). However, in the context of reduced overall budgets, substitution and disinvestment become paramount. Previous studies have found that explicit priority setting tends to have an additive effect on overall spending (Sabik and Lie 2008) suggesting that for priority setting to become an effective tool for reducing overall activity and spend, more work needs to be done.

Insights from the broader public policy literature suggest that implementation is most challenging when decisions are surrounded by high levels of ambiguity and conflict (Matland 1995). This may help to explain some of the difficulties priority setters face. We have seen that the ethical complexity of rationing heightens the sense of decision ambiguity (i.e. what are we trying to achieve?). Furthermore, the highly politicized context of healthcare resource allocation increases the likelihood of conflict ensuing from decisions to invest and disinvest. In these circumstances, implementation of setting decisions will be subject to the interplay of coalitions of local interest groups – including those involved in the provision and receipt of healthcare.

Addressing these barriers can therefore be understood as the attempt to *reduce* ambiguity and conflict. We have discussed the role of public engagement, and to that should be added the importance of soliciting support for the priority setting process from clinical, governmental and other stakeholders. Explicit priority setting also implies the need for a sophisticated media and communications strategy and skills in areas of sense-making and leadership.

Conclusion

This chapter has summarized some key themes from the literature on resource allocation and priority setting in healthcare, focusing in particular on the management function. As research, policy and practice in this area have matured, there has been an increasing acceptance that a single prescription (whether ethical, analytical or structural) is unlikely to emerge as a solution for all the problems priority setters face. At this stage, therefore, we are confined to identification of some key 'ingredients' of a priority setting process which stands a reasonable chance of success.

First, it is clear that evidence and analysis have an important role to play but cannot on their own replace the messy business of ongoing engagement and deliberation. The terms and parameters of this deliberative component therefore should be formally agreed to ensure accountability in decision-making. If we accept that, in this process, the public (as opposed to, for example, professionals, stakeholders and patients) should be the primary arbiters of values and ends, then there is also a strong case for meaningful and ongoing citizen engagement, despite the difficulties associated with this. Allied to process models such as A4R, such activities can help to alleviate the legitimacy deficits currently experienced by those seeking to set priorities in an explicit fashion. Similarly, those leading the priority setting enterprise at local levels will benefit from adding political acumen and relationship management to the traditional management skill set, however difficult these are to codify. Finally, the best-laid priority setting plans will founder if not clearly embedded in organizational systems, cultures and processes. For the manager or strategic decision-maker, these ingredients can be summarized in terms of the need to align the three imperatives of the strategic triangle: maximizing value through the deployment of scarce resources in a process which reflects the authority of political overseers and bolsters public trust in the institutions of care. However, it is unlikely that this daunting challenge can be met by the management function alone. Rather, the nettle of priority setting will need to be grasped by government, interest groups and wider civic society if substantial progress is to be made.

Some suggestions for priority setters

- **Explore and debate the ethical underpinnings of resource allocation:** Even though resolution of the tensions involved may not always be possible, this will help to make explicit the moral concerns informing decisions.

- **Involve the public in these discussions:** Engaging citizens is difficult and problematic but is essential if decisions over resource allocation are to be considered legitimate. Public engagement can also help to raise awareness of the difficulties decision-makers face.
- **Attend to the procedural dimensions of decision-making:** Adopting process-based models (such as A4R) can improve quality, consistency and legitimacy of decisions.
- **Draw on the evidence base:** Although decision analysis cannot replace debate and deliberation, it can provide an invaluable aid to inform priority setting.
- **Clarify the functions of your decision-making bodies:** It is essential that clarity is achieved over: the remit of decision-making bodies; the roles and responsibilities of those involved; the budgets implicated in determinations, and the link to other organizational strategies and priorities.
- **Manage the authorizing environment:** Many of the above strategies can help garner legitimacy for the priority setting enterprise. However, as rationing remains a highly politicized activity, those involved should deploy all available means to maximize public trust and stakeholder commitment, and create a coalition of support for the decision-making processes of resource allocation.

Summary box

- Resource scarcity in healthcare is a universal and long-standing problem which has intensified following the recent economic downturn.
- In many systems, responsibility for negotiating the gap between demand and resources falls on healthcare managers.
- Explicit approaches to priority setting and rationing are increasingly advocated as an alternative (or supplement) to other cost containment strategies.
- Explicit approaches require attention to a range of factors if they are to be successful. These include consideration of: ethics; processes and accountability; evidence generation and analysis; public engagement; legitimacy and politics; and decision implementation.
- In this context, leadership, political acumen and change management expertise are likely to be beneficial, alongside more established prescriptions for population-level decision-making.
- Ultimately, managers cannot implement explicit approaches to resource allocation in public healthcare systems without support from stakeholders such as government, the clinical community and the wider public.

Self-test exercises

1 Do formal processes for setting priorities for resource allocation exist in your organization/area?

2 Is decision-making informed by an ethical framework and, if so, how is this applied?

3 What is the role of citizens in establishing decision processes, criteria and outcomes in your health system?

4 What is the role of other stakeholders in decision-making processes?

5 Is decision-making informed by evidence and analysis and, if so, how is this applied?

6 How do decision-making processes perform against the four conditions of accountability for reasonableness?

7 Are those involved in decision-making given a clear understanding of their remit and responsibilities?

8 How do priority setting decisions connect to actual resource allocation processes?

9 How is implementation of decisions managed and recorded?

10 What is the perception of the priority setting process from the broader population and the local media?

References and further reading

Abelson, J., Forest, P., Eyles, J., Smith, P., Martin, E. and Gauvin, F. (2003) Deliberations about deliberative methods: issues in the design and evaluation of public participation processes. *Social Science & Medicine*, 57: 239–51.

Austin, S.E. (2001) *Medical Justice: A Guide to Fair Provision*. New York: Peter Lang.

Birch, S. and Gafni, A. (2006) The biggest bang for the buck or bigger bucks for the bang: the fallacy of the cost-effectiveness threshold. *Journal of Health Services Research and Policy*, 11(1): 46–51.

Blank, R.H. and Burau, V. (2008) *Comparative Health Policy*, 2nd edn. Basingstoke: Palgrave Macmillan.

Calltorp, J. (1999) Priority setting in health policy in Sweden and a comparison with Norway. *Health Policy*, 50: 1–9.

Daniels, N. and Sabin, J. (1998) The ethics of accountability in managed care reform. *Health Affairs*, 17(5): 50–64.

Daniels, N. and Sabin, J. (2008) *Setting Limits Fairly: Learning to Share Resources for Health*. Oxford: Oxford University Press.

Department of Health (DH) (2007) *World Class Commissioning: Competencies*. London: DH.

Dolan, P. and Tsuchiya, A. (2009) The social welfare function and individual responsibility: some theoretical issues and empirical evidence. *Journal of Health Economics*, 28: 210–20.

Drummond, M.F.B., O'Brien, G., Stoddart, G. and Torrance, G. (1997) *Methods for the Economic Evaluation of Healthcare Programmes*. Oxford: Oxford University Press.

Elshaug, A.G., Hiller, J.E., Tunis, S.R. and Moss, J.R. (2007) Challenges in Australian policy processes for disinvestment from existing, ineffective health care practices. *Australia and New Zealand Health Policy*, 4(23). doi: 10.1186/1743-8462-4-23.

Florin, D. and Dixon, J. (2004) Public involvement in health care. *British Medical Journal*, 328: 159–61.

Friedman, A. (2008) Beyond accountability for reasonableness. *Bioethics*, 22(2): 101–12.

Gibson, J., Mitton, C., Martin, D., Donaldson, C. and Singer, P. (2006) Ethics and economics: does programme budgeting and marginal analysis contribute to fair priority setting? *Journal of Health Services Research and Policy*, 11(1): 32–7.

Gold, M.R., Siegel, J.E., Russell, L.B. and Weinstein, M.C. (eds) (1996) *Cost-effectiveness in Health and Medicine.* Oxford: Oxford University Press.

Ham, C. and Coulter, A. (2000) International experiences of rationing (or priority setting). In A. Coulter and C. Ham (eds) *The Global Challenge of Health Care Rationing.* Buckingham: Open University Press, pp. 1–13.

Ham, C. and Robert, G. (eds) (2003) *Reasonable Rationing: International Experience of Priority Setting in Health Care.* Maidenhead: Open University Press.

Heifetz, R.A. and Laurie, D.L. (2001) The work of leadership. *Harvard Business Review*, Reprint R0111.

Holm, S. (1998) Goodbye to the simple solutions: the second phase of priority setting in health care. *British Medical Journal*, 317: 1000–2.

Hope, T. (2001) Rationing and life-saving treatments: should identifiable patients have higher priority? *Journal of Medical Ethics*, 27: 179–85.

Jacobs, L.R., Marmor, T. and Oberlander, J. (1998) The Political Paradox of Rationing. The Case of the Oregon Health Plan. The Innovations in American Government Program. John F. Kennedy School of Government, Harvard University, Occasional Paper 4.

Jonsen, A.R. (1986) Bentham in a box: technology assessment and health care allocation. *Law, Medicine and Health Care*, 14(3): 172–4.

Kapiriri, L., Norheim, O.F. and Martin, D.K. (2009) Fairness and accountability for reasonableness: do the views of priority setting decision makers differ across health systems? *Social Science & Medicine*, 68: 766–73.

Klein, R. (2006) *The New Politics of the NHS: From Creation to Reinvention*, 5th edn. Oxford: Radcliffe Medical Publishing.

Lord, J., Laking, G. and Fischer, A. (2004) Health care resource allocation: is the threshold rule good enough? *Journal of Health Services Research & Policy*, 9(4): 237–45.

McPake, B., Kumaranayake, L. and Normand, C. (2003) *Health Economics: An International Perspective*, 2nd edn. New York: Routledge.

Martin, D. and Singer, P. (2003) A strategy to improve priority setting in health care institutions. *Health Care Analysis*, 11(1): 59–68.

Matland, R.E. (1995) Synthesising the implementation literature: the ambiguity-conflict model of policy implementation. *Journal of Public Administration Research and Theory*, 5(2): 145–57.

Mitton, C. and Donaldson, C. (2004) Doing health care priority setting: principles, practice and challenges. *Cost Effectiveness and Resource Allocation*, 2(3). doi: 10.1186/1478-7547-2-3.

Mitton, C., Smith, N., Peacock, S., Evoyd. and Abelson, J. (2009) Public participation in health care priority setting: a scoping review. *Health Policy*, 91: 219–28.

Mooney, G. (1998) 'Communitarian claims' as an ethical basis for allocating health care resources. *Social Science and Medicine*, 4(9): 1171–1180.

Moore, M. (1995) *Creating Public Value: Strategic Management in Government.* Cambridge, MA: Harvard University Press.

Newdick, C. and Derrett, S. (2006) Access, equity and the role of rights in health care. *Health Care Analysis*, 14: 157–68.

Nord, E. (2005) Concerns for the worse off: fair innings versus severity. *Social Science and Medicine*, 60: 257–63.

Øvretveit, J.A. (1997) Managing the gap between demand and publicly affordable health care in an ethical way. *European Journal of Public Health* 7(2): 128.

Rawls, J. (1972) *A Theory of Justice.* Oxford: Oxford University Press.

Reeleder, D., Goel, V., Singer, P.A., and Martin, D.K. (2006) Leadership and priority setting: the perspective of hospital CEOs. *Health Policy*, 79: 24–34.

Rhodes, R.A.W. and Wanna, J. (2008) Stairways to heaven: a reply to Alford. *Australian Journal of Public Administration*, 67(3): 367–70.

Richardson, J. (2002) The poverty of ethical analysis in economics and the unwarranted disregard of evidence. In C.J.L. Murray, J.A. Salomon, C.D. Mathers, and A.D. Lopez (eds) *Summary Measures of Population Health.* Geneva: World Health Organisation, pp. 627–40.

Rivlin, M.M. (2000) Why the fair innings argument is not persuasive. *BMC Medical Ethics*, 1: 1.

Russell, J. and Greenhalgh, T. (2009) *Rhetoric, Evidence and Policy Making: A Case Study of Priority Setting in Primary Care.* London: University College London

Sabik, L.M. and Lie, R.K. (2008) Priority setting in health care: lessons from the experiences of eight countries. *International Journal for Equity and Health*, 7: 4.

Schmidt, H. and Kreis, J. (2009) Lessons from abroad. *Hastings Center Report*, 39(6): 20–2.

Shani, S., Siebzehner, M.I., Luxenburg, O. and Shemer, J. (2000) Setting priorities for the adoption of health technologies on a national level – the Israeli experience. *Health Policy*, 54(3): 169–85.

Singer, P.A. and Mapa, J. (1998) Ethics of resource allocation: dimensions for healthcare executives. *Hospital Quarterly*, 1(4): 29–31.

Sorenson, C., Kanavos, P. and Drummond, M. (2007) Ensuring value for money in health care: the role of HTA in the European Union. In *Financing Sustainable Health Care in Europe.* Luxembourg: Luxembourg Ministry of Health.

Stevens, A. and Gillam, S. (1998) Needs assessment: from theory to practice. *British Medical Journal*, 316: 1448–52.

Syrett, K. (2003) A technocratic fix to the 'legitimacy problem'? The Blair government and health care rationing in the United Kingdom. *Journal of Health Politics, Policy and Law*, 28(4): 715–46.

Tauber, A.I. (2002) Medicine, public health and the ethics of rationing. *Perspectives in Biology and Medicine*, 45(1): 16–30.

Williams, A. (1997) Intergenerational equity: an exploration of the fair innings argument. *Health Economics*, 6(2): 117–32.

Williams, A. (1998) Economics, QALYs and medical ethics: a health economist's perspective. In S. Dracopoulou (ed.) *Ethics and Values in Health Care Management.* London: Routledge, pp. 29–38.

Williams, I. and Bryan, S. (2007) Cost-effectiveness analysis and formulary decision making in England: findings from research. *Social Science and Medicine*, 65(10): 2116–29.

Williams, I., McIver, S., Moore, D. and Bryan, S. (2008) The use of economic evaluations in NHS decision-making: a review and empirical investigation. *Health Technology Assessment*, 12(7): 1–175.

Yeo, M., Williams, J.R. and Hooper, W. (1999) Incorporating ethics in priority setting: a case study of a rational health board in Canada. *Health Care Analysis*, 7: 177–94.

Websites and resources

Health Economic Evaluations Database (HEED): HEED contains information on studies of cost-effectiveness and other forms of economic evaluation of medicines and other treatments and medical interventions:
http://onlinelibrary.wiley.com/book/10.1002/9780470510933.

The International Network of Agencies for Health Technology Assessment (INAHTA): The purpose of this network is to share information on Health Technology Assessment across countries and cultures: www.inahta.org.

International Society on Priorities in Health Care: The purpose of this society is to strengthen the theory and practice of priority setting in healthcare by providing a forum in which researchers, practitioners and others involved in priority setting can come together to exchange ideas and experience:
http://org.uib.no/healthcarepriorities/.

NHS Institute for Innovation and Improvement. Guide to tackling tough choices in health care: The purpose of this toolkit is to assist in the tough choices associated with resource allocation and priority setting in health care:
http://www.institute.nhs.uk/world_class_commissioning/tackling_tough_choices/tackling_tough_choices_creating_public_value_homepage.html.

NHS programme budgeting tools and data: The purpose of this resource is to provide analysis of expenditure in healthcare programmes, such as cancer, mental health and cardiovascular diseases across the NHS:
http://www.dh.gov.uk/en/Managingyourorganisation/Financeandplanning/Programmebudgeting/index.htm.

CHAPTER 5

Research, innovation and health technology assessment

James Raftery

Introduction

One of the reasons for the steady growth in healthcare expenditure across the developed world is the continuing process of scientific and medical innovation. Our ability to diagnose, treat and manage major healthcare problems has advanced through the discovery, testing and introduction of new technologies, pharmaceuticals, devices and equipment. This chapter explores how science, industry and healthcare combine to produce those innovations. The pathway from research to healthcare delivery has, it has been suggested, eight steps between basic scientific discovery and routine delivery in healthcare systems (Cooksey 2006), set out in Box 5.1.

The interconnected roles of private and public sectors are characteristic of the process of innovation. While most basic research is funded by the public sector and undertaken in universities and other public institutions, steps 2 to 4 are mainly carried out by the pharmaceutical and medical device companies in pursuit of profit on behalf of their shareholders. Steps 5 to 8 are largely public sector activities again, certainly in those health systems where the delivery of healthcare is wholly or mainly in the hands of the state. The contrast is striking with other sectors and markets such as those for consumer goods where all the steps between research and product delivery are carried out by the private sector, and the state plays little or no role in controlling or managing the uptake of scientific innovation.

This characterization above of research and innovation as mainly public sector activities is open to challenge, particularly from pharmaceutical companies. This debate has been played out in the USA, as recounted by Goozner (2004), who showed that the basic science for almost all new drugs had been carried out largely in the public sector. While this seems to be true for pharmaceuticals, it may be less so for other relevant companies, such as those making medical devices or diagnostics.

While this research, development and implementation pathway applies most clearly to drug development, in which companies are legally required to carry out clinical trials before they are allowed 'market authorization', other health-related products such as devices or service innovations face the same challenges. The precise pathway and the balance between public and private sector inevitably vary by product and by degree.

Box 5.1: *Translation of health research to healthcare delivery*

Step	Mainly done by
1 Basic research	Publicly funded research
2 Prototype discovery and design	Pharmaceutical companies
3 Preclinical development	Pharmaceutical companies
4 Early clinical trials	Pharmaceutical companies
5 Late clinical trials	Pharmaceutical companies
6 Health technology assessment	Public sector
7 Knowledge management	Public sector
8 Healthcare delivery	Public sector

Source: Adapted from Cooksey (2006).

The mixture of public and private roles in healthcare innovation outlined in Box 5.1 has evolved largely to promote innovation, rather than necessarily to serve the needs of the healthcare system. Pharmaceutical companies have financial incentives to discover and develop new products by patent protection, which gives them 20 years of highly profitable monopoly production on any new drug. Imagine what would have happened to drug development if it had been left wholly to the publicly funded research and health system. It seems inconceivable that the range of novel drugs now available would have been developed. However, exceptions do exist, and some important healthcare innovations have emerged from the public sector. One striking example of NHS-led innovation in the UK was the invention of the artificial hip joint, which was first developed by the orthopaedic surgeon John Charnley, who worked in the NHS in Manchester. Charnley, however, was a maverick whose success was probably more despite of than because of the NHS – see Box 5.2, and the wonderful account of the development of artificial hips (Anderson et al. 2007). This chapter first discusses the processes of research and innovation in healthcare, and the parts played in them by institutions and stakeholders. It goes on to explore how health systems have developed methods for trying to manage the introduction of innovations, through systems such as health technology assessment, and to control the cost and other consequences for health systems and for healthcare spending. The chapter looks at how health systems have dealt with the challenges of unprecedentedly high priced drugs. It reviews methods that have evolved to support decision-making. It also considers how this appears to the life sciences industries and to governments keen to promote particular healthcare industries. It concludes by discussing the future role of research and innovation, particularly in the context of globalization in health systems.

Research and innovation

Government policy on research and development and innovation is concerned not only with individual sectors such as health and industry but also with

---

Box 5.2: *The development of the artificial hip joint*

The artificial hip joint was developed by John Charnley (1911–82), a maverick orthopaedic surgeon in Manchester in 1960. Charnley was a self-taught engineer with his own lathe and workshop who set up his own department in a former TB hospital after working on his hip joint in his attic at home. He had small-scale funding from the Manchester Hospital Board.

His key breakthrough was the use of ultra high molecular weight polyethelene in 1961. Charnley never patented his prosthesis as he continued to modify it, so it was widely copied in the USA and Europe. The Charnley hip remained one of the most widely used hip prostheses in the NHS when NICE reviewed the hundreds of prostheses in use in 2000. Following NICE's recommendation, a National Joint Register was established which contains details of all hip and knee artificial joints used in both public and private healthcare, with a view to establishing their clinical and cost effectiveness.

Source: www.njrcentre.org.uk.

---

macroeconomic growth. Research and development policy is seen as a key factor that generates long-term economic growth. Since the health sector comprises an important part of research and development, tensions can arise between health industry policies, on one hand, and healthcare policies, on the other. For instance, industrial policy might stimulate R&D which leads to the development of a new expensive drug which the public healthcare system considers too expensive or not cost-effective and declines to purchase.

The role played by R&D in economic growth has undergone major changes since around 1990. Up till then technological change was seen as exogenous – since then it has been seen as endogenous. This means that instead of technological change being seen as external to the economic system, it is seen as internal to the economic system and amenable to manipulation or management. Hence the importance governments now attach to spending on research and development. International comparisons of expenditure on R&D show the UK close to the OECD average in terms of proportion of GDP, and sixth overall in size of spending in the G7 in 2005, down from third in 1985 (ONS 2008). The decline in the relative ranking of the UK has been due to a decline in private as opposed to public spending but this is complicated by the mix of industries. The two most research-intensive industries in the UK are pharmaceuticals/biotechnology and aerospace/defence (or colloquially, drugs and arms), whether measured in terms of size or contribution to export earnings. These two sectors account for almost 80 per cent of UK private expenditure on R&D. Within pharmaceuticals, two companies accounted for the bulk of the spend in the UK: Glaxo Smith Kline and AstraZeneca.

The UK strategy under the Labour government (1997–2010) was to increase the total national spending on R&D from around 1.8 per cent GDP to 2.8 per cent by 2014. Between 2005 and 2008 this increased from 1.6 to 1.8 per cent. The increase was to be achieved partly by increasing the publicly funded element but also by ensuring optimal linkages and the encouragement of privately funded spend. Publicly funded R&D makes up around 40 per cent (ONS 2008) of the total spend.

The Cooksey (2006) review of UK health research funding provided a useful overview as well as rationale for coordinating and increasing spending on health research. Produced at the request of the government's Treasury rather than the Department of Health, this report explicitly had the goal of keeping the UK at the forefront of health research and making it the location of choice for the pharmaceutical industry to locate its R&D. It found the UK at risk of failing due to lack of any overarching health research strategy and identified two gaps, the first in translating ideas from basic and clinical research into new products, the second to do with implementing those new products into clinical practice. The first gap had to do with linking prototype discovery and design to preclinical development and early clinical trials, which Cooksey proposed needed improved coordination, appropriate skills, better access to capital and arrangements for technology transfer. The second gap, between the development of new products and their use in healthcare delivery, Cooksey saw as requiring the identification and evaluation of the clinical and cost effectiveness of these new products. This involved health technology assessment, health services research and knowledge management.

Healthcare institutions and the healthcare professions, particularly medicine, have historically been highly resistant to change and innovation. *Bad Medicine: Doctors Doing Harm Since Hippocrates*, Wooton's (2006) provocatively entitled book, provides numerous examples of the way that conservative patterns of clinical practice have perpetuated the use of ineffective treatments (or delayed the introduction of effective ones) for decades or even longer. For example, blood letting was a mainstream medical therapy from 1500 to 1850 and the discovery of the circulation of the blood (1628), of oxygen (1775), and of the role of haemoglobin (1862) made no difference. In fact, these discoveries were adapted to the therapy but not vice versa (Wooton 2006: 17). Other examples of failures to innovate include the treatment of scurvy with vitamin D, the prevention of puerperal fever through control of infection measures, and the use of antiseptics. Wooton considers that medicine only began to improve health in the last 150 years, from around 1850, with most of the improvements in recent periods. The understanding that medicine could do harm or good contributed to the demand for health technology assessment.

The large pharmaceutical companies typically spend 20 per cent of turnover on research and development, a figure which may be higher for some of the other life science industries. As global firms they can determine the R&D spend of any particular country. But their R&D spending is largely determined and directed by regulation – due to past high-profile disasters with new drugs, market authorization requires proof of safety and efficacy (better than placebo) as demonstrated by randomized clinical trials. It is the cost of these trials that comprises the major part of the cost of bringing a new drug to market (Goozner 2004).

The relevant industries extend beyond pharmaceuticals to cover the 'life sciences' and life science firms are also major research spenders. The mapping of the human genome in 2000 (which was subject to competition then cooperation between public and private sectors) led to a proliferation of attempts to develop marketable products. Success has been less that hoped but has been most notable in linking diagnostic tests to particular treatments. For example, herceptin (trastuzumab) for advanced breast cancer is effective only in those women who test positive for HER2, which is a genetic test marketed by Roche who also supply trastuzumab.

Personalized medicine, which links treatment success to patient sub-groups (such as breast cancer HER2 positive patients) looks at restructuring the existing research and development processes (Parliamentary Office of Science and Technology 2009). Genomics, customized diagnostics, information technology and targeted drugs could change the way healthcare is organized in ways that are difficult to predict. Increased 'consumerism' points towards more private sector arrangements while improved risk estimation could mean the end of the risk sharing that underpins systems of health insurance. In the USA, genetic discrimination in terms of healthcare insurance (but not life insurance) has been ruled illegal. In the UK and other countries with universal coverage through tax-funding or social insurance, genetic discrimination is not an important issue for health insurance. For life assurance, applicants are required to disclose if they had genetic tests but are not required to disclose the results (House of Lords Science and Technology Committee 2009).

The development of new health technologies poses many challenges for policy-makers and health systems. The escalating costs particularly of pharmaceuticals have necessitated increasing consideration of value for money and have sometimes resulted in healthcare insurers or funders refusing to purchase some high cost innovations. From an industrial policy viewpoint, healthcare is a highly dynamic sector, in which new technologies promise not only life and well-being, but also high profit. Pharmaceutical companies rank among the largest and most profitable companies worldwide and in countries with large pharmaceutical sectors, governments often face trade-offs between industrial and health policy.

The conflict between health and industrial policy can be put in terms of supply and demand. Industrial policy has to do with supply, that is encouraging or facilitating expansion and growth among companies that are either national or based in the relevant nation-state. Health policy has to do with the demand of the health system for technologies such as drugs, and the ability of the healthcare system, and of the funders of that system, to keep pace with, manage, and – in some cases – limit demand. However, this is not purely a national concern, because of the globalization of research and innovation, and especially of the pharmaceutical sector, the health and industrial policy of any one country has effects on others. Perhaps the most significant example of this is the impact that policy in the United States of America has on Europe and the rest of the developed and developing world.

The sheer size of the USA matters. It devotes a higher share of its economy (16 per cent of GDP) to healthcare than any other country in the world, and is home to a large part of the research and innovation infrastructure both through its huge government investment in publicly funded research and through its thriving and dynamic life sciences and pharmaceuticals sector. Over 50 per cent of global pharmaceutical sales are in the USA. Pharmaceutical companies set prices for the less regulated US market which then apply worldwide, partly driven by the threat of parallel importing. Health systems in poorer countries must either spend more on drugs than they can afford or limit their access through rationing in some form or other.

Health technology assessment

'Health technology' tends to be defined broadly. The UK Department of Health (Department of Health 1992) defined health technologies as: 'all methods used by health professionals to promote health, prevent and treat disease, and to improve rehabilitation and long term care'. And in the USA, the Office of Technology Assessment (1976) defined health technologies as: 'the set of techniques, drugs, equipment and procedures used by health care professionals in delivering medical care to individuals and the systems within which such care is delivered'. These definitions are so broad as to include almost any aspect of healthcare. Furthermore, interventions in healthcare often comprise a bundle of technologies. For instance, a surgical procedure may involve drugs, equipment and care procedures which could be carried out in various settings, along with the training and competencies of staff such as surgeons, anaethestists, nurses and laboratory staff.

Technologies that are regulated by law tend to have fuller, more precise definitions. Pharmaceuticals constitute a specific class of health technologies, due to having long been subject to licensing in most countries, both to ensure quality and to prevent harm. The regulation of pharmaceuticals, which tend to be manufactured and marketed by private enterprises, reflects a history of harm and subsequent litigation. The thalidomide and opren scandals in the 1960s (Stephens and Brymer 2001) led to tighter controls in many industrialized countries. Within pharmaceuticals, different regulations apply depending on whether drugs are available only on prescription, over-the-counter in pharmacies only, or in all shops.

Medical and surgical devices tend to be less regulated, but since they are often privately manufactured, they are also subject to litigation (the extent of which varies internationally). Litigation has led to the establishment of registers of patients who have had certain devices implanted (for example, cardiac pacemakers, silicone breast implants, and hip and knee prostheses). The main regulation of other services such as diagnostic testing has to do with quality control, such as the external quality schemes for pathology laboratories in many countries.

Other health technologies are subject to less regulation and tend to be less well defined. Surgical procedures are recorded in routine datasets for inpatient and day cases (but often not as well recorded if they are carried out in outpatient or primary care settings) and are not regulated other than by clinical audit of outcomes (both in general and of adverse events), and voluntary registers, though some professional bodies (such as the medical Royal Colleges in the UK) set training standards and competencies for particular types of surgery – one example being endoscopic procedures. A list of UK health-related databases originally developed in the London School of Hygiene is held by the Department of Health (Information Centre 2010).

Changes in the settings or organization of healthcare are less regulated again, and innovations such as the redesign of care pathways, the transfer of work from a hospital to an outpatient or community setting, or the shifting of work from one group of healthcare professionals to another in skillmix or workforce redesign often require little or no regulatory approval or authorization.

Health technologies differ from technologies in other industries in one crucial respect: they generally increase cost. The price of most technologies falls over time, with computers, mobile phones and cars providing some obvious examples. Not only does price fall but quality often improves. However, in healthcare, new technologies, particularly drugs, come at increased prices often without proven quality gains. Overall technological change is seen as cost increasing in healthcare (Sheldon and Faulker 1996). Whether the increased cost provides value for money is a key question which health technology assessment attempts to answer.

Types of health technology assessment

Three kinds of health technology assessment have been identified (Raftery et al. 2005) – those to do with efficacy or effectiveness, those to do with equity or diffusion and those to do with costing health technologies and their impact. Each type of health technology assessment is described below. These assessments are of interest principally to those responsible for funding or organizing healthcare systems – in most developed countries, a role that government generally fulfils with the result that health technology assessment is largely a public sector activity, often undertaken by or on behalf of government agencies.

The efficacy of a health technology can be defined as that which demonstrates patient benefit outweighing harm in scientifically robust, usually experimental, studies. Effectiveness has to do with demonstration of patient benefit outweighing harm when the technology is actually applied in uncontrolled everyday practice, rather than in the context of research. Often efficacy is regarded as the maximal effectiveness because technologies often achieve greater benefits when they are used within the very controlled setting of research studies than they subsequently demonstrate when used in everyday practice.

Efficacy-orientated HTAs place particular emphasis on randomized clinical trials (RCTs) and systematic reviews of trials. The conventional wisdom is that only trials can provide the requisite data on efficacy/effectiveness and perhaps on cost effectiveness. Clinical trials are rightly a core part of medical research and may be the only way of assessing efficacy/effectiveness in many instances but have limits (Rawlins 2008).

Effectiveness studies require data on the degree to which a particular intervention retains its efficacy in everyday practice. This requires data on the patients on whom it is carried out, in some instances how the technology was delivered (if different from trial data) and the degree to which the same outcomes (both benefit and harm) are achieved.

In contrast, equity can be defined in terms of which groups of patients or citizens use particular health technologies, and whether their use is fairly distributed across such different groups. Studies of equity require data on which particular groups receive a health technology, and such groups can be defined in many ways (age, sex, ethnicity, socio-economic group, disease severity, geography, etc.). Studies of diffusion are concerned with the factors influencing the uptake of health technologies by place and time. Studies of equity and diffusion often draw on broadly similar information sources.

Only some health technologies are priced – such as pharmaceuticals and particular packages of healthcare, depending on the country, and the way that healthcare financing is organized. The cost impact of health technologies often extends well beyond their price, to include effects on services used or not. Since not all technologies are priced, costing often involves estimating unit costs for health technologies and for the range of personal costs and benefits. Furthermore, prices vary, depending on patent, industrial processes, and competition.

Cost-related HTAs employ a range of economic approaches including cost efficacy, cost effectiveness, 'cost of illness', cost consequences and cost impact studies. Costing is complicated by several factors, including the wide definition of cost used by economists and the lack of prices or unit costs for many health technologies. Economists define costs in terms of societal opportunity costs, which often requires data on the consequential effects of particular health technologies (both in terms of the full range of personal costs and benefits, and over the entire life of the patient). Cost effectiveness analysis combines several of these elements of HTA to assess the relative value of one technology against another. It has been used by several countries to help to decide whether or not to fund particular technologies, notably drugs.

Eddy (2009) has identified four stages of health technology assessment: (1) systematic review of evidence; (2) outcomes analysis including benefits and risk; (3) assessing the effect of the technology on costs; and (4) cost effectiveness analysis combining the costs and benefits to enable choices to be made. These stages, Eddy suggests, are ordered, not only methodologically in terms of the sequence in which they are undertaken but socio-economically, in terms of their political and social acceptability. This explains, he suggests, the differences between countries, some of whom are not ready for the difficult choices implied by full health technology assessments based on cost-effectiveness analysis. A fifth stage of HTA was discussed by Eddy to do with analysis of the ethical and legal implications of the technology. This might be extended to include making a decision on the appropriate use of a health technology. The development of appraisal in the UK by the National Institute for Health and Clinical Excellence (NICE) is discussed below.

The use of health technology assessment in health systems

The high prices of drugs described earlier have led to reactions by funders of healthcare and governments, especially in countries with mainly tax-based systems for healthcare funding. No less than 33 countries have published guidelines for economic evaluation of health technologies (ISPOR 2010).

Five countries have led in the use of HTA to decide on purchase of new health technologies include, in chronological order: Australia (Pharmaceutical Benefits Advisory Commission, established 1954), Sweden (Swedish Council on Health Technology Assessment (SBU), established 1987), New Zealand (PHARMAC, established 1993) Canada (Canadian Coordinating Office for Health Technology Assessment, later Canadian Agency for Drugs and Technologies in Health, 1989), UK (National Institute for Clinical Excellence, 1999). INAHTA, the international organization of public sector HTA agencies had 46 members in 2010. Full HTA (stage 4, according to Eddy) is more common in health systems with a centralized payor.

At one extreme is the UK with NICE which, though it was established relatively late in the chronology outlined above, is one of the larger and better documented agencies. It has a brief to appraise health technologies and issue mandatory guidance to the NHS on their use. The term 'appraisal' is distinguished from 'assessment' in that the former makes recommendations based on health technology assessments and other relevant factors. The NICE appraisal process is explicitly informed by cost effectiveness analysis in the form of cost per QALY.

Raftery (2006) showed that although NICE recommendations have largely been positive and permissive, it had recommended against the use of several high cost drugs, notably zanamivir, a flu antiviral from Glaxo Smith Kline (and later against other similar drugs from other companies). This led to GSK threatening to quit the UK, a threat which was not realized. This provides a dramatic example of the conflict that can arise between health and industrial policy, since GSK is one of the foremost UK pharmaceutical companies.

At least as important was the recommendation by NICE against new drugs for multiple sclerosis (beta interferon and glatimer acetate). The political implications of this refusal led the then Labour government to establish a Multiple Sclerosis Risk Sharing Scheme which aimed to enable patients to access the drugs with prices to be reduced in line with their effectiveness if less than promised. The failure of that scheme is recounted elsewhere (McCabe et al. 2010; Raftery 2010).

At the other extreme from the UK is the USA which abolished the one federal agency that assessed health and other technologies (the Office for Technology Assessment which was disestablished in 1993). As part of the Obama healthcare reforms, in 2010, the USA has recently established the Patient Outcomes Research Institute. (Tunis and Pearson 2010). In terms of the stages of health technology assessment outlined earlier, the new centre will be limited to the first two stages – the USA, despite having the most costly healthcare system in the world, does not allow the government to explore cost-effectiveness which, extraordinarily, is statutorily forbidden (Sullivan et al. 2009; Neumann and Weinstein 2010).

Important methodological developments have occurred at each of the four stages of health technology assessment outlined above. Formal methods for evidence review have been pioneered by the Cochrane Collaboration, which employs a hierarchy of evidence with randomized clinical trials at the top. Analysis of the magnitude of the effect of particular technologies on outcomes has been taken forward by meta analysis of randomized trials. The effects on costs have led to clarifications as to which perspective is to be adopted, with choices from societal through public sector to payor. Estimation of the cost effectiveness of one technology compared to another has required mathematical modelling to deal with the complexities of synthesizing disparate data, extending time frames beyond those of clinical trials to patients' entire lifetimes and exploring the uncertainty of the resulting estimates.

The focus on cost effectiveness modelling has had implications for the earlier stages. Evidence reviews have had to extend beyond clinical trials to provide data on generic outcomes and on costs. Disease-specific outcomes in clinical trials have had to be translated into generic outcome measures such as Quality Adjusted Life Years (QALYs) to enable comparisons to be made between disparate technologies. The sheer complexity of these models has led to a need for guides to good practice (Philips et al. 2004).

Bayesian analysis has been particular important, because it enables indirect comparisons of outcomes and the quantification of uncertainty in modelling. Probabilistic sensitivity analysis has led to cost effectiveness acceptability curves which deal with the difficulty of fitting confidence intervals to ratios. Value of information takes this further by estimating the value of meeting particular information gaps (Tappenden et al. 2004). Method development has been driven by the requirements of health technology assessment as used to aid decision-making.

While health technology assessment has often been assumed to do with the analysis of existing data, an important extension has been to do with generating new data. While this has often been small-scale such as the collection of data on costs or outcomes, in some instances it has led to the funding of randomized clinical trials. Acceptance of the hierarchy of evidence implies that such trials may be required when the relevant comparisons are absent. Health systems have begun to fund clinical trials to meet the evidence gaps. An example is provided by the difficulties regarding drugs for age-related macular degeneration, which has led to randomized clinical trials in several countries including IVAN in the UK and CATT in the USA, as well as in several European countries (Steinbook 2006; Raftery et al. 2007) (see Box 5.3).

Health technology assessment is seen by the pharmaceutical companies as an unwelcome 'fourth hurdle' in addition to quality, safety and efficacy for new pharmaceuticals. The ability of companies to charge unprecedentedly high prices for new drugs is challenged by the increasing use of institutionalized health technology assessment. High drug prices often originate in the US market which comprises 50 per cent of the global market. New products which offer to extend life are sometimes priced at extraordinarily high levels. For example, the drug ceredase which is used to treat Gauchers disease was developed by Genzyme in 1991 through what was initially a complex process to derive the enzyme from placentas (Goozner 2004). Genzyme set an important precedent by its pricing – set at $350k a year for the dose needed by an average-sized male adult. Although this extraordinary high price led to criticism, it set a standard for the

---

Box 5.3: *Case study of Avastin, Lucentis and blindness*

Age-related macular degeneration (AMD) is the leading cause of blindness in the over-75s. Two drugs provide effective treatment, reversing the vision loss in some patients. Lucentis (ranibizumab) was licensed by Roche for AMD in the USA in 2006 and in Europe in 2007. Avastin (bevacizumab), its close relative, was licensed by Roche for colorectal cancer but not for wet AMD despite being used widely off-label for this condition. Lucentis costs almost US$2,000 per injection compared to US$17–50 per injection for Avastin (Steinbrook 2006). Lucentis was recommended by NICE for treatment of wet AMD. NICE could not appraise Avastin for AMD as it was not licensed for this. If Avastin were to replace Lucentis, the NHS would save almost £300m annually. The IVAN (UK) and CATT (US) trials will compare Avastin and Lucentis head-to-head.

industry. Soon the drug was synthesized (making its manufacture cheaper) and patented but the price remained extremely high, making Genzyme one of the most profitable companies in the world (Goozner 2004).

The refusal by some countries to agree to purchase these very highly priced drugs has led to tensions between pharmaceutical companies, patient groups, clinicians and healthcare funders. In the UK, some of NICE's more controversial decisions have been challenged in the courts, and although the legal challenges have in general been unsuccessful, they have led to more detailed, rigorous and bureaucratic processes for health technology assessment which are designed to be proof against judicial review.

Faced with decisions to refuse to fund some drugs, pharmaceutical companies have resorted to various ways of selling their products without being seen to publicly reduce list prices. These have varied from providing discounts on other products (Raftery 2006) to schemes which link costs to patient response or outcomes known as patient access schemes.

The application of health technology assessment to genomics and linked diagnostic testing has been slower for reasons that include the less-developed regulations surrounding these technologies, the place of direct sales to consumers, as well as the paucity of effective therapies. These factors imply different future relationships between public and private sectors.

Conclusion

Perhaps the single biggest challenge for the future is that health technology assessment is still largely practised at national level while the companies supplying health technologies are global in nature. Take, for example, the funding and management of the trials of Roche's two drugs, Avastin versus Lucentis, which was described earlier in Box 5.3. In the unlikely event that Roche decided to run such a trial, it would almost certainly be a single multinational trial. This could probably have been done quickly as recruitment, the greatest barrier, would be eased by including several countries. However, the best that public sector research funders have been able to do is to fund separate, individual trials in each country. While a long list of the barriers to a single public sector trial can be readily listed (different timescales, preparedness of clinical research teams, access to, and distribution of, unlicensed Avastin, etc.), the cost of the delay may be very high should the trial demonstrate the equivalence of the two drugs. National uniqueness applies also to health technology assessment agencies like NICE. Each has its own methods and procedures. Worse, the list of topics each has considered shows more differences than commonalities. Inevitably all have had to consider some of the 'hot' topics, specifically those new high cost drugs with some evidence of effectiveness. While the agencies have tended to reach similar conclusions about some high cost and controversial drugs (beta interferon for multiple sclerosis, herceptin for breast cancer, Lucentis for macular degeneration, Imatinib for leukaemia), their decisions vary in part because of the place that national politics plays in what are overtly technocratic determinations.

The sheer 'cussedness' of the USA poses a major challenge to the ability of the rest of the world to use health technology assessment to achieve efficiencies in healthcare.

Not only is health technology assessment in the USA largely confined to the first two stages of evidence review and outcome analysis, the latter stages to do with cost and cost effectiveness are expressly forbidden by law. The USA spends the largest share of domestic income on healthcare in the world and seems likely to continue to pay very high prices for health technologies. As long as it does, the rest of world will have to bear the impact of high US prices on their own health systems. Ironically the political unacceptability of health technology assessment in the USA makes it all the more necessary for the rest of the world.

While individual countries in Europe have embraced health technology assessment, the European Union has been much slower to engage in part because the EU has a limited mandate to act in health policy and health systems, while it does have a mandate to work on industrial policy, trade and research and development. However, this situation has been increasingly challenged by developments in EU law which have made it far easier for patients to access services outside their own country, leading to a rise in 'medical tourism' and more formally, a growing international trade in healthcare provision (Smith et al. 2009). EU rules have permitted citizens of one member country to be treated in another, at the cost to the public sector in the citizen's home country. But much medical tourism outside the European Union is privately funded and key areas include elective and cosmetic surgery, and reproductive services. The prices for such services vary widely, unlike the prices for drugs which companies set globally. Such health services are relatively cheaper in Asia than in Europe and, as a result, India and Thailand have become important destinations for European citizens seeking low-cost healthcare. Similarly, South America and New Zealand cater for US medical tourists. And Europe and the United States also receive inflows of wealthy patients from elsewhere able to afford the treatments available in the private sector of these countries.

The rise of consumerism in healthcare has meant that some decisions that were once those of the clinician are increasingly of the individual patient or consumer. This applies least to services with least choice such as emergency care and most for those in which choice exists, such as elective surgery or treatments for long-term conditions. Consumerism means that patients who are denied any treatment may well protest, campaign and receive sympathetic media attention. This has happened in the UK in response to guidance issued by NICE on the adoption of some high cost drugs used at the end of life with marginal benefits in terms of extending life.

In conclusion, conflicts between the needs of health and industrial policies will continue, particularly for those countries with sizeable healthcare industries, and conflicts between the policies of different countries arising from differences in healthcare funding levels and approaches are also likely to endure. The relentless pace of healthcare innovation, paired with the globalizing and democratizing effects of information technology which make it easy for people everywhere to access and learn about new health technologies, will continue to create huge pressures on healthcare costs. As long as the bulk of healthcare funding continues to come from government (through tax or social insurance schemes) or through other third parties (such as health or employer insurance) rather than from the individual consumer, society will need ways to manage the pace and process of healthcare innovation and its consequences.

Summary box

- The continuing progress of medical and scientific innovation is one of the key reasons for increasing healthcare costs across the developed world. Because our ability to diagnose, treat and manage health problems is increased by healthcare innovation, it expands demand and drives up overall health system costs even though it may sometimes improve productivity and efficiency.

- Healthcare innovation is a shared responsibility between government, healthcare funders and providers, and private entities such as pharmaceutical companies. Much basic medical research is directly funded by government, and industrial policy often promotes investment in research and development because it is believed to lead to macroeconomic growth. However, government health policies are often concerned with managing or constraining healthcare innovation, because of its impact on healthcare expenditure.

- Health technology assessment involves the structured analysis of the efficacy, effectiveness, equity and cost effectiveness of health technologies, which include pharmaceuticals, medical devices, diagnostic technologies, surgical procedures, and other innovations in the way healthcare is organized and delivered. Usually, most attention is focused on the assessment of new drugs both because their development is more closely regulated and because of their high costs.

- In the past two decades, over 30 countries have established systems, guidelines or institutions for undertaking health technology assessment. While the actual processes vary in the extent to which they implement a full cost-effectiveness analysis of health technologies and the choice of technologies which they assess, their overall effect has certainly been to bring much greater rigour to the processes by which healthcare innovations are taken up by healthcare providers.

- For the future, the increasing globalization of healthcare innovation processes and health systems combined with the increased availability of information about healthcare innovation mean that the cost and other pressures will grow on national governments and institutions concerned with managing research and development and managing the adoption of healthcare innovations. This means that as long as healthcare costs are mainly funded collectively, by governments or by systems of social or other insurance, there will be an increasing need for strong systems for health technology assessment.

Self-test exercises

1 What are the stage of health technology assessment? How might countries be classified? At what stage would you put: (1) the UK; (2) the USA; (3) your own country (if not the UK or the USA)?

2 What proportion of pharmaceutical sales are to the USA? What implications does this have for health technology assessment?

3 Why are pharmaceutical companies required to carry out clinical trials before being allowed to market their products? Is this a form of health technology assessment?

4 What is the impact of globalization on health technology assessment?

5 What is meant by 'medical tourism'? What are its likely effects?

References and further reading

Anderson, J., Neary, F. and Pickstone, J.V. (2007) Surgeons, manufacturers and patients: a transatlantic history of total hip replacement. In *Science Technology and Medicine in Modern History*. Basingstoke: Palgrave Macmillan.

Cooksey, D. (2006) *Review of UK Health Research Funding*. London: HM Treasury.

Department of Health (1992) *Assessing the Effects of Health Technologies: Principles, Practice, Proposals*. London: Department of Health.

Eddy, D. (2009) Health technology assessment and evidence based medicine: what are we talking about? *Value in Health*, S2:S6–S7.

Goozner, M. (2004) *The $800 Million Pill: The Truth Behind the Cost of New Drugs*. Berkeley, CA: University of California Press.

Greenhalgh, T., Stramer, K., Bratan, T., Byrne, E., Russell, J. and Potts H.W.W. (2010) Adoption and non-adoption of a shared electronic summary record in England: a mixed-method case study. *BMJ* 340:c3111, doi: 10.1136/bmj.c3111.

House of Lords Science and Technology Committee (2009) *Genomic Medicine*. London: House of Lords. Available at: www.publications.parliament.uk/pald20089.

Information Centre (2010) NHS DoCDat. Available at: www.icapp.nhs/docdat/default.aspx.

ISPOR (2010) Available at: http://www.ispor.org/PEguidelines/index.asp.

Kennedy, I. (2009) Appraising the benefits of innovation and other benefits: a short report. Available at: http://www.nice.org.uk/media/98F/5C/KennedyStudyFinalReport.pdf.

McCabe, C., Chilcott, J., Claxton, K., Tappenden, P., Cooper, C., Roberts, J., Cooper, N. and Abrams, K. (2010) Continuing the multiple sclerosis risk sharing scheme is unjustified. *BMJ* 340:doi:10.1136/bmj.c1786.

Neumann, R. (2009) Lessons for health technology assessment: it is not only about the evidence. *Value Health*, 12(Suppl. 2): S45–S48.

Neumann, R. and Weinstein, M. (2010) Legislating against the use of cost effectiveness information. *NEJM* 363: 16. Oct. 14.

Office of National Statistics (2008) *UK Gross Domestic Expenditure on Research and Development*. Available at: www.statistics.gov.uk/pdfdir/gerd0310.pdf.

Office of Technology Assessment (1976) *Development of Medical Technologies: Opportunities for Assessment*. Washington, DC: US Government Publishing Office.

Parliamentary Office of Science and Technology (2009) *Personalised Medicine: Post-note.* April. 329. Available at: www.parliament.uk/documents/post/postnote329.pdf.

Philips, Z., Bojke, L., Sculpher, M., Claxton, K. and Golder, S. (2004) *Good Practice Guidelines for Decision-Analytic Modelling in Health Technology Assessment: A Review and Consolidation of Quality Assessment.* HTA Monograph.

Raftery, J. (2006) Review of NICE recommendations on use of health technologies, 1999-2005. *BMJ*, 332:1266–68.

Raftery, J. (2008) Paying for cost pharmaceuticals: regulation of new drugs in Australia, England and New Zealand. *Medical Journal of Australia.* 188(1): 26–8.

Raftery, J. (2010) Multiple sclerosis risk sharing scheme: a costly failure. *BMJ*, 340:doi:10.1136/bmj.c1672.

Raftery, J., Jones, J., Clegg, A. and Lotery, A. (2007) Ranibizumab (lucentis) versus bevacizumab (avastin): modelling cost effectiveness. *British Journal of Ophthalmology*, 91:1244–46.

Raftery, J., Stevens, A. and Roderick, P. (2005) *The Potential Use of Routine Data for Health Technology Assessment.* HTA Monograph.

Rawlins, M. (2008) De Testimonio: on the evidence for decisions about the use of therapeutic interventions. *RCP.* Available at: www.rcplondon.ac.uk.

Sheldon, T. and Faulkner, A. (1996) Vetting new technologies. *BMJ* 31 August 1996.

Smith, R., Chandra, R. and Tangcharaoensathien V. (2009) Trade in health related services. *Lancet*, 373: 593–600.

Steinbrook, R. (2006) The price of sight: ranibizumab, bevacizumab and the treatment of macular degeneration. *NEJM,* 355: 1409–12.

Stephens, T. and Brymer, R. (2001) *Dark Reality. The Impact of Thalidomide and its Revival as a Vital Medicine.* Cambridge, MA: Perseuss Publications.

Sullivan, S. et al. (2009) Health technology assessment in health care decisions in the in the US. *Value in Health* S2, S39–S44.

Tappenden, P., Chilcott, J.B., Eggington, S., Oakley, J. and McCabe, C. (2004) Methods for expected value of information analysis in complex health economic models: developments on the health economics of interferon-beta and glatiramer acetate for multiple sclerosis. *Health Technology Assessment* 8(27): 1–78.

Tunis, S. and Pearson, S. (2010) US moves to improve health decisions. *BMJ* 23 August 2010 341:c3615.

Wootton, D. (2006) *Bad Medicine: Doctors Doing Harm since Hippocrates.* Oxford: Oxford University Press.

Websites and resources

EU Health Technology Assessment Network: http://www.eunethta.net/.

European Commission Directorate General for Research and Innovation: http://ec.europa.eu/research/home.cfm.

European Observatory on Health Systems and Policies: http://www.euro.who.int/observatory.

HTAi, Health Technology Assessment International: http://www.htai.org/.

INAHTA, International Network for Health Technology Assessment: http://www.inahta.org/.

National Institute for Health and Clinical Excellence: www.nice.org.uk.

National Institute for Health Research, UK: www.nihr.ac.uk.

WHO HEN, World Health Organization Health Evidence Network: http://www.euro.who.int/HEN.

CHAPTER 6

Health and well-being: the wider context for healthcare management

Ann Mahon

Introduction

This chapter looks at the social and cultural context within which health and illness are defined and experienced by people in different cultures and countries around the world. It also considers which strategies to improve health and prevent or treat illness and disease have been developed and implemented. It begins with an exploration of how health, illness and disease are defined and how such definitions influence health and illness behaviours. Patterns of health and illness across different countries and between different socio-economic groups are described and explanations for the existence of inequalities in health are also explored. The contribution of formalized systems of healthcare is thus set in context and the implications of this for healthcare managers now and in the future are briefly discussed.

Definitions of health and illness

Health is an elusive concept. There is no single, definitive and objective definition of what it means to be healthy. It is well established in the sociological literature – and increasingly recognized in health policy and management – that definitions of health, illness and disease are socially constructed through the various social, cultural, political and economic contexts within which people live their daily lives. Health and well-being are therefore not merely biological or physiological notions but linked inextricably to the social environment that people live in. Dubos, for example, argues:

> Health and disease cannot be defined merely in terms of anatomical, physiological or mental attributes. Their real measure is the ability of the individual to function in a manner acceptable to himself and to the group of which he is part.
>
> (Dubos 1987: 261)

This more social or 'holistic' perspective contrasts with what has come to be known as the 'medical model', whereby medical knowledge is seen as based on a universal and generalizable science and illness and disease can be located in specific parts of the human body. This is in contrast to lay knowledge derived from 'unscientific' folk knowledge or individual experience. Thus medical and social medical models of health and illness are often set apart and viewed as distinct, mutually exclusive and even opposing perspectives. However, Mildred Blaxter argues that this dichotomy, set between biomedical, scientific models of healthcare and looser more holistic models, does not reflect reality and in practice an intermixing is inevitable. First, lay people have been taught to think in biomedical terms and second 'holistic' concepts are also a part of medical philosophy (Blaxter 1990). Cecil Helman (2001), an anthropologist and a general practitioner in the UK, looked at the relationship between medical and lay or folk beliefs surrounding health and illness. His focus was on the impact of health education, television programmes and increased access to healthcare, on folk beliefs. His findings suggested that folk beliefs about illness and healthcare not only survive the impact of scientific medicine but in some cases may even be perpetuated by this contact. For example, he argues that doctors do not or cannot differentiate between bacteria and viruses and so neither do their patients. The distinction may be reinforced through overprescribing of antibiotics in general and for viral illnesses in particular. It strengthens the lay view that all germs are bad and similar in nature. Helman concludes that, in the UK, free access to health and medicine does not seem to have altered some of the traditional folk beliefs about health and illness – medical concepts like the germ theory of disease, while being widely known to the lay public, may be understood in an entirely different way and often in terms of a much older folk view of illness (Helman 2001).

Kleinman (1985) identified three sectors found in any modern healthcare system. These are the professional sector, the folk sector and the popular sector. The professional sector consists of professional scientific 'Western' medicine and also professionalized indigenous healing traditions such as chiropractice and acupuncture. The folk sector represents non-professionalized healing specialists. The popular or lay sector comprises wellness activities performed in the family and community context. Given that most illness in all countries and cultures is managed (at least in the early stages) outside of formalized systems of healthcare (Kleinman's professional sector), conceptions of health and illness and how people manage their health and illnesses are of particular significance. For decades numerous epidemiological enquiries have estimated the proportion of symptoms presented to the professional sector (Wadsworth et al. 1971; Dunnell and Cartwright 1972). More recently Hughner and Kleine (2004) cite evidence that suggests between 70 per cent and 90 per cent of sickness is managed solely within the lay domain in Western society.

Blaxter's (1990) work describes how the way in which health is conceived differs over the life course. Young men tend to speak of health in terms of physical strength and fitness. Young women think in terms of energy, vitality and the ability to cope. In middle age, concepts of health become more complex, with older people thinking in terms of function as well as ideas about contentment and happiness.

It is common for the terms 'illness' and 'disease' to be used interchangeably and for health to be viewed in simple terms as the absence of illness or disease. By looking more closely at how terms are defined, we gain greater understanding of the social context of health and illness. The way lay people think about health and wellness influences their health and wellness-related behaviours – in other words, what we do or do not do to become or remain healthy and how we interpret and respond to symptoms of illness. There has been a lot of research into lay people's understanding of health – most of it in the 1970s and 1980s and much of it based in the UK and the USA. Typically these studies have looked at how health and illness are defined according to age, gender, specific disease categories, social class and ethnicity. Hughner and Kleine (2004) synthesized this research and identified 18 themes (set out in Table 6.1) that fall into four categories. The four categories are definitions of health (themes 1–5), explanations for health (themes 6–13), external and/or uncontrollable factors impinging on health (themes 14–16), and the place health occupies in people's lives (themes 17–18). Hughner and Kleine (2004: 397) conclude that popular worldviews about health and wellness are 'complex interweavings of information drawn from different sources including lay knowledge, folk beliefs, experiences, religious and spiritual practices and philosophy'.

More recently, particularly in countries with significant indigenous populations such as New Zealand, Australia, Canada, India and others, there has been an increased recognition and acceptance of how indigenous peoples define health. For example, the 1999 Declaration on the Health and Survival of Indigenous Peoples proposed the following definition of indigenous health:

> Indigenous peoples' concept of health and survival is both a collective and an individual inter-generational continuum encompassing a holistic perspective incorporating four distinct shared dimensions of life. These dimensions are the spiritual, the intellectual, physical and emotional. Linking these four fundamental dimensions, health and survival manifests itself on multiple levels where the past, present and future co-exists simultaneously.
>
> (Durie 2003a: 510)

Healthcare changes and develops at an increasingly fast pace. The rise in 'alternative' therapies, changes in technological interventions and access to information about health and health-related issues, particularly through the internet, are *inter alia* likely to be having an impact on health and illness beliefs and behaviours. At the same time the provision of healthcare and doctor–patient interactions continue to change – not least in response to technological advances and the implications of 'high tech' medicine whereby electronic patient records and magnetic resonance imaging may start to 'privilege the image over the actual body and its experience' (Blaxter 2009: 762). There has also been a decline in trust and confidence in health professionals and public services and, as a consequence, we are witnessing a shift in the balance of power between patients and professionals with a concomitant increase in the expectations and the role of patients in the consultation process (Henderson 2010). Globally, populations are becoming more mobile, leading to a diversity of health status, beliefs and behaviours within a community. It has been estimated, for example, that 11 per cent of the total UK population in 2008 was born outside of the UK (Jayaweera and Quigley 2010).

How these and other changes are influencing definitions and experiences of health and illness provide fertile grounds for future research, as well as having important implications for policy and practice. It is outside the scope of this chapter to give a comprehensive and critical account of studies conducted in different countries and

TABLE 6.1 Lay views of health: themes and associated statements

Theme	Example statement
Definitions of health	
1 Health is the absence of illness	'If I am not sick (for example, running a fever). I generally consider myself healthy.'
2 Health is functional ability	'As long as I am able to carry out my daily functions (e.g. going to work, taking care of the household), I consider myself healthy.'
3 Health is equilibrium	'The mind, body and spirit are all connected; all need to be in sync for good health.'
4 Health is freedom	'Good health is freedom; with it comes the ability to do what I want to do, to live how I want to live.'
5 Health is constraining	'Good health is constraining; with it individuals have to conform to the demands of society.'
Explanations for health	
6 Health through meditation or prayer	'Health and wellness can be maintained through meditation or prayer.'
7 Health is dependent upon mental attitude	'The power of a positive outlook or attitude can prevent sickness.'
8 Health through working	'As long as I keep going, I tend not to get sick – keeping busy doesn't allow one to have the time to get sick.'
9 Religious and supernatural explanations	'God works in mysterious ways; health and sickness is part of the divine plan.'
10 Health maintained through rituals	'The use of certain rituals is helpful in the maintenance of health (for example, reciting a prayer or psalm).'
11 Health is a moral responsibility	'I have a responsibility to my family to maintain my health.'
12 Health is maintained through internal monitoring	'I believe visiting a medical doctor for regular check-ups is important to maintain good health.'
13 Self-blame	'Many people suffer illnesses caused by their own bad habits.'
External uncontrollable factors	
14 Health as policy and institutions	'I believe good health is in part the product of governmental institutions that ensure the health of citizens.'
15 Modern way of life	'Many diseases of modern life result from the stressful and polluted environment in which we live.'
16 Health is genetics	'Often getting sick just happens and little can be done about it.'
Place of health in life	
17 The value and priority placed on health	'I have more important goals in my life than the pursuit of optimal health.'
18 Disparity between health beliefs and behaviours	'I know a lot about how to keep healthy (e.g. which type of eating and activity behaviours are considered healthy); however, I often do not practise this health knowledge.'

Source: Hughner and Kleine (2004: 419).

cultures and the ways in which the provision of healthcare has changed. Nevertheless it can be argued from this perspective that the 'medical model' is severely limited. Health is more than the absence of disease. Our beliefs about what causes our health influence our beliefs about how to behave when ill. Health beliefs interact with health behaviours, which has major implications for the relationship between individuals and providers of care.

Patterns of health and illness

There are both similarities and differences in the patterns of health, illness and disease across different countries and between different socio-economic and cultural groups within countries. Typically, health and illness are measured by three main indicators: those that measure life expectancy, mortality and morbidity. Tables 6.2 to 6.5 present a range of health and illness indicators for 15 World Health Organization (WHO) member states. Life expectancy and the probability of dying under the age of 5 and between the ages of 15 and 60 are presented in Table 6.2. Death rates for the three major causal categories – communicable diseases, non-communicable diseases and injuries – are given in Table 6.3. Table 6.4 reports the number of reported cases for selected infectious diseases in the six WHO-defined regions of the world. Finally, Table 6.5 presents data on performance relating to the achievement of selected WHO millennium development goals for each of the 15 selected countries.

The data shown in Tables 6.2 to 6.5 illustrate the following themes and trends:

- Health inequalities between the different countries exist for all of the selected measures of health and disease.

- Although considerable advances in life expectancy have been achieved in many countries in recent decades, there are significant differences between countries in life expectancy at birth. When a child is born in South Africa, he or she can be expected to live for 53 years. The same child born in India would live for an additional 11 years and at least a further 27 years if born in the UK, Sweden, the Netherlands, Germany, Australia and New Zealand.

- Women live longer than men in all of the countries selected, reflecting a global trend. In recent years, although the gap in life expectancy between men and women has reduced, the overall trend remains.

- The stage of economic, social and political development in countries is reflected in their patterns of health and illness. The populations of the poorest countries and those in political conflict typically have lower life expectancy, greater probability of dying prematurely and greater mortality and morbidity from infectious diseases.

- The relative burden of the three major diseases categories varies considerably between different countries. Poorer developing countries continue to suffer high death rates from infectious diseases while richer countries have experienced the epidemiological transition from infectious diseases to the non-communicable chronic diseases.

TABLE 6.2 Global Health Indicators: life expectancy and probability of dying, 2008

Member state and population (000)	Life expectancy at birth (years, both sexes)	Life expectancy at birth (males)	Life expectancy at birth (females)	Probability of dying (per 1000) under 5 years of age (males)	Probability of dying (per 1000) under 5 years of age (females)	Probability of dying (per 1000) 15–60 years of age (males)	Probability of dying (per 1000) 15–60 years of age (females)
Australia (21,512)	82	79	84	6	5	81	46
China (1,354,146)	74	72	76	18	24	140	84
Cuba (11,204)	77	76	79	7	6	122	81
France (62,637)	81	78	85	5	3	119	55
Germany (82,057)	80	77	83	5	4	101	54
Guatemala (14,377)	69	65	72	34	35	302	159
India (1,214,464)	64	63	66	65	73	250	173
Indonesia (232,517)	67	66	69	44	37	226	185
The Netherlands (16,653)	80	78	82	5	4	78	57
New Zealand (4,303)	81	78	83	7	5	88	57
Papua New Guinea (5,586)	62	61	64	73	65	292	235
South Africa (50,492)	53	52	55	70	58	563	479
Sweden (9,293)	81	79	83	3	3	76	48
UK (59,068)	80	78	82	6	5	96	59
USA (317,641)	78	76	81	9	7	135	79

Source: Data drawn from World Health Statistics (2010) Part II Global Health Indicators. http://www.who.int/whosis/whostat/2010/en/index.html.

Note: Member state population estimates are based on the United Nations World Population Prospects: The 2008 Revision Population Database. http://esa.un.org/UNPP/p2k0data.asp.

- Access to basic public health amenities is vital in population health. Populations in rural regions are most vulnerable to a lack of a reliable and clean supply of water so that only a third of people in the rural regions of Papua New Guinea and two-thirds in the rural regions of China have access to clean water.

TABLE 6.3 Cause of specific mortality and morbidity: age standardized mortality rates, 2004, per 100,000

Member state and population (000)	Communicable diseases	Non-communicable disease	Injuries
Australia (21,512)	21	355	32
China (1,354,146)	86	627	73
Cuba (11,204)	49	437	50
France (62,637)	26	387	45
Germany (82,057)	22	429	28
Guatemala (14,377)	279	515	103
India (1,214,464)	377	713	116
Indonesia (232,517)	272	690	233
The Netherlands (16,653)	31	425	24
New Zealand (4,303)	14	398	39
Papua New Guinea (5,586)	468	772	100
South Africa (50,492)	965	867	159
Sweden (9,293)	22	372	32
UK (59,068)	37	441	26
USA (317,641)	36	450	50

Source: Data drawn from World Health Statistics (2010) Part II Global Health Indicators http://www.who.int/whosis/whostat/2010/en/index.html.
Note: Member state population estimates are based on the United Nations World Population Prospects: The 2008 Revision Population Database. http://esa.un.org/UNPP/p2k0data.asp.

While these data illustrate the patterns of health and illness and some stark inequalities *between* different countries, they tend to conceal the considerable inequalities between different socio-economic, cultural and ethnic groups *within* countries, as well as inequalities based on geographic location (urban versus rural). This is well documented in the UK and other European countries in terms of social class or social status where it has become common to talk about the 'social gradient' present in health and illness data, where the poorest and most deprived groups experience the poorest health while the more affluent members of society experience both better social and environmental

TABLE 6.4 Selected infectious diseases: number of reported cases by WHO region

WHO Region	Cholera (2008)	Diptheria (2009)	HSN1 Influenza (2009)	Japanese encephalitis (2008)	Leprosy (2008)	Malaria (2008)	Measles (2008)	Meningitis (2008)
African Region	160801	–	–	–	29814	60835731	37010	82312
Region of the Americas	–	102	–	–	41891	719783	203	–
South-East Asia Region	4168	6502	–	1642	167505	100743491	75770	–
European Region	–	184	–	1	–	–	8883	–
Eastern Mediterranean Region	–	133	–	–	3938	8291229	12120	–
Western Pacific Region	1228	95	13	3428	5835	2604165	147986	–

Source: Data drawn from World Health Statistics (2010) Part II Global Health Indicators. http://www.who.int/whosis/whostat/2010/en/index.html.

conditions and better health status on a range of indicators (Marmot 2010). While the inequalities in health that exist in developed countries are not as extreme as those evident in the poorest countries of the world, they are nevertheless important, reflect societal inequalities and need to be addressed (Marmot 2010). In England, for example, people in the poorest areas die on average seven years earlier than those in the most affluent areas (Marmot 2010).

In New Zealand, Australia, India, Canada and other countries with indigenous populations, national data conceal the poorer health status of their indigenous people. It has been estimated that there are between 350 and 370 million indigenous people representing over 5000 cultures in more than 70 countries on every continent (Smith 2003; UN 2010). Indigenous peoples tend to have higher mortality and morbidity rates right across the disease spectrum and much of the excess arises from non-communicable chronic diseases. In all four countries cited above, cardiovascular and respiratory diseases and endocrine illnesses (mainly diabetes) and neoplasm account for most of the excess deaths among indigenous people. These conditions collectively account for 70 per cent or more of excess mortality in indigenous people. This is significant because of the avoidable nature of much chronic disease (Ring and Brown 2003). Indigenous populations generally have a lower life expectancy than non-indigenous populations, a higher incidence of most diseases including diabetes, mental disorders and cancers and experience Third World diseases, like TB and rheumatic fever, in developed countries (Durie 2003a). So while indigenous peoples represent a diversity of cultures, traditions and histories, they also represent the most marginalized populations in the world (UN 2010). The degree of marginalization and social injustice is rather graphically illustrated by the gaps in life expectancy between indigenous and non-indigenous people which is a staggering 20 years in Australia, 13 years in Guatemala and 11 years in New Zealand (UN 2010).

TABLE 6.5 Millennium development goals: selected health indicators for selected WHO member states, based on data from 2000–2008

Member state and population (000)	Children under 5 years of age under-weight for age (latest available figures between 2000-2008 (%)	One-year-olds immunized against measles (2008) (%)	Maternal mortality ratio (2005) (per 100 000 live births)	HIV prevalence among 15–49-year-olds (2008) %	Tuberculosis mortality rates (2008) (per 100 000 population)	Population with sustainable access to an improved water source % Urban	% Rural
Australia (21,512)	–	94	4	0.2	0.4	100	100
China (1,354,146)	6.8	94	45	0.1	12	93.7	66.1
Cuba (11,204)	3.9	99	45	0.1	0.4	99	95
France (62,637)	–	87	8	0.4	0.4	N/A	N/A
Germany (82,057)	1.1	95	4	0.1	0.3	N/A	N/A
Guatemala (14,377)	17.7	96	290	0.8	12	98	88
India (1,214,464)	43.5	70	450	0.3	23	95	79
Indonesia (232,517)	19.6	83	420	0.2	27	90	69
The Netherlands (16,653)	–	96	6	0.2	0.4	100	100
New Zealand (4,303)	–	86	9	0.1	0.5	100	N/A
Papua New Guinea (6,888)	18.1	54	470	1.5	21	88	32
South Africa (50,492)	–	62	400	18.1	39	99	73
Sweden (9,293)	–	96	3	0.1	0.4	100	100
UK (61,899)	–	86	8	0.2	0.7	100	100
USA (317,641)	1.3	92	11	0.6	0.3	100	100

Source: Data drawn from World Health Statistics (World Health Organization 2010) Part II Global Health Indicators. http://www.who.int/whosis/whostat/2010/en/index.html.

Note: Member State population estimates are based on the United Nations World Population Prospects: The 2008 Revision Population Database. http://esa.un.org/UNPP/p2k0data.asp.

How can these patterns of health and illness be explained? How can the relationship between where we live, how long we live for and the quality of our lives be explained? The next section looks at the factors that determine health.

The determinants of health

A number of different perspectives can be employed to explain inequalities in health. Historical and cultural analyses will shed light on the history surrounding the health status of a population or a social group. See, for example, Friedrich Engels on the social and economic conditions of Victorian England and Mason Durie on the experiences of Māori in New Zealand (Engels 1999; Durie 1994, 2003a, 2003b), and Myrna Cunningham on the indigenous concept of health and health systems (Cunningham 2010). Political, sociological, biological and genetic explanations will yield different explanations.

Compared to many other countries, the UK has a strong tradition of producing robust data over time to describe patterns of inequalities and these data have been compiled in a number of high-profile sources over many decades. However, the evidence in relation to why these patterns exist is less robust and raises political questions about the relative roles and responsibilities of individuals, families, the community and society and the state (Baggott 2010). The authors of the UK Black Report describe four theoretical explanations of the relationship between health and inequality. These are artefact explanations, theories of natural/social selection, materialist/structuralist explanations and cultural/behavioural explanations. They conclude that the most significant causes are those relating to materialist/structuralist explanations and base their recommendations for action on this perspective (Townsend and Davidson 1982). Durie argues that explanations for current indigenous health status can be grouped into four main propositions: genetic vulnerability, socio-economic disadvantage, resource alienation and political oppression. All four propositions can be conceptualized as a causal continuum. Short distance factors at one end (such as the impact of abnormal cellular processes) and at the other end long-distance factors such as government policies. Midway factors include values and lifestyles (Durie 2003a).

Wilkinson and Marmot (2003) focus upon the social determinants of health that affect populations and distinguish this perspective from the role that individual factors, such as genetic susceptibility, play in health and illness. The key social factors, a brief summary of the evidence base and the implications of this for public policy, based on Wilkinson and Marmot, are presented in Table 6.6. The research evidence for the summaries of 'what is known' and the 'policy implications' are fully sourced in the original publication, which is available on the European Public Health Alliance (EPHA) website (see useful websites at the end of this chapter).

The relative influence of these factors is influenced by economic and political factors. Economic growth and improvements in housing brought with them the epidemiological transition from infectious to chronic diseases – including heart disease, stroke and cancer. With it, came a nutritional transition when diets, particularly in Western Europe, changed to over-consumption of energy-dense fats and sugars, producing more obesity (Wilkinson and Marmot 2003: 26).

TABLE 6.6 The social determinants of health

What is known: key points	Policy implications
Health inequalities	
• Poor social and economic circumstances affect health status from birth to old age.	• Policy should address social and economic circumstances in policy areas such as housing and minimum wages.
• Differences between social and economic groups exist for most disease categories and causes of death.	• Critical transitions in life – for example, starting school and moving from primary to secondary school – can affect health and should be the focus of policy interventions.
• The effects upon health accumulate during the life cycle.	
Stress	
• Poor social and psychological circumstances can cause long-term stress.	• As well as managing the biological changes associated with stress, attention should be focused 'upstream', i.e. on the causes and not just on the effects.
• Anxiety, insecurity, low self-esteem and social isolation affect health status due to the physiological effects of stress on the immune and cardiovascular system.	• The quality of the social environment and material security in schools, workplaces and the wider community are important.
Early life	
• Infant experience is important to later health for biological, social and psychological reasons.	• Improved preventive healthcare before the first pregnancy and for mothers and babies in pre- and postnatal services and through improvements in the educational levels of parents and children.
• Insecure emotional attachment and poor stimulation can lead to low educational attainment and problem behaviour.	• Policies for improving health in early life should aim to increase the general level of education, provide good nutrition, health education and health and preventive care facilities and adequate social and economic resources before and during pregnancy and in infancy and support parent–child relationships.
• Slow or retarded physical growth in infancy is associated with reduced cardiovascular, respiratory, pancreatic and kidney development and function, which increase the risk of illness in adulthood.	
Social exclusion	
• Poverty, relative deprivation and social exclusion have a major impact on health and premature death.	• All citizens should be protected by minimum income guarantees, minimum wages legislation and access to services.
• The unemployed, many ethnic minority groups, guest workers, disabled people, refugees and homeless people are at particular risk of both absolute poverty (a lack of the basic material necessities of life) and relative poverty (being much poorer than most people in society).	• Interventions to reduce poverty and social exclusion at both the individual and the neighbourhood levels.
	• Legislation can help protect minority vulnerable groups from discrimination and social exclusion.
	• Public health policies should remove barriers to health and social care, social services and affordable housing.
	• Labour market, education and family welfare policies should aim to reduce social stratification.

TABLE 6.6 The social determinants of health

What is known: key points	Policy implications
Work	
• In general having a job is better for health than having no job. • Stress at work plays an important role in contributing to inequalities in health, sickness absence and premature death. • Health also suffers if people have little opportunity to use their skills and low decision-making authority. • The psychosocial environment at work is an important determinant of health and contributor to the social gradient in ill health.	• Improved conditions at work will lead to a healthier workforce, which will lead to greater productivity. • Appropriate involvement in decision-making is likely to benefit employees at all levels of an organization. • Good management involves ensuring appropriate rewards (money, status and self-esteem). • Workplace protection includes legal controls and workplace healthcare.
Unemployment	
• High rates of unemployment cause more illness and premature death. • Unemployed people and their families suffer a substantially increased risk of premature death. • The health effects of unemployment are linked to psychological and financial consequences. • Job insecurity has been shown to increase effects on mental health, self-reported ill health and heart disease.	• Policy should aim to prevent unemployment and job insecurity; to reduce the hardship suffered by the unemployed and to restore people to secure jobs.
Social support	
• Social support provides people with emotional and practical resources. • Supportive relationships may also encourage healthier behaviour patterns. • Social isolation and exclusion are associated with increased rate of premature death and poorer chances of survival after a heart attack. • The amount of emotional and practical social support people get varies by social and economic status. • Social cohesion (quality of social relationships, trust and respect in wider society) helps to protect people and their health.	• Good social relations can reduce the physiological response to stress. • Reducing socio-economic inequalities can lead to greater social cohesiveness and better standards of health. • Improving the social environment in schools, at work and in the community will help people feel valued and supported. • Designing facilities to encourage meeting and social interaction in communities could improve mental health. • Practices that treat some groups as socially inferior or less valuable should be avoided, as they are socially divisive.

TABLE 6.6 The social determinants of health (continued)

What is known: key points	Policy implications
Addiction	
• Drug use is both a response to social breakdown and an important factor in worsening the resulting inequalities in health.	• Support and treatment of addictions.
• Alcohol dependence, illicit drug use and cigarette smoking are all closely associated with social and economic disadvantage.	• Address underlying social deprivation.
	• Regulate availability of drugs.
	• Health education about less harmful forms of administration.
	• The broad framework of social and economic policy must support effective drug policy.
Food	
• A good diet and adequate food supply are central for promoting health and well-being.	• Local, national and international government agencies, non-governmental organizations and the food industry should ensure:
• A shortage of food and lack of variety cause malnutrition and deficiency diseases.	• The integration of public health perspectives into the food system to provide affordable and nutritious fresh food, especially for the most vulnerable.
• Excessive intake of food is also a form of malnutrition – obesity contributes to a number of diseases including cardiovascular disease, diabetes and cancer.	• Democratic, transparent decision-making and accountability in all food regulation matters.
• More deprived people are more likely to be obese. In many countries the poor substitute cheaper processed foods for fresh foods. Dietary goals to prevent chronic diseases emphasize eating more fresh vegetables, fruits and pulses and more minimally processed starchy foods but less animal fat, refined sugars and salt.	• Support for sustainable agriculture.
	• A stronger food culture for health, for example, through school education.
Transport	
• Healthy transport means less driving and more walking and cycling supported by better public transport systems.	• Improve public transport and change incentives to encourage use of public transport.
• Cycling, walking and using public transport provide exercise, reduce fatal accidents, increase social contact and reduce air pollution.	• Encourage cycling.

Source: Wilkinson and Marmot (2003).

108

Michael Marmot's strategic review of health inequalities in England, published in 2010, identified six areas as being particularly significant in determining health and inequalities and which incorporate most of those discussed here (Marmot 2010). His review considered the evidence in relation to the following:

- health and early years
- health and education
- health and work
- health and unemployment
- health and income
- health and communities.

Social and economic inequalities play a key role in determining the health of the population. Wilkinson and Pickett detail not just the negative impact that inequalities have on health but develop the thesis that, for a whole range of indicators, outcomes are worse where inequalities are greater. Where the income differences between the richest and the poorest in a society are small (as in Sweden and Japan), the whole population experience better health. Conversely, where income differences are greatest (as in the USA), then health is poorer. The existence of inequalities in itself exerts a negative social, psychological and ultimately physical effect on the population (Wilkinson and Pickett 2009). The implications are clear – reducing income inequalities within a society improves health for the whole population – we all do better in a more equal society. These analyses encourage a more critical perspective on the role of formalized healthcare systems. The next section in this chapter briefly considers the contribution of healthcare to health.

The contribution of healthcare to health status: healthcare in perspective

Until the 1970s, it was commonly assumed that the improvements in health experienced in many countries during the past century had occurred as a consequence of advances in medical care. Marmot and Wilkinson's work summarizes the evidence demonstrating that the health of people, patients and populations is influenced by many factors that exist outside of formalized systems of healthcare (Wilkinson and Marmot 2003). The amount of money spent on healthcare, measured by the proportion of GDP spent on health (see Table 6.7) within a system is not in itself a direct and causal contributor to the health profile of the nation. Spending on health reflects economic affluence which in turn influences population health.

During the 1970s, there was a fundamental change in Western societies' attitudes to medicine and the 'self-evident' efficacy of medicine. The validity of medical knowledge has also been increasingly challenged. These challenges came from a number of sources both within and outside of medicine (Cochrane 1972; Illich 1977a, 1977b; McKeown 1979; Kennedy 1983). However, some recent publications have suggested the need for a reappraisal of the role of medical and heathcare (Bunker 2001; Nolte and McKee 2004; Craig et al. 2006). As Craig et al. (2006: 1) states: 'The idea that successfully

TABLE 6.7 Expenditure on health expressed as percentage of GDP and percentage of government and private expenditure 2000–7, for a selection of WHO member states

Member State	Total expenditure on health as % of gross domestic product		General government expenditure on health as % of total expenditure on health		Private expenditure on health as % of total expenditure on health	
	2000	2007	2000	2007	2000	2007
Australia (21,512)	8.3	8.9	66.8	67.5	33.2	32.5
China (1,354,146)	4.6	4.3	38.7	44.7	61.3	55.3
Cuba (11,204)	6.7	10.4	90.9	95.5	9.1	4.5
France (62,637)	10.1	11	79.4	79	20.6	21
Germany (82,057)	10.3	10.4	79.7	76.9	20.3	23.1
Guatemala (14,377)	6.2	7.3	39.8	29.3	60.2	70.7
India (1,214,464)	4.4	4.1	24.5	26.2	75.5	73.8
Indonesia (232,517)	2.0	2.2	36.6	54.5	63.4	45.5
The Netherlands (16,653)	8.0	8.9	63.1	82	36.9	18
New Zealand (4,303)	7.7	9.0	78	78.9	22	21.1
Papua New Guinea (5,586)	4.0	3.2	81.7	81.3	18.3	18.6
South Africa (50,492)	8.5	8.6	40.5	41.4	59.5	58.6
Sweden (9,293)	8.2	9.1	84.9	81.7	15.1	18.3
UK (59,068)	7.0	8.4	79.3	81.7	20.7	18.3
USA (317,641)	13.4	15.7	43.2	45.5	56.8	54.5

changing society and the environment will result in improved health is uncontentious. However, it does not follow that healthcare has little role to play.'

Access to appropriate, acceptable and good quality healthcare is an important contributor to health and this is the case across all social and ethnic groups. Even where this is demonstrated, there is not a direct relationship between the availability of effective healthcare and health because of inequalities in access where those in greatest need of healthcare have least access (Tudor-Hart 1971). Wilkinson and Marmot suggest:

> Health policy was once thought to be about little more than the provi-
> sion and funding of medical care: the social determinants of health were

discussed only among academics. This is now changing. While medical
care can prolong survival and improve prognosis after some serious diseases, more important for the health of the population as a whole are
the social and economic conditions that make people ill and in need of
medical care in the first place. Nevertheless, universal access to medical
care is clearly one of the social determinants of health.

(2003: 7)

Many healthcare systems across the world are making fundamental changes to the
management and delivery of healthcare in attempts to reduce inequalities in both
health status and access to health services and in recognition of the influence of the
social determinants of health. In addition, after a period of unprecedented growth and
in an era of economic downturn in many countries, there is now increasing concern
about productivity, efficiency and the quality of care. It is outwith the scope of this
chapter to provide a full and systematic account of such changes. Instead, a number of
strategies that have attempted to incorporate the social determinants of health into the
design and delivery of healthcare, alongside a concern to improve health outcomes,
will be described. These include examples of addressing health inequalities in Europe,
attempts to improve the health of indigenous populations and targeting services at
vulnerable populations who are high-users of health services.

Addressing health inequalities: examples of European experiences

In an analysis of policy developments on health inequalities in different European countries, Mackenbach and Bakker (2003) found that countries are in widely different phases
of awareness of and willingness to take action on inequalities in health. Their international comparisons suggest that the UK is ahead of continental Europe in developing
and implementing policies to reduce socio-economic inequalities in health and is 'on
the brink of entering a stage of comprehensive, coordinated policy'. They identified
factors that supported or inhibited action on inequalities, including the availability of
descriptive data, the presence or absence of political will and the role of international
agencies such as WHO. Innovative approaches were identified in five main areas:
policy steering mechanisms, labour market and working conditions, consumption and
health-related behaviour, healthcare, and territorial approaches:

1 **Policy steering mechanisms** such as quantitative policy targets and health inequalities impact assessment. In the Netherlands, for example, quantitative policy targets
   were set for the reduction of inequalities in 11 intermediate outcomes including
   poverty, smoking and working conditions.
2 **Labour market and working conditions** can be addressed universally or in a targeted approach. An example of a universal approach comes from France where
   occupational health services offer annual check-ups and preventive interventions
   to all employees. An example of a targeted approach is job rotation among dustmen
   in the Netherlands.

3 **Consumption and health-related behaviour**. Again universal and targeted approaches are identified. In the UK, women on low income are targeted using multi-method interventions to reduce smoking. In Finland a universal approach is adopted by serving low-fat food products through mass catering in schools and workplaces.

4 **Healthcare**. Examples of innovative practices here include working with other agencies. In the UK, for example, there are community strategies led by local government agencies but integrating care across all the local public sector services.

5 **Territorial approaches** include comprehensive strategies for deprived areas such as the health action zones in the UK (Mackenbach and Bakker 2003).

Although there were some similarities, for example, the UK, Netherlands and Sweden have comprehensive strategies to reduce inequalities informed by national advisory committees, their analysis found considerable variations in approaches which, they suggest, is a symptom of intuitive as opposed to rigorous evidence-based approaches to policy-making. They conclude: 'Further international exchanges of experiences with development, implementation and evaluation of policies and interventions to reduce health inequalities can help to enhance learning speed' (Mackenbach and Bakker 2003: 1409).

Addressing the health status of indigenous peoples

Mason Durie identifies two broad directions for improving health services for indigenous health in New Zealand: increasing the responsiveness of conventional services and establishing dedicated indigenous programmes. In New Zealand, both these approaches are endorsed in legislation and government health policy. Section 8 of the New Zealand Public Health and Disability Act (2000) requires health services to recognize the principles of the Treaty of Waitangi – the 1840 agreement that saw sovereignty exchanged for Crown protection (Durie 2003b). The New Zealand strategy is broad in its approach, seeking to influence macro policies such as labour market policies, public health population approaches to health, and personal health services. In this respect, it is consistent with the Māori holistic approach to health and intersectoral determinants of health.

Indigenous health services provide a range of healing methods, including conventional professional services and traditional healing. Durie argues that their most significant contribution is improved access to health services for indigenous people, enabling earlier intervention, energetic outreach, higher levels of compliance and a greater sense of community participation and ownership. Indigenous services tend to be built around indigenous philosophies, aspirations, social networks and economic realities (Durie 2003b). For Durie, coexistence of conventional and indigenous healthcare is not problematic:

> While there is some debate about which approach is likely to produce the best results, in practice conventional services and indigenous services can exist comfortably together. More pertinent is the type of service that

> is going to be most beneficial to meet a particular need. In general indige-
> nous health services are more convincing at the level of primary health
> care. Higher rates of childhood immunisation, for example, seem to be
> possible with services that are closely linked to indigenous networks, and
> early intervention is embraced with greater enthusiasm when offered by
> indigenous providers.
>
> (Durie 2003b: 409)

The importance of partnership and collaborative working is identified as a crucial component for success:

> Conventional health services and indigenous services need, however, to
> work together within a collaborative framework. Clinical acumen will
> be sharpened by cultural knowledge and community endeavours will be
> strengthened by access to professional expertise. It makes sense to build
> health networks that encourage synergies between agencies, even when
> philosophies differ.
>
> (Durie 2003b: 409)

Devadasan et al. (2003) describe an initiative working with tribes in India where a health system specifically targeted at tribal people had a remarkable impact on infant and maternal mortality. Over 10 to 15 years, immunization coverage increased from 2 per cent to over 75 per cent. Use of hospital services was three times the national average in a population that initially refused to go to hospital because 'only dead spirits circulate there'. They identified the main features that characterized the success of this initiative:

- It was nested within larger development services, such as agriculture, education and housing.
- It was owned by the people. From the beginning, tribal communities participated in planning and implementing the scheme. Most of the staff were from the tribal community.

The health system was developed with the worldview of the tribal community in mind. For example, initially the hospital did not have beds, as patients found it more comfortable to sleep on mats on the floor (Devadasan et al. 2003). Culturally sensitive strategies can be applied to a range of problems experienced by indigenous communities with demonstrable improvements in health outcomes (Cunningham 2010).

Focusing on vulnerable people

Findings from a series of studies of health and illness behaviour suggest that we need to rethink aspects of healthcare delivery, health education and health promotion and the role of providers and communities. An innovative series of initiatives at McMaster University in Ontario, Canada, has found that social factors are greater predictors of health than clinical factors. Vulnerability is defined as being caused by the interaction between biological factors (for example, genetic predisposition), personal resources (such as resilience, cognitive and intellectual capacities) and environmental factors (such as the availability of social support). Through a series of clinical trials that have been ongoing since 1991, they have found that targeting vulnerable people and offering pro-active and integrated care is more effective and usually less expensive than on-demand care. In this context holistic and integrated care are crucial (KPMG 2010).

The role of healthcare managers

Managers and leaders must understand the wider context that shapes health and illness as increasingly the strategies being adopted by many countries are broad public policies, in recognition that progress in health outcomes depends on a wide range of social determinants. Managers can no longer work in organizational isolation and need to be externally focused in order to both make sense of and implement health policies that may be so broad-based that the proximity of interventions to specific illness in individuals may not be apparent to their workforce. In response, new paradigms of leadership emphasize the need to bring together diverse networks, adopt cross-boundary working, innovation and entrepreneurship, and focus on outcomes. Here Mintzberg's three distinct aspects of managerial work are useful in exploring the implications of the wider context of health for managers – managers have important interpersonal roles, informational roles and decisional roles (Mintzberg 1989) that are increasingly performed in a system of interdependence rather than in organizational isolation.

Interpersonally, managers are figureheads for their organization both internally and externally. One key aspect of this role is to develop effective and enduring relationships with partners outside of their organization and to be able to communicate the importance and significance of this to the workforce within their organizations. Thus the interpersonal role is also important in carrying out the informational role where managers are responsible for collecting, analysing and disseminating information from a range of different sources. This includes both sense-making in policy terms but also an appreciation of effective, evidence-based mechanisms to implement and evaluate change. The evidence supporting the effectiveness of health service interventions needs to be better understood by managers, healthcare professionals, the public health community and individual users of services. Finally managers must make decisions and act as negotiators, resource allocators and entrepreneurs – all with a firm eye on maximizing the use of scarce resources to improve the health of the population. At the same time, the relevance of interventions outside the health service such as welfare reforms, agricultural polices and pollution control needs to be understood by the same key stakeholders. Change requires cultural changes within the healthcare workforce and organization but also a recognition and acceptance of the significance of culture to definitions and experiences of health and illness.

To meet the challenge of implementing broad-based public policies, the development of an appropriate and effective workforce is essential. A number of developments are apparent here, ranging from joint appointments between local government and healthcare organizations for the public health workforce in the UK (Fotaki et al. 2004) to New Zealand where the development of the workforce is a common theme in the development of indigenous health. The similarities and contrasts between different countries suggest the value to be had from sharing good practice and developing research through international links.

The interpersonal, informational and decisional challenges facing healthcare managers are becoming more complex. Understanding the wider context within health systems work is vital to effective execution of their role.

Conclusion

This chapter has argued that health is much more than the absence of disease by providing evidence in support of the WHO's (1946) definition of health: 'Health is a state of complete physical, mental and social wellbeing and not merely the absence of disease or infirmity.' The responsibility for health and healthcare extends beyond formalized systems of healthcare. Nevertheless the role of healthcare and healthcare managers is crucial in ensuring access to healthcare interventions that improve the health of their populations alongside wider public policies that address the social determinants of health:

> The evidence that health is determined by social, environmental and economic influences throughout a person's life is not at issue. What is lacking is secure evidence that many broad public health interventions are effective. Priority must be given to addressing this lack of evidence. In the meantime, instead of polarized positions, an appropriate balance needs to be struck between the contrasting strategies of developing health services and intervening outside the health system.
>
> (Craig et al. 2006: 1)

Summary box

- Definitions of health and illness are the product of the complex interaction of the individual with cultural, social and political factors within their environment.
- The relative burden of the three major disease categories varies considerably between different countries. Poorer developing countries continue to suffer high death rates from infectious diseases while richer countries have experienced the epidemiological transition from infectious diseases to the non-communicable chronic diseases.
- Routine data conceal considerable inequalities between different socio-economic, cultural and ethnic groups within countries.
- The key social factors determining health are inequalities in health, stress, early life, social exclusion, work, unemployment, social support, addiction, food and transport.
- More equal societies are healthier. Countries with small differences between highest and lowest incomes are healthier than those with greater social distance.

- Access to appropriate, acceptable and good quality healthcare is also an important determinant of health.

- The evidence supporting the effect of health services interventions needs to be better understood by managers, healthcare professionals, the public health community and individual users of services.

- Change requires cultural changes not only within the healthcare workforce and organization but also a recognition and acceptance of the significance of culture to definitions and experiences of health and illness.

- The interpersonal, informational and decisional challenges facing healthcare managers are becoming more complex. Understanding the wider context within health systems work is vital to effective execution of their role.

Self-test exercises

Describing and explaining inequalities in health

1 Using the data presented in Table 6.2, describe the relationship between sex and life expectancy for each country. What are the similarities and differences in this data for the 15 countries listed?

2 Now consider why women live longer than men. Using Wilkinson and Marmot's list of the ten social determinants of health, develop your own hypotheses about why women live longer than men.

3 Do your hypotheses suggest that the disparities in life expectancy between men and women are *inequities* that are unfair and unjust or *differences* that are inevitable and acceptable at a societal level?

The role of healthcare managers

4 Using Mintzberg's framework, how do you think that the role of healthcare managers and leaders will develop in the next five to ten years? How do you think these roles will develop differently in the different organizations that form the health system in your country?

References and further reading

Baggott, R. (2010) *Public Health: Policy and Politics*. 2nd edition. Basingstoke: Palgrave Macmillan.

Blaxter, M. (1990) *Health and Lifestyles*. London: Tavistock-Routledge.

Blaxter M. (2009) The case of the vanishing patient? Image and experience. *Sociology of Health and Illness*, 31(5): 762–78.

Bunker, J.P. (2001) *Medicine Matters After All: Measuring the Benefits of Primary Care, a Healthy Lifestyle and a Just Social Environment*. London: Nuffield Trust for Research and Policy Studies in Health Services.

Cochrane, A.L. (1972) *Effectiveness and Efficiency: Random Reflections on Health Services*. London: Nuffield Provincial Hospitals Trust.

Craig, N., Wright, B., Hanlon, P. and Galbraith, S. (2006) Does health care improve health? Editorial. *Journal of Health Services Research*, 11(1): 1–2.

Cunningham, M. (2010) Health. In United Nations *State of the World's Indigenous Peoples*. Available at: http://www.un.org/esa/socdev/unpfii/en/sowip.html.

Davey, B., Gray, A. and Seale, C. (eds) (2001) *Health and Disease: A Reader*, 3rd edn. Maidenhead: Open University Press.

Devadasan, N., Menon, S., Menon, N. and Devadasan, R. (2003) Use of health services by indigenous population can be improved. Letters. *British Medical Journal*, 327: 988.

Dubos, R. (1987) *Mirage of Health*. New Brunswick, NJ: Rutgers University Press.

Dunnell, K. and Cartwright, A. (1972) *Medicine Takers, Prescribers and Hoarders*. London: Routledge and Kegan Paul.

Durie, M. (1994) *Whaiora: Māori Health Development*. Auckland: Oxford University Press.

Durie, M. (2003a) The health of indigenous peoples. *British Medical Journal*, 326: 510–11.

Durie, M. (2003b) Providing health services to indigenous peoples. *British Medical Journal*, 327: 408–9.

Engels, F. (1999) *The Condition of the Working Class in England*. Oxford: Oxford University Press.

Fotaki, M., Higgins, J. and Mahon, A. (2004) *The Development of the Public Health Role in Primary Care Trusts in the North West*. Manchester: Centre for Public Policy and Management, University of Manchester.

Helman, C. (2001) Feed a cold, starve a fever. In B. Davey, A. Gray and S. Seale (eds) *Health and Disease: A Reader*, 3rd edn. Maidenhead: Open University Press.

Henderson, J. (2010) Expert and lay knowledge: a sociological perspective. *Nutrition and Debate*, 67: 4–5.

Hughner, R.S. and Kleine, S.S. (2004) Views of health in the lay sector: a compilation and review of how individuals think about health. *Health*, 8(4): 395–422.

Illich, I. (1977a) *Disabling Professions*. London: Boyars.

Illich, I. (1977b) *Limits to Medicine: Medical Nemesis – the Expropriation of Health*. New York: Penguin.

Jayaweera, H. and Quigley M.A. (2010) Health status, health behaviour and healthcare use among migrants in the UK: evidence from mothers in the Millennium Cohort Study. *Social Science and Medicine*, 71: 1002–10.

Kennedy, I. (1983) *The Unmasking of Medicine: A Searching Look at Healthcare Today*. St Albans: Granada.

Kleinman, A. (1985) Indigenous systems of healing: questions for professional, popular and folk care. In J. Salmon (ed.) *Alternative Medicines: Popular and Policy Perspectives*. London: Tavistock.

KPMG (2010) *A Better Pill to Swallow: A Global View of What Works in Healthcare.* Case Study. Ontario: McMaster University, pp. 24–7.

Mackenbach, J.P. and Bakker, M.J. (2003) Tackling socio-economic inequalities in health: analysis of European experiences. *The Lancet*, 362: 1409–14.

McKeown, T. (1979) *The Role of Medicine: Dream, Mirage or Nemesis?* Princeton, NJ: Princeton University Press.

Marmot, M. (2010) *Fair Society, Healthy Lives: The Marmot Review. Strategic Review of Health Inequalities Post-2010.* London: The Marmot Review. Available at: http://www.marmotreview.org/AssetLibrary/pdfs/Reports/FairSocietyHealthyLives ExecSummary.pdf.

McDermott, R. et al. (2003) Sustaining better diabetes care in remote indigenous Australian communities. *British Medical Journal*, 327: 428–30.

Mintzberg, H. (1989) *Mintzberg on Management.* New York: Free Press.

Nolte, E. and McKee, M. (2004) *Does Healthcare Save Lives? Avoidable Mortality Revisited.* London: Nuffield Trust.

Ring, I. and Brown, N. (2003) The health status of indigenous peoples and others. *British Medical Journal*, 327: 404–5.

Smith, R. (2003) Learning from indigenous people. *British Medical Journal*, 327. doi: 10.1136/bmj.327.7412.O-f.

Townsend, P. and Davidson, N. (eds) (1982) *Inequalities in Health: The Black Report.* Harmondsworth: Penguin.

Tudor-Hart, J. (1971) The inverse care law. *The Lancet*, 1: 405–12.

United Nations (2010) *State of the World's Indigenous Peoples*, United Nations. Available at: http://www.un.org/esa/socdev/unpfii/en/sowip.html.

Wadsworth, M., Butterfield, W.J.H. and Blaney, R. (1971) *Health and Sickness: The Choice of Treatment.* London: Tavistock.

Wilkinson, R. and Marmot, M. (eds) (2003) *Social Determinants of Health: The Solid Facts*, 2nd edn. Geneva: World Health Organisation.

Wilkinson, R. and Pickett, K. (2009) *The Spirit Level: Why More Equal Societies Almost Always Do Better.* London: Allen Lane.

World Health Organization (2010) *World Health Statistics.* Geneva: World Health Organisation.

World Health Organization (1946) Preamble to the Constitution of the World Health Organisation as adopted by the International Health Conference, New York, 19–22 June 1946; signed on 22 July 1946 by the representatives of 61 States (Official Records of the World Health Organization, 2: 100) and entered into force 7 April 1948.

Websites and resources

Association of Public Health Observatories (APHO). The Association of Public Health Observatories (APHO) represents a network of 12 public health observatories (PHO) working across the five nations of England, Scotland, Wales, Northern Ireland and the Republic of Ireland. They produce information, data and intelligence on people's health and health care for practitioners, policy-makers and the wider community. Their expertise lies in turning information and data into meaningful health intelligence: http://www.apho.org.uk/.

Department of Health. The Public Health link on the Department of Health website provides detailed summaries of policies and good practice in addressing inequalities in health in the English NHS: http://www.dh.gov.uk/en/Publichealth/index.htm.

European Public Health Alliance (EPHA). Represents over 100 non-governmental and other not-for-profit organizations working in public health in Europe. EPHA's mission is to promote and protect the health of all people living in Europe and to advocate for greater participation of citizens in health-related policy-making at the European level: http://www.epha.org/.

The System-Linked Research Unit on Health and Social Service Utilization, Ontario, Canada, was launched in 1991 and funded by the Ontario Ministry of Health and Long Term Care to compare the effects and costs of innovative, intersectoral, comprehensive services with the usual sectoral, fragmented approaches of serving vulnerable populations. Details on their research programme can be found on: http://fhs.mcmaster.ca/slru/unit.htm.

World Health Organization (WHO) is the directing and coordinating authority for health within the United Nations system. It is responsible for providing leadership on global health matters, shaping the health research agenda, setting norms and standards, articulating evidence-based policy options, providing technical support to countries and monitoring and assessing health trends. Extensive data on a range of health topics for WHO Member States is accessible on their website: http://www.who.int/.

Global health policy: governing health systems across borders

Scott L. Greer

Introduction: What is global health?

More often than not, discussions of 'international health', or 'global health', amount to discussions held in rich countries of projects in aid of poor countries. Almost a species of development studies, it is called international health. But to think of it that way – as development, or charity – disguises the extent to which factors outside the borders of one's country affect health and healthcare systems. Health and healthcare are global and are increasingly affected by global factors.

This chapter focuses on global health (Table 7.1): the structures, organizations, and issues that directly or indirectly affect health and transcend borders. It first looks at the issues that transcend borders, then the structures and organizations, and then the challenges that they present and the opportunities to affect them. While in a sense any issue or governance structure can affect health, the focus here is on the ones that relatively directly affect the inputs and outputs of healthcare, e.g. workforce, finance, and patients.

What internationalization means in and for health policy

If global health means causes of ill health that transcend borders, then the issues in global health are not hard to identify: they are the ones that cross borders. This section reviews the most important ones with clear effects on health systems and does not discuss larger global changes such as South–North migration or climate change.

Infectious diseases

Infectious diseases are the oldest global health issue, and policies to deal with diseases that cross borders are almost as old as the state itself. The fear of the plague arriving on the next boat, or caravan, rightly haunted Eurasian polities for centuries. Today, in the aftermath of HIV/AIDS, SARS, H5N1 and H1N1 influenza, the need to pay attention to the health and healthcare of distant countries is clear (Kaufmann 2009). The medieval Venetian Republic invented the concept of quarantine by making boats wait 40 days to dock, but modern states lack that luxury and, as a result, often create the capacity to

TABLE 7.1 Definitions in global health governance

Term	Definition
Public health	The overarching field of study and practice concerned with improving population health and creating more equal health outcomes by a variety of evidence-based means, at any territorial scale
Global health	Study and practice of issues that directly or indirectly affect heath but transcend boundaries
International health	Study and practice of health issues of countries other than one's own, with a focus on low– and middle-income countries
Comparative health	Study and practice of comparing different systems' and states' approaches to healthcare and public health
Healthcare management and policy; Health services research	Study and practice of the financing and delivery of healthcare services

Source: Heavily modified by author from Koplan et al. (2009) and Fried et al. (2010).

cope with outbreaks on their borders and monitor events elsewhere. Even if the burden of disease in the rich world, and increasingly the whole world, is in non-communicable and chronic diseases, the fear of a pandemic and the need for vigilance mean that the policy area remains a constant preoccupation. In practice, it calls for states to have domestic bureaucracies that can identify and deal with outbreaks, and international surveillance to identify emerging diseases as quickly as possible.

Medical tourism and patient mobility

Causes of illnesses cross borders, and so do the ill. Patient mobility, also known as medical tourism, is the practice of the patient going to a doctor or facility in another country to seek treatment.

There are three broad reasons reasons why patients would want to do this (Laugesen and Vargas-Bustamente 2010). One is *primary* exit, in which patients cross borders because they lack access to healthcare. The most-publicized examples of this are in the United States, which has phenomenally expensive healthcare and a large uninsured population (Turner 2010), but there are a few marginal groups in the EU who use it (such as workers from outside the EU, or new accession states, whose eligibility for healthcare in some states is unclear). Within the European Union, where patients enjoy near-universal healthcare, some patient mobility is *complementary*: travelling to get specific treatments that are not available at home. The other system, in this model, complements their own system by offering specific treatments or lower co-payments. Most who travel within the EU, travel for *duplicative* reasons, in which they use a healthcare service that is available within their own country. They usually do this for comfort and convenience, like patients who live in border regions where the nearest hospital is on the other side of the frontier, or retirees who move to another EU member state but prefer to get their healthcare at home, in their own language. Some do it because they feel that higher quality healthcare is available elsewhere. Finally, a few states choose to send patients abroad, taking advantage of other countries' excess capacity (Glinos et al. 2010).

The scale of patient mobility within Europe, let alone around the world, is largely unknown, and what data are available are not well publicized (Carrera and Lunt 2010). Overall, it seems that about 2 per cent of European healthcare is cross-border, and it is mostly duplicative care in border regions or areas with large settlements of migrants (such as Spanish coasts and islands) (Legido-Quigley et al. 2007).

Patient mobility potentially allows patients a better deal, but it is a very problematic subject. Not only does it create serious legal issues within the EU (see 130–133); it also, in the EU or worldwide, creates problems of quality assurance, redress and health service planning. For example, what happens to healthcare in a poor country if medical tourists from a rich country use up its healthcare capacity? What can the patient who suffers from a medical error do? The effects of healthcare mobility have mostly been framed, by policy-makers and the press alike, as being about cost. The effects on quality and access are much more ambiguous and neither scholars nor policy-makers have fully grasped them (Jarman et al. 2011).

Professional mobility

Sometimes the patient goes to the doctor or nurse; the older and more common dynamic involves the doctor or nurse going to the patient. This is professional mobility. The basic dynamic of professional mobility worldwide is the export of professionals from poor and middle-income countries to richer countries. Rich countries 'shop' for professionals on a 'spot market'; the rich countries that import the most are English-speaking, pay doctors and nurses well, and do not train as many as they need. This affects the UK because it is such a country, though the United States is by far the biggest importer with the worst professional workforce planning and the highest professional pay (Aiken 2007). That said, professional mobility is increasing within the EU (Young et al. 2010).

Professional mobility solves problems for rich countries that need doctors and nurses, and for the professionals from poor countries who can enjoy a mixture of higher pay, better professional conditions and opportunities, and opportunities for their families. It usually works to the detriment of the poorest countries, which lose their extremely scarce professionals. If the poor countries have educated and trained those professionals, then they have actually subsidized the richest countries! Middle-income countries, such as India, are the biggest exporters and are in a more stable situation; their professional education system has outpaced their creation of good professional posts, and so they export. Such exports tend to fall off as demand for care grows at home. The fact that India exports the bulk of doctors, and that it will over time be able to employ them at home, means that it is not as much of a problem as the export of any professionals from the poorest states. A dozen doctors from Ghana or Ethiopia have no significant impact on healthcare in a big, rich European country, but their departure can hugely diminish the medical workforce in their home country (Box 7.1).

Box 7.1: *Professional mobility*

Edward Okeke, London School of Hygiene and Tropical Medicine

Dr Charles is a doctor at a private hospital in Lagos, Nigeria, where he earns approximately $450 a month. From 9a.m.–3p.m., he is a medical officer there. From 4p.m.–9p.m. he is still a medical officer, but at another private clinic on the other side of town. There he earns another $350. He does this every day, Monday to Friday, and is on call the entire weekend, twice a month. He cannot wait to move to the UK or the USA where he knows classmates who earn $10,000 a month. He has tried several times to travel to the UK but has been unsuccessful. One day he hears from a classmate that doctors are needed in East Timor (this classmate has just gotten a visa for Ireland) and that from there, after a while, it is possible to make one's way to the UK. This is in August. By October, Dr Charles is gone.

Dr Charles is one of thousands of doctors who every year try to leave the country. Their motto: 'Anywhere but here.' These doctors end up in South Africa, Botswana, Trinidad and Tobago, even East Timor. The true end goal, the golden prize, a work permit for the USA or the UK.

In the discussion on health professional migration, we often highlight the statistics on migration, the proportion of doctors/nurses produced in African country X that are in a developed country. What is sometimes forgotten is that this number only tells part of the story. There are many thousands of health professionals who would like to migrate but cannot, because they cannot afford the high fixed costs of migration, because they are unable to get a visa, etc. In a 2004 survey of nearly 2400 health professionals in six countries in Africa, half of the surveyed professionals expressed an intention to migrate. This is arguably still an underestimate; some who wish to migrate prefer to keep their plans to themselves. Why are so many health professionals so desperate to migrate? That is a question that deserves far more attention than it is presently getting. Some early work by Okeke (2009a, 2009b) suggests that economic factors are indeed important, but a lot more work remains to be done before we can make meaningful policy in this area.

In the short term, any country experiencing outward professional mobility can suffer serious problems. After EU accession in 2004, a number of states lost a large proportion of their nursing and medical staff. The effect of EU enlargement was that countries such as the UK or Germany, which pay doctors and nurses well, could compete with native Eastern European health systems that lacked the resources to offer anything like competitive professional environments or pay.

Cross-border healthcare businesses

One of the major reasons why health never was parochial, and never will be, is that it is involved with global businesses. Some of the biggest names in the world economy make much of their revenue from health systems: not just healthcare sector firms like the pharmaceutical companies, but also insurers, information technology firms such as IBM, and engineering firms such as GE and Siemens.

Some firms are interested in the health systems themselves; public and quasi-public healthcare (not counting 'wellness' such as spas or putative health food) is about 6-10 per cent of most EU economies. That is an enormous amount of money with more than enough scope for return on private investment. Of the firms who directly seek to enter public systems, the most common sell products or services: pharmaceuticals, medical devices, and perhaps services such as construction. These are often very political businesses, with pharmaceutical firms in particular known for their large profit margins, enormous investment in politics and often tough tactics against politicians and states that cross them. Generally, they are interested in preserving their intellectual property (i.e. reducing competition), reducing regulatory burdens, and increasing their pricing power: all entirely reasonable goals for profit-making companies. These firms occupy a profitable and growing global segment that depends on public money, and they take a keen and well-resourced interest in the developing structure of global health governance. They also have the increasingly remarked tendency to conduct clinical trials in poor countries, a politically and ethically complex issue.

A few firms sell services in multiple countries or across borders, such as the South African healthcare services firm Netcare or the UK-based BUPA, or the various American elite institutions opening up operations in Europe, Asia and the Middle East. These companies occupy a miniscule part of international healthcare, and most of that in the jurisdictions whose governments court them (England under Labour, Madrid region, Dubai, etc.). Their small size, depending on the analyst, means that they are in a marginal niche, or that they have enormous room to grow. The next few years will tell which is the case.

Finally, there are firms that try to provide healthcare finance. They deserve special attention in a discussion of global health because their presence is much more significant in global than in domestic health policy. In general, liberalizing finance is very dangerous for healthcare systems because it risks adverse selection, i.e. 'cream-skimming' (Evans 1999). Private insurance offers the promise of reduced state liability for healthcare, but generally leaves public systems stuck with the worst risks, least lucrative customers, and the same or worse capacity constraints. Private insurers, aware that few health policy-makers will voluntarily risk their systems' equity, stability and financial sustainability by letting them play a major role, have increasingly sought to use international economic governance such as the EU and GATS (see Boxes 7.2 and 7.4) to penetrate health systems and lock in their commercial positions.

Outside healthcare, many companies are interested in international health governance and try to shape it. The most notorious, after pharmaceutical companies, are tobacco firms, another sector whose profits, and indeed core business models, depend on a particular regulatory environment. Thus, just as the pharmaceutical industry tried to use the US-Australia free trade agreement to introduce language that would make it difficult to control drug prices, the tobacco industry lobbies worked hard to make sure that Chinese accession to the World Trade Organization would require China to open up its cigarette market to their products (Holden et al. 2010 discuss how one company lobbied, showing the different techniques they use).

Governance mechanisms

What are the bodies and rules that try to shape these issues? What kinds of governance transcend borders and influence health as the issues in the previous section transcend borders and influence health? This section discusses the important organizations, loosely arranged by their age. It is not a history of international health governance (Birn 2009).

World Health Organization (WHO)

The World Health Organization is the only truly global organization with the mission of improving health and healthcare for all. With 193 states as members – almost every government in the world – it is the obligatory reference point for international health debates and governance. While its antecedents date back to before the First World War, the WHO was formed after the Second World War with a broad remit – not just to coordinate communicable disease control, but also to promote health. It has two key components. One is the World Health Assembly, which is made up of representatives of all 193 states. Each state gets one vote. The other is the WHO itself, which is an international organization of about 8,000 staff answerable to the Assembly and divided into regions with distinctive cultures, problems, and organizations.[1]

Over time, this has meant influential statements such as the 1978 Alma Ata Declaration, which called for putting primary care at the center of healthcare, the 1981 'Health for All' movement, which advocated for basic healthcare as a universal right, and the 2008 Tallinn Charter, which, if it achieves the fame of the others, will be a reference point for the argument that good health is both a value in itself and the basis of a strong economy. Less visibly, its working groups and assemblies also influence policy on a host of medical, regulatory, and public health issues. Anybody can make statements, but the global nature of the WHO and the legitimacy of the UN system to which it belongs mean that such statements become reference points for debate. Advocates for primary care, basic needs, or health investment can point to WHO declarations to buttress their cases. More concretely, WHO has been a key node in the global networks coordinating the identification and response to emerging diseases such as SARS.

Despite these advantages, and its successes in giving some shape to global campaigns, the WHO has many faults. It is rigid, highly political, decentralized so that it often shows different faces to different parts of the world, and above all underfunded. Because, like most UN agencies, it depends on grants from donors, it can often act like an NGO trying to raise money for funders' goals. Such dependence makes stable policy harder. It also undercuts the World Heath Assembly's one-state-one-vote kind of democracy by giving far more influence to the big states that can fund its activities.

Clubs: Organisation for Economic Co-operation and Development (OECD), the G8 and the G20

International economic governance influences health in two ways. First, it affects the world economy by helping states coordinate their macroeconomic policies. Second,

TABLE 7.2 Memberships of the G8, the G20, and the OECD, June 2010

G8	G20	OECD
Canada	Argentina	Australia
France	Australia	Austria
Germany	Brazil	Belgium
Italy	Canada	Canada
Japan	China	Chile
Russia	France	Czech Republic
United Kingdom	Germany	Denmark
United States	India	Finland
(EU representatives attend)	Indonesia	France
	Italy	Germany
	Japan	Greece
	Mexico	Hungary
	Russia	Iceland
	Saudi Arabia	Ireland
	South Africa	Italy
	South Korea	Japan
	Turkey	Luxembourg
	United Kingdom	Mexico
	United States	The Netherlands
	European Union	New Zealand
		Norway
		Poland
		Portugal
		Slovakia
		South Korea
		Spain
		Sweden
		Switzerland
		Turkey
		United Kingdom
		United States

it often involves states or the organization commenting on each other's spending. The experience of international governance is, however, different for rich and poor states.

This specific set of groups, which I call 'clubs', are different from the biggest international organizations because they are a subset of the richest, or at least most powerful, states. The G8 was originally formed in 1975 to allow the leaders of the biggest six, then seven western states to discuss and sometimes coordinate economic policy. After the fall of the Soviet Union, they added Russia to make the G8. It has in good part been superseded by the newer G20, which emerged as a forum for international economic coordination in the 2008–present economic crisis; what was originally a forum for technical cooperation turned into probably the leading forum for economic coordination. The G8 is now much less important and might well cease to meet within a few years. The differences are worth considering, because they are a handy summary to changes in world power and autonomy (Table 7.2). First, they are testament to the declining relative role of European, indeed G8, states in the world. Second, the European Union is now a full member, alongside EU member states.

For the student of health policy, these clubs are worth watching because their summits both force consensus and sharpen debate about economic policy, above all, spending. They show us what consensus there is among the world's most powerful elites on the basic issues of policy, such as whether government spending should go up or down.

The OECD is the most specifically interested in health, with substantial publications and reviews of the health and public policies of its members. It is a club of rich countries small and large, with (unlike the others) a secretariat in Paris. Its comparative health data, especially *Health at a Glance*, is probably the most influential source for information on how much countries spend on various parts of healthcare. Its membership, for most scholars, makes it an adequate basis for generalizations about how rich countries allocate money and make policy, as well as a basis for comparison. When Americans want to show the flaws of their healthcare system, all they have needed to do is use the *Health at a Glance* graphs showing the US spending to be double most of the other countries and leaving the largest percentage of its population uninsured. While it is nowhere near as neoliberal as it is sometimes painted, the OECD does have a tendency to support smaller welfare states, private finance, means testing, and market mechanisms in health and most other policy.

The International Monetary Fund (IMF) and the World Bank

The IMF and the World Bank are among the most visible international organizations. Both are shareholding organizations, governed by the states who put a larger share of the money in; both have very significant European influence. Both are influential because of their money, but they are also influential because of their resources: their staff, their deep connections with the profession of academic economics in rich countries, and their central position in economic debates.

The IMF is a sort of central bank, or lender of last resort. When a state cannot issue debt (get loans), the IMF will give it loans. But the IMF, in order to ensure that it gets the money back, applies conditions, i.e. reforms that it insists the debtor state must make in order to make it a good prospect for paying back the loans and staying out of trouble. These reforms often have damaging effects on health; directly, when they force cuts in health budgets, and indirectly through changes in subsidies and other programs (such as reduced food subsidies) or through their broader effects on economies that are, by definition, in trouble when they encounter the IMF.

The World Bank is somewhat different. It is also a lender to states that cannot raise enough money on the global markets, but for longer-term development. It works essentially in poor countries. Even though amounts of money that it allocates are relatively small, World Bank involvement in a poor country is a sign to other investors that the country is reasonably trustworthy and a good investment opportunity.

These organizations both live in a constant political storm. It is partly their jobs as bankers and partly because they are constantly trying to change the public policies of various countries. But the sensible basis on which to discuss their work, and their activities, is to question the ways in which they determine their decisions: how does the IMF decide what would be a good fiscal strategy for a country in crisis? How does the

World Bank decide what kind of state, and what kind of projects, merits a loan? These questions directly touch on health: should the IMF let a country in a foreign exchange crisis protect health spending? Is investment in community health a good development strategy, or should the World Bank focus on building roads or schools?

They must use some criteria, and that means some theory of effective public administration, public sector reform and priorities. Those theories, generally drawn from basic academic economics, shape their advice on key issues such as the desirability of private heath finance, or redistributive taxation, or even small issues like school meals, hospital co-payments, and the appropriate staffing of community clinics.

Unsurprisingly given their focus on policy advice, both organizations routinely start campaigns advocating, for example, for privatization of pensions and some aspects of healthcare (Lee and Goodman 2002; Weyland 2007; Orenstein 2008). Their international profile and position at the hub of development and economics resources, including their substantial funding to the economics profession, give them great power over policy debates and advice. As a result, some quite debatable ideas that they sponsor have received wide discussion and implementation in rich and poor countries alike.

The European Union (EU)

For EU member states, the European Union is by far the most important international organization. Unlike the clubs and international organizations, whose power is usually confined to debates and declarations or is exercised against poor countries, the EU shapes every aspect of life, and health policy.

The European Union is both complex and well-established; there are a variety of good textbooks on its politics (Peterson and Shackleton 2006), policy-making (Richardson 2011) and impact on states (Bulmer and Lequesne 2005) as well as its health politics (Greer 2009; Mossialos et al. 2010) that underpin this section. It is effectively a new part of the government of each member state, interacting with all parts of society and government in each member state and wielding considerable power in areas as diverse as trade, agriculture, product safety, environmental policy and health. Understanding its structures (Box 7.2) is just as important as understanding the parliament or courts of one's own country.

The treaties that constitute the European Union give it minimal health policy powers; the member states never intended the EU to have a significant health, let alone healthcare, policy. They did, however, support its work to create a unified internal market with standard regulations and laws preventing member states from discriminating against each other's citizens. They also harmonize professional qualifications and eased professional mobility in the 1970s, but this had relatively limited effects because few professionals saw cause to move and member states did not make it easy to do so.

From 1998, however, the European Court of Justice began applying internal market laws to health. Initially, its decisions were about patient mobility, making it more difficult for EU member states to restrict patients who went to a different country, received treatment, and then sought to have their home country pay for it (as in the case of a Dutch citizen who wanted treatment in Austria, paid by Dutch insurance funds,

---

Box 7.2: *European Union institutions*

The **European Commission** is the executive of the European Union. It is a small body concerned with high level policy, based in Brussels. Its leadership (the President and the Commissioners, equivalent to ministers in a state) are nominated by member states and confirmed by the European Parliament. They are responsible for both executing and proposing EU legislation. For all practical purposes, the Commission must propose legislation if there is to be legislation.

The **European Council** is the representative body for the member states in the EU. It must approve any legislation. It meets in 'formations', such as the EPSSCO council that deals with Employment, Social Policy, and Health and brings together those ministers from the different EU member states to decide on legislation and other issues. Heads of state of the EU can also meet and take decisions as the Council.

The **European Parliament** is a directly elected body representing the citizens of Europe. It must approve a large part of EU legislation jointly with the Council, though its powers are weak in some policy areas. It is a much derided body, but has been gaining both power and credibility since at least the 1980s.

The **European Court of Justice** (ECJ), along with the Commission, is the engine of European integration and the source of most EU health policy initiative. It takes 'references' from member state courts that think they are faced with a question of EU law that it should decide. It was originally created as an internal oversight body to make sure that the other EU institutions behaved correctly, but over time created and implemented the principles of 'direct effect', which means that EU law applies even if it is not translated into member state law, and 'supremacy', which means that EU law overrides member state law. These principles, and the Court's ability to apply EU law in areas where member states never intended it (such as healthcare) have made it a powerful agent of European integration.

There are also two advisory bodies. One is the **Committee of the Regions**, which represents subnational governments. While its opinions do not seem to influence the Council and Parliament, both of which view their own legitimacy as governments and elected MEPs as superior, the Commission takes it increasingly seriously as a source of information and means of interacting with and learning about the many subnational governments in Europe that actually carry out so much policy. The other is the **Economic and Social Committee** (ECOSOC), which represents employers and unions and is largely irrelevant.

---

or an English woman who received treatment in France to avoid waiting for her procedure in England and then wanted the NHS to pay for it) (see the chapters in Mossialos et al. 2010, or for a shorter version, Greer 2009).

Given that the European Court of Justice and the European Commission are relatively isolated from democratic oversight, member states were unable to simply reverse the decisions that progressively expanded rights to patient mobility (at any given time, only a couple of member states have supported expanded patient mobility). The only way for member states to respond to the potential threats to their systems' equality, stability, and quality was with EU legislation that would put a framework of their liking around the principles that the Court had created. The obvious option of reversing the new EU powers was not available because there is no way for member states to thus override the Court. This is the key paradox of European integration. Once it has started, the only response to the problems it creates is . . . more of it.

The politics of EU healthcare services policy since then have mostly been about developing awareness of the issue and the slow search for EU-level policies that will satisfy the many states, professional groups, interest groups, MEPs, Commission officials and others who are now engaged in debating the proper shape and nature of EU health policy (Greer 2008, 2009). There are also a large number of areas in which the EU tries to play a supportive role in promoting health and healthcare. Box 7.3 summarizes a few.

Of all the organizations discussed here, the EU is the one that is most determined and likely to actually change health services and systems. It collects and distributes

---

Box 7.3: *European Union policies supportive of health: examples*

- **Health Impact Assessment (HIA)** is part of the movement for 'Health in All Policies', which focuses on the ways in which policies outside the health policy world, such as transportation, education, food or environmental policy affect health. HIA is one of the tools that the EU has introduced, without overwhelming success. Modelled on Environmental Impact Assessment, this means that every new EU policy, regardless of its purpose, should be assessed for its good or bad impact on health, and ideally amended to maximize its beneficial health effects.

- **The European Centre for Disease Control and Prevention** is a small centre in Stockholm that coordinates reporting on diseases and threats to health by member states. It is both a reference for developing European good practice and an educational force, promoting the development of communicable disease control capacity in the many EU states that have poor communicable disease control infrastructure.

- The **Open Method of Coordination** (OMC) is a form of 'peer review' that tries to pursue goals that matter to citizens and policy-makers in health, i.e. the quality, accessability, and economic sustainability of healthcare systems. It is therefore something of a reaction to an EU that more often seems to threaten those values (directly, via ECJ decisions, and indirectly, via the ECB). In the OMC, member states agree indicators of their goals and then self-report on how they are performing and what they could do better. The Commission and the rest of the states evaluate these and offer comments. Its effects in health will be slow and possibly difficult to identify (Greer and Vanhercke 2010).

- **Networks of Reference** try to take advantage of patient mobility to enhance the quality and efficiency of care for people with rare diseases (occurring less than 5 per 10,000). They provide Commission support for networks that would concentrate resources in particular centers, allowing them to treat a higher volume of patients with those rare cases.

increasingly convincing comparative data; funds and supports networks that develop detailed guidelines and codes on issues such as blood and organ donation, cancer care, and alcohol control. The EU is by no means a full government. It cannot and will never be able to finance healthcare services; its budget is 1 per cent of the EU GDP (most EU states' budgets are about half of their GDPs) and most EU spending goes on agricultural subsidies. But it can fund networks that develop and exchange practice, support data collection that allows comparison, and above all regulate states' decisions about healthcare services and finance in the name of the European Union internal market. All of these are serious issues for health policy and management. Fortunately, the EU is also the most democratic and responsive and has the most sophisticated policy-making mechanisms of the organizations here (no great compliment); the directly elected European Parliament represents citizens, as does the Council in which their member states vote. The European Commission is not democratically elected or very accountable, but its desire for legitimacy and relevant information means that it consults widely and supports groups that give it information and support its policies.

The European Central Bank (ECB)

The European Central Bank, the bank responsible for issuing and setting interest rates for the Eurozone, deserves a separate mention from the EU. First, while it is constituted by the same treaties as the EU institutions, its governance is wholly separate from the other EU institutions such as the Council and Commission. Second, the Euro is easily the most significant EU policy for health and healthcare. Qualification involved a long period of budgetary austerity, which had effects on health and healthcare as well as the balance of power within governments (empowering finance ministries at the expense of spending ministries such as health) (Featherstone 2004). Euro membership had major economic effects, creating property or other speculative bubbles in some member states, while contributing to low growth on the part of other member states for the better part of the decade. Finally, Euro membership meant that states such as Greece and Spain lacked the autonomy to adjust without major budget changes when they hit the economic crisis of 2008–present. In other words, the Euro shapes healthcare spending, spending on policies that affect health such as education, the balance of power within governments, the shape of the economy (e.g. the oversize building sector in Ireland or Spain), and the economic fortunes of the population, which affect their health. Furthermore, the ECB is obliged by treaty to focus on only one objective, which is low inflation (rather than health, or employment), and it is very difficult for member states or anybody else to affect its decisions. No specific EU health policy has had anything like such consequences (Martin and Ross 2004).

The World Trade Organization and trade agreements

The EU is not the highest level of law to which European states have bound themselves. They are also participants in negotiations about and signatories to trade agreements, above all the General Agreement on Trade and Tariffs (GATT) and the newer General Agreement on Trade in Services (GATS). In these trade agreements, states bind

Box 7.4: *The GATS and the public services debate*

Holly Jarman, State University of New York, Albany

The General Agreement on Trade in Services (GATS) covers some of the most complex issues ever negotiated, from transnational communications and sales of financial products to cross-border provision of water, social services and healthcare.

While services make up a large proportion of total economic activity in most developed countries, they are only a modest part (approximately 20 per cent) of trade across borders. Aiming to 'achieve progressively higher levels of liberalization of trade in services through the reduction or elimination of the adverse effects on trade in services of measures' (GATS 2000 guidelines), the states participating in the agreement hope to replicate previous successes in breaking down barriers to trade in goods, promoting economic growth.

But how can we determine which government 'measures' are actually barriers to trade, and which protect legitimate public interests? Will publicly funded services be construed as trade barriers, and will this lead to their privatization? Uncertainty over the status of public services under the GATS agreement, combined with a perceived lack of democratic process during the negotiations, caused NGOs, public sector unions and public health professionals in the EU to voice their opposition. Facing this pressure, EU Trade Commissioner Pascal Lamy declared in 2003 that the EU would not make any new commitments to liberalize public services such as healthcare and education during the Doha Round.

Opposing this moratorium, countries such as India (which has large numbers of trained medical professionals and low labor costs) are keen to see health liberalized in order to allow more of their citizens to practice medicine abroad and more patients from countries where healthcare is expensive to seek out cheaper care elsewhere. With rapidly rising medical costs in countries like the United States increasing the profile of medical tourism worldwide, it may soon no longer be feasible for developed countries to deny emerging economies the ability to access their domestic health markets.

themselves to eliminate restrictions on trade such as requirements that given services be provided by citizens, or restricting insurance sales to tightly regulated domestic firms. They operate under the umbrella of the World Trade Organization, which helps trade liberalization talks (known as 'rounds') and organizes 'adjudication panels' to decide complaints from one state about another's policies.

What does this have to do with health? Most directly, the GATS creates a rudimentary legal framework for liberalization of trade in healthcare services (Box 7.4). Patient mobility, and cross-border patient mobility, stand to benefit from removing restrictions on cross-border healthcare services. Equally or more importantly, trade law restricts states' policy autonomy. Just as EU member states that contravene EU law can be sued and forced to change their ways and pay damages, states that contravene their ratified trade agreements can be sued and forced, by a WTO disputes panel, to change their policy and perhaps pay damages. Much health regulation, such as licensing or negotiated medical payments, can look like a barrier to trade to trade lawyers.

Even if the actual scale of cross-border business or patient mobility is small, the regulatory framework is important. The world trade system is a framework for any of the major players discussed on p.126 to seek their objectives. Private insurance companies can challenge restrictions on their health insurance business, providers can demand the right to compete for government contracts, and supply providers can try to defeat cost containment or technology assessment initiatives. Pharmaceutical companies are already aggressive users of these laws in their efforts to increase their pricing power. One example is the US-Australia free trade agreement, which, thanks to an effective lobbying operation, now includes provisions designed to let pharmaceutical companies segment markets and avoid price negotiations. This will undermine the Australian pharmaceutical pricing system to the benefit of suppliers and to the detriment of Australian taxpayers and patients (Drahos et al. 2004). The pharmaceutical companies' further objective was to create replicable trade language that would bind the United States (their most lucrative market) (Fox 2010).

Another example is given in Box 7.5, discussing a case in which Dutch and German authorities seized a shipment of Indian medicines bound for Latin America because they believed that they violated intellectual property law. Finally, the tobacco industry has

---

Box 7.5: *Transit of pharmaceutical products*

Elize Massard da Fonseca, Edinburgh University

In 2008 and 2009, Dutch and German customs authorities seized cargoes of generic medicines in transit from India to Latin American countries, arguing this violated intellectual property rights in the country in transit. These drugs were used to treat AIDS, Alzheimer's disease and heart conditions and were not protected by patent either in India or in the country of destination. Mobility of medicines soon became a problem of health diplomacy. European officials pointed to the risk of counterfeit medicines, citing substandard drugs and the worrying level of the current trade in illegal medicines. In contrast, developing countries such as India and Brazil pointed out that the concept of generic drugs must not be confused with counterfeit products, and argued that the seizures and shipping delays affect their capacity to provide prompt access to affordable medicines.

This contest highlights a possible gap between the World Trade Organization (WTO) and European Union law. The intellectual property architecture in the WTO's Agreement on Trade-Related Aspects of Intellectual Property Rights (TRIPS) defines patents as territorial, that is protected according to each country's patent system. However, a regulation issued by the European Council in 2003 allows customs officials to seize and destroy goods that infringe intellectual property rights, including goods in transit through the EU territory (Regulation number 1383).

The key message is that shipping of medicines, which is an ordinary trade procedure, became a problem of global health governance that is far from being solved. Although there is an increasing concern with intellectual property rights enforcement, little is agreed on how to formulate enforcement mechanisms that secure public health interests.

used these frameworks, as in the case of tobacco companies influencing the conditions for China's WTO membership.

Framework Convention on Tobacco Control (FCTC)

The FCTC is an example of a distinctive kind of international governance. It is what the name suggests: a framework for thinking and acting on tobacco use. It specifies a series of actions that signatories promise to take in order to reduce tobacco use (Box 7.6).

Like all treaties, there is a difference between participating in negotiations, signing, and ratifying. Participating involves a diplomatic decision to participate, signing indicates satisfaction with the precise language, and ratification means formally agreeing to it. The EU and EU states ratified it in 2004 or 2005; the United States signed it in 2004

Box 7.6: *Framework Convention on Tobacco Control*

The aim of this Convention and its protocols is to protect present and future generations from the devastating health, social, environmental and economic consequences of tobacco consumption and exposure to tobacco smoke by providing a framework for tobacco control measures to be implemented by the Parties at the national, regional and international levels in order to reduce continually and substantially the prevalence of tobacco use and exposure to tobacco smoke.

The core demand reduction provisions in the WHO FCTC are contained in Articles 6–14:

- Price and tax measures to reduce the demand for tobacco.
- Non-price measures to reduce the demand for tobacco, namely:
  - protection from exposure to tobacco smoke;
  - regulation of the contents of tobacco products;
  - regulation of tobacco product disclosures;
  - packaging and labelling of tobacco products;
  - education, communication, training and public awareness;
  - tobacco advertising, promotion and sponsorship;
  - demand reduction measures concerning tobacco dependence and cessation.

The core supply reduction provisions in the WHO FCTC are contained in Articles 15–17:

- illicit trade in tobacco products;
- sales to and by minors;
- provision of support for economically viable alternative activities.

Source: Quotations from Foreword and Article 3, FCTC. Available at: http://www.who.int/fctc/text_download/en/index.html.

but, saddled with a legislature that is suspicious of treaties and requires a two-thirds majority to ratify treaties, did not ratify it. With 168 signatories, the FCTC is one of the most widely accepted international treaties. It does what international organizations and agreements often do: provide a norm that activists can often point to when they advocate for policies at home.

NGOs and international charities

As might be imagined, this set of organizations can look cumbersome, rigid, unrepresentative and ineffective. Combine the obvious problems of formal international organizations with the early twenty-first century's scepticism about public sector initiatives, and we explain the rise of specialist NGOs focused on international health issues (see the list of websites at the end of the article). The largest and most exciting is the Bill and Melinda Gates Foundation, sponsored by the personal wealth of Microsoft's co-founder Bill Gates and buttressed by the wealth of investor Warren Buffett. The Gates Foundation's immense wealth and tight focus give it considerable influence over any field it enters. More conceptually interesting is the Global Fund for Aids, Tuberculosis and Malaria. This was the highest profile example of the vaunted 'public–private partnerships' in international health (Buse and Walt 2009). Charities, donors and recipient countries formed the board of an NGO focused on those diseases and able to operate outside the usual constraints of the WHO or bilateral aid.

Finally, there is the intervention by rock musicians such as Bob Geldof and Bono (of U2), who use their high public profiles to draw attention to poverty in developing countries and related health issues. Organizations such as the One Campaign and Make Poverty History, which called for a fairer international trading system, the cancellation of developing country debt, global financial reform and action to prevent the spread of HIV among other issues, were made possible in part by the political activism of such celebrities (Jarman 2006). The financial crisis of 2008 spoiled much of rich countries' interest in poorer countries, while the simultaneous rise of Brazil, China and India shifted definitions of poor and gave poor (African) countries new strategic alternatives to reliance on Western aid.

Challenges in global health policy and politics

As the chapter so far should have shown, global health is a thick jungle, with all manner of different species, ecosystems, and interactions. Policy-makers who not long ago would have just worried about doctors' payment regimes or obesity now must also keep an eye on European Union legislation, bilateral free trade agreements, Indian hospitals competing for plastic surgery, cross-border process outsourcing, patients travelling for complementary care, and all sorts of other issues. In this jungle, though, there are two main threats. They both come from the mismatch between the issues that transcend borders and the institutions that transcend borders.

Insufficient governance

The first problem is insufficient governance. This is when the institutions are inadequate to cope with the issues, and as a result the quality, equity, or sustainability of healthcare is endangered. A clear example is the issue of international professional mobility. There is no mechanism to ensure that poor states keep the professionals that they have trained. At best, some states have codes of conduct for ethical recruitment, which is nice in the UK, but is not always followed and is anyway swamped by US recruitment. The result contributes to the health crises in areas such as Sub-Saharan Africa. Another example is the difficulty that the EU member states have faced in passing legislation to respond to European Court of Justice's decisions on patient mobility. The Court created a destabilizing right to challenge member state health systems. The rigid and limited EU legislative process only passed legislation in early 2011 – thirteen years later.

In each case, the problem is that the institutions we have do not equip states to act together to solve the problems. Even when the developments are good, we might not have a way to cushion any negative side-effects. One simple answer is to say that we should have greater international integration: a bigger EU budget to fund a European welfare state, or a more democratic United Nations, or a more important WHO. This is not something states agree to easily; policy-makers trust themselves more than international organizations. But such answers, even if they were politically simple (and they are not) are not always clearly desirable. Most international organizations have long track records of disappointment, with various problems including rigidity, corruption, sluggishness and dogmatism. The European Union is the quickest, cleanest, and most democratic of any, and the Lisbon Treaty's reforms to its voting procedures enhanced its democratic accountability. But it remains deeply unsatisfactory to many Europeans.

Excessive governance

The other kind of problem is the reverse: a form of international governance that is too effective. International organizations are almost all restricted to a few purposes; even the EU, easily the most broad-ranging effective organization, is at its core a device for integrating Europe's single market. This means that when one develops power and autonomy, it runs the risk of providing too much of whatever it provides. Furthermore, the isolation of international organizations, which depend on states' agreeing to rein them in, means that they can be difficult to stop once they are doing something.

This is often the case with the IMF and the World Bank, which have crusaded effectively for policy schemes (such as co-payments or privatized pensions) whose value is highly debatable. This probably was the case with the EU, where unhelpful interventions in healthcare services antedated helpful ones by a decade. It could well be the case with GATS, which is creating frameworks with little sense of how they might affect health and healthcare.

What kinds of solutions exist? The European Union is one kind of model. It is important to remember the distinctions between health governance in the European Union and health governance worldwide (Jarman and Greer 2010). In essence, all the problems of democratic deficits, political paralysis, and threats to the equity and sustainability of health systems that are serious issues in the EU are much worse in the world environment. The European Union has democratic mechanisms that can rein in the problems of excessive governance – its 2011 legislation on patient mobility tries to balance other health systems' needs against patient mobility and provider rights. It can also, thanks to that level of democracy and legislative capacity, address problems such as harmonizing professional training. The purpose of representative democracy and a strong state is to avoid both excessive and inadequate governance. The EU is an imperfect democracy and a patchy sort of state, but compared to most other international governance, it is a great success.

The problem, for the EU and for any other initiative, is to constrain international organizations from imperialism and dogmatism, without letting them succumb to the clientelism and immobility that afflict many of them. The charm of a foundation such as the Gates Foundation, or of a public–private partnership with a private company, or even of international organizations with simpler accountability such as the IMF, is that they can act decisively. This charm rapidly dissipates for those who disagree with the organizations. The result is that all the advocacy and complaint of domestic politics also takes place at the international level, but can seem even more puerile because the claims to address global problems are so grand and the resources generally so poor.

Conclusion

Nigel Crisp, who was once Chief Executive of the English NHS, noted that somebody in his job in 1980 or even 1990 would not have needed to pay attention to global or international health issues, but that by 2001, running the English NHS meant understanding and successfully engaging with global health issues such as professional mobility, emerging infectious diseases, and EU law (Crisp 2010).[2]

This chapter has been written from the point of view of rich countries; the (undeniably serious) issues affecting poor and middle-income countries sometimes distract global health debates from the fact that the problems and governance truly transcend borders. Global health is not just an issue for poor countries. Nor is it what it once was – a system in which poor countries exported problems and rich countries exported volunteers, advice or orders. It is an issue for all of us, and one that demands understanding of the increasingly even balance between the capacity and knowledge of different peoples around the world.

Summary box

- Global health, the issues and governance structures that transcend borders, are increasingly important to domestic policy in rich and poor countries alike.
- Workforce, infectious diseases, patients, economic trends and law (both European and international) shape health system policy options in different countries.
- A wide variety of international structures purportedly guide or govern global health issues. They range from the EU to the WTO and the OECD.
- There are two serious policy problems in global health. One is too little governance: international governance structures that are too patchy or weak to address

major global issues. The other is too much governance: international governance structures with too much of a focus on one objective (such as trade liberalization) and too little willingness or ability to balance different priorities.

- No healthcare system will go unaffected by global health issues. The question is whether its leaders will be policy-makers or policy-takers.

Self-test exercises

1 The Framework Convention on Tobacco Control is a treaty that obliges signatories to enact a series of anti-tobacco policies. Its apparent success has led others to propose similar framework conventions on alcohol control, or obesity, or health promotion. What are the advantages and disadvantages of pursuing such policy initiatives through a treaty, rather than through domestic politics?

2 How much autonomy do rich countries have to make health policy changes? What are the significant constraints on them?

3 What are the most important global health issues facing the UK health systems? Divide your answer into health challenges and governance responses, and explain your answer.

4 What are two key issues on which the United Kingdom could strengthen global health governance? What would be the objectives and how could it be done?

5 There is a trade-off between autonomy and accountability in any organization, including international organizations. Discuss the trade-offs for the organizations in this chapter, ranging from highest to lowest levels of accountability to states, and their consequences.

Notes

1 Europe, which includes Israel and the former Soviet Union; Africa; Western Pacific (running from Japan to Australia); Eastern Mediterranean (North Africa and the Middle East minus Israel), and Southeast Asia (from India to Indonesia, and including North Korea in order to prevent the diplomatic issues that would arise if North and South Korea were both in the Western Pacific region). The 'Region of the Americas' is actually the old Pan-American Health Organization, which was a precursor of the WHO and just became a WHO region.
2 Talk at LSE Health, 22 June 2010.

References and further reading

Aiken, L.H. (2007) U.S. nurse labor market dynamics are key to global nurse sufficiency, *HSR: Health Services Research*, 42(3, pt. II): 1299–320.

Awases, M., Gbary, A., Nyoni, J. and Chatora, R. (2004) *Migration of Health Professionals in Six Countries: A Synthesis Report. Tech. Report.* World Health Organization (WHO) Regional Office for Africa.

Birn, A.E. (2009) The states of international (global) health: histories of success or successes of history? *Global Public Health,* 4(1): 50–68.

Bulmer, S. and Lequesne, C. (eds) (2005) *The Member States of the European Union.* Oxford: Oxford University Press.

Buse, K., Hein, W. and Drager, N. (eds) (2009) *Making Sense of Global Health Governance: A Policy Perspective.* Basingtoke: Palgrave Macmillan.

Buse, K. and Walt, G. (2009) The World Health Organization and global public–private health partnerships: in search of 'good' global health governance. In N. Yeates and C. Holden (eds) *The Global Social Policy Reader.* Bristol: Policy.

Carrera, P. and Lunt, N. (2010) A European perspective on medical tourism: the need for a knowledge base. *International Journal of Health Services,* 40(3): 469–84.

Cooper, A.F. and Kirton, J.J. (eds) (2009) *Innovation in Global Health Governance.* Aldershot: Ashgate.

Cooper, A.F., Kirton, J.J. and Schrecker, T. (2007) *Governing Global Health: Challenge, Response, Innovation.* Aldershot: Ashgate.

Crisp, N. (2010) *Turning the World Upside Down: The Search for Global Health in the 21st Century.* London: Royal Society of Medicine Press.

Drahos, P., Lokuge, B., Faunce, T., et al. (2004) Pharmaceuticals, intellectual property and free trade: the case of the US-Australia free trade agreement. *Prometheus,* 22(3): 243–57.

Evans, R.G. (1999) Health reform: public success, private failure. In D. Drache and T. Sullivan (eds) *Health Reform: What 'Business' Is it of Business?* London: Routledge.

Featherstone, K. (2004) The political dynamics of external empowerment: the emergence of EMU and the challenge to the European social model. In A. Martin and G. Ross (eds) *Euros and Europeans: Monetary and the European Model of Society.* Cambridge: Cambridge University Press.

Financial Times (2009) India warns EU on generic drugs seizure. 7 August.

Fox, D.M. (2010) *The Convergence of Science and Government: Research, Health Policy, and American States.* Berkeley, CA: University of California Press.

Fried, L.P., Bentley, M.A., Buekens, P., et al. (2010) Global health is public health. *The Lancet,* 375: 535–7.

Glinos, I.A., Baeten, R. and Maarse, H. (2010) Purchasing health services abroad: practices of cross-border contracting and patient mobility in six European countries, *Health Policy,* 95(2): 103–12.

Greer, S.L. (2008) Choosing paths in European Union health policies: a political analysis of a critical juncture. *Journal of European Social Policy,* 18(3): 219–31.

Greer, S.L. (2009) *The Politics of European Union Health Policies.* Buckingham: Open University Press.

Greer, S.L. and Vanhercke, B. (2010) The hard politics of soft law. In E. Mossialos, G. Permanand, R. Baeten and T. Hervey (eds) *Health Systems Governance in Europe. The Role of EU Law and Policy.* Cambridge: Cambridge University Press.

Hansen, S.B. (2006) *Globalization and the Politics of Pay.* Washington, DC: Georgetown University Press.

Holden, C., Lee, K., Gilmore, A., et al. (2010) Trade policy, health and corporate influence: British American Tobacco and China's accession to the World Trade Organization. *International Journal of Health Services*, 40(3): 421–41.

Jarman, H. (2006) Bring back Bono: the successful failure of the UK Movement for Debt Cancellation. Paper presented at Society for the Advancement of Socioeconomics Annual Meeting, University of Trier, 30 June–2 July 2006. Available at: www.hollyjarman.com.

Jarman, H. and Greer, S.L. (2010) Crossborder trade in health services: lessons from the European laboratory. *Health Policy*, 94(2): 158–63.

Jarman, H., Kowalski, K. and Amodeo, J. (2011) *Medical Tourism: The Implications of European Union Debates for Healthcare Quality and Access in the United States.* Albany, NY: Rockefeller College of Public Affairs.

Kaufmann, S. (2009) *The New Plagues: Pandemics and Poverty in a Globalized World.* London: Haus.

Koplan, J.P., Bond, C., Merson, M.H., et al. (2009). Towards a common definition of global health. *The Lancet*, 373: 1993–5.

Labonté, R., Schrecker, T., Packer, C. et al. (eds) (2009) *Globalization and Health: Pathways, Evidence and Policy.* London: Routledge.

Laugesen, M.J. and Vargas-Bustamente, A. (2010) A patient mobility framework that travels: European and United States-Mexican comparisons, *Health Policy*, 97(2): 225–31.

Lee, K., Buse, K. and Fustukian, S. (eds) (2002) *Health Policy in a Globalising World.* Cambridge: Cambridge University Press.

Lee, K. and Goodman, H. (2002) Global policy networks: the propagation of health care financing reform since the 1980s. In K. Lee, K. Buse and S. Fustukian (eds) *Health Policy in a Globalising World.* Cambridge: Cambridge University Press.

Legido-Quigley, H., McKee, M., Glinos, I. et al. (2007) Patient mobility in the European Union. *BMJ (Clinical Research ed.)*, 334(27): 188–90.

Martin, A. and Ross, G. (eds) (2004) *Euros and Europeans: Monetary Integration and the European Model of Society.* Cambridge: Cambridge University Press.

Mossialos, E., Permanand, G., Baeten, R. et al. (eds) (2010) *Health Systems Governance in Europe: The Role of EU Law and Policy.* Cambridge: Cambridge University Press.

Okeke, E.N. (2009a) African Doctor Migration: Are Economic Shocks to Blame? SSRN Working Paper. Available at: http://ssrn.com/paper=1588604.

Okeke, E.N. (2009b) Doctors Across Borders: Do Higher Salaries Lead to Less Physician Migration? Mimeo.

Orenstein, M.A. (2008) *Privatizing Pensions: The Transnational Campaign for Social Security Reform.* Princeton, NJ: Princeton University Press.

Peterson, J. and Shackleton, M. (eds) (2006) *The Institutions of the European Union.* Oxford: Oxford University Press.

Reuters (2009) Developing states attack EU on generic drug seizure. 4 February.

Richardson, J.J. (ed.) (2011) *Policy Dynamics in the European Union.* Oxford: Oxford University Press.

Turner, L. (2010) 'Medical tourism' and the global market in health services: U.S. patients, international hospitals, and the search for affordable health care. *International Journal of Health Services*, 40(3): 443–67.

Weyland, K. (2007) *Bounded Rationality and Policy Diffusion*. Princeton, NJ: Princeton University Press.

Young, R., Weir, H. and Buchan, J. (2010) *Health Professional Mobility in Europe and the UK: A Scoping Study of Issues and Evidence*. London: SDO.

Websites and resources

Bill and Melinda Gates Foundation: www.gatesfoundation.org.

Euractiv, a helpful and free news aggregator for EU politics and policy: www.euractiv.com.

European Bank for Reconstruction and Development (similar to a World Bank for Europe): www.ebrd.org.

European Central Bank: www.ecb.int.

European Observatory on Health Systems and Policies, the gold standard for work on health systems in the WHO European region and a major source of information about EU policy: www.euro.who.int/en/home/projects/observatory.

European Union general portal 'Europa': http://europa.eu/index_en.htm.

European Union health page: http://europa.eu/pol/health/index_en.htm.

Financial Times, easily the best media source for following developments in international politics and economics: www.ft.com (many institutions have subscriptions through their libraries).

Global Fund to Fight AIDS, Tuberculosis and Malaria: www.theglobalfund.org.

IMF: www.imf.org.

OECD: www.oecd.org.

Observatoire Social Européenne, a highly credible think tank working on healthcare politics and policy in the EU: www.ose.be.

ONE campaign: www.one.org.

WHO: www.who.int/en/.

World Bank: www.worldbank.org.

PART 2

Healthcare services

CHAPTER 8

Healthcare services: strategy, direction and delivery

Mirella Cacace and Ellen Nolte

Introduction

The provision of healthcare services is a key function of health systems, along with financing, resource generation and what has been broadly described as governance (Roemer 1991; World Health Organization 2000, 2007). But the overall strategies to organize the delivery of services differ among healthcare systems. There is thus a need to better understand different systems in their political, institutional, social and historical context. All modern healthcare systems are facing common challenges caused by globalization, medical and technological progress, and demographic change. This requires systems to adjust and change their ways of how service provision is organized. In this chapter, we use the examples of four countries, Canada, England, Germany and the United States, as a means to illustrate typical system features and the most fundamental directions of change in the governance of healthcare provision. We begin by setting out the evolution of the healthcare systems in these four countries. We then examine the principles of governance in healthcare provision, using the four countries to illustrate the key issues such as the role of the public and private sectors, regulation and direction, and the separation or integration of financing and provision. A third section explores the structure of healthcare provision and how patients access health services, again using Canada, England, Germany and the United States as our main examples. The final section examines how health service reconfiguration is enacted in different healthcare systems in response to the rising burden of chronic disease, again highlighting different ways that countries are responding to this challenge.

The historical context of health systems

Organized health systems as understood in the modern sense, namely to benefit the population at large, are relatively recent. Today's health systems are broadly modelled on system design features that have emerged and developed from the late nineteenth century onwards. At the risk of simplification, universal healthcare systems as they are characteristic for most OECD countries can be distinguished into those that are dominated by elements of social health insurance, in which coverage is tied to employment and where the provision of healthcare is through both public and private providers;

and those predominantly financed through tax revenues, with mostly public health-care provision. Examples of the former include Germany, France, Belgium, Austria, and the Netherlands; examples of the latter are England[1]/the United Kingdom, the Nordic countries, Italy, Spain and New Zealand, while Australia and Canada bring together elements of both types. A third type of system involves those where state involvement is also considerable but coverage under the public is limited to certain population groups and provision and ownership of facilities are largely private. An example of this type of system is the USA.

This section briefly outlines the evolution of the healthcare system in four countries: Canada, England, Germany and the United States, highlighting some of the key features considered relevant in relation to the principles of the provision of healthcare services as described in subsequent sections. These countries were selected to represent the basic types of healthcare system. While England is a typical example of a centralized National Health Service (NHS) with mainly public service providers, Canada is strongly decentralized with a high proportion of private providers. Germany represents a typical social health insurance system while the US is the only country within the OECD mainly relying on private insurance.

Canada

Health policy in Canada is shaped by the governments of the ten provinces and three territories ('the provinces'). The federal government has some regulatory power by providing funding and attaching conditions to it (Tuohy 1999). Emerging from a rudimentary private insurance scheme, public coverage has a long tradition in the Canadian healthcare system. Thus, in Ontario, from 1874, not-for-profit municipal, charitable and religious hospitals were obliged to accept patients on the basis of medical need in return for a per diem reimbursement (Marchildon 2005). This excluded private-for-profit hospitals so their (already small) number declined further while voluntary hospitals, which were under the tight oversight of state governments, proliferated (Boychuk 1999). In 1947, Saskatchewan implemented a universal hospital services plan, which placed no utilization limits for medically necessary services and offered a comprehensive benefit package. By the end of the 1950s, encouraged by federal co-funding, all provincial governments had established similar plans.

Saskatchewan also was the first province to adopt a comprehensive, government-sponsored health insurance scheme in 1962. By 1971, Medicare was established in all provinces as federally co-funded programmes. Attached to this commitment was the requirement to adhere to the criteria of universality, public administration, comprehensiveness and portability. This, however, caused doctors to go on strike for guarantees of contractual autonomy for the medical profession (Marchildon 2005), following which several provinces allowed hospitals to introduce user fees and gave physicians the right of extra billing, that is to charge patients on top of public Medicare reimbursement. As a consequence of these developments, most doctors in Canada have remained self-employed private providers operating on a fee-for-service basis. The only exception is Quebec, where primary care also became organized in government-sponsored health centres with salaried GPs (Naylor 1986).

In 1977, due to fiscal pressure, the federal government altered its cost-sharing arrangement to a block grant, thereby *de facto* cutting transfers to the provinces (Banting 2005), followed by the introduction of the Canada Health Act in 1984, which guaranteed that all medically necessary services would be covered under the universal public system. This, however, excluded some goods and services, such as prescription drugs and dental care, some long-term care and home care, which have to be funded from private sources. As these sectors grew, the Canadian healthcare system experienced a 'passive privatization' (Flood and Archibald 2001). Recessions in the early 1990s led to another freeze of federal spending, which then was one of the most expensive systems among OECD countries (OECD 2009).

Starting with Quebec in the late 1980s, some major decentralization set in. In order to allocate financial resources based on regional needs, funding was devolved from the provincial government to regional health authorities (RHAs). RHAs also had the effect of centralizing the management from individual health facilities, thus facilitating the horizontal integration of hospitals and the downsizing of acute care facilities (Marchildon 2005). However, there has been a reversal of this trend recently, such as in the province of Alberta (Lewis 2008).

England

In the United Kingdom, the healthcare system initially followed a social health insurance model, introduced under Lloyd George in 1911, which, as in many other systems at that time, covered industrial workers only and not their families, and was limited to primary care and drugs (Terris 1978). This system was replaced in 1948 by the National Health Service to provide a full range of services to all residents. Healthcare services were provided by hospitals in public ownership with doctors and nurses as state employees. Primary care was delivered by general practitioners (GPs) tied to the NHS through exclusive contracts, so bringing the state and the professionals together as principal and agent (Greer 2004). While the central state confined its role to setting budgets, the medical profession maintained its influence on decisions at each level of the system, with free clinical decision-making at the individual level.

In 1974, the NHS underwent a major reorganization that unified all NHS services, except general practice, into a new organizational structure so as to better coordinate the system and to give clinicians a greater say in the management of services. The reform involved the creation of three administrative tiers, in addition to the Department of Health and Social Security, at the regional (Regional Health Authorities), area (Area Health Authorities and Family Practitioner Committees) and district level to enable a balanced decentralized decision-making process (Paton 1975).

Further fundamental change was introduced in the late 1980s, following the publication of the 1989 White Paper *Working for Patients,* by the then Conservative government. At the core of these reforms were the purchaser–provider split and the newly established 'internal markets' introducing GP fundholders and hospital trusts. GP practices with 11,000 or more patients could apply for their own NHS budgets (GP fundholders) to purchase a set of hospital services on behalf of their patients, together with, and also in lieu of, the then newly established District Health Authorities. Acute hospitals could apply for self-governing status to become NHS trusts, which, as providers of specialist care, were to compete for contracts with districts and GP fundholders. To address the pressing issue of waiting times, GP fundholders could also purchase certain procedures from the private sector as well as the NHS, increasingly blurring the idea of an 'internal market' (Le Grand et al. 1998).

By the late 1990s, with the incoming Labour government, a further set of reforms was introduced, paving the way for the 'third way' between state hierarchy and market competition as set out in the 2000 NHS Plan (Grimmeisen and Frisina 2010). This involved the abolition of GP fundholding and the creation of Primary Care Groups in 1999, subsequently to become Primary Care Trusts (PCTs) (2002), with Strategic Health Authorities introduced in 2002 to provide local strategic leadership. Primary care trusts were made responsible for organizing the delivery of care locally through a mix of direct service provision and commissioning of services from others, with the latter having been devolved further to the level of general practices, although PCTs typically hold the resultant contracts and retain ultimate financial responsibility (Ettelt et al. 2008). The NHS Plan also introduced activity-based payments of hospitals (Payment by Results, PbR), which was implemented in 2003. From a regulatory perspective, the NHS provides the classical model of a hierarchical, geographically organized system under the aegis of the state, while at the same time allowing physicians an effective veto power at each level of the system (Tuohy 1999).

Germany

The German statutory social health insurance (SHI) (*Gesetzliche Krankenversicherung*, GKV), introduced under Bismarck in 1883, initially only covered blue-collar workers but coverage was extended successively, both in terms of membership and benefits, with almost 90 per cent of the population covered by SHI by the late 1980s. According to its basic principles, SHI is mainly financed through insurance contributions, collected from employers and employees. Framework regulation is set by the federal government and enshrined in the Social Code Book (SGB 5) (Ettelt et al. 2007). Specifications within this framework have been delegated to self-governing corporate actors, which are represented at each level of the federalist political system. This corporate structure involves associations of sickness funds, provider associations and also includes representatives of employers and the insured members.

Right from the inception of the SHI, physicians in private practice began to lobby for autonomy and higher incomes and, in 1931, were granted the legal monopoly to provide services outside hospital ('ambulatory care') through regional SHI physicians' associations (Alber 1992). This monopoly meant that with the exception of university hospitals, until recently, acute hospitals were not permitted to provide outpatient care services (Busse and Riesberg 2004). Further separation between the ambulatory and inpatient care sectors was induced by the continuous expansion and specialization of acute care hospitals.

While autonomy of providers and self-governance were temporarily suspended during National Socialism (1933–45), legislation in the early 1950s basically restored the pre-war system (Wasem et al. 2005). As a consequence, steering became particularly complex through the interaction of governmental (federal and state) regulation and self-regulation on the part of corporate actors (Alber 1992; Rothgang et al. 2010b). This 'institutional sclerosis' was also responsible for a lack of structural reforms in the German healthcare system for some decades (Cacace et al. 2008). The 1960s and 1970s witnessed a series of rapid expansion of healthcare services. Hospitals were reimbursed covering all expenses, with little or no incentives for cost containment. Ambulatory care physicians' remuneration is determined in a two-tier process, with sickness funds and regional SHI physicians' association negotiating a total reimbursement and the latter allocating the funds to each individual physician according to a fee schedule. As free choice of provider is a well-established principle, the delivery of services tends to be particularly resource-intensive.

By the end of the 1970s, triggered by the worldwide economic crisis following the oil price shocks, cost-containment became a political issue. In line with the basic structure of the healthcare system, the government strengthened the bargaining power of sickness funds vis-à-vis the SHI physicians' associations (Rothgang et al. 2010b). Further developments included German unification of 1990, which essentially involved modelling the East German healthcare system according to the structures in place in the western part (Nolte 2004).

Fundamental change in the German healthcare system only occurred in 1993, when the Healthcare Structure Act introduced free choice of sickness funds, so introducing market elements that led to a considerable decline in the number of sickness funds, from just over 1200 in 1993 to about 400 in 2000 and to 169 in 2010 (GKV Spitzenverband 2010). In contrast, the provider side was largely exempted from market principles although the 1993 reform already marked the beginning of changes in the hospital financing system, eventually leading to the introduction of activity-based funding using diagnosis-related groups (DRG) in 2004. As contracts between insurer and provider have to be made uniformly, selective contracting is not permitted, with the exception of a few selected areas (Götze et al. 2009). Following further reform, the 2003 SHI Healthcare Modernisation Act established the Joint Federal Committee (2004) as the highest decision-making body of self-regulating corporate actors to improve coordination in decision-making across sectors. The (so far) latest series of reforms was phased in from 2007. Recent developments led to an increasing role of the state, particularly through moving the right to set contribution rates from corporate actors to the federal government.

The United States of America

Private health insurance in the United States was established as a consequence of the Great Depression, when a private non-profit hospital offered coverage of inpatient treatments to a selected group in 1929. The private scheme gained ground particularly after the Second World War, when employers, following a mandatory wage freeze, offered insurance as a voluntary 'fringe benefit' to reward employees. Federal and state governments also supported private, employer-sponsored insurance with tax subsidies. With the 1945 McCarran–Ferguson Act, the states assumed overall responsibility for health insurance regulation, resulting in considerable variation among the states. In 1965, the public health insurance programmes Medicare and Medicaid were introduced to cover specific population groups, mainly the elderly, the disabled and the indigent. As a concession to the American Medical Association (AMA), which lobbied against the introduction of public insurance, the 'Prohibition against Any Federal Interference' clause prohibited the federal government from interfering in the autonomy of medical service providers, particularly with regards to the payment method. As a consequence, prices for medical care rose rapidly (Marmor and McKissick 2000). Effective provider regulation within the public programmes did not set in before activity-based payment using DRGs were introduced in 1983.

In the private insurance market, employers who self-insured their employees were exempted from state taxation and control through the 'Employee Retirement Income Security Act Employee', introduced in 1974. There was little control by federal or state government of providers, particularly in the private market (Stone 2000), an issue only addressed with the introduction of private managed care organizations from the 1980s. Health Maintenance Organizations (HMOs) in particular, which integrate financing and service provision vertically within one organization, exert hierarchical control on providers and patients through gatekeeping requirements and utilization reviews. From the mid-1990s, however, due to the so-called 'backlash' against managed care, HMO-enrolment declined and was replaced by more loosely structured, network-based models, such as Preferred Provider Organizations (PPOs) (Kaiser/HRET 2010), giving way to virtually integrated managed care models, which primarily rely on long-term selective contracting, with elements of negotiation between medical care providers and insurers. As more beneficiaries of the public programmes (have to) join managed care plans, these governance structures also spread into the public programmes (Cacace 2010b).

Over time, the state expanded public coverage, thereby assuming a more important role in healthcare financing and also in regulation. If tax exemptions are considered as public spending, more than half of total healthcare expenditures today come from public sources. In contrast, as relates to the provision of healthcare services, the state has steadily retreated over time. Medical doctors are mainly self-employed, private providers (De Alessi 1989), while hospital care is dominated by private non-profit facilities. In exchange for their tax-exempt status, public and private non-profit hospitals have to offer community benefits and provide care for the indigent.

Today, the American healthcare system is fragmented with many sub-systems, which partly overlap and in addition leave a considerable part of the population un- or underinsured. A major move to improve this situation came with the Patient Protection and Affordable Care Act, signed into law in March 2010. The core provisions of the legislation are an expansion of coverage by making health insurance mandatory for most population groups and several measures for improving the performance of the healthcare system.

TABLE 8.1 Organizing healthcare service delivery: approaches

Criteria	Sources
Structural and institutional dimensions at the system level	Rothgang et al. (2010a); Tuhoy (1999); Rico et al. (2003); Cacace (2010a)
Direct versus indirect control	Abel-Smith (1992)
Selective versus collective contracting	White (1999)
Modes of financing and provider payment	Chernichovsky (2000); Hurst (1991)

Principles governing healthcare provision

This section explores some of the fundamental principles of governing the provision of healthcare services. At a system level, the regulatory structure distinguishes the public/private mix of actors involved as well as different coordination mechanisms. At the level of the micro-regulation, it focuses on the principal relationships between funders and service providers and specific features such as ownership, the way how providers are paid, or, more generally, how contractual relationships between providers and payers are specified. Table 8.1 illustrates the different approaches that have been discussed in the literature.

As noted above, at the system level, the regulatory structure is characterized by the public/private mix of actors combined with different modes of interaction (Rothgang et al. 2010a). The modes of interaction can be classified according to the traditional markets–networks–hierarchies distinction applied by institutional economists (Williamson 1985). In healthcare, these differentiate between the market, collegiality and hierarchical control (Tuohy 1999; Rico et al. 2003), with a more recent classification distinguishing between market coordination, long-term contracts and hierarchy (Cacace 2010a). Markets are characterized by decentralized contracts and financial compensation while hierarchies rely on centralized directions and plans. In contrast, networks governance is characterized by common socialization processes and the high salience of reputation and shared value systems (Rico et al. 2003). It is important to note that an array of public, societal, and private actors are involved in healthcare governance. This means that regulatory functions may also be assumed by non-governmental bodies. Table 8.2 provides an overview of the most typical regulatory structures.

The purest types of regulatory structure can be described as a simple combination of actors and modes of interaction, that is, by linking state with hierarchy, collective actors with bargaining elements, and market actors with competition. These correspond to the basic regulatory structures in so-called 'ideal type' healthcare systems. State-led hierarchical control, for example, is a typical element of the English NHS. Regulation in the German social insurance system relies on collective negotiation in a self-regulatory structure, which is dominated by corporate actors. The predominately private insurance scheme in the USA, by contrast, is traditionally based on competition as a coordination mechanism. Similarly, as illustrated in Table 8.3, applying a distinction along the structural and institutional dimension, classifies England as a hierarchical state-led system, the market-based US healthcare system as dominated by private finance, and Canada as a public healthcare system with particular professional dominance.

TABLE 8.2 Types of regulatory structures

		Actors		
		State	**Self-governing actors**	**Market participants**
Form of coordination	Hierarchy	State-hierarchical regulation		
	(Collective) negotiation/ bargaining		Social self-regulation	
	Competition			Private competitive regulation

Source: Rothgang et al. (2010a).

Over time, systems have evolved into more mixed structures, away from their initial 'pure' structure (Tuohy 1999; Rothgang et al. 2010a). For example, pro-cooperative reforms, such as the delegation of purchasing functions to GP fundholders in England in the 1990s described earlier, are indicative of the strengthening of the network principle (Rico et al. 2003). In contrast, in Germany, the state has begun to interfere through hierarchical regulation, for example, through setting contribution rates centrally and by mandating the corporate actors to introduce a DRG-based payment of hospitals in the early 2000s (Woerz and Busse 2005). In the USA, albeit with growing state regulation, the most important development has been increasing interference by private actors to hierarchically steer providers and patients through capitation payment and utilization reviews. In Canada, passive privatization increasingly limits state regulation, so permitting market elements to take hold of the healthcare system.

Turning to the level of micro-regulation, authors have classified the interaction of providers and funding bodies according to the ownership relation (Abel-Smith 1992). In direct systems of control, the government (as the funder) or the main health insurers own healthcare facilities and employ healthcare workers on a salaried basis. This vertically integrated form of ownership implies a strong degree of hierarchical control. Systems in which healthcare providers are in a contractual relationship with the government or the main insurers are referred to as indirect systems of control. Several payment mechanisms are possible here, i.e. fee-for-service, capitation, or salary. The degree of

TABLE 8.3 Structural and institutional parameters in selected healthcare systems

		Institutional parameter		
		Hierarchical control	**Collegiality**	**Market**
Structural dimension	State	Britain		
	Medical profession		Canada	
	Private finance			United States

Source: Adapted from Tuohy (1999).

concentration in the insurance market, or of centralization of government respectively, is also relevant as it determines the monopsony power of the payer/s. Depending on the degree of organization on the provider side, the payer largely determines the rules.

Vertical integration of the financing and provision function is the dominant form of service delivery in the English NHS in its original set-up and in the early forms of managed care in the USA, where private insurers in Health Maintenance Organizations (HMOs) employed providers and acquired hospitals. As HMOs not only integrated vertically, but also horizontally by incorporating primary, secondary and tertiary care providers,[2] they had considerable potential to increase the coordination of care based on their particular governance structure. In Germany, where social health insurers are not permitted to own facilities or to employ providers, vertical integration is rare or absent.

A further distinction is made between contractual relationships based on selective versus collective contracting, also referred to as 'coordinated payment' (White 1999). Under collective contracting, all providers are paid according to the same terms. Coordinated payments therefore bring the payers' collective power to bear on providers. In contrast, within selective contracting, individual payers can choose the providers they wish to contract with. In a competitive context, selective contracting can be an effective tool to steer provider behaviour. As providers have an interest not to be delisted from the panels, selective contracting is means to govern providers in line with the payer's objectives (Rich and Erb 2005).

In Germany, selective contracting is only possible in a restricted integrated care setting. In general, contracts must not discriminate between providers, meaning that social health insurance funds are obliged to contract with all providers authorized to deliver care under the public scheme by the self-governing bodies on equal terms and therefore have to apply the same fee-schedule. Similarly, in England and Canada, service providers are generally contracted collectively. However, selective contracting plays an important role in the American healthcare system where the dominant form of managed care mainly relies on provider networks (Kaiser/HRET 2010).

Hurst (1991) distinguishes at least seven subsystems of organizing financing and delivery of healthcare, which can also coexist within one healthcare system (Table 8.4).

Public financing systems differ from private insurance and out-of-pocket payments systems in that they pool resources and thus allow the spreading of risk and access to healthcare services for broader part or all or the population. The governance of healthcare providers is also influenced by reimbursement methods, which can be differentiated into direct and indirect methods. Indirect payment separates the insurer from the providers in that the patient is reimbursed by the insurer. Direct payment of providers can be further classified into contract-based forms, usually involving fee-for-service payments or capitation, and reimbursements based on global budgets and salaries.

The subsystems identified by Hurst (1991) differ in their effectiveness to steering providers. The public contract model, involving public health insurance on the financing side and contract-related, direct payments, has been proposed as the most promising means to promote efficiency and cost containment in healthcare systems. For that

TABLE 8.4 Subsystems of organizing the financing and delivery of healthcare

Financing	Payment of providers	Model
Out-of-pocket payment		Self-medication
Private (voluntary) insurance	Indirect payment of providers through reimbursement of patients (insurers and providers are not connected)	Private reimbursement model
	Direct, contract-based payment of (mainly independent) providers through fee-for-service or capitation payments	Private contract model
	Direct payment of providers through global budgets and salaries (vertical integration)	Private integrated model
Public insurance	Indirect payment of providers	Public reimbursement model
	Direct payment through fee-for-service or capitation	Public contract model
	Direct payment through global budgets and salaries	Public integrated model

Source: Adapted from Hurst (1991).

reason, at the time the model was developed, this was thought to be the dominant way of organizing financing and delivery in healthcare. The public contract model was further specified by Chernikovsky (2000). Accordingly, public contract models comprise all contractual relationships between financing bodies, collecting public funds either through mandatory contributions or taxation, and offering a well-defined basket of services in exchange. Providers and/or contractors do not have to be 'public' in the sense of public ownership; they can be for-profit or not-for-profit organizations.

Public contract models are indeed quite common in healthcare systems, also in the countries we explored, although this is of course not sufficient proof for its efficiency. The public contract model is the dominant form of health insurance and delivery in the German social health insurance scheme and in the English NHS. GPs practices in England are paid using a blended system comprising capitation, fee for service and pay-for-performance, while hospitals are paid according to activity based on contracts, in line with the public contract model. In Canada's public health system, only physicians are paid on a fee-for-service basis, while hospitals are paid under global budgets (integrated model). In the USA, public contracts play a limited role only in the subsystem of network-related managed care models for beneficiaries of the public Medicare and Medicaid programmes. As these examples show, there is also considerable variation within the public contract model to organize financing and delivery in healthcare. Thus, far from convergence on *one single* common model of organizing healthcare delivery systems, diversity remains.

Structure of healthcare provision

Traditionally, healthcare services have been classified according to the level within the hierarchy of services into primary, secondary and tertiary care. Conceptualized as a pyramid, primary care constitutes the base, secondary care forms the middle layer and tertiary care is situated at the top, while informal, or lay, care is an unspecified area below the pyramid (Boerma 2006).

Primary care has been defined as 'the first port of call for the sick' (Porter 1997: 669); it is general rather than specialized, the response to unspecified and common health problems (Black and Gruen 2005; Boerma 2006). Secondary care refers to specialized care that is usually provided in (local) hospitals or in outpatient care settings; secondary care is frequently, although not always, accessible following referral through a primary care practitioner only (see below). Tertiary care comprises highly specialized care services and is usually provided in regional or national hospitals (Black and Gruen 2005). In the UK, 'specialized services' are defined as those that require a planning population catchment area of more than a million people (National Commissioning Group for Highly Specialised Services 2010), with nationally designated services those that are very low volume or require rare skills, e.g. heart transplants.

Healthcare services can be further classified according to the set of functions and activities provided (e.g. information, reassurance or advice; health promotion and prevention; diagnostic procedures; therapeutic and surgical interventions; rehabilitation; palliation) or according to a set of characteristics of their organization. For example, primary care has been described as care that is directly accessible to patients, with a generalist character that is provided within the community it serves and that is oriented towards the individual in their social context (Boerma 2006).

Although this conceptualization is useful, boundaries are not clear-cut. For example, the term 'primary care' is often used interchangeably with the notion of general practice, referring to the common characteristic of providing first contact care that is of a generalist nature, i.e. addressing a wide range of unselected health problems. Yet, these concepts are not necessarily equivalent, depending, as Boerma (2006) has argued, on the functions and characteristics of what is being defined as general practice, and this differs among countries. In several European countries, general practitioners have claimed specialist status so as to achieve recognition as a separate discipline (Heath et al. 2000). Other systems use the term 'family medicine', partly to circumvent negative connotations associated with poorly trained general practitioners. In some settings, the notion of primary care as care that is of a generalist nature is difficult to conceptualize. For example, in Germany, about 50 per cent of office-based doctors (physicians in private practice) work as family physicians (*Hausarzt*) (Busse and Riesberg 2004). Of these, about half hold a specialist qualification in family medicine, around 25 per cent are specialists in internal medicine or paediatricians while the remainder comprises physicians without any specialist qualification who practise family medicine. A similar structure has been described for the primary care system in the USA (Bindman and Majeed 2003).

Systems also differ in relation to the actual setting within which the different levels of care are being provided. Thus, in NHS-type systems, such as England/the UK, specialized care services are typically provided in hospital, a model also in place in Canada. In contrast, in Germany and other social health insurance systems such as France, such services are also accessible through office-based, specialist doctors outside hospital, an arrangement that is also characteristic of the United States.[3] Indeed, in Germany, about 50 per cent of office-based doctors work as specialists, most frequently in gynaecology, neurology, ophthalmology, orthopaedics, dermatology and ENT (ear, nose and throat) (Busse and Riesberg 2004).

Accessing care

Where countries offer universal healthcare, entitlement to publicly funded services in tax-based systems is usually granted by virtue of being resident in the country, such as those provided through the NHS in England and Canada's public insurance system Medicare. In social health insurance systems, entitlement to publicly funded care is through statutory social health insurance, which, in Germany, covers about 85 per cent of the population (GKV Spitzenverband 2010).[4] The range of services covered under the public system varies, with most providing a comprehensive basket of services that, in the NHS in England and the German statutory social health insurance system, offers access to a wide range of preventive services, physician and hospital services, prescription drugs, mental healthcare, dental care and rehabilitation. Healthcare is largely free at the point of use although certain co-payments apply, for example, for prescription drugs and dental care. Canada's Medicare system provides universal coverage for physician and hospital services. Access to other services including prescription drugs is generally through a mix of public programmes and supplementary private insurance; provinces vary widely in the extent to which they fund or subsidize services outside those offered under Medicare (Jiwani and Dubois 2008).

In contrast, in the United States, access to care is through a range of mechanisms, reflecting the multiple payer character of the system described earlier, with around 56 per cent of the population covered by employment-based private insurance, about 14 per cent covered by the federal Medicare programme for those aged 65 and over, and just under 16 per cent by Medicaid, while, in 2009, just over 16 per cent of the population were without any insurance coverage (DeNavas-Walt et al. 2010).[5] The range of services offered varies by type of coverage but typically includes physician and hospital services, with many also including access to preventive services and prescription drugs (The Commonwealth Fund 2010). Co-payment and user charges are typical for a range of services; those without insurance will have to pay part or all of physician charges.

Countries also differ in the ways in which patients enter the system of primary, or non-urgent, first-contact care. Some systems require patients to register with a general practitioner. This is often, although not always, the case in tax-funded systems such as in England, where patients have to register with a general practitioner in the area in which they live; other examples are Denmark and Finland (Ettelt et al. 2006). The Netherlands, which, in 2006, has moved to a mandatory, regulated private insurance system[6] (Schäfer et al. 2010) also requires registration with a general practitioner, although patients can principally choose any practitioner, as is the case in Italy (Lo Scalzo et al. 2009). In contrast, in the tax-funded Canadian system, patients can see any general practitioner as is the case in Germany (and France) as an example of a social health insurance system (Ettelt et al. 2006).

Most OECD countries operate some form of gatekeeping to control access to specialist care in non-urgent cases, although systems vary to the degree with which this is implemented. Thus, in England, a referral from a general practitioner is usually the only means for patients to consult a specialist, and a similar system applies to Denmark, Italy, the Netherlands and New Zealand (Ettelt et al. 2006; Schoen et al. 2009). However, among these, several countries have introduced mechanisms to facilitate access to certain specialists. For example, in Italy, patients may access gynaecologists, dental care, paediatrics, optometric services and psychiatric services for children directly through a central booking point (*centro unico di prenotazione*, CUP) (Lo Scalzo et al. 2009). Similarly, Denmark allows direct access to selected specialist services including ENT (ear, nose and throat) and ophthalmology (Strandberg-Larsen et al. 2007).

Where the primary care system does not have a formal gatekeeping function, countries have introduced incentives to encourage patients to see their primary care provider first. For example, in Sweden, while some counties operate a gatekeeping system, patients may choose to access specialists directly and without referral but will then have to make a co-payment (Ettelt et al. 2006). Germany, which traditionally offers direct access to medical specialists outside hospital has recently introduced measures to strengthen the gatekeeping and coordinating role of the primary care physician. Thus, since 2004, statutory social health insurance funds are required to offer their members GP-centred care ('*Hausarztmodell*' or gatekeeper model) in which patients voluntarily sign up with a family doctor as first point of contact for a period of at least one year, tied to financial incentives for both patients and the joining doctor (Kassenärztliche Bundesvereinigung 2008).

A similar system is in place in France where, since 2005, residents are encouraged to sign up with a '*médecin traitant*' ('preferred doctor', mainly general practitioners), a voluntary gatekeeping system, incurring higher co-payments for those patients who choose to directly access a specialist without a referral from their preferred doctor (Naiditch and Dourgnon 2009). Uptake of the scheme has been high, with about 80 per cent of patients having signed up with a preferred doctor by mid-2007, believing it to be compulsory. In contrast, uptake has remained low in Germany, at only about 20 per cent of those covered by social health insurance since the introduction of the scheme (Kassenärztliche Bundesvereinigung 2010; Lisac et al. 2010). In the USA, primary care physicians generally do not have a formal gatekeeping function, except within some managed care plans, which embraced the idea of gatekeeping as a means to improve the quality of care and reduce resource use (Bindman and Majeed 2003). Studies in both Germany and the USA point to an improved coordinating role of the family physician/general practitioner (Bindman and Majeed 2003; Lisac et al. 2010), however, evidence of the impact of optional gatekeeping on patterns of use remains inconclusive (Forrest et al. 2001; Or et al. 2010).

It is noteworthy that in both Germany and the USA, low uptake of gatekeeping has been linked, at least in part, to reluctance among patients to 'trade in' choice of specialist care provider and leave this decision to the primary care physician (Bindman and Majeed 2003; Lisac et al. 2010). This observation appears important against the background that many systems that had traditionally limited choice of specialist care provider have begun to introduce measures to enable patients to choose where and when to access specialist services. Thus, countries such as Denmark, England and Sweden have introduced user choice of hospital provider as a means to relieve pressure on waiting times in secondary care and to increase the responsiveness of the system (Thomson and Dixon 2006). In Denmark, patients have been able to choose a hospital provider since 1993, subsequently reinforced by a waiting time guarantee (2002, 2007) for patients to be seen within one month from referral through a general practitioner (Strandberg-Larsen et al. 2007). Likewise in Sweden, patients are formally entitled to freely choose their specialist care provider throughout the country, a policy initially introduced in 1991 and further extended from 2003 (Or et al. 2010).

In England, patient choice of hospital was principally introduced in the late 1980s, coinciding with the market-based reforms of that period although, in practice, decision-making was left with the general practitioners (Thomson and Dixon 2006). The policy of patient choice of hospital was renewed in the 2000s, with successive stages first introducing choice of four to five local hospitals from 2006, subsequently extended to any provider of hospital treatment nationally (2008) through to becoming a patient right with the 2009 NHS Constitution (Dixon et al. 2010).

Health service reconfiguration

The previous section has shown how different health systems vary in relation to the provision of primary and secondary care and the ways patients and users access these. Yet, the nature of the delivery of healthcare services itself is changing, slowly in some instances and more rapidly in others, increasingly blurring the traditional boundaries between what used to be considered as primary and secondary care. For example, new developments in medical technology have made it possible to provide many services closer to the patient, with diagnostic or therapeutic interventions that would previously have required a hospital environment now being carried out in ambulatory settings (Rosen 2002). Elsewhere, advances in the medical device and telemonitoring technology allow the monitoring and control of many chronic conditions in people's homes.

While the acute hospital will always play an important role in the provision of healthcare, both as a key locale for teaching, training and research as well as in the management of complex and rare disorders, there have been increasing concerns about health systems' dependence on hospital-based delivery and the efficiency of such services, given the changing disease burden and related demand for services (Rechel et al. 2009). There are also concerns about the (perceived) high costs of hospital care and the notion of moving care into the community as a means to increase accessibility of services and so the responsiveness of the system, and, potentially, to reduce costs.

In consequence, healthcare systems have been experimenting with new ways of shifting specialist services from hospital into the community, for example, by transferring or relocating diagnostic services, access to which is often considered a crucial bottleneck in NHS-type systems in particular, into the primary care setting (Ettelt et al. 2006). An example is the 'Closer to Home' initiative in England which sought to substitute community for hospital care through making greater use of specially trained community staff ('Practitioners with Special Interests') and through the increased provision of diagnostic and treatment facilities in community settings (Sibbald et al. 2008). Approaches such as this have been found to be effective in improving access to specialist care for patients and to reduce the demand on acute hospitals (Sibbald et al.

2007). However, there is concern about the quality of care which may decline while evidence of the impact on cost remains, at best, inconclusive. Conversely, countries such as Germany which traditionally offer direct access to specialist services, including diagnostic services, outside hospital have introduced measures to extend hospital capacity to also provide these in acute hospitals (Ettelt et al. 2006). This reflects, in part, a concern about possible inefficiencies of provision of these services by office-based doctors, who are paid on a fee-for-service basis, and the notion of supplier-induced demand. At the same time, hospitals have been granted permission to provide selected outpatient services in areas that are underprovided outside hospital such as pneumology and rheumatology (Busse and Riesberg 2004).

However, one of the greatest challenges facing healthcare systems is the rising burden of chronic disease. This requires healthcare services to transform from the traditional model of acute, episodic care that focuses on individual diseases and is based on a relationship between an individual patient and a doctor towards one that involves coordinated inputs from a wide range of health professionals over an extended period of time and that places patients at the centre as co-producers of care to optimize health outcomes (Nolte and McKee 2008a). There is thus a need for new service delivery models that are characterized by collaboration and cooperation among professions and institutions that have traditionally worked separately.

The growing recognition of this need is causing many countries to explore new approaches to healthcare delivery that can bridge the boundaries between professions, providers and institutions and so provide appropriate support to patients with long-standing health problems. However, countries vary in their attempts to do so with strategies and approaches that are being implemented reflecting the characteristics of individual health systems as it relates to the relationships between, and responsibilities of, different stakeholders in the regulation, funding and delivery of healthcare (Nolte et al. 2008).

Strategies that have been implemented include the introduction of new roles and competencies in primary care, in particular nurse-led strategies such as nurse-led clinics, discharge planning and case management. Such approaches are common in systems with a tradition in multidisciplinary team working involving physicians, nurses and other health professionals such as England/the UK, Sweden and, more recently, the Netherlands. For example, in Sweden, nurse-led clinics are now common at primary healthcare centres (PHCC) and in hospital policlinics, managing a wide range of chronic conditions including diabetes and hypertension, with some also managing allergy/asthma/Chronic Obstructive Pulmonary Disease, psychiatric disorders, and heart failure (Karlberg 2008). In England, from the mid-2000s, case management of people with complex needs involving so-called 'community matrons' became central to the government's policy for supporting people with chronic health problems and complex needs (Singh and Fahey 2008). Community matrons tend to be senior nurses or therapists based in primary care settings, tasked with coordinating primary and secondary care and social services. In the Netherlands, from the early 1990s specialized nurses have been playing an increasingly important role that sought to bridge the divide between secondary care and alternative settings ('transmural care'), while more recently there has been a move towards disease management models, with nurse-led clinics at their core (Klein-Lankhorst and Spreeuwenberg 2008).

In contrast, systems where primary care is traditionally provided by doctors in solo practice, paid on a fee-for-service basis of individual providers and that operate with few support staff, have found it more challenging to develop and implement new roles and competencies. This is in part because of legal provisions, as in France, where redefining roles and delegating tasks to non-medical personnel requires changes in the law on professional responsibilities (Durand-Zaleski and Obrecht 2008), along with professional concerns among physicians about delegating tasks (Nolte et al. 2008). As a consequence, there has been a trend towards the development of, usually physician-led, structured disease management programmes as a means to strengthen the coordination of care for selected conditions, following the model developed in the USA, such as in Germany and, more recently, Denmark and France (Nolte et al. 2008). Thus, in Germany, the nationwide introduction of structured care or disease management programmes (DMPs) from 2003 has been viewed as a key means to improve the quality of care for those with diabetes type I and II, coronary heart disease, breast cancer, asthma and COPD (Siering 2008).

Systems are also experimenting with elements of delivery system re-design, including models to improve the management of the primary/secondary care and/or secondary care/rehabilitation interface. For example, in Germany, the 2004 healthcare reform enabled social health insurance funds to designate financial resources, up to a total of 1 per cent of their income, for selective contracting with single providers or network of providers to promote intersectoral care, many of which focus on the secondary care/rehabilitation interface (Busse and Riesberg 2004). However, although this opportunity has been taken up quite widely, it was noted that, by the end of 2008, when the start-up funding ceased, less than half of these contracts had indeed incorporated elements of intersectoral care (Sachverständigenrat zur Begutachtung der Entwicklung im Gesundheitswesen 2009). In Canada, provinces which are responsible for health service organization have developed different strategies with, for example, Quebec launching a range of initiatives to enhance chronic care, including the creation of local services networks (health and social services centres, CSSS) which bring together all care providers in a region to develop partnerships of relevant groups (such as physicians and community organizations) (Jiwani and Dubois 2008).

It is important to note that strategies to address chronic disease are constantly evolving and this chapter could, in the space available, only provide a brief illustration of the many approaches that are being tested and implemented in countries in Europe and elsewhere. At the risk of generalization it is, however, fair to conclude that different systems are at different stages of the process and with different degrees of comprehensiveness. Moreover, the evidence of what works best in what circumstances remains uncertain. This is in part because of the lack of investment in sound evaluation of many of the innovations or, where evaluation has taken place, the premature adoption of new approaches even before evaluation results are available (Nolte and McKee 2008b). However, what seems to be emerging is that those health systems with a tradition of patient choice of any provider, little or no enrolment with particular providers that use fee-for-service as main payment method in primary care, face the greatest challenges in implementing system-wide strategies to provide care for patients with chronic illness (Busse and Mays 2008).

Conclusion

The provision of healthcare services is a core component of healthcare systems. It is characterized by its own dynamics and at the same time is closely intertwined with other dimensions such as financing and regulation. This chapter set out from a highly aggregated level of the healthcare system and its regulatory structures to describe the strategy, direction and delivery of healthcare services. We find that although all healthcare systems face common challenges, calling their dominant approach to organizing the delivery of services into question, systems' responses are highly diverse. One of these common challenges is the changing burden of disease, requiring a move towards a more coordinated system involving multi-professional working across sectors and along a longer timeframe as well as actively involving patients. We find that countries differ markedly in the ways in which patients access the care system. Similarly, there are considerable differences in the setting within which different levels of care are being provided. Thus, in contrast to what has been suggested in literature, there is no dominant way to organize healthcare service delivery. Consequentially, there is no evidence for one single model, neither within nor across healthcare systems.

Summary box

- The provision of healthcare services is organized and structured quite differently across countries even though their healthcare systems face similar challenges, and are often apparently similar in their aims, levels of funding and other characteristics.

- There are four main models – illustrated in this chapter by Canada, England, Germany and the USA – which vary in the way health services are funded (taxation, social insurance, or employer insurance) and provided (by the state, by quasi-governmental institutions and agencies, by private not-for-profit entities, or by the private for-profit sector including companies and corporations.

- Understanding the current structures for healthcare provision in any country requires an understanding of their past history and development, and the culture and social values and ideologies which have shaped it.

- Different healthcare systems have different modes or methods of governance. Four key types can be identified – bureaucratic direction in state-owned and state-run systems; collective negotiation and regulation in systems where large non-profit quasi-public agencies are responsible for funding and provision; and straightforward regulation, contracting and competition in systems where private not-for-profit or for-profit entities predominate.

- Health services are often described as a pyramid or hierarchy – from self-care, through primary care, to secondary and tertiary care. Most care is provided at the bottom of the pyramid, and the most expensive and specialist services exist at the apex of the pyramid. Key features of healthcare provision include the way services are distributed across the pyramid of care; how the interfaces between these levels (for example, between primary and secondary or secondary and tertiary care) are organized; and how patients access the different levels of care, often through 'gatekeeping' or control mechanisms.

- In many countries, health service reconfiguration is being driven by changes in the burden of disease, the expectations and needs of service users, and the development of healthcare technology. It is both allowing some services to move down the pyramid (out of secondary care and into primary care), and is creating pressures to centralize and further specialize in other areas (out of secondary care and into tertiary care).

- Service reconfiguration often challenges the long-standing arrangements for healthcare provision in countries and the interests of groups such as physicians, hospital associations and the like, and is most difficult to enact in systems where provision is fragmented, regulatory oversight is weak, and control of financing is poor.

Self-test exercises

1 Think about the healthcare system in the country you live in. How would you describe its main constituent parts? Think of the difference between the notion of a system and the elements it is made of. Who are the main actors and how do they relate to each other in terms of ownership and control?

2 Describe a typical journey of a patient through a healthcare system you are familiar with. Please contrast pathways for patients with different needs: elective surgery and acute complication of a chronic disease (e.g. diabetes). What are the main differences and challenges at what transition points? How can observed challenges be overcome and who should take charge of changing these?

3 Think about the following description of a typical (older) patient in primary care:

> [L]ater she developed diabetes ... we controlled her blood pressure with tablets which worsened her renal function. A statin lowered her cholesterol, but her liver function went haywire ... Beta blockers made her breathing worse and her warfarin had to be stopped after a gastric bleed ... there always seemed to be a new symptom or drug side effect to deal with.[7]

How well does the system you have described in (1) meet the needs of this patient? What would need to change to improve the care provided to this type of patient and where would you start to introduce such changes? Please also consider the role of the patient as a key actor.

Notes

1 The responsibility for healthcare in the United Kingdom is devolved to England, Scotland, Northern Ireland and Wales. Consequently, the organization of healthcare differs in the devolved countries.
2 It is important to note that this conceptualization of vertical and horizontal integration differs from that commonly used in the integrated care literature, which classifies vertical integration as that between organizations at different levels of a hierarchical structure (i.e. primary, secondary and tertiary care) while horizontal integration takes place between organizations or organizational units that are on the same level in the delivery of healthcare or have the same status (see Nolte and McKee 2008a).
3 With the exception of the USA, country examples provided in this section refer to healthcare services that are funded through the statutory system only; these may include both public and private providers.
4 Since 2009, health insurance has been mandatory for all people legally resident in Germany. The large majority of the population (have to) take out social health insurance; about 10 per cent are privately insured.
5 Types of insurance in the USA are not mutually exclusive; people may be covered by more than one scheme during a given year.
6 The Dutch healthcare system is (still) considered as a social health insurance system to emphasize that the core principle of solidarity is being upheld as private for-profit health insurers have to accept new applicants and are not permitted to differentiate their premiums on the basis of age, sex or health risks (see e.g. Schäfer et al. 2010).
7 Adapted from Jelley (2006).

References and further reading

Abel-Smith, B. (1992) Cost containment and new priorities in the European Community. *The Milbank Quarterly*, 70(3): 393–416.

Alber, J. (1992) *Das Gesundheitswesen der Bundesrepublik Deutschland. Entwicklung, Struktur und Funktionsweise*. Frankfurt a.M.: Campus.

Banting, K.G. (2005) Canada: nation-building in a federal welfare state. In H. Obinger, S. Leibfried and F.G. Castles (eds) *Federalism and the Welfare State*. Cambridge: Cambridge University Press, pp. 89–137.

Bindman, A. and Majeed, A. (2003) Primary care in the United States: organisation of primary care in the United States. *BMJ*, 326: 631–4.

Black, N. and Gruen, R. (2005) *Understanding Health Services*. Maidenhead: Open University Press.

Boerma, W. (2006) Coordination and integration in European primary care. In R. Saltman, A. Rico and W. Boerma. *Primary Care in the Driver's Seat?*

Organizational Reform in European Primary Care. Maidenhead: Open University Press, pp. 3–21.

Boychuk, T. (1999) *The Making and Meaning of Hospital Policy in the United States and Canada*. Ann Arbor, MI: University of Michigan Press.

Busse, R. and Mays, N. (2008) Paying for chronic disease care. In E. Nolte and M. McKee (eds) *Caring for People with Chronic Conditions: A Health System Perspective*. Maidenhead, Open University Press, pp. 195–221.

Busse, R. and Riesberg, A. (2004) *Health Care Systems in Transition: Germany*. Copenhagen: WHO Regional Office for Europe on behalf of the European Observatory on Health Systems and Policies.

Cacace, M. (2010a) *Das Gesundheitssystem der USA: Governance-Strukturen staatlicher und privater Akteure*. Frankfurt a.M.: Campus.

Cacace, M. (2010b) The US healthcare system: hierarchization with and without the state. In H. Rothgang, M. Cacace, S. Grimmeisen and C. Wendt (eds) *The State and Healthcare: Comparing OECD Countries*. Basingstoke: Palgrave Macmillan.

Cacace, M., Goetze, R. et al. (2008) Explaining convergence and common trends in the role of the state in OECD healthcare systems. *Harvard Health Policy Review*, 9(1): 5–16.

Chernichovsky, D. (2000) The Public-Private Mix in the Modern Health Care System: Concepts, Issues and Policy Options Revisited. NBER Working Paper Series. Working Paper 7881. NBER.

De Alessi, L. (1989) The effect of institutions on the choices of consumers and providers of health care. *Journal of Theoretical Politics*, 1: 427–58.

DeNavas-Walt, C., Proctor, B. et al. (2010) *Income, Poverty, and Health Insurance Coverage in the United States: 2009*. Washington, DC: U.S. Government Printing Office.

Dixon, A., Robertson, R. et al. (2010) The experience of implementing choice at point of referral: a comparison of the Netherlands and England. *Health Econ Policy Law*, 5: 295–317.

Durand-Zaleski, I. and Obrecht, O. (2008) France. In C. Knai, E. Nolte and M. McKee. (eds) *Managing Chronic Conditions: Experience in Eight Countries*. Copenhagen: European Observatory on Health Systems and Policies.

Ettelt, S., Nolte, E. et al. (2006) *Health Care Outside Hospital: Accessing Generalist and Specialist Care in Eight Countries*. Copenhagen: World Health Organization on behalf of the European Observatory on Health Systems and Policies.

Ettelt, S., Nolte, E. et al. (2007) *A Review of the Role and Responsibilities of National Ministries of Health in Five Countries*. London: London School of Hygiene and Tropical Medicine.

Ettelt, S., Nolte, E. et al. (2008) *Capacity Planning in Health Care: Reviewing the International Experience*. Copenhagen: World Health Organization on behalf of the European Observatory on Health Systems and Policies.

Flood, C. and Archibald, T. (2001) The illegality of private health care in Canada. *Canadian Medical Association Journal*, 164(6): 825–30.

Forrest, C., Weiner, J. et al. (2001) Self-referral in point-of-service health plans. *JAMA*, 285: 2223–31.

GKV Spitzenverband (2010) Kennzahlen der gesetzlichen Krankenversicherung. Available at: http://www.gkv-spitzenverband.de/Presse_Zahlen_und_Grafiken .gkvnet (accessed 28 September 2010).

Götze, R., Cacace, M. et al. (2009) Von der Risiko- zur Anbieterselektion. Eigendynamiken wettbewerblicher Reformen in Gesundheitssystemen des Sozialversicherungstyps. *Zeitschrift für Sozialreform*, 55(2): 149–75.

Greer, S. (2004) *Territorial Politics and Health Policy*. Manchester: Manchester University Press.

Grimmeisen, S. and Frisina, L. (2010) The role of the state in the British healthcare system: between marketization and statism. In H. Rothgang, M. Cacace, L. Frisina **et al.** (eds) *The State and Healthcare: Comparing OECD Countries*. Basingstoke: Palgrave Macmillan.

Heath, I., Evans, P. et al. (2000) The specialist of the discipline of general practice. *BMJ*, 320: 326–7.

Hurst, J.W. (1991) Reforming health care in seven European nations. *Health Affairs*, 10(3): 7–21.

Jelley, D. (2006) Which patients with which needs are leading the patient-led NHS? *BMJ*, 332: 1221.

Jiwani, I. and Dubois, C. (2008) Canada. In E. Nolte, C. Knai and M. McKee (eds) *Managing Chronic Conditions: Experience in Eight Countries*. Copenhagen: World Health Organization on behalf of the European Observatory on Health Systems and Policies, pp. 161–81.

Kaiser/HRET (2010) The Kaiser Family Foundation and Health Research & Educational Trust: Employer Health Benefits 2010, Annual Survey. Available at: http://ehbs.kff.org/pdf/2010/8085.pdf (accessed 24 September 2010).

Karlberg, I. (2008) Sweden. In E. Nolte, C. Knai and M. McKee (eds) *Managing Chronic Conditions: Experience in Eight Countries*. Copenhagen: European Observatory on Health Systems and Policies.

Kassenärztliche Bundesvereinigung (2008) Vertragsmöglichkeiten. Hausarztzentrierte Versorgung. Available at: http://www.kbv.de/koop/8790.html (accessed 26 August 2010).

Kassenärztliche Bundesvereinigung (2010) *Versichertenbefragung der Kassenärztlichen Bundesvereinigung 2010*. Berlin: FGW Forschungsgruppe Wahlen Telefonfeld GmbH/Kassenärztliche Bundesvereinigung.

Klein-Lankhorst, E. and Spreeuwenberg, C. (2008) The Netherlands. In E. Nolte, C. Knai and M. McKee. (eds) *Managing Chronic Conditions: Experience in Eight Countries*. Copenhagen: European Observatory on Health Systems and Policies.

Le Grand, J., Mays, M. et al. (1998) *Learning from the NHS Internal Market: A Review of the Evidence*. London: King's Fund.

Lewis, S. (2008) De-regionalizing Alberta: the road to reform or collateral political damage? And then there was one (commentary). *Healthcare ISSUES*, Available at: http://www.longwoods.com/view.php?aid=19806 (accessed 23 August 2010).

Lisac, M., Reimers, L. et al. (2010) Access and choice: competition under the roof of solidarity in German health care: an analysis of health policy reforms since 2004. *Health Econ Policy Law*, 5: 31–52.

Lo Scalzo, A., Donatini, A. et al. (2009) Italy: health system review. *Health Systems in Transition*, 11(6): 1–216.

Marchildon, G. (2005) *Health Systems in Transition: Canada*. Copenhagen: WHO Regional Office for Europe on behalf of the European Observatory on Health Systems and Policies. Available at: http://www.euro.who.int/Document/E87954.pdf.

Marmor, T.R. and McKissick, G.J. (2000) Medicare's future: fact, fiction and folly. *American Journal of Law and Medicine*, 26(2–3): 225–53.

Naiditch, M. and Dourgnon, P. (2009) The Preferred Doctor Scheme: A Political Reading of a French Experiment of gate-keeping. Working Paper DT no. 22. Paris: IRDES.

National Commissioning Group for Highly Specialised Services (2010) Specialised services. available at: http://www.ncg.nhs.uk/ (accessed 21 August 2010).

Naylor, C. (1986) *Private Practice, Public Payment: Canadian Medicine and the Politics of Health Insurance, 1911–1966*. Montreal: McGill-Queen's University Press.

Nolte, E. (2004) Integration of East Germany into the EU: investment and health outcomes. In M. McKee, L. MacLehose and E. Nolte (eds) *Health Policy and European Union Enlargement*. Maidenhead: Open University Press, pp. 73–81.

Nolte, E. and McKee, M. (2008a) Integration and chronic care: a review. In E. Nolte and M. McKee (eds) *Caring for People with Chronic Conditions: A Health System Perspective*. Maidenhead: Open University Press, pp. 64–91.

Nolte, E. and McKee, M. (2008b) Making it happen. In E. Nolte and M. McKee (eds) *Caring for People with Chronic Conditions: A Health System Perspective*. Maidenhead: Open University Press, pp. 222–44.

Nolte, E., McKee, M. et al. (2008) Managing chronic conditions: an introduction to the experience in eight countries. In E. Nolte, C. Knai and M. McKee (eds) *Managing Chronic Conditions: Experience in Eight Countries*. Copenhagen: World Health Organization on behalf of the European Observatory on Health Systems and Policies, pp. 1–14.

OECD (2009) *Health Data*, 1st version, July 2009. Paris: OECD.

Or, Z., Cases, C. et al. (2010) Are health problems systemic? Politics of access and choice under Beveridge and Bismarck systems. *Health Econ Policy Law*, 5: 269–93.

Paton, A. (1975) Reorganisation: the first year: how it strikes a contemporary. *BMJ*, 2: 729.

Porter, R. (1997) *The Greatest Benefit to Mankind: A Medical History of Humanity from Antiquity to the Present*. London: HaperCollins Publishers.

Rechel, B., Wright, S. et al. (2009) Introduction: hospitals within a changing context. In B. Rechel, S. Wright, N. Edwards, B. Dowdeswell and M. McKee (eds) *Investing in Hospitals of the Future*. Copenhagen: World Health Organization on behalf of the European Observatory on Health Systems and Policies, pp. 3–26.

Rich, R.F. and Erb C.T. (2005) The two faces of managed care – regulation and policy-making. *Stanford Law and Policy Review*, 16(1): 233–75.

Rico, A., Saltman, R.B. et al. (2003) Organizational restructuring in European health systems: the role of primary care. *Social Policy and Administration*, 37(6): 592–608.

Roemer, M.I. (1991) *National Health Systems of the World*. New York: Oxford University Press.

Rosen, R. (2002) Introducing new technologies. In M. McKee and J. Healy (eds) *Hospitals in a Changing Europe*. Buckingham: Open University Press, pp. 240–51.

Rothgang, H., Cacace, M. et al. (2010a) *The State and Healthcare: Comparing OECD Countries*. Basingstoke: Palgrave Macmillan.

Rothgang, H., Schmid, A. et al. (2010b) The self-regulatory German healthcare system between growing competition and state hierarchy. In H. Rothgang, M. Cacace, S. Grimmeisen and C. Wendt (eds) *The State and Healthcare: Comparing OECD Countries*. Basingstoke: Palgrave Macmillan.

Sachverständigenrat zur Begutachtung der Entwicklung im Gesundheitswesen (2009) *Koordination und Integration: Gesundheitsversorgung in einer Gesellschaft des längeren Lebens*. Bonn: Sachverständigenrat zur Begutachtung der Entwicklung im Gesundheitswesen.

Schäfer, W., Kroneman, M. et al. (2010) The Netherlands: health system review. *Health Systems in Transition*, 12(1): 1–229.

Schoen, C., Osborn, R. et al. (2009) A survey of primary care physicians in eleven countries, 2009: perspectives on care, costs, and experiences. *Health Affairs*, 28: w1171–83.

Sibbald, B., McDonald, R. et al. (2007) Shifting care from hospitals to the community: a review of the evidence on quality and efficiency. *J Health Serv Res Policy*, 12: 110–17.

Sibbald, B., Pickard, S. et al. (2008) Moving specialist care into the community: an initial evaluation. *J Health Serv Res Policy*, 13: 233–9.

Siering, U. (2008) Germany. In C. Knai, E. Nolte and M. McKee (eds) *Managing Chronic Conditions: Experience in Eight Countries*. Copenhagen: European Observatory on Health Systems and Policies.

Singh, D. and Fahey, D. (2008) England. In E. Nolte, C. Knai and M. McKee (eds) *Managing Chronic Conditions: Experience in Eight Countries*. Copenhagen: European Observatory on Health Systems and Policies.

Stone, D. (2000) United States. *Journal of Health Politics, Policy and Law*, 25(5): 953–8.

Strandberg-Larsen, M., Nielsen, M. et al. (2007) Denmark: health system review. *Health Systems in Transition*, 9(6): 1–164.

Terris, M. (1978) The three worlds systems of medical care: trends and prospects. *American Journal of Public Health*, 68(11): 1125–31.

The Commonwealth Fund (2010) *International Profiles of Health Care Systems*. New York: The Commonwealth Fund.

Thomson, S. and Dixon, A. (2006) Choices in health care: the European experience. *J Health Serv Res Policy*, 11: 167–71.

Tuohy, C.H. (1999) *Accidental Logics: The Dyamics of Change in the Health Care Arena in the United States, Britain, and Canada*. New York: Oxford University Press.

Wasem, J., Greβ, S. et al. (2005) Gesundheitswesen und Sicherung bei Krankheit im Pflegefall. In Bundesministerium für Arbeit und Soziales und Bundesarchiv (ed.) *Geschichte der Sozialpolitik in Deutschland seit 1945, Band 7: 1982–1989*. Baden-Baden: Nomos.

White, J. (1999) Targets and systems of health care cost control. *Journal of Health Politics, Policy and Law*, 24(4): 653–96.

Williamson, O. (1985) *The Economic Institutions of Capitalism: Firms, Markets, Relational Contracting*. New York: Free Press.

Woerz, M. and Busse, R. (2005) Analysing the impact of health-care system change in the EU member states – Germany. *Health Economics*, 14: 133–49.

World Health Organization (2000) *The World Health Report 2000: Health Systems: Improving Performance*. Geneva: World Health Organization.

World Health Organization (2007) *Everybody's Business: Strengthening Health Systems to Improve Health Outcomes: WHO's Framework for Action*. Geneva: World Health Organization.

Websites and resources

European Observatory on Health Systems and Policies: provides detailed health system profiles of countries in the European Region of the World Health Organization and other OECD countries and comparative analyses of selected health policies and systems aspects in a range of countries:
http://www.euro.who.int/en/home/projects/observatory.

'On-call' Facility for International Healthcare Comparisons: provides timely, targeted, relevant and concise information on a range of health policy themes from Europe, Australia and New Zealand to inform health policy developments in England: www.international-comparisons.org.uk.

Organisation for Economic Co-operation and Development (OECD): undertakes performance measurement and analysis of health systems for international comparison through data projects and analytical projects:
http://www.oecd.org/topic/0,2686,en_2649_33929_1_1_1_1_37419,00.html.

The Commonwealth Fund International Health Policy Center: resource for information on health systems and policies in a range of OECD countries including an annual international survey of health policy issues, covering 11 OECD countries (2010): http://www.commonwealthfund.org/Topics/International-Health-Policy-2009.aspx.

World Health Organization Regional Office for Europe Health Evidence Network: information resource and platform on health evidence primarily for public health and healthcare policy-makers in the WHO European Region:
http://www.euro.who.int/en/what-we-do/data-and-evidence/health-evidence-network-hen.

For readers with an interest in middle- and low-income settings:

Alliance for Health Policy and Systems Research: an international collaboration with the aim of promoting the generation and use of health policy and systems research as a means to improve the health systems of developing countries:
http://www.who.int/alliance-hpsr/en/.

World Health Organization Health Systems programme: resource for data and tools relating to core health systems components (service delivery, health workforce, health systems financing, health information systems, leadership and governance, vaccines and technologies): http://www.who.int/healthsystems/en/.

CHAPTER 9

Primary healthcare

Judith Smith

Introduction

The defining moment in contemporary history of primary healthcare is generally considered to have been the declaration, at a World Health Organization conference in 1978, of what primary healthcare should provide to people in communities and nations. This declaration, known as the Alma Ata Declaration after the name of the town in the Russian Federation where the conference took place, sets out the following statements about the nature of primary healthcare:

> [Primary healthcare] . . . forms an integral part of both the country's health system of which it is the central function and the main focus of the overall social and economic development of the community.
>
> (WHO 1978: Section VI)

> Primary health care addresses the main health problems, providing preventive, curative, and rehabilitative services accordingly . . . but will include at least: promotion of proper nutrition and an adequate supply of safe water; basic sanitation; maternal and child care, including family planning; immunization against the major infectious diseases; education concerning basic health problems and the methods of preventing and controlling them; and appropriate treatment of common diseases and injuries.
>
> (WHO 1978: Section VII)

Thirty years later, the WHO's annual report focused on primary healthcare as its core theme 'Primary health care: now more than ever' and, as the title suggests, sought to revisit 'the ambitious vision of primary health care as a set of values and principles for guiding the development of health systems' (WHO 2008: 2). The report asserted the critical importance of primary care on the basis that it is able to 'accelerate the transformation of health systems so as to yield better and more equitably distributed health outcomes' (2008: 13).

These definitions are striking in their holistic assessment of primary healthcare as being what Tarimo (1997) has termed an 'approach to health development', namely, all those elements of care and community development that together enable people to lead healthy and meaningful lives. A view of primary healthcare as an approach to health development holds that it is central and foremost within a healthcare system, comprising all those activities and conditions that go towards ensuring the public health. 'Primary' therefore implies that this area of care is fundamental, essential and closest to people's everyday lives and experiences. The Alma Ata Declaration goes on to call for countries of the world to address the structural causes of ill health and in this way the WHO declaration defines primary healthcare as a central part of a strategy for social action.

The Alma Ata conception of primary care as an approach to health development is striking in its difference from what is traditionally considered to be 'primary care' in many health systems, and particularly in countries in the more developed world where hospitals and more technical forms of care tend to dominate people's understanding of a health system. In these countries, primary care tends to be viewed as one part of the biomedical spectrum of health services provided to people who are ill, with primary care being the point of 'first contact' with the health system. Thus primary care is often viewed as what Tarimo has termed 'a level of care', in contrast to the broader understanding of primary healthcare as an approach to overall health development.

The work of Barbara Starfield draws together these two main conceptions of primary care, viewing primary care as a level in a healthcare system, but at the same time considering it to be crucial and central to that system and to the health of populations:

> Primary care is that level of a health service system that provides entry into the system for all new needs and problems, provides person-focused (not disease-orientated) care over time, provides for all but very uncommon or unusual conditions, and co-ordinates or integrates care provided elsewhere by others.
>
> (Starfield 1998: 8–9)

Starfield set out what she considered to be the four central features of effective primary care:

1 The point of first *contact* for all new needs.

2 Person-focused rather than disease-focused *continuous* care over time.

3 Providing *comprehensive* care for all needs that are common in the population.

4 *Coordinating* care for both those needs and for needs that are sufficiently uncommon to require special services.

These 'four Cs' were asserted by Starfield to define what is essential about primary care, and she used these dimensions as a way of assessing the degree of effectiveness of a country's primary care system. Indeed, Starfield's research into the quality and nature of primary care in the international context suggests a link between the strength of a country's primary care system (as measured against the four Cs) and the degree of cost effectiveness of that system, and the level of health outcomes achieved for the population (Starfield 1998; Macinko et al. 2003). Having ranked the primary care systems of 12 industrialized nations, Starfield noted that 'countries with a better primary care orientation tend to have better rankings on health indicators than countries with a poor primary care orientation' (1998: 355).

On the thirtieth anniversary of the Alma Ata Declaration, Gillam (2008) argued that the principles of the declaration were as relevant as ever and that ensuring adequate community participation in health and healthcare, together with intersectoral action, remained key priorities if inequalities in health were to be addressed. He noted:

> Effective primary health care is more than a simple summation of individual technological interventions. Its power resides in linking different sectors and disciplines, integrating different elements of disease management, stressing early prevention, and the maintenance of health.
>
> (2008: 538)

Managing in primary care

Given the acknowledged importance of having a strong primary healthcare orientation to a health system, it is striking that relatively little has been written about the management (as opposed to the delivery) of primary care, particularly in comparison with the amount of analysis accorded to the management of hospital services. However, the management of primary care has in recent years been given greater prominence in both academic and practitioner communities, as people have increasingly come to view primary care as the main locus for seeking to improve health and control health system costs, and hence a key priority within health system reform (e.g. Tarimo 1997; WHO 2002; Peckham and Exworthy 2003; Shi et al. 2003; Starfield et al. 2005; Smith and Goodwin, 2006; WHO 2008). For example, in 2008, the WHO asserted:

> Reorienting a health system is a long-term process, if only because of the long time lag to restructure the workforce and because of the enormous inertia stemming from misaligned financial incentives and inadequate payment systems. Given the countervailing forces and vested interests that drive health systems away from PHC [primary health care] values, reform requires a clear vision for the future. Many countries have understood this and are developing their strategic vision of public policies for health with a perspective of 10 to 20 years.
>
> (WHO 2008: 100)

The rationale for placing a strong emphasis on primary care as the central function and value base within a health system is that primary healthcare can play a particular role in improving people's health, and thus in preventing illness and the need for hospital and other medical care (see Chapter 7). In order to bring about this stronger health improvement element within a health system, it is acknowledged that primary care itself needs to be strengthened and developed, including the provision of a wider range of services in community settings outside hospitals and extending access to primary care for disadvantaged communities (Starfield 1998; Hefford et al. 2005; Starfield et al. 2005).

A further role ascribed to primary care in some health systems, and one seen as being a lever to enable health improvement and primary care development, is that of primary care-led commissioning. This function, whereby primary care practitioners and organizations assume a role in the funding, planning and purchasing of healthcare on behalf of populations registered with local general practices, has been used most enthusiastically by state policy-makers in England and by managed care insurers in the United States, and also in more limited ways in experiments with primary care budget holding in Sweden, New Zealand, Australia and Canada.

In more recent times, this role has been extended to the development in a number of countries of primary care-based organizations that assume a capitated health service budget for a population, with the primary care organization taking responsibility for developing better integrated care for local people. A budget-holding organization of this nature typically assumes responsibility for the health outcomes of the local population, the quality of health services that people receive, and appropriate use of the budget itself. These bodies are known by names such as 'accountable care organisations' (Fisher et al. 2007), 'integrated care organisations' (Lewis et al. 2010), or 'clinical commissioning groups' (Department of Health 2011).

Taken together, the use of primary care as a locus for health improvement, primary care development, service commissioning, and the development of integrated care points to a general policy intention on the part of many governments to bring about a more primary care-based health system. Such a system embodies the principles of the Alma Ata Declaration and more recent interpretations of WHO and other international health policy, namely that health managers should seek to develop strong primary care as a way of bringing about improved public health and community well-being. Thus we can identify the following four functions for the management of primary care:

- managing for health improvement;
- managing for primary care service development;
- managing for primary care led commissioning;
- managing for a primary care-based health system.

These functions reflect an increasing international trend towards viewing primary care as a part of the health system that can be used to manage and influence change in health and health services, one that has been coined 'managed primary care' (Smith and Goodwin 2006), or increasingly, 'integrated care' (see Chapter 10 for more about integrated care). These functions associated with the management of primary care (or of primary care as the basis for developing better integrated care) are used here as the basis for exploring what is distinctive and important about managing in primary care.

Managing for health improvement

As noted above, a robust primary care system has been argued as important to the delivery of good and equitable health outcomes (e.g. Starfield 1998; Macinko et al. 2003; Davis and Stremikis 2010). Shi et al. (2003) similarly assert that managing and improving primary care is a key strategy for policy-makers seeking to reduce health

> ## Box 9.1: *Starfield's four Cs as an organizing framework*
>
> 1 Point of first contact – system of primary care gatekeeping, a single point of access to most services provided by the health system.
>
> 2 Person-focused continuous care over time – registration of patients with a single primary care practitioner or practice.
>
> 3 Comprehensive care for all common needs – multidisciplinary primary care and community health services that can assess, diagnose and treat common conditions.
>
> 4 Coordination of care provided elsewhere – role as the individual's advocate and guide through the wider health system, including the guardian of overall patient information.
>
> *Source:* Adapted from Starfield (1998).

inequalities but lacking the political power or mandate to influence factors outside the health sector. These authors point to evidence that an improvement in people's primary healthcare can, to some extent, act as a counterweight to health-damaging environmental conditions. Thus, the point is made that the management and development of primary care are crucial to improving people's health, and in turn to the amelioration of some of the inequalities in health status that exist in most if not all countries. In order to identify the key areas for action by primary care managers seeking to manage for health improvement, Starfield's 'four Cs' provide a useful organizing framework. These functions are set out in Box 9.1.

Primary care 'gatekeeping' is considered by many researchers and analysts (Starfield 1998; Peckham and Exworthy 2003; Wilson et al. 2006; Davis and Stremikis 2010) as being crucial to the management of an effective health system, both in relation to cost and clinical effectiveness. What gatekeeping entails is the identification of a single point of access to the health system for most of the health needs that people experience and traditionally this has been a general practice staffed by family doctors and their teams. Within a system of primary care gatekeeping, patients cannot access hospital specialists or associated diagnostic services unless they have first consulted their family doctor. The strength of such a system is seen as being the ability of the family doctor to take a holistic view of a person's care, assuring only appropriate referrals to more specialist services, and thus avoiding unnecessary expensive and possibly invasive tests and care in hospital settings. Gatekeeping is a function typically associated with tax-funded health systems such as those in the UK, New Zealand, Denmark, Italy and Sweden. Critics of gatekeeping assert that it limits patients' rights and choices within a health system.

Countries that have a strong libertarian tradition such as France, Israel and the United States typically baulk at the concept of limiting people's choice of point of access to care in this way, although for reasons of medical cost inflation, all three of these countries have been experimenting with pilot projects of gatekeeping. One such experiment in the United States – *the primary care medical home* – is increasingly being seen as a way of offering patient-centred and integrated care in a manner that is affordable, high quality and accessible to a majority of the population (Rosenthal 2008; Davis and Stremikis 2010). The model entails patients being enrolled with a primary care practice that holds a capitated budget for its patients, taking responsibility for referrals to specialist and other care, and coordination of the individual's care from the 'primary care home'. The primary care medical home is arguably an example of a well-functioning general practice as understood in countries such as the UK, New Zealand, Denmark, the Netherlands and Canada, albeit it does imply a strong system leadership and care coordination role for the primary care physician which is not always a feature of day-to-day general practice in the countries cited above.

The *registration of patients* with a single practice or practitioner is viewed by public health practitioners and policy-makers as being vital in relation to both individual and population health. For individuals, it is considered to enable the development of a long-term and continuous relationship between patient and family doctor (or medical practice), meaning that the doctor can have an overview of a person's medical history, firmly located within a knowledge and understanding of their broader social context, including family situation, employment status, housing provision and education. For populations, a system of registration provides managers in a health system with a register of people that sets out key health data (e.g. age, sex, any chronic ill-health problems, family situation) and thus represents the basis for carrying out population-focused health interventions such as calls for health screening, immunization campaigns, child health surveillance and health monitoring associated with specific age categories. The importance of a system of registration has been powerfully demonstrated by the experience of New Zealand, where from 2001, the government explicitly developed a Primary Health Care Strategy (Minister of Health 2001) that sought, among other things, to develop a system of patient registration, and where, just a few years later, there was evidence that levels of access to care and health promotion services had shown an improvement from their previously low base in comparison with other developed countries (Hefford et al. 2005; Cumming and Gribben 2007).

The provision of *comprehensive and multidisciplinary primary and community services* is a goal that is clearly set out in the Alma Ata Declaration as being a key element in enabling effective primary healthcare. This underlines the WHO vision of primary care as being the centre of a health system, and not the bottom of a pyramid of care as is often implied or asserted in management and clinical circles. The specific nature of comprehensive primary care differs both within and between countries, but typically entails a locally based practice or health centre that offers (or can easily refer to) community-based services such as:

- general practice (family medicine)
- primary care nursing
- public health nursing
- child health surveillance
- chronic disease management

- community mental health
- physiotherapy
- speech and language therapy
- community dietetics
- dentistry
- pharmacy.

Together with the role of gatekeeping and patient registration, comprehensive provision of services in a community setting is seen as a key element in supporting people in maintaining good health and managing much of their ill health and longer-term conditions. Despite the common perception among the populations of many countries that a health system is synonymous with hospitals, the majority of people's healthcare takes place within primary care, at least in those countries where there is effective gatekeeping of the wider health system, and restrictions on direct access to specialist care.

The role of *coordinating a person's care* within the health system is perhaps the most problematic function that is ascribed to 'ideal' primary care, given the ever more complex nature of healthcare interventions. For example, many approaches to chronic disease management are founded on the principle of a clinical professional taking responsibility for the coordination of care for an individual, this role encompassing needs assessment, monitoring of health, organization of care and advocacy for the individual if admitted to hospital care. There is a body of research evidence that points to the difficulties in achieving effective coordination of care for people with complex needs (whether in community or hospital settings), and an analysis of the associated issues is set out in Chapter 10 (chronic disease and integrated care). Nevertheless, analysis of primary healthcare in the international context highlights primary care as the most appropriate location for the coordination of care for individuals, especially when combined with effective gatekeeping and patient registration (e.g. Starfield 1998; Macinko et al. 2003; Davis and Stremikis 2010).

When managing for health improvement, policy-makers and managers face a dilemma in relation to how far they focus on the concerns and priorities of individual patients or citizens, and how far they address the health needs of the wider population. For example, a system of primary care gatekeeping (or in the US context, based on a primary care medical home) enables cost-effective use of a nation's health resources, but compromises an individual's ability to choose their care provider. Similarly, the development of a system of individual care managers for people with long-term conditions may enable personal choice in care management, but could lead to fragmentation of overall care, unless there is careful integration of the activity of care managers within an overall local health plan (see Chapter 10 for a more detailed discussion).

This patient/population tension is a further manifestation of Tarimo's two alternative approaches to understanding primary healthcare – as a level in the health system (that provides care to patients) or as an approach to health development (that seeks to improve public health). Others see this tension as an expression of the fact that two medical disciplines, general practice and public health, seek to own and manage what is typically understood as primary care. On the one hand, general practice traditionally sees its role as providing medical care for individual patients, whereas public health seeks to improve the health of whole populations. One example of how such tensions can play out in practice is the New Zealand Primary Health Care Strategy, where implementation of reform focused more on the development of population health within a public health view of primary care, with arguably less management and policy attention being paid to the development of better integrated primary care services for individual patients within general practice (Smith 2009).

One management and organizational solution to this patient/population tension in recent years has been the development of 'primary care organizations', bodies that are set up to manage and develop primary care services in order to both improve population health and enable effective and high quality general practice provision (Ham 1996; Malcolm et al. 1999; Mays et al. 2001; Dowling and Glendinning 2003; Smith and Goodwin 2006). Primary care organizations are a specific manifestation of the move towards more managed primary care in a number of health systems, and represent a managerial solution to the dilemma of how to draw together often diverse and autonomous general practices and other community services into a coherent local plan for improving health. Further analysis of the role of primary care organizations is set out below.

Managing for primary care service development

The management of primary care service delivery and development continues to be, in many health systems, the most pressing and time-consuming challenge for primary care managers. This typically takes the form of planning, funding and managing two main areas of service delivery: general practice (family medicine) and associated services such as practice nursing and chronic disease care; and community health services including public health nursing, child health surveillance, continuing care of older people and health promotion. The relative importance of these two areas of primary care service provision varies between countries.

For example, in Australia, general medical practice continues to represent the primary form of care provision outside of hospitals, albeit that there are moves towards greater use of community health teams incorporating nursing, physiotherapy and other allied health professions. In the UK, although general medical practice continues to feature in most people's mind as the first point of entry to the health system, in reality, more and more primary care services are delivered directly by community nurses, public health nurses, community pharmacists and social care staff, and in some cases through new organizations such as nurse-led walk-in centres, the phone and internet-based NHS Direct/NHS Choices, and GP-led health centres that do not require patients to be registered with the organization.

At the other end of the general practice–public health spectrum, in some countries, for example, Tanzania, some New Zealand Māori or Canadian Inuit communities, local health workers or nurses form the backbone of the primary care system, acting as public health and health promotion advisers, signposting people towards medical and nursing services as and when they need them. In the context of the Alma Ata definition of primary healthcare, it can be argued that a community health approach to the provision of primary care, and based on strong public health nursing, is more appropriate to developing overall community health than a system based on medical practice. However, general medical practice has dominated the provision of primary care in many industrialized countries and the challenge for managers is how they can make a system of general practice work in such a way that it achieves wider public and community health goals.

General medical practice is often organized on the basis of independent self-employed doctors working in small groups (or singly), and contracting with local health authorities to provide services to a registered local population. This system operates in the UK, the Netherlands, Denmark and Canada. In other countries, doctors similarly work in independent practices but levy fees directly from patients who can in some cases seek reimbursement of fees from their state or private health insurance. General practitioners levy fees from patients in countries such as New Zealand, France, Australia and the USA. The practice-based system of primary care is not confined to general medical practice, but is also commonly found in community dentistry, optometry and pharmacy.

A system of independent practice in primary care poses a range of challenges to those seeking to manage primary care service delivery and development. There is a fundamental decision for a health system to make in respect of how it will structure its relationship with general practice and thus seek to bring about change with that part of the health sector. Options available for managing the relationship between the health system and general practice include the following:

- managing through *a system of contracts* between the health system and individual general practices or practitioners, thus using financial incentives and/or quality indicators as a way of bringing about desired changes to services (e.g. UK, Danish, and Australian general practice);
- letting a *market* develop whereby fee-paying patients (or their insurers) choose their practice or practitioner, and services are developed in response to patient (or insurer) demand, and prices regulated largely by the market (e.g. traditional New Zealand general practice, French general practice, US family medicine);
- providing centrally run (by the state or by insurance organizations) *primary care centres* with salaried doctors and associated staff, with standards and services defined by the state or insurer (e.g. Swedish health centres, US managed care organizations);
- developing *primary care organizations* as intermediary bodies that seek to influence primary care provision using options such as letting contracts with providers of services; making specific payments to practices or others to develop or extend services; establishing specialized services; shifting resource from other parts of the

health system in order to facilitate service development in primary care (e.g. clinical commissioning groups in England, New Zealand primary health organizations and independent practitioner associations, Australian divisions of general practice and Medicare Locals, Californian physician networks and independent practice associations).

- establishing other non-governmental organizational forms such as *community or social enterprises* as a vehicle for developing and providing care in innovative ways that are appropriate to specific population groups, in particular those traditionally excluded from general practice (e.g. in New Zealand by Māori for Māori, or Pasifika healthcare organizations; community health enterprise organizations in the UK; US care organizations for people with long-term conditions).

The choice as to how to structure the relationship between the health system and primary care providers is likely to involve multiple and 'blended' payment solutions as a means of influencing the behaviour of practitioners (Gosden et al. 2001; Ham 2010). In health systems that are increasingly complex, and with more and more patients living to an older age and with long-term conditions, managers need to find solutions that not only assure the development of primary care services for different groups of the population, but also ensure the achievement of wider health system goals. In addition to the structuring of the relationship with primary care as set out above, they may also seek to use other tools in developing primary care services including: the establishment of new community health centres that provide a wide range of health and social care for local communities; walk-in assessment centres for emergency primary care; telehealth and telecare monitoring and care delivery services; and out-of-hours care centres that involve paramedic, nursing, general practice and perhaps hospital emergency room practitioners.

What is clear is that health systems are increasingly seeking to coordinate and manage a diverse range of providers of primary care, trying at once to develop and improve primary care services, while improving the public health, and assuring overall better integration of care and health outcomes.

This poses specific management challenges, including assuring the quality of services provided to patients and the public, delivering value for money for taxpayers and insurers, enabling continuity and coordination of care for individuals and their carers, and finding ways of developing a workforce for current and future community health services. These management challenges are now finding their way into the health strategies of many countries, with primary care being seen as a key element in wider health plans. Examples of countries that are taking a more primary healthcare-focused approach to strategy development include New Zealand with its Primary Health Care Strategy, Wales and Northern Ireland with their clearly public-health oriented plans for national health, and Australia with its strategy for primary healthcare and new investment in developing integrated local primary care organizations (e.g. health 'superclinics'). At an international level, as noted earlier, the WHO continues to press for a stronger primary healthcare orientation to health systems, and for the development of primary care to be seen as the heart and not on the periphery of a healthy care system (WHO 2008).

Managing for primary care-led commissioning

Primary care-led commissioning (or purchasing or budget-holding, as it is often known) is a key management function at the disposal of primary care managers and has been defined as follows:

> Commissioning led by primary health care clinicians, particularly GPs, using their accumulated knowledge of their patients' needs and of the performance of services, together with their experience as agents for their patients and control over resources, to direct the health needs assessment, service specification and quality standard setting stages in the commissioning process in order to improve the quality and efficiency of health services used by their patients.
>
> (Smith et al. 2004: 5)

In other words, it concerns the use of primary care practices (or clusters of practices) for the planning and funding (or purchasing through the placing of contracts) of health services for a defined population, for example, the people registered with a practice or living in a specific locality. Primary care-led commissioning typically takes the form of a total or partial delegated budget that is managed by GPs, nurses and primary care managers, with the intention of using this resource as a means of buying services that will support the achievement of local (and perhaps national) primary care development and health improvement goals. In this way, it offers a further tool for primary care managers seeking both to develop primary care and improve health. Its particular potential is considered to be the ability for primary care budget holders to redesign health services in such a way that they are refocused on community and primary care, with less of a reliance on hospital care.

Primary care-led commissioning is an area of primary care management that is regarded as a key feature of some health systems, while being eschewed or not even considered in others. The English NHS is the system that has most consistently held faith with primary care-led commissioning, seeking to use primary care practices and organizations as the main location for the planning and purchasing of health services. This has been further emphasized by the announcement, in the plans of the Coalition Government elected in May 2010, of a move to make groups of GPs the main statutory funders and purchasers of some 60 per cent of health services in England (Department of Health 2010).

Other countries that continue to pursue or have experimented with primary care purchasing or budget holding include New Zealand (independent practitioner associations, community-governed organizations, and primary health organizations); Australia (divisions of general practice, and proposals for Medicare Locals); the United States (independent practice associations, health maintenance organizations, accountable care organizations); Sweden and Estonia (GP budget holding); Scotland, Wales and Northern Ireland (GP fundholding in the 1990s).

There is a significant base of research evidence concerning the management challenge posed by primary care-led commissioning, particularly in relation to the process of implementing and developing such approaches. An analysis of this evidence base

---

Box 9.2: *Factors facilitating effective primary care-led commissioning*

- Stability in the organization of healthcare, especially the structure of commissioning bodies.
- Sufficient time to enable clinicians to become engaged, and strategies for commissioning to be developed and implemented.
- A policy that supports offering patients and commissioners a choice of providers.
- A policy that enables resources to be shifted between providers and services.
- A local service configuration that enables commissioners to choose between providers.
- A local primary care system that is sufficiently developed to provide additional services.
- Incentives that engage general practitioners and practices in seeking to develop new forms of care across the primary–secondary care interface.
- Effective management and information support for practice-based commissioners.
- Appropriate regulation to minimize conflicts of interest arising from general practitioners being both commissioners and providers.

Source: Smith et al. (2005: 1398).

---

points to the following factors known to facilitate effective primary care-led commissioning, as set out in Box 9.2.

Where some or all of the above conditions are met, research evidence suggests that a health system is likely to experience: demonstrable improvements in the delivery of primary and intermediate care services; some marginal changes to the quality and responsiveness of secondary care; greater engagement of doctors, nurses and other professionals in the planning and funding of care; and a stronger overall primary care orientation in the health system (Mays et al. 2001; Smith et al. 2004; Curry et al. 2008; Smith et al. 2010).

There will, however, remain some apparently intractable problems for managers of primary care including: trying to make a significant or strategic impact on the delivery of secondary and tertiary (i.e. hospital) services; shifting resources from hospital to community settings; and reshaping the pattern of delivery of emergency and unscheduled care (Mays et al. 2001; Smith et al. 2004; Smith et al. 2010). These challenges (as examined in Chapter 14) are not unique to primary care-led approaches to commissioning, and are faced by planners and funders of care in almost all health systems. They are, however, significant for managers of primary care who, in their attempts to improve the quality and range of primary care services as part of an overall attempt to develop the public health, might consider primary care-led commissioning as a tool in their armoury. What is clear is that primary care-led commissioning has real and evidence-based potential as a means of developing primary care (and thus, over time, in enabling improvements to health as envisaged by Starfield and others), but that it remains to be proven as to whether it can play a significant role in wider redesign of health services across health systems.

One such attempt to use primary care as the basis for bringing about more radical change in the delivery of health services is a concept developed in the USA by Fisher and others (2007) – the accountable care organization. This describes local organizations that are led by clinicians, and take responsibility for a health budget for a local population for which all preventative, primary and community healthcare services, as well as some or all acute care, is purchased. The accountable care organization thus assumes the financial risk associated with the healthcare of a local population, and is incentivized to try and keep its patients as healthy as possible, focusing on preventative and community-based care and avoiding unnecessary admissions to hospital. In England, this idea is being developed through pilots of 'integrated care organizations' (see Lewis et al. 2010, for more details), and in New Zealand through 'integrated family health centres' (The Office of the Leader of the Opposition 2007). There are also examples of new integrated care networks in Spain, Canada, Germany and the Netherlands to name a few – more exploration of the concept and practice of integrated care is set out in Chapter 10 (chronic disease and integrated care).

Managing for a primary care-based health system: what are the main challenges?

In line with WHO policy, many countries are seeking to develop less of a sickness and more of a health-focused system, based on strong primary healthcare. In so doing, they espouse the research of Starfield, Shi and others that advocates strong primary care as a vital prerequisite for improved health outcomes that are achieved in a manner that is cost effective for overall health systems. While the WHO's assertion of primary care as the centre of a health system, with secondary care playing an important (but essentially secondary in both senses of the word) role, can seem somewhat idealistic, there is international evidence of countries seeking to redress the balance of health funding, activity and management effort away from hospital care in favour of primary care.

For example, the Welsh Assembly specified the strengthening and development of family health services as a key health priority, including improvements to community health services and the extension of availability of free eye care and prescriptions along with other public health measures (Welsh Assembly Government 2005). The policy pursued in Wales during the early-mid 2000s was strikingly more primary care focused than that of its neighbour England where improvements in access to secondary care services were arguably the main target of policy and management attention (King's Fund 2010). Likewise, Australia has, since 2007, embarked on a process of health reform which includes a primary healthcare strategy and an intention to develop local primary care planning agencies to be known as 'Medicare Locals' (Commonwealth of Australia, 2010). This approach is similar to the policy adopted by the New Zealand government over the period 1999–2008, when a primary healthcare strategy was used as a guiding force in seeking to improve access to primary care, reduce health inequalities, improve care for people with chronic disease, and enhance community participation in health (Minister of Health 2001).

This indicates the possibility of countries adopting a specific policy focus on primary healthcare (in its widest Alma Ata Declaration sense) as the guiding framework for health policy. As can be seen in both cases, the management response to such a policy direction requires a range of tools and approaches including: the use of health improvement goals and activities that aim to reduce health inequalities; the development of policies directed at improving primary care services (use of incentives for practices and practitioners, establishing contracts for services, establishment of new forms of service); and a commitment to shift resources from elsewhere in the system to support improvements to primary care. Primary care-led commissioning is not being used to any significant extent in New Zealand and Wales, but research evidence would suggest that it has the potential to further incentivize improvements to and extensions in the range of services provided outside of hospitals, as is believed by English policy-makers who are introducing a policy of 'GP commissioning' (Department of Health 2010) as a way of making GPs directly accountable for healthcare purchasing in the hope that this will result in improved management of the demand for secondary care services.

The major challenges faced by those seeking to manage primary care are therefore those related to the two dimensions of primary care that were considered at the start of this chapter – namely trying to improve the relative strength and power of primary care within the health system and realize its potential as an approach to health development (Tarimo 1997). Primary care, although being targeted as an area for specific policy and management attention in many health systems, typically remains the poor relation in respect of attracting significant investment, particularly in comparison with the power of large hospitals that attract political and public visibility and support. There are many reasons for this disparity, including the somewhat diffuse and networked nature of primary care providers in comparison with the institutional power and status of hospitals. Likewise, GPs have traditionally been perceived to wield less power within health systems compared with hospital specialists, mainly on account of their commonly held status as self-employed business people working in small groups or as individuals, while specialists operate in larger clinical teams.

There are, however, significant potential health and cost effectiveness gains to be made if health systems can become more primary care focused. This is even more the case in the context of rising incidence of chronic disease in developed countries, and infectious diseases such as HIV/AIDS and malaria in developing countries (see Chapter 7), for these public health trends are particularly amenable to primary healthcare solutions. However, if the potential of primary care-based approaches to health policy and management are to be realized by those with the power to influence resource allocation and future policy development, managers need to have in place robust measures that can demonstrate the degree to which more managed primary care can deliver improvements to both primary care itself and to the wider public health (Box 9.3).

Box 9.3: *The main challenges for managing in primary care*

- Putting in place an effective system of primary care gatekeeping.
- Ensuring the registration of the public for primary care and public health purposes.
- Developing primary care provision that is comprehensive and multidisciplinary in nature.
- Having a clear primary care-based coordination function for individual patients being cared for elsewhere in the health and social care system.
- Developing an appropriate balance between the provision of family medicine (general practice) and community health services.
- Working out the appropriate blend of approaches and techniques for managing the relationship between general practice and the wider health system.
- Determining the degree to which primary care-led commissioning or budget holding is relevant to the wider achievement of primary care and public health goals.
- Exploring ways of using primary care as the basis for developing new forms of integrated care.
- Working to ensure that the system-wide strategy is primary care focused.
- Seeking to strengthen the overall position and power of primary care within the health system.
- Having measures in place that can demonstrate progress towards the achievement of primary care and public health goals.

Conclusion

For managers in primary care, as has been demonstrated, the main challenges relate to how they can act in order to improve health, develop primary and community care, enable primary care-led commissioning, and thus have a more clearly primary care-based health system. In so doing, they need to find ways of meeting the main challenges of managing in primary care.

Summary box

- Primary healthcare is concerned with enabling and improving healthy communities and societies.
- In many countries, however, primary healthcare has been seen as synonymous with first contact care in the healthcare system and with general practice in particular.
- Primary healthcare is fundamental to both healthcare and health improvement, and the existence of a strong primary care orientation in a health system has been shown to improve health outcomes and cost effectiveness.

- The management of primary care is increasingly receiving policy and research attention, in particular with reference to improving health, developing primary care services and as a basis for commissioning services elsewhere in the health system.

- In managing primary care for health improvement, key functions include the development of effective gatekeeping, patient registration and care coordination.

- In managing primary care for the development of primary and community services, there is a balance to be struck between the emphasis on family medicine and community health services.

- The management of the relationship between a health system and family medicine is crucial for primary care managers and can be achieved through various means including the use of contracts, financial incentives, and the development of primary care organizations.

- Primary care-led commissioning is a management function used by some primary care managers as a means of developing primary care, improving service integration, and increasing overall primary care influence within a health system.

- Ultimately, the main challenge for the management of primary care is to increase its influence in a health system in relation to the power and resources of hospital services.

- If this shift in influence can be achieved, primary healthcare can become a route to improving health and developing stronger and more sustainable communities.

Self-test exercises

1 Make an assessment of your own country's health system in relation to its degree of primary care orientation according to Starfield's 'four Cs'. In so doing, assess on a scale of 1–10 (where 1 = not at all, and 10 = completely) your health system's

- degree of gatekeeping in primary care
- extent of primary care and public health registration
- provision of comprehensive primary care and community health services
- ability to provide primary care-focused coordination of care for individuals.

2 Make the same assessment for the health system of another country with which you are familiar through personal experience or your studies. How do the two countries' health systems compare in respect of primary care orientation?

3 Find out how these same two countries compare in relation to health outcomes data and cost effectiveness of the overall health system. Is there any relationship between what you have observed in relation to primary care orientation and system health and cost outcomes?

4 Examine the concept of the 'accountable care organization' and consider how such an idea might be enacted within your own health system, with a primary care-based entity taking responsibility for health outcomes, service quality, and value for money associated with the healthcare resource for a local patient population.

References and further reading

Commonwealth of Australia (2010) *A National Health and Hospitals Network for Australia's Future – Delivering the Reforms*. Canberra: Commonwealth of Australia.

Cumming, J. and Gribben, B. (2007) *Evaluation of the Primary Health Care Strategy: Practice Data Analysis 2001–2007*. Wellington: Health Services Research Centre and CBG Research.

Curry, N., Goodwin, N., Naylor, C. and Robertson, R. (2008) *Practice-based Commissioning: Replace, Reinvigorate or Abandon*? London: The King's Fund.

Davis, K. and Stremikis, M. (2010) Preparing for a high-performance health care system. *Journal of the American Board of Family Medicine*, 23(supplement): 11–16.

Department of Health (2000) *The NHS Plan: A Plan for Investment, a Plan for Reform*. London: The Stationery Office.

Department of Health (2004) *Practice Based Commissioning: Promoting Clinical Engagement*. London: Department of Health.

Department of Health (2010) *Equity and Excellence: Liberating the NHS*. London: Department of Health.

Department of Health (2011) *Government Response to the NHS Future Forum Report*. CM 8113, London: Department of Health.

Dowling, B. and Glendinning, C. (eds) (2003) *The New Primary Care, Modern, Dependable, Successful*. Maidenhead: Open University Press.

Fisher, E., Staiger, D., Bynum, J. and Gottlieb, D. (2007) Creating accountable care organisations: the extended hospital medical staff, *Health Affairs*, 26(1): w44–w57.

Gillam, S. (2008) Is the Declaration of Alma Ata still relevant to primary health care? *British Medical Journal*, 336: 536–8.

Gosden, T., Forland, F., Kristiansen, I., Sutton, M., Leese, B., Giuffrida, A., et al. (2001) Impact of payment method on behaviour of primary care physicians: a systematic review. *Journal of Health Services Research and Policy*, 6(1): 44–55.

Ham, C. (1996) Population centred and patient focused purchasing: the UK experience. *Milbank Quarterly*, 74(2): 191–214.

Ham, C. (2010) *GP Budget Holding: Lessons from Across the Pond and from the NHS*. Birmingham: Health Services Management Centre.

Hefford, M., Crampton, P. and Macinko, J. (2005) Reducing health disparities through primary care reform: the New Zealand experiment. *Health Policy*, 72: 9–23.

King's Fund (2010) *A High Performing NHS? A Review of the Evidence, 1997–2010*. London: The King's Fund.

Lewis, R.Q., Rosen, R., Goodwin, N. and Dixon, J. (2010) *Where Next for Integrated Care Organisations in the English NHS*? London: The Nuffield Trust and The King's Fund.

Macinko, J., Starfield, B. and Shi, L. (2003) The contribution of primary care systems to health outcomes within Organisation for Economic Co-operation and Development countries, 1970–1998. *Health Services Research*, 38: 831–65.

Malcolm, L., Wright, L. and Barnett, P. (1999) *The Development of Primary Care Organizations in New Zealand: A Review Undertaken for Treasury and the Ministry of Health*. Lyttelton: Aotearoa Health.

Mays, N., Wyke, S., Malbon, G. and Goodwin, N. (eds) (2001) *The Purchasing of Health Care by Primary Care Organisations: An Evaluation and Guide to Future Policy*. Buckingham: Open University Press.

Minister of Health (2001) *The New Zealand Primary Health Care Strategy*. Wellington: Ministry of Health. http://www.moh.govt.nz/ (accessed 14 July 2011).

Peckham, S. and Exworthy, M. (2003) *Primary Care in the UK: Policy, Organisation and Management*. Basingstoke: Palgrave Macmillan.

Rosenthal, T.C. (2008) The medical home: growing evidence to support a new approach to primary care. *Journal of the American Board of Family Medicine*, 21(5): 427–40.

Shi, L., Macinko, J., Starfield, B., Wulu, J., Regan, J. and Politzer, R. (2003) The relationship between primary care, income inequality and mortality in US states, 1980–1995. *Journal of the American Board of Family Practice*, 16(5): 412–22.

Smith, J.A. (2009) *Critical Analysis of the Primary Health Care Strategy Implementation and Framing of Issues for the Next Phase*. Wellington: Ministry of Health.

Smith, J.A., Curry, N., Mays, N. and Dixon, J. (2010) *Where Next for Commissioning in the English NHS?* London: The Nuffield Trust and The King's Fund.

Smith, J.A., Dixon, J., Mays, N., Goodwin, N., Lewis, R., McClelland, S. et al. (2005) Practice-based commissioning: applying the evidence. *British Medical Journal*, 331: 1397–9.

Smith, J.A. and Goodwin, N. (2006) *Towards Managed Primary Care: The Role and Experience of Primary Care Organizations*. Aldershot: Ashgate.

Smith, J.A., Mays, N., Dixon, J., Goodwin, N., Lewis, R., McLelland, S. et al. (2004) *A Review of the Effectiveness of Primary Care-Led Commissioning and its Place in the NHS*. London: Health Foundation.

Starfield, B. (1998) *Primary Care: Balancing Health Needs, Services and Technology*. Oxford: Oxford University Press.

Starfield, B., Shi, L. and Macinko, J. (2005) Contribution of primary care to health systems and health. *Milbank Quarterly*, 83: 457–502.

Tarimo, E. (1997) *Primary Health Care Concepts and Challenges in a Changing World: Alma-Ata Revisited*. Geneva: World Health Organization.

The Office of the Leader of the Opposition (2007) Better, Sooner, More Convenient. Discussion Paper by Hon. Tony Ryall MP. Wellington: Office of the Leader of the Opposition.

Welsh Assembly Government (2005) *Designed for Life: Creating World Class Health and Social Care for Wales in the 21st Century*. Cardiff: Welsh Assembly Government.

Wilson, T., Roland, M. and Ham, C. (2006) The contribution of general practice and the general practitioner to NHS patients. *Journal of the Royal Society of Medicine*, 99: 24–8.

World Health Organization (1978) *Declaration of Alma Ata*. Geneva: WHO.
World Health Organization (2002) *Innovative Care for Chronic Conditions: Building Blocks for Action*. Geneva: WHO.
World Health Organization (2008) *Primary Health Care: Now More Than Ever: The World Health Report 2008*. Geneva: WHO.

Websites and resources

Australian Primary Health Care Research Institute: www.anu.edu.au/aphcri.

Canadian Health Services Research Foundation (see primary healthcare policy pages): www.chsrf.ca.

European Forum for Primary Care: www.euprimarycare.org.

King's Fund: www.kingsfund.org.uk.

National Primary Care Research and Development Centre, Manchester: www.npcrdc.man.ac.uk/.

New Zealand Ministry of Health (see primary health care and PHOs pages): www.moh.govt.nz.

The Commonwealth Fund: www.commonwealthfund.org.

The Nuffield Trust: www.nuffieldtrust.org.uk.

World Association of Family Doctors: www.globalfamilydoctor.com/.

World Health Organization: www.who.int/about/en.

Chronic disease and integrated care

Vidhya Alakeson and Rebecca Rosen

10

Introduction

Chronic diseases are the leading cause of morbidity and mortality in OECD countries and are an increasing problem in low-income and middle-income countries. They include a wide range of conditions, such as ischaemic heart disease, asthma, diabetes and chronic kidney disease that cannot be cured, but can be managed with medications and other therapies. Increasingly, conditions such as HIV/AIDS, mental health disorders (such as depression, schizophrenia and dementia) and cancer – which can be driven into remission with drug treatments, but may recur at a later date – are also thought of as chronic conditions. Table 10.1 shows the burden of chronic disease in several high-income countries.

Although the overall prevalence of chronic disease is greater in high-income countries, 80 per cent of deaths from chronic disease occur in low- and middle-income countries (WHO 2005). The challenge for these countries is to continue to address infectious disease at the same time as tackling the growing burden of chronic disease. Table 10.2 shows the ten countries with the largest number of people with diabetes in 2000 and projections for 2030, indicating the steady rise of diabetes in low-income countries such as Bangladesh and Pakistan.

The proportion of people living with chronic conditions rises with age, with older people typically living with more than one condition, and the number of co-existing conditions rising with age. Figure 10.1 illustrates the proportion of English people reporting different numbers of chronic conditions (described in Figure 10.1 as 'long-term conditions' or LTCs) at different ages. In low- and middle-income countries, individuals develop chronic diseases at younger ages, suffer longer – often with preventable complications – and die younger than in high-income countries. Figure 10.2 shows the projected age standardized death rates from chronic disease for individuals between 30 and 69 in high-, middle- and low-income countries. Death rates for this younger age cohort in the United Kingdom and Canada are dwarfed by death rates in India, Nigeria, Tanzania and the Russian Federation.

As well as ageing, many chronic diseases are linked to lifestyle factors such as obesity, smoking, lack of physical activity and risky sexual behaviour. Smoking prevalence is falling across OECD countries, with an average of 23 per cent of adults reporting

TABLE 10.1 Selected disease causes of death as percentage of all causes of death in high-income countries, 2004

Causes of death	High-income countries	Australia	Germany	UK	USA
HIV infection	0.3	0.1	<0.1	0.1	0.7
Diabetes mellitus	3.0	2.7	2.9	1.1	3.1
Chronic lower respiratory disease	6.4	4.4	0.6	4.5	5.1
Cerebrovascular disease	9.5	9.1	8.4	10.3	6.3
Ischaemic heart disease	17.0	18.5	18.7	18.0	27.2
Malignant neoplasm	26.2	28.7	25.6	26.2	23.1

Source: Anderson et al. (2007).

daily smoking, but with rates as low as 17 per cent in some countries (Sweden, Austria and the USA). This compares to a prevalence rate of 33.2 per cent in the USA in 1978 (National Cancer Institute 1991).

In contrast, obesity rates are rising globally. Obesity and being overweight increase blood pressure, cholesterol, triglycerides and insulin resistance, exacerbating the risk of developing certain chronic diseases, including type 2 diabetes, cardiovascular disease, hypertension, stroke, and certain forms of cancer. Figure 10.3 shows the prevalence of obesity in a range of high-income countries. It is important to note that obesity rates in low- and middle-income countries are also rising, with obesity in some parts of Northern India, for example, reaching 9 per cent among women (Agrawal 2002). Of particular concern is the increase in childhood obesity which predicts significant future growth in the population with chronic conditions. In the USA, obesity among children under 5 increased from 5 to 10.4 per cent between 1976-1980 and 2007-2008 and from 6.5 to 19.6 per cent among 6–11-year-olds. Among adolescents aged 12–19, obesity increased from 5 to 18.1 per cent during the same period (CDC 2010).

TABLE 10.2 Top ten countries for number of persons with diabetes

	Year 2000			Year 2030	
Rank	Country	People with T2DM (million)	Rank	Country	People with T2DM (million)
1	India	31.7	1	India	79.4
2	China	20.8	2	China	42.3
3	USA	17.7	3	USA	30.3
4	Indonesia	8.4	4	Indonesia	21.3
5	Japan	6.8	5	Pakistan	13.9
6	Pakistan	5.2	6	Brazil	11.3
7	Russia Fed.	4.6	7	Bangladesh	11.1
8	Brazil	4.6	8	Japan	8.9
9	Italy	4.3	9	Philippines	7.8
10	Ukraine	3.2	10	Egypt	6.7

Source: http://sancd.org/uploads/pdf/Vipin%20on%20diabetes%20[6].pdf.
Wild et al. (2004).
Note: T2DM = Type 2 Diabetes Mellitus.

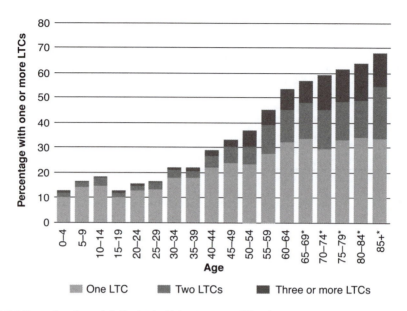

FIGURE 10.1 Proportion of people in England with long-term conditions by age.
* For those aged 65 or over as adjustment has been made using 2001 census data to account for those living in commercial establishments
Source: General Household Survey 2005 and populations census estimates 2004 for England.

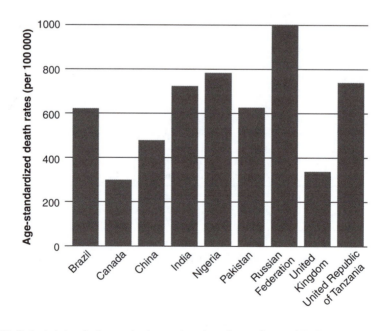

FIGURE 10.2 Projected chronic disease death rates for selected countries, aged 30–69 years, 2005
Source: http://www.who.int/chp/chronic_disease_report/contents/part1.pdf.

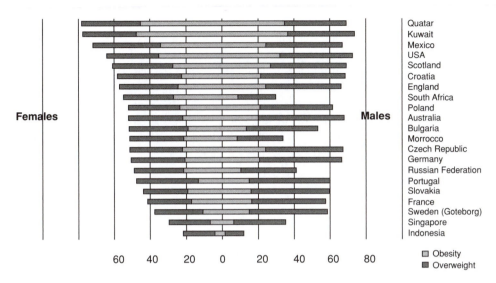

FIGURE 10.3 Percentage of overweight and obesity around the world since 2000

Note: With the limited data available, prevalences are not age standardized. Prevalences are based on the best available data for the country, in some circumstances the data may be based on subnational surveys. Sources and references are available from IASO. © International Association for the Study of Obesity, London, October 2010.

The concept of ambulatory-care sensitive (ACS) conditions was developed by John Billings, Professor of Health Policy at New York University (Billings and Teicholz 1990). An ACS condition is one where admission to hospital is potentially avoidable through good quality primary and preventative care. This is the case for many chronic conditions. As well as treatment, ambulatory care also includes preventive measures such as screening and the management of risk factors such as cholesterol and blood pressure. When patients are admitted to hospital for treatment of an ACS condition, this can be thought of as an avoidable hospital admission. Rates of ACS admissions are, therefore, often used as a measure of the quality of primary care in a local area, as has been the case in New Zealand.

Chronic diseases underlie a high proportion of healthcare resource consumption. High healthcare costs often stem from avoidable hospitalizations as a result of poorly co-ordinated primary and ambulatory care. The wider economic and social costs from lost productivity and foregone national income attributable to chronic conditions amount to hundreds of billions of dollars in the USA (DeVol et al. 2007).

- US estimates attribute 76 per cent of overall Medicare health expenditure (government spending on people over 65 years) to people living with five or more chronic diseases (Swartz 2007).

- In Canada, 42 per cent of total, direct healthcare expenditure and an estimated 65 per cent of indirect costs (due to lost productivity) are related to chronic conditions (Mirolla 2004).

- In England, up to 80 per cent of GP consultations are with people with chronic conditions. Furthermore, the 15 per cent of people with three or more chronic conditions account for almost 30 per cent of inpatient days in hospitals. These people are among the most intensive users of inpatient services, for whom 55 per cent of inpatient days are attributable to 10 per cent of inpatients, and 42 per cent of inpatient days are attributable to just 5 per cent of people (Wilson 2005).

- Overall diabetes prevalence in an age and sex standardized census of six large sickness funds in Germany was 6.45 per cent. The cost of diabetes for sickness funds including hospital cost, medication and sickness benefits, and excluding ambulatory doctor care, was € 3.69bn. The total cost of diabetes from a societal perspective was calculated as € 5.71bn for 1999 (Stock et al. 2005).

Organization and delivery of services for chronic diseases

What is the problem that services have to tackle?

People living with one or more chronic diseases typically receive care from multiple providers and hence fragmentation, duplication and poor coordination of care are significant problems. Transfers between care settings can be confusing, with one survey of American patients concluding that the system was 'a nightmare to navigate' due to the limited or conflicting information given to patients about medications and care plans and poor handovers between health and care professionals (Picker Institute 2000).

These problems have been well described and are international in nature (Shoen et al. 2008), and Vrijhoef and Wagner (2009) characterize their causes as multi-factorial, with a mixture of consequences ranging from less severe to very severe.

The organization of care delivery varies significantly between countries, depending on the characteristics of each national healthcare system, and can create its own barriers to effective chronic disease management. For example, chronic disease management is mediated by GPs in some places (e.g. UK, Holland, Australia, New Zealand, Canada and Denmark) but directly accessed through specialists in many other countries. Individuals with more than one chronic disease in America will typically be under the care of multiple specialists who may not communicate with each other and may, therefore, duplicate investigations or inadvertently prescribe duplicate or incompatible medications. By contrast, in the UK, GPs act as a central repository of medical information, coordinating the advice from different specialists, yet duplication of care and poor communication when patients transfer between different settings are still widespread problems in the NHS (Rosen and Ham 2008).

Alongside these effects of different health systems, there is evidence of less use of hospital services (Gibson et al. 2004; Newman et al. 2004) and better outcomes associated with support for self-care in people with chronic conditions (Lorig et al. 1999). Yet surveys have shown that many patients are not helped to self-care. Figure 10.4 shows the percentage of primary care doctors in 11 countries who report routinely giving chronically ill patients written instructions about how to manage their care at home.

At a population level, the challenges of preventing, diagnosing and treating chronic diseases are considerable. Strategies for prevention extend well beyond the health

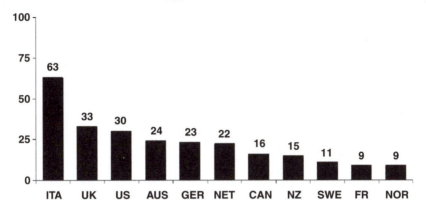

FIGURE 10.4 Commonwealth Fund international survey results of primary care physicians, 2009
Source: Commonwealth Fund International Survey, 2009. http://www.commonwealthfund.org/Content/Publications/In-the-Literature/2009/Nov/A-Survey-of-Primary-Care-Physicians.aspx.

policy arena to include leisure, transport, food and housing policy, requiring strategic collaboration between different government sectors.

Organizing services for better chronic disease management

The chronic care model offers a synthesizing approach through which to address the problems of fragmentation, duplication and poor coordination described above and to enhance the involvement of patients in decisions about their care (see Figure 10.5).

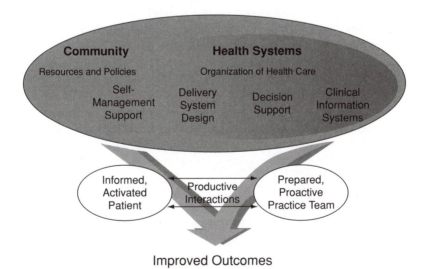

FIGURE 10.5 The chronic care model
Source: http://www.improvingchroniccare.org/index.php?p=The_Chronic_Care_Model&s=2).

Developed by Wagner and colleagues (Bodenheimer et al. 2002) the model is a guide to higher-quality chronic illness management. The model predicts that improvement in its six inter-related areas can produce system change in which informed, activated patients interact with prepared, proactive practice teams. These six areas are:

- the overall health system;
- delivery system design;
- decision support;
- clinical information systems;
- self-management support; and
- the local community.

The model is predicated on the idea that improved outcomes result from productive interactions between patients and their care team. For these interactions to be productive, professional practice must be redesigned in the four areas shown in the centre of the model: self-management (teaching patients how to manage and live with their condition); delivery system design (who is part of the healthcare team and how they interact with patients); decision support (what is the best care and how can care be delivered in this way every time); and clinical information systems (capturing and using critical information for clinical care). Together, these four areas promote systems that enable clinicians to proactively manage populations of patients, to practise evidence-based medicine and encourage collaborative consultations between health professionals and patients. In addition, the model acknowledges that clinician–patient interactions take place in the wider context of the overall healthcare system that shapes the ways in which clinicians are trained, provides incentives for better care, etc., and that local health systems operate within a community context. This recognizes that patients spend most of their time away from health services and encourages links with community groups and facilities to support self-management and risk factor reduction.

Redesigning services for better chronic care

There are numerous ways in which service redesign can support implementation of the chronic care model and contribute to better chronic care. Two such approaches are described briefly in relation to self-management support and the role of information technology. We then consider the potential contribution to chronic care of integration.

Self-management support

A variety of professional roles are emerging to support people living with chronic diseases, and their carers, to self-manage their conditions. These roles include health coaches, educators, care navigators and expert patients (Coleman 2009). They are typically focused on increasing people's ability to cope with and manage their own symptoms and to engage more effectively with their clinicians. Boxes 10.1 and 10.2 provide two examples of ways in which these new professionals are being deployed: the

Box 10.1: *The Expert Patient Programme*

The English Expert Patient Programme is a nationwide programme in which participants attend six group sessions led by trained lay people who themselves live with one or more chronic conditions. The sessions are not condition-specific but focus on self-care issues commonly faced by individuals living with chronic conditions, such as communicating with friends, family and professionals and dealing with pain and extreme tiredness (www.expertpatient.co.uk). The programme is adapted from the self-management model developed by Lorig (1999) and was first piloted in the NHS in 2002. A randomized control trial of the pilot phase found the programme to be moderately effective in improving self-efficacy and energy levels in people with chronic conditions. It was also found to be cost effective because an overall reduction in service utilization offset the cost of the intervention (Rogers et al. 2006).

Expert Patient Programme in England and the Techniker Krankenkasse's Health Coach programme in Germany.

Health information technology

The Commission on High Performing Health Systems created by the Commonwealth Fund in the USA (2007) describes the central role of health information technology (HIT) in improving the quality and safety of care. Several developments that enable

Box 10.2: *Health coaching, Techniker Krankenkasse, Germany*

Techniker Krankenkasse (TK), Germany's second largest statutory health insurer, introduced health coaching in January 2008 for patients with heart failure. The programme has now expanded to type II diabetes, myocardial infarction and ischaemic heart disease. Coaches initially contact patients weekly and then on a monthly basis. Coaches focus on behaviour change, including nutrition, exercise, alcohol consumption, smoking and adherence to medications. In early 2010, TK employed 15 coaches and had 5000 beneficiaries involved in the programme. The programme is popular with patients, with 80 per cent reporting high levels of satisfaction. Analysis of the coaching data for 1300 heart failure patients taking part in the programme found a patient-reported improvement in health status irrespective of age, gender, socio-economic status or severity of illness and a positive correlation between the number and frequency of coaching contacts and improvements in patient-reported health. Compared to patients with congestive heart failure receiving usual care, those in the coaching programme show significantly lower in-patient costs (KPMG International 2010).

better chronic care have been made possible by the ability to combine data from individual health records into population profiles. Powerful health information systems can extract data from individual health records on diagnoses, medications, hospital admissions, emergency department attendances, GP use and personal risk factors such as smoking and obesity. When combined in a data warehouse, this information can be used to describe the distribution of chronic illness and of risk factors for future illness throughout a population – identifying patient sub-groups or geographic areas in which specific conditions are concentrated and where extra services are needed. It can also be used to identify gaps in care for individual patients, sending prompts to clinicians (during a consultation) about tests or treatments that are needed. In addition, data linking socio-demographic characteristics, clinical diagnoses and past use of health services can be used to predict the likelihood of future use of healthcare (Curry et al. 2005).

This approach is particularly useful for adjusting the intensity of services delivered to individual patients in line with their level of need, targeting high intensity services such as community matrons (see p. 201) to people at highest risk of hospital admission. Further developments in this type of risk prediction are combining health and social care data to predict future use of both health and social care services (Lewis et al. 2008), allowing better planning and targeting of health and social care.

Personal access to medical records and health information is increasingly common and is becoming an important feature in self-management support. An example can be seen in the *My Geisinger* website run by the Geisinger Health System in America (see www.geisinger.org). These systems allow individual patients to track blood results (e.g. HbA1C for diabetics or liver function results for arthritis patients taking toxic drugs) and submit biometric data (e.g. blood pressure and weight) that enable health professionals to track clinical progress. They support email contact between patients and clinicians and provide general and condition-specific health advice and information. With access to this range of information, patients, carers and their wider supporters begin to have the resources to monitor their own conditions, understand how to stay well and to seek timely advice from health professionals when needed.

Delivery system redesign and the role of integration

Despite almost a decade of publicity about the chronic care model, research shows that many of its components are yet to be implemented (Wu et al. 2003; Pearson et al. 2005). In addition, there is strong evidence that many patients do not receive all the evidence-based interventions for selected chronic conditions from which they would benefit. A seminal study of healthcare quality by the Rand Corporation found that adults with chronic conditions received only 56.1 per cent of recommended care. Care requiring an encounter or other intervention, such as the annual visit recommended for patients with hypertension, had the highest rates of adherence to recommended care at 73.4 per cent, and care involving counselling or education, such as advising smokers with chronic obstructive pulmonary disease to give up smoking, had the lowest rates of adherence at 18.3 per cent (McGlynn et al. 2003).

Lack of progress on delivery system reform has led to a focus on 'integrated care' as a possible route to realizing the vision of delivery system redesign set out in the chronic care model. There is no straightforward definition of the term 'integrated care', although the following section explores the many ways in which the term is used. However, it implies a level of organization and coordination between services and this has been linked by some authors to higher quality care and better implementation of the chronic care model. Casalino, for example, has studied associations between organized medical groups which use a range of integration processes, and quality of care, concluding that while the evidence base remains relatively weak, in general, they have more infrastructure to improve quality and perform better in chronic disease management (Casalino 2009). And there is some evidence that large medical groups – bringing together multiple physicians under a coordinating umbrella organization – score higher on process measures and use more care management processes (Solberg et al. 2009).

Defining integration

It is helpful to distinguish between 'integrated care' and 'integration'. *Integrated care* is an organizing principle for care delivery with the aim of achieving improved patient care through better coordination. *Integration* is the combined set of methods, processes and models that seek to bring about this improved coordination of care. Accordingly, where the result of efforts to improve integration benefits patient groups, so the outcome can be called integrated care (Kodner and Spreeuwenberg 2002).

A recent review of the literature on integrated care revealed some 175 definitions and concepts (Armitage et al. 2009). Such diversity reflects what one commentator refers to as 'the imprecise hodgepodge of integrated care' (Kodner 2009). Various taxonomies of the 'methods and models' that comprise integrated care have been summarized by Nolte and McKee (2008) who argue that the term can be differentiated by *type, breadth, degree* and *process*. Nolte and McKee identify four 'types' of integration:

- *functional* (e.g. support systems such as financial management and strategic planning);
- *organizational* (e.g. networks, mergers and strategic alliances;
- *professional* (e.g. professional networks);
- *clinical* (relating to the coordination of care across teams and institutions).

Fulop et al. (2005) further developed this work, adding two additional 'types' of integration, to create a typology with the six elements illustrated in Figure 10.6.

Breadth of integration

Breadth of integration refers to the range of services within the healthcare economy involved in efforts to coordinate care. A distinction is commonly made between horizontal and vertical integration (Gillies et al. 1993).

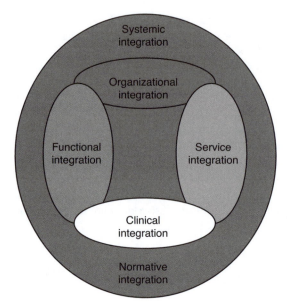

FIGURE 10.6 Typology of healthcare integration
Source: Fulop et al. (2005), adapted from Shortell (2000) and Contandriopoulos et al. (2001).

- **Horizontal integration:** integration between services within a level of care, e.g. primary and community services which are both based in community settings.
- **Vertical integration:** integration between services at different levels in the healthcare economy, e.g. community and hospital services.

Degree of integration

Degree of integration describes the extent of the relationships between participants involved in integration. Based on work by Leutz (1999), Table 10.3 presents a continuum from linkage in which participating organizations are loosely connected to full integration in which participant organizations are integrated into a single organizational entity.

Process of integration

Finally, the process of integration relates to the ways in which teams and organizations come together. This may be through structural arrangements and the development of shared infrastructure (organizational mergers, aligned tasks and functions, integrated information technology); through cultural integration based on convergence of values, norms and working methods; or through social integration, drawing together the social networks and relationships between key actors.

TABLE 10.3 Levels of integration: how do you work with the 'other side'?

Operations	Linkage	Coordination	Full integration
Screening	Screen or survey populations to identify emergent needs	Screen flow at key points (e.g., hospital discharge) to find those who need special attention (e.g., CM)	Not important except to receive good referrals (changing needs identified and met through team members)
Clinical practice	Understand and respond to special needs of PWDs in primary care, LTC, education, etc.	Know about and use key workers (e.g., discharge planners) to link	Multidisciplinary teams manage all care
Transitions/service delivery	Refer and follow up	Smooth the transitions between settings, coverage, and responsibility	Control or directly provide care in all key settings
Information	Provide when asked; ask when needed	Define and provide items/reports routinely in both directions	Use a common record as part of daily joint practice and management
Case management	None	Case managers and linkage staff	Teams or 'super' case managers manage all care
Finance	Understand who pays for each service	Decide who pays for what in specific cases and by guidelines	Pool funds to purchase from both sides and new services
Benefits	Understand and follow eligibility and coverage rules	Manage benefits to maximize efficiency and coverage	Merge benefits; change and redefine eligibility
Need dimensions			
Severity	Mild/moderate	Moderate/severe	Moderate/severe
Stability	Stable	Stable	Unstable
Duration	Short- to long-term	Short to long term	Long term or terminal
Urgency	Routine/non-urgent	Mostly routine	Frequent urgency
Scope of services	Narrow-moderate	Moderate-broad	Broad
Self-direction	Self-directed or strong informal care	Varied levels of self-direction and informal care	May accommodate weak self-direction and informal care

Notes: CM, care management; LTC, long-term care; PWD, person with disabilities.
Source: Leutz (1999).

Practical approaches to improving integration

This section illustrates some of the diverse initiatives and services that seek to achieve integration between teams and institutions and considers how they relate to the typologies described above. Their unifying characteristic is in seeking to improve alignment and coordination and to deliver more integrated care to patients.

Organizational integration

Organizational integration occurs when two or more institutions are brought together to improve coordination and support the delivery of integrated care. At one end of the spectrum, organizational integration involves the formal merger of two or more separate organizations into a single entity with one chief executive. At the other end, organizations remain separate entities and form a virtual network for the purposes of coordinating care or agree on intra- and inter-organizational governance arrangements to support integration, such as memoranda of understanding. Organizational integration can also be stimulated by purchasers through financial incentives or reimbursement mechanisms such as episode-based payments or capitation which require more than one service provider to work together in a coordinated way (Box 10.3).

Functional integration

Functional integration involves integrating non-clinical, back office functions, such as human resources management, across organizations. It is often undertaken to support small practices with limited resources to coordinate care more effectively. Functional

---

Box 10.3: *Local Health Integration Networks, Ontario, Canada*

In 2006, Ontario created 14 Local Health Integration Networks (LHIN) with the aim of moving from a collection of fragmented services to a coordinated healthcare system at the local level. LHINs oversee $20.3 billion and are responsible for planning, funding and integrating health services to meet the needs of their local population, including hospitals, community care access centres, community support services, long-term care, mental health and addictions services and community health centres.

LHINs seek to drive the delivery of integrated care through their role as convenors and purchasers. They have the convening power to bring together all the parts of the healthcare delivery system to plan how best to meet local needs. As purchasers, LHINs can contractually drive greater coordination between providers, both horizontally and vertically. In its annual report, the Ontario Health Quality Council rates the performance of each LHIN against the provincial average, according to a set of quality measures. This includes measures related to hospital and emergency department discharge that act as a proxy for the level of integration achieved by the LHIN (Ontario Health Quality Council 2010).

For further information: www.lhins.on.ca (accessed 19 September 2010).

integration can also involve staff from umbrella organizations being seconded to support clinicians and joint education and training across professional groups and organizations.

In their case studies of organizations seeking to improve integration Rosen et al. (2011) describe the many ways in which regional networks in the US state of North Carolina support small, independent, physician practices to improve the quality and continuity of care they provide to low-income patients who are funded through the US government Medicaid programme (www.communitycarenc.com). The support they offer is diverse, including the development of evidence-based resources to enable good clinical practice; education and training for participating clinicians; centralized data collection and analysis to monitor and provide peer feedback on the standard of care provided to Medicaid patients; and the provision of peripatetic clinicians (pharmacists, care coordinators, community nurses and others) to coordinate and support the care of patients with complex health problems (McCarthy and Mueller 2009).

Clinical integration

Arguably the most important level at which integration can operate is at the clinical level, closest to the patient. Two of the most common approaches to clinical integration are care coordination and disease management. Care coordination involves adding a nurse care coordinator to the primary care team or developing a stand-alone care coordination function that operates in-person or by telephone. Disease management is a structured programme built on evidence-based protocols and focused on a particular condition such as diabetes. Other tools that can be used to facilitate clinical integration include: data-driven clinical prompts and gap analyses; population-focused preventive care; peer review and professional incentives to change clinical practice; and care transition interventions to support discharge from hospital.

Integral to clinical integration are changes in the professional skill mix of services for people with chronic conditions. An example of the evolving chronic disease workforce is seen in the English NHS and Social Care model *Supporting People with Long Term Conditions* (Department of Health 2005), which outlines the role of community-based nurses (called community matrons) as care coordinators, advisors, navigators and supporters of people with long-term conditions and their carers. These nurses have advanced training and work with patients identified to be at high risk of hospital admission and often with multiple chronic conditions. Their focus is *generic* and does not concentrate on specific conditions. In contrast, cadres of nurse specialists are also emerging who provide clinical support when patients experience an exacerbation of a condition such as diabetes or heart failure (Blue et al. 2001; Avery 2008). The use of care teams including nurses and medical assistants in the management of patients with chronic conditions is now widespread in Sweden, the UK, the Netherlands, Australia, New Zealand, Germany (Box 10.4) and Norway (Schoen et al. 2008).

Systemic integration

Systemic integration frequently relies on supportive financial, regulatory and policy environments (Burns and Muller 2008). Examples of supportive financial arrangements

---

Box 10.4: *Disease management programmes, Germany*

Disease management programmes (DMPs) were introduced in Germany in 2002. Individuals with chronic conditions who are enrolled by statutory insurance funds into a DMP attract an additional payment from the risk equalization scheme, creating a strong incentive for insurers to recruit individuals with chronic conditions.

Disease management programmes currently exist for six major chronic conditions: type 1 diabetes, type 2 diabetes, breast cancer, coronary heart disease, asthma and chronic obstructive pulmonary disease. In October 2009, 5.4 million were enrolled in disease management programmes, including 2.8 million people enrolled in DMPs for type 2 diabetes and 1.3 million in DMPs for heart disease. Participation is voluntary for patients and providers, although incentives exist for both: patients are exempt from outpatient co-payments; physicians receive a lump sum payment for coordination and documentation activities (Schlette et al. 2009).

---

include: capitated, whole system budgets with physician risk and gain sharing; integrated condition-specific budgets; and micro incentives aligned across practices and organizations. The best known and most extensively evaluated examples of systemic integration are the integrated delivery systems in the USA, for example, Kaiser Permanente in Southern California and Geisinger Health System in Pennsylvania (Box 10.5). These bring an insurer function, medical group and hospital group into a single health system.

Box 10.5: *Geisinger Health System, Pennsylvania*

Geisinger is a physician-led, not-for-profit integrated delivery system based in mainly rural, western Pennsylvania (PA), USA. It employs 800 physicians through its physician practice group and contracts with a further 18,000 doctors across the state to provide care for enrolees in Geisinger insurance plans. It provides health maintenance organization (HMO) insurance plans for 235,000 enrolees and it runs a state-wide network of hospitals and clinics. In addition to its integrated organizational structure, Geisinger drives clinical integration in multiple ways, including adherence to evidence-based guidelines and clinical pathways; systematic identification of gaps in preventive care; and the use of extensive IT infrastructure for secure communication between doctors supporting new forms of generalist-specialist integration (McCarthy et al. 2009).

Geisinger has a well-established track record of high quality and efficiency. Data from the Dartmouth Atlas of Health Care, which examined care at the end of life for Medicare patients with chronic illness, indicate that those who received the majority of their care at Geisinger Medical Center from 2001 to 2005 had relatively lower Medicare spending per person (83 per cent) and fewer hospital days (64 per cent) and physician visits (73 per cent) compared with the US average (Wennberg et al. 2008).

For further information: www.geisinger.org (accessed 19 September 2010).

Box 10.6: *Integration for rehabilitative care in Copenhagen, Denmark*

Bispebjerg University Hospital, the City of Copenhagen (the municipal government) and GPs in Copenhagen have created a virtually integrated network based on the chronic care model to improve the rehabilitation care pathway for four chronic conditions: chronic obstructive pulmonary disease (COPD), type 2 diabetes, chronic heart failure and falls in older people.

Working groups developed clinical tools to support coordination. This included disease management programmes that were developed collaboratively and used by all three parties. The three parties also agreed stratification guidelines to identify which patients would get referred for rehabilitation to the hospital and which would go to the municipal health centre. In addition, performance measures were developed for each condition and used across all three sites of care.

Collaboration between leadership across the three parties and the adherence to jointly agreed protocols and performance measures were identified as important success factors. The absence of a shared clinical information system across the different sites of care was noted as a barrier (Frøhlich et al. 2010).

Degree of integration

A care pathway describes the recommended stages in treatment and condition management that a patient with a particular condition should receive (Box 10.6). Each care pathway includes multiple services provided by different organizations within the healthcare system. For example, the care pathway for type 2 diabetes includes patient education services, dietician services, retinal screening, foot care and regular monitoring of blood glucose and lipid profile. The professional teams involved in providing the different components of care do not merge into a single group or organization. Rather their work is coordinated through a network or chain of care (Box 10.6).

Breadth of integration: horizontal integration between health and social care

The majority of social care services (i.e. services offering personal care such as bathing and domestic support such as household cleaning) are provided in community settings and can make an important contribution to preventing avoidable hospital admissions and enabling people with chronic diseases to continue to live independently in the community (Lewis 2007). However, many emergency hospital admissions are still associated with failures in social support and poor coordination between health and social care providers remains a common problem (Blunt et al. 2010).

> ### Box 10.7: *Health and social care integration in Torbay Care Trust*
>
> Torbay Care Trust serves a population of 140,000 and is divided into five integrated health and social care teams, each of which serves a defined geographical area which is aligned with local general practice boundaries. Each team has a single manager (of health and social care staff); a single point of contact for patients and their carers; a single assessment process and a shared, electronic health and care record. There are pooled budgets that can be used by any of the integrated team members to commission services for which a need has been assessed.
>
> Recent evaluations of the care trust suggest that it has one of the lowest emergency admission rates in the South West of England for the over-65 age group (Ham 2010). Some of the reported success of the care trust has been attributed to changes in front-line working arrangements for the integrated health and social care teams; the introduction of care coordinators; the allocation of social workers to GP practices rather than geographic areas and the role of the care trust itself in managing the whole system (Ham 2009).

One approach to overcoming fragmentation between health and social care services was the introduction of 'care trusts' into the UK NHS in the early 2000s. Care trusts exemplify full organizational integration described in the right-hand box of Table 10.3, and were created through formal mergers between local government directorates of adult social care and NHS health authorities. Some of the main challenges faced by these new organizations were developing shared structures and accountabilities and overcoming the differences in culture, working practices and employment terms and conditions between the two organizations (Glasby and Peck 2003). However, over time, these problems have been successfully addressed, as illustrated in the example of Torbay Care Trust (Box 10.7).

Common characteristics of integrated services for chronic disease management

These above examples illustrate just how varied are the initiatives that seek to improve integration and to deliver more integrated care to patients. However, it is possible to identify some common characteristics within and between organizations, teams and group of professionals that strive to strengthen coordination and alignment between services. Drawing on the findings of international case studies of integrated care organizations, Rosen et al. (2011) identified numerous systems, processes, and clinical arrangements that contributed to greater coordination and alignment within and between services and which were termed 'integrative processes'. These build on earlier conceptual work by Fulop (2008), Nolte and McKee (2008) and others describing different types of integration, but place greater emphasis on how they are operationalized within and between organizations. Six groups of integrative processes were identified, with professional leadership, trust and clear communications found to be enabling factors that were essential for the viability of the integrative processes

- **Organizational integrative processes** – relating to organizational design and the governance arrangements within and between participating teams and institutions. Examples include:
  - structural integration in integrated delivery systems;
  - virtual integration through an 'umbrella organization' to form a network or association;
  - intra- and inter-organizational governance arrangements to support integration.
- **Informational integrative processes** – related to the role of clinical information systems and shared access to clinical information to support aligned practice across different clinical settings. Examples include:
  - clinical information systems and data integration between practices to support clinical and administrative functions such as needs assessment, risk stratification, outcomes monitoring and performance management;
  - population registries to identify gaps in care and preventive care opportunities;
  - patient access to selected parts of their medical record.
- **Clinical integrative processes** – related to the delivery of consistent clinical care to patients along the whole continuum of care. These were exemplified by the following:
  - care coordination delivered by multi-professional teams;
  - population-focused preventive care;
  - peer review and professional incentives to change clinical practice.
- **Functional integrative processes** – providing administrative and functional links (such as human resource management and seconded staff) to support small practices and build links with the case study organization. Examples include:
  - shared administrative functions;
  - staff employed by case study organization and seconded to clinicians;
  - joint education and training across professional groups and organizations.
- **Financial integrative processes** – relating to budgetary arrangements and payment systems in place across organizations participating in integration. Examples include:
  - capitated, whole system budgets with physician risk and gain sharing;
  - integrated condition-specific budgets;
  - micro incentives aligned across practices and organizations.
- **Normative integrative processes** – relating to efforts to achieve a shared vision and shared goals and values across individuals and organizations involved in integration. Examples include:
  - role of professional leaders in establishing and communicating goals and values;

- techniques such as job shadowing to understand different professional roles;
- social events to unite participating individuals.

Conclusion

Chronic diseases are the leading cause of morbidity and mortality in OECD countries. They are also the single biggest driver of health system costs, with a substantial amount of the costs stemming from unplanned emergency and inpatient care as a result of poor coordination between different healthcare providers and between health and social services.

The proportion of people living with chronic disease rises with age, with many older adults living with multiple chronic conditions. Life-style factors such as obesity and smoking are major contributors to chronic disease and the growing trend in childhood obesity indicates that chronic disease can only become a bigger, more costly problem in the future. Add to this the steady growth of chronic disease in low- and middle-income countries and it is clear that chronic disease management will soon be the biggest global healthcare challenge, outweighing the burden of communicable disease in low- and middle-income countries.

There is broad agreement that coordinating care across healthcare providers is critical to delivering high quality, efficient care for individuals with chronic conditions and to ensuring that patients who require care from multiple providers, often at different levels of the healthcare economy, have as joined up an experience of care as possible. Delivering more coordinated care requires many changes in the organization of healthcare systems, as outlined in the chronic care model. These include greater emphasis on patient self-management; a team-based approach to healthcare delivery with an increased role for nurse care coordinators; and additional investment in informational technology to support clinical decision-making and the sharing of data between clinicians and across organizations.

Theoretical models of how to bring about these changes in the delivery of healthcare have led to the development of an extensive literature and different typologies for the integration of care, focusing on the breadth, degree, process and types of integration. These theoretical approaches provide a useful framework within which to understand the range of activities being undertaken internationally. In practice, there is no single model for the organization and delivery of integrated care for chronic diseases, and nor would one be desirable. Local context is critical in determining which approach might work best in a particular country, region or delivery system and the case studies illustrate the diversity of international practice.

Improving the coordination and alignment of care between organizations, whether by creating a single organization or a virtual network, requires supportive policy frameworks, regulation and financial incentives. For example, reimbursement models that make physicians accountable for episodes of care or for the care of patients as a whole are more likely to stimulate integration than fee-for-service models. However, much depends on intra- and inter-organizational mechanisms to support integration, notably information technology to facilitate clinical information exchange and support consistent, evidence-based clinical decision-making. These processes need to be supported, in turn, by the development of relationships and values shared by participating professionals. Case studies of organizations, teams and groups of professionals that have succeeded in strengthening coordination and alignment between services indicate that, while there is no single model, successful approaches do share some common characteristics or 'integrative processes' as described above. These six groups of processes – organizational, informational, clinical, functional, financial and normative – underpin a model of high performance healthcare for the management of chronic conditions in which care is coordinated and aligned between services, ensuring a less fragmented experience for patients.

Summary box

- Chronic diseases are the leading cause of morbidity and mortality in OECD countries and are an increasing problem in low- and middle-income countries.

- As well as ageing, many chronic diseases are linked to lifestyle factors such as obesity, smoking and lack of physical activity and risky sexual behaviour.

- Chronic diseases underlie a high proportion of healthcare resource consumption. High healthcare costs often stem from avoidable hospitalizations as a result of poorly coordinated primary and ambulatory care.

- People living with one or more chronic diseases typically receive care from multiple providers, and fragmentation, duplication and poor coordination of care are significant problems, irrespective of the characteristics of the national healthcare system.

- The chronic care model offers a synthesizing approach to address the problems of fragmentation, duplication and poor coordination. Developed by Wagner, the model is a guide to higher-quality chronic illness management based on interactions between informed, activated patients and prepared, proactive practice teams.

- Fulop et al. (2005), building on Contandriopoulos and Denis (2001), have developed a typology of six 'types' of integration process: organizational integration, functional integration, service integration, clinical integration, normative integration and systemic integration.

- While there is some evidence that integration improves the quality of care, in general, evidence related to the impact of integration on efficiency remains patchy.

- To thrive, integration needs supportive policy frameworks, regulation and financial incentives. Much also depends on intra- and inter-organizational mechanisms to support integration and the development of relationships and shared values between participating organizations and professionals.

Self-test exercises

1 You are the operational manager for respiratory medicine at a 300-bed general hospital. Emergency admission rates for chronic obstructive pulmonary disease (COPD) at your hospital are the highest in your region. The community COPD specialist nurse, who treated people with symptom exacerbations in the community, recently retired and has not been replaced and a local audit by a public health trainee reported poor adherence by GPs and hospital doctors to best practice guidelines. In addition, there have been several complaints by patients with COPD about the quality of hospital care they received during recent exacerbations of their condition with disjointed follow-up and no information on the medicines they were meant to take. What can you do?

2 You have been asked to develop proposals for improving the hospital service and working collaboratively with community nurses and GPs. Revisiting the chronic care model, identify changes that you could make (assuming you have start up funding for new ways of working) which would support the development of a high quality, integrated COPD service.

3 You are a practice manager in a large primary care clinic (with 20,000 patients) and have been asked to work with three local cardiologists (who work in solo practices in the local community) to develop a new way of managing patients with possible heart failure. The patients have only mild symptoms and do not need hospitalization, but do need diagnostic tests linked to advice to their primary care doctor on how to manage their condition. You are trying to set up a new care pathway to keep them in community-based specialist clinics rather than refer them into specialist clinics in hospital. What integrative processes would you use to develop an integrated care pathway between GP and community cardiologists that delivered cost effective care with good outcomes and good patient experience (you do not need to use all of the integrative processes described in the chapter)?

References and further reading

Agrawal, P. (2002) Emerging obesity in Northern Indian States: a serious threat for health. Paper presented to the IUSSP Conference, Bangkok, 10-12 June.

Andersen, P. and Jensen, J. (2009) Healthcare reform in Denmark. *Scand J Public Health*, 38: 246.

Anderson, G., Frogner, B. and Reinhardt, U. (2007) Health spending in OECD countries 2004: an update. *Health Affairs*, 25(5): 1481–9.

Armitage, G., Suter, E. and Oelke, N. (2009) Health systems integration. The state of the evidence. *International Journal of Integrated Care*, 9(17), 1–11.

Avery, L. (2008) An evaluation of the role of diabetes nurse consultants in the UK. (Report). *Journal of Diabetes Nursing*, 12(2): 58–63.

Billings, J.A. (1998) What is palliative care? *Journal of Palliative Medicine*, 1: 73–81.

Billings, J.A. (2000) Recent advances in palliative care. *BMJ*, 321: 555–8.

Billings, J. and Teicholz, N. (1990) Uninsured patients in District of Columbia hospitals. *Health Affairs*, 9(4): 158–65.

Blue, L., Lang, E., McMurray, J. et al. (2001) Randomised controlled trial of specialist nurse intervention in heart failure. *BMJ*, 323: 715–18.

Blunt, I., Bardsley, M. and Dixon, J. (2010) *Trends in Emergency Admissions in England 2004–2009: Is Greater Efficiency Breeding Inefficiency?* London: Nuffield Trust.

Bodenheimer, T., Wagner, E.H. and Grumbach, K. (2002) Improving primary care for patients with chronic illness. *JAMA*, 14: 1775–9.

Burns, L. and Muller, R. (2008) Hospital-physician collaboration: landscape of economic integration and impact on clinical integration. *The Milbank Quarterly*, 86(3): 375–434.

Casalino, L. (2009) What does the evidence say about high-performing organizations that deliver integrated care? About systems versus the challenge of small group practices? Presentation to the Commonwealth Fund-Nuffield Trust, 10th International Meeting on Quality of Health Care: Strategies for Improving Integration of Care for People with Chronic Illness. Woking, Surrey.

Centers for Disease Control (2010) *Childhood Overweight and Obesity*. Available at: www.cdc.gov/obesity/childhood/index.html (accessed 6 August 2010).

Centers for Medicare and Medicaid Services (2009) Medicare physician group practice demonstration. Available at: https://www.cms.gov/DemoProjectsEvalRpts/downloads/PGP_Fact_Sheet.pdf. (accessed 6 August 2010).

Christakis, N.A. and Lamont, E.B. (2000) Extent and determinants of error in doctors' prognoses in terminally ill patients: prospective cohort study. *BMJ*, 320: 469.

Chu, B. (2009) Presentation to the Commonwealth Fund-Nuffield Trust, 10th International Meeting of Quality of Healthcare. Woking, Surrey.

Coleman, E. (2009) Encouraging patients and family caregivers to assert a more active role during care hand-offs: The Care Transitions Intervention™, *International Journal of Integrated Care*, ISSN 1568-4156.

Commission on a High Performance Health System (2007) *A High Performance Health System for the United States: An Ambitious Agenda for the Next President*. New York: Commonwealth Fund.

Contandriopoulos, A.P. and Denis J.L. (2001) Intégration des soins: concepts et mize en oeuvre. Montreal: Groupe de recherche interdizciplinaire en santé, Université de Montréal.

Curry, N., Billings, J., Darin, B., et al. (2005) *Predictive Risk Project: Literature Review*. London: The King's Fund.

Dean, M. (2008) End of life care for COPD patients. *Primary Care Respiratory Journal*, 17(1): 46–50.

Department of Health (2005) *Supporting People with Long Term Conditions: An NHS and Social Care Model to Support Local Innovation and Integration*. London: HMSO.

DeVol, R., Bedroussian, A., Charuworn, A. et al. (2007) *An Unhealthy America: The Economic Burden of Chronic Disease – Charting a New Course to Save Lives and Increase Productivity and Economic Growth*. Santa Monica, CA: Milken Institute.

Field, M.J. and Cassel, C.K. (eds) Committee on Care at the End of Life. Institute of Medicine (1997) *Approaching Death: Improving Care at the End of Life*. Washington, DC: National Academy Press.

Flory, J., Young-Xu, Y., Gurol, I. et al. (2004) Place of death: US trends since 1980. *Health Affairs*, 23: 194–200.

Frøhlich, A., Høst, D., Schnor, H. et al. (2010) Integration of healthcare rehabilitation in chronic conditions. *International Journal of Integrated Care*, ISSN 1568-4156.

Fulop, N. (2008) Integrated care: what can the evidence tell us? Paper presented to the Nuffield Trust, London, 11 November.

Fulop, N., Mowlem, A. and Edwards, N. (2005) *Building Integrated Care: Lessons from the UK and Elsewhere*. London: The NHS Confederation.

Gibson, P.G., Powell, H., Coughlan, J. et al. (2004) Self-management education and regular practitioner review for adults with asthma. *The Cochrane Library Issue 2*. Chichester: John Wiley & Sons.

Gillies, R., Shortell, S., Anderson, D. et al. (1993) Conceptualizing and measuring integration: findings from the Health Systems Integration study. *Hospital and Health Services Administration*, 38(4): 467–89.

Glasby, J. and Peck, E. (eds) (2003) *Care Trusts: Partnership Working in Action*. Oxford: Radcliffe Publishing.

Ham, C. (2009) *Removing the Policy Barriers to Integrated Care: The Torbay Experience*. London: Nuffield Trust.

Ham, C. (2010) *Working Together for Health: Achievements and Challenges in the Kaiser NHS Beacon Sites Programme*. Birmingham: Health Services Management Centre.

Institute of Innovation and Improvement (2010) *Quality and Service Improvement Tools Web Page. Plan, Do, Study Act (PDSA)*. Available at: http://www.institute.nhs .uk/quality_and_service_improvement_tools/quality_and_service_improvement_ tools/plan_do_study_act.html (accessed 14 July, 2011).

King's Fund (2002) *Partnerships Under Pressure*. London: King's Fund.

KMPG International (2010) *A Better Pill to Swallow: A Global View of What Works in Healthcare*. London: KPMG International.

Kodner, D. (2009) All together now: a conceptual exploration of integrated care. *Healthcare Quarterly*, 13(Sp): 6–15.

Kodner, D.L. and Spreeuwenberg, C. (2002) Integrated care: meaning, logic, applications, and implications – a discussion paper. *International Journal of Integrated Care*, 2: e12.

Lewis, G. (2007) *Predicting Who Will Need Costly Care: How Best to Target Preventive Health, Housing and Social Programmes*. London: King's Fund.

Lewis, G., Georghiou, T. and Bardsley, M. (2008) Developing a model to predict the use of social care. *Journal of Care Services Management*, 3(2): 164–75.

Leutz, W.N. (1999) Five laws for integrating medical and social services: lessons from the United States and the United Kingdom. *Milbank Quarterly*, 77(1), 77–110.

Lorig, K., Sobel, D. and Stewart, A. (1999) Evidence suggesting that a chronic disease self-management program can improve health status while reducing utilization and costs: a randomized trial. *Medical Care*, 37(1): 5–14.

Lurito, K. (2007) Mercer Government Human Services Consulting, Letter to Mr. Jeffrey Sims, State of North Carolina Division of Medical Assistance. Available at: www.communitycarenc.com. (accessed 6 August 2010).

Marie Curie Palliative Care Institute (2010) *Liverpool Care Pathway for the Dying Patient.* Available at: http://www.mcpcil.org.uk/liverpool-care-pathway/index.htm (accessed 8 August 2010).

McMarthy, D. and Mueller, K. (2009) *Community Care of North Carolina: Building Community Systems of Care Through State and Local Partnerships.* New York: Commonwealth Fund.

McCarthy, D., Mueller, K. and Wrenn, J. (2009) *Geisinger Health System: Achieving the Potential of System Integration Through Innovation, Leadership, Measurement, and Incentives.* New York: Commonwealth Fund.

McGlynn, E., Asch, S., Adams, J. et al. (2003) The quality of health care delivered to adults in the United States. *New England Journal of Medicine,* 348: 2635–45.

Mirolla, M. (2004) *The Cost of Chronic Disease in Canada.* Ottawa: The Chronic Disease Prevention Alliance of Canada.

Murray, S., Boyd, K. and Sheik, A. (2005) Palliative care in chronic illness. *BMJ,* 330: 611–12.

National Audit Office (2008) *End of Life Care.* Norwich: The Stationery Office.

National Cancer Institute (1991) *Tobacco Control Monograph.* Available at: http://cancercontrol.cancer.gov/TCRB/monographs/1/m1_3.pdf (accessed 6 August 2010).

Newman, S., Steed, L. and Mulligan, K. (2004) Self-management interventions for chronic illness. *Lancet,* 364: 1523–37.

Nolte, E., Knai, C. and McKee, M. (2008) *Managing Chronic Conditions: Experience in Eight Countries.* Geneva: World Health Organization.

Nolte, E. and McKee, M. (2008) *Caring for People with Chronic Conditions: A Health System Perspective.* Maidenhead: Open University Press.

Ontario Health Quality Council (2010) *Quality Monitor: 2010 Report on Ontario Health System.* Toronto: Ontario Health Quality Council.

Ouwens, M., Wollersheim, H., Hermens, R. et al. (2005) Integrated care programmes for chronically ill patients: a review of systematic reviews. *International Journal for Quality in Health Care,* 17(2): 141–6.

Paull, G. (2007) Palliation in heart failure: improving end of life care. Presentation available at: http://www.acra.net.au/images/news/Website%20Glenn%20Paull%20NSW%20CRA%20HF%20End%20of%20Life%20Care.ppt.pdf?PHPSESSID=f0e3933b5109a439114ed52393994f11, cited in Johnson, M. (2007) Management of end stage cardiac failure. *Post graduate Journal,* 83: 395–401.

Pearson, M., Wu, S., Schaefer, J. et al. (2005) Assessing the implementation of the chronic care model in quality improvement collaboratives. *Health Services Research,* 40(4): 978–96.

Picker Institute (2000) *Eyes on Patients.* Report by the Picker Institute for the American Hospital Association. Boston: Picker Institute.

Rogers, A., Bower, P., Gardner, C. et al. (2006) *The National Evaluation of the Pilot Phase of the Expert Patient Programme. Final Report.* Manchester: National Primary Care Research & Development Centre, Manchester University.

Rosen, R. and Ham, C. (2008) *Integrated Care: Lessons from Evidence and Experience.* London: The Nuffield Trust.

Rosen, R., Mountford, J., Lewis, G., Lewis, R., Shand, J. and Shaw, S. (2011) *Integration in Action: Four International Case Studies.* London: The Nuffield Trust.

Schäfer, I., Küver, C. and Gedrose, B. (2010) The disease management program for type 2 diabetes in Germany enhances process quality of diabetes care – a follow-up survey of patients' experiences. *BMC Health Services Research*, 10:55doi:10.1186/1472-6963-10-55.

Schlette, S., Lisac, M. and Blum, K. (2009) Integrated primary care in Germany: the road ahead. *International Journal of Integrated Care*, ISSN 1568-4156.

Schoen, C., Osborn, R., How, S. et al. (2008) In chronic condition: experiences of patients with complex health care needs in eight countries. *Health Affairs* Web Exclusive, November 13, w1–w16.

Shaw, S., Rosen, R. and Rumbold, B. (2011) *What is Integrated Care?* London: Nuffield Trust.

Solberg, L., Ashce, S., Shortell, S. et al. (2009) Is integration in large medical groups associated with quality? *Am J Managed Care*, 15(6): e34–e41.

Shortell, S.M. (2000) Remaking Health Care in America: the evolution of organised delivery systems. San Francisco: Jossey Bass.

Stock, S., Redaelli, M., Wendland, G. et al. (2005) Diabetes – prevalence and cost of illness in Germany: a study evaluating data from the statutory health insurance in Germany. *Diabetic Medicine*, 23(3): 299–305.

Swartz, K. (2007) Projected costs of chronic diseases. *HealthCare Cost Monitor.* Available at: http://healthcarecostmonitor.thehastingscenter.org/kimberlyswartz/projected-costs-of-chronic-diseases/ (accessed 6 August 2010).

Vrijhoef, B. and Wagner, E. (2009) Fragmentation of chronic care: a call for clarity. *Journal of Integrated Care*. Oct.–Dec., e172. Published online 31 December 2009.

Wagner, E.N. et al. *The Chronic Care Model.* Available at: http://www.improving chroniccare.org/index.php?p=The_Chronic_Care_Model&s=2 (accessed July 2010).

Wennberg, J., Fisher, E., Goodman, D. et al. (2008) *Tracking the Care of Patients with Severe Chronic Illness: The Dartmouth Atlas of Health Care 2008.* Hanover, NH: Dartmouth Institute for Health Care Policy and Clinical Practice.

Wild, S., Roglic, G., Green, A., Sicree, R. and King, H. (2004) Global prevalence of diabetes: estimates for the year 2000 and projections for 2030. *Diabetes Care*, 27: 1047–53.

Wilson, T. (2005) Rising to the challenge: will the NHS support people with long term conditions? *BMJ*, 330: 657–61.

World Health Organization (2005) *Preventing Chronic Diseases: A Vital Investment. WHO Global Report.* Geneva: WHO.

Wu, S., Pearson, M. and Schaeffer, J. (2003) Assessing the implementation of the Chronic Care Model in quality improvement collaboratives: does baseline system support for chronic care matter? *Human Factors in Organizational Design and Management*, VII: 595.

Websites and resources

Chronic care model: http://www.improvingchroniccare.org/index.php?p=The_Chronic_
    Care_Model&s=2.
Community Care of North Carolina: www.communitycarenc.com.
Geisinger Health System: www.geisinger.org.
Integrated Care Network resource page:
    http://www.dhcarenetworks.org.uk/Integration/icn/ICNPublications/.
International Journal of Integrated Care: www.ijic.org/.
Local Health Integration Networks: www.lhins.on.ca.
UK Department of Health Integrated Care Network:
    www.dhcarenetworks.org.uk/Integration/icn/?.

CHAPTER 11

Acute care: elective and emergency, secondary and tertiary

Anthony Harrison

Introduction

Acute hospitals play a central role in all advanced healthcare systems. In most countries they absorb a major share of the health budget: over 60 per cent in some eastern European countries, over 40 per cent in the UK, Italy and Austria, and over 30 per cent in most other EU countries.

Acute hospitals provide care for the seriously ill or injured, as well as a wide range of less critical but important treatments. They are also teaching institutions for the medical workforce and research institutions where new procedures are developed and new drugs trialled.

This chapter considers a number of the issues that acute hospitals raise for policy-makers.

The changing hospital

Although in most countries the hospitals' share of total healthcare spending has fallen, the absolute level of spend has risen, as total health budgets have expanded and the share of health spending in GDP has risen.

The primary driver for the expansion of the role of the hospital in the international context has been growth in medical knowledge, leading to the introduction of new treatments and surgical procedures. Although some, particularly new, medicines are the results of private sector research by pharmaceutical companies, many have been discovered within the hospital system itself.

These developments have enabled hospitals to expand the range of treatments they offer and to develop new ways of treating them. Improvements in anaesthesia and the introduction of less invasive treatments have made it possible to carry out operations on elderly people who would at one time have been judged too risky to treat.

At the same time, the way in which hospitals provide treatments and care has changed. While all activity indicators continue to show a rise, the number of beds and the time patients spend in them continue to fall despite the fact that the inpatient population consists largely of elderly people with complex conditions. In contrast to earlier decades when hospitals often provided long-term and terminal care, now only a

TABLE 11.1 Average length of stay: days

	2000	2001	2002	2003	2004	2005	2006	2007	2008
France	13.2	13.3	13.3	13.3	13.3	13.3	13.0	13.0	12.9
Germany	11.4	11.2	10.9	10.6	10.4	10.2	10.1	10.1	9.9
Japan	39.1	38.7	37.5	36.4	36.3	35.7	34.7	34.1	33.8
UK	9.9	10.3	9.9	9.7	9.4	9.1	8.8	8.2	8.1
USA	6.8	6.7	6.6	6.5	6.5	6.5	6.4	6.3	6.3

Source: OECD Health Data 2010 – Version: June 2010.

TABLE 11.2 Percentage of day cases

	2000	2001	2002	2003	2004	2005	2006	2007
Australia	43.5	44.4	47	46.9	47.1	47.1	47.1	47.7
Canada	60.6	62.8	64.8	64.1	64.6	65.4	65.3	65.8
Germany			9.5	11.2	16.7	21.9	22.8	23.6
Italy	20.8	24.1	28.7	32.8	34.8	35.9	35.8	35.1
Netherlands	43	44.7	46.2	47.3	48.2	49	49.5	50.5
UK	54.0	54.4	54.3	54.2	54.8	55.8	55.4	54.4

TABLE 11.3 Acute care beds per 1,000 population

	2000	2001	2002	2003	2004	2005	2006	2007	2008
France	4.1	4.0	3.9	3.8	3.7	3.7	3.6	3.6	3.5
Germany	6.4	6.3	6.1	6.1	5.9	5.9	5.7	5.7	5.7
Japan	9.6	9.3	8.9	8.5	8.4	8.2	8.2	8.2	8.1
Netherlands	3.2	3.1	3.2	3.1	3.1	3.1	3.0	2.9	2.9
UK	3.1	3.1	3.1	3.1	3.1	3.0	2.8	2.8	2.7

Source: OECD Health Data 2010 – Version: June 2010.

few severely ill or injured patients remain in hospital for long periods. For many surgical procedures such as cataract or hernia, patients are treated on a day basis and lengths of stay for those surgical patients who are admitted to a hospital ward are vastly reduced. As a result, the number of hospital beds has steadily fallen in nearly all advanced health systems (Tables 11.1, 11.2, 11.3).

Whereas at one time hospitals were full of surgical and other patients recovering, often for lengthy periods, from the treatment they received, now patients are discharged to home or to community settings for rehabilitation if they require it. The net result of the changes described here is that the acute hospital has become a rapid turnover institution.

Hospital hierarchies

All hospital systems embody some degree of hierarchy. Most hospitals treat a range of patients and hence are commonly called general hospitals. But within this group a distinction can usually be drawn between general hospitals and tertiary centres. Both carry out a wide range of procedures and treatments but the tertiary centres provide, in addition, more specialized care to smaller client groups. In some countries, such as Sweden, France and parts of the UK a third tier can be identified, consisting of small local hospitals carrying out a limited range of surgical procedures, diagnostics and rehabilitation services. Major national institutions may provide services to small client groups perhaps of only a few hundred and are therefore sometimes called quaternary centres.

While hospital hierarchies are common, where the line should be drawn between the tertiary centres and other hospitals is open to debate. It depends critically on the perceived advantages of the extent of hospital specialization, i.e. the scale of hospital activity in each area of treatment. Evidence bearing on this issue is discussed on p. 237.

Specialist hospitals

Some hospitals specialize in one client group such as children or the mentally ill or the treatment of a specific disease such as cancer or heart disease. Other hospitals may carry out only elective procedures. These are so-called focused factories such as the surgi-centres developed in some parts of the USA or similar facilities in the Netherlands, Australia and England (Bredenhoff et al. 2010). A prime example is the Shouldice Centre in Canada which only repairs hernias and claims an almost 100 per cent success rate in that operation.

Even if greater scale does promise better results, it inevitably creates disadvantages in terms of poorer access as smaller hospitals are closed and their activity transferred to larger centres. The debate on this issue is discussed on p. 220.

The concept of a hospital hierarchy emphasizes the upward process of referral from primary to secondary to tertiary care. Patients that a lower tier cannot treat are referred upwards to the level appropriate to their needs. In many countries, however, hospital networks have been developed which emphasize horizontal links between hospitals as much as vertical ones. These are discussed on p. 221.

Finally, we consider how the balance of care between hospitals and community services should be determined. Some services can be provided safely and effectively in both hospital and community. In addition, effective community services may reduce hospitals' workload and improve the efficiency and effectiveness of the healthcare system as a whole.

Hospitals and public policy objectives

The rising cost of hospitals and health services as a whole has focused the minds of policy-makers on ways of containing the growth of spending and improving the efficiency with which resources are used. Many countries have turned to reform the way that hospitals are paid to promote these and other objectives. These payments systems are discussed on p. 224.

At the same time, particularly in countries where hospitals are largely publicly funded and budgets tightly constrained, there has been concern at the inability of hospitals, evidenced by long waiting lists for treatment, to provide a timely response to patients' needs. How these have been addressed is considered on p. 225.

Structure and roles

Specialization and scale

Hospital hierarchies have largely developed as a result of increasing specialization among clinical staff. Fifty years ago hospitals were staffed by a handful of specialists: now, depending on exactly what counts as a specialty, they may have over 40 and their consultant specialist staff number in the hundreds.

The presumption has been that specialization in a particular disease or set of procedures is essential to the provision of high quality care. If a hospital is to have all specialities on site with fully staffed departments in each, then inevitably it must be a very large institution serving a large catchment area.

For some rare conditions, there may be a very small number of treatment centres so that even large tertiary hospitals have to refer patients on to them. Some patient groups number less than 1000 for the whole of England. For this reason, arrangements are in place at national level to ensure that they are served by only a small number of centres that can be appropriately staffed and equipped (see Table 11.4).

The development of specialization has occurred naturally as the growth in medical knowledge has made it impossible for doctors and other staff to be up-to-date across the full range of conditions that patients present with. Over the past 30 years, however, evidence has accumulated that tends to suggest that larger hospitals whose staff treat larger numbers of patients provide, on average, better care.

Starting in the USA, studies have emerged that link the volume of activity carried out by an individual surgeon or a hospital to the outcome of cases (usually measured by 30-day mortality or, in the case of orthopaedic procedures, the need for revision of

TABLE 11.4 Some rare conditions and number of treatment centres

Condition	No. of treatment centres: England
Amyloidosis	1
Bladder exstrophy	2
Bridge to heart transplant (adults)	3
Bridge to heart transplant (children)	2
Choriocarcinoma	2
Complex tracheal	1
Craniofacial	4
Epidermolysis bullosa	4
Extra corporeal membrane oxygenation (adults)	1
Extra corporeal membrane oxygenation (neonates, infants, children)	3

Source: National Commissioning Group, Department of Health. (http://www.specialisedservices.nhs.uk).

TABLE 11.5 Leapfrog Referral Standards: minimum activity levels per annum for some procedures

Procedure	Minimum number
CABG	450
PCI	400
Aortic valve replacement	120
Bariatric surgery	125

Source: www.leapfrog.org).

the original operation). This evidence has been used as a guide to commissioners of care or as the basis of direct prohibitions on smaller hospitals from carrying out certain procedures.

In the USA, for example, the Leapfrog Association has set out a number of minimum volume requirements as a guide to purchasers (see Table 11.5). A similar approach has been adopted in a number of European countries. In France and in the Netherlands, smaller hospitals are banned from carrying out certain procedures such as complex cancer operations. In Germany, minimum treatment volumes have been introduced for liver and kidney transplantation and complex pancreatic and oesophegal procedures. In England, the National Commissioning Group limits the number of hospitals treating small client groups such as those listed in Table 11.4.

Use of the evidence from volume/outcome studies has, however, been challenged on a number of grounds. Systematic reviews (Gruen et al. 2009; Co-operation and Competition Panel 2010) have concluded that the quality of many of the studies reporting a volume/outcome relationship is low on several grounds: poor data, inappropriate analytic methods and a wide scatter in the results. Some studies show, for example, that while on average larger hospitals may perform better, some perform less well than some smaller ones. As a consequence, simply closing small ones or setting arbitrary minimum activity levels may do as much harm as good.

The pressures for the creation of larger units have also come from concerns about the proper treatment of the severely injured and other patients requiring rapid treatment, such as those suffering from stroke. The capacity to treat any severely injured patient requires the full range of specialities on site and the capacity to treat at any time of day or week requires large clinical teams to provide expert cover, and for diagnostic services to be available for the full 168 hours. Although most hospitals are open 24 hours and every day of the week, some specific facilities such as rapid imaging/scanning may not be, and at night and weekend medical cover can consist of inexperienced trainees. There is evidence suggesting that this leads to some patients receiving sub-optimal care at off-peak times (Aylin et al. 2010).

Such concentrations of human and physical resources are expensive to provide, so if such facilities are to be economic, they must be heavily utilized, i.e. attract patients from a wide geographical area including the 'natural' catchment area of other hospitals. This economic logic has underpinned the case for superacute stroke centres (Box 11.1).

> ## Box 11.1: *Rapid access for stroke patients*
>
> The need for a rapid response at all times is a requirement of effective care for other types of patient. In the case of stroke, for example, it has been recognized worldwide that treatment has been poor and that hospitals must organize themselves to ensure that treatment is offered promptly when patients arrive at hospital. Subsequently they should receive a structured programme of care along a defined pathway specific to their needs so as to increase their chances of full recovery. This requirement has led to the establishment of stroke units within acute hospitals. Some countries have established superacute units (sometimes called comprehensive stroke centres) to which all patients over a large area (in terms of population or geography) are sent for initial diagnosis and if appropriate treatment as well. These units provide round-the-clock services to ensure high quality of care, particularly diagnosis, at all times.

For a hospital to offer 24-hour availability of all facilities and experienced clinical staff represents a large fixed cost that can only be justified at a high level of utilization. In practice, therefore, it is not economic for small institutions to do so and as a result many smaller hospitals' emergency departments have closed, and their activities have moved elsewhere. The closure of an A&E department makes it harder for other activities to take place on the same site and hence a snowball effect develops which can lead to loss of all emergency facilities or to total closure. In most European countries the number of hospitals has fallen as the benefits of larger units have been realized (HOPE 2009).

The introduction of the European Working Time Directive from 2003 onwards has made it even harder or more expensive to maintain continuous medical cover for the full 168 hours in hospitals in European Union countries. Hospitals have traditionally ensured 24-hour medical cover by having juniors, i.e. doctors in training, on call overnight and at weekends. Nominal working hours were therefore very long. The Directive limits the number of hours doctors can work or be on call to 48, making it impossible for medical cover to be provided in this way unless staffing levels are substantially increased.

In response to these developments, the UK Department of Health launched a Hospital at Night programme which defined ways in which hospitals could be safely operated at night-time, without a complete complement of experienced medical staff. Typically these arrangements involve trying to minimize the load on the medical staff at night by shifting part of their work, particularly that of doctors in training, to other professionals, and shifting some other tasks to daytime hours. Similar programmes have been adopted in other countries including Australia, New Zealand, Hong Kong and the USA, in their case, in response to an overall shortage of doctors.

In parts of the world, hospitals have had to adapt because of an overall shortage of doctors or of doctors willing to work in particular locations (Jones et al. 2008). Financial incentives may form part of the solution and a number of countries, including some

American states, Japan, Canada, New Zealand and South Africa, have used these to encourage clinical staff to work in remote areas. But changes in clinical practice may also be required. The next section describes some of the options available.

Specialization versus access

In some countries or parts of countries, geography dictates that not all patients can have easy access to specialist centres. This is particularly true of countries such as the USA and Australia with vast rural hinterlands or the less densely populated areas of countries such as Scotland or Wales.

Even if specialization does lead to better outcomes, longer journeys to hospital may discourage people from travelling to them. Studies have shown for example that patients in rural areas may be reluctant to travel to regional centres (Jones et al. 2008) in part because of the cost and in part due to the discomfort of the journey itself.

In addition there is evidence that every extra 10 km distance to a hospital increases the risk of dying of patients with life-threatening conditions by 1 per cent (Nicholl et al. 2007). A study in the USA found that the benefits of centralizing stroke care were offset by the risks imposed by longer journeys to specialist centres (Votruba and Cebul 2006). In addition to the trip itself, there are also risks arising from the handover process if patients have to transfer to ICUs in another hospital (Singh and MacDonald 2009).

Given this tension between concentration and access, a key question is whether there are ways of obtaining the benefits of specialization while preserving easy access. There are a number of possibilities:

- Move the individual surgeon to the patient: this may be appropriate where a large hospital is surrounded by smaller satellites without in-house surgical staff. A number of English acute hospitals provide surgery to small localities in this way. Similarly eye services in a number of London's smaller district general hospitals are provided by Moorfields, a specialist eye hospital, on a 'franchise' basis. For the staff involved, this system has the advantage of being part of a large clinical group. In Australia, models of cooperative care between generalists and specialists have been developed which involves surgeons travelling to remote communities without any form of hospital facility (Carson 2009).

- Use IT or telemedicine to allow local clinicians to seek advice from specialized units on the basis of electronic transfer of imaging. This is particularly appropriate in areas of low population density. A telemedicine system for stroke patients was introduced in Catalonia in 2007 (Perez dela Ossa et al. 2009): the result was fewer transfers to a large hospital and doubling of the rate of thrombolyis and reductions in the time between stroke onset and the initiation of treatment. Alternatively telemedicine may be used to support direct contact between clinicians and patients, e.g. in the case of mental health (Pyne et al. 2010).

- Transfer through agreed protocols, the care systems developed in tertiary hospitals to smaller units. This has been shown to be effective in Finland (Paimela et al. 2005) and the USA (Schell et al. 2008).

A further possibility is the introduction of care networks linking smaller hospitals to larger ones: these are discussed in the next section.

The most fundamental solution is to ensure that the small local hospital is able to match the performance of larger units. Studies from a number of countries have shown this to be feasible, even for complex procedures, provided that they have well-trained staff, both medical and nursing, as well as the right physical facilities.

There is evidence from Norway and Finland, for example, that small units can match the performance of larger ones (Paimela et al. 2005; Debes et al. 2008). An even more striking example comes from Japan. A recent study (Miyata et al. 2008) has shown that none of its hospitals carrying out CABGs come anywhere near the Leapfrog benchmark – the typical activity level was below 50 cases a year – but they nevertheless achieve comparable results. These studies do not, however, show that they can match the cost levels of the larger units.

The evidence bearing on hospital size and costs on balance suggests that the cost advantages of larger scale are soon exhausted, i.e. at around 200 beds (Posnett 1999) and there is some evidence that diseconomies may occur in the largest institutions (Wang et al. 2006). But if there is a cost penalty attached to small scale, it may of course still be worth paying for the access benefits that local provision offers.

Hospitals within systems of care

For some hospital services, particularly simple elective procedures, the care pathway is simple: GP referral, consultation, treatment and then perhaps a check or aftercare. But some services form part of what can be a lengthy (in terms of time) pathway involving a wide range of services, many outside the hospital itself. In addition, as noted above, the creation of networks around a major hospital linking in smaller units may allow a compromise between the need to centralize and easy access for most patients.

The case for networks has been promoted for a wide range of conditions, including trauma, cancer, cardiac care and stroke. Trauma centres dealing with the most severely injured may form part of a network of hospitals, with varying degrees of capacity for treating patients needing immediate care. For the network as a whole to work effectively, protocols must be in place which determine which patients are transferred 'upwards' to the trauma centre and provide an effective (air) ambulance service able to effect the transfers required or increasingly, to take patients directly to the appropriate place of care. Such networks have been introduced in whole or in part in countries such as Canada, Australia, Germany, Norway and Denmark, and England is in the process of doing so. In 2009, the UK Department of Health encouraged the NHS to introduce trauma centres, 'within regionally organised major trauma networks' with the aim of 'delivering the patient rapidly and safely to a specialist hospital capable of delivering definitive care as early as possible' (Department of Health 2009a: 1).

Effective cancer care also requires systems of care to be developed for the whole of the care pathway from initial symptoms through to rehabilitation or end of life care. For these systems to work efficiently from the health system's and the patient's viewpoint, there must be agreement on the division of work between hospitals and effective links between them so that patients are treated in the most appropriate setting. The same applies to hospitals and community institutions such as general practice, social care and hospices. Such arrangements have also been introduced in a number of countries including France, Australia, New Zealand and England.

The terms used to describe such arrangements vary: in some cases they are termed coordinated care systems, care chains, hub and spoke models, regional systems, networks or managed clinical networks (MCNs). The way they operate also varies: there is no standard model. The key feature of all of them is they work across the organizational boundaries of the hospitals and community service providers involved, as this definition of the managed clinical networks introduced in Scotland makes clear:

> Linked groups of health professionals and organisations from primary, secondary, and tertiary care working in a coordinated manner, unconstrained by existing professional and organisational boundaries to ensure equitable provision of high quality effective services.
>
> (Scottish Executive 2002)

Evidence on the effectiveness, in terms of impact on patient care, is limited. In the case of trauma networks, evidence from the USA suggests that they can lead to an increase in the proportion of severely injured patients whose lives are saved (Celso et al. 2006; Cameron et al. 2008).

But in other areas the benefits are less easily identified. A recent study found it hard to identify clear evidence of their impact although overall it concluded it had been favourable (Guthrie et al. 2010). Professionals identified benefits such a better inter-professional and inter-organizational working while patients considered that co-ordination across services had improved. Similarly Ferlie et al. (2010) found that while networks were an appropriate form of organization for dealing with complex issues crossing organizational and professional boundaries, there was also a risk that they would degenerate into talking shops that excluded outsiders.

Similarly a systematic review in Australia (CanNET National Support and Evaluation Service 2008) found little research evidence to support the value of MCNs in practice but substantial evidence that they take time to set up and produce useful results.

Despite these findings, the need for effective inter-organizational links between hospitals and between hospitals and community services is clear both from a professional and patient viewpoint (Ham 2007). As we see in the next section, such links may also be necessary if a health system is to get the best balance between the hospital and community sectors.

Hospitals and community services

Just as the boundaries between hospitals are flexible, according to considerations of cost, access and clinical quality, so too is the boundary between hospitals and community services. Historically, hospitals have accumulated functions because they were in the best position, given their human and physical resources, to carry them out. But cost considerations, on the one hand, and concerns about access, on the other, have led to policies designed to shift some hospital activities to other settings. Hospitals are expensive facilities: they have high overheads and hence there is a presumption that they should focus on those categories of care that they alone can provide.

Attempts have been made in a number of countries to test the scope for shifting care out of hospitals to other settings. In France, the concept of a *hôpital sans murs* (hospital without walls) was developed more than 30 years ago. This involved providing hospital standard care in the home environment. It was imitated in England in Peterborough (Mowat and Morgan 1982) but not widely adopted.

Recently, however, there has been interest in less radical schemes focused on rapid discharge after an acute episode. The primary aim has been to move patients out of expensive hospital beds to other cheaper settings in the community, often run by social care authorities. In England, there has been substantial investment in intermediate care facilities designed both to reduce hospital use and to prepare patients to return to their own homes (Department of Health 2009b).

To provide a further incentive to the rapid transfer of patients out of the acute sector, Sweden introduced a system, later adopted in England, which allowed hospitals to charge local authorities for any time patients spent in hospital after they were declared fit for discharge. Subsequent research (McCoy et al. 2007) suggests, however, that although discharge delays have been reduced, the contribution of the charging system has been small. Other factors such as the scale of investment in intermediate facilities and the degree of cooperation between healthcare providers and social care services run by local authorities have also been critical.

Reviews of the evidence worldwide (Shepperd et al. 2009a, 2009b) have tended to show that hospital at home and early discharge schemes can match the quality of acute hospital care, and that patients often prefer care in their own homes, but they cannot be relied upon to produce cost savings on a like-for-like basis. In addition, there is some evidence (Taylor and Dangerfield 2005) that shifts in care may stimulate demand because services are more accessible.

The case for considering the hospital as part of a wider care system goes beyond examining the potential for transferring particular services. Most healthcare systems embody a range of responses to patients' perceived need for urgent treatment, including the hospital's emergency department or emergency room and emergency bed and treatment capacity as well as services outside the hospital such as general practice, together with telephone advice, ambulance and other mobile resources such as community responders and nurse-run facilities for minor conditions.

The hospital's role in emergency care depends critically on the services available outside it, including preventive services. Two main groups of patients have been identified who do not need hospital emergency services but who may nevertheless use them, creating a *prima facie* case for attempting to shift the balance of care away from the hospital.

The first group consists of those who seek care for minor conditions that do not need the resources of the hospital to resolve. Surveys of users of emergency departments typically find many who could be treated by a GP or nurse. Some hospitals have responded to this by putting GPs into emergency departments or siting them nearby (Carson et al. 2010). Some local health economies have established alternative facilities such as nurse-run minor injuries centres, some with IT links to a main hospital, that make it possible to seek expert advice where the diagnosis is not clear. Others have established advice lines in the expectation that this would reduce visits to emergency departments, particularly out of hours. However, experience in England suggests that some of these facilities may lead to more people seeking advice or treatment (Maheswaran et al. 2007).

The second consists of people whose need for admission can at least in principle be avoided. As the population has grown older, the importance of chronic as opposed to acute conditions has also grown. From the viewpoint of the healthcare system as a whole, it is important that patients with chronic conditions are given adequate support in the community so as to minimize the risks of their requiring admission to hospital (see Chapter 10).

Analysis of hospital admissions in the USA and elsewhere has identified patients termed frequent flyers who are admitted several times within a year. This work has led to attempts to identify such patients in advance of their actually presenting and to provide care programmes that, it is hoped, obviate the need for hospital admissions (Billings et al. 2006). There have been experiments with such programmes in a number of countries but the evidence has been mixed, both on their impact and the best way of organizing them, in particular how best to achieve effective links between hospital and community services, i.e. whether these can be achieved by informal or contractual arrangements or whether they require complete organizational mergers.

Managing hospital performance

Acute hospitals remain powerful institutions enjoying a large degree of discretion. But in recent years there have been important changes in the context in which they operate that have led to policies designed to influence how they function.

Policy-makers concerned about the cost of healthcare have sought to reduce spending on hospital services by encouraging more efficient operation and by reducing demand for their services. Many countries have introduced new forms of payment that make a closer link between what hospitals do and what they are paid.

In addition, governments, particularly those which fund their hospitals from taxation, have introduced policies designed to reduce the time that patients wait for treatment in response to public pressures and clinicians concerned about the implications of delay for their patients' hopes of successful treatment. This section examines two issues common to most healthcare systems: how hospitals should be paid for, and how waiting for hospital treatment should be addressed.

Paying the hospital

Hospitals in publicly funded systems have typically been funded through block allocations increased annually in the light of factors such as inflation or demographic change or through loosely worded contracts for broad categories of service. Such methods can constrain spending effectively – though in some cases payment has followed expenditure rather than limited it. But however effectively total spending is controlled, such arrangements do not directly promote broad health policy objectives such as greater efficiency in the use of resources or reductions in waiting times.

In the past 20–30 years, many countries have introduced payments systems for at least some hospital services linked directly to the level of their activity – the number of operations, consultations, etc. they carry out – with a view to exercising greater control over hospitals' performance. Such systems were initially developed in the USA but are now in place in many European countries and elsewhere (HOPE 2009). However, they differ a great deal at the detailed level (Street et al. 2007) so it is not straightforward to compare the experience of one country to another with an apparently similar system.

Payment systems of this type have been introduced to promote a number of policy objectives including:

- incentives for efficient/low cost providers to expand activity and in this way either promote competition or imitate the effect of it by setting tariff levels that only efficient providers can achieve;
- encouraging hospitals to reduce waiting lists;
- promoting good quality care by 'rewarding' good performance by setting higher tariffs when outcomes are judged to be better than average.

Studies of the impact of such systems in Denmark, Norway and Australia (Street et al. 2007), England (Sussex and Farrar 2010) and Eastern Europe (Moreno-Serra and Wagstaff 2009) have found some evidence that they do lead to lower costs or shorter lengths of stay and have made some contribution to shorter waiting times. But in respect of quality, difficulties of measurement mean that only limited moves have been made in this direction although it is firmly on the agenda of American purchasers (Shah 2009) and also in England (Department of Health 2008b).

The most fundamental issue, however, is that there may be conflicts between objectives. Linking payment to activity encourages more activity – a good outcome if the aim is to reduce waiting times for elective treatment. But if the aim is to shift emergency care away from the hospital, the opposite incentive is required. In the case of emergency medical admissions, for example, the English tariff has been modified so that admissions over a threshold level are paid at 'half price'. Similarly there is a risk if the payment regime is too tight, i.e. embodies over-stringent assumptions about the scope for reducing costs, that hospitals will cut quality.

In summary: activity-based payment systems seem set to continue as the main instrument for paying hospitals. It seems likely, however, that the precise form they take will continue to change, in response to changes in the overall objectives they are used to promote.

Reducing treatment delays

Hospital activity has increased steadily in recent decades as new operations have been developed and improvements in anaesthesia and post-operative care have allowed more people to be treated. At the same time, however, waiting lists have developed in a number of countries, as hospitals have been unable to deal promptly with all those capable of benefiting from treatment.

By its nature, elective care can usually be deferred, at least for a limited period, without harm to the patient. Hence if resources are tight because of overall budgetary constraints or the pressure on emergencies, allowing queues to develop for elective treatment makes sense.

 However, waiting is unpopular with patients and can be fatal. In the case of some heart conditions, research has identified the scale of this effect. A study by Sobolev and colleagues (2008) in Canada found that for every month on the waiting list, a patient's chances of dying increased by 5 per cent. Patients waiting incur a wide range of other costs including loss of income, higher home care costs and reduced ability to perform day-to-day tasks (Harrison and Appleby 2009).

Surprisingly, given the political salience of waiting times, reported measures of delay are usually inadequate. In most countries, measurement has focused on the period between when decision to treat has been made to the date of the treatment itself. This measurement has been shown to be deficient. Special surveys carried out in England, in 2005, showed that some patients waited for very long periods before their diagnostic tests were carried out, prior to the decision to treat. These waits were ignored in the targets in force at the time and continue to be ignored in countries setting waiting time reduction targets.

In England, a new target of 18 weeks was introduced that took all waits into account, i.e. an end-to-end target. A similar form of target had already been introduced for cancer but in this case the maximum wait allowed was 7 weeks from initial referral to a hospital specialist to the start of definitive treatment.

In response to the emergence of waiting lists, a wide range of measures have been introduced across most OECD countries, designed to reduce the time patients spend waiting for care. A recent OECD study (Siciliani and Hurst 2005) identified a range of measures that are currently in use. The former include redesign of funding systems on the lines discussed above to encourage more activity at lower cost and measures to raise hospital productivity such as redesign of care pathways. Such measures may be initially expensive in terms of management time: they may also involve small amounts of capital investment. But on balance they seem to lead to lower costs/higher productivity once they are introduced (Tey et al. 2007). Given the variety of ways in which health systems are organized, there can be no single 'best set' of measures but some lessons can be drawn from recent attempts to reduce time spent waiting.

First, experience suggests that a strong incentive to improve performance is critical and that the pressure for improvement must be maintained (Kreindler 2010). In Sweden, targets were introduced for some procedures and then relaxed, after which waiting returned to its former level (Hanning and Lundstrom 2007). In the UK, the evidence suggests that the introduction of 'performance managed targets' in England from 2000 onwards led to better performance than in other countries in the UK that did not introduce targets at that time (Harrison and Appleby 2006; Connolly et al. 2010). Against this background it seems likely that the decision by the incoming UK Coalition Government to scrap the 18-week target will lead to increases in waiting times.

Second, experience has shown that for hospitals to meet targets required them not simply to increase the number of operations they carry out but also change in the way that they deliver care. In some cases, this has involved a shift from inpatient to outpatient care. In some areas, inpatient treatment has remained the norm but, as the data quoted above shows, the time people spend in hospitals has been reduced and hence this has freed up beds for other patients.

The pressure to reduce waiting times has had implications for the internal structure of hospitals. To some extent, the needs of elective and emergency patients interact. At times of peak demand for emergency care during winter months, hospitals may have to cancel operations to free up bed and nursing capacity. The pressure of targets, however, has led some hospitals to separate elective from emergency care so as to ensure that the operation of the elective pathway is not disturbed by emergencies and hence that productivity of staff and facilities can be maximized. In some areas, emergency and elective care are provided in separate hospitals. Such a division, however, poses the risk that any gains on the elective side may be at the expense of greater cost for emergency care where some other way must be found of providing capacity to meet variations in demand. Evidence of the effect on total hospital productivity, however, is unclear: studies carried out in Norway (Kjekhus and Hagen 2005) suggest that there may be some loss of overall efficiency, but the results are not clear-cut.

Future challenges

The dynamic nature of hospitals poses a number of continuing issues and dilemmas:

- how to ensure that services are appropriately structured and linked together in a seamless way;
- how to balance access and quality and access and cost;
- how to ensure that the hospital performs in line with the expectations of the public in terms of value for money, timeliness, quality and cost;
- how to ensure that the different policy instruments bearing on hospitals are effective and mutually consistent.

These questions will continue to engage those responsible for promoting higher standards of hospital care. Different countries will find different answers and the answers will change over time as new technologies are developed for treating patients in hospitals and in alternative settings.

Conclusion

For the foreseeable future, the hospital sector will continue to absorb a major share of the resources devoted to the provision of healthcare. But how those resources are used and how the balance will be struck between the different levels in the hospital hierarchy and between the hospital and other providers are much less clear. The only certainty is that change will continue in the way that hospital services are provided and where they are provided.

Summary box

- Hospitals are dynamic institutions: their roles change in response to changes in medical technology and also wider changes in society.
- There are conflicts between increasing specialization and patient access: there are, however, a number of ways in which the scale of the conflict can be reduced.
- Hospitals are best seen, not as free-standing institutions, but rather as the focus for a series of care pathways linking their services to those in the community.
- Governments and other payers will seek to impose payment regimes for hospital services that encourage efficiency and quality.
- Information on how best to structure hospital services is still weak in many areas.

Self-test exercises

1 What do you think are the best ways of ensuring that patients in all parts of a country have good access to the full range of hospital services? How might you go about designing a strategy to put such measures into place?

2 What obstacles can you identify in your health system to effective linkages between hospitals and other care providers? How can they be overcome?

3 What are the risks and benefits of paying hospitals according to the number of treatments they provide?

4 What do you think will be the nature of the 'hospital of the future' in your country? What will need to happen in the wider healthcare system for this to be put into place?

References and further reading

Academy of Medical Royal Colleges (2007) *Acute Health Care Services: Report of a Working Party*. London: Academy of Medical Royal Colleges.

Albright, K.C., Raman, R., Emstrom, K. et al. (2009) Can comprehensive stroke centers erase the 'weekend effect'? *Cerebrovascular Disease*, 27(2): 107–13.

Argent, V.P. (2010) Pre-hospital risks of the reconfiguration of obstetric services. *Clinical Risk*, 16: 52–5.

Aylin, P., Yunus, A., Bottle, A., Majeed, A. and Bell, D. (2010) Weekend mortality for emergency admission: a large multi-centre study. *Quality and Safety in Health Care*, 19: 213–17.

Barnighausen, H.T. and Bloom, D.E. (2009) Financial incentives for return of services in underserved areas. *BMC Medicine*, 9: 86.

Billings, J., Mijanovich, T., Dixon, J. et al. (2006) *Case Finding Algorithms for Patients at Risk of Re-hospitalisation: PARR1 and PARR2.* London: King's Fund.

Bodenant, M., Leys, D., Debette, S. et al. (2010) Intravenous thrombolysis for acute cerebral ischaemia: comparison of outcomes between patients treated at working versus nonworking hours. *Cerebrovascular Diseases*, 30(2): 148–56.

Bredenhoff, E., van Lent, W.A.M. and van Harten, W.H. (2010) Exploring types of focused factories in hospital care: a multiple case study. *BMC Health Services Research*, 10: 154.

Cameron, J.I. and Marsell, A. (2008) Optimising stroke systems of care by enhancing transitions across care environments. *Circulation*, 39: 2637.

Cameron, P.A., Gabbe, B.J., Coper, J. et al. (2008) A statewide system of trauma care in Victoria: effect on patient survival. *Medical Journal of Australia*, 189(10): 546–50.

CanNet National Support and Evaluation Service (2008) *Managed Clinical Networks – A Literature Review.* Canberra: Cancer Australia.

Carson, D., Clay, H. and Stern, R. (2010) *Primary Care and Emergency Departments.* Lewes: Primary Care Foundation.

Carson, P.J. (2009) Providing specialist services in Australia across barriers of distance and culture. *World Journal of Surgery*, 33: 1562–7.

Celso, B., Tepas, J., Langland-Orban, B. et al. (2006) A systematic review and meta-analysis comparing outcome of severely injured patients treated in trauma centers following the establishment of trauma systems. *The Journal of Trauma, Injury, Infection and Critical Care*, 60(2): 371–8.

Commonwealth Fund (2010) *International Profiles of Care Systems.* New York: Commonwealth Fund.

Connolly, S., Bevan, G. and Mays, N. (2010) *Funding and Performance of Health Systems in the Four Countries of the UK Before and After Devolution.* London: Nuffield Trust.

Cooperation and Competition Panel (2010) *The Impact of Hospital Treatment Volumes on Patients' Outcomes.* London: Cooperation and Competition Panel.

Cowie, M.R. (2010) 'Hospital at home' care shows similar mortality and subsequent hospital admissions to hospital care for older patients with decompensated chronic heart failure. *Evidence Based Medicine*, 15: 9–10.

Crowley, R.W., Yeoh, H.K., Stukenborg, G.J. et al. (2009) Influence of weekend versus weekday hospital admission on mortality following subarachnoid hemorrhage. *Journal of Neurosurgery*, 111(1): 60–6.

Debes, A.J., Storkson, R.H. and Jacobsen, M.B. (2008) Curative rectal cancer surgery in a low volume hospital: a quality assessment. *The Journal of Cancer Surgery*, 34: 382–9.

Department of Health (2008a) *Using Commissioning for Quality and Innovation (CQUIN): Payment Framework.* London: Department of Health.

Department of Health (2008b) *High Quality Care for All: NHS Next Stage Review Final Report.* London: Department of Health.

Department of Health (2009a) *Improving Acute Care for Major Trauma Patients.* London: Department of Health.

Department of Health (2009b) *Intermediate Care: Halfway Home.* London: Department of Health.

Ferlie, E., Fitzgerald, L., McGivern, G., Dopson, S. and Exworthy, M. (2010) *Networks in Health Care: A Comparative Study of their Managements, Impact and Performance.* Report for the National Institute for Health Research Delivery and Organisation Programme. London: HMSO.

Freeman, J., Nicholl, J. and Turner, J. (2006) Does size matter? The relationship between volume and outcome in the care of major trauma. *Journal of Health Services Research and Policy,* 11(2): 1015.

Frick, K.D., Burton, L.C., Clark, R. et al. (2008) Substitutive hospital at home for older persons: effect on costs. *The American Journal of Managed Care,* 15: 49–56.

Gruen, R.L., Pitt, V., Green, S., Parkhill, A., Campbell, D. and Jolley, D. (2009) The effect of provider case volume on cancer mortality; systematic review and meta analysis. *CA: A Cancer Journal for Clinicians,* 59: 192–211.

Guthrie, B., Davies, H., Greig, G. et al. (2010) *Delivering Health Care through Managed Clinical Networks: Lessons from the North.* London: HMSO.

Hall, R.W. (ed.) (2006) *Patient Flow: Reducing Delay in Healthcare Delivery.* New York: Springer.

Ham, C. (2007) *Clinically Integrated Systems: The Next Step in English Health Reform.* London: Nuffield Trust.

Ham, C., York, N., Sutch, S. and Shaw, R. (2003) Hospital bed utilisation, Kaiser Permanante, and the US Medicare programme: analysis of routine data. *BMJ,* 327: 1257.

Hanning, M. and Lundstrom, M. (2007) Waiting for cataract surgery: effects of a maximum waiting time guarantee. *Journal of Health Services Research and Policy,* 12: 5–10.

Harris, R., Ashton, T., Broad, J., Connolly, G. and Richmond, D. (2005) The effectiveness, acceptability and costs of a hospital-at-home service compared with acute hospital care: a randomised control trial. *Journal of Health Services Research & Policy,* 10: 156–66.

Harrison, A. and Appleby, J. (2006) *The War on Waiting for Hospital Treatment.* London: King's Fund.

Harrison, A. and Appleby, J. (2009) English NHS waiting times: what next? *Journal of the Royal Society of Medicine,* 102: 260–4.

Hogan, A.M. and Winter, D.C. (2008) Does practice make perfect? *Annals of Surgical Oncology,* 15(5): 1267–70.

HOPE (2009) *Hospitals in the 27 States of the European Union.* Paris: Dexia.

Intercollegiate Group on Trauma Systems (2009) *Regional Trauma Systems: Interim Guidance for Commissioners.* London; Royal College of Surgeons.

Jones, A.P., Haynes, R., Sauerzapf, V. et al. (2008) Travel time to hospital and treatment to breast, colon, rectum, lung, ovary and prostate cancer. *European Journal of Cancer,* 44: 992–9.

Kjekhus, L.E. and Hagen, T.P. (2005) Ring fencing of elective surgery: does it affect hospital efficiency? *Health Services Management Research,* 18: 186–97.

Knowelden, J., Westlake, L., Wright, K.G. and Clarke, S.J. (1991) Peterborough Hospital at Home: an evaluation. *Journal of Public Health*, 13(3): 182–8.

Kreindler, S.A. (2010) Policy strategies to reduce waits for elective care: a synthesis of international evidence. *British Medical Bulletin*. doi:10 1093/bmb/dq014/.

Liaw, S.-T. and Kilpatrick, S. (eds) (2008) *A Textbook of Australian Rural Health*. Canberra: Australian Rural Health Education Network.

Maheswaran, R., Pearson, T., Munro, J. et al. (2007) Impact of NHS walk-in centres on primary care access: ecological study. *BMJ*, 334: 838.

Mahon, A., Harris, C., Tyrer, J. et al. (2005) *The Implementation and Impact of Hospital at Night Pilot Projects: An Evaluation Report*. London: Department of Health.

McCoy, D., Godden, S., Pollock, A.N. and Bianchessi, C. (2007) Carrot and sticks? The Community Care Act (2003) and the effect of financial incentives on delays in discharge from hospitals in England. *Journal of Public Health*, 29(3): 281–7.

McKee, M. (2004) *Reducing Hospital Beds: What Are the Lessons to be Learned?* Copenhagen: European Observatory of Health Systems and Policies.

McHugh, G.A., Campbell, M., Silman, A.J., Kay, P.R. and Luker, K.A. (2008) Patients waiting for a hip or knee joint replacement: is there any prioritization for surgery? *Journal of Evaluation in Clinical Practice*, 14: 361–7.

Miyata, H., Motomura, N., Ueda, Y., Matsuda, H. and Takamoto, S. (2008) Effect of procedural volume on outcome of coronary artery bypass graft surgery in Japan: implications toward public reporting and minimum volume standards. *Journal of Thoracic and Cardiovascular Surgery*, 135: 1306–12.

Moreno-Serra, R. and Wagstaff, A. (2009) *System-Wide Impacts of Hospital Payments Reforms: Evidence from Central and Eastern Europe and Central Asia*. Washington, DC: World Bank.

Mowat, I.G. and Morgan, R.T.T. (1982) Peterborough Hospital at home. *BMJ*, 294: 62–6.

Moynihan, B., Davis, D., Pereira, A., Could, G. and Markus, H.S. (2010) Delivering regional thrombolysis via a hub and spoke model. *Journal of the Royal Society of Medicine*, 103: 363–9.

National Audit Office (2010) *Major Trauma Care in England*. London: TSO.

NHS Confederation (undated) *Why We Need Fewer Hospital Beds*. London: NHS Confederation.

NHS Confederation (2010) *Implementing Trauma Systems: Key Issues for the NHS*. London: NHS Confederation.

Nicholl J., West, J., Goodacre, S. and Turner, J. (2007) The relationship between distance to hospital and patient mortality in emergencies. *Emergency Medicine Journal*, 24: 665–8.

Paimela, H., Lindstrom, O., Tomminem, T. et al. (2005) Surgery for colorectal cancer in a low volume unit. *International Journal of Gastrointestinal Cancer*, 35(3): 205–10.

Paiser, T.R., Cromwell, D.A., Hardwick, R.H.G. et al. (2009) Reorganisation of oesophago-gastric cancer care in England: progress and remaining challenges. *BMC Health Services Research*, 9: 204.

Parker, H. (2006) *Making the Shift: A Review of NHS Experience*. Birmingham: University of Birmingham.

Pedragosa, A., Alvarez-Sabin, J., Molina, C.A. et al. (2009) Impact of a telemedicine system on acute stroke care in a community hospital. *Journal of Telemedicine and Telecare*, 15: 260–3.

Perez dela Ossa, N., Millan, M., Arenillas, J.F. et al. (2009) Influence of direct admission to comprehensive stroke centers on the outcome of acute stroke patients treated with intravenous thrombolysis. *Journal of Neurology*, 256(9): 1270–6.

Posnett, J. (1999) Is bigger better? Concentration in the provision of secondary care. *BMJ*, 319: 1063–5.

Propper, C., Sutton, M., Whitnall, C. and Windmeijer, R. (2008) Did 'targets and terror' reduce waiting times in England for hospital care? *The BE Journal of Economic Analysis and Policy*, 8: 2.

Purdy, S. and Griffin, T. (2008) Reducing hospital admissions. *BMJ*, 336: 4.

Pyne, J.M., Fortney, J.C., Tripathi, S.P. et al. (2010) Cost-effectiveness analysis of a rural telemedicine collaborative care intervention for depression. *Archives of General Psychiatry*, 67(8): 812–21.

Rechel, B.W., Wright, S., Edwards, N., Dowdeswell, B. McKee, N. (2002) *Investing in Hospitals of the Future*. Copenhagen: European Health Observatory on Health Care Systems.

Royal College of Paediatrics and Child Health (2006) *A Guide to Understanding Pathways and Implementing Networks*. London: Royal College of Paediatrics and Child Health.

Royal College of Physicians (2008) *Teams Without Walls: The Value of Medical Innovation and Leadership*. London: Royal College of Physicians.

Schell, M.T., Barcia, A., Spitzer, A.L. and Harris, H.W. (2008) Pancreatico duodenectomy: volume is not associated with outcome within an academic health care system. *HPB Surgery*, Article ID 825940.

Scottish Executive (2002) *Promoting the Development of Managed Clinical Networks in Scotland*. HDL (2002) 10. Edinburgh: Scottish Executive.

Scottish Executive Health Department: National Planning Team (2005) *Drivers for Change in Health Care in Scotland*. Edinburgh: Scottish Executive.

Scottish Executive Health Department (2007) *Strengthening the Role of Managed Clinical Networks*. Edinburgh: Scottish Executive.

Shah, J.J. (2009) Quality and payment: the US experience of tying inpatient and outpatient caremix payments to quality measures and reporting. *BMC Health Services Research*, 9: 1.

Sheldon, T.A. (2004) The volume-quality relationship: insufficient evidence for use as a quality indicator. *Quality and Safety in Health Care*, 13: 325–6.

Shepperd, D., Doll, H., Angus, R.N. et al. (2009a) Avoiding hospital admission through provision of hospital care at home: a systematic review and meta-analysis of individual patient data. *Canadian Medical Association Journal*, 180(2): 175–82.

Shepperd, S., Doll, H., Broad, J. et al. (2009b) Early discharge hospital at home, *Cochrane Database Systematic Review*, Jan. 21 (1): CD000356.

Siciliani, L. and Hurst, J. (2005) Tackling excessive waiting times for elective surgery: a comparative analysis in 12 OECD countries. *Health Policy*, 72: 201–15.

Singh, J.M. and MacDonald, R.D. (2009) Pro/con debate: do the benefits of regionalized critical care delivery outweight the risks of interfacility patient transport? *Critical Care*, 13: 219.

Sobolev, B.G., Fradet, G., Hayden, R. et al. (2008) Delay in admission for elective coronary bypass grafting is associated with increased mortality. *BMC Health Services Research*, 8: 185.

Stewart, G.D., Long, G. and Tulloh, B.R. (2006) Surgical service centralisation in Australia versus choice and quality of life for rural patients. *The Medical Journal of Australia*, 185(3): 162–3.

Street, A. and Maynard, A. (2007a) Activity based financing in England: the need for continual refinement of payment by results. *Health Economics*, 2: 419–27.

Street, A. and Maynard, A. (2007b) Payment by results: qualified ambition? *Health Economics*, 2: 445–8.

Street, A., Vitikainen, K., Bjorvatn, A. and Hvenegaard, A. (2007) *Introducing Activity-Based Financing: A Review of Experience in Australia, Denmark, Norway and Sweden*. York: Centre for Health Economics, University of York.

Sussex, J. and Farrar, S. (2010) Activity-based funding for National Health Service hospitals in England: managers' experience and expectations, *The European Journal of Health Economics*, 10(2): 197–206.

Taylor, K. and Dangerfield, B. (2005) Modelling the feedback effects of reconfiguring health services. *Journal of the Operational Research Society*, 56: 659–75.

Tey, A., Grant, B., Harbison, D. et al. (2007) Redesign and modernisation of an NHS cataract service (Fife 1997-2004): multi-faceted approach. *BMJ*, 334: 148–52.

Ting, H.H., Rihal, C.S., Gersh, B.J. et al. (2007) Regional systems of care to optimise timeliness of reperfusion therapy for ST-elevation myocardial infarction. *Circulation*, 116: 729–36.

University of Birmingham Health Services Management Centre (2006) *Reducing Unplanned Hospital Admissions: What Does the Literature Tell Us?* Birmingham: HSMC.

University of Birmingham Health Services Management Centre (2009) *Acute Services in the Community*. Birmingham: HSMC.

Votruba, M.E. and Cebul, R.D. (2006) Redirecting patients to improve stroke outcomes. *Medical Care*, 44(12): 1129–35.

Wang, J., Zhao, Z. and Mahmood, A. (2006) *Relative Efficiency, Scale Effect and Scope Effect of Public Hospitals: Evidence from Australia*. Bonn: Institute for Study of Labor.

Ward, D., Drahota, A., Gal, D., Severs, M. and Dean, T.P. (2008) Care home versus hospital and own home environment for rehabilitation of older people. *Cochrane Database of Systematic Reviews*, 8(4).

Websites and resources

A number of international bodies have produced data or reports on the development of hospitals.

Cochrane Collaboration: this Publishes reviews of clinical topics including issues bearing on the role of the hospital: www.cochrane.org.

The Commonwealth Fund covers the USA and the UK and other European and Commonwealth countries. The precise coverage varies between reports: www. Commonwealth Fund.org.

European Hospital and Healthcare Federation: this produces both special reports and statistics on hospitals in Europe: www.Hope.be.

The International Hospital Federation produces an annual publication and a journal covering hospitals topics across the world: www.ihf-fhi.org.

The Organisation for European Co-operation and Development covers both Europe and major countries outside it including the USA and Japan: www.OECD.org.

For specific topics such as volume and outcome relationship, specialization or hospital-at-home, healthcare database such as Pub Med are useful: www.ncbi.nlm.nih.org. There are some national versions of this such as: ukpmc.ac.uk for the UK and www.pubmed.nl for the Netherlands.

Think-tanks, professional bodies and central government departments at national or regional/state/provincial level are also useful sources of information and analysis.

The World Bank covers all parts of the world and produces occasional reports on hospital topics: www.World Bank.org.

The World Health Organization's European arm produces reports on individual countries and health topics, including hospitals. Its definition of Europe is, like the OECD's, an elastic one, comprising substantial parts of Asia:
http://www.euro.who.int/en/home/projects/observatory.

CHAPTER 12

Mental health

Andrew McCulloch and Matt Muijen

Introduction

This chapter offers an overview of the state of and challenges facing mental health services today, and the key management issues arising. These services and issues are highly complex in every country, interfacing with many public and independent sector services, and with very different issues and responses in high-, middle- and low-income countries. There is great diversity around the world in terms of the location, content, style, purpose and history of mental health services. This chapter focuses on the major points, but concentrates on the European experience with particular emphasis on United Kingdom/English NHS services. In doing so, we have attempted to use the UK as an example of a highly developed and complex service, and to draw out wider lessons that managers of health services need to be aware of. UK mental health policy has a clear international context, drawing on experiences in the United States and Australia, for example, and many countries have in turn drawn on UK work, a recent example being current Spanish mental health policy.

This chapter is divided into six main sections. The first three give background on the scope, history, size and nature of mental health services. The fourth discusses the role and coverage of mental health services and variations across countries. The fifth and most substantial looks at key management issues within the sector that are of relevance across developed countries, supplemented with a discussion in the sixth part of international variations.

Background, subject and scope of mental health services

Mental illness is a leading cause of suffering, economic loss and social problems worldwide. It accounts for over 12 per cent of the disease burden, i.e. the proportion of the burden of morbidity and mortality attributable to diseases and disorders, as measured by disability adjusted life years (DALYs) in the world. This is unevenly spread across developed and underdeveloped countries. But even in poor countries, with their high prevalence of communicable diseases, the burden attributable to mental disorders is still around 10 per cent. In developed countries such as Germany, mental disorders are the leading cause, at 26 per cent, compared to cardio-vascular disease at 20 per cent and cancers at 17 per cent (Lopez et al. 2006). In the European Union at least 83 million people (27 per cent) suffer from mental health problems (Wittchen and Jacobi 2005). The most common mental health problem is depression which is typically experienced by 8–12 per cent of the adult population (Üstun et al. 2004). In addition, about 10 per cent (nearly 850,000) of children and young people aged between 5–16 years have mental health problems (Green et al. 2005). In the United Kingdom, for example, up to 1 in 6 people have a mental health problem at any one time and the costs, including loss of earnings and personal suffering exceed £100bn per annum (equivalent to the costs of providing all healthcare – Mental Health Foundation 2007).

Mental disorders can arbitrarily be divided into five main groups. All occur globally, although epidemiology is variable, especially for old age disorders and eating disorders.

1 **Common mental health problems, of which depression and depression with anxiety are most important.** A study of prevalence of mental disorder in Europe reported a lifetime incidence of mood disorders of 14 per cent and anxiety disorders of 13.6 per cent. In one year prevalence was much lower at 4.2 per cent and 6.4 per cent respectively, with women reporting double the rates of men (Alonso et al. 2004a). Most sufferers will have mild to moderate depression which does not require specialist input but it does create a large economic and social burden. In some countries this part of the disease burden is increasing, for example, in England common mental health problems affected 17.6 per cent of the adult population in 2007 as opposed to 15.5 per cent in 1993 (NHS Information Centre 2008).

2 **Severe mental health problems such as schizophrenia and bi-polar illness.** Schizophrenia has a median incidence of 0.15/1000, and a prevalence of 0.7 per cent. The variation between countries and differences between rural and urban areas are considerable, and this is likely to be due to a range of biological, social and environmental factors (McGrath et al. 2008). Typically two-thirds of sufferers may require ongoing specialist interventions as well as a range of social and other support.

3 **Eating disorders, primarily anorexia,** are rarer than the other groups of disorders, with great variation in incidence between developed and developing countries, although important in some countries as mortality is high and expensive specialist services are needed.

4 **Dementias** are common in countries with ageing populations, with age the main predictor of incidence. An estimated 5.4 million people in the European Union currently have dementia. One in every 20 people over the age of 65 has Alzheimer's disease, the most common form of dementia. Some 20 per cent of people over 85 have dementia in many developed countries. This is probably an underestimate, since about 30 per cent of people do not receive a diagnosis. For developed countries this is the largest direct cost burden for mental health services of all the disease groups, mainly due to the residential care required.

5 **Personality disorders,** which is a controversial 'disease group', affect perhaps 4 per cent of the population. Some sub-groups create heavy burdens for society and for

the criminal justice system, and this group is heavily over-represented in prisons. The group is very underserved by mental health services but has significant and long-term mental health needs.

The primary task of mental health services is to promote mental health and prevent mental health problems, treat mental ill health and to provide specialist input including reintegration into society for people with severe and enduring mental health problems (WHO 2001, 2005). Mental health services also have an 'asylum' or place of safety function and a social control function, and the balance of these functions varies from country to country. In the twentieth century, the legitimacy of these functions was widely debated but this chapter is not the place for a review of this debate. However, it is an important point that the politics of mental health and mental health services impact on management of services, especially the risk management agenda.

The public health function, i.e. the aim to promote mental health and prevent mental illness, is of growing importance to governments due to the cost of mental health problems associated with preventable work absence, and the awareness that many mental disorders have their origins in childhood (WHO 2004).

Current thinking is that mental health is a somewhat different concept to the absence of mental illness because some people will enjoy good general mental health while having a specific diagnosis. Others do not enjoy good general mental health but have no diagnosis – this is an important group from a public health perspective (the languishing or struggling group). In one study it was found that of all people who went to see health staff for mental health reasons, one-third went to GPs only, another third to mental health staff only, and a final third consulted both. However, 4 per cent of the sample without a disorder also consulted for mental health problems, and a slightly higher proportion saw GPs only (Alonso et al. 2004). This can be interpreted as an appropriate gatekeeping role by primary care, but it also indicates a heavy burden on the health service imposed by people who are struggling yet do not have a diagnosable psychiatric disorder.

At the opposite end is the problem of the treatment gap (Kohn et al. 2004). Many people with mental health problems do not access any services. In European countries, only 25 per cent of people with mental disorders receive specialist mental health services (Alonso et al. 2004). Only 50 per cent of persons diagnosed with depressive disorders receive any care, and 90 per cent of those with alcohol dependence do not receive any intervention.

A management challenge is to organize mental health services in such a way that the people with the greatest needs receive the most effective and resource intensive services. In developing countries, this challenge is accentuated by the lack of specialist staff and absence of service structures that are taken for granted in most Western countries, such as community teams and day hospitals. This will be discussed later.

History of mental health services

There is some evidence that people with major mental health problems have been segregated either for care or containment for centuries. There are various accounts of the development of the psychiatric hospital in the 'dark' ages. For example, Howells (1975) refers to psychiatric care developing as part of general hospitals in Islamic countries from the eighth century and in India from the tenth century. Dedicated hospitals for people with mental health problems and other conditions in England go back at least as far as the Middle Ages (the Bethlem Hospital was founded in 1247).

The story of modern psychiatric care is well known. The emergence of the Victorian asylum in England has been documented by many distinguished historians such as Roy Porter (Porter 2002). This approach was paralleled in most if not all developed countries to a greater or lesser extent, including France, Italy, the United States and the countries of the former Soviet Union. The asylums provided long-term residential care for a wide mixture of people including people with severe mental health problems, dementias such as those resulting from tertiary syphilis, learning disabilities, epilepsy and 'moral defectiveness' (e.g. having an illegitimate child out of wedlock). At their height, asylums in England accommodated 150,000 people (0.4 per cent of the total population).

This remained the main model of psychiatric care until the mid-twentieth century when a combination of advances in psychiatry, greater emphasis on human rights, and advances in social science and philosophy including labelling and institutionalization theory combined to start the deinstitutionalization movement that is not yet complete today. In England, this became explicit government policy in the 1960s and this was paralleled in other countries which used administrative policy to gradually close institutions. Some countries such as Italy took stronger action through legislation (in this case Nuova Legge 180) to abolish the mental asylum.

Deinstitutionalization has therefore been one of the primary drivers behind the development of modern care. It has been defined as

> the process of moving patients from large scale psychiatric institutions towards the community, where alternative psychiatric services strive to provide care and support in the client's community, together with more modern and appropriate treatment with better outcomes. Its main goal is to empower and emancipate people with psychiatric and social problems, enabling them to be fully participating members of society.
>
> (Bauduin et al. 2002)

Deinstitutionalization and community care are also at the heart of international policy development (WHO 2001, 2005).

The development of modern care

Since the 1960s, governments, municipalities and healthcare systems across the developing world have worked to a greater or lesser extent towards the goal of implementing community-based mental health services. Reform started early in a number of countries including the United States, Italy, England, Australia, New Zealand and the Scandinavian countries. Some of the most comprehensive models have been developed in countries like Australia where complex sets of teams interact to provide treatment and support for different groups of people with different age and need profiles, supported by some inpatient and residential care and housing and welfare benefits packages. This 'comprehensive model of care' is necessary to support deinstitutionalization, because of the complexity of need with the mental healthcare group. The many functions provided in the traditional asylums including healthcare, housing, food, occupation and leisure, arguably none very satisfactorily (Goffman 1961), had to be unpacked, and to be offered after individual assessments by many different agencies in community settings.

In most European countries, including the United Kingdom, the initial aim has been to develop a model of care based on a combination of some long-term provision, often still based in the old mental hospitals, with acute psychiatric units in District General Hospitals and community mental health teams within the community (McCulloch et al. 2000). This was seen to fail as it neither completed the deinstitutionalization process fully, nor did it provide comprehensive care in the community, especially for the most vulnerable, leading to a loss of public confidence. A comprehensive model had to be adopted instead, closing the mental hospitals and creating a range of community facilities teams, each with complementary functions (see p. 244).

At present, there is a strong divide between service provision across the world. All countries in Europe have hospital beds, but bed numbers do not reflect GDP or the stage of development of the other sectors (Figure 12.1). Many countries, both in the high- and middle-income categories, are struggling to complete or even initiate the deinstitutionalization process. Community teams are the exclusive domain of high-income countries, with the occasional isolated teams that are struggling to sustain themselves in mid-income countries. Some low-income countries have only very limited services, with very rudimentary hospital facilities, and are struggling to provide any basic hospital care that meets human rights standards.

A risk to mental health services in times of economic pressure is that they are a tempting target for cuts, even though population mental health needs and problems such as alcohol abuse, violence and depression increase as a consequence of rising unemployment and growing insecurity (Muijen 2010). Countries that have advanced the most are struggling to defend the resources they have in order to deal with emerging issues such as substance misuse and demographic increases in dementia. Countries with lagging services find it hard to allocate the resources to deal with even the most basic needs.

Funding of the mental health sector

The mental health sector is of course largest in high-income countries. This effect is disproportionate, since there is an association between GDP, investment in health and proportion of the budget allocated to mental health (WHO 2005). High-income countries such as the United Kingdom, France or Germany spend about 10 per cent of their health budget on mental healthcare. In contrast, most low-income countries spend less than 1 per cent of their low health budget on mental health services.

Organization of mental health services is dependent upon the organization of healthcare generally, so that countries with largely state-funded systems have universal state-funded mental health services (e.g. the United Kingdom and Italy), those

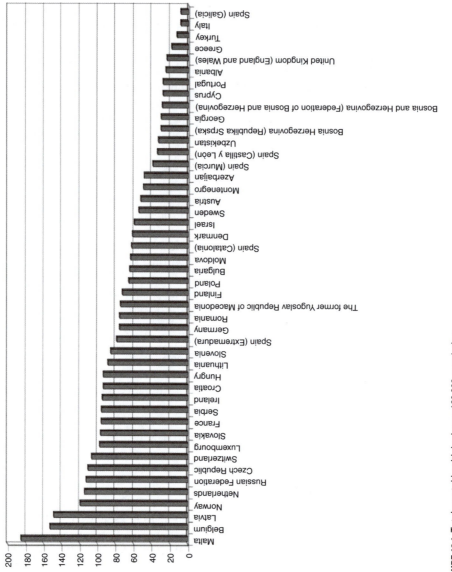

FIGURE 12.1 Total mental health beds per 100,000 population
Source: WHO Regional Office for Europe (2008).

with comprehensive insurance systems may use private or not-for-profit providers but offer universal access (most continental European countries including France and Germany), and those without comprehensive insurance systems have varied access routes to providers according partly to the ability to pay (e.g. the USA). In many countries in the last group informal carers provide the bulk of care for people with mental health problems depending on the availability and cost of provision. Many low-income countries rely heavily on co-payment, i.e. funding by the individual or often their families. This can have disastrous consequences on the financial state of families and continuity of care for chronic conditions, which can be unaffordable.

Funding systems may include charitable or faith-based services and international aid. Mental health services in low-income countries can rely on such funding sources, but some of these sources are also important in developed countries too. For example, in the United Kingdom the charitable/not-for-profit sector now provides some £1bn worth of mental health services funded largely by municipalities and housing benefits but also by the NHS and individuals. Almost all countries have a mixed economy of mental healthcare and many will have slightly different boundaries between what is considered health provision, social care and housing, for example, all of which are needed for people with severe mental health problems.

A major issue is the coverage of mental disorders, particularly by private insurers. It cannot be assumed that parity exists between mental and physical disorders in conditions such as length of coverage of care or inclusion of benefits. Gradually legislation is being introduced in countries to impose parity.

Mental health staff

Mental health services all around the world employ a range of professionals including psychiatrists and mental health nurses, although in widely varying numbers. The provision of occupational therapists, clinical psychologists, psychotherapists and social workers is standard practice only in high-income countries. Even in the high- and middle-income countries of Europe, the rates of psychiatrists and mental health nurses per head of population differ greatly (Figures 12.2 and 12.3). Rates of psychiatrists and nurses only correlate moderately (0.45), suggesting that the roles and responsibilities of psychiatrists and mental health nurses vary. Figures cannot simply be compared, since in some countries psychiatrists work mostly in the public sector, whereas in others many are privately employed, including a high proportion in psychotherapy. Nurses are almost always employed publicly, but their roles and responsibilities vary from independent clinicians active in hospital and community settings to custodians in asylums (WHO Regional Office for Europe 2008).

What is covered by 'mental health services'?

Considering the diversity of service provision, it is not possible to describe the coverage of mental health services in a meaningful generalized way. Therefore, this section will start by using England as an example of what is covered by mental health services and then offer some international comparisons to illustrate differences and commonalities.

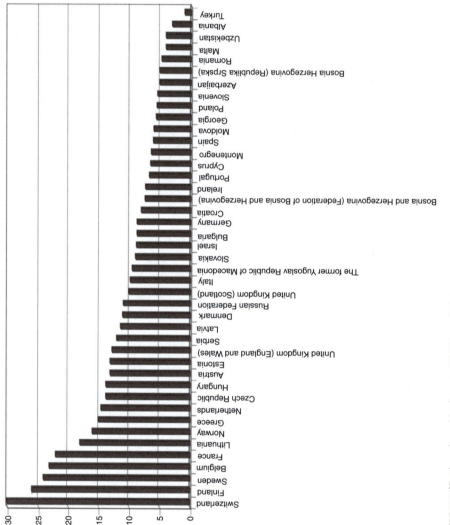

FIGURE 12.2 Number of psychiatrists per 100,000 population
Source: WHO Regional Office for Europe (2008).

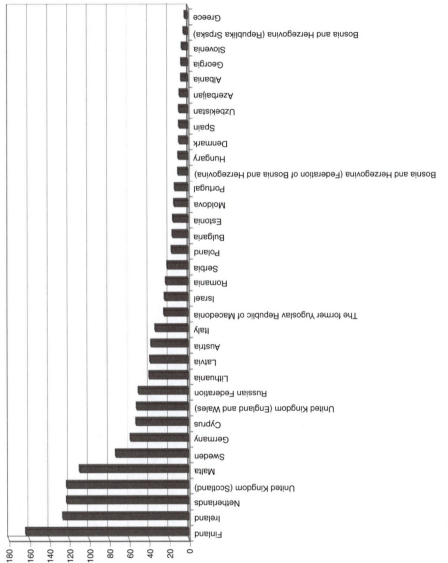

FIGURE 12.3 Number of nurses working in mental health care per 100,000 population
Source: WHO Regional Office for Europe (2008).

The main providers of mental health interventions in England are:

- Primary care physicians and their staff which provide the vast majority of primary mental healthcare (although some is provided by direct access counselling services, for example) and a proportion of chronic care. Around a third of GP consultations are mental health related and they also provide the care for about one-third of all people with severe mental illnesses. GPs in the United Kingdom are self-employed but paid for by the NHS.

- Specialist mental healthcare is provided by NHS mental health Foundation Trusts (90 per cent) and the private sector (10 per cent, although with a much bigger part of some markets such as secure care). Tertiary mental healthcare is provided by the same agencies with the private sector having a larger role.

- Social care is provided by municipalities (local authorities) but often this distinction is blurred as there is scope for pooling budgets across health and social care and there are many examples of joint commissioning. It is normal practice for social workers to be employed by social services and funded by local authorities but integrated into mental health teams.

- A great deal of housing and support is provided by specialist housing associations on behalf of municipalities and using central government grant aid.

- There is an extensive not-for-profit sector providing services such as employment rehabilitation, housing and counselling, mostly funded by contracts with local authorities.

- Significant public mental health interventions are also emerging provided by agencies such as educational establishments and large employers.

- Mental healthcare is commissioned by Primary Care Trusts (local NHS commissioning agencies) and municipalities, but the current government wishes to shift much of this commissioning responsibility to consortia of GPs – a concept with which England has experimented before and which has some similarities to HMOs in the United States.

- Services for older people and especially children are differently organized. It is beyond the scope of this chapter to describe these differences but it is worth noting the added complexities, particularly in regard to age transitions.

The multiple agencies, sometimes several involved simultaneously, create an intricate network of pathways. Priorities are ease of access, particularly for those at greatest needs, and an efficient allocation of resources. The gatekeeping roles of primary care for health and social workers for social care are essential for identification and appropriate referral and allocation. However, the role of commissioning is crucial, since sufficient services need to be available to address the local need, based on survey data, epidemiological research and local service demand. Services also need to be comprehensive, in combination covering all the functions required to address the diverse needs of people with mental health problems. Both the agreement on what are valid needs and essential services are related to culture, funding and evidence, and variations from one area to a neighbouring one can be striking.

Services in England are particularly complex, characterized by functional special-ization, and are seen by many countries as an aspirational example. They cover the following functions:

- Inpatient care in different settings: general adult, low secure/intensive care, medium secure, high secure and sub-speciality units (e.g. for eating disorders). These units accounted for about 126,000 admissions in 2008/9 in England with just over 21,000 available beds (The Health and Social Care Information Centre 2009). These included 48,000 compulsory admissions under the Mental Health Act (NHS Information Centre 2009).
- Community-based crisis care delivered by specialist crisis teams: 280 people per 100,000 adults receive crisis resolution in England each year (Glover et al. 2007).
- Community teams providing the first level of specialist response for a wide range of problems for people with a range of mental health issues.
- Assertive outreach teams delivering a specialist service to people with severe mental illness who are hard to engage. Some 60 people per 100,000 receive assertive outreach (Glover et al. 2007).
- Early intervention teams that deal with the onset of psychosis in young people and young adults to attempt to limit the lifetime impact of the illness.
- 24-hour nursed care for people with severe mental health problems and permanent cognitive impairment.
- Residential care for similar groups but with lower-intensity healthcare needs.
- Supported housing.
- Daytime activities directed at rehabilitation and social inclusion.
- Social support.

The strength of the English model is the range of specialist interventions available. The risks of the model are the potential of fragmentation and the cost.

Only a few of the wealthiest countries in the world aim to offer such a range of specialist services. Most developed countries are developing community-based men-tal health services, but limit the structural diversity. Typically they will have a single community team covering a population of between 100,000 and 250,000 people, re-sponsible for crisis intervention and continuing care. Only developed countries are able to offer a choice of residential facilities. Middle- and low-income countries are burdened by their mental hospitals which consume up to 90 per cent of mental health budgets, and lack the workforce and infrastructure to initiate mental health reform (WHO Regional Office for Europe 2008).

Management issues in the mental health sector

Managing mental health services, by which we primarily mean specialist mental health services, presents many challenges which blend issues related to the running of health-care services generally with those specific to mental healthcare. The latter relate to the service implications of the nature of mental ill health and especially severe mental disorders. Features of mental health services which create distinct management challenges include:

- the fact that some patients do not or cannot consent to treatment, i.e. lack capacity, and in some cases need to be treated against their will in order to protect themselves or the community they live in – this creates a different dynamic and accountability for the service as well as extra, necessary, administrative requirements;
- the stigma of mental illness which discourages people from seeking help, and communities and carers from engaging;
- the association in many people's mind of modern services with the old asylums and abusive practice;
- the contested nature of the concept of mental illness both outside and inside services (e.g. between psychiatrists and psychologists);
- the chronic and recurring nature of some conditions;
- the extent of co-morbidity of mental and physical health problems;
- the association or perceived association of mental ill health with other social problems such as poverty, homelessness, substance misuse, offending and even homicide. In England, the latter is of great importance even though the proportion of homicides committed by psychiatric patients has fallen.
- the prevalence of suicide within the patient population – about 15 per cent of people with severe disorders end their own lives.

To put it another way, it is the social politics of mental illness which often impacts on managers both when working strategically, e.g. deciding what services to commission or where to build a new unit, or even in day-to-day work such as liaison with the local community.

At a broader level we have identified seven key challenges facing mental health service managers which are of wider relevance:

1 policy implementation
2 finance
3 partnership working
4 age transitions
5 special groups and settings
6 security and incident management
7 patient involvement and empowerment

Policy implementation

Mental health is an area of healthcare where there is often significant public policy involvement. Most developed countries have both mental health specific law and administrative policy, and for good reason, since this group is at high risk of stigma, discrimination and human rights abuse as pointed out above (see also Muijen and McCulloch 2009). There is a tendency for some government policy to be aspirational and ahead of public opinion, or even 'ahead' of clinical opinion, and this means that managers must reconcile these conflicts within local services. Sometimes, as in England, policy is very complicated, so that managers must choose priorities and which parts of policy should be implemented urgently. And often policy is not fully funded or the workforce requirements are not fully worked out. This can lead to a massive challenge for managers to look both ways – to satisfy the centre (the regional or national agencies to which they are accountable) – while working with local clinicians, patients and communities. Where policy is weak, the reverse applies because managers then have no mandate from the centre for any changes they wish to make and have to exercise leadership locally. In both sets of circumstances, alliances with opinion leaders, particularly respected psychiatrists, are essential to succeed. Best practice is almost without exception the product of a local clinical champion supported by managerial leadership.

Finance

Even in countries with well-funded mental health services such as England, France and the Nordic countries, there is a huge level of unmet need, as specified earlier. The treatment gap differs by conditions, but disorders that pose major public health challenges such as depression or substance misuse disorders have a coverage of only 5–10 per cent (Kohn et al. 2004). There are always gaps in the local services which could be filled with more resource, whether the service is measured against the international evidence base or against the aspirations of local patients, carers and communities. However, the health economic evidence of the benefits of psychiatric treatment in the short term is not always as dramatic as it is for physical healthcare, despite the very high burden of disease. Cancer treatment is measured and publicized by mortality, schizophrenia and depression by functioning.

In addition to this common problem, the multi-agency nature of mental healthcare can create perverse incentives and complex resource flows. In some countries there is an incentive for clinicians to admit patients since the reimbursement system funds every admission. The consequence is a very high number of admissions, despite a relatively low number of beds. Moreover, this hinders the development of community services that do not receive sufficient reimbursement. In other countries there is an incentive to admit under compulsory powers as this may release resources or make beds available. In every system, as a consequence of separate funding streams, there will be cost shifting between health and social care and other funders, for example, by discharging early to residential facilities, or the reverse, refusing transfer. Few of these tactics are in the clinical interest of patients, as well as posing significant challenges for managers to secure resources, establish efficient funding and transaction methodologies and eliminate perverse incentives and boundary disputes.

Internationally, a range of solutions have been attempted for some of these problems, for example:

- In Sweden, municipalities have to repay healthcare costs if patients cannot be discharged from hospital when they are ready.

- In the United States, some social and healthcare maintenance organizations have constructed pooled budgets based on maintaining the mental and physical health of their client base as a whole.

- In England, use of a payment by results mechanism for mental health is in a pilot phase that would aim to reduce the tendency of providers to hold onto patients with moderate problems for whom further treatment has diminishing effect.

Every funding system will have its strengths and weaknesses, and the variety of funding systems in place across the world indicates the frustration with current systems and search for improvements. Internationally a gradual move towards DRG systems can be observed in mental health, despite the problems of the poor link between diagnosis and cost and the lack of evidence of increased efficiency (Burgess et al. 1999; Lien 2003).

Partnership working

A typical psychiatric patient with complex needs will require support with all aspects of life such as money, relationships, physical and mental health and well-being, housing, social care and employment. Problems in any one of these areas could trigger relapse due to the bio-psychosocial nature of mental illness. A key problem with managing mental health services is that the inputs into many of these life domains will come from other agencies such as welfare benefits, housing and social care agencies (often linked to municipalities) as well as wider civil society including family carers, charities and faith communities, for example. While health service managers are not expected to manage across all these boundaries, effective care requires the development of strong partnerships with the large number of agencies involved locally.

A key issue in many countries is links between local authorities or municipalities and mental health providers, whether in the public or private sector. In England, there are a number of complications in this relationship which are mirrored in other countries:

- Mental health providers in England cover large populations, often circa 1m, whereas many local authorities are smaller, creating a lack of co-terminosity.

- Local authorities are politically accountable to the local electorate whereas Mental Health NHS Foundation Trusts are accountable to non-political governors and also to different national oversight bodies. In many countries mental hospitals will be state-owned.

- Local authorities have very wide remits – with many mental health relevant issues such as education and elder care – Trusts and hospitals are very focused on health services.

- The concepts and language used about mental health are very different in each type of agency, as local authorities focus more on public mental health and well-being and Trusts on high-level needs.

- Financial arrangements are different as is expertise, e.g. local authorities are more expert at commissioning.

Yet to provide excellent mental healthcare, good partnerships between the NHS and local authorities are essential. Leadership in establishing and maintaining such partnerships and clarifying mutual expectations is a key part of the mental health manager's role.

Age transitions

It is a key aspiration in many countries that good mental healthcare is provided across the life span, dealing equally well with childhood disorders, which are generally behavioural, adult disorders, and the diseases, usually dementia, that particularly emerge in old age. A critical challenge within this is not only to provide the appropriate skills and knowledge to treat the particular disorders at each stage of life but also to manage the transitions, especially between adolescence and adulthood and adulthood and old age. The former is of strategic importance because the typical age of onset of schizophrenia is in the period 16–25, yet during this period many healthcare systems transfer responsibility for care from child and adolescent services to adult services. This can create great difficulties for patients and their families.

The typical age of transfer of a young person from Child and Adolescent Mental Health Services (which are not necessarily located in the same provider agency as adult services) to adult services in England is 18, but this can vary somewhat. It can take one to two years to satisfactorily complete a transfer and this can be made more difficult by differences in care pathways, treatment thresholds and philosophy (which can even extend to differences in terminology and diagnosis) applying to adolescent and adult teams. This is unfortunate as this transition coincides not only with the onset period for adult disorders but also other key stressful transitions such as exams, and starting university or jobs, and this leads to many missed opportunities for services to treat and ameliorate illness at this critical phase of life.

Solutions that have been attempted include:

- specialist early intervention teams that operate over transitional age range e.g. 16–30;
- the development of youth mental health services;
- use of transition workers that place young people in adult services and stay with them for up to two years;
- age flexibility in criteria for the use of services;
- youth services managing the interface with mental health providers at street level or within educational institutions;
- the development of separate primary mental healthcare services for young people by specialist workers with direct access from schools or youth work (i.e. not using GPs).

All these have their merits but the management challenge of making the boundaries work – which is one of the key overarching challenges in mental health – remains.

Special groups and settings

There are strong links between physical and mental health, e.g. as in medically unexplained illness, cardiovascular disease and Type 2 diabetes (Vieweg et al. 2010), and also between a range of conditions such as learning disabilities and physical disabilities and mental health. Many sub-groups within society also suffer from a raised prevalence of mental disorder for a variety of reasons including social stressors. These include recent immigrants, sexual minority groups, prisoners and those who misuse substances. This requires mental health services to develop strong links with:

- other health services. Despite the obvious requirement for such a link, interfaces are sometimes poor. The provision of physical healthcare in mental healthcare settings, both primary and specialist care, and the availability of mental health assessments and care in general medical facilities by liaison psychiatry is often inadequate;

- minority groups and their representatives. The large number of cultures and languages, and in particular people who do not speak the national language can pose a major challenge to services, particularly in inner cities.

- disability service providers and representative groups;

- prisons and the criminal justice system. A high number of prisoners suffer from psychotic disorders and personality disorders, with insufficient capacity and competence to provide adequate mental healthcare internally. The formation of in-reach services provided by the health sector can help, but will rarely be sufficient (Singleton et al. 1998).

Patient involvement and empowerment

Patient empowerment is central to modern mental health provision, forming as it does part of the rationale for deinstitutionalization and a current understanding of rehabilitation, increasingly referred to as recovery (Shepherd et al. 2008). It also relates to modern ideas of citizenship and consumerism. It is important to understand that patient involvement and empowerment have a number of goals which may include:

- service improvement through continuous quality assurance;

- strategy formulation by gearing of new services to patient's needs;

- rehabilitation of the individual patient – i.e. therapeutic goals in which recovery is almost synonymous with empowerment;

- improving access to the labour market for patients and reducing reliance on the state;

- fulfilling political and philosophical goals;

- encouraging patients to take a role in self-managing conditions such as bipolar disorder or families to manage childhood disorders.

Balancing the competing components and motivations for empowerment activity is a challenge, but so too are the practicalities of involving patients in the right way and making this sustainable. This may require compromise, shifts in power and changes in the way meetings are conducted, for example; and it may be hard to ensure the right patients are involved and that issues such as representativeness are properly addressed. However, if addressed well, this can create a powerful driver for service change as well as individual recovery, and in practice the experience is that involvement results in constructive empowerment and co-ownership of issues.

Security and incident management

A critical issue in the past 20 years in mental health services has been a focus on safety of patients and staff but particularly of the general public. In England in the early 1990s there were a number of incidents in which psychiatric patients killed members of the general public which created huge media publicity and led to a series of high profile administrative inquiries which generated a series of recommendations, not necessarily coherent or consistent, for services (McCulloch and Parker 2004). Similar incidents occurred in many other countries, preoccupying policy-makers. This wave of publicity and pressure was out of all proportion to the prevalence of such homicides which form only a small minority of the overall homicide rate nationally. These inquiries were necessary in principle, but in practice became bureaucratized, expensive, demoralizing and stigmatizing.

Nonetheless, there have been benefits and lessons learnt, and important management issues have been raised. Key areas of management practice that have been improved over the past 20 years in England include:

- risk management;
- follow-up and documentation of incidents;
- liaison with other agencies and most importantly between primary and secondary care which has proven to be an important factor in many care breakdowns in the United Kingdom;
- giving feedback to carers and relatives which many clinicians and managers seem to find difficult;
- reducing access to means for self-harm, suicide or harm to others in inpatient units;
- creating formal inter-agency review and learning opportunities following on from incidents.

International challenges in service development

A key challenge of mental health service management is to create and sustain effective mental health services that provide evidence-based interventions. Principles of community-based services are available (WHO 2003), and most countries have now drafted adequate mental health strategies. However, many countries that have adopted mental health policies are faced with the challenge of moving towards implementation.

In international meetings the points described above regularly emerge as concerns. In addition, the frequent changes in leadership of the ministries of health often cause disruption of initiatives and projects, and new decision-makers are seldom aware of commitments made by their predecessors. This is equally true of politicians or directors of agencies at lower levels.

Several additional points are of particular concern in middle- and low-income countries:

1 **Policy.** Shifting service provision from large psychiatric hospitals to community-based services is the core of mental health reform in these countries. National policies and legislation have been adopted to support this process, but there is still confusion about what community care should entail. There is a need for clarification of the concept of community-based care and a better understanding of the interface between hospital care and care available at community level.

2 **Deinstitutionalization.** The number of psychiatric beds in hospitals is decreasing in most countries, while there are no community-based services and no mental health services are provided in primary care. Private facilities rarely exist (they are often not allowed by law). Cuts in psychiatric beds and funds traditionally allocated to hospitals, without proper investments in services and infrastructure at community level, can lead to decreasing, rather than improving the quality of mental health services.

3 **Workforce.** The number of mental health professionals is low. Psychiatry is not a popular profession due to low salaries and stigmatization. There are not enough clinical psychologists, and often there are no educational institutions for social work. There is also no training in mental health for doctors of other specialities and no training in management and leadership is available. In general, there is no tradition of evidence-based training. Retaining staff is increasingly a challenge in these countries, and young generations of professionals need to be incentivized not to leave their countries.

4 **Quality.** Apart from the poorest, most countries have information on activity data such as admissions, discharges and treatment episodes. This is often due to health insurance demands, and reimbursement depends on such information. Little information is available on outcomes, quality of care and service satisfaction.

Conclusion

The challenges facing the managers of mental health services are daunting. There are commonalities and key differences across countries. However, the authors have often observed that when mental health service managers meet in international fora, it is the shared experiences which come across most strongly. Often mental health service managers are motivated by the challenge of weaving together the complex web of services required for this vulnerable and neglected client group. These challenges will evolve as the evidence base develops, as users become more empowered and as resource pressures change. However, in essence, mental health services remain a complex human service, requiring management of the highest technical competence coupled with humanity and vision.

Summary box

- Mental illness accounts for about 12 per cent of overall disease burden in the world, and in developed countries can be the cause of up to 26 per cent of overall ill health. The commonest problem is depression and/or anxiety, but other key conditions include schizophrenia and bipolar disorder, dementia, and personality disorders.

- Mental health services are different in many ways from other health services because, as well as treating people, they provide protection or a place of safety or 'asylum' and they engage in social control, treating some people involuntarily and constraining or detaining some because of the risk of harm to themselves, to others or to the wider public.

- In many countries, there was a tradition of isolating people with mental health problems in large institutions, separated from wider society, where standards of care and treatment were often very poor. This 'asylum' model of service provision has been challenged widely through a greater emphasis on human rights, advances in psychiatry and the emergence of new therapies, and greater acceptance and understanding of mental illness in wider society (or less social stigma).

- Deinstitutionalization has led to the wholesale transfer of mental health services and their users into the community, though a mixture of models of care exist with different staffing arrangements (between specialists and generalists; doctors, nurses, social workers and psychologists, and care workers).

- Mental health provision is often a mixture of inpatient hospital services, day care, primary care, social care and specialist services with important input from non-health sectors such as housing, education, criminal justice, and the like. Services are often segmented for children and adolescents, adults and older people and the transitions between these three areas can be problematic.

- Key management challenges include the public protection function and its consequences, the stigma still associated with mental illness, the chronic and recurring nature of much mental illness, the contested nature of diagnosis and therapy, and the embeddedness of mental health problems in the wider social and economic difficulties of what are often very vulnerable and hard-to-reach user populations.

Self-test exercises

1 Take one of the five main groups of mental disorders set out in the chapter and examine how services for that group are organized in your healthcare system or in a particular healthcare organization. For example, explore how services are funded or financed, what is known about the burden of disease or levels of need,

and investigate the way services are structured and delivered. Identify strengths and weaknesses, and make some recommendations for improvement.

2 Investigate how the issues of risk and public protection from people with a serious mental illness are managed in your healthcare system. Specifically, research the legislative provisions governing detention and involuntary treatment for people with mental health problems, and how they work. Consider how incidents of serious harm (such as suicides or homicides involving people who are undergoing treatment for a mental illness and are known to mental health services) are dealt with both by service providers and regulators/government and by the media and the public.

References and further reading

Alonso, J., Angermeyer, M.C., Bernert, S., Bruffaerts, R., Brugha, T.S., Bryson, H. et al. (2004a) Prevalence of mental disorders in Europe: results from the European Study of the Epidemiology of Mental Disorders (ESEMeD) project. *Acta Psychiatr Scand Suppl.* (420): 21–7.

Alonso, J., Angermeyer, M.C., Bernert, S., Bruffaerts, R., Brugha, T.S., Bryson, H. et al. (2004b) Use of mental health services in Europe: results from the European Study of the Epidemiology of Mental Disorders (ESEMeD) project. *Acta Psychiatr Scand Suppl.* (420): 47–54.

Bauduin, D., McCulloch, A. and Liegeois, A. (2002) *Good Care in the Community: Ethical Aspects of de-institutionalisation.* Utrecht: Netherlands Institute of Mental Health and Addiction.

Burgess, P., Pirkis, J., Buckingham, W. et al. (1999) Developing a casemix classification for specialist mental health services. *Casemix.* 4.

Glover, G., Arts, G. and Babu, K.S. (2007) *Crisis Resolution Teams and Impatient Mental Health Care in England.* Durham: Centre for Public Mental Health, University of Durham.

Goffman, E. (1961) *Asylums: Essays on the Social Situation of Mental Patients and Other Inmates.* New York: Anchor Books.

Green, H., McGinnity, A., Meltzer, H., Ford, T. and Goodman, R. (2005) *Mental Health of Children and Young People in Great Britain 2004.* London: Palgrave. Available at: http://www.statistics.gov.United Kingdom/.

Health and Social Care Information Centre (2009) *Mental Health Bulletin.* Health and Social Care Information Centre.

Howells, J. (ed.) (1975) *A World History of Psychiatry.* New York: Bailliere Tindall.

Kohn, R., Saxena, S., Levav, I. and Saraceno, B. (2004) The treatment gap in mental health care. *Bull World Health Organ,* 82(11): 858–66.

Lien, L. (2003) Financial and organisational reforms in the health sector: implications for the financing and management of mental health care services. *Health Policy,* 63(1): 73–80.

Lopez, A., Mathers, C. and Ezzati, M. et al. (2006) *Global Burden of Disease and Risk Factors.* Washington, DC, Oxford: Oxford University Press and World Bank.

McCulloch, A. and Cohen, A. (2008) Mental health policy and primary mental health care. In A. Cohen (ed.) *Delivering Mental Health in Primary Care: An Evidence Based Approach*. London: Royal College of General Practitioners.

McCulloch, A., Muijen, M. and Harper, H. (2000) New developments in mental health policy in the United Kingdom. *Int. J. of Law and Psychiatry*, 23(3-4): 261–76.

McCulloch, A. and Parker, C. (2004) Compliance, assertive community treatment and mental health inquiries. In N. Stanley and J. Manthorpe. *The Age of Inquiries*. London: Routledge.

McGrath, J., Saha, S., Chant, D. and Welham, J. (2008) Schizophrenia: a concise overview of incidence, prevalence and mortality. *Epidemiological Reviews*, 30: 67–76.

Mental Health Foundation (2007) *The Fundamental Facts*. London: The Mental Health Foundation.

Muijen, M. (2010) Challenging times for mental health services. *International Psychiatry*, 7(1): 3.

Muijen, M. and McCulloch, A. (2009) Public policy and mental health. In M. Gelder *et al. New Oxford Textbook of Psychiatry*. Oxford: Oxford University Press.

NHS Information Centre (2008) *Psychiatric Morbidity in England, 2007*. London: NHS Information Centre.

NHS Information Centre (2009) *In-patients Formally Detained in Hospitals under the Mental Health Act 1983 and Patients Subject to Supervised Community Treatment: 1998–99 to 2008–09*. London: Department of the Health.

Porter, R. (2002) *Madness: A Brief History*. Oxford: Oxford University Press.

Shepherd, G., Boardman, J. and Slade, M. (2008) *Making Recovery a Reality*. Sainsbury Centre for Mental Health.

Singleton, N., Meltzer, H. and Gatward, R. (1998) *Psychiatric Morbidity among Prisoners in England and Wales*. London: The Stationery Office.

Üstun, T.B., Ayuso-Mateos, J.L., Chatterji, S., Mathers, C. and Murray, C.J. (2004) Global burden of depressive disorders in the year 2000. *Br J Psychiatry*, 184: 386–92.

Vieweg, W.V., Hasnain, M., Pandurangi, A.K. and Lesnefsky, E.J. (2010) Major depression and coronary artery disease. *Arch Gen Psychiatry*, 67(6): 653.

WHO (2001) *World Health Report (2001): Mental Health: New Understanding, New Hope*. Geneva: World Health Organization.

WHO (2003) *WHO Mental Health Policy and Service Guidance Package: Organization of Services for Mental Health*. Geneva: World Health Organization.

WHO (2004) *Prevention of Mental Disorders: Effective Interventions and Policy Options*. Geneva: World Health Organization.

WHO (2005) *WHO Atlas: Mental Health Resources in the World 2005*. Geneva: World Health Organization.

WHO Regional Office for Europe (2005) Mental Health Declaration for Europe. Paper presented at WHO European Ministerial Conference on Mental Health: Facing the Challenges, Building Solution, 12–15 January 2005, Helsinki.

WHO Regional Office for Europe (2008) *Policies and Practices for Mental Health in Europe: Meeting the Challenges*. Copenhagen: WHO Regional Office for Europe.

Wittchen, H.U. and Jacobi, F. (2005) Size and burden of mental disorders in Europe: a critical appraisal of 27 studies. *European Neuropsychopharmacology,* 15(4): 357–76.

Websites and further resources

Centre for Mental Health: http://www.centreformentalhealth.org.uk/.
Department of Health, England: mental health:
    http://www.dh.gov.uk/en/Healthcare/Mentalhealth/index.htm.
European Commission: mental health:
    http://ec.europa.eu/health/mental_health/policy/index_en.htm.
Mental Health America: http://www.mentalhealthamerica.net/.
Mental Health Foundation: http://www.mentalhealth.org.uk/.
MIND: the largest mental health charity for England and Wales: www.mind.org.uk.
National Mental Health Development Unit: http://www.nmhdu.org.uk/nmhdu/.
Rethink: charity focused on severe mental illness: http://www.rethink.org/.
World Health Organization: mental health: http://www.who.int/mental_health/en/.

CHAPTER 13

Social care

Helen Dickinson and Jon Glasby

Introduction

It has long been acknowledged that providing good health to populations needs the input of more than just healthcare organizations. Considering health in its widest sense requires going beyond simply the actions of healthcare organizations and professionals to include other agencies such as education, leisure services, criminal justice bodies, communities, families and individuals. Although the exact language and focus vary from country to country, a key partner for health services has often been 'social care' (sometimes described as 'personal social services'). While more detailed definitions are provided below, this often includes practical support with activities of everyday living via services such as home care, day care, short breaks and residential care.

By their very nature, adult health and social care tend to work with people at their most vulnerable and distressed. In social care in particular, many of the groups supported – for example, people with mental health problems or people with learning difficulties – often experience considerable stigma, and can be the recipients of negative publicity and commentary. As a result, the quality and responsiveness of such services are paramount and of fundamental importance to the individuals concerned. Similarly, adult health and social care are also often key issues in the media and in national and local politics. In many countries large sums of public money are invested in public health and social services, so politicians, the public and the media alike all have a strong interest in how well such services perform.

Yet, regardless of how social care services are organized, most care systems are presently coming under increasing pressure due to demographic changes and rising public expectations. Most developed countries are experiencing changes in the make-up of their population, with people living longer and family structures changing. In many parts of the developed world, countries are becoming older and more frail with diminished traditional family care structures to support these individuals (Kröger 2003; European Foundation for the Improvement of Living and Working Conditions 2006). However, it is not just the increased demand for social care that is fuelling such interest in this sector – expectations of what kinds of services individuals want and are entitled to are also undergoing something of a transformation, with people demanding better quality and more individualized services than have traditionally been provided.

This has significant implications in terms of funding, the workforce, the types of agencies involved in providing support and the voice of service users, among an array of other factors. This raises a number of management challenges, some of which health and social care managers will face together.

The chapter starts out by examining what social care is and the many different types of terminology that are associated with this. This section argues that what is classed as social care has significant implications in practice and that in interpreting social care in its widest sense it is important that we pay attention to the role of informal care which provides a significant proportion of social care around the world. The next section goes on to set out a case study where we examine the ways in which social care in the UK has been defined and understood over time. While each country has its own unique history and context, we look at the history and evolution of UK social care as one example of the factors that have influenced the development of social care, using this to start to tease out the main management challenges for health and social care, now and in the future. These are further discussed in detail in the final substantive section of the chapter. We suggest that countries are engaged in very similar debates, and arguably all recognize the importance of social care in being able to provide high quality welfare services to their populations. The final section provides some tentative conclusions and pulls together the key lines of argument set out in this chapter.

What is 'social care' and how is it delivered?

Different national models of social care

Social care is defined and delivered in different ways in a range of countries – making it difficult to provide a clear picture of the nature, size and scope of the social care sector (see Payne 2005, for an overview of the nature and history of social care). Most developed countries have universal social care arrangements, meaning that regardless of the income or the age of an individual, those with levels of need or care that meet defined criteria should be eligible for care. Exceptions to this rule are England and the USA, where those with the appropriate levels of need are often means- or asset-tested before they are able to access publicly funded services. Although countries like Japan and France have universal systems for social care, in accessing some aspects of social care individuals might be assessed to decide if they should make a co-payment for that service. If we look internationally, there are different types of funding systems for social care arrangements and also different definitions and conditions of eligibility for social care but the state generally plays a fairly major role. Regardless of this, most of the care for sick and disabled adults and older people is provided informally, rather than by the state (see below for further discussion).

In terms of who provides social care and where individuals receive social care, this is again a very mixed picture internationally. For example, in Finland, home-help services are provided in individuals' homes, available from municipalities, as is institutional care (although its quality often varies). In Italy and Portugal, access to publicly provided domiciliary care services is much more difficult, as is access to long-term institutional care. Finland, France and the UK all have different combinations of public, commercial and voluntary organizations who provide social care. In Portugal and Italy, social care is mostly provided by the state, but in some places may be provided by the voluntary sector using subsidies from the state (Kröger 2003).

What is clear when looking at social care around the world is that even in universal systems, social care is often organized and delivered at a local level. So although eligibility criteria may be set at a national level, taxes raised nationally might be devolved to federal/municipal/local governments to deliver social care (and some systems have additional locally-based tax systems). In practice, this means that many countries experience tensions between the national and local levels and debates over matters of equity between local areas (Canada and Australia are good examples of where these debates have arisen recently – see Joseph Rowntree Foundation 2008). Box 13.1 sets out the different models of European social services and how we might characterize these services, while Box 13.2 summarizes some of the key roles of social care.

Box 13.1: *Different models of European social services*

The **Scandinavian** model of public services (e.g. Sweden, Denmark, Norway and Finland) is based on the principle of universalism, offering services for groups such as older people, people with disabilities and children, which are paid for from general taxation. Local government often plays a strong role in planning and delivery with limited commercial and voluntary sector involvement. This type of model is seen as being strong on service user rights compared to other models, but has come under challenge in recent years due to economic and political factors in relation to the notion of universalism.

The **family care** model (e.g. Greece, Spain, Portugal, Italy, Cyprus, Malta) tends to be based on limited state provision and an emphasis on family responsibility for care often linked to the Catholic tradition and some use of established voluntary organizations. This model is criticized for relying on female informal carers and lacking voice for service users.

The **means-tested** model (e.g. the UK and to some extent Ireland) has a limited role for the state in terms of direct service provision, with this being delivered on contract with providers from other sectors. Resources predominantly go to individuals with limited resources and the heaviest needs.

The **northern European subsidiarity model** (e.g. Germany, Austria, the Netherlands and to some extent France and Belgium) provides, services mainly through commercial and voluntary organizations and the state plays a major role in financing these. The family also often has a strong primary responsibility for care, although there are variations between countries. strong primary responsibility for care, although there are variations between countries.

Source: Based on Munday (2003).

Box 13.2: *Key roles of social care*

- **Protection** – of children, older people and disabled people that might be at risk in some way.

- **Provision of care and support** – this is a central role of social care in most countries, although the form it might take and who might provide this vary from region to region.

- **Care coordination and brokerage** – linked to the previous point, in many areas of the world, care is not simply provided by the state but a range of other different statutory and non-statutory bodies and social care has a role in coordinating these activities. With the advent of personal budgets this is becoming even more pronounced in some areas (see below for further discussion).

- **Regulation** – again, linked in part to mixed economies of care, social care may have a role in overseeing and regulating providers of care services.

- **Community development and social integration** – social care traditionally has played a role in attempting to halt social exclusion and in developing communities. This is becoming an increasing concern in the face of increased globalization and social mobility.

As Box 13.1 shows, countries vary dramatically in the types of care that they provide as a result of different economies, cultures, histories, politics and religious backgrounds. This is particularly important in relation to the arena of social care. As the European Foundation for the Improvement of Living and Working Conditions (2006: 11) argues,

> Cultural factors mediate between the individual and social behaviours that develop in response to demographic, social and economic trends and pressures. These produce different approaches to and preferences in the ways that people deal with major life course decisions. Resolving the problem of 'who should do what' in social care will become an ever larger moral, political and economic question in policy debates in the near future: care work extends into cultural values, different public services, technological advancements and the public media.

The role of informal carers

Whatever formal services exist, informal carers are the main providers of care for frail or disabled adults in most areas of the developed world and this looks set to increase, given that demand outstrips supply in most areas. Munday (2003: 10) argues that:

> A combination of demographic and attitudinal changes to family care will impact heavily on the demand for formal social services for elderly people in the 21st century. Providing sufficient affordable care for elderly citizens is identified as probably the highest priority for the European public service sector, together with the need to learn from the experience

of other countries in this field. An additional factor is that trend for more women – the traditional family carers – to enter the labour market and so become less available to care for dependent family members. The 'traditional family' model is also changing, with increasing numbers of one-parent families and families affected by divorce and re-marriage. These are complex subjects with major consequences for the future of family care and social services.

Despite the different systems and structures in different countries, the level of informal care across European countries has been found to be similar (Cangiano et al. 2009). It is estimated that around 6 per cent of citizens carry out daily care for older people in most EU member states (European Commission 2000) and women are far more likely to be informal carers than men. Further, it is often people with worse health who devote most of their time caring for other adults (European Commission, 2000: 82). These European patterns seem to be reflected in most other developed countries (Glendinning 2010).

Social care then is often predominantly provided by informal carers and yet is increasingly more crucial to the effective delivery of health and welfare services. Even in countries where health and social care are provided alongside each other, there is growing awareness of the role that social care can play in stopping the health/medical element of the system from spending money on expensive institutional care or older people being admitted to hospital as a result of falls or inappropriate support in the community (Jöel and Dickinson 2009). Arguably, if hospital and primary healthcare services of the future are to be effective, they will need to work ever more closely with social care in its widest sense to support the population with its changing demographic characteristics. However, in this there may be one further obstacle. What have broadly been referred to as the 'social' and 'medical' models have quite different values, perspectives and ways of seeing the issue of health.

The social model of care

Medical services have tended to focus predominantly on biomedical models of health and seek causes that have distinct causes and find solutions to these through medical treatments. Social care traditionally takes a rather different look at issues of impairment and disability, adopting a more holistic perspective on health. The social model was developed by disabled people as a direct response to the medical model and the impact that this had on their lives. The social model sees disability not just as a biomedical issue, but as caused in part by the society we live in – as a product of the physical, organizational and social worlds that lead to discrimination (Oliver 1996; French 1993; Oliver and Barnes 1993). Those in favour of a social model have advocated the removal of barriers (physical, attitudinal and behavioural) that stop disabled people having the same sorts of opportunities as others. These types of values and beliefs have tended to be more associated with social care than medical services (although by no means exclusively) and are important in understanding why different agencies and professionals may have difficulty in working together (see Table 13.1 for some of the structural and attitudinal barriers that can lead to conflict when trying to promote more effective inter-agency/professional working).

TABLE 13.1 Differences in characteristics of medical and social models

Medicine	Social care
Treatment	Care
Focus on the individual	Focus on the individual in context
Strong professional identity	Newer profession
Universal services	Focus on vulnerable
Procedurally regimented/top-down style	Practical focus and more bottom-up
Looks to the sciences/medicine	Looks to the social sciences

As we have already alluded to in this chapter, many areas of the world are experiencing significant shifts in terms of their demographics, compounded with changes in attitudinal factors, and this is fundamentally changing the types of demands that are put on care services (Escobedo et al. 2002). Regardless of the model of social care that different countries have, they are increasingly re-opening debates about the most appropriate ways to design and deliver social care. There are key tensions around whose responsibility social care should be (in terms of funding and in terms of who delivers care), where this should be provided, when and in what ways. Although the specific context is clearly different between countries, these debates tend to coalesce around very similar themes. The following section sets out a history of social care in the UK and the following section then compares the key features of debates to those in other countries. As suggested above and in the introduction to this chapter, each country will have a slightly different system and different historical and contextual factors influencing service development and delivery. However, the more detailed case study below provides an example on which to draw out some more general themes and challenges that are also evident in many other developed countries.

History and evolution of social care in the UK

The formalization of social care

While the history of social care in the UK is complex, a key contribution comes from a series of nineteenth-century voluntary organizations and philanthropists. Prior to this, much social support had been provided (as is still the case today) by families and local communities. In Tudor times, much of the assistance available was religious in nature and delivered via the monasteries. Following the dissolution of the monasteries and stimulated by rapid urbanization and industrialization, a number of more formal services began to develop via the notorious Poor Law. While this included outdoor relief (payments to people in financial need), the main source of 'support' was typically the workhouse, with conditions deliberately made as harsh as possible so as to ensure that only the most needy applied for state help (an approach known as 'the workhouse test' and the principle of 'less eligibility'). Over time, workhouses became increasingly focused on different groups of people, with different approaches emerging for the able-bodied poor (often seen as lazy and capable of supporting themselves) and for frail older people, people with mental health problems and people with learning difficulties (who were increasingly seen as not to blame for their plight and hence deserving of assistance).

During the latter part of the nineteenth century, two prominent voluntary organizations were important in developing new approaches to the alleviation of poverty and in pioneering many of the approaches that later became associated with modern social work:

1 Founded in response to a proliferation of almsgiving following the depression of the late 1860s, the Charity Organisation Society (COS) promoted principles of 'scientific charity' – assessing those in need and providing charitable support only to those deemed deserving (with those deemed undeserving left to rely on the Poor Law and the workhouse). In this way, COS hoped to coordinate the provision of financial support and to give individuals an incentive to be self-sufficient (guarding against the danger that generous support would only encourage the feckless and thriftless).

2 Founded in 1884 with the creation of Toynbee Hall in Whitechapel, the Settlement movement had considerable overlaps with COS (and the same individuals were often involved in both movements), but increasingly diverged over time. Settlements were colonies of educated people living in poor areas of large cities, with the dual purpose of using the education and privilege of 'settlers' to help the poor, but also of getting to know the poor as neighbours and hence understanding more about the nature of poverty. Over time, it became increasingly apparent to many settlers that poverty was not the result of individual failings, but the product of wider social forces, and a number of settlers (for example, Clement Attlee and William Beveridge) made significant contributions to the advent of a welfare state.

In many ways, these different perspectives continue to influence current practice, with social work approaches such as care management continuing to focus on the assessment of individual need to ascertain entitlement to support, and community development and neighbourhood renewal focusing much more on community empowerment and on the individual in a broader social context.

Following the Second World War, an increasing amount of social work activity came to be subsumed within two local government departments: specialist children's departments and health and welfare departments. These were later combined into generic social services departments (SSDs) following the 1968 Seebohm Report. By bringing together a range of adult and children's social care services, Seebohm argued, there was scope to create a more comprehensive and coordinated approach, to attract greater resources and to plan ahead to identify and meet the needs of a local area more effectively. SSDs were soon boosted by a growing national infrastructure, including a more unified system of social work education and the creation of a new National Institute of Social Work Training (which was later subsumed into a new Social Care Institute for Excellence).

In many ways, this system was to remain intact until the late 1980s, when a review of community care services by Sir Roy Griffiths (managing director of Sainsbury's supermarket) led to the 1990 NHS and Community Care Act. Henceforth, social workers were to be 'care managers', responsible for assessing individual need and arranging care packages from a combination of public, private and voluntary services. Consistent with the ideological commitments of the then Conservative government (1979–1997), this changed social workers into 'purchasers' rather than providers, and much of the new funding that accompanied the changes was to be spent in the independent sector.

New Labour and social care

Under New Labour (1997–2010), much of this ethos remained, but with a growing emphasis on modernization (often portrayed as a 'third way' between the market-based ideology of the New Right and the public sector values of the traditional Labour Party). Unfortunately, such a concept tends to be better at defining what a 'third way' is not (i.e. not the market and not the state), and the result was arguably a rather eclectic series of different policies and approaches. The 'third way' has also been an important influence in Australian policy and in Germany under the name of the *'neue Mitte'* (Clasen 2002: 67). Central to recent UK policy has been an emphasis on:

- greater **choice and control** (with people who use services having greater say over what they receive and how money is spent on their behalf). Perhaps the best example is the increasing role played by direct payments, with social care service users receiving the cash equivalent of directly provided services with which to purchase their own care or hire their own staff;
- greater **partnership working** (with health and social care in particular becoming increasingly inter-related over time);
- a stronger emphasis on **citizenship** and **social inclusion** (with a growing tendency – slow at first – to look beyond traditional health/social care to more universal services, and various attempts to tackle discrimination and promote human rights).

In structural terms, the key change under New Labour was the abolition of generic SSDs, and the creation of new integrated services for children and for adults. Thus, Directors of Children's Services are now responsible for both education and children's social care. Similarly, Directors of Adult Social Services are charged with developing partnerships with NHS colleagues and broader services, and often oversee both adult social care and other services (such as housing or adult education). In recognition of such changes, many SSDs have split into a Directorate of Children's Services and various configurations of adult care (termed 'Social Care and Health', 'Social Inclusion and Health', Social Care and Housing', 'Adults and Communities', etc). In many ways, this takes social care back to pre-Seebohm days (without necessarily stating why the need for generic SSDs which Seebohm placed at the heart of his vision for social care is now no longer relevant).

The Coalition Government and social care

With the election of a new Coalition Government, there is less clarity in terms of what future policy developments might emerge. The one big issue that will remain – and which is presently also being echoed in most other countries around the world – is that of long-term care funding. While dissatisfaction has been growing with the current system for some time, any future government will have to find ways of responding to the growing mismatch between the money available to fund community care services and increasing levels of need in an ageing society.

A second enduring issue is that of personal budgets, again a trend that is increasingly growing internationally (O'Brien and Duffy 2009) in countries such as the USA, Germany, Sweden, Australia and Canada among others. Although all three main political parties in the UK seem supportive of the roll-out (and potential extension) of personal budgets, there remain a series of ambiguities about the motives of different stakeholders. One of the reasons why both direct payments and personal budgets enjoyed such initial support was partly because they appealed to a range of groups across different parts of the political spectrum – with different people supporting these concepts for potentially different reasons. Whereas some people are supportive of these ways of working because they see them as part of a campaign for greater civil rights, choice and control for disabled people, others see them as an essentially market-based mechanism for rolling back the boundaries of the welfare state and as a form of 'privatization by the backdoor' (see Glasby and Littlechild 2009, for further discussion).

In many ways, this links to a third issue about the future of welfare services more generally, particularly in a period where there may well be much greater need as the population ages, but much tighter public finances with which to respond. To date, many have seen self-directed support and personal budgets as a potential means of starting to square this circle – possibly achieving better outcomes for either the same or sometimes less money. Essentially this revolves around what we will be expected to prepare for and pay for ourselves and what the state will provide on our behalf. Answers to these issues are often highly personal, philosophical and political – with scope for any government to make itself extremely unpopular.

Key enduring and emerging issues for management

The UK case study set out above provides a detailed overview of one social care system and is designed to illustrate a series of broader themes that are also evident in other developed countries (albeit in different cultures and national contexts). We argue that several of these are enduring and will continue to be 'hot topics' going forward and set out the key features of these debates in this section. A key driver of these debates in most countries seems to be the combination of demographic and economic contexts. This in turn has implications for notions of equity and most developed countries are having debates around the types of inequalities that are endemic in their systems. As part of debates over economics and equity, discussions over who are the providers of care have also come to the fore. Here we discuss these in terms of challenges arising in relation to mixed economies of care and the workforce.

The economic context

Social care is an area that is in flux in most countries and will continue to be so going forward into the future. We cannot get away from the fact that more people than ever before will be seeking support and within a context that seems set to get only more financially constrained. Managers are being challenged to do 'more with less' and in a way that will deliver more effective and more efficient services that people want and need.

As Glendinning (2010) illustrates, in response to financial pressures in recent years, Germany and Austria have both introduced caps on social care funding on individual service users. In the Netherlands, the range of help funded through mainstream universal schemes has been restricted through the transfer of responsibility for domestic help services from social insurance to municipalities. The Netherlands, Germany, Austria and Italy have also cut the prices that they pay for services which will clearly have implications on the well-being of the social care workforce (more on which below). Australia has restricted the coverage of state-funded social care to those on middle and higher income, focusing care on those who cannot pay. Although different mechanisms are arising to deal with a constrained economic context, clearly all countries are having to think carefully about the impacts of the economic context and their shifting demographics and the implications for social care.

Equity

As set out in the Introduction, one major point of debate in a number of countries is the issue of equity. This debate cuts across a number of different levels. We might think of equity in terms of what kinds of services individuals have access to in particular areas. As already touched upon, the delivery of social care is often done at a local level, while social care policy is a more national issue. This means that the same kinds of services might not be delivered in all areas, creating what is sometimes known as a 'postcode lottery'. In addition to the examples already given, one example of this debate from the UK is in terms of Scotland where older people are eligible for free personal care while their English neighbours are means-tested and may have to pay for the equivalent care (Dickinson et al. 2007).

Equity is not only a geographical issue and also stretches across different types of client groups (older people, children, people with mental health issues, etc.). There is the issue of the types of services which different groups receive and whether these are equitable. Diagnostic equity is the 'principle that people with similar levels of impairment are treated equally, regardless of medical condition or the reason for needing social care' (Glendinning 2010: 6). Some countries (e.g. Germany) do not take into account family context when making decisions on access to care, while others (e.g. the Netherlands) consider this as part of the decision over what care will be provided.

The final issue of equity we will discuss here is of intergenerational equity. As outlined above, people are living longer and having fewer children than in the past in most developed countries. A consequence of this is that younger generations are paying proportionally more to support older generations. In countries such as Germany and Japan, new mechanisms are being tried out where different age groups are paying contributions based on their age banding.

Mixed economy of care

One of the main challenges that a number of countries are struggling with is in developing mixed economies of care. Most countries are attempting to do this for economic and political reasons; particularly in terms of reducing the financial contribution of the state. Many countries are attempting to find a suitable mix in terms of the amount of services provided by the state and those which come from commercial, voluntary and also informal care. The key message seems to be is that there is not an easy answer to this conundrum and that services need to be designed in a way that is sympathetic to the local cultural and social needs of that area. While this is easier to some extent in urban areas where there are larger critical masses of populations, this may prove more challenging in rural areas where limited numbers of people seek support. The degree to which people are able to be offered real choice in these areas is to some degree still not clear. One area where this issue is particularly true is in terms of individual budget schemes.

Cash benefits schemes operate in varying ways in the Netherlands, Austria, Germany, France, Sweden, the USA, Canada, Australia and the UK among others (Carr 2009). One implication of devolving responsibility of purchasing decision to the individuals themselves is that some people are choosing to purchase very different types of services, and from non-state bodies, or different from those that have been traditionally purchased in the past (Carr 2009). In countries such as France, Germany, Italy and Sweden, competitive-based social care markets already existed to varying degrees but these have been extended with the introduction of cash allowances which have resulted in greater mixes between different types of care providers.

Increasingly constrained finances have led to a trend in introducing practices from the commercial sector into the management of the public sector. Essentially this is an attempt in many places to make the public sector more 'business-like' (Ferlie et al. 1996). In many cases this has seen social care aiming to concentrate on service user outcomes and adopting more formal systems of performance management. In many areas this is posing significant cultural challenges to services that have traditionally focused on inputs and processes. How to set meaningful outcomes and evidence these effectively is clearly a key challenge for managers (Dickinson 2008). How can we ensure that we set the right sort of outcomes that are meaningful to service users and then how might we go about trying to measure these, improve performance and commission on the basis of quality and outcomes? In principle at least, an outcomes-based approach to inspection and performance management could lead to some searching questions about the contribution of social care and to a move away from notions of equality of input (treating everyone the same) to equality of outcome (working with different groups differently to achieve similar outcomes). In might also boost joint working between health and social care, ensuring that future partnerships are designed with a much greater sense of what they are trying to achieve, why and for whom.

Workforce

The issue of workforce brings us on to our final point. We have argued that this area is to continue to be characterized by change and reform and keeping a workforce engaged while such change is occurring will be a challenging task. Many of those in the social care workforce are low paid and, as we have illustrated, beyond this formal care, informal carers are more often not paid at all. In some countries this low pay seems set to continue and even become more pernicious in some cases. An example of this is the Netherlands where recent reforms have resulted in purchasers simply paying less for services (Glendinning 2010). This kind of downwards pressure inevitably makes conditions worse for those who are already working under difficult conditions.

Although the advent of personal budgets (cash for care) is a welcome advent in a number of ways, we also need to ensure that those delivering this care are also supported. In the UK there are currently very limited mechanisms of support for personal assistants, and individuals employed in these roles may not be afforded the same sorts of employment protection that they would have previously been, had they been employed directly by the state. Similar patterns have also been observed in many of the other countries who are also employing cash for care schemes (Carr 2009).

A number of countries are struggling to fulfil the full array of social care positions that are available and find that many within their own population reject these types of low-paid jobs. Some developed countries are seeing an influx of migrant workers to take up these types of positions which clearly brings with it a range of challenges for the host country but also those countries where these workers come from (Cangiano et al. 2009). Many developed countries are seeing an influx of workers from less developed countries who are willing to take on roles that the host population sometimes see as less appealing but there can be issues over training, regulation and safety. There is also a further ethical dimension to this debate in the sense that we are drawing workers from countries where these people would likely have provided some sort of caring role within their own families. Not only are these individuals often displaced from their friends and families (which might provoke challenging social issues), but this could potentially leave families in other countries with less support for their needs. As yet it is far from clear what impact migrant workers might have, but in developed countries such as Canada, the USA, Australia and Germany, it is clear without these migrant workers, we would often find it very difficult to recruit sufficient staff to provide some care services. In the future it may be that we should try to think very differently about how we draw on workforces, particularly in terms of those who have reached retirement age but are still active and willing to become engaged with their local community in some way.

Conclusion

Health and social care are essential features of welfare systems, providing practical, crisis and ongoing support to millions of people each year. However, perhaps because they are so important, they are frequently a source of discussion, debate and controversy – for politicians, the media and members of the public alike. Most countries in recent years have made attempts to reform health and social care and modernize it in some ways.

During these changes, there have been ongoing difficulties and frequent discussion of particular 'hot topics'. However, underlying many of these debates is a deeper and often unspoken issue about the basis on which health and social care should be provided and reformed. As this chapter has illustrated, social care is an incredibly complex area of practice, but is an important partner to health in being able to deliver high quality care. Arguably social care will become an even more important partner in coming years if the health service is to tackle the types of pressures that arise from changing demographics and rising expectations. However difficult working together can sometimes be, not working together simply is not an option, given current financial and demographic pressures.

Summary box

- Social care is a key partner to the health service and is crucial to achieving a number of joint priorities.
- It is organized and has developed in very different ways, raising a series of practical barriers to joint working.
- An important distinction is often drawn between a 'social' and 'medical model'.
- Key hot topics include issues such as the future funding of long-term care, equity and the development of the personalization agenda.
- Changing demographics and rising expectations mean that joint working between health and social care will be even more important in future.

Self-test exercises

1 How is social care organized in your country and what debates are taking place about issues such as equity, funding, workforce and the relationship between the state, the family and the individual?

2 What impact are changing demography, technological advances and rising public expectations having on current services?

3 What could and should formal services be doing to support informal carers?

4 How well do health services and professionals work with social care and what could be done to improve this relationship?

References and further reading

Barnes, C. and Mercer, G. (2006) *Independent Futures: Creating User-led Disability Services in a Disabling Society.* Bristol: Policy Press/British Association of Social Worker.

Cangiano, A., Shutes, I., Spencer, S. and Leeson, G. (2009) *Migrant Care Workers in Ageing Societies: Report on Research Findings in the UK.* Oxford: Compas.

Carr, S. (2009) *The Implementation of Individual Budget Schemes in Adult Social Care.* London: Social Care Institute for Excellence.

Clasen, J. (2002) Modern social democracy and European welfare state reform. *Social Policy and Society,* 1: 67–76.

Dickinson, H. (2008) *Evaluating Outcomes in Health and Social Care.* Bristol: Policy Press.

Dickinson, H., Glasby, J., Forder, J. and Beesley, L. (2007) Free personal care in Scotland: a narrative review. *British Journal of Social Work*, 37: 459–74.

Duffy, S. (2003) *Keys to Citizenship*. London: Paradigm Consultancy and Development Agency.

Escobedo, A., Fernandez, E., Moreno, D. and Moss, P. (2002) *Surveying Demand, Supply and Use of Care Consolidated Report: Care Work in Europe*. London: Thomas Coram Research Unit, Institute of Education, University of London.

European Commission (2000) *Long-Term Care*. Luxembourg: European Commission.

European Foundation for the Improvement of Living and Working Conditions (2006) *Employment in Social Care in Europe*. Dublin: European Foundation for the Improvement of Living and Working Conditions.

Ferlie, E., Pettigrew, A., Ashburner, L. and Fitzgerald, L. (1996) *The New Public Management in Action*. Oxford: Oxford University Press.

French, S. (1993) Disability, impairment or something in between? In J. Swain, V. Finkelstein, S. French and M. Oliver (eds) *Disabling Barriers – Enabling Environments*. London: Sage.

Glasby, J. and Littlechild, R. (2009) *Direct Payments and Personal Budgets: Putting Personalisation into Practice*. Bristol: Policy Press.

Glendinning, C. (2010) *Dartington Review on the Future of Adult Social Care: What Can England Learn from the Experiences of Other Countries?* Totnes: Research in Practice for Adults.

Jöel, M.-E. and Dickinson, H. (2009) The economics of integrated care. In J. Glasby and H. Dickinson (eds) *International Perspectives on Health and Social Care: Partnership Working in Action*. Oxford: Wiley-Blackwell.

Joseph Rowntree Foundation (2008) *Rethinking Social Care and Support: What Can England Learn from Other Countries?* York: Joseph Rowntree Foundation.

Kröger, T. (2003) *Families, Care and Social Work in Europe: SOCCARE*. Available at: http://www.uta.fi/laitokset/sospol/soccare/ (accessed 1 September 2010).

Lymbery, M. (2005) *Social Work with Older People*. London: Sage.

Means, R., Richards, S. and Smith, R. (2008) *Community Care: Policy and Practice*, 4th edn. Basingstoke: Palgrave Macmillan.

Means, R. and Smith, R. (1998) *From Poor Law to Community Care*. Basingstoke: Macmillan.

Munday, B. (2003) *European Social Services: A Map of Characteristics and Trends*. Council of Europe, available at: http://www.coe.int/...ocialrights/source/SocServ Eumap_en.doc (accessed 17 July 2010).

O'Brien, J. and Duffy, S. (2009) Self-directed support as a framework for partnership working. In J. Glasby and H. Dickinson (eds) *International Perspectives on Health and Social Care: Partnership Working in Action*. Oxford: Wiley-Blackwell.

Oliver, M. and Barnes, C. (1993) Discrimination, disability and welfare: from needs to rights. In J. Swain, V. Finkelstein, S. French, and M. Oliver (eds) *Disabling Barriers – Enabling Environment*. London: Sage.

Oliver, M. (1996) Defining impairment and disability: issues at stake. In C. Barnes and G. Mercer (eds) *Exploring the Divide: Illness and Disability*. Leeds: The Disability Press.

Oliver, M. and Barnes, C. (1998) *Disabled People ad Social Policy: From Exclusion to Inclusion.* Harlow: Longman.

Oliver, M. and Sapey, B. (1993) *Social work with Disabled People*, 3rd edn. Basingstoke: Palgrave Macmillan.

Payne, M. (2005) *The Origins of Social Work: Continuity and Change.* Basingstoke: Palgrave.

Pilgrim, D. and Rogers, A. (2010) *A Sociology of Mental Health and Illness*, 4th edn. Buckingham: Open University Press.

Rogers, A. and Pilgrim, D. (2001) *Mental Health Policy in Britain*, 2nd edn. Basingstoke: Palgrave Macmillan.

Rogers, A. and Pilgrim, D. (2003) *Mental Health and Ineqalities.* Basingstoke: Palgrave Macmillan.

Websites and resources

Key national websites include:

The European Interprofessional Education Network in health and social care. The network focuses on interprofessional education (IPE) in health and social care because this is of international interest, and a specific concern of partners: http://www.eipen.org/.

The European Social Network (ESN) brings together people who are key to the design and delivery of local public social services across Europe to learn from each other and contribute their experience and expertise to building effective social policy and practice: http://www.esn-eu.org/home/index.htm.

The General Social Care Council – responsible for registering social workers and maintaining appropriate professional standards: www.gscc.org.uk.

In Control – a national social innovation network responsible for developing the concept of personal budgets: www.in-control.org.uk.

The National Centre for Independent Living – the national organization of disabled people supporting the development of direct payments: www.ncil.org.uk.

Social Care Institute for Excellence – tasked by government to identify and disseminate good practice in social care (website includes free access to the Social Care Online database): www.scie.org.uk.

For the history and development of social care, Payne (2005) describes the origins of social work (with helpful international material and a detailed list of relevant references and relevant websites).

For more recent social care developments, Means and Smith (1998) and Means et al. (2008) are key sources.

Key texts on specific user groups include:

- Lymbery's (2005) *Social Work with Older People*.
- Books by Rogers and Pilgrim (2001, 2003; Pilgrim and Rogers 2010) on mental health services.

- Textbooks by disabled academics and campaigners such as Michael Oliver (Oliver 1996; Oliver and Sapey 2006) and Colin Barnes (Barnes and Mercer 2006; Oliver and Barnes 1998) for services for disabled people.
- Duffy's (2003) *Keys to Citizenship* for services for people with learning difficulties.

Healthcare organizations

Purchasing healthcare

Judith Smith and Juliet Woodin

Introduction

Purchasing and contracting (also sometimes described as commissioning) are complex and much debated features of many healthcare systems today. This chapter initially explores purchasing, contracting and commissioning through an account of the healthcare policy context within which they have developed, as a backcloth to understanding how the terms are commonly defined and understood. The key elements of purchasing and contracting will then be described, and the technical difficulties of implementing such systems in healthcare discussed. The chapter then considers how purchasing is designed and organized within health systems to deliver this complex role. Next, the chapter examines the evidence about purchasing as a lever for change and in achieving health system goals. In conclusion, an examination is made of the overall challenges for health purchasing within health systems.

The health policy context

Organized healthcare systems are complex entities and include a number of fundamental functions and roles, which are shown in Box 14.1. In insurance-based systems, such as the United States of America (USA), Germany and the Netherlands, the insurance organization (the third party payer) is usually separate from the provider of services, although there are also examples of integration in the USA (Enthoven and Tollen 2005). In tax-funded, publicly run systems such as the United Kingdom, Sweden and New Zealand, third party payers and service providers have traditionally been located largely within the same organization.

During the last decades of the twentieth century healthcare reforms took place in many developed healthcare systems, which made changes to the third party payer role and its relationship with the provider role. These trends during the 1970s to 1990s can be seen as consisting of two phases: during the late 1970s and early 1980s a focus on cost containment at the macro level; then during the late 1980s and early 1990s, a focus on micro efficiency and responsiveness to users, including the introduction of market-like mechanisms, management reforms and budgetary incentives (Ham 1997, 2008). The development of purchasing as a function was a key part of this second phase and

---

Box 14.1: *Roles in the healthcare system – a conceptual framework*

Principal funder   The citizen or consumer of healthcare who provides the funds – directly or indirectly – to pay for healthcare.

Third party payer   The organization that buys healthcare on behalf of the individual citizen or consumer. This may be the government itself, a public body such as a health board, physician network or an insurance fund, an employer, or some other form of association. Where the individual buys their own care direct from a healthcare provider, there is no third party payer. This role is often referred to as the 'purchasing' or 'commissioning' role.

Provider   The organization or clinician delivering care to the patient.

Government   The generator of the national health strategy and priorities which form the framework within which the healthcare system operates.

Source: Adapted from Figueras et al. (2005a).

---

illustrates well the phenomenon known as the new public management (Ferlie 1996). NPM embodies the ideas of 'disaggregation of units in the public sector', 'greater competition in the public sector' 'explicit standards and measures of performance' and 'greater emphasis on output controls' (Hood 1991), all of which are features of a commissioning or contracting system.

In the UK, in 1991, an internal market was introduced into the formerly integrated, directly managed healthcare system (DH 1989). Health authorities and general practitioner (GP) fundholders took on a purchasing role and provision was strengthened through the creation of NHS trusts. After the devolution of political power to Scotland, Wales and Northern Ireland in 1999, the UK systems diverged, with Scotland and eventually Wales returning to a more integrated system, but England developed the internal market even further (Lewis et al. 2009). Similar developments can be observed in the New Zealand health system over the period of the 1990s and 2000s (Ashton et al. 2004; Barnett et al. 2009).

In Europe, there is considerable diversity among healthcare systems but purchasing or commissioning has become a feature of many (Dixon and Mossialos 2002; Figueras et al. 2005a). In the USA, purchasing was well established in a system based predominantly on insurance arrangements and private provision, but many initiatives attempted to strengthen the purchasing function, through the introduction of health plans and managed care, and through experimentation with new funding and contracting mechanisms, such as capitation funding (Rodriguez 1990; Enthoven 1994; Hughes et al. 1995; Light 1998; Chambers et al. 2004; Hummel and Cooper 2005).

More recently, debate in the USA has shifted to focus on the need for integrated delivery systems which are funded by payers who place the provider systems at risk for health outcomes, patient experience of services, and financial performance (e.g. Enthoven and Tollen 2005; Casalino 2011). This is being explored in the USA within the concept of an 'accountable care organization' (Fisher et al. 2009; 2007) which entails a group of clinicians (or a healthcare organization and its clinicians) taking on a budget for the health needs of an enrolled population, and being accountable for health outcomes of those people, together with budgetary and health service performance.

There have been a number of drivers for these reforms. In most industrialized countries, public spending has become a focus of attention, and particularly so in the context of a world economic recession. Added to this there has been a view, supported by survey evidence, that healthcare systems are often unresponsive to the needs of patients and public and need reform (Commonwealth Fund 2010). In some countries, political ideas were also a driver, with New Right politicians providing an ideological justification for a reform process which introduced market-type arrangements (Walsh 1995; Le Grand et al. 1998).

Whatever the underlying drivers, there has been burgeoning policy and academic interest in commissioning and contracting roles and processes, against the background of expectations that they will improve the efficiency and responsiveness of healthcare systems. The NHS in England has introduced a number of experiments with commissioning and contracting, which have been studied and reported on, and this chapter draws on research evidence from the NHS, as well as using examples from other health systems.

Definitions of commissioning, purchasing and contracting

The interest by health policy-makers in the role of the third party payer has given rise to a vocabulary of terms such as commissioning, contracting, purchasing and procurement. The dynamic and evolving nature of the role has, unsurprisingly but confusingly, led to different terminology being used in different contexts, or the same terms being given slightly different meanings. These differences appear in policy documents and academic literature alike. This chapter will in the main use the terms commissioning, purchasing and contracting, and will define commissioning as the broadest and most strategic set of activities and contracting as the narrowest. The definitions are given in Box 14.2.

Box 14.2: *Definitions*

- **Commissioning** is the set of linked activities required to assess the healthcare needs of a population, specify the services required to meet those needs within a strategic framework, secure those services, monitor and evaluate the outcomes.

- **Purchasing** is the process of buying or funding services in response to demand or usage.

- **Contracting** is the technical process of selecting a provider, negotiating and agreeing the terms of a contract for services, and ongoing management of the contract including payment, and monitoring variations.

- **Procurement** is the process of identifying a supplier and may involve, for example, competitive tendering, competitive quotation, single sourcing. It may also involve stimulating the market through awareness raising and education.

Commissioning is a term used most in the English NHS context and tends to denote a proactive strategic role in planning, designing and implementing the range of services required, rather than a more passive purchasing role. A commissioner decides which services or healthcare interventions should be provided, who should provide them and how they should be paid for, and may work closely with the provider in implementing changes. A purchaser buys what is on offer or reimburses the provider on the basis of usage.

Procurement and contracting focus on one specific part of the process – the selection, negotiation and agreement with the provider of the exact terms upon which the service is to be supplied. Procurement usually refers to the process of provider sourcing and selection, and contracting to the establishment and negotiation of the contract documentation.

These definitions are similar to those offered by Øvretveit, although his definition of commissioning is even wider, incorporating activities which do not involve payment for services, such as influencing other agencies to promote the health of the population (Øvretveit 1995). These broader activities are indeed very likely to be undertaken by organizations designated as 'commissioners', for it is in their interests to encourage others to undertake health-promoting activities and thus reduce the call on healthcare services.

Finally, it should be noted that in much of the literature describing the US, European and New Zealand health systems the term most frequently used for third party payers is 'purchasing'. Yet the role described increasingly displays the more strategic proactive characteristics associated with 'commissioning' in the English NHS context. When referring to international experience the term 'purchasing' will inevitably hold a wider meaning.

Commissioning and contracting in theory and practice

As experience and evidence have accumulated about the implementation of internal market reforms to public services during the 1990s and 2000s, a number of books have been published which provide a comprehensive analysis of the theory and practice of commissioning and contracting, primarily in the UK context (for example, Øvretveit 1995; Flynn and Williams 1997; Le Grand et al. 1998; Bamford 2001; Mays et al. 2001; Smith et al. 2010). There is not space in this chapter to cover the breadth and detail of these texts, but a brief overview of the tasks and processes involved in commissioning and contracting follows.

The commissioning cycle

As described above, commissioning consists of a set of linked activities. There are many ways of modelling the commissioning process, such as cycles, task lists and levels (Øvretveit 1995: 71–3). The presentation of commissioning as a cycle of activity has become well established, especially in England where it has been used by the Department of Health to describe the intention of the commissioning function, so this will be adopted as the starting point for this section, as illustrated in Figure 14.1.

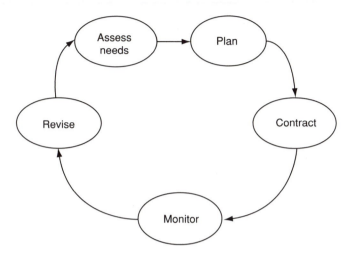

FIGURE 14.1 The commissioning cycle
Source: Adapted from Department of Health (2003).

This cycle is a simplified model of a process which is in reality far more complex, containing many tasks and activities which cannot always be addressed sequentially as the cycle suggests, and often take place concurrently with each other. Box 14.3 illustrates some of the more specific tasks that go to make up the main stages of the cycle.

Contracts

Contracts fulfil a number of functions within a commissioning or purchasing system: they bring together details of the services required (the specification), the price to be paid, quality standards to be met, information to be collected and supplied, monitoring arrangements, mechanisms for variation and review of the contract, the duration of the agreement and so on. Their purpose has been summed up as follows:

> Contracts are the most visible and practical part of purchasing. They are a key tool that defines the relationship between principals (purchasers) and agents (providers). They can be used to reflect the purchaser's health objectives and the health needs of the population, and to make clear what services are to be provided and under which terms. They also have an important function in specifying the risk-sharing arrangements that apply to either the purchaser of provider in the event of unplanned events.
>
> (Duran et al. 2005: 187)

The different types of contract typically used within healthcare are summarized in Box 14.4.

Box 14.3: *Commissioning and contracting activities*

Main stage of cycle	Activities
Assess needs	• Quantification of need based on epidemiological studies, census data, mortality and morbidity rates and other population data • Quantification of need based on health records of registered population/members • Identification of evidence-based interventions • Patient surveys and focus groups • Professional and stakeholder views.
Plan	• Review of current provision • Gap analysis • Prioritization • Assessment of market capacity • Specification of services required including quality standards
Contract	• Educating the market • Competitive tendering • Determination of contract currency • Negotiation with providers on volume quality and price • Terms and conditions of contract • Arrangements for variations • Determination of routine monitoring requirements.
Monitor	• Reconciliation of invoices • Payment • Analysis of information provided • Reporting and investigation of trends and variances • Contract monitoring meetings • Agreement to variations • Payment.
Revise	• Adjust contract volumes, price and other aspects in accordance with terms and conditions • Feed trend and usage information through to longer-term needs assessment and planning cycle.

How best should services be specified?

It is perhaps self-evident that in order to place a contract, it is necessary to define the product to be purchased. The specification forms the basis of the contract and monitoring of delivery. Designing service specifications in healthcare is one of the most challenging parts of the commissioning cycle because the product is in many cases

Box 14.4: *Types of contract*

Type of contract	Description	Use
Block	Like a budget for a service. The purchaser or commissioner agrees to pay a fee in exchange for access to a broadly defined range of services. Volumes may not be mentioned or may only be indicative	When costing and activity information is scarce
Cost and volume	Payment is related to treatment of a specified number of patients in a given specialty or service. Payment arrangements for activity above or below the specified volume are defined in the contract.	When reliable information is available to monitor activity and volumes are relatively high
Cost per case	A cost is set for an individual item of service or care package.	For high-cost care which occurs relatively infrequently.

Source: Adapted from Savas et al. (1998).

difficult to define and describe in a precise way (Flynn and Williams 1997). These difficulties relate to:

- definition of services at a macro level;
- the currency used to describe activity and interventions;
- the pace of change of healthcare technology;
- provider dominance.

The first difficulty is defining healthcare provision at a macro level. For the purposes of policy, strategy and planning, healthcare is traditionally subdivided or categorized largely on the basis of the professional expertise that delivers the services (e.g. by medical specialty such as general surgery, or ophthalmology, or professional group such as district nursing or physiotherapy). These descriptions reflect the way in which services are conventionally organized and delivered, and not necessarily how a commissioner may wish services to be designed for the future.

Health system reform seeks to streamline patient care, removing inefficiencies that occur at organizational and professional boundaries and becoming more responsive to patient experience. Other ways of specifying services have therefore become attractive to commissioners. For example, they may design service specifications by reference to the client group to be served (e.g. mental health services, children's services, older people's services), or as disease or condition based (such as diabetes services, cancer services, coronary heart disease services, long-term medical conditions). These categorizations enable all the relevant service elements for that client or disease group to be included, whether they are supplied by primary, community, secondary or tertiary care organizations. Specifying services in this way raises new boundary issues, for many people, especially those who consume most health resources, and experience multiple health conditions.

The second difficulty is in finding a common and meaningful currency in which service activity and interventions can be described. There are many options: diagnosis-related groups; consultant or specialist treatment episodes; hospital stays; outpatient attendances; specific operations; complex care packages; capitation (i.e. the number of individuals for whom comprehensive care must be provided); patient pathways (where the specification describes the care process for a given condition which providers must follow); and outcomes of care in terms of improved health status.

Commentators have debated the merits and feasibility of some of these (Buckland 1994; Soderland 1994; Kindig 1997). It is generally agreed that some aspects of healthcare activity are more straightforward to specify than others; in particular, elective hospital inpatient activity as opposed to community health services, where interaction between professional and patient is key to the service (Flynn et al. 1996).

The rapid pace of change of healthcare technology provides a further challenge for service specification. New drugs and medical technologies, research evidence about existing treatments and new disease patterns are all part of the fluid environment in which healthcare systems operate. It is not possible therefore to specify service requirements with certainty very far into the future. Service specifications date rapidly and this contains risks for the contracting parties.

A further issue related to service specification, which probably compounds the difficulties referred to above, is that in many systems knowledge and expertise about healthcare provision are concentrated in the supplier organizations, a factor often termed 'asymmetry of information'. Commissioners may not have the detailed understanding of services to specify them fully, and incomplete or flawed contract documentation may result. Alternatively, as case studies of the early years of the internal market in the UK showed, purchasing organizations may rely upon providers to write their service specifications, which not only reinforces the tendency towards passive purchasing rather than active strategic commissioning but also undermines the credibility of the purchaser (Dopson and Locock 2002; Short and Norwood 2003).

Making contracts effective

The contract is a key part of any commissioning or purchasing process, but its value is not as an end in its own right but as a means of implementing the strategies and plans of the commissioner. Although contracts are in place in many healthcare systems today, they suffer from number of limitations (Ferlie and McGivern 2003). Among these are two areas which will be commented on here:

- information deficits
- enforcement issues.

The information deficits affecting contracts largely mirror those related to service specifications. The problem in many systems is that data collection systems are not sufficiently developed to support the monitoring of activity through contracts. Although some commentators argue that data are available but not systematically used (Soderland 1994), there is agreement that many aspects of healthcare are simply not covered by current systems in a meaningful way.

Costing systems contain similar difficulties, especially in tax-funded healthcare systems. A further issue is the management of risk within the contract. The introduction of formal contracts requires arrangements to be agreed about how increases in activity over and above the contracted volume are to be dealt with. The reduction of this risk through predictive modelling is an established technique in predominantly privatized insurance systems such as the USA (Chambers et al. 2004), but is now being used more extensively in systems such as the UK (Billings et al. 2006).

Effective contracts contain mechanisms such as financial incentives, penalties, and the ultimate possibility of termination, which can be used to steer the provider in the direction required or to move to an alternative supplier, a feature that has been termed 'contestability' (Ham 1996). Healthcare contracts may be commercial, legally enforceable contracts – as in the USA, New Zealand in the early years of the reforms there (Ashton et al. 2004), and between English NHS commissioners and foundation trusts or independent providers – or may be internal service agreements. In principle, both types are enforceable: the former with recourse to the courts if necessary and the latter through managerial action. However, there is evidence that in the UK commissioners have been discouraged from enforcement action that would destabilize an NHS provider and that this has impeded the use of contract-type instruments to achieve change (Walsh 1995; Smith et al. 2010). Finally, the extent to which a real market exists will affect a commissioner's scope to enforce contract penalties. If there are no alternative suppliers in the market, the threat of termination will be hollow.

Relational contracting

Although it can be argued that better constructed, written and legally enforceable contracts would have benefits for health systems (Ferlie and McGivern 2003), the real problems and constraints associated with formal or 'hard' contracting in a healthcare context suggest that there are likely to be ongoing obstacles to the achievement of this aim. In addition, there are significant transaction costs associated with establishing a contractual environment which must be set against any benefits gained (Light 1998; Light and Dixon 2004).

These issues point to the importance of recognizing the role that the wider context of relationships, including trust, common values and established and new networks, play in the operation of healthcare systems (Lapsley and Llewellyn 1997; Shaw et al. 2006). Some writers identify the potential for conflict when commissioner–provider relationships and formal contracting are introduced into pre-existing trust-based relationships, for example:

> The development of trust is central to the maintenance of social systems, and the danger of contract is that it undermines trust, through basing contracts on punishment for failure. If we undermine trust then we may

find that the making of agreements, and ensuring that they are kept, will become very costly. The value of trust is that it is cheaper to trust people, and to develop institutions that will ensure trust, rather than to watch them. Control and influence over producers may go along with trust and the development of distrust make efficient public service impossible to attain.

(Walsh 1995: 255)

However, a number of other writers (Bennett and Ferlie 1996; Ferlie 1996; Flynn et al. 1996; Hodgson and Hoile 1996; Dopson and Locock 2002; Ferlie and McGivern 2003; Ashton et al. 2004; Forder et al. 2005) have observed trust and informal contact continuing to play an important part in commissioner–provider relationships in healthcare alongside a formal contract or service agreement.

A caveat to the discussion about relational contracting is that such relationships cannot be understood without reference to the distribution of power within the system (Cox et al. 2003). Reference has already been made to the dominance of providers in the design of service specifications and this is a broader issue:

Purchasing in health care is highly vulnerable to provider capture. After all, they control the technology, make the diagnosis, control what is ordered, and control the information that the buyers need. Thus it has been a long struggle for American commissioning groups of employers to learn how to do it effectively.

(Light 1998: 14)

The application of relational contracting ideas to healthcare is an interesting area but one which as yet has not been subjected to systematic analysis or development, taking account of the relative power of the parties.

The commissioning organization

Discussion of the practical realities of commissioning and contracting for healthcare begs the question of who, or what type of organization, should be charged with this challenging and difficult role. There is considerable debate about the effectiveness of the variety of types of purchasing organization found in different healthcare systems. Employers, commercial insurance companies, sick funds, mutual associations, groups of healthcare professionals and the national or local state in various forms all take on the purchasing or commissioning role (Dixon and Mossialos 2002).

The NHS in England has seen a vigorous debate about the appropriate organizational model for commissioning, which has been accompanied by frequent restructuring (Walshe et al. 2004; Smith et al. 2010). Locality-based models have been favoured since the mid-1990s, including small-scale, GP-led ones, largely because of the opportunities to build on the traditional strengths of UK primary care in demand management and the potential for joint commissioning with local government (Balogh 1996; Le Grand et al. 1998; Smith and Goodwin 2006).

However, the benefits of an approach based on programmes for specific client groups or conditions, which often need a larger population base, have also been argued

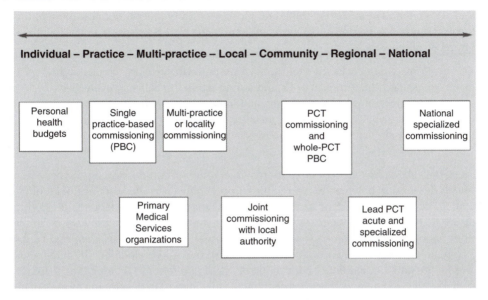

FIGURE 14.2 Continuum of commissioning in the NHS in England in 2010
Source: Adapted from Smith et al. 2004.

(Chappel et al. 1999). The evidence and arguments about the effectiveness of different organizational models are fully examined by Smith and colleagues (2004, 2010) who conclude that a mix of approaches is needed in each health economy in the light of the services involved and context, resulting in a 'continuum of commissioning' rather than any 'one size fits all' solution. A worked example of the continuum of commissioning for the NHS in England in 2010 is set out in Figure 14.2.

The concept of the purchaser–provider split implies a clear separation of roles and functions. However, as noted earlier in our discussion about accountable care organizations, many systems display some degree of integration of the two. In the USA, the growth of managed care has resulted in organizational forms which provide some services in-house and purchase others externally (Enthoven 1994; Fisher et al. 2007; Light and Dixon 2004). In the UK, GP fund holding, then primary care groups, practice-based commissioning and, from 2012, GP commissioning build on the gatekeeping role of primary care by giving general practitioners a central role in commissioning, and displaying only a partial separation of functions (given that GPs are at once providers and commissioners of care). Similar approaches have been developed in Canada and New Zealand (Peckham 1999; Smith and Mays 2007).

Linked with this debate about separation or integration is a related one about whether commissioning should be primary care-led or not. In the UK, the introduction of GP fundholding from 1991 onwards paved the way for further development of primary-care led commissioning, so that by 2005 the majority of services in England were commissioned by primary care organizations. A number of studies of primary care-led purchasing have identified an impact on services, albeit modest (Le Grand et al. 1998; Smith et al. 2004; Smith and Goodwin 2006). Internationally, though, this is not a common approach and Light commenting from a US perspective, has identified a number of drawbacks:

> Primary care lacks the clout to take on powerful specialty groups and hospitals; the technical skills and infrastructure to challenge ineffective or inefficient practices; the time and training to carry out this complex task; the ability to address inequalities and wasteful practices in primary care itself.
>
> (1998: 72)

The debate about the extent of separation or integration of commissioning and provision reflects the tension between two principles: impartiality and independence of commissioning, versus integration of care. In a market situation, independence is needed to ensure that the commissioner selects the most cost-effective service provision. On the other hand, managing some services directly (usually at the primary care end of the care pathway) may enable commissioners to improve micro-efficiency by integrating care for the patient, and better controlling demand and referrals (Forder et al. 2005).

In the NHS in England, there has been increasing interest in developing models of integrated provision and commissioning along the lines of accountable care organizations in the USA, with authors arguing that such arrangements are not anti-competitive, but rather that they offer the possibility of patients being able to choose between providers who offer care that is integrated across primary and secondary care (e.g. Smith et al. 2009; Lewis et al. 2010; Curry and Ham 2010).

Wherever commissioning is located, the organization must possess sufficient capacity and capability to commission effectively. Smith et al. (2010: 8–9) identify the following features which affect commissioners' ability to exert influence:

- incentives for clinicians to be involved in commissioning (real budgets and responsibility);
- size of commissioning organization;
- management and analytical capability and capacity;
- sophisticated information systems;
- involvement of secondary care as well as primary care clinicians;
- appropriate accountability to local people and patients;
- financial flexibility in relation to payment approach;
- careful risk-adjustment of budgets; and
- an acceptance that there is no one optimal model of commissioning.

Some of these characteristics are matters of policy (for example, whether or not a budget is held) but others flow from the size and characteristics of the commissioning organization, particularly from the information at its disposal and the skills and capabilities of its staff. Many commissioning organizations in tax-funded systems have evolved from their more bureaucratic and hierarchical predecessors with little attention paid to whether they are appropriately staffed or skilled for their new role. Casalino (2011:19) in a study reflecting on the experience of independent practice associations (IPAS) in the USA and the lessons they hold for primary care-led commissioning in the UK comments:

> Successful IPAs have skilled leaders and invest in leadership, management, and infrastructure (Thorlby et al. 2011). . . . Physicians in the U.S. tend to grossly underestimate the amount of investment that is necessary; focus on their current income and dislike reducing their current income to pay for things that they do not value, that is leadership, management, and infrastructure.

Other writers have endorsed this point about management support, and added competencies such as negotiation, political sensitivity, knowledge of needs and demands of the population, quality management, service improvement, awareness of evidence on effectiveness and cost effectiveness of different interventions, team working, understanding of ethics, and leadership (Mays and Dixon 1996; Jackson 1998; Bamford 2001; Kaufman 2002; Velasco-Garrido et al. 2005; Smith et al. 2010; Thorlby et al. 2011). While some of these are general management skills, and not inherently lacking in the evolving purchasing or commissioning organizations, others are more commercially oriented and may not be present in public sector bodies. Little investment has been made by governments into providing training and development which could ameliorate this.

The frequent restructuring of commissioning organizations mentioned earlier has not been confined to England, and other systems such as New Zealand and Sweden have experienced requirements to change commissioning arrangements. Organizational restructuring has impeded the development of a cohort of skilled and experienced commissioning staff, changed the flow of information, and caused a loss of organizational knowledge.

The impact of commissioning

Having considered the theory and the practice of commissioning and contracting, this section discusses the evidence on the strategic impact and effectiveness of commissioning.

The goals of commissioning reflect health system goals. Efficiency, responsiveness, health improvement and quality, while not a comprehensive list and not always mutually compatible, are relevant to most systems and form a basis for the evaluation of the effectiveness and impact of commissioning (Le Grand et al. 1998; Figueras et al. 2005b; Smith and Curry, forthcoming).

Commissioning for efficiency

The evidence as to whether commissioning has improved system efficiency in any sense is mixed. The OECD states: 'In systems where both financing and delivery of care is a public responsibility, efforts to distinguish the roles of health-care payers and providers, so as to allow markets to function and generate efficiencies from competition, have proved generally effective' (2004: 17). The purchaser–provider separation appeared, in the 1990s and 2000s, to be widely accepted and little challenged in the English NHS, although Scotland and later Wales have abandoned such a split in favour of integrated funder/provider health boards.

Le Grand and colleagues, examining the NHS internal market of the 1990s, noted an increase in efficiency as measured by the cost per unit of activity, but found little evidence to demonstrate whether this had been caused by the reforms or by other factors (Le Grand et al. 1998). Ham made similar observations about the complexity involved in ascribing specific achievements to commissioning, as opposed to the wider set of policy mechanisms, in a review of international experience of health purchasing (Ham 2008: 7):

> Commissioning is only one element in the programme of health reforms and its impact will be affected by how other elements are taken forward. ... much will hinge on providers having autonomy over their own affairs and the ability to respond rapidly to changing market conditions. Similarly, the impact of commissioners will be influenced by the payment systems that are in place, the strengths of the incentives contained within these payment systems, the arrangements for market management and regulation ... , and the degree to which politicians are willing to 'let go' and allow commissioners to exercise their leverage, even if the consequences are unpopular with the public.

However, Ashton and colleagues (2004) found no evidence of major efficiency gains in the hospital sector following the introduction of market reforms in New Zealand. A review of purchasing in the US system in 1996 concluded that 'it is too soon to conclude that purchasers in every market are in the driver's seat guiding changes in the health market' and 'despite some impressive reductions in the rate of health care premium growth, it remains unclear whether these lower annual growth rates are the result of purchaser pressure or are due to exogenous factors at work in the health care market place' (Lipson and de Sa 1996: 75–6).

Several commentators identify the transaction costs incurred by systems that separate purchasers from providers, and Light points to a range of new inefficiencies, including 'managerialism, datamania, accountability as an end, disruptions and inefficiencies of underused losers and overused winners and an ethos of commercialism replacing ethos of service' (Light 1997: 322).

Commissioning for responsiveness

Purchasing or commissioning organizations are by definition third-party payers acting on behalf of a population or membership. Where purchasing or commissioning has been introduced as a system reform, there have been formal expectations that commissioning organizations will engage with their populations or membership and demonstrate responsiveness to their requirements. The mechanisms for doing this can be categorized as 'voice' and 'exit' (den Exter 2005); the former broadly meaning the use of administrative and managerial techniques for hearing what patients and the public want, and the latter building in market-type mechanisms which give patients maximum opportunity to choose their care.

A review of international experience identified many examples of initiatives which facilitate patients or members of the public to influence purchasers, either through the exercise of 'voice' or 'choice'. However, it was not clear how far these mechanisms resulted in changes in the purchaser's policies or improvements in services in response to the issues raised (den Exter 2005). Similar conclusions were drawn in relation to the UK health reforms of the 1990s (Le Grand et al. 1998) and the 2000s (Smith and Curry forthcoming).

There are a number of reasons why this may be the case. Commissioning organizations in systems with strong national direction are constrained by nationally determined policies and targets and the scope to respond to the priorities of local populations may be limited. Purchasers may have concerns about the legitimacy of the views of those members of the public who engage in consultation and involvement exercises, and there are costs involved in the proper organization of patient and public involvement which purchasers may not consider justified (see Chapter 18 about user involvement for more discussion).

The emphasis on clinical involvement in commissioning in many healthcare systems (e.g. Siverbo 2005) may be in tension with public involvement, in terms both of beliefs and understandings about what constitutes valid evidence of need and benefit, the clinical focus on the individual patient as opposed to the population or group focus, and in terms of established patterns of collaborative or non-collaborative behaviour (Peckham 1999). Finally, poor information systems impede the ability of commissioners to provide precise and meaningful accounts of their activities to the public on whose behalf they are acting.

Commissioning for health improvement

The tendency of contracting to focus on the available measures of activity, which are usually rather limited input measures as described earlier, has stimulated calls for a greater focus on the desired end product of health services: improved outcomes based on the commissioning of evidence-based services (Kindig 1997; Ham 2008; Smith et al. 2009; Department of Health 2010). Studies of commissioning in the UK illustrate that in practice, however, there have been difficulties in translating strategies for health improvement into action through contracts. Case studies of the implementation of a strategy for stroke services (North 1998) and maternity services (Dopson and Locock 2002) demonstrate that in practice there has been a discontinuity between the needs assessment and planning stages of the cycle and the contracting stage. Contracts departments tended to focus on annual negotiation of volumes and prices of activity, while public health and planning functions considered the changes in services required in the longer term to meet the needs of the population (Milner and Meekings 1996). Implementing service change was not the main focus of contracting activity, and where it did occur, change tended to be at the margin.

Studies of GP fundholding do show that fundholders used contracting to achieve service changes but again this tended to be small scale and localized rather than strategic (Croxson et al. 2001; Propper et al. 2002; Smith et al. 2004).

Commissioning for quality

There has been a growing interest across European health systems in improving the quality of health services through more effective purchasing (Figueras et al. 2005a). Reviews of quality in the early stages of the NHS internal market comment on the limited attention paid to quality in the purchasing process, as opposed to the focus on activity and price (Gray and Donaldson 1996; Thomson et al. 1996; Glennester 1998; BRI Inquiry Secretariat 1999). However, a later review of international experience identified a range of examples in France, Germany, Italy and the UK of quality being made an issue in contracts (Velasco-Garrido et al. 2005). The development in the NHS of the Quality and Outcomes Framework (DH 2004) as part of the new General Medical Services contract for GPs, has provided a mechanism for linking payment to the achievement of defined quality standards, both clinical and organizational, albeit that its appropriateness in relation to be able to influence key health priorities and improve the quality of primary care is subject to some international debate.

In terms of the effectiveness of commissioning in achieving the goal of improved quality, evidence is mixed. Le Grand and colleagues (1998) and Smith and colleagues (2004) concluded that GP fundholders obtained greater provision of outreach services, quicker admission for their patients and generally more response from providers, compared with those non-fundholding GPs whose services were commissioned for them by health authorities.

Despite a major focus on quality improvement in the USA, a review found little evidence of impact (Goldfarb et al. 2003). An international review of quality-based purchasing concluded that 'there is some evidence of public-sector purchasers acting as agents to improve quality, but there is almost no documentation of either formal-sector private insurers, or community-based health financing schemes promoting quality through purchasing' and highlighted the 'large knowledge gaps concerning the results of initiatives taken' (Waters et al. 2004).

Conclusion

Commissioning and contracting have been introduced into health systems against a background of high expectations and within an environment of significant social and economic challenge. There has been little sustained and systematic evaluation of their impact, and in any case evaluation of such policy interventions is fraught with difficulties, including the regular reorganization of commissioning arrangements in countries such as England, and the difficulties in ascribing improvements in health or health services to commissioning as opposed to wider reform mechanisms (Le Grand et al. 1998; Figueras et al. 2005a; Ham 2008; Smith and Curry forthcoming).

Such evidence as exists of the success or otherwise of commissioning and contracting is mixed. This is unsurprising given the complexity of the task, the relative youth of the roles and organizations and the limited attention paid to organizational development. What is clear is that commissioning organizations have struggled to assert their authority vis-à-vis provider organizations, which are able to exert influence through their detailed knowledge of services, their control of information, the power and influence vested in their medical staff and the public support which they enjoy. In the context of this imbalance of power, the commissioning role needs further investment and development in order to realize its potential, especially at a time when health services internationally need to be transformed in ways that enable them to meet the challenge of rising chronic disease (see Chapter 10) and a tighter economic context (see Chapter 3) .

Summary box

1 The separation of purchasing and providing roles and the establishment of contractual relationships between health commissioners and providers have been features of healthcare system reform in many countries during the past two decades.

2 This separation is typically expected to provide a means of controlling costs and generating greater efficiency and to make healthcare systems more responsive to public requirements.

3 Commissioning and contracting are relatively straightforward concepts in theory, but there are technical difficulties associated with implementing contracting in the healthcare context. In particular, there are a number of problems with the design of meaningful service specifications and contracts.

4 Perhaps the most significant constraint on purchasing in healthcare is the imbalance of power and information between commissioners and providers.

5 The constraints on formal contracting and other features associated with healthcare systems suggest that commissioning and contractual relationships in healthcare display many of the characteristics of relational contracting.

6 The challenges of commissioning and contracting in all healthcare systems require strong and competent commissioning bodies, and extensive management support. The development of such bodies has been slow, impeded, especially in England, by frequent restructuring.

7 There is limited evidence that commissioning and contracting have successfully impacted on system efficiency and responsiveness. There has been considerable interest in their impact on other connected health system goals such as quality, and health improvement, but again evidence is limited.

8 This is hardly surprising given the relative youth of commissioning and contracting for health, the lack of consistent attention to the development of the function, and the inherent difficulties of evaluation.

Self-test exercises

1 Obtain a copy of a health service specification. Review it with the following points in mind:

- How adequate is the description of services?
- Does it link to the strategic objectives of the commissioning body?
- Is the service's activity described in relation to inputs, outputs or outcomes?
- Will data be available with which to monitor whether the service is being delivered?
- Generally, do you feel this specification provides a satisfactory basis for a contract?

2 Imagine you are the chief executive or clinical lead of a healthcare commissioning organization setting up a five-year prospective evaluation of the effectiveness of your commissioning process. Make a list of the dimensions and indicators you would ask the evaluators to monitor in order to provide the evidence you require.

3 Consider the advantages and disadvantages of operating a purchaser–provider split within a publicly funded health system, and set out a 'balance sheet' of these. What conclusions do you draw from this assessment? Would you recommend such a split of funding and provision for your own health system? If not, what would you suggest as an alternative approach to planning, funding and assuring the quality of health and health services?

References and further reading

Ashton, T., Cumming, J. and McLean, J. (2004) Contracting for health services in a public health system: the New Zealand experience. *Health Policy*, 69: 21–31.

Balogh, R. (1996) Exploring the role of localities in health commissioning: a review of the literature. *Social Policy and Administration*, 30(2): 99–113.

Bamford, T. (2001) *Commissioning and Purchasing*. London: Routledge.

Barnett, P., Tenbensel, T., Cumming, J. et al. (2009) Implementing new modes of governance in the New Zealand health system: an empirical study. *Health Policy*, 93: 118–27.

Bennett, C. and Ferlie, E. (1996) Contracting in theory and in practice: some evidence from the NHS. *Public Administration*, 74: 49–66.

Billings, J., Dixon, J., Mijanovich, T. and Wennberg, D. (2006) Risk stratification in the NHS. *BMJ*, 333: 327–30.

BRI Inquiry Secretariat (1999) *BRI Inquiry Paper on Commissioning, Purchasing, Contracting and Quality of Care in the NHS Internal Market*. London: The Stationery Office.

Buckland, R.W. (1994) Healthcare resource groups. *British Medical Journal*, 308(23): 1056.

Casalino, L. (2011) *GP Commissioning in the NHS in England: Ten Suggestions from the United States*. London: The Nuffield Trust.

Chambers, N., Kirkman-Liff, B. and Cassidy, M. (2004) Raising Arizona. *Health Service Journal*, 114(5920): 24–5.

Chappel, D., Miller, P., Parkin, D. and Thomson, R. (1999) Models of commissioning health services in the British National Health Service: a literature review. *Journal of Public Health Medicine*, 21(2): 221–7.

Commonwealth Fund (2010) *International Health Policy Survey in Eleven Countries*. New York: Commonwealth Fund.

Cox, A., Londsdale, C., Watson, G. and Qiao, H. (2003) Supplier relationship management: a framework for understanding managerial capacity and constraints. *European Business Journal*, 15(3): 135–45.

Croxson, B., Propper, C. and Perkins, A. (2001) Do doctors respond to financial incentives? *Journal of Public Health Economics*, 79: 375–98.

Curry, N. and Ham, C. (2010) *Clinical and Service Integration: The Route to Improved Outcomes*. London: The King's Fund.

den Exter, A.P. (2005) Purchasers as the public's agent. In J. Figueras, R. Robinson and E. Jakubowski (eds) *Purchasing to Improve Health Systems Performance*. Maidenhead: Open University Press.

Department of Health (1989) *Working for Patients*. London: The Stationery Office.

Department of Health (2003) *The NHS Contractors' Companion*. London: Department of Health.

Department of Health (2004) *Quality and Outcomes Framework Guidance*. London: Department of Health.

Department of Health (2010) *Equity and Excellence: Liberating the NHS*. London: Department of Health.

Dixon, A. and Mossialos, E. (2002) *Healthcare Systems in Eight Countries: Trends and Challenges*. London: European Observatory on Healthcare Systems.

Dopson, S. and Locock, L. (2002) The commissioning process in the NHS: the theory and application. *Public Management Review*, 4(2): 209–29.

Duran, A., Sheiman, I., Schneider, M. and Øvretveit, J. (2005) Purchasers, providers and contracts. In J. Figueras, R. Robinson and E. Jakubowski (eds) *Purchasing to Improve Health System Performance*. Maidenhead: Open University Press.

Enthoven, A.C. (1994) On the ideal market structure for third-party purchasing of health care. *Social Science and Medicine*, 39(10): 1413–24.

Enthoven, A.C. and Tollen, L. (2005) Competition in healthcare: it takes systems to pursue quality and efficiency. *Health Affairs*, 7 September.

Ferlie, E. (1996) *The New Public Management in Action*. Oxford: Oxford University Press.

Ferlie, E. and McGivern, G. (2003) *Relationships between Health Care Organisations: A Critical Overview of the Literature and a Research Agenda*. London: National Coordinating Centre for NHS Service Delivery and Organisation R&D.

Figueras, J., Robinson, R. and Jakubowski, E. (2005a) *Purchasing to Improve Health Systems Performance*. Maidenhead: Open University Press.

Figueras, J., Robinson, R. and Jakubowski, E. (2005b) Purchasing to improve health systems performance: drawing the lessons. In J. Figueras, R. Robinson and E. Jakubowski (eds) *Purchasing to Improve Health Systems Performance*. Maidenhead: Open University Press.

Fisher, E.S., McClellan, M.B., Bertko, J. et al. (2009). Fostering accountable health care: moving forward in Medicare. *Health Affairs*, 28(2): w219–w231.

Fisher, E., Staiger, D., Bynum, J. and Gottlieb, D. (2007) Creating accountable care organizations: the extended hospital medical staff. *Health Affairs* 26(1): w44–w57.

Flynn, R. and Williams, G. (1997) *Contracting for Health: Quasi-Markets and the National Health Service*. Oxford: Oxford University Press.

Flynn, R., Williams, G. and Pickard, S. (1996) *Markets and Networks: Contracting in Community Health Services*. Maidenhead: Open University Press.

Forder, J., Robinson, R. and Hardy, B. (2005) Theories of purchasing. In J. Figueras, R. Robinson and E. Jakubowski (eds) *Purchasing to Improve Health Systems Performance*. Maidenhead: Open University Press.

Glennester, H. (1998) Competition and quality in health care: the UK experience. *International Journal for Quality in Health Care*, 10(5): 403–10.

Goldfarb, N.I., Maio, V., Carter, C.T., Pizzi, L. and Nash, D.B. (2003) *How Does Quality Enter into Health Care Purchasing Decisions?* New York: Commonwealth Fund.

Gray, J.D.G. and Donaldson, L.J. (1996) Improving the quality of health care through contracting: a study of health authority practice. *Quality in Health Care*, 5: 201–5.

Ham, C.J. (1996) Contestability: a middle path for health care. *British Medical Journal*, 312: 70.

Ham, C.J. (1997) *Healthcare Reform: Learning from International Experience*. Maidenhead: Open University Press.

Ham, C.J (2008) *Health Care Commissioning in the International Context: Lessons from Experience and Evidence*. Birmingham: Health Services Management Centre.

Hodgson, K. and Hoile, R.W. (1996) *Managing Health Service Contracts*. London: W.B. Saunders.

Hood, C. (1991) A public management for all seasons? *Public Administration*, 69: 3–19.

Hughes, D., Stolzfus Jost, T., Griffiths, L. and McHale, J.V. (1995) Health care contracts in Britain and the United States: a case for technology transfer? *Journal of Nursing Management*, 3: 287–93.

Hummel, J.R. and Cooper, S.J. (2005) The managed care contract: the blueprint for monitoring agreements. *Healthcare Financial Management*, 55(6): 49–52.

Jackson, S. (1998) Skills required for healthy commissioning. *Health Manpower Management*, 24(1): 40–3.

Kaufman, G. (2002) Investigating the nursing contribution to commissioning in primary health-care. *Journal of Nursing Management*, 10: 83–94.

Kindig, D.A. (1997) *Purchasing Population Health*. Ann Arbor, MI: University of Michigan Press.

Lapsley, I. and Llewellyn, S. (1997) Statements of mutual faith: soft contracts in social care. In R. Flynn and G. Williams (eds) *Contracting for Health: Quasi-Markets and the National Health Service*. Maidenhead: Open University Press.

Le Grand, J., Mays, N. and Mulligan, J-A. (1998) *Learning from the NHS Internal Market: A Review of the Evidence.* London: King's Fund.

Lewis, R., Rosen, R., Goodwin, N. and Dixon, J. (2010) *Where Next for Integrated Care Organizations in the NHS in England?* London: the Nuffield Trust and the King's Fund.

Lewis, R., Smith, J.A. and Harrison, A. (2009) From quasi-market to market in the National Health Service in England: what does this mean for purchasing of health services? *Journal of Health Services Research and Policy,* 14(1): 44–51.

Light, D.W. (1997) From managed competition to managed cooperation: theory and lessons from the British experience. *Milbank Quarterly,* 75(3): 297–341.

Light, D.W. (1998) *Effective Commissioning: Lessons from Purchasing in American Managed Care.* London: Office of Health Economics.

Light, D.W. and Dixon, M. (2004) Making the NHS more like Kaiser Permanente. *British Medical Journal,* 328: 763.

Lipson, D.J. and de Sa, J.M. (1996) Impact of purchasing strategies on local health care systems. *Health Affairs,* 15(2): 62–76.

Mays, N. and Dixon, J. (1996) *Purchaser Plurality in Healthcare: Is a Consensus Emerging and Is It the Right One?* London: King's Fund.

Mays, N., Wyke, S., Malbon, G., and Goodwin, N. (eds) (2001) *The Purchasing of Health Care by Primary Care Organizations.* Buckingham: Open University Press.

Milner, P. and Meekings, J. (1996) Failings of the purchaser–provider split. *Journal of Public Health Medicine,* 18(4): 379–80.

North, N. (1998) Implementing strategy: the politics of healthcare commissioning. *Policy and Politics,* 26(1): 5–14.

OECD (2004) *Towards High Performing Health Systems.* Paris: OECD.

Øvretveit, J. (1995) *Purchasing for Health: A Multidisciplinary Introduction to the Theory and Practice of Health Purchasing.* Maidenhead: Open University Press.

Peckham, S. (1999) Primary care puchasing: are integrated primary care provider/purchasers the way forward? *Pharmacoeconomics,* 15(3): 209–16.

Propper, C., Croxson, B. and Shearer, A. (2002) Waiting times for hospital admissions: the impact of GP fundholding. *Journal of Health Economics,* 21: 227–52.

Rodriguez, A.R. (1990) Directions in contracting for psychiatric services managed care firms. *The Psychiatric Hospital,* 21(4): 165–70.

Roland, M., Dusheiko, M., Gravelle, H. and Parker, S. (2005) Follow up of people aged 65 and over with a history of emergency admissions: analysis of routine admission data. *British Medical Journal,* 330(7486): 289–92.

Savas, S., Sheiman, I., Tragakes, E. and Maarse, H. (1998) Contracting models and provider competition. In R.B. Saltman, J. Figueras and C. Sakellarider (eds) *Critical Challenges for Health Care Reform in Europe.* Maidenhead: Open University Press.

Shaw, S.E., Ashcroft, J. and Petchey, R.P. (2006). Developing sustainable relationships for health improvement: the case of public health and primary care in the UK. *Critical Public Health,* 16(1): 7388.

Short, D. and Norwood, J. (2003) Why is high-tech healthcare at home purchasing underdeveloped and what could be done to improve it? *Health Services Management Research,* 16(2): 127–35.

Siverbo, S. (2005) The purchaser–provider split in principle and practice: experiences from Sweden. *Financial Accountability and Management*, 20(4): 401–20.

Smith, J. and Curry, N. (forthcoming) Commissioning. In A. Dixon and N. Mays (eds) *Review of the Evidence of the NHS under Labour, 1997–2010*. London: the King's Fund.

Smith, J., Curry, N., Mays, N. and Dixon, J. (2010) *Where Next for Commissioning in the English NHS?* London: the Nuffield Trust and the King's Fund.

Smith, J. and Goodwin, N. (2006) *Towards Managed Primary Care: The Role and Experience of Primary Care Organizations*. Aldershot: Ashgate Publishing.

Smith, J. and Mays, N. (2007) Primary care organizations in New Zealand and England: tipping the balance of the health system in favour of primary care? *International Journal of Health Planning and Management*, 22: 3–19.

Smith, J., Mays, N., Dixon, J. et al. (2004) *A Review of the Effectiveness of Primary Care-Led Commissioning and its Place in the UK NHS*. London: Health Foundation.

Smith, J., Wood, J. and Elias, J. (2009) *Beyond Practice-Based Commissioning: The Local Clinical Partnership*. London: the Nuffield Trust and the NHS Alliance.

Soderland, N. (1994) Product definition for healthcare contracting: an overview of approaches to measuring hospital output with reference to the UK internal market. *Journal of Epidemiology and Community Health*, 48: 224–31.

Starfield, B. and Mangin, D. (2010) An international perspective on the basis of pay for performance. *Quality in Primary Care*, 18(6): 399–404.

Thomson, R., Elcoat, C. and Pugh, E. (1996) Clinical audit and the purchaser–provider interaction: different attitudes and expectations in the United Kingdom. *Quality in Health Care*, 5: 97–103.

Thorlby, R., Rosen, R. and Smith, J. (2011) *GP Commissioning: Insights from Medical Groups in the United States*. London: The Nuffield Trust.

Velasco-Garrido, M., Borowitz, M., Øvretveit, J. and Busse, R. (2005) Purchasing for quality of care. In J. Figueras, R. Robinson and E. Jakubowski (eds) *Purchasing to Improve Health Systems Performance*. Maidenhead: Open University Press.

Walsh, K. (1995) *Public Services and Market Mechanisms: Competition, Contracting and the New Public Management*. Basingstoke: Macmillan.

Walshe, K., Smith, J., Dixon, J. et al. (2004) Primary care trusts. *British Medical Journal*, 329(7471): 871–2.

Waters, H.R., Morlock, L.L. and Hatt, L. (2004) Quality-based purchasing in health care. *International Journal of Health Planning and Management*, 19: 365–81.

Websites and resources

Commonwealth Fund. A private foundation supporting independent research on health and social issues. While US focused, it conducts and publishes international comparative surveys of health systems performance and policy approaches: www.cmwf.org.

Department of Health. Official UK government site. The commissioning pages provide access to policy documentation, guidance and resources for the National Health Service on commissioning and contracting: http://www.dh.gov.uk/en/index.htm.

National Committee for Quality Assurance. The NCQA accredits US Health Plans for quality. The website explains the quality rating system, the Health Plan Employer Data and Information Set (HEDIS) which is the NCQA's data collection tool, and provides information about the quality ratings of individual health plans. It gives a useful insight into the US health system of managed care: www.ncqa.org.

Organisation for Economic Co-operation and Development. Health pages give access to key statistics and publications about the health systems of the OECD's 30 member countries:
http://www.oecd.org/topic/0,2686,en_2649_37407_1_1_1_1_37407,00.html.

World Health Organization Regional Office for Europe. Health systems pages provide details of WHO projects and programmes on all aspects of health systems, and access to publications and reports: http://www.euro.who.int/en/home.

CHAPTER

15

Buildings, facilities and equipment

Barrie Dowdeswell and Steve Wright

Introduction

The context for capital planning is changing dramatically and irrevocably. A combination of the global credit crisis and subsequent calls for austerity in the management of public finances has come at a time when there were already growing international doubts about the efficacy, efficiency and sustainability of a hospital-centric model of service delivery, in particular for the chronic ill and elderly. Across Europe, there is evidence of change which, despite differences in the structures of health systems, appears to be strongly convergent. Two distinct trends are emerging. First, a shift from centralization of guidelines and planning to greater local control and flexibility; second, a move from bed-based normative planning to a more integrated and responsive system which is activity-based and perhaps looks towards care (disease) pathways as the principal planning influence, a trend that is explored in more depth in Chapter 10 (chronic disease management and integrated care).

Concurrent with this shift is an intent by many governments to 'outsource' capital debt incurred for public services. Government funding as a source of new capital has all but dried up in many countries and is unlikely to return in the foreseeable future. This opens avenues for different forms of public–private partnerships (PPP), which notably include direct transactions between local (hospital) providers and the commercial banking sector for investment capital. There is now a greater emphasis on what many regard as the more technical dimensions of the capital agenda but which are nevertheless critical in contributing towards economic and functional sustainability. This includes factors such as lifecycle investment planning, a better alignment between workforce process and building design, asset performance value and the carbon agenda. This is an exciting if challenging time for those concerned with capital asset strategy for healthcare; new opportunities are opening up but conversely capital investment mistakes have a long shelf life.

This chapter highlights factors likely to influence significantly capital asset strategy in healthcare. Many commentaries on 'capital' tend towards translating and explaining how to make the best of extant processes, guidelines and practices, and can prove parochial and introspective in nature and application. What is now emerging is the globalization of capital policy, and hence there is a need for practitioners and managers to develop fresh perspectives necessary for the greater freedoms and self-reliance that lie ahead.

The chapter starts with the changing context within which capital is likely to operate in future, examining issues associated with investment funding. This is followed by a consideration of concept development, referencing contemporary research evidence from Norway. It then moves to an exploration of the role of commercial funding sources, including public–private partnerships. Attention is also drawn new thinking about hospital design to address issues around the increasingly rapid and unpredictable changes in models of care. Finally, there is a compendium of 'quick access' information, with extensive web referencing.

Context

The healthcare landscape is undergoing profound change. For example, the impact of the interlinked dimensions of the credit crisis and an almost universal reappraisal of public service spending priorities by governments throughout Europe is already generating problems in accessing new capital and sustaining revenue flexibility to pay off existing capital debt. Even where health budgets appear to be ring-fenced from direct cuts, leverage to improve cost-efficiency is inevitable and will challenge cash flow assumptions that underpinned previous judgements about the affordability of capital projects. Furthermore, these factors are set within a changing ideological viewpoint of many governments which see the introduction of some form of market (choice) orientated autonomy and freedoms as creating the stimulus and opportunity to devolve operational accountability for service delivery and capital assets.

What has been exposed by this comparatively sudden change in outlook is the prior tendency over recent decades for capital investment to have become dominated by an emphasis on the short-term tactical positioning of capital assets. Many health systems have been caught out by these unexpected shifts, and are finding that their capital asset models look increasingly out of step with the future longer-term needs of the services they house and the workforce they accommodate. This is perhaps unsurprising. Government political cycles cluster around five years, health is, as we noted in Chapter 2, heavily politicized, and the public is apt to regard the physicality and proximity of hospital buildings as an investment in their future well-being. Pressures to deliver immediate results became almost irresistible.

A more realistic appraisal of the future shape of healthcare suggests a trend towards a more diverse yet integrated and intersectoral focus for care delivery (see Chapters 8 and 10). Thus far, capital investment has usually remained locked within tight sectoral boundaries and with a short horizon; its DNA predisposed to incremental replication rather than rapid evolution. This is now set to change.

Health systems convergence

The Semashko system in Eastern European countries relied heavily on a hospital-centric care model and centrist planning regimes. Standardization was central to its philosophy and practice and its legacy can be seen in the monolithic buildings that dominate the healthcare landscape across many new EU Member States, these dating from the 1950s, 1960s and 1970s, and now outmoded and in a state of disrepair. Some Western health systems have buildings that similarly display many of these characteristics.

Beveridgean health systems tended towards the 'free goods' equity model, with the state supplying capital funds and often not even nominally charging for this. Capital investment policy was built around balancing spending across competing needs. Planning was mostly formulaic, a trait that often remains today. However, one of the notable characteristics was the extent to which capital investment decisions were influenced by building condition deficit recovery, as opposed to long-range strategic planning. In other words, there was short-termism concerned with making good a legacy of lack of maintenance and investment, without large-scale capital reappraisal.

In contrast, the Bismarckian Social Health Insurance (SHI) model provided separation between the commissioner (SHI sickness fund) and provider (primary care or hospital) of healthcare. In SHI systems, the public sector remains the regulator, and may at various levels be a commissioner or provider or both; but there is a split in the roles. In many SHI systems, there are clear separations between the primary and secondary health sectors and sometimes between the secondary and tertiary hospital sector. This could in principle lead to poorer integration of care compared with Bevridgean unitary health systems; although even there, a lack of integration is manifest in some systems (see Chapter 10). In the case of Germany, there is also a specific separation (the Duales System) of financing provision, in that the public sector at least nominally provides the capital in the hospital sector even if the insurance funds provide the revenue funding; these two parties need to coordinate on hospital projects but arguably have not always done so closely enough.

At the limit, it should be observed that all European healthcare models are universal, and are essentially risk-pooling mechanisms, at least compared to a US-style private market. Evidence suggests an increasing degree of convergence, including in capital investment terms, between the different types of European health systems.

The overarching trends

In all systems, the current harsh economic climate is provoking a deeper questioning of capital investment conventions. Furthermore, health systems are having to face up to the demographic and epidemiological transitions evident throughout Europe. These transitions are increasingly well mapped, documented, and understood, but in capital investment terms are as yet hardly accounted for. They will transform future demands on acute care facilities, but not necessarily in the direction of further growth in scale of the large institutions; almost certainly the reverse. Other trends affecting capital planning and development include: the expansion in new clinical and information technology innovations (Chapter 16); more sophisticated health technology assessment (Chapter 5); the availability of new forms of care delivery as a result of such technological and clinical innovations; and a move towards care being delivered in community settings with concomitant concentration of specialist services in tertiary centres. The middle ground province of the acute general hospital therefore looks set to feel the squeeze; capital will be in demand to facilitate this change ('disinvest to invest').

Finally, there is the need for economic sustainability – successful hospitals of the future will be those that get the balance right between short-term tactical responsiveness and delivering longer-term sustained strategic value, namely those with better synergy between service and capital performance. Access to future capital supply will no longer be so dependent on patronage (the political element in prioritizing capital), compliance with tick box formulae or building condition deficit recovery, but rather more on the commercial principle of return on investment. Collateral for the future supply of capital will be the income stream of the institution, resulting from the fact that many healthcare economies now have activity-based budgeting (see Chapter 22).

Transcending this daunting agenda is the problem of health inequalities. As public resources continue to be squeezed, policy-makers will naturally question the contribution that capital investment in health facilities makes in tackling this problem. A recent comprehensive review of the state of capital strategy in Europe (Rechel et al. 2009a), confirmed the shortcoming. A survey of literature on the quality of care outcomes, Legido-Quigley et al. 2008), also highlights that there is little mention of the 'capital' contribution to care. It is remarkable that in a service dominated by evidence-based principles, good and reliable evidence to guide policy-makers in the capital domain is so under-developed.

There are nevertheless significant reference points across Europe. The recently-released EU strategic document, *Europe 2020: A Strategy for Smart, Sustainable and Inclusive Growth*, aims to promote a more central role for public–private partnerships as a means of transforming public services – put simply, outsourcing. In the Netherlands, 95 per cent of hospitals are owned and managed by not-for-profit wholly independent trusts that raise capital privately. In Finland, there is at least one example of a public hospital (Coxa Hospital, Tampere Region) opting out of direct state control, to deliver better public services by using the greater freedom independence confers. In France, many elective medicine units, including new specialized high technology hospital developments are privately financed and owned. It is worth noting that many of these private companies have an annual capital refreshment/replacement rate far above public hospitals and they do not have to queue for capital.

The 'Concept' project in Norway draws attention to the need to focus more on 'quality at entry' of projects into the design, financing and procurement cycles. Finally, there is the move to greater autonomy and diversity in hospital and healthcare provision in the (English) NHS as new government reforms are unveiled (Department of Health 2010).

Improving the focus on strategic capital planning

The principal elements of strategic capital planning are often embedded in centrist capital planning practice. The UK Welsh Office, for example, has a Strategic Capital Investment Cabinet Committee that 'will agree, direct and keep under review, the new Strategic Capital Investment Framework designed to strengthen our approach to prioritising and managing our capital investment and deliver sustainable benefits for Wales'. It aims to take a whole systems approach 'which begins with making effective, well-justified and strategic investment decisions and extends to the management of the assets throughout their lifetime'.

In practice, a growing number of Continental European countries are moving away from top-down overview and control of capital. One significant example is the Netherlands, which, as a potential template for the future, is worth examining. The Health Ministry of the Netherlands until recently looked to its specialist capital planning agency, 'Bouwcollege', to set and monitor health facility building guidelines and standards, and advise on the strategic positioning of capital investment. Although almost all Dutch hospitals are independent (usually not-for-profit trusts), their capital debt was underwritten by a government-controlled institution, and as such they received preferential risk-free loan rates from the commercial banking sector. To obtain this benefit, the investment strategy of hospitals was necessarily governed by the overarching strategic planning system. This has all changed as part of the current health reform programme (Daley and Gubb 2007).

The first step taken by the Dutch was the withdrawal of mandatory health sector building guidelines, and putting in place a light-touch advisory support service from Bouwcollege, with greater freedom for hospitals to become more innovative in responding to their local needs. The second stage in the process of loosening the reins on capital governance was the wider consequences of the move towards a market economy in the health insurance and hospital sectors. Social insurance funds have new freedoms to tender for services from providers, and hospitals have the freedom to bid for contracts based on their future business strategy. The third element was the removal of the underwriting safety net for bank loans; lending is now at negotiated commercial rates, influenced by the security of future income streams and 'at-risk' to the hospitals. Banks in the Netherlands have always had a good understanding of the macro risks implicit in health policy, but are now also focusing on the micro levels, namely the adequacy of individual hospital business plans and the institutions' ability to manage effectively in the marketplace. This is proving a steep learning curve for many hospitals. The role of Bouwcollege (now renamed the Dutch Centre for Health Assets, DUCHA) has also changed and it has become an autonomous organization (outside government control) free to offer research and development and consultancy advice to all those concerned with capital investment in the health sector.

Implicit in this approach is an acceptance that the rapidity of change in healthcare, uncertainty of resource flow of a market system, and the need to stimulate innovation within the capital sector all lead towards shifting accountability for strategic planning and management of capital assets from the centre to those who ultimately carry the risk.

This shift releases hard-pressed governments to focus on overarching health policy, free of the encumbrance of accountability for capital assets. For example, more German Länder and municipalities are 'selling off' their hospitals to the private sector. There is a shift towards regionalization in France, coupled with a more liberal approach to Public–Private Partnership diversity. There are also indications of growing interest across most EU new member states in PPP development, a recent illustration here is Slovakia transferring its major hospitals into joint stock companies. There are, however, counterpoint views: Italy seems for the moment to be retaining its regional structural planning model for capital; and Finland is increasing the degree of regionalization of healthcare planning and investment. The picture in Finland is far from straightforward on this issue as described by Rechel et al. (2009a), where Coxa Hospital (see above) has created the precedent for more hospital services in the Tampere Region to move to independent status in coming years.

Overall, the tide appears to be turning in favour of devolution of decision-making about capital development in healthcare. However, provider scope for investment will inevitably be influenced by the commissioners because (indirectly at least) they will be the source of the income stream to service capital cost. Whether commissioners will develop a population-based strategic planning stance in their funding policy remains unclear.

Rechel et al. (2009a) provide evidence to suggest that devolving accountability in this manner can transform asset performance. Furthermore, in place of assumptions that strategic capital investment needs to be based on high degrees of certainty about future healthcare needs and trends, it appears that the opposite may become the norm. The new strategic approach is likely to lean more towards one that assumes and plans for high levels of uncertainty and unpredictability. Figure 15.1 from a presentation given by David Clarke at 'Design and Health Canada 2010' demonstrates the problem. Given that hospital buildings have a lifespan of around 30 to 40 years, predictions at the time of project development proved very wide of the mark, and the danger in such circumstances of locking in operating or finance contracts is clear.

The picture becomes even more interesting when set against the corollary to this illustration; the impact of an ageing population (Figure 15.2).

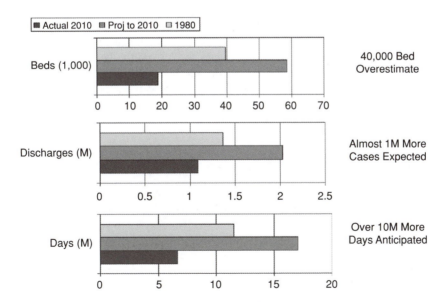

FIGURE 15.1 Health capital in Ontario – projections made in 1980 for 2010
Source: Clarke (2010).

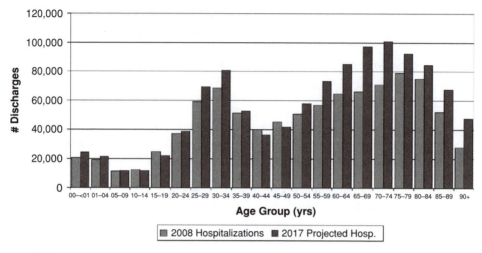

FIGURE 15.2 Ontario current and projected acute care hospitalizations by age group
Source: Clarke (2010).

What can be seen here is the potential increase in demand for some form of hospital care as a consequence of demographic transition. Many current hospital designs are not only wrongly (over-)sized but are configured for the conventional acute, short stay, interventional and episodic care patient, and wholly unsuited for this potentially growing class of frail older patient.

The future approach therefore may be much more about building against a more speculative outlook where emphasis on flexibility and adaptability in design, construction, functionality and intrinsic value are the watchwords. This carries risk, but it may also prove a critical factor in the further evolution of capital strategy. Risk assessment of this nature can sharpen the focus and stimulate change, particularly when government safety nets are removed. This will prove a new and disturbing fact of life for those institutions in transition from state ownership and control to various forms of autonomy and self-governance. The safety net of handed-down guidelines (no matter how frustrating) is likely to diminish or disappear altogether.

Concept development

Most evaluation of capital projects tends towards reviewing the effectiveness of project delivery – the 'on-cost, on-time' dimension or its shorter-term technical performance. An example of this is the recent UK National Audit Office report on PFI. But even here the reviewers indicated awareness of the short time horizon. The Audit Office, in introducing the report, commented, 'There continue to be risks, however, to the long-term value for money of these contracts'. The Norwegian Ministry of Finance, in establishing the Concept project in that country sought an answer to this type of question in asking why so many major public service capital projects seem to under-perform over time.

The deceptively simple answer was that the roots of most failures are embedded at the concept development stage of the project. This can result from a variety of reasons but one of the most significant is what can be described as the rush to certainty. Pressure to move ahead with project planning is usually considerable. This can trigger a familiar cycle, where past hospital activity and extrapolation of perceived trends are used to build up a profile of potential service demand which can be translated into a capacity and functional map. It is an easy option, often facilitated by advisory agencies offering a wealth of high quality, if at times theoretical, knowledge. The problem is that this rush to build an early degree of 'certainty' into the scoping and scaling of projects often denies the reality that predicting future patterns of healthcare need with any degree of certainty is illusory, as illustrated in the example from Ontario above. There are numerous examples where new clinical technologies and models of care render some capital projects out of date even before they are commissioned, as evidenced by the rapid development of specialist wards for AIDS patients before anti-retroviral drug treatment rendered dedicated inpatient facilities obsolete.

The Concept findings from Norway promote two solutions to help achieve 'quality at entry' of projects into the subsequent more detailed design, financing and procurement phases:

1 Adopting a more realistic time scale for project development to test fully all options, preferably with some form of wide-ranging scenario planning – but avoiding the rather meaningless 'do nothing' option that in truth only serves to emphasize the preferred option. To be effective, project development must be rigorous and realistic and without prejudgement. This may include periodic and independent 'gateway' reviews – a process of examining projects at key decision points in their lifecycle (see www.ogc.gov.uk for an example of this approach). However, as the shift towards local autonomy in capital planning accelerates, what form and who should undertake independent reviews remain uncertain. In the Netherlands, hospitals now voluntarily submit proposals for expert review by DUCHA, welcoming the rigour of a second opinion from this now independent organization. A marked feature of the new-style Dutch reviews is the acceptance of unpredictability as a normative element, unlike many such review processes that still look for high degrees of certainty and precision.

2 Aligning projects more closely with the main purpose of the investment – improving the quality and scope of healthcare delivery. This may sound obvious, but the means of achieving it often lacks a reliable, rigorous and proven methodology and too frequently relies on the looser process of iterative discussion and negotiation between the key players, with attendant dangers of specialism or territorial bias in the eventual project outcome.

Both of these recommendations seem almost too simple, and this may betray a further problem in many current capital planning models. In most bureaucratic (public) systems of capital provision, compliance with process – ticking the right boxes – often dominates over project quality as does the mantra of delivery 'on-cost and on-time' beloved of treasuries.

Healthcare delivery flow and developing the appropriate capacity

Capital investment must necessarily relate to its primary function of supporting health-care delivery, and should, as far as possible, be able to adapt to the trajectory of future clinical needs. Increasingly, clinical protocols are framed within care (disease) pathways which promise tangible improvement in safety, quality and effectiveness. It would therefore seem axiomatic that they should also provide a reliable foundation on which to build capital models for the future. A notable feature of some of the most effective and innovative hospital projects in Europe (Rechel et al. 2009a) is the adoption of care pathways as the foundation for infrastructure planning.

A survey by the European Health Property Network (EuHPN) on the adoption of care pathways for capital planning purposes (Hindle et al. 2004) found that, while there was growing expectation that pathways would provide the basis for a more systemalised approach to future planning and delivery, the response from capital planners when asked about their intentions to adopt care pathways for project planning purposes was disappointingly limited. Far too few had knowledge of the principles and benefits of care pathway planning (Hindle et al. 2004). However, since the time of the survey, more hospitals seem to be turning to this approach as the basis of their future capital asset planning, for example, Orbis Medical Centre, Sittard, the Netherlands, the Rhoen Klinikum Hospital Group, Germany, and Karolinska Solna Hospital, Stockholm, Sweden. Nevertheless, progress is slow and sporadic despite the logic of this approach. Panella and Vanhaecht (2010a) describe the defining characteristics of care pathways in the following terms:

- an explicit statement of the goals and key elements of care based on evidence, best practice, and patients' expectations and their characteristics;
- the facilitation of communication among the team members and with patients and families;
- the coordination of the care process by coordinating the roles and sequencing the activities of the multidisciplinary care team, patients and their relatives;
- the documentation, monitoring, and evaluation of variances and outcomes; and
- the identification of the appropriate resources.

It is, however, a major jump from using individual patient pathways for operational planning to go to generic care pathways that can be aggregated and used for capital planning purposes. Those hospitals that have made this transition have done so necessarily through implementation of comprehensive information and communication technology (ICT) support systems, invariably embedded as part of the core design of the facility. This is not always the case, as, in many capital planning systems, ICT seems to run on a parallel track with little cross-over integration.

One test here is the almost certain shift away from the decades-old anchor point of planning by bed ratios towards new thinking about patient flow as the new determinant of capacity within hospitals and across the diverse range of care delivery agencies

(Rechel et al. 2010). 'The bed' is more a storage concept, perhaps relevant in the days when hospitals were oriented particularly towards 'watchful waiting' with built-in 'waiting' space, but less relevant now that the patient typically experiences more intensive treatment over much shorter time scales. The ideas of 'lean' organizational processes, imported from manufacturing and other industries, emphasize the importance of quality for the final consumer (the patient) and avoidance of waste including time. 'Lean' strategies, however, must be supported by adequate information systems so that at every treatment stage the provider of the treatment has total knowledge of the patient, previous stages and outcomes and the required treatment. This component is often under-developed or misunderstood by advocates of lean principles.

The hospital can now be better thought of as a network than a linear process. It can be conceptually difficult to calculate the capacity of a network in healthcare or elsewhere, particularly one faced with variable volume and types of patient flow. However, this simply reveals that hospitals may need to be designed, and run, through the use of simulation modelling techniques.

The 'layers' model breaking the hospital's facilities down into a limited number of key 'processing' elements such as 'hot floor' (operating theatres, intensive care and imaging), 'hotel' accommodation, utilities and 'offices' (consulting rooms and administration) developed by DUCHA and TNO in the Netherlands, may help overcome the level of complexity in this modelling, as is discussed later in this chapter.

The private sector, and public–private partnerships (PPPs)

There has been a marked trend in the past decade towards the use of a PPP mechanism to deliver public infrastructure. This now appears in many countries to have reached a pause, as discussed by Barlow et al. (2010). These authors observe that, at a time when governments face financial constraints because of high levels of borrowing and taxation and should be increasingly turning to the private sector to meet the infrastructure funding gap, the financial markets are in turmoil due to the credit crunch and are often unresponsive to demand.

The requirement for modern healthcare infrastructure will outlast any short-term impact of the current economic crisis. How to pay for such infrastructure, in the course of a trajectory towards large ageing-related healthcare and pension commitments, which will be of the order of several percentage points of GDP in their own right for most or all countries, is a major challenge for governments and health services across the world. The economic crisis, and need for governments in countries where healthcare infrastructure is essentially publicly-funded to rein in expenditure will without doubt reinforce moves towards an increased role for the private sector.

PPP is often proposed as offering private sector efficiencies, accessing cheap finance or taking expenditure off government balance sheet. In fact, as an instrument it is primarily about risk management – both reduction of risk premia and risk transfer between parties with different degrees of risk aversion. This risk management is achieved by bundling activities across project phases (through-life management), and securing private finance. Because the destination, not the path, becomes the organizing theme around which a project is built suggests that this principle enables the public sector to focus to greater extent on the outcome-based public value they are trying to create rather than the inputs required to get there.

PPPs in so-called 'economic infrastructure' sectors (transport or energy, etc.) usually involve a transfer of much of the demand or market risk. In 'social infrastructure' such as health and education, the demand risk is so heavily controlled by the government, even within social fund models, that the private sector is often unwilling to accept this risk. Instead, the risk transfer usually ends up limited to the performance of the buildings and asset availability, and future building cost control, although some models do use capitation payments as a limited version of demand risk. In healthcare, there are a number of archetypal PPP models:

- accommodation-only (the physical buildings, and sometimes equipment, like the UK private finance initiative (PFI), and also used in Italy, France, Spain and some Portuguese projects);
- accommodation and clinical services via separate companies (four Portuguese 'Wave 1' projects);
- 'regulated privatization', such as in Germany, where for-profit hospital companies are buying facilities from the non-profit sector or state organizations, but having to run them according to the Krankenhausplan licence which ensures that hospitals must provide full and open access to all public patients, or in Finland, with the Coxa Project;
- 'full population service' structures, with integrated hospital facilities and community medical services (Alzira and several other Valencia region services, Spain).

Payment systems can be closely and directly linked to the PPP structure, e.g. performance and availability fees paid for the physical space provided. The major alternative is indirect – the appropriation of some proportion of income generated by standard health sector measures, such as fee for service and case-mix/diagnostic-related group linked. Most interestingly among the latter examples is population capitation. This seems to offer the best prospects of aligning short- and long-term incentives between the two sides of a capital planning and funding agreement. It is worth trying to structure the arrangement so that it is not purely a contractual agreement, to be characterized by an adversarial relationship between the two sides with recourse if necessary to litigation, but rather a true partnership oriented to problem-solving during the project life. This is the approach chosen for the new Karolinska Solna (Stockholm) Hospital development. The scheme, an accommodation model and one of the largest healthcare projects in Europe, with a total investment of EUR 1.42 billion at 2007 prices, seeks to incorporate in its PFI structure a more adaptable functional design concept, including much greater contract flexibility to allow for wider variations in demand and functional use than has been the case so far. It looks to be the start of a second generation PPP model; detailed contract negotiations are now underway (at time of writing).

Governments around the world need to be aware of future challenges in increasing the role of PPP arrangements in healthcare infrastructure and service provision. For instance, it is clear that cost control often is achievable, for the private sector partner. However, quality for the public sector (capacity variation, performance improvements, and innovation) is often not easily contractible at least on a sufficient scale to meet likely future needs. The maximization of innovation and flexibility throughout the contract period is desirable. But as observed by McKee and Healy (2000), in order to minimize risks, both public and private organizations are often incentivized to enter into a contract which is specified in great and stifling detail. All too often there is a lack of what Luo Y (2002) called 'contingency adaptability', where private and public sectors work together in partnership to resolve the inevitable changes in circumstances during the contract life.

Design and adaptability; the 'layers' model

A feature of the European Congress, Healthcare Planning and Design, Rotterdam 2010, was the depth of new thinking about designing health facilities that are more responsive to the changing nature of healthcare delivery. Prominent are approaches which favour a disaggregation of normally adjacent departments and functions, and redesign and reposition these elements in a new and potentially more efficient, cost-effective and sustainable way. The principle is to design hospitals around the multi-disciplinary team concept emerging through the care pathway movement, and which undoubtedly responds well to flow modelling.

One of the most promising ideas is the 'layers' concept mentioned above. In place of the conventional modular building design with distinct territorial separation based on patients' illness or body system type, the layers approach questions the future of these functional divisions. It proposes a new way of defining and segregating functional content, as noted on p. 307 above. Design follows the form dictated by each functional categorization. The different functions are then arranged according to the care pathway, work process systemization, and flow concepts proposed by the institution as its preferred model of care delivery. The following sequence set out in Figures 15.3 to 15.5 illustrates the principles.

These diagrammatic representations can ideally form the basis of scenario testing the alignment between work processes and design configurations, and to provide the stimulus for new concepts in hospital design. The benefits of this design concept suggest that:

- The principle of 'form following process function' facilitates clearer differentiation between the design characteristics of each element, recognizing that each will have a substantially different profile as regards building and functional cost, and rate of decay of functional effectiveness. For example, the hot floor will house technologies that are high capital (and operating) cost, generally will have a relatively short optimal lifespan, need constant upgrading and replacement, and will thus generate a high rate of depreciation. The ability to constantly refresh this 'layer' without wholesale disruption of the hospital as whole can be a design requirement that can add measurably to lifecycle sustainability and functional value.

- It avoids the embedded dispersal of different functional 'layers' throughout hospital buildings in a pattern which, although reflective of work practice at time of design,

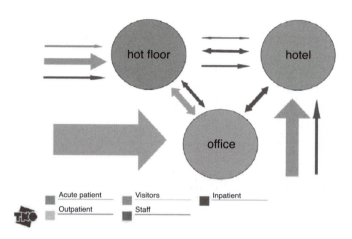

FIGURE 15.3 Layers approach analysis flows
Principal workforce and patient flows are mapped across the principal layers. 'Industry' (diagnostic areas, catering, laundry, stores, utilities, etc.) tends not to generate significant cross-site people flow. The analysis can be used to present an indication of scale and scope of translation of an existing configuration to a layers model.

is likely to change considerably over the lifespan of the building and may render the design dysfunctional or obsolete and costly to correct.

- Building cost comparisons suggest it can unlock significant savings. For example, a comparison between the 'monolith' and 'extreme model' illustrated above demonstrates an 11 per cent reduction in favour of the extreme model in Figure 15.6. Furthermore, it is possible to compare the rate of return of each 'layer' of the different models shaped by differential lifespan considerations as shown in Figure 15.7.

A key element of this concept is that it facilitates the shift towards a flow model of capacity planning and service delivery. This is the principle that underpins the Rhoen

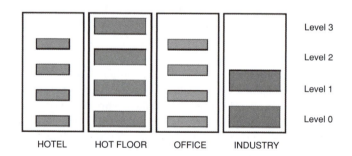

FIGURE 15.4 Layers approach.
Alternative design strategies can be adopted – shown here as a vertical modular approach

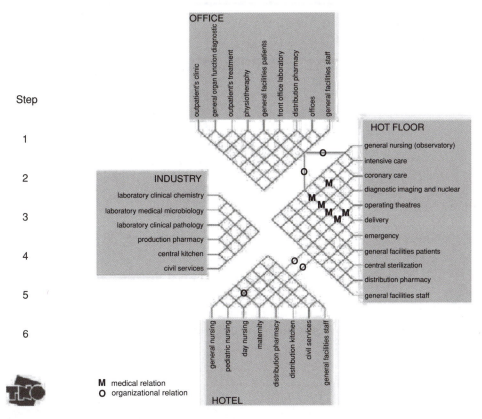

FIGURE 15.5 Relations extreme model.
A more extreme approach is adoption of a campus-style physical separation of layers

Klinikum approach to aligning (multi-disciplinary) work practices and hospital design in Germany. It also supports the flow principles adopted by three Dutch Hospitals: Sittard – Maaaslandzeikenhuis; Deventer – Deventer Zeikenhuis; and Utrecht – Mesos Medisch Centrum.

Taken further, the layers model promotes the idea that many elements of the conventional hospital can be reconfigured and relocated within local and more accessible community settings (Boluijt and Hinkema 2005). However, elsewhere the principles are being applied in more limited form, for example, the integrated capital investment strategy spanning primary, secondary and social care in Northern Ireland.

Quick access reference information

The following provides a 'quick access' section that highlights other important contemporary trends and shifts in approach to future capital design and investment.

Properties and construction costs extreme model (C)

Step		Model A	Model C	Difference	Hotel	Hot floor	Office	Industry
	useful floor area (m²)	29.597	29.597		7.938	7.191	10.708	3.760
1	gross / useful	160%	156%		163%	158%	152%	147%
	gross floor area (m²)	47.355	46.075	−1.280	12.923	11.372	16.270	5.510
	floors				5	3.3	5	2
2	height of floor (m)	3.75			3.3	3.75	3.4	3.75
	footprint		11.630		2.570	3.350	3.110	2.600
	€/m²	1.500	1.377		1.351	1.669	1.085	1.693
3	costs (min.)	71.0	63.4	−7.6	17.5	19.0	17.7	9.3
4								
5								
6								

−(11%)

Price level February 2007, exclusive of VAT and premises

FIGURE 15.6 Comparative cost analysis between the vertical modular model (Figure 15.4) and the campus model (Figure 15.5)

Step		Monolith*	Extreme	Hotel	Hot floor	Office	Industry
	gross floor area (m²)	46.075	46.075	12.923	11.372	16.270	5.510
1	building costs (mln.)	68.0	43.4	17.5	19.0	17,5	9,3
	investments cost (mln.)	99.1	42.4	25.4	27.7	25,4	13,6
	life span (yrs.)	40		50	20	50	20
2	Internal Rate of Return (IRR)	6,00%		4,49%	6,92%	7,47%	7,33%
	increase return			25%	15%	25%	22%

* = for comparison the gross floor areas are equal and the monolith costs 7% more

3							
4							
5							
6							

Price level February 2007, exclusive of VAT and premises

FIGURE 15.7 A comparative view of the rate of potential rate of return on floor space of the relative designs (Figures 15.4 and 15.5)

Evidence-based design (EBD)

Evidence-based design (EBD) promotes the adoption of hospital design characteristics that have a sound evidence base and which can demonstrate measurable improvement in patient outcomes involving the direct patient environment, for example, décor, noise, room size and access to outside views. Kirk Hamilton in his evidence-based design study series (Malone et al. 2008), suggests, 'Evidence-based design is the conscientious, explicit and judicious use of current best evidence from research and practice in making critical decisions, together with an informed client, about the design of each individual and unique project.'

What we talk about here is the proposition that a healing environment is the result of a design that has demonstrated measurable improvements in the physical and/or psychological states of patients and/or staff, physicians, and visitors. A healing environment is therefore a complementary treatment modality that makes a therapeutic contribution to the course of care. A tangible and still one of the best demonstrations is a pioneering study, conducted by Roger Ulrich in 1984 (reported in his paper 'A view through a window may influence recovery from surgery') that linked hospital design to better clinical outcomes. However, this remains an area of significant 'work-in-progress'.

Where the evidence-based design approach is conclusively becoming more topical and moving rapidly up the design agenda is as part of the armoury to combat hospital-acquired infection (HAI). In the USA, the American Institute of Architects has called for a universal transition to single rooms in publishing its 2006 *Guidelines for Design and Construction of Health Care Facilities*. In Europe, there is a similar groundswell of opinion but there are some notable differences of opinion on this issue. Many new hospital projects in mainland Europe and France, in particular, have moved firmly in favour of a single bed patient room configuration. Furthermore, rooms are now designed at a larger scale for multi-functional purposes ('acuity adaptable'), as is also the case of the US studies: bedroom, treatment room, visitors' room – thus minimizing patient movement and errors, and axiomatically it would seem reducing the risk of cross-infection.

Clearly, more research is needed to evaluate different design options, both in regard to reducing the risk of HAI, improving patient quality and understanding the impact on workforce effectiveness and cost. Studies into current practices within existing facilities are examining cross-contamination from a range of perspectives: different room configurations for intensive care; the implied traffic and movement patterns; consequential compliance with hand washing; the division between clean and dirty spaces; cleaning regimes; and the use of statistical process control to improve cleaning efficiency. An evidence base is being developed through research and will eventually be integrated into a risk assessment and training tool kit for each discipline in a healthcare working space (see www.HACIRIC.org).

Lifecycle costing

Lifecycle costing (LCC) is simply a tool that offers improved insight into the full financial effects of owning and running a building. LCC is a systematized means of planning and developing the lifetime costs of projects, in which it is important to estimate and compare the costs of the investment project itself, the acquisition of property, and sustaining the capital project during its period of use. It may also include disposal of assets. In the new market-related and more competitive environment in which hospitals operate, this knowledge – prior to capital investment commitment – will become vital.

LCC is not new; it is already used in many other sectors, e.g. manufacturing. Nevertheless, LCC in its more complete 'industrial' form is relatively new to the healthcare sector. This may be because a number of healthcare sector-specific characteristics (e.g. the rapid and unpredictable nature of change) have not been adequately factored into the models until now. Progress is, however, being made, for example, the accelerated hospital building programme generated by the private finance initiative in the NHS in England has furthered understanding of the links between space, operational functionality and lifecycle maintenance needs. It is in essence a starting point for investigating how different project planning scenarios score, and is an important factor in avoiding the 'rush to certainty' phenomenon described earlier.

Asset utilization

The term 'sweating the assets' has become commonplace in many health systems. This approach is often based on quite simple comparisons of ratios relating to patient throughput per defined asset unit, for example, beds and operating theatres. Many centrist health systems maintain some form of performance assessment using this principle. It may have served well in the past as a means of comparing relative hospital performance but is far removed from what will be needed in the future, including the ability for hospitals to improve substantially their costing and pricing methodologies.

Some of the most progressive development work in this field is being undertaken at the Karlsruhe Institute of Technology in Germany (www.kit.edu – Institute for Technology and Management in Construction), based on the OPIK project (Optimization and Analysis of Processes in Hospitals). This project analysed the asset performance of 33 hospitals with an aggregate of 27,000 beds and related asset utilization to the German diagnostic-related group (DRG) classification system. The project looked at the tactical application of assets and facilities management, and displayed wide variations in performance. This data and classification system has been used to develop an extremely sensitive methodology that can be used reliably for costing and pricing asset consumption at DRG level and benchmarking efficiency and effectiveness – and simulation and scenario assessment, as shown in Figure 15.8.

This project has now moved on to considering the strategic dimensions of asset and Facilities Management (FM) related to future planning needs. The DRG model is first used to model potential as against actual patient utilization of the hospital, along with market share penetration. From this, it is possible to extrapolate future capital asset and FM need against different planning scenarios. This will be an important tool to enable hospitals to make decisions about future business strategy, including the cost effectiveness of chasing increased market share. It is at present a large and under-developed field for most hospitals.

FIGURE 15.8 Diagnosis related strategies for hospital planning and operation

The carbon agenda

Finally, a demanding growth area in hospital planning, design and construction is responding to the need for reduced carbon emissions. The EU is calling for a 20 per cent reduction (based on 1990 levels) by 2020. The WHO, in launching its discussion draft, *Healthy Hospitals, Healthy Planet, Healthy People: Addressing Climate Change in Health Care Settings 2009,* observed that 'No one knows the precise size of the health sector's global climate footprint but we know that it is substantial – reducing the (sector's) climate impact is as complex as the broad diversity of health systems that exist in the world'. The draft addresses, among other issues, what it describes as the 'seven elements of a climate-friendly hospital': 'energy efficiency; green building design; alternative energy generation; transportation; food sourcing; and waste and water'.

Illustrative and typical of the 'green' building design approach is the model adopted for the new Meyer's Children's Hospital, Florence, Italy. A combination of new principles of natural ventilation flow coupled with the extensive use of solar panels has resulted in significant improvement in its carbon footprint. This is one example of new design principles stimulated by moving on from the energy-demanding deep plan designs of the 1980s and 1990s towards the lower carbon footprint models represented

Flexible integrated capital and revenue budgeting

Healthcare
impact

Clinical process systematization   Adaptable capital assets

FIGURE 15.9 Investing for sustainable value

by new contemporary 'narrow-plan' principles. A model design brief encompassing many of these sustainability principles has been produced by the Health Estates Agency, Northern Ireland (see http://www.euhpn.eu/resource/sustainable-design-brief-health-estates-agency-northern-ireland). Comprehensive advice on the wider carbon agenda including national pilots and mutual learning opportunities is available through the EU portal at www.lowcarbon-healthcare.eu.

Conclusion

A notable feature of this overview of capital asset strategy is not only the complexity and rate of change but also the degree of convergence, across Europe and globally, in terms of recurring themes and strategies. Successful hospitals of the future will be those that recognize the need for change, and that it is a remorseless, never-ending process. Planning must remain dynamic, and, wherever possible, evidence based, and keep in view key interactions within the healthcare domain, as illustrated in Figure 15.9.

Almost all health systems are moving towards models of healthcare delivery that stimulate greater efficiency and effectiveness. Globalization will come into play in a different way – capital planning and investment in healthcare facilities have tended to be largely parochial and lack international perspectives, but this will change. At the time of writing, some of the most progressive ideas are emerging in the Indian sub-continent in the shape of what some describe, unkindly but accurately, as health process factories. Notable here are the two pioneering institutions: the Aravind Eye Hospitals, and a more recent development the Narayana Hrundayala (NH) Heart Hospital, Bangalore, (Bhattacharyya et al. 2008; Barak et al. 2008). An analysis of their structure and operation lies outwith the scope of this chapter, nevertheless their performance, including building design, construction cost and asset utilization and efficiency, markedly exceed their Western counterparts. One of these enterprises, Narayana Hrundayala, has recently started to consider entry into Europe in response to the more open and liberal marketplace that is opening up. This is the other side of the coin for those European providers clamouring for independence, it may bring unexpected and for some, unwelcome challenges from beyond Europe. This will raise the bar even further for those driving forward new standards for capital asset strategy in the health sector.

Summary box

- Healthcare capital planning is in transition from having been a largely centralized activity where governments issued detailed guidelines, to one where there is much more local control and flexibility.

- There is a move from bed-based planning of hospitals towards a more activity and care pathway approach, and assuming uncertainty and change for the long term.

- There is now much more outsourcing of capital debt within healthcare capital planning and development, with public–private partnerships, and the direct use by hospitals, and other healthcare providers, of commercial banking.

- The technical dimensions of capital planning are being increasingly developed in many countries – examples include the use of lifecycle investment planning, the alignment of workforce and building plans, asset performance value, and addressing the carbon agenda.

- These shifts within capital and building planning reflect wider healthcare and societal changes related to patterns of disease, ageing, technological developments, and emerging assumptions about what constitute appropriate forms of care.

Self-test exercises

The following self-test headlines have emerged as consensus views of participants from various workshops and masterclasses, on capital asset strategy, from across Europe.

1 Capital projects are often evaluated against 'on-time, on-cost' project delivery outcomes. What other models might you use to evaluate how well a project functions against projected service, economic and societal needs? How might you disseminate this knowledge for the benefit of others?

2 Demographics and epidemiological prevalence and trend data provide critical input to the future development of models of care. How might you develop clinical care pathway modelling as a basis of capital project planning to reflect these needs?

3 Rapidity of change in clinical technologies and models of care is a feature of the new healthcare landscape. What design strategies are available to help ensure buildings remain functionally responsive and economically sustainable?

4 'Evidence-based design' is a corollary to evidence-based medicine. What do you consider to be the principles and benefits of this? How might you factor in the contribution that nature/art/environmental-related aspects of building design can make to the therapeutic care of patients? If challenged on any potential additional project cost this may incur, how would you seek to justify it?

5 What do you consider to be the advantages and disadvantages of using a PPP approach to funding the development of new healthcare facilities within your country? Can you identify real-life examples and research evidence to support your assertions?

References and further reading

American Institute of Architects (2006) *Guidelines for Design and Construction of Health Care Facilities*. New York: American Institute of Architects/Facility Guidelines Institute.

Barak, D., Richman, P. et al. (2008) Lessons from India in organizational innovation: a tale of two heart hospitals. *Health Affairs*, 27(5).

Barlow, J., Roehrich, J. and Wright, S. (2010). De facto privatization or a renewed role for the EU? Paying for Europe's healthcare infrastructure in a recession. *J. R. Soc Med*, 103: 51–5.

Bhattacharyya, O., McGahan, P., Dunn, D., Singer, P. and Abdallah, D. (2008) Innovative Health Service Delivery Models for Low and Middle Income Countries 'Technical partner paper 5, University of Toronto, Rockefeller Foundation and Results Development Institute.

Boluijt, P. and Hinkema, M.J. (eds) (2005) *Future Hospitals: Competitive and Healing*. Utrecht: College Bouw Ziekenhuisvoorzieningen.

Clarke, D. (2010) Presentation given at Design and Health Canada 2010. Health Analytics Branch, Ontario Ministry of Health and Long-Term Care.

Daley, C. and Gubb, J. (2007) Health Reforms in the Netherlands. Available at: www.civitas.org.uk/nhs/download/netherlands.pdf.

Department of Health (2010) *Equity and Excellence: Liberating the NHS*, White Paper. London: TSO.

European Commission (2010) *Communication from the Commission. Europe 2020, A Strategy for Smart, Sustainable and Inclusive Growth*. Available at: ec.europa.eu/economy. . ./europe_2020/index_en.htm.

Hindle, D., Dowdeswell, B. and Yasbeck, A.-M. (2004) *Report of a Survey of Clinical Pathways and Strategic Asset Planning in 17 EU Countries*. Utrecht: Netherlands Board for Hospital Facilities.

Kent, J., Richter, L., Keller, A. et al. (2009) *Integrating Evidence-Based Design: Practicing the Healthcare Design Process (EDAC Study Guide Three)*. Center For Health Design.

Legido-Quigley, H., McKee, M., Walshe, K. et al. (2008) How can quality of care be safeguarded across the European Union? *British Medical Journal*, 336: 920–3.

Luo, Y. (2002) Contract, cooperation and performance in international joint ventures. *Strategic Management Journal*, 23: 903–19.

Malone, E., Harmsen, C., Reno, K. et al. (2008) *An Introduction to Evidence-Based Design: Exploring Healthcare and Design. The Center for Health Design*. Building the Evidence-Base: Understanding Research in Healthcare Design (EDAC Study Guide Two).

McKee, M. and Healy, J. (2000) The role of the hospital in a changing environment. *Bull World Health Organ*, 78: 803–10.

Nolte, E. (2010) *International Benchmarking of Healthcare Quality: A Review of the Literature*. Rand Corporation, Europe. Available at: www.rand.org/pubs/technical_reports/2010/RAND_TR738.pdf.

Panella, M. and Vanhaecht, K. (2010a) Care pathways and organizational systems: the basis for a successful connection. *International Journal of Care Pathways*, 14: 45,46.

Panella, M. and Vanhaecht, K. (2010b) Is there still need for confusion about pathways?. *International Journal of Care Pathways* 14: 1–3.

Quan, X., Geboy, L., Ginsberg, R., Bosch, S., Joseph, A. and Keller, A. (2009) *The Center for Health Design. Integrating Evidence-Based Design.*

Rechel, B., Erskine, J., Wright, S., Dowdeswell, B. and McKee, M. (eds) (2009a) *Capital Investment for Health: Case Studies from Europe.* Copenhagen: World Health Organization, on behalf of the European Observatory on Health Systems. Available at: http://www.euro.who.int/InformationSources/Publications/Catalogue/20090908_1

Rechel, B., Wright, S., Edwards, N., Dowdeswell, B. and McKee, M. (eds) (2009b) *Investing in Hospitals of the Future.* Copenhagen: World Health Organization, on behalf of the European Observatory on Health Systems. Available at: http://www.euro.who.int/observatory/Publications/20090323_1.

Rechel, B., Wright, S., Barlow, J. and McKee, M. (2010) Hospital capacity planning: from measuring stocks to modelling flows. *Bull World Health Organ*, 88: 632–6.

Sackett, D., Rosenberg, W., Muir Gray J., Haynes, B. and Scott Richardson, W. (1996) Evidence based medicine: what it is and what it isn't, *BMJ*, 312: 71.

Ulrich, R. (1984) View through a window may influence recovery from surgery. *Science*, 224(4647): 420–1.

Welsh Office, Cabinet sub-committees (2010) *Capital Investment.* Available at: http://wales.gov.uk/about/cabinet/cabinetsubcommittees/previous/capitalinvestment/?lang=en.

Web resources

The following are web resources (including reports) reflected in this chapter that provide useful capital-related information.

Care Pathways: http://www.isip.nhs.uk/library/care-models.

The Center for Health Design, Texas, USA, has produced a compendium of credible reference projects: http://www.healthdesign.org/.

Design and Health Canada 2010:
http://www.designandhealth.com/Events/Canada-2010.aspx.

EU Public–Private Partnership perspectives – European Commission – "Europe 2020": A strategy for smart, sustainable and inclusive growth" Brussels, European Commission (COM(2010) 2020. http://ec.europa.eu/eu2020/index_en.htm.

Gateway principles – Office of Government Commerce support for public service capital procurement: http://www.ogc.gov.uk/what_is_ogc_gateway_review.asp.

Healthcare design – European Congress, Healthcare Planning and Design, Rotterdam 2010:
http://www.tno.nl/downloads/European%20Congress%20Healthcare%20Planning%20and%20Design_DuCHA10.pdf.

Italy, Structural Planning:
   http://www.euhpn.eu/resource/stewardship-and-governance-decentralised-health-systems-italian-case-study.
Karolinska Solna, Stockholm: http://www.nyakarolinskasolna.se/en.
The 'Layers' design principles:
   http://www.bouwcollege.nl/smartsite.shtml?id=6726.
   And http://kennisplein.zorgenbouw.nl/smartsite.dws?ch=KEN&id=8724.
Northern Ireland, Integrated planning:
   http://www.euhpn.eu/resource/euhpn-annual
   workshop-belfast (The service vision in Northern Ireland).
PFI, UK National Audit Office Reports:
   http://www.nao.org.uk/publications/1011/pfi_hospital_contracts.aspx.
Public–Private Partnerships PWC, as reported by PWC, December 2009.
Strategic Capital Planning – Welsh Office Strategic Capital Investment Framework, May
   2008, National Assembly for Wales: www.assemblywales.org/qg10-0011.pdf.

The following organizations provide libraries of capital-related information and/or broader health policy issues:

CABE (Commission for Architecture and the Built Environment): www.cabe.org.uk/.
European Centre for Health Assets and Architecture, ECHAA, the Netherlands: www.echaa.eu.
EHMA (European Health Managers Association): www.ehma.org.
European Union Health Property Network: www.euhpn.org.
HaCIRIC, UK: www.haciric.org.
LSHTM (London School of Hygiene and Tropical Medicine, Department of Public Health): www.lshtm.ac.uk.
TNO/DUCHA (Dutch Centre for Health Assets), the Netherlands: www.tno.nl/ducha.

Recommended reading for a contemporary compendium view of capital asset strategy in Europe, including case study analysis:

Rechel, B., Erskine, J., Wright, S., Dowdeswell, B. and McKee, M. (eds) (2009a) *Capital Investment for Health: Case Studies from Europe*. Copenhagen: World Health Organization, on behalf of the European Observatory on Health Systems; http://www.euro.who.int/InformationSources/Publications/Catalogue/20090908_1.
Rechel, B., Wright, S., Edwards, N., Dowdeswell, B. and McKee, M. (eds) (2009b) *Investing in Hospitals of the Future*. Copenhagen: World Health Organization, on behalf of the European Observatory on Health Systems. http://www.euro.who.int/observatory/Publications/20090323_1.

CHAPTER 16

Informatics for healthcare systems

Iain Buchan

Introduction

This chapter explores the role of Informatics in managing healthcare systems, emphasising innovation and future trends. It begins with definitions of Health Informatics as an academic discipline and emerging profession. The Informatics approach centres on health problems rather than technologies or organizations – a direction of translational thinking that healthcare managers should consider when dealing with information and communications technologies. Subsequent sections take a journey from the maintenance of well-being to specialist medical care, and consider the information systems requirements at each stage. The chapter then brings together different systems in creating a population-wide picture of health and healthcare to enable well-informed management of the whole system. The concluding section demonstrates the need for perpetual innovation of both Informatics and healthcare systems, in a tightly coupled and sometimes disruptive way.

Definitions of health informatics

The term 'Informatics' is variably used to describe academic disciplines and professions, usually specified to a domain of application, such as Health Informatics or Business Informatics (Wikipedia 2011a). The academic diaspora of Informatics has one thing in common across different domains – namely that it brings technically focused science and engineering together with research that is focused on human factors. This union of approaches has a common purpose to inform discovery and decision-making in any given field. Information systems are common to all fields of Informatics, but the balance between technical and human focus varies. To emphasize the importance of human factors, the term 'eHealth' is sometimes used interchangeably with Health Informatics (Wikipedia 2011b).

Definitions and terms for Health Informatics vary. Broadly, Health Informatics comprises the knowledge, skills and tools which enable information to be collected, managed, used and shared safely to support the delivery of healthcare and promote health (UK Council for Health Informatics Professions 2011). The International Medical

Informatics Association pulls the various threads together and organizes a four-yearly conference 'Medinfo'.

The professionalization of some Informatics specialities has arisen from the spread of information systems into most business processes. In order to manage the risks and opportunities posed by modern information systems, which are too complex to be addressed properly without specialist knowledge, it is necessary to set professional standards. The Health Informatics profession is emerging. In the UK, for example, the Council for Health Informatics Professions was formed in 2002, but registration is still voluntary (UK Council for Health Informatics Professions 2011). Healthcare systems around the world are exploring various levels of Informatics competence for: (1) all health professionals; and (2) specialist Health Informaticians. In the USA and parts of continental Europe, there are career paths, with recognized specialist qualifications, for people intending to manage information systems in clinical settings – some of these paths are open to clinicians and form clinical sub-specialities. It is interesting to note that in the UK, where there is no clinical career path in Informatics and there has been the world's largest healthcare IT programme, that the technical infrastructure produced by the programme was found to be largely successful (Payne et al. 2011) while the clinical application was poor (Hendy et al. 2005; Robertson et al. 2010). It could be argued that any large healthcare organization should have a Board member capable of translating healthcare needs into Informatics requirements.

Translational Informatics thinking for healthcare management

Informatics concerns information systems, which in turn comprise people, organizations and technologies. The most challenging part of developing *health* information systems is overcoming cultural, political and organizational barriers – the engineering is more predictable (Coiera 2009). It is therefore wise for healthcare managers to take a problem-oriented approach to Informatics, prioritized by the potential public health gain from informating specific aspects of healthcare systems. In addition, information technologies can uniquely enable timely collective decision-making. So those managing healthcare should keep Informatics in mind as a way of coordinating care and understanding the whole system. Proactive healthcare managers will ensure that their Informatics and clinical teams are thinking ahead about requirements for information systems. More often there is a reactive approach, with boards being asked to approve business cases written by IT managers for expensive technology. This chapter takes a translational approach, from health problems to information systems, and encourages general managers to do the same in any healthcare organization. This approach can be taken for all aspects of the health of a defined population, from maintenance of well-being to end-of-life care. The need for a problem-oriented approach is illustrated by considering the problem of tackling the obesity epidemic (Roux and Donaldson 2004) and avoiding acute escalations of long-term conditions (Purdy 2010). Both of these are priority areas in many healthcare systems in terms of reducing costs and suffering. Maintenance of a healthy body weight is common to both problems, and information systems might be used to help control body weight (Gibbons et al. 2009). An organization-centred approach might consider the information systems requirements for the health promotion, diabetes care, cardiology, rheumatology, etc. services separately. But there is an economy of scale in considering Informatics for supporting a healthy weight for patients across these organizational units.

Translational Informatics thinking like this is common among those tackling *information infrastructure* problems such as appointment booking systems, but it is uncommon among those in a position to drive *healthcare innovation* through informatics. Such innovation is where Informatics has the greatest potential to improve healthcare systems. General managers have oversight of this translation and need to make sure it happens proactively.

A common need for innovation is to improve the coordination of care between healthcare organizations, with relevant information following the patient/citizen. In order to translate information needs across organizational boundaries, we will consider the citizen's journey from maintaining well-being to receiving care for multiple conditions. Figure 16.1 illustrates this journey and shows the personal health record as the single common information system.

Citizen-led well-being and 'pre-primary' care

Reviews of the affordability of healthcare in society consistently emphasize the lack of sustainability (Medearis and Hishow 2010), and the need for more prevention (Wanless et al. 2007). In the United States, some Health Maintenance Organizations actively engage with their clients over managing health risks such as obesity, as part of a contractual obligation of the insured person to make their best efforts to maintain their

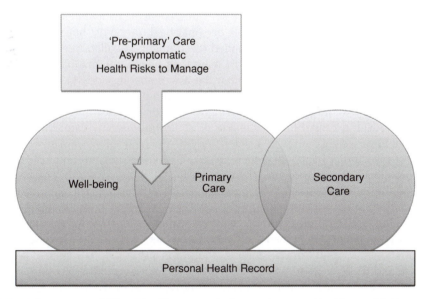

FIGURE 16.1 Convergence of different healthcare organizations on the personal health record, linking healthcare and well-being sectors as 'Pre-primary' Care

health (Steinbrook 2006). In some cultures, such as Singapore, social programmes al-most mandate citizens to tackle their own health risks (Toh et al. 2002). In more liberal nations with state-funded healthcare, such as the UK, there is a tension over avoiding 'nanny state' approaches to the public health vs. meeting the escalating costs of health-care (Department of Health 2010). Irrespective of the political or organizational issues, the daily choices an individual makes, which may affect their health, are becoming easier to collate through networked data sources about transactions, and through mo-bile technologies. The recent emergence of mobile or 'm' health as a sub-speciality of Health Informatics or eHealth emphasizes the importance of mobile technologies in linking the consumer healthcare and well-being market with clinical healthcare (Wikipedia 2011c). Consider the position and motion sensing capability of the latest mobile phones – this can be harnessed to track an individual's unstructured physical activity. In addition, a local network connection between the mobile phone and gym equipment might record structured physical activity. It is likely to be attractive to the individual citizen to be at the centre of information systems that 'persuade' them into greater well-being – thus there is a case for developing this kind of health promotion in the well-being market. But the same technologies might also be used to monitor physical activity as part of a healthcare contract with an insurer or state healthcare organization. There is room for experimentation to develop the most safe, effective, efficient and acceptable means of health promotion through mobile technologies. The balance between consumer freedom and responsibility will vary from culture to culture but the information opens up a new interface with primary healthcare in general.

Given a growing well-being market and the emergence of on-line personal health records, healthcare information will start to accumulate at much earlier stages of disease than is the case with present medical records. This creates an opportunity for primary care to reach 'upstream' in its preventive activities, engaging with individuals who have mounting health risks apparent in their personal health records, but who might not otherwise seek primary care. The extended reach might be called 'pre-primary' care. Furthermore an individual who elects to share their health information with a trusted primary care professional might find that the act of sharing adds to the motivation they need, for example, to take more exercise. So, pre-primary care might become an important vehicle for targeting primary care resources.

The following potential future scenario illustrates pre-primary care: Mr Smith is a 43-year-old overweight man with a sedentary job, and he is an ex-smoker with family history of myocardial infarction under age 65. His blood pressure and lipid profiles were in a slightly raised risk zone when he saw his GP three years ago, and he would like to be able to find the motivation to reduce his risk of a heart attack. His wife bought him a motion and position tracking wrist watch for his birthday to encourage him to exercise. The device required him to register with the company's website and create a profile. From his profile he had the option to connect with social networks such as Facebook to get support from his friends. There was also a link to a general personal health record (PHR) system, where he decided to create a profile. His primary care organization had an agreement with the PHR provider to advertise a linkage scheme between medical records and PHRs. So he made an appointment with his GP and arranged for the records to be linked. Mr Smith and his GP discussed cardiovascular risk reduction strategies. Scenarios of lifestyle change vs. risk were available for Mr Smith to reflect via his PHR on the Web following the consultation. The act of sharing his physical activity achievements with his friends and GP motivated Mr Smith to keep taking regular exercise. The treatment for high blood pressure that had been considered at the first consultation was no longer necessary after three months of regular exercise. The primary care organization had engaged actively in health promotion with a person who, in times before the PHR and connected devices, might not otherwise have presented until they had symptomatic disease. First contact in this case had been made by the consumer of a well-being product. First contact might otherwise be made by the healthcare provider running population based cardiovascular screening for the over-40s. Both of these approaches are pre-primary care.

Patient co-produced primary care information

As patients engage with primary care there is a need for information: (1) to support the decision whether or not to seek primary care; (2) to provide the primary care professional with all relevant information; and (3) to maximize the concordance with treatment. The Informatics focus in this area since the mid-1990s has been on the quality of medical information available to the public via the Internet (Eysenbach and Diepgen, 1998), and on triage services such as algorithm-driven telephone and Web-based help-lines like NHS Direct (Bunn et al. 2005). Such initiatives assume that individuals will (1) seek the information issued by the main healthcare provider; and (2) act on high quality information predictably. Neither of these assumptions may hold true. With the advent of personal health records (Tang et al. 2006), there is an opportunity to engage with patients over the information they are bought into rather than the information that is being offered to them. Consider the individual who has a health record that is linked to sources of advice over managing illness – it is easier for the healthcare provider's information system to give personalized advice with this kind of system than via Web search engines, which lack contextual information about the individual, and which have a multitude of competing websites that may drown out the most relevant one. In addition to reducing unnecessary clinical appointments, personal health records could considerably improve the exchange of information during and around the clinical encounter. Early initiatives to open up primary care records to patients are proving popular with patients – where patients can add information to records, the majority choose to do so (Hannan and Fitton 2011). Thus there is an opportunity to engage with patients as co-producers of primary care (information). This might be another vehicle for encouraging individuals to take a more active part in their own healthcare. A by-product of the co-produced healthcare record might be an increase in knowledge about medical interventions 'in the wild', outside the rarefied environments of clinical trials – the results of trials predicting as little as a quarter of what will happen to a patient given the treatment in question (Fortin et al. 2006). An example of a potentially important missing signal might be a daily quality of life score filled in by the patient as part of their 'contract' in being prescribed a course of antibiotics. The current signal from medical records that a patient has or has not tolerated therapy is much less detailed, is often missing and is subject to multiple biases, i.e. unusable. Mobile technologies connected to personal health records could further enhance the capture of new signals about responses to treatment. Indeed the aspiration of 'personalized medicine', usually discussed in the context of genomics, depends on more accurate and detailed capture of personal health information. The same information is likely to be important for targeting primary care resources. Co-production of care through a shared record is illustrated in the following potential future scenario: Mrs Jones is a 53-year-old woman with a ten-year history of rheumatoid arthritis, requiring occasional hospital admissions during flare-ups. She has also been treated for clinical depression. Since the introduction of access to her care records through a Personal Health Record (PHR), Mrs Jones has been able to share daily pain and quality of life scores with her care team. Both the specialist rheumatology services and primary care are able to see when Mrs Jones is running into problems and intervene early to help avoid hospital admission – which is particularly important for avoiding healthcare associated infection as Mrs Jones is immune-compromised by the treatment for her arthritis. In addition, she joined a social network of people with arthritis, finding rewarding ways to increase physical activity, in spite of their disease, to offset the increased risk of cardiovascular diseases in rheumatoid arthritis and its treatment – she brought up this risk with her primary care team for the first time and discussed the management options. An Informatics researcher studying Mrs Jones' experience of care before and after she took up the PHR found that she felt a greater sense of control over her own care, specifically the coordination between generalist and specialist care, which she felt was lacking previously.

Informing self-care

Given the patient, or the patient's immediate carer, as an active co-producer of the healthcare record, the information systems that link patient/carer, professional and personal health records can provide a new vehicle for informing self-care. The Informatics of self-healthcare, however, is usually considered in respect of 'information prescriptions', telemedical consultations with patients, or monitoring physical parameters such as blood glucose in the community (Nijland et al. 2008). In healthcare management terms there is a more subtle, and potentially more influential, Informatics phenomenon around the communication loop between patient, professional and information system.

Consider the patient with schizophrenia in relation to community psychiatric nursing, primary care and inpatient psychiatric services. The cost to the patient and the healthcare service of relapse requiring inpatient admission is large. So the monitoring and adjustment of therapy in the community to prevent relapse are important. Patients respond best to such monitoring when they are actively involved (May et al. 2009). Information systems that send text messages to a patient's mobile phone and analyse responses could help to detect when a patient is going off their mediation and at risk of relapse, thus triggering self-adjustment of medication and enhanced contact with clinical services. Early results from studies of the use of text message loops between service user, care team and information system are showing reduced relapse in schizophrenia and bipolar disorder (Merz 2010; Lewis 2011).

A new form of healthcare organization comprising patient, clinical service and algorithm/information system is emerging. This is effectively a triangle of information between patient, clinician and technology – more usually considered in the context of medical devices. Regulatory agencies are gradually catching up with this. For example EU Directive 2007/47/EC now classifies algorithms/software as medical devices if the information produced is used to support diagnostic or prognostic decisions (European Union 2007). Consider the many software applications that are used to calculate risks such as the risk of a cardiovascular event within X years given a set of information about an individual's characteristics. Such applications, which have not been validated as medical devices, may now contravene laws in the EU. There is a need to bring Informatics into the mainstream of healthcare management to maximize the benefits of such systems while managing the risks.

Coordinating care for patients with multiple conditions

With an ageing population, improved care outcomes and the persistence of multiple disease risk factors such as obesity, the number of people with multiple long-term conditions is set to rise (Nolte and McKee 2008). At the same time advances in medical knowledge have produced more interventions, and services have become more specialized. The increasing specialization adds to the complexity of healthcare organizations with a greater number of organizational units and the need for coordination between them.

One mechanism for managing the quality of care of patients as they flow between generalist and specialist services, and between different health professions, has been the introduction of clinical guidelines and integrated care pathways (Kitchiner et al. 1996). This has been informed by a branch of Health Informatics concerned with representing medical knowledge and supporting clinical decisions (Peleg et al. 2003). But there is a fundamental problem with condition-specific care pathways – namely a person with multiple conditions is not the sum of multiple specialist care pathways (Valderas et al. 2009). For example, a patient with type 2 diabetes, chronic kidney disease, high blood pressure and coronary heart disease might have an over-emphasis on control of blood sugar by diabetic services at the expense of increasing body weight, pushing up blood pressure and making the kidney disease more difficult to control. At a simpler level, scheduling of blood tests in one visit rather than three would increase efficiency and convenience, and decrease the risk of healthcare-associated infection. Informatics in sectors such as transport has developed workflow optimization techniques that tackle challenges similar to coordinating healthcare for a person with multiple conditions. As care pathways are central to the body of knowledge that defines clinical professions, there is a need for more clinical engagement in Health Informatics if workflow is to be optimized within healthcare systems. At a socio-technical level, the central Informatics problem for improving care for people with multiple conditions is the lack of interoperability of the knowledge of patients, generalist clinicians and specialist clinicians. Simply connecting all parties to a conventional medical record on-line will not solve this problem. Indeed, it has been argued that the natural evolution of the medical record will produce an avatar representation of a person's health, with different personalities depending on who is interacting with it – in other words, neither like clinical case-notes

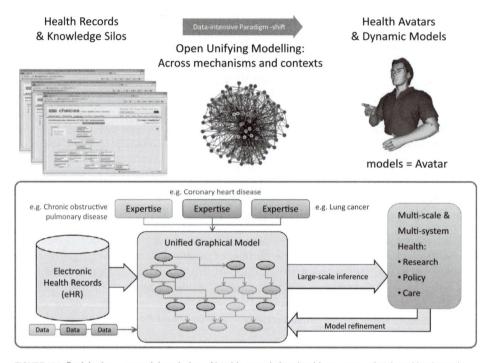

FIGURE 16.2 Envisioning a potential evolution of health records into health avatars underpinned by dynamic models, frequently updated data, and more useful complexity of healthcare knowledge

nor the early attempts at personal health records (Buchan et al. 2009). Figure 16.2 illustrates this concept.

It would be easy to get lost in the technical details here, and for managers to delegate the responsibility for this to a technical department. Instead, managers might usefully keep oversight and return frequently to ask how the evolving clinical information systems in their organizations are leading to a common understanding of care between patients, generalist clinicians and specialist clinicians. In part, the impetus may come from patients directly, as they become co-producers of health records shared with healthcare organizations. The danger is that a two-tier record may develop, one tier for health professionals, the other for patients, translating a paper-based barrier to communication into a digital barrier. The early signs of primary care record sharing are encouraging that this obstacle may be overcome sooner rather than later (Fisher et al. 2007).

Using Informatics to help manage health systems

Improving the coordination of care for individuals across multiple parts of a healthcare system is effectively a generalization of patient level Health Informatics to the population level. In other words, titrating healthcare resources to deliver maximum population health gain can be seen as a Public Health Informatics problem (Ainsworth and Buchan 2009). This area is usually the preserve of Management and Economics. In some countries, such as the UK, however, the Public Health Service helps to inform healthcare resource allocation, adding an epidemiological perspective to the corporate and comparative approaches to healthcare needs assessment (Wright et al. 1998). Management information for health systems usually focuses on strategy rather than tactics. For example, the resource allocation decisions that are made infrequently may be supported by deep analyses while the subsequent implementation of services is barely monitored. Commissioners may return to examining this service in a cycle of, say, three years, therefore the oversight relies on summary evaluation covering long periods. Tactical management is under-informed in most health systems – this is particularly apparent when healthcare is compared with dynamically adapting sectors such as e-commerce. Business intelligence solutions and 'dashboards' are marketed to healthcare organizations as ways to produce more timely management information (Mettler and Rohner 2009). These information systems range from clinically oriented summaries of process or outcome across multiple care records to financially centred intelligence. All such systems are limited by: (1) the quality of the underpinning data; and (2) the engagement of staff with the information. Typical databases of healthcare transactions are fraught with errors. For example, a clinician using the code for a heart attack may edit the code's rubric with 'MI r/o' meaning heart attack has been ruled out – so the dashboard may count this as an event that did not occur. Non-coded and miscoded clinical information is common. This problem will not be resolved until clinical and personal healthcare records have evolved to capture and check the relevant information at source. However, there are subsets of care data captured for clinical audit and performance management purposes that are important for benchmarking. Such information is most advanced where clinicians drive the comparisons at national scale – for example, the publications on survival rates after heart surgery by the Society of Cardiothoracic Surgery of Great Britain and Ireland (Care Quality Commission 2011). A different approach is commissioner/insurer-driven benchmarking, for example, the 'Spend and Outcomes' tools from the NHS in England where mortality and spend data are analysed leading to an 'information pack' for each locality with slides declaring, for example, 'Bolton PCT has a higher spend and worse outcome for CVD when compared to PCTs nationally' (NHS Information Centre for Health and Social Care 2011). Such benchmarking may fail to adjust for factors such as case-mix differences or time-limited investments. In future, there may be more value in creating social networks of benchmarking clubs over live information than in managing responses to intermittent publication of comparisons. The same principle applies to intra-organization benchmarking, say, over rates of healthcare-associated infections between different wards of a hospital. Given what is envisioned above about the evolution of medical records into dynamic, interactive information systems co-produced with patients, there is a need to plan to adapt services according to more detailed and contemporary assessments of the health needs of populations. Even before such systems are developed, there is a vast amount of unused information about population health needs that could be produced now by linking and analysing databases across health systems. The Informatics challenge in providing this information is not about linking databases, that is the easy part. The central challenge is one of social computing – to generate collective insight across information silos such as finance, public health, clinical quality improvement, service performance management, etc. The tipping point is more likely to be a cultural shift through increased visibility of actors than a technical achievement of a certain quality of information.

Imagine Amazon-like prompts for clinical audit, whereby the information system prompts the user with '... colleagues who selected the variables you have selected from the audit system also selected these ... might they be relevant to your analysis?' Further, imagine a needs-assessment for bariatric surgery services for population X, where instead of starting from scratch the analyst can search an information system for a template needs assessment conducted in population Y, populate it with data from population X, refine the methods, publish the template back up and get professional development credits for sharing this knowledge. The bottleneck for generating population health intelligence is not the supply of data, nor is it the supply of methods for analysing the data. The enduring bottleneck is, and will continue to be, the supply of people with the skills to contextualize and interpret the analyses. The ideal Informatics approach here is to connect such people with social computing methods so that their insights collectively are greater than the sum of parts.

With the right information systems, health services management and public health approaches to understanding the healthcare needs of populations can reinforce one another. A substantial amount of research and sharing of data and expertise will be needed to build such systems, creating dynamic, localized models of population health needs vs. services.

Harnessing disruption: synchronous innovation and implementation

Commissioning a data warehouse is an example of an investment in part of an information system, which, if the data simply gathers (digital) dust, is inadequate. There is a need to link such investments to clear requirements for generating information from the data, particularly in areas of unmet need for informing healthcare decisions. But healthcare IT policies tend to stop at data management and information *infrastructure*. This is not sufficiently disruptive (Christensen et al. 2009) to engage the relevant staff and service users to become part of the information *system* – taking ownership and bringing essential tacit knowledge to bear.

Informatics management needs to tread a careful line between not getting enough clinical engagement and getting too much. An example of 'too much' would be where a clinician diverts more Informatics resource into their own specialist area of interest at the expense of other areas with equal or greater needs. A core competence of an Informatician is to be able to abstract requirements, say, from diabetes to another service such as rheumatology, so that one system can serve both needs and an economy of scale is realized. Furthermore, the smart Informatician will try to seed innovation in the rheumatology service from what is observed in the diabetes care service, and vice versa. With the dawn of personal health records, a new ally in this cross-fertilization of innovation is the patient.

The *trained* Health Informatician workforce is in short supply and the degree of professionalization varies around the world (Hersh 2008). So it is difficult for many healthcare organizations' boards to keep oversight both of what is needed and of what is technically possible of healthcare information systems. The scarcest resource is clinically-trained Informaticians. Healthcare IT policies and activities have therefore focused on technical infrastructure, and are often under the management of a Director of Finance.

Conventional healthcare IT policies focus on large infrastructure and long procurement cycles. As already noted, this can fail to engage clinicians and patients sufficiently to make best use of the infrastructure. A knee-jerk response to this problem might be to get clinical and patient groups to suggest priorities for care information and then fund various pilot initiatives. Such responses usually fail to recognize generic Informatics problems, for example, that the different priority areas selected share a common Informatics requirement to close the loop between the production and use of information. A clear oversight of what is needed and what is technically possible might be generated by managing the *innovation* much more closely with the *implementation* of health information systems.

Looking ahead, a greater supply of data and analytical tools, combined with social networks of sense-making, will generate complex models of healthcare. The use of such models will need to be managed – their limitations understood and accountabilities for monitoring them made clear. Under-use will also need to be managed, which is more often the case at present. For example, a patient requiring coronary revascularization (unblocking coronary arteries to prevent a heart attack) needs to consider the risk of dying during the procedure, the risk of having a coronary event within X years without the procedure, and the risk of requiring another revascularization within Y years. The treatment options are: (1) stay on current drug treatment and observe; (2) revascularize using a catheter and stents; or (3) revascularize using open surgery and bypass grafts. Then there are optional variations on the procedure such as the number of blocked vessels to target. Currently, patients are given risk information based on models developed using data from when the indications for treatment were different (Grayson et al. 2006). So the models need updating. Furthermore, the modelling is done separately by cardiologists and cardiac surgeons, working on speciality-specific audit databases, precluding the kind of modelling that might help a patient choose between surgery and stenting. It could be argued that healthcare managers have a duty to ensure that the relevant data is shared and models are kept up to date, in order that patients are properly informed about the treatment options relevant to local services.

The introduction of new information systems into healthcare usually disrupts a clinical or administrative workflow. If the disruption is led by those driving the relevant clinical or administrative work, then the system is likely to succeed. If not, it may be wasteful or directly harmful. The long procurement cycles that have come to characterize healthcare IT initiatives have disconnected technical infrastructure development from healthcare innovation. Many large healthcare IT initiatives have failed because they treated innovation to implementation as a one-way process over a long time period. Other sectors have benefited from a more participative, user-centred approach, harnessing the beneficial effects of disruptive technologies. Managers of healthcare in an ever more data-intensive and socially-networked world, might bring together the innovation in care with innovation in Informatics to achieve the participation needed to deliver the best healthcare information.

Conclusion

Most businesses and public sector organizations are becoming more data intensive. In this chapter we have shown that healthcare has particular needs: (1) to engage with service-users to provide additional data and co-produce their care information; (2) to generate more complex understanding of healthcare across conventional organizational boundaries; (3) to harness the insights of networks of health professionals using complex information about services and social computing techniques; (4) to increase workforce capacity in Health Informatics; and (5) to integrate Informatics operations with all parts of healthcare organizations, particularly clinical leadership and innovation.

Summary box

- Health Informatics comprises the knowledge, skills and tools which enable information to be collected, managed, used and shared safely to support the delivery of healthcare and promote health.
- Health Informatics is an academic discipline and emerging profession.
- Human factors are core to health information systems.
- Healthcare managers should oversee a translational approach to Health Informatics, with coordinated clinical engagement and needs-led planning.
- Consumers of well-being products and services, linked to primary care through Personal Health Records, may form a new sector 'pre-primary care', through which preventive healthcare measures can be enhanced.
- Patients can usefully co-produce their care record via access to clinical systems, and might add further information through Personal Health Record systems and devices.
- The communication loop between patient, healthcare professional and information system can provide mobile information that supports self-care.
- Analysis of data from aggregated care records is essential for filling gaps in medical knowledge, particularly for people with multiple conditions.
- Healthcare record extracts are easily misused in benchmarking performance – clinical coding and case mix adjustment are commonly problematic.
- Social networks of 'sense-making' are as important as databases for informing the management of health systems.
- The disruptive effects of IT might be harnessed within healthcare innovation initiatives: this requires the early participation of patients and professionals.

Self-test exercises

1 Consider the life course of a person from birth to death and all of the information required to help make decisions about their health and healthcare. Arrange those decisions in a Venn diagram with sets: self-care; primary care; and secondary care. Compare and contrast the information systems required to support those decisions and explore the overlap between them. How might that overlap be managed efficiently?

2 Choose five hospital departments and describe their possible responses to a central request to increase the amount of secondary prevention and self-care that they promote. How can each department co-produce healthcare information with patients in a coherent manner, and what are the common information systems requirements? Describe the information experience of a person with multiple conditions interacting with more than one department. How might social computing technologies be harnessed to help the departments to coordinate their responses?

3 Describe the potential for personal health records to form the aggregation hub for healthcare information from multiple providers. Draw a map of trust for this arrangement and describe the management issues for: maintaining privacy and confidentiality; and quality assurance of decision support. Outline an Informatics workforce development plan to help manage the change from organization-centred to patient-centred management of healthcare information.

References and further reading

Ainsworth, J. and Buchan, I. (2009) e-Labs and work objects: towards digital health economies. In R. Mehmood, E. Cerqueira, R. Piesiewicz, and I. Chlamtazc (eds) *Communications Infrastructure: Systems and Applications in Europe. Lecture Notes of the Institute for Computer Sciences, Social Informatics and Telecommunications Engineering*. Berlin: Springer, 16: 206–16. DOI: 10.1007/978-3-642-11284-3.

Buchan, I., Winn, J. and Bishop, C. (2009) A unified modelling approach to data intensive healthcare. In *The Fourth Paradigm: Data-intensive Scientific Discovery*. T. Hey, S. Tansley, K. Tolle (eds) Microsoft Research. Available at: http://research.microsoft.com/en-us/collaboration/fourthparadigm/4th_paradigm_book_part2_buchan.pdf.

Bunn, F., Byrne, G. and Kendall, S. (2005) The effects of telephone consultation and triage on healthcare use and patient satisfaction: a systematic review. *British Journal of General Practice*, 55: 956–61.

Care Quality Commission. (2011) *Rates of Survival after Heart Surgery in the UK*. Available at: http://heartsurgery.cqc.org.uk/Survival.aspx.

Christensen, C., Grossmab, J. and Hwang, J. (2009) *The Innovator's Prescription: A Disruptive Solution for Health Care*. Maidenhead: McGraw-Hill Professional.

Coiera, E. (2009) Building a national health IT system from the middle out. *Journal of the American Medical Informatics Association*, 16: 271–73. doi:10.1197/jamia. M3183.

Department of Health (2010) *Healthy Lives, Healthy People: Our Strategy for Public Health in England*. White Paper. Available at: http://www.dh.gov.uk/en/Publichealth/ Healthyliveshealthypeople/index.htm.

European Union (2007) Directive 2007/47/ec of the European Parliament and of the Council. *Official Journal of the European Union*, L 247/21.

Eysenbach, G. and Diepgen, T. (1998) Towards quality management of medical information on the internet: evaluation, labelling, and filtering of information. *BMJ*, 317: 1496.

Fisher, B., Fitton, R., Poirer, C. and Stables, D. (2007) Patient record access: the time has come! *British Journal of General Practice*, 57(539): 507–11.

Fortin, M., Dionne, J., Pinho, G., Gignac, J., Almirall, J. and Lapointe, L. (2006) Randomized controlled trials: do they have external validity for patients with multiple morbidities? *Annals of Family Medicine*, 4: 104–8.

Gibbons, M., Wilson, R., Samal, L., Lehmann, C., Dickersin, K., Lehmann, H. et al. (2009) *Impact of Consumer Health Informatics Applications*. Evidence Report/ Technology Assessment Number 188. U.S. Department of Health and Human Services. AHRQ Publication No. 09(10)-E019.

Grayson, A., Moore, R., Jackson, M., Rathore, S., Sastry, S., Gray, T. et al. (2006) Multivariate prediction of major adverse cardiac events after 9914 percutaneous coronary interventions in the North West of England. *Heart* 92: 658–63.

Hannan, A. and Fitton, R. (2011) Study on patient access to the GP electronic health record Haughton Thornley Medical Centres. Available at: http://www.htmc.co.uk/ pages/pv.asp?p=htmc0147.

Hendy, J., Reeves, B., Fulop, N., Hutchings, A. and Masseria, C. (2005) Challenges to implementing the national programme for information technology (NPfIT): a qualitative study. *BMJ*, 331: 331 doi: 10.1136/bmj.331.7512.331.

Hersh, W. (2008). Health and biomedical informatics: opportunities and challenges for a twenty-first century profession and its education. *Yearbook of Medical Informatics*, 2008: 157–64.

Kitchiner, D., Davidson, C. and Bundred, P. (1996) Integrated care pathways: effective tools for continuous evaluation of clinical practice. *Journal of Evaluation in Clinical Practice*, 2(1): 65–9.

Lewis, S. (2011) Personal communication.

May, C., Mair, F., Finch, T., MacFarlane, A., Dowrick, C., Treweek, S. et al. (2009) Development of a theory of implementation and integration: Normalization Process Theory. *BMC Implemetation Science*, 4: 29.

Medearis, A. and Hishow, O. (2010) *Narrowing the Sustainability Gap of EU and US Health Care Spending*. Working Paper FG 1, SWP Berlin. Available at: http://www .swp-berlin.org/fileadmin/contents/products/arbeitspapiere/HealthDebt_EU_USA_ formatiert_neu_KS.pdf.

Merz, T.A. (2010) Using cell/mobile phone SMS for therapeutic intervention. In K. Anthony, D.M. Nagel and S. Goss (eds) *The Use of Technology in Mental Health: Applications, Ethics and Practice*. Illinois: Charles Thomas.

Mettler, T. and Rohner P. (2009) Performance management in health care: the past, the present, and the future. In *Proceedings of the 9th International Conference on Business Informatics*, pp. 699–708.

NHS Information Centre for Health and Social Care (2011) *Right Care: Health Investment Pack*. Available at: http://www.ic.nhs.uk/services/in-development/right-care.

Nijland, N., van Gemert-Pijnen, J., Boer, H., Steehouder, M. and Seydel, E. (2008) Evaluation of internet-based technology for supporting self-care: problems encountered by patients and caregivers when using self-care applications. *Journal of Medical Internet Research*, 10(2) e13.

Nolte, E. and McKee, M. (2008) *Caring for People with Chronic Conditions: A Health System Perspective*. European Health Observatory on Health Systems and Policies, World Health Organization. Maidenhead: Open University Press.

Payne, T., Detmer, D., Wyatt, J. and Buchan, I. (2011) National-scale clinical information exchange in the United Kingdom: lessons for the United States. *Journal of the American Medical Informatics Association*, 18(1): 91–8.

Peleg, M., Tu, S., Bury, J., Ciccarese, P., Fox, J., Greenes, R.A. et al. (2003) Comparing computer-interpretable guideline models: a case-study approach. *Journal of the American Medical Informatics Association*, 10(1): 52–68.

Purdy S. (2010) *Avoiding Hospital Admissions: What Does the Research Evidence Say?* London: Kings Fund. Available at: www.kingsfund.org.uk/document.rm?id=8877.

Robertson, A., Cresswell, K., Takian, A., Petrakaki, D., Crowe, S., Cornford, T. et al. (2010) Implementation and adoption of nationwide electronic health records in secondary care in England: qualitative analysis of interim results from a prospective national evaluation. *BMJ*, 341: c4564.

Roux, L. and Donaldson, C. (2004). Economics and obesity: costing the problem or evaluating solutions? *Obesity Research*, 12(2): 173–9.

Steinbrook, R. (2006) Imposing personal responsibility for health. *New England Journal of Medicine*, 355: 753–6.

Tang, P., Ash, J., Bates, D., Overhage, J. and Sands, D. (2006) Personal health records: definitions, benefits, and strategies for overcoming barriers to adoption. *Journal of the American Medical Informatics Association*, 13: 121–6. doi:10.1197/jamia.M2025.

Toh, C., Cutter, J. and Chew, S. (2002) School based intervention has reduced obesity in Singapore. *BMJ*, 324: 427.

UK Council for Health Informatics Professions. (2011) Available at: http://www.ukchip.org.

Valderas, J.M., Starfield, B., Sibbald, B., Salisbury, C. and Roland, M. (2009) Defining comorbidity: implications for understanding health and health services. *Ann. Fam. Med.*, 7(4): 357–63.

Wanless, D., Appleby, J., Harrison, A. and Patel, D. (2007) *Our Health Future Secured? A Review of NHS Funding and Performance*. London: King's Fund. Available at: www.kingsfund.org.uk/document.rm?id=7700.

Wikipedia (2011a) Informatics. Available at: http://en.wikipedia.org/wiki/Informatics.

Wikipedia (2011b) eHealth. Available at: http://en.wikipedia.org/wiki/EHealth.

Wikipedia (2011c) mHealth. Available at: http://en.wikipedia.org/wiki/MHealth.

Wright, J., Williams, R. and Wilkinson, J. (1998) Development and importance of health needs assessment. *BMJ*, 316: 1310.

Websites and resources

The International Medical Informatics Association is an association of Health Informatics associations. The website acts as a portal to the lead Health Informatics association in each member country and coordinates the four yearly international conference: www.imia-medinfo.org.

The main Health Informatics Journals provide objective evidence:

Journal of the American Medical Informatics Association has a North American focus but carries many international articles: jamia.bmj.com.

Journal of Internet Medical Research focuses on Web-based medical intervention: www.jimronline.net.

Methods of Information in Medicine carries more technical articles: www.schattauer.de/en/magazine/subject-areas/journals-a-z/methods.html.

Health Affairs focuses on policy: www.healthaffairs.org.

The Web can present a blizzard of information about healthcare information systems sponsored by vendors or other organizations who might take a biased viewpoint. The reader exploring the healthcare management implications of an Informatics problem is advised to search for scholarly articles via Google Scholar: scholar.google.com.

CHAPTER 17

The healthcare workforce

Paula Hyde and Anne McBride

Introduction

Healthcare services depend upon the knowledge, expertise and work of staff members, making staffing a major budget item for any healthcare organization. We rely upon the ability of healthcare organizations to train and develop, then deploy, manage and engage the healthcare workforce as effectively as possible. In addition, there continues to be on-going shortages of healthcare workers and uneven distribution of these workers within and between countries. This has been described as a global health workforce crisis; not least because health organizations struggle to sustain their workforce (World Health Organization 2010a). Thus, healthcare managers need to be able to find suitable staff to provide high quality services as efficiently as possible. The challenges managers face in achieving this remain a central feature of healthcare management. Demands for health services continue to rise regardless of financial constraints or workforce supply. Managers around the world, therefore, share a common desire to manage people in ways that enable the workforce to perform at their best.

This chapter looks at four key workforce issues which all have a role to play in ensuring the organization has 'the right people with the right skills in the right place at the right time to deliver the organisation's objectives' (CIPD 2010). Each workforce issue is covered in subsequent sections of this chapter. The first issue, having the right people, concerns workforce planning and ensuring that the organization has the people resources in place to deliver short- and long-term objectives. The second issue concerns workforce training and development, i.e. ensuring staff have the 'right skills'. The third is workforce modernization, whereby organizations rethink the labour process as a means of enabling high quality services to be delivered as efficiently as possible. The fourth issue relates to how organizations coordinate and manage these three issues. While numerous authors (Boxall and Purcell 2003; Vere 2005; Boaden et al. 2007; Sparrow et al. 2008) indicate the need to link workforce issues to business strategy, research in the NHS in England indicates the challenge of ensuring a meaningful interaction between financial planning, service planning and workforce planning and the implications of failure in this regard.

Thus this chapter will be presented in four main sections: workforce planning; training and development; workforce modernization; and strategic workforce management.

Each section is grounded in the international experience and informed by research findings from initiatives in the NHS in England and elsewhere. This analysis also acknowledges that '"modernisation" is not a neutral step forward but a highly coloured version of progress rooted in market-style efficiency' (Seifert and Sibley 2005: 226). These four sections are preceded with an outline of the characteristics of the international healthcare workforce.

Characteristics of the international healthcare workforce

There are about 60 million health workers worldwide. Two-thirds provide health services and one-third is made up of management and support workers, moreover, demand for health workers is increasing in high-income countries (World Health Organization 2010b). Health workers form a significant proportion of most national employment statistics and hospitals often play an important role in local economies. Healthcare is one of the largest industries in the USA, providing 14.3 million paid jobs in 2008 (Bureau of Labor Statistics 2010). Equally, the NHS is by far the largest UK employer with 1.43 million employees in 2009 (NHS Information Centre 2010).

Healthcare organizations are characteristically made up of a large proportion (around 50 per cent) of professionally qualified staff providing frontline services to recipients of healthcare. Table 17.1 gives the relative proportions of clinical, support and infrastructure staff groups in the NHS. Support staff refers to clinical support workers and infrastructure refers to managerial, administrative and hotel service workers. This type of organizational arrangement has been called a 'professional bureaucracy' (Daft 1992). Such organizations are characterized by having high proportions of professionally qualified staff organized around clients or services. Decision-making takes place around the operating core (professional frontline staff) and management and administration take place by mutual agreement.

Healthcare is a rapidly growing industry sector. For example, the US healthcare workforce is projected to rise by 22.4 per cent between 2008 and 2018, an increase of 3.2 million paid jobs (Bureau of Labor Statistics 2010). In support of these figures, ten of the most rapidly growing occupations are healthcare related (Bureau of Labor Statistics 2010). While the global economic downturn since 2009 may have slowed down

TABLE 17.1 Professionally qualified, support and infrastructure staff in the NHS, 2009

Staff group	Percentage of NHS workforce
Professionally qualified clinical staff	54.1
Support to clinical staff	28.2
Infrastructure support (management, administration and hotel services)	17.6

Source: NHS Information Centre (2010).

projected growth in this sector, the populations of most Western countries continue to age. Increasing demand is closely related to increasing numbers of older people in the population. A combination of rapid expansion, high staff turnover and an increasingly ageing workforce has contributed to significant projected staff shortfalls of registered professionals and other skilled staff in countries such as the USA, the UK and Australia (Wanless 2002; National Center for Workforce Analysis 2004; Australian Government Productivity Commission 2005). Migration of healthcare workers away from poorer countries and towards richer countries also makes staff shortages a global problem.

The World Health Organization (2006: xvii) identified the key factors shaping national healthcare workforces: *health needs* such as demographic changes and epidemiology shape demand for services while *health systems* and *national context* provide infrastructure for development and deployment of the healthcare workforce. Challenges to providing the right people with the right skills are affected by *numbers of workers*, *skill mix*, *distribution of workers* and the *attractiveness of health work* (working conditions) (see Self-test exercise 1).

As one of the world's largest healthcare workforces, the UK NHS provides an example of workforce changes and challenges. The NHS workforce has experienced an annual staff growth rate in the UK of around 2.7 per cent per year since 1997 (NHS Information Centre 2010). Doctors and other professionals traditionally work long hours and absence rates in the NHS are high. The average time lost per year in the health service is around 4.5 per cent (NHS Information Centre 2010), compared to 3.3 per cent elsewhere (CIPD 2009). Turnover rates are lower in the health sector (13.2 per cent) than the public sector generally (13.5 per cent) and considerably lower than in the private sector (20.4 per cent), nevertheless, health sector staff can be costly to replace (Dawson et al. 2009). In some countries unplanned losses of staff through illness, death and migration threaten workforce stability (WHO 2006). In Western countries, management style, poor communication, poor working conditions and stress have been cited as reasons for staff attrition (Leveck and Jones 1996; Cangelosi et al. 1998; Newman and Maylor 2002). In the UK, successful recruitment has been hampered by poor public perceptions of the NHS as an employer because of poor pay, lack of flexible hours and pressures associated with low staff numbers (Arnold 2004). The last decade, however, has seen increased emphasis on tackling these issues and making the NHS a better place to work (Department of Health 2002). Given that the UK NHS is the third largest employer in the world, these initiatives provide useful case studies to illustrate both the challenges facing healthcare managers today, and possible strategies for addressing them.

Workforce planning

Using similar terminology as CIPD (2010) cited above, the World Health Organization (2006) identifies getting the 'right workers with the right skills in the right place doing the right things' (2006: xx) as *the* simple workforce goal to tackling world health problems.

The report identifies three key ways in which policy-makers and management can pursue this goal (2006: xx):

- active planning and management of the health workforce production pipeline (entry);
- improvements in performance (workforce);
- limiting workforce attrition (exit).

The complexity of such a simple goal can be illustrated through determining an appropriate model for workforce planning. As indicated by Birch et al. (2007), the general approach to workforce planning (or Health Human Resources Planning in Canada), has been to focus almost exclusively on calculating sizes of training programmes (i.e. entry) with scant attention paid to productivity improvements (often referred to as supply-based models). Another regular omission has been a more nuanced identification of need. While these omissions might be understandable in the context of indistinct social and political choices about access and delivery of care, they can result in the over-estimation of workforce requirements and healthcare service costs (Birch et al. 2007: 2,45). An extended (needs-based) analytical framework would go beyond calculations based on demography and current level of providers and consist of demography; epidemiology; standards of care and provider productivity (Birch et al. 2007). At what level, however, are such calculations to be made? Workforce planning flows from organizational strategy (CIPD 2010: 2) but within a national healthcare system with large occupational groups and independent providers, whose business is workforce planning?

The UK House of Commons Health Committee has reported several times on the NHS workforce (House of Commons Health Committee 1999, 2007). In 1999, the Health Committee concluded that the NHS was in the middle of a staffing crisis and in 2007 it indicated that there had been a 'disastrous failure of workforce planning' (2007: 3). After reviewing evidence from a number of witnesses during 2006–07, the Committee concluded that insufficient thought had been given to long-term or strategic planning; too few people had the ability and skills to do the work; there was a lack of coordination between workforce and financial planning; and none of the NHS organizations at national, regional or local level made workforce planning a priority (2007: 3–4). Although a national plan of action had been published (Department of Health 2000) and regional Workforce Development Confederations dedicated to workforce planning had been established, the Committee indicated that a huge growth in funds (and associated targets) had led to an unanticipated increase in staff exacerbated by the constant reorganization and later abolition of the Workforce Development Confederations.

The Health Committee argued that organizations at the regional level (Strategic Health Authorities (SHAs)) should take the lead in creating a better workforce planning system, with the integration of workforce, financial and service planning being a key priority. A year later, the Next Stage Review (Darzi 2008) indicated that workforce planning should reflect service planning and be based on pathways of care (reflecting complex co-morbidities). This model envisaged workforce planning starting at the local provider level (with the involvement of social care) so that the local purchasers of care would produce combined service and workforce plans for their local health economies, SHAs would combine these plans into a single integrated service and workforce regional plan, and a new Centre of Excellence would synthesize the plans for professional advisory board review.

A change in the UK Government since the publication of the Darzi Report is likely to impact the shape of workforce planning within NHS in England but the establishment of the national *Centre for Workforce Intelligence* has continued, with three objectives:

- the provision of workforce intelligence to enable better short- and long-term decisions;
- the support of senior leaders in health and social care to drive workforce planning;
- the provision of support to enable more effective workforce planning at local, regional and national levels.

Established for five years, this model is similar to the *Australian Health Workforce Institute*, which is separate from government and receives commissions for workforce research projects from the National Health Workforce Taskforce (itself established by state governments in Australia). The US Health Resources and Services Administration (HRSA) originally funded six regional workforce analysis centres but while these still operate in their own right, their federal funding ceased in 2006. All these models are different to *Health Workforce New Zealand* which has similar objectives but is part of government. A common driver for the establishments of such centres is the need for accurate information.

While not specific to healthcare, the CIPD (2010: 13) usefully identifies two dimensions of information used in workforce planning: quantitative or qualitative; and internal or external. Thus, qualitative internal information is that derived from strategic planners, senior management, line managers and HR; qualitative external includes social trends; developments in technology; lifestyle patterns; and social attitudes. Quantitative internal relates to workforce data and organizational data and quantitative external includes information on labour markets, migratory trends, population and benchmarking information. Particular to healthcare is the need for accurate information about national (occupational) workforces and global labour markets, and the capacity for analysis, workforce modelling and scenario building. The WHO identifies seven areas of expertise required in the development of policy in national health workforce planning (2006: 142):

- policy and planning
- institutional and management development
- legal frameworks and policies
- health workforce economics
- education
- workforce management systems and tools
- professional focused workforce development

As indicated, workforce planning may be pursued centrally through a 'bottom-up' or 'top-down' approach or decentralized to individual healthcare organizations and this will be determined by the healthcare system itself. As indicated above, integral to any planning is the management of workforce education and training. At the last count, the world had 1600 medical schools, 6000 nursing schools and 375 schools in public health, and was not producing sufficient numbers of graduates, nor was it taking sufficient account of the role of support workers (WHO 2006). It is not the intention of this chapter to discuss national strategies for the education and training of the 'health workforce production pipeline' (WHO 2006: xx), rather, it outlines a concept developed in NHS in England for organization-wide workforce training and development (see Self-test exercise 2).

Workforce training and development

Grugulis (2007: 15) begins her critical text on skills, training and human resource development by reminding us that while 'skill' is an elusive concept, workforce skills play a key role in quality and productivity levels, pay determination and labour market dynamics. This is particularly pertinent to the NHS. By 2004, the NHS was spending over £4 billion a year on workforce training and development. Historically such funding was spent on registered staff (pre- and post-registration) rather than on non-qualified, non-registered staff. The review of workforce planning, above (Department of Health 2000) indicated the need to increase equity of opportunity to training and development and thereby capitalize on latent talent within organizations and beyond. The result was the development of what was termed a 'Skills Escalator'. As noted elsewhere (McBride et al. 2006), the concept of the Skills Escalator reflected a number of objectives, but at its heart it is an organization-wide workforce development strategy.

The Skills Escalator is depicted in Table 17.2. As indicated, the model divides NHS staff into seven categories with the purpose of making explicit the means of career progression from each level: socially excluded; the unemployed; roles requiring fewer

TABLE 17.2 The Skills Escalator framework

Level	Category	Means of career progression
1	Socially excluded individuals	6-month employment orientation programmes
2	The unemployed	6-month placements in 'starter' jobs
3	Jobs/ roles requiring fewer skills and less experience	National Vocational Qualifications (NVQs), Learning Accounts, appraisal, Personal Development Plan (PDP)
4	Skilled roles	NVQs or equivalent
5	Qualified professional roles	Appraisal and PDP to support career progression
6	More advanced skills and roles	As above, role development encouraged in line with service priorities/personal career choices
7	'Consultant' roles	Flexible 'portfolio careers' informed by robust appraisal, career and PDP

Source: Adapted from Department of Health (2001: 18).

skills and less experience; skilled roles; qualified professional roles; more advanced skills and roles; and 'consultant' roles (Department of Health 2001: 18). The idea is to attract new entry level recruits to the service (through Levels 1 and 2), while simultaneously encouraging flexibility and movement within the current workforce (at Levels 3 to 7), so that existing staff take on different jobs or delegated tasks. Expected outcomes are increased recruitment and retention and efficiency gains from workload passing down the escalator. The Skills Escalator thus encompasses the practice of being a 'good employer'; providing attractive careers; developing latent talent; providing lifelong learning; widening participation; and enabling more flexible working.

A study of the Skills Escalator in practice (McBride et al. 2006) provides evidence of how employers can effectively use intermediate labour markets to encourage new recruits into the organization, and use internal labour markets to capitalize on the latent talent within their existing staff. These cases also indicate that the development of new pathways to qualifications, the use of vocational training and the provision of state funding for individual learning accounts and nurse secondment can facilitate women's progression at work (McBride et al. 2005). This study indicates too, however, the rarity of such activity. Of seven case study sites, six were implementing it in an opportunistic, piecemeal manner.

Only one was implementing the Skills Escalator as an explicit organization-wide approach to developing the capacity and capability of their staff. Recruitment to entry level vacancies was tackled through pre-employment and volunteering schemes (Levels 1 and 2). In partnership with the local authority, and using external community development monies, the organization had set up an on-site job brokerage service. This had saved £300,000 through reducing recruitment costs in an 18-month period. The organization was providing training to sub-contracted staff as a recruitment avenue (Level 3). It was also 'growing' its own staff (e.g. Housekeepers: Level 3, Assistant Practitioners: Level 4 and Advanced Practitioners: Level 6). These jobs were enabling the delegation of tasks down the Skills Escalator to someone coming up the Skills Escalator into a new, intermediate role.

This approach was being used to revitalize the organization's internal culture and external reputation. In the short term, the organization needed to fill skills shortages through improving recruitment in a labour market area that had high unemployment and skill needs among potential recruits. It also wanted to develop multi-skilled staff and new 'treatment pathways' for its new treatment centre. In the long term, it wanted to build its reputation as a model employer and fulfil a broader role as a 'Health Village'. These objectives were operationalized through the work of the Transformation and Redesign Team (TRT), set up as part of organization's modernization programme, and the remit of the Service and Organisational Development Directorate. This team, employing about ten staff, works with clinical staff and managers to review and redesign clinical, managerial and support services. Even in this integrated strategy, however, it is to be noted that the senior management team decided not to locate TRT in the HR Directorate, but the latter Directorate still held responsibility for workforce planning.

Overall the research indicated that healthcare organizations acted in a contingent manner based on their perceptions of the supply of and demand for skills within the workforce. Research indicated that without an overarching, organization-wide approach to workforce development, organizations are in danger of developing their staff within groups, rather than across the organization, and of reacting to short-term localized 'hot spots', rather than addressing longer-term needs. Thus the contribution of the Skills Escalator is as a useful conceptual framework for reviewing the systemic and systematic development of the future workforce and encouraging organizations to capture latent talent through new career pathways and intermediate jobs.

Workforce modernization

As indicated above, workforce modernization is ideally part of an overarching organization-wide workforce development strategy. However, for the purposes of grounding it within a broader set of literatures, it will be discussed separately in this chapter. The growing trend towards changes in workforce configuration and skill mix in healthcare has been driven by a range of environmental pressures and challenges (Davies 2003). These drivers include: the need to respond to skills shortages; pressure for better management of labour costs (which account for much of overall healthcare cost); a desire to enhance organizational effectiveness; and changes in professional regulation (Adams et al. 2000; Sibbald et al. 2004). Central to such initiatives have been ideas borrowed from two overlapping traditions: first, business process re-engineering, which includes emphasis on worker responsibility, multi-skilling and job variety (Leverment et al. 1998; McNulty and Ferlie 2002); second, role redesign, which focuses on skill variety, task identity and significance, autonomy and feedback (Parker and Wall 1998).

Role redesign 'concerns the way jobs are designed or configured within the overall organization of production' (Bélanger et al. 2002: 17) and dates back to the 1960s. Such initiatives took place against a background of trade union activism and labour shortages and were part of an attempt to deal with rising absenteeism and high staff turnover often linked with Taylorist production systems (Payne and Keep 2003). Role redesign initiatives were claimed to improve outcomes by increasing the meaningfulness of work while encouraging employees to experience responsibility for outcomes and to have active knowledge of the results of work activities. Moderating factors included knowledge and skills of the workers and motivation to adapt the role (Parker and Wall 1998).

In the 1980s, with labour surpluses and declining union power, role redesign was focused on improving organizational performance. Kelly (1992) proposed that role redesign led to improved performance through: employees negotiating changes in content (and increased output) in exchange for increased pay; employees perceiving closer links between effort, performance and valued rewards; increased goal setting motivating better performance; and improved efficiency of work methods leading to performance improvements. However, improved efficiency can come at a price. Within the NHS, work by Thornley (1996: 165) illustrates how 'the state was able to play on the nebulous character of "skill" in nursing' and substitute cheaper labour for more expensive grades in a process that Thornley calls 'grade dilution'. A change in approach came with the election of the Labour Government in 1997 which had a focus on role redesign programmes involving revised pay and staff structures and redesigned roles. Introducing the latter was the responsibility of the Changing Workforce Programme (CWP). The example given in the following section examines one attempt to introduce different ways of working.

Introducing different ways of working: the CWP example

Beginning in 2001, 13 CWP pilot sites were established within NHS organizations or health economies across England. The intention was that roles would be redesigned locally under the guidance of CWP who provided project managers and workforce designers to each pilot site for the period of the pilot programme. Potential roles were identified and redesigned through the Role Redesign Workshop (a set of materials aimed at supporting local staff in redesigning their own roles) where local stakeholders came together to redesign roles around a particular patient pathway. A phase of testing was planned to precede anticipated implementation and national spread throughout the NHS, should the redesigned role be judged a success.

CWP employed a contingent, emergent approach to workforce design that could be adapted and used locally. Project managers and workforce designers worked locally with staff from organizations to initiate role redesign. Nationally, the CWP team worked with professional bodies and education institutions to overcome barriers to change. CWP established a national database of information on new and redesigned roles in health and social care and printed materials and guides (Modernisation Agency 2002a, 2002b). They established Accelerated Development Programmes to support speedier implementation of new roles in areas where the benefits had been tested and proven models were available to guide implementation (Hyde et al. 2005).

Hyde et al.'s (2004) evaluation of CWP led them to conclude that nationally CWP played a key role in developing capacity in the health service for workforce modernization through role redesign – providing training across the UK, national level support to 'join up the dots' between different initiatives and bodies, and disseminating learning. Locally, CWP led to personal development and job satisfaction for staff; service improvements and strengthened organizational partnerships through the development of roles that involved cross-boundary working.

Hyde et al. indicate important issues for workforce managers by illustrating the inextricable links between workforce management and different ways of working. Remuneration provides one such illustration. A large number of redesigned roles were staffed through extensions of existing staff roles (53 per cent). This testing of extended roles through existing staff raised concerns about future recognition and remuneration. For example, one role redesign was delayed because the staff group 'wouldn't do it without remuneration'. Settling pay in advance was an important factor. Not discussing pay in advance of role development led to limitations in the numbers involved (Hyde et al. 2005). Difficulties were also found in roles that crossed professional boundaries where there were existing pay disparities. One example of this was the emergency care worker who could be a paramedic or a nurse who were performing the same new role but who received substantially different remuneration. Difficulties in determining pay settlements faced by healthcare organizations are not unique to this programme (see Bach 1998) and the importance of pay for successful policy implementation has already been noted (Sibbald et al. 2004: 34). Parker and Wall (1998) argued that remuneration should be settled prior to implementation of role redesign and some pilot sites managed this while others did not. Increased pay has been linked to increased performance, especially where the employee is involved in negotiating changes of role (Kelly 1992).

Where the links between workforce management and different ways of working operate successfully, new practices may become embedded in the organization. Successful role redesign, while developed at a service delivery level, was successful only where strong, explicit support of senior managers was obtained along with associated funding. This meant that roles that had been redesigned by the frontline staff providing the service could be examined at a higher level in the organization for sustainability by addressing a series of key questions:

- Could the role be financed if expanded to include other workers?
- What arrangements were needed for managerial accountability of roles that crossed traditional boundaries?
- Would it be possible to offer the necessary training and development to a wider group of staff?
- Would the role fit with organizational strategy?

Each of these questions requires health service managers to understand different ways of working. CWP roles that did not continue beyond the testing phase were often impractical in terms of one of the questions above and had proceeded without explicit involvement or commitment of senior managers. Although not stated explicitly, Hyde et al. imply that lack of senior management involvement made it more likely that role redesigns would be singular examples, for one or two people, and that they would not be fully funded on a permanent basis (see Self-text exercise 3).

Strategic workforce management

The chapter, as a whole, is structured around four key aspects of workforce development: having 'the right people with the right skills in the right place at the right time to deliver the organisation's objectives' (CIPD 2010). We have broadly discussed ways in which health organizations can obtain the right staff (through workforce planning) with the right skills (through training and development) in the right place at the right time (through new ways of working). However, what is often overlooked is the fourth aspect – how the development and deployment of people are organized to deliver organizational objectives – what we term strategic workforce management.

Much research has focused upon how people management affects organizational performance. This research has tended to focus on particular management activity

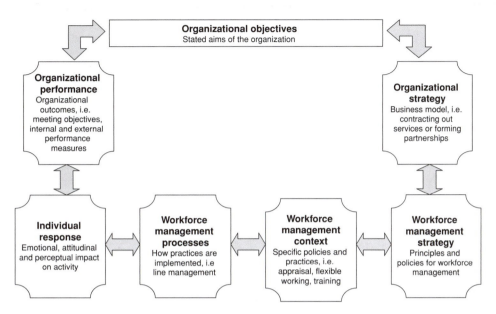

FIGURE 17.1 Strategic workforce management process

(see, for example, West et al. 2002, who link reduced patient mortality to improved staff appraisal) or on psychological aspects of individual performance (see, for example, Purcell et al. 2003; Hyde et al. 2006; Hyde et al. 2009). As the examples above have illustrated, workforce development and deployment do need managing and Boaden et al. (2007) identified a process of workforce management in high performing healthcare organizations that seemed to align aspects of people management with organizational objectives. Building on this work, we delineate a process of strategic workforce management (see Figure 17.1). The two-way arrows in Figure 17.1 illustrate reciprocal relationships between aspects of organizational functioning in high performing organizations. Organizational objectives set the direction for organizational activity and organizational strategy develops a business model that shapes the way healthcare is delivered. Workforce management strategy needs to be able to realize organizational strategy so that the workforce are developed and deployed in ways that enable organizational objectives to be achieved.

The examples earlier in this chapter of role redesign and workforce development strategies illustrate the scope and contribution of government workforce initiatives alongside the challenge to healthcare managers wishing to implement them. As depicted in Figure 17.1, unless workforce initiatives (such as the Skills Escalator and role redesign activities) fit with organizational objectives, they will not become embedded or sustained. This is despite such activities being effective, addressing patient needs and giving staff high levels of job satisfaction and greater commitment to the organization. McBride et al. (2005) argue that this is further explained by competing logics that are geared around the needs of the customer at the same time as being geared around the need for rationality and efficiency. With role redesign, these logics are frequently so much in contradiction that a nurse (taking over a task from the junior doctor and thereby saving 20 hours per week) may wish to spend (more) time taking consent from a patient commensurate with patient need, not productivity concerns. If this additional time cannot be absorbed into the overall workforce plan, or become part of a new 'premium fee' business model, then such role redesign will not proceed past the testing stage. As noted by one interviewee, 'Directorates are very good at saying they want more, but not that good at saying we are going to fund it by stopping doing Y' (Hyde et al. 2004: 66). Attention to the interface between organizational objectives, organizational strategy, workforce management strategy and workforce management context would offer one way of counteracting the tensions between providing patient-centred care and providing efficient services.

Strategic workforce management requires health service managers to perform three distinct functions to support workforce deployment and development; first, there needs to be alignment between organizational objectives and strategy, workforce strategy, context and processes so that the workforce being developed and deployed are in a position to help the organization realize its objectives. Second, managers need to act as translators of strategy into action, and third, they need to be able to communicate across strategic and operational boundaries (see Self-test exercise 4).

Conclusion

Managing the healthcare workforce presents several challenges. Demand for workers often exceeds supply, requiring constant attention to mitigating strategies such as improved recruitment and retention and the changing of skill-mix requirements. In addition, the workforce is often the most expensive budget cost, thus attracting attention in times of recession and budgetary constraints. While managers can go some way towards mitigating shortages and containing costs through workforce planning, training and development and establishing new ways of working, these are sophisticated procedures that require strategic and operational coordination in order that workforce developments might improve organizational performance. Research in one of the largest healthcare workforces has indicated the vital role that managers at all levels play in ensuring effective and efficient development and deployment of the workforce.

Through strategic workforce management, health managers should be able to align the development of workers to the needs of the organization. This requires, however, a clear commitment by senior management to an embedded and sustainable organizational-wide workforce development strategy, which integrates workforce planning, workforce modernization and workforce training and development. Without such an overarching framework, smaller groupings within organizations (such as departments and professional groups) are apt to develop narrowly focused workforce development activity among themselves which, while beneficial to their specific cohort of patients, may contradict or overlap with what others are attempting elsewhere.

Summary box

- There are approximately 60 million health workers worldwide, of which approximately half are professionally qualified.

- Managers face challenges obtaining the right people with the right skills to deliver organizational objectives because of shortages of health workers. Options include workforce planning, training and development, different ways of working and strategic management.

- Workforce planning needs to be integrated across a number of levels in a healthcare system and take account of, at a minimum, demographics, epidemiology, standards of care and provider productivity.

- An organization-wide workforce development strategy with an emphasis on progression encourages organizations to capture latent talent in their organizations.

- Different ways of working can lead to improved performance, but care must be taken that changes are embedded and sustainable.

- Strategic management of the healthcare workforce which pays attention to integrating planning, training, deployment and management can deliver performance improvements.

Self-test exercises

1 Consider the factors shaping the healthcare workforce and the workforce challenges (see Figure 17.1). Consider the circumstances of your organization. How are these factors shaping the workforce in your organization? Which factors, or combination, are creating the most pressure on your organization at the moment? Is this likely to change in the future? Which challenge(s) is your organization dealing with? Are they dealing with them using an integrated approach?

2 Does your organization have a workforce plan? What are the planning assumptions which underpin it? Does it take account of demographics, epidemiology, standards of care and provider productivity? Is it based on timely, robust quantitative and qualitative information which is derived from the internal and external environment, e.g. do you know whether labour is scarce? Does the plan relate to service and financial planning in your organization? How does the plan relate to other organizations within the healthcare system?

3 Do you have an organization-wide strategy for developing the latent talent within your organization? Does this involve the development of new roles or different ways of working? If these are separate functions, why is this, could they be integrated?

4 In your organization, consider the extent to which the workforce is managed strategically. Could managers at all levels be involved more? If so, what could facilitate this change? What is your role in building these links?

References and further reading

Adams, A., Lugsden, E., Chase, J. and Bond, S. (2000) Skill–mix changes and work intensification in nursing. *Work, Employment and Society*, 14(3): 541–55.

Arnold, J. (2004) Cut to the chase. *Health Service Journal*, 22: 36–7.

Australian Government Productivity Commission (2005) *Australia's Health Workforce*. Melbourne: Productivity Commission.

Bach, S. (1998) NHS pay determination and work re-organization: employment relations reform in NHS trusts. *Employee Relations*, 20(6): 565–76.

Bélanger, J., Giles, A. and Murray, G. (2002) Towards a new production model: Potentialities, tensions and contradictions. In G. Murray, J. Bélangen, A. Giles and P. Lapointe (eds) *Work and Employment Relations in the High-Performance Workplace*. Londeon: Continuum.

Birch, S., Kephart, G., Tomblin-Murphy, G. et al. (2007) Human resources planning and the production of health: a needs-based analytical framework. *Canadian Public Policy*, xxxiii, supplement: 1S–16S.

Boaden, R., Marchington, M., Hyde, P. et al. (2007) *Improving Health Through Human Resource Management: The Process of Engagement and Alignment*. London: Chartered Institute of Personnel and Development.

Boxall, P. and Purcell, J. (2003) *Strategy and Human Resource Management*. New York: Palgrave Macmillan.

Bureau of Labor Statistics (2010) *Healthcare Career Guide to Industries, 2010–2011. Edition*. Available at: http://bls.gov.oco/cg/cgs035.htm (accessed 30 July 2010).

Cangelosi, J.D., Markham, F.S. and Bounds, W.T. (1998) Factors related to nurse retention and turnover: an updated study. *Health Marketing Quarterly*, 15(3): 25–43.

CIPD (2009) *Absence Management: Annual Survey Report 2009*. London: CIPD.

CIPD (2010) *Workforce Planning: Right People, Right Time, Right Skills*. London: CIPD.

Daft, R. (1992) *Organization Theory and Design*, 4th edn. New York: West Publishing Company.

Darzi, A. (2008) *High Quality Care for All: NHS Next Stage Review Final Report*. London: Department of Health.

Davies, C. (2003) *The Future Health Workforce*. London: Palgrave Macmillan.

Dawson, J., Chu, C., Kaur, M. et al. (2009) *Health and Wellbeing of NHS Staff: A Benefit Evaluation Model*. London: The Work Foundation.

Department of Health (2000) *A Health Service of All the Talents*. London: DH.

Department of Health (2001) *Working Together, Learning Together: A Framework for Lifelong Learning for the NHS*. London: Department of Health.

Department of Health (2002) *HR in the NHS Plan*. London: Department of Health.

Department of Health (2008) *NHS Next Stage Review: A High Quality Workforce*. London: Department of Health.

Grugulis, I. (2007) *Skills, Training and Human Resource Development: A Critical Text*. Basingstoke: Palgrave Macmillan.

House of Commons Health Committee (1999) *Future NHS StaffingRequirements, Third Report of Session 1998-99, HC 38-1*. London: The Stationery Office.

House of Commons Health Committee (2007) *Workforce Planning, Fourth Report of Session 2006-7, Volume 1, HC 171-1*. London: The Stationery Office.

Hutchinson, S. and Purcell, J. (2003) *Bringing Policies to Life: The Vital Role of Front Line Managers in People Management*. London: Chartered Institute of Personnel and Development.

Hyde, P., Boaden, R., Cortvriend, P. et al. (2006) *Improving Health through HRM: Mapping the Territory*. London: Chartered Institute for Personnel and Development.

Hyde, P., Harris, C., Boaden, R. and Cortvriend, P. (2009) Human Relations Management, expectations and health care: a qualitative study. *Human Relations*, 62(5) 701–25.

Hyde, P., McBride, A., Young, R. and Walshe, K. (2004) *A Catalyst for Change: The National Evaluation of the Changing Workforce Programme*. Manchester: Manchester Centre for Healthcare Management, Manchester Business School.

Hyde, P., McBride, A., Young, R. and Walshe, K. (2005) Role redesign: introducing new ways of working in the NHS. *Personnel Review*, 34(6): 697–712.

Kelly, J.E. (1992) Does job re-design theory explain job re-design outcomes? *Human Relations*, 45: 753–74.

Leveck, M. and Jones, C. (1996) The nursing practice environment, staff retention and quality of care. *Research in Nursing and Health*, 19(4): 331–43.

Leverment, Y., Ackers, P. and Preston, D. (1998) Professionals in the NHS – a case study of business process re-engineering. *Work and Employment*, 13(2): 129–39.

McBride, A. (2007) How is NHS 'modernisation' affecting gender equality? Paper presented at Gender Work and Organization Conference, Keele University, June.

McBride, A., Cox, A., Mustchin, S. et al. (2006) *Developing Skills in the NHS*. Manchester: The University of Manchester Press.

McBride, A., Hyde, P., Young, R. and Walshe, K. (2005) Changing the skills of frontline workers: the impact of the embodied customer. *Human Resource Management Journal*, 15(2): 35–49.

McNulty, T. and Ferlie, E. (2002) *Re-engineering Healthcare: The Complexities of Organizational Transformation*. Oxford: Oxford University Press.

Modernisation Agency (2002a) *Workforce Matters: A Good Practice Guide to Role Redesign in Primary Care*. London: Department of Health.

Modernisation Agency (2002b) *Workforce Matters: A Guide to Role Redesign for Staff in the Wider Healthcare Team*. London: Department of Health.

National Center for Workforce Analysis (2004) *Effects of the Workforce Investment Act of 1998 on Health Workforce Development in the States*. Washington, DC: Department of Health and Human Services. Available at: http://bhpr.hrsa.gov/healthworkforce/reports/factbook.htm (accessed 5 December 2005).

Newman, K. and Maylor, U. (2002) The NHS Plan: nurse satisfaction, commitment and retention strategies. *Health Services Management Research*, 15: 93–105.

NHS Information Centre (2010) NHS Hospital and Community Health Service (HCHS) and General Practice Workforce 1999–2009. Available at: http://www.ic.nhs.uk/statistics-and-data-collections/workforce/nhs-staff-numbers/nhs-staff-1999–2009-overview (accessed 30 July 2010).

Parker, S. and Wall, T. (1998) *Job and Work Redesign: Organizing Work to Promote Well-being and Effectiveness*. London: Sage.

Payne, J. and Keep, E. (2003) Revisiting the Nordic approaches to work reorganization and job redesign: lessons for UK skills policy. *Policy Studies*, 24(4): 205–25.

Procter, S. and Currie, G. (1999) The role of the personnel function: roles, perceptions and processes in an NHS Trust. *International Journal of Human Resource Management*, 10(6): 1077–91.

Purcell, J., Kinnie, N., Hutchinson, S., Rayton, B. and Swart, J. (2003) *Understanding the People and Performance Link: Unlocking the Black Box*. London: Chartered Institute of Personnel and Development.

Seifert, R. and Sibley, T. (2005) *United They Stood: The Story of the UK Firefighters' Dispute 2003–2004*. London: Lawrence and Wishart.

Sibbald, B., Shen, J. and McBride, A. (2004) Changing the skill mix of the healthcare workforce, *Journal of Health Service Research and Policy*, 9(1): 28–38.

Sparrow, P., Hesketh, A., Hird, M., March, C. and Balain, S. (2008) *Reversing the Arrow: Using Business Model Change to Tie HR into Strategy*. Lancaster: Lancaster University Management School.

Thornley, C. (1996) Segmentation and inequality in the nursing workforce: reevaluating the evaluation of skills. In R. Crompton, D. Gallie and K. Purcell (eds) *Changing Forms of Employment*. London: Routledge.

Vere, D. (2005) *Fit for Business: Building a Strategic HR Function in the Public Sector* London: Chartered Institute of Personnel and Development.

Wanless, D. (2002) *Securing our Future Health: Taking a Long-term View – The Wanless Report*. London: HM Treasury.

West, M., Borrill, C., Dawson, J. et al. (2002) The link between the management of employees and patient mortality in acute hospitals. *International Journal of Human Resource Management*, 13(8): 1299–310.

World Health Organization (2006) *Working Together for Health: The World Health Report 2006*. Geneva: World Health Organization.

World Health Organization (2010a) *Migration of Health Workers*. Fact Sheet 301, updated July 2010. Available at: http://www.who.int/mediacentre/factsheets/fs301/en/print.html (accessed 30 July 2010).

World Health Organization (2010b) *Health Workforce*. Available at: http://www.who.int/hrh/en (accessed 30 July 2010).

Websites and resources

Australian Health Workforce Institute. Provides advice to state, national and international policy-makers on health workforce issues: http://www.ahwi.edu.au/.

Centre for Workforce Intelligence. NHS-funded, provides advice and information to NHS on workforce planning and development: http://www.cfwi.org.uk/.

Chartered Institute of Personnel and Development (UK). Includes information about workforce management and development: http://www.cipd.co.uk/.

Department of Health (UK). Information for managers:
http://www.dh.gov.uk/en/Managingyourorganisation/.

Healthcare People Managers Association (UK). Provides a network for healthcare managers: http://www.hpma.org.uk/.

Health Resources and Services Administration (US). Workforce information in the US health sector: http://www.ask.hrsa.gov.

Health Workforce New Zealand. Leads and coordinates planning and development of the health and disability workforce: http://www.moh.govt.nz/healthworkforcenz.

Industries Skills Council (Australia). Details from industry skills council for community services and health industry, Australia: http://www.cshisc.com.au/.

King's Fund (UK). Publications and resources on health workforce issues: http://www.kingsfund.org.uk/.

NHS Confederation (UK). Policy information and networks for NHS organisations: http://www.nhsconfed.org/.

NIHR Service Delivery and Organization Programme (UK) Research reports about service organization and management:.
http://www.sdo.nihr.ac.uk/newspublicationsandevents.html.

Skills for Health (UK). Details of skills development in the UK health sector: http://www.healthcareworkforce.nhs.uk/.

World Health Organization (Global). For publications and information on international health and workforce matters: http://www.who.int/hrh/en.

CHAPTER 18

User perspectives and involvement

Shirley McIver

Introduction

The relationship between those who provide health services and the people who use them is a changing one. Most writers link this to other economic and social changes, such as a rise in consumerism associated with the growth of market-based societies which produces rising expectations in the context of scarce resources (Abercrombie 1994; Mechanic 1998; Mays 2000). Falling levels of public trust due to increased media coverage of healthcare scandals, such as the lack of appropriate screening of blood products in France in the 1980s or the Bristol cardiac surgeons in the UK, and greater explicitness about the way care is resourced or rationed have also been cited (Davies 1999).

Within this context, many governments have introduced health policy that increases the importance of user perspectives and involving patients in decisions. The form this policy takes varies between countries but there are some common elements. For example, many countries have developed policies to protect patients' rights. Finland was the first in 1992 but many countries now have laws or charters of this kind although the extent to which these are enforced varies. For example, research conducted by Abekah-Nkrumah, Manu and Atinga (2010) into the impact of the Patients' Charter in Ghana, that was established in 2002, suggested that few people were aware of its existence. Other countries have carried out national consultation about health priorities (e.g. New Zealand, England) or have direct citizen involvement in local health organizations (e.g. Israel, New Zealand, Wales) and in most countries there have been surveys to find out users' views (Calnan 1995, 1998). In many countries, regional elected bodies, county or local municipal councils have a responsibility for health decisions. This can vary from an oversight role to one of commissioning or managing services. Where power has been decentralized to a greater extent (e.g. Finland), citizens are more likely to be able to influence local health policy (WHO, 2006a).

The issue of user involvement is complex but in this chapter it will be broken down into four main areas. The first section examines evidence about whether user perspectives are different from those of the health professionals and managers and what is known about influences on these perspectives. It also considers the different aims and objectives of user involvement and the advantages of taking a strategic overview to ensure that involvement is integrated into the organization.

The second section looks at the involvement of users in choices about treatment and care, identifying the reasons why this is considered important and ways of helping users to make these decisions such as better information, decision aids and education programmes.

The third section examines the involvement of users in service improvement, looking specifically at the involvement of users in clinical research, service planning and evaluation. The importance of the wider context of quality management is emphasized to overcome a common tendency to collect users' views without working out the implications for practice so that changes to services can be produced as a result.

The fourth section concentrates on the involvement of the public or local communities and identifies a number of different approaches while arguing for the value of community involvement because it has a clearer conceptual foundation than other approaches and is supported by the World Health Organization.

Identifying users and objectives

The first question that it is important to address is 'why involve users?' This question can be answered in a number of ways. One argument is that health professionals and service users have different interests. Rudolf Klein, for example, argues that where there are scarce resources, then different groups will come into conflict about how these resources should be shared out. Some healthcare systems institutionalize the power of the professional expert and so this voice is dominant and other voices become repressed, which results in the interests of users being overlooked (Klein 1984).

There is evidence that health professionals and service users have different views on what are the most important indicators of good quality care. For example, research by Wensing and colleagues (1996) with chronically ill patients and general practitioners, utilizing panels, focus group discussions and a written consensus procedure, showed such differences. These included the finding that general practitioners stressed the importance of answering patients' needs, whereas patients wanted to be listened to and taken seriously. Patients valued involvement in decisions, whereas general practitioners thought that patients' capacities should not be overestimated. The findings led the researchers to comment about indicators that are relevant for patients but not for general practitioners:

> To use such indicators as part of quality improvement initiatives might therefore cause resistance among general practitioners and reduce the likelihood of achieving improvement. On the other hand, as many indicators as possible that patients consider relevant should be included to get a full picture of patients' views. Clearly a balance has to be found.
>
> (Wensing et al. 1996: 80)

Another argument is that healthcare decisions cannot be based on technical information alone but will also include values and beliefs. This means that those involved will weigh options differently. This can result in two doctors disagreeing about which treatment is best for a patient. Rakow (2001) found that doctors treating children with congenital heart disease varied in their preferred management for the same patient, leading the researcher to comment: 'Ultimately, it is the outcome and time preferences of patients (or arguably, of parents when they act as proxy decision makers) that should determine choice' (2001: 149).

A third argument is that patient involvement in decisions about treatment and care produces better health outcomes. Some studies have shown that patients who are informed are more likely to comply with treatment and to have improved outcomes (Kaplan et al. 1989). However, although there is plenty of evidence that failures in communication of information about illness and treatment are the most frequent source of patient dissatisfaction, the evidence about the extent to which patients want choice and control over treatment decisions is more mixed. Desire for involvement can vary, depending on the nature of the illness and the characteristics of the patient (Coulter and Ellins 2006).

These arguments have a number of consequences. The first is that different interests and values can be found among different types of users, as well as between users and health professionals (and also among different types of health professionals). This suggests that there is value in distinguishing between regular and occasional users, current and potential users, user advocates and representatives, and carers. It also raises the importance of differential access to 'voice'. Disempowered and vulnerable people are less likely to be able to get their views across.

Another consequence is consideration of the degree of influence that users should have over decisions. This raises questions about the mechanisms and methods for listening to users and involving them in decisions. Clearly the implications will be different if the decision takes places at the micro level of an individual, the meso level of a health organization, or the macro level of a health system. This presents a complicated set of issues to consider and so it is useful to summarize them into a framework.

Various analytical frameworks are available (e.g. Charles and DeMaio 1993; Saltman 1994) but most make distinctions between the individual patient, service users in general and the local community, and between the different types or focus of involvement. One of the most practically relevant conceptual frameworks has been developed by the World Health Organization (WHO 2006a) based upon an analysis of different measures being used by European health systems to support user involvement in decision-making. This divides the different measures into *choice*, *voice* and *representation*.

Initiatives to support an individual in choosing between service providers, treatment options and similar fall into the first category of *choice*. Those measures designed to help individuals and groups provide feedback on services or engage in redesigning services fall into the category of *voice*. Mechanisms to help members of the public or communities engage in health decisions at the more strategic level, such as on governing boards and committees, fall into the category of *representation* (WHO 2006a). Most European countries have put in place structures and policy that supports these different types of involvement. (The self-test exercise at the end of the chapter provides a guide to identifying relevant policy and initiatives and the implications for

TABLE 18.1 Framework for examining public and patient involvement

Level	Focus	Methods
Micro	Patient information	Different media, link workers
	Patient education	Patient self-management programmes, self-help groups
	Patient choice of provider	League tables and performance data
		Facilitators
	Patient involvement in treatment and care decisions	Patient consultation aids
	Complaints and redress	Decision aids
		Complaints system
		Patient's advocates
		Patient's rights
Meso	Evaluation of local services	Patient surveys and other methods
		Inspection and scrutiny of services
	Planning changes to local services	Membership of decision-making groups and organizations
	Allocating resources locally	
	Local accountability	Role of voluntary and community sector organizations
		Press
Macro	Influencing national health policy and government agenda	National voluntary sector organizations and patient committees and groups
	Input into clinical research agenda	Members of Parliament
		Lobbying, protest and direct action

evaluating interventions within these initiatives. Examples of initiatives in different European countries can be found in WHO 2006a.)

There may also be a connection between the focus and the method. Table 18.1 provides a summary showing the connections between these different elements. Mechanisms to aid choice, voice and representation can occur at all three levels.

It is important that managers involved in health and social care organizations are clear about the three different strands of patient, user and community involvement, understand the arguments for and against involvement and are aware of some of the difficulties that can occur and how they might be overcome. These issues will be covered in more depth in the following three sections. It is also important that a manager new to the area of user involvement knows where to start. If an organization does not have a user involvement strategy, it can be useful to develop one. (The self-test exercise on p. 368 presents some key stages to work through.)

Involving users in choices about treatment and care

There are two main arguments for the importance of involving users in treatment choices. The first relates to the ethical principle of autonomy which states that individuals have a right to exercise control over decisions which affect their lives. In many countries this has led to legislation to support the clinical duty to obtain informed consent for treatment and participation in research. This means that if users believe that health professionals have abused their right to make informed choices about their care, they can seek redress in court. However, legal standards and procedures differ between countries.

The second argument is that better information and greater involvement in decisions produce improved health outcomes. Evidence to support this argument is not clear-cut. The findings from research in this area present a complex picture because different types of outcomes can be measured, for example, patient satisfaction; health status; and patient–provider communication. Likewise, different kinds of interventions can be tested, and a range of illnesses and conditions can be involved. However, a Cochrane Review (Gibson et al. 2002) found that education alone does not improve health outcomes, suggesting that involvement was likely to be an important element of successful treatment, particularly in the case of chronic conditions which require greater patient self-management. A review by Marshall, Haywood and Fitzpatrick (2005) of methods for involvement of patients in decisions about chronic conditions suggested that there was some encouraging evidence available for short-term changes in outcomes. There is strong evidence that users value information. Lack of information and poor communication are a frequent source of patient dissatisfaction (McIver 1993; Coulter and Ellins 2006). This means that the argument for improving information for patients is more straightforward than the argument for greater participation in treatment decisions. A number of authors have pointed out that the extent to which users desire involvement will vary depending on factors such as whether or not it is an emergency situation, or whether they have a chronic condition and have built up knowledge about it. Research has also shown that younger and more highly educated people express a greater desire to be involved in treatment decisions than older people (Charles et al. 1997; Coulter 1997).

The main arguments against providing patients with better information and giving them more opportunity to get involved in treatment and care decisions are the difficulties and the resource implications. As Coulter and Ellins (2006: 79) point out:

> Despite strong organisational commitment in favour of the policy and fairly strong evidence of benefit, widespread implementation of innovations designed to improve clinical decision-making and promote greater patient involvement has yet to occur. Barriers include lack of awareness, lack of knowledge and skills, concerns about time and resource pressures, and negative attitudes among some clinicians because of possible loss of power, loss of face, or loss of income.

Difficulties lie not just in conveying complex information about the risks and benefits of one course of action over another, but also in establishing what is actually happening in a consultation and then changing patterns of established behaviour. For example, research carried out by Fiona Stevenson and colleagues (2000) showed that although the majority of patients in the study believed that talking to their doctors about the medicines they were taking was useful and that they were encouraged to do so, observations of the consultations showed that in reality this did not happen. Even when information was shared, patients' beliefs were not generally taken seriously. Solutions to these problems lie in creating standard treatment information packages that can be adapted for individual use, usually know as 'decision aids' and providing alternative methods of informing, educating and supporting users.

A Cochrane Database Systematic Review (O'Connor et al. 2003) identified 34 trials that looked at decision aids. In comparison to usual care, decision aids were found to increase patient involvement in decision-making by 30 per cent and the proportion of patients with realistic perceptions of the chances of benefits and harms improved by 40 per cent. A decision aid has the following features that distinguish it from more general patient information:

- information tailored to patients' health status;
- values classification;
- examples of other patients;
- guidance or coaching in shared decision-making;
- different modes of delivery;
- not educational materials that inform about health issues in general way;
- not passive informed consent materials;
- not designed to promote compliance with recommended option.

Although decision aids may not be useful in all situations, they are valuable when the options have major differences in outcomes or complications, decisions require trade-offs between short-term and long-term outcomes, one choice can result in a small chance of a grave outcome or there are marginal differences in outcomes between options.

There have also been developments in providing alternative ways of educating and supporting patients. One of these is the chronic disease self-management programme developed by Professor Kate Lorig and colleagues at the University of Stanford in the USA. This is a community-based patient self-management education course that uses trained people who have a chronic condition to deliver the programme. It covers topics such as exercise and nutrition, use of cognitive symptom management techniques, fatigue and sleep management, dealing with emotions of anger, fear and depression, communication and problem-solving and decision-making. A randomized controlled trial showed that treatment subjects, when compared with controls, demonstrated improvements at six months in weekly minutes of exercise, frequency of cognitive symptom management, communications with physicians, self-reported health, health distress, fatigue, disability and social/role activities limitations. Also they had fewer hospitalizations and days in hospital, but no differences were found in physical/pain discomfort or psychological well-being (Lorig et al. 1999). Limitations have, however, been identified in Lorig's research and in more recent research into lay-led self-management programmes and this has led to discussion about the features of such programmes that are of most benefit to patients. Taylor and Bury (2007: 41), for example, argue that the lay-led element may not be as important as other elements and 'finding ways of adapting mainstream professional practice to facilitate more patient confidence in health- and illness-related problem solving' may be a more cost effective way to achieve these benefits.

One of the main ways in which managers can help in the development of greater user involvement in treatment and care decisions is to make sure that the organization is helping clinicians to provide good quality information (see Box 18.1: Checklist for developing good quality information).

The linked task of making sure that informed consent procedures are clear and monitoring the implementation of these procedures is also vital. Other important steps include the provision of advocates and interpreters to help vulnerable people and those who have difficulty communicating, facilitating access to self-help and support groups and the establishment of resources to enable local access to chronic disease self-management programmes.

Involving users in service improvement

The literature on business approaches to quality management emphasizes the importance of focusing on the customer to achieve services that meet their needs (Pollitt 1996; Buetow and Roland 1999; Berwick 2009). The health sector has adopted many of the approaches used in manufacturing and other sectors to manage and improve service quality, including carrying out market research to find out users' views. The most important point to be made about involving users in quality improvement initiatives such as service planning and evaluation is that this involvement must not be carried out as a separate activity. The quality management context, including the systems for assuring and accounting for quality in an organization, should be linked together. This principle has been promoted in many countries and internationally by the World Health Organization (WHO).

An example of this is the World Alliance for Patient Safety which was established by the WHO in 2004 to coordinate, disseminate and accelerate improvements in patient

---

Box 18.1: *Checklist for developing good quality information*

1 Identify sources of up-to-date evidence that can be used in the information.

2 Find out from users what they want to know and when they need to know it.

3 Review what information is already available and look for sources that might be adapted or used.

4 Work with clinicians and users to develop draft information and test it out on users, improving the clarity of the language and presentation as required.

5 Think about using a variety of different media to make it accessible to different types of users at different times.

6 Make sure that all professionals involved are referring to the same information and are consistent in what they say to users.

7 Consider whether the information could be taken further to educate patients to better manage their condition and, if so, look for or set up a self-management programme.

8 Consider whether users might benefit from information about sources of support.

9 Evaluate the effectiveness of the information in fulfilling the aims.

safety. This has led to a number of initiatives including 'Action on Patient Safety', a project led by the Joint Commission on Accreditation of Healthcare Organizations and its affiliate Joint Commission International. The project, which is operating in seven countries, involves the implementation of five standardized patient safety solutions, including prevention of hand-over errors, wrong site/procedure/person surgical errors, continuity of medication errors, high concentration of drug errors and the promotion of effective hand hygiene practices. (www.jointcommission.org).

There is also evidence that the importance of the user's perspective on what comprises good quality care has gained widespread acceptance. A seminar entitled 'Through the Patient's Eyes', which was attended by 64 individuals from 29 countries in Salzburg in 1998, adopted the guiding principle of 'nothing about me without me' and created the country of PeoplePower. This set out a vision for the future that included the principles of production, governance and accountability created by patients and health professionals working closely together (Delbanco et al. 2001).

There are a number of stages in health and social care service development when users can be involved, but three are particularly important and have received most attention:

1 during research to find out which treatments and services are most effective;
2 during the planning, development and redesign of services;
3 during the evaluation of services.

This section will briefly examine each of these areas in turn before considering some of the particular difficulties encountered in this sector.

The value of consumer involvement in health research is a relatively recent activity but one that has been acknowledged internationally through organizations such as the Cochrane Collaboration, the Consumers Health Forum of Australia and the UK Health Technology Assessment Programme (Telford et al. 2004). This stretches beyond issues around the involvement of users as research subjects into their involvement at all stages in the design, conduct and dissemination of clinical and health services research. For example, the Planning and Evaluation Unit for Canary Islands Health Authority, Spain, involved patients using the Delphi Method, in the design of a systematic review on the effectiveness of treatments for degenerative ataxias (Serrano-Aguilar et al. 2009).

As Charlotte Williamson has pointed out, consumer groups have for some time lobbied governments and professional bodies over their concerns about the lack of investigation of certain topics, of poorly designed and unsafe research and a disregard of research evidence from other countries, and this had some impact. Members of consumer groups have pressed research organizations to include consumers on their research committees, or they have initiated research themselves and invited clinicians and researchers to join them (Williamson 2001).

Most countries have identified a need for the training of users if they are to be able to take part in research a meaningful way. A US course called LEAD (Leadership, Education and Advocacy Development) is now seen as a prerequisite for women participating in breast cancer research activities funded by the US Department of Defense and the

National Cancer Institute, and this is being attended by consumers from other countries such as Australia (Goodare and Lockwood 1999). In the UK, the Department of Health has set up an organization called Involve, to support and promote public and user involvement in health and social care research and this funds research and produces a newsletter. In 2004, a project to assess training provision and participants' experiences was carried out and this confirmed the value of training, leading the researchers to comment: 'We recommend that training should be an integral, vital part of any research activity if service user involvement is to be effective and meaningful' (Lockey et al. 2004).

User involvement in the planning and development of health services is also a relatively recent activity. A systematic review of the literature on this subject identified reports going back to the 1980s (Crawford et al. 2002, 2003). Very few of these assessed the subsequent impact on quality of care although the researchers were careful to point out that the absence of evidence should not be mistaken for the absence of effect and they were able to identify a number of improvements to services that resulted from user involvement, such as improved sources of information for patients and improved access. The Social Care Institute for Excellence (SCIE) carried out a review examining the impact of service user participation on social care services and came to similar conclusions – there was plenty of information about ways to involve users and what constituted good practice in involvement but less information about the effects of participation (Carr 2004).

Users can be involved either indirectly or directly in planning and development. They can be involved indirectly by providing their views through a market research technique such as focus group discussions, interviews or a questionnaire survey, which are then taken into consideration along with other information by health professionals making the planning decisions. Alternatively they can be directly involved on committees or in workshops where decisions are made. Little research has been carried out on which methods are the most effective for involving users. Reviews highlight difficulties such as lack of consensus over outcome measures (Coulter and Ellins 2006). However, some reviews suggest that the method is not the most important factor in determining effectiveness. For example, Rose et al. (2002) in their review of user and carer involvement in change management in mental health, identified a facilitative organizational culture as the most important factor, followed by a strategy for providing information and the provision of resources.

Of the three main stages of health and social care service development, the one with the longest history is that of user evaluation of services. Patient and user 'satisfaction' surveys have been carried out in many countries since the 1970s. Despite this, 'satisfaction' is a complex and little understood concept in the health sector. As Williams (1994 p. 510) writes: 'we do not currently know how patients evaluate and, because of this, inferences made from many satisfaction surveys may not accurately embody the true beliefs of service users.'

Some of this complexity is due to the different types of information that can be collected from users. Wensing and Elwyn (2002) summarize this along two dimensions: whether users are evaluating their own health outcome or whether they are evaluating the service provided, and whether they are reporting their experiences or rating them in some way. There has been progress in recent years, however. A systematic review of the literature on the measurement of satisfaction with healthcare and the implications for practice was carried out by Crow et al. (2002) This provides a good summary of the key issues and makes a number of methodological recommendations. There is also a survey advice centre run by the Picker Institute Europe, an organization that produces a newsletter dedicated to sharing good practice on improving the patient's experience. The Picker Institute Europe is working with the Organisation for Economic Co-operation and Development (OECD) to identify and develop a common set of patient experience indicators to compare the performance of healthcare systems internationally.

A focus on the patient experience (rather than reports, ratings, satisfaction, or outcomes) is a major part of initiatives incorporating ideas from the design sciences into healthcare. Advocates of 'experience-based design' argue that healthcare has been better at some aspects of design, namely performance (evidence-based practice, pathways and process) and engineering (clinical governance and standards and safeguards for patients) but not so good at designing human experiences. As a result of this, as Bate and Robert comment:

> One wonders what is the point of a great process and a terrible experience ... We suggest that designing services, environments, interactions and processes for the human experience – literally targeting experience – poses a formidable, but highly worthwhile, challenge for healthcare improvement professionals.
>
> (2006: 308)

One of the most important difficulties experienced in the health and social care sector is that of involving groups of people who are vulnerable or who have communication problems, such as those with learning disabilities, autism or dementia, but examples can be found:

- Researchers at the Norah Fry Research Centre at the University of Bristol, UK, involved service users with learning difficulties in a project on gender issues in service provision that used a questionnaire survey approach (Towsley 2000).

- Researchers at the Department of General Practice, Maastricht University, the Netherlands, carried out focus group discussion and interviews with people with intellectual disability (ID) to find out their views on how communication with their GP could be improved (Wullink et al. 2009)

- Talking Mats is an approach to involving people with communication difficulties including children with social and emotional difficulties and people with dementia. It is used in a wide range of countries, including India, the USA, Australia, Brazil and South Africa. This approach was developed by the Augmentation and Alternative Communication (AAC) Research Unit at the University of Stirling (www.talkingmats.com).

- The Alzheimer's Society (in the UK) won an award in 2001 for its involvement of users in all aspects of its research programme using a Consumer Network approach.

- Potter and Whittaker (2001) explored the way in which children with a diagnosis of autism communicated and how the environment could enable them.

Tailoring approaches to capture the views of these groups of people is still a methodologically underdeveloped area but the research so far suggests that indirect approaches to questions using stimuli such as singing, pictures, reminiscence and questions during everyday activities work best, although advocates, interpreters and people with special skills may be needed (McIver 2005). A key task for managers lies in making sure that patient surveys and similar activities designed to get users' views about services are linked to other mechanisms to assure and improve the quality of services. A common failing of patient surveys has been an inability to use the findings to improve services (see self-test exercise p. 368).

Involving potential users and communities

This final section examines the involvement of 'the public' or local communities in health and social care decisions. This can encompass a range of different activities at both the national and local level such as: lay representation on professional bodies or national inspectorates; national consultation exercises; lay representation on the governing boards of local organizations; and consultation with local communities. Three main types of approaches can be identified: public representation on committees and governing boards; market research and opinion polls; and community involvement. These approaches have different aims and serve different purposes although there is a general lack of clarity about the role and function of involving the public in these different ways. The most developed approach is that of community involvement and several arguments can be put forward for why it is important.

First, it can be seen as a basic right for citizens. Many countries have signed up to the World Health Organization Alma-Ata Declaration 1978 that stated: 'the people have the right and duty to participate individually and collectively in the planning and implementation of their health care'.

A second reason linked to this is that it gives people an enhanced sense of self-esteem and capacity to control their own lives and reaffirms the role of people in managing their own health (Annett and Nickson 1991). More typically, health services providers have seen community consultation as a way of finding out local needs and priorities for resource allocation. Associated with this is the fact that involvement can enhance accountability to local communities through more open decision-making and participative democracy. Community involvement is a rather broad and general concept that can include a wide range of activities. A useful definition is provided by Zakus and Lysack (1998: 2):

> Community or public participation in health, sometimes called citizen or consumer involvement, may be defined as the process by which members of the community, either individually or collectively and with varying levels of commitment:
>
> **(a)** develop the capability to assume greater responsibility for assessing their health needs and problems
>
> **(b)** plan and then act to implement their solutions
>
> **(c)** create and maintain organisations in support of these efforts
>
> **(d)** evaluate the effects and bring about necessary adjustments in goals and programmes on an ongoing basis

Community participation is therefore a strategy that provides people with the sense that they can solve their problems through careful reflection and collective action.

This is a helpful definition because it makes very clear the different stages involved. That is, it emphasizes the fact that local communities are not necessarily aware of their own health needs and so health planners cannot expect to find out needs by just asking people. Public health doctors and others will have information that they can share with local communities to help inform their discussions. It also identifies the importance of establishing and resourcing community organizations that can support communities during the process of assessing, identifying and implementing solutions. Finally, it highlights the need for regular evaluation to assess the impact of activities and measure progress towards objectives.

One of the advantages of taking a community development approach is that it provides a framework that can encompass a range of methods for listening to the views of local people and can coordinate this information collection. A systematic literature review to establish evidence for what is successful in community involvement identified the following key elements (Home Office 2004):

1 Understand the geography and socio-demographic features of the local community, identify local circumstances that may present barriers (e.g. transport) and act to overcome these.
2 Engage the community in project management.
3 Develop targeted and universal strategies to reach all members of the local community.
4 Engage in training and capacity building.
5 Provide information and publicity.
6 Evaluate progress and identify barriers.
7 Work in partnership with the local voluntary sector and other agencies.

The NHS National Institute for Health and Clinical Excellence has produced guidance on how to engage the community to improve health (NICE 2008). This is based on a review of relevant evidence and includes recommendations relating to the prerequisites for effective community engagement, the infrastructure required for effective practice, the approaches to encourage involvement, and evaluation of the different approaches used. The international literature on community engagement in rural health has been reviewed by Kilpatrick (2009), and the World Health Organization has produced a review of the literature examining the evidence on the effectiveness of empowerment and community participation to improve health (WHO 2006b).

The involvement of the public in priority setting and rationing in healthcare has become of particular interest in many countries in recent years, and the context for this is explored in more detail in Chapter 4. A range of different methods has been used including surveys, meetings, focus groups and panels and rapid appraisal, as well as various techniques to elicit values or rank and rate different options (Mullen and Spurgeon 2000). A number of deliberative methods have also been piloted. The best-known is the citizens' jury or planning cell, an approach used in the USA, the UK and

Europe to involve citizens in planning decisions (Stewart et al. 1994). The key features of deliberative methods are: the provision of information to participants in a way that does not rely on a high literacy level (e.g. through presentations or role play); the opportunity for participants to ask questions to get the information they need; time for discussion and debate between participants to enable them to work through the implications of the information. The assumption is that this approach will enable participants to develop a more informed view and that this will be more stable than that produced in response to questions in a survey (Dolan et al. 1999). Box 18.2 summarizes the findings of an evaluation of citizens' juries in the UK.

Box 18.2: *Findings from an evaluation of citizens' juries in healthcare in the UK*

The citizens' juries enabled local people to contribute to debates about funding priorities within service areas for five reasons:

1 **Clarity and focus:** The method requires a specific question. This ensures that there is a focus to the issue which enhances a person's ability to get to grips with it. Also jurors were given a definite task to perform so expectations were clear.

2 **Information provision:** Witness presentations enable jurors of all literacy levels to hear about the issues in an interesting and accessible way. Questioning of witnesses allows people to get information relevant to their needs.

3 **Discussion and deliberation:** Time allowed for discussion in small and large groups enabled people to exchange views, share ideas and work together as a team. This enhanced their understanding of issues, broadened their perspective and maintained their commitment to working hard on the task.

4 **Recommendations:** The process enabled local people to formulate a number of practical recommendations about what action the organization should take to address the issue. This was useful for the organization because the implications were clear and it facilitated project planning.

5 **Accountability:** The citizens' jury process made clear what was expected of the organization. The recommendations went to a public board meeting and this made sure they were put on the organization's agenda. Local publicity and observers ensured that the organization had to respond.

Source: McIver (1998).

An important task for managers is to make sure that community involvement takes places within a framework that improves networking and coordination between different agencies in order to minimize the duplication of information collection and maximize the effective use of resources. A difficult but necessary aspect of this is to assess the impact of community involvement activities to measure progress against goals and account for the use of resources (see self-test exercise p. 369 on measuring the impact of community involvement).

Conclusion

Managers can have an important role to play in facilitating the development of user involvement through making sure that a strategic approach is adopted that covers different aspects of involvement, including patient involvement in choice of treatment, user involvement in service improvement and community involvement in tackling local health problems. They can help to create an organization that values the user's voice as an integral part of its activities and one which learns from its experiences and develops the skills of its staff by evaluating user involvement initiatives and mechanisms.

Summary box

- Different interests and values can be found among different types of users, as well as between users and health professionals so it is important to distinguish between groups of users to make sure that they are involved.

- Disempowered and vulnerable people are less likely to be able to get their views across.

- It is important that managers involved in health and social care organizations are clear about the three different strands of patient, user and community involvement, understand the arguments for and against involvement and are aware of some of the difficulties that can occur and how they might be overcome.

- There is strong evidence that users want better health information because lack of information and poor communication are a frequent source of patient dissatisfaction. This means that the argument for improving information for patients is clearer than the argument for greater participation in treatment decisions and is a good place to begin to develop patient choice.

- Decision aids and self-management programmes are ways of helping users to become more informed and better able to take part in decisions about choice of treatment.

- There are many examples of ways in which users have been involved in clinical research, service planning and evaluation, but it is important that this involvement is set within the wider context of quality management so that improvements in services can be produced as a result.

- The public have been involved as members of committees and groups at both national and local level through market research techniques and opinion polls and through deliberative methods which are thought to facilitate the development of a more informed view.

- Many writers argue that a community involvement approach should be adopted because this is supported by the World Health Organization and concentrates on the benefits brought by enabling people to solve their own problems through collective action.

Self-test exercises

1 Developing a user involvement strategy

1 Has there been any mapping of current user involvement activities? What kind of information is being produced for users? Is it coordinated? Is there user involvement in service improvement? Are there mechanisms to ensure users' views are heard at all levels in the organization? How diverse is the range of views heard? Are some groups of users overlooked, such as the vulnerable, children or people with communication difficulties? What relationships exist with local communities? Are there networks linking different organizations representing users and community interests?

2 How would you analyse the internal environment? Who would you involve? What are the strengths and weaknesses of the current mechanisms to involve users?

3 How would you analyse the external environment? What are the pressures supporting user involvement or creating barriers to it?

4 What other information would be useful? Policy documents and/or evidence of what works? What are other similar organizations doing?

5 How would you identify priorities from the list of possible activities?

6 How would you develop a consensus among stakeholders on what are the priorities for action?

7 How would you identify the resources to address the priorities?

8 Who will lead on developing and overseeing the implementation of an action plan?

9 Is there a way of reporting on the progress of the action plan to the governing board of the organization?

10 When will progress against achievements be assessed?

2 Using the findings of patient surveys to improve services

Your organization wants to listen to the views of its service users in order to improve services and it recently carried out a self-completion questionnaire survey of patients about their satisfaction with services. Unfortunately the response rate was only 10 per cent and the questionnaires have not been analysed as the project manager is on extended sick leave. You have been given the job of working out what to do next.

1 What might be reasons why the response rate was so low?

2 Would it be worth analysing the findings?

3 What could you do to increase the response rate in future surveys?

4 What other methods could you adopt to get users' views?

5 What other sources of information could you use together with the findings to help you identify areas that might be causing problems for users?

6 What would you do when you had identified a problem area? What method could you adopt to investigate the root cause of the problem?

7 How would you develop ideas for overcoming the problem? Who would you involve?

8 How would you report back to users about what had been the findings and impact of the survey?

3 Measuring the impact of community involvement activities

1 How would you measure the impact on services (e.g. changes in uptake, new services being offered, changes in location of services)?

2 How would you measure the impact on service users (e.g. greater or more appropriate use of services, more diverse range of users, greater willingness to get involved or provide their views)?

3 How would you measure the impact on staff (e.g. greater staff satisfaction, less sickness leave)?

4 How would you measure the effect on other agencies (e.g. better networking, more appropriate referrals from and to other agencies, greater level of activities)?

5 How would you measure the impact on community health (e.g. greater uptake in screening programmes and other services; greater uptake of sport, leisure and recreation facilities; improvements to the local environment, decline in crime rates)?

4 Identifying policies and initiatives relating to choice, voice and representation

1 What policies and initiatives are you aware of that promote the following?

- patient choice (for example, a facility to select a social health insurer, or choice of hospital);

- voice (for example, a patient survey, patient panel, or patient advocacy group);

- representation (for example, patients or community members on the board of a local hospital or health centre). What are the different aims of these initiatives (e.g. greater flexibility and control; improving services; making sure the views of different sections of the community are heard)?

2 What are the implications of the different aims for evaluating the effectiveness of these initiatives? For example, is control over hospital and appointment date important to patients and did they achieve it? Do the findings from patient surveys result in improvements to services? Do members of hospital boards contribute the views of wider sections of the local community at Board meetings?

References and further reading

Abekah-Nkrumah, G., Manu, A. and Atinga, R.A. (2010) Assessing the implementation of Ghana's Patients' Charter. *Health Education*, 110(3): 169–85.

Abercrombie, N. (1994) Authority and consumer society. In R. Keat, N. Whiteley and N. Abercrombie (eds) *The Authority of the Consumer*. London: Routledge.

Annett, H. and Nickson, P. (1991) Community involvement in health: why is it necessary? *Tropical Doctor*, 21: 3–5.

Bate, P. and Robert, G. (2006) Experience-based design: from redesigning the system around the patient to co-designing services with the patient. *Quality and Safety in Health Care*, 15: 307–10.

Berwick, D. (2009) What 'patient-centred' should mean: confessions of an extremist. *Health Affairs*, 28(4): w555–w565.

Buetow, S.A. and Roland, M. (1999) Clinical governance: bridging the gap between clinical and managerial approaches to quality of care. *Quality and Safety in Health Care*, 8: 184–90.

Calnan, M. (1995) Citizens' views on health care. *Journal of Management in Medicine*, 9(4): 17–23.

Calnan, M. (1998) The patient's perspective. *International Journal of Technology Assessment in Health Care*, 14(1): 24–34.

Carr, S. (2004) *Has Service User Participation Made a Difference to Social Care Services?* SCIE (Social Care Institute for Excellence) Position Paper 3.

Charles, C. and DeMaio, S. (1993) Lay participation in health care decision making: a conceptual framework. *Journal of Health Politics, Policy and Law*, 18(4): 881–904.

Charles, C., Gafni, A. and Whelan, T. (1997) Shared decision-making in the medical encounter: what does it mean? (or it takes at least two to tango). *Social Science and Medicine*, 44: 681–92.

Coulter, A. (1997) Partnerships with patients: the pros and cons of shared clinical decision-making. *Journal of Health Services Research Policy*, 2(2): 112–21.

Coulter, A. and Ellins J. (2006) *Patient Focused Interventions: A Review of the Evidence*, The Health Foundation. Available at: www.health.org.uk.

Crawford, M.J., Rutter, D., Manley, C. et al. (2002) Systematic review of involving patients in the planning and development of healthcare. *British Medical Journal*, 325(7375): 1263–4.

Crawford, M., Rutter, D. and Thelwall, S. (2003) *User Involvement in Change Management: A Review of the Literature*. London: National Co-ordinating Centre for NHS Service Delivery and Organisation Research and Development.

Crow, R., Gage, H., Hampson, S. et al. (2002) The measurement of satisfaction with healthcare: implications for practice from a systematic review of the literature. *Health Technology Assessment*, 6(32): 1–244.

Davies, H. (1999) Falling public trust in health services: implications for accountability. *Journal of Health Services Research and Policy*, 4(4): 193–4.

Delbanco, T., Berwick, M.D., Boufford, J.I. et al. (2001) Healthcare in a land called PeoplePower: nothing about me without me. *Health Expectations*, 4: 144–50.

Dolan, P., Cookson, R. and Ferguson, B. (1999) Effect of discussion and deliberation on the public's views of priority setting in health care: focus group study. *British Medical Journal*, 318: 916–19.

Entwistle, V., Andrew, J., Emslie, M. et al. (2003) Patients' views on feedback to the NHS. *Quality and Safety in Healthcare*, 12: 435–42.

Gibson, P.G., Powell, H., Coughlan, J. et al. (2002) Limited (information only) patient education programs for adults with asthma. *Cochrane Database of Systematic Reviews*, Issue 1. Art. No.: CD001005.

Goodare, H. and Lockwood, S. (1999) Involving patients in clinical research. *British Medical Journal*, 319: 724–5.

Home Office (2004) *Facilitating Community Involvement: Practical Guidance for Practitioners and Policy-Makers*. Home Office Development and Practice Report 27. London: Home Office. Available at: www.homeo.ce.gov.uk.

Kaplan, S.H., Greenfield, S. and Ware, J.E. (1989) Assessing the effects of physician–patient interactions on the outcomes of chronic disease. *Medical Care*, 27(suppl): S110–S127.

Kilpatrick, S. (2009) Multi-level rural community engagement in health. *Australian Journal of Rural Health*, 17(1): 39–44.

Klein, R. (1984) The politics of participation. In R. Maxwell and N. Weaver (eds) *Public Participation in Health*. London: King Edward's Hospital Fund for London.

Lockey, R., Sitzia, J., Millyard, C. et al. (2004) *Report Summary. Training for Service User Involvement in Health and Social Care Research: A Study of Training Provision and Participants' Experiences*. Eastleigh: INVOLVE. Available at: www.invo.org.uk.

Lorig, K.R., Sobel, D.S., Stewart, A.L. et al. (1999) Evidence suggesting that a chronic disease self-management programme can improve health status while reducing hospitalization: a randomized trial. *Medical Care*, 37(1): 5–14.

Mays, N. (2000) Legitimate decision making: the Achilles' heel of solidaristic health care systems. *Journal of Health Services Research and Policy*, 5(2): 122–6.

Marshall, S., Haywood, K.L. and Fitzpatrick, R. (2005) *Patient Involvement and Collaboration in Shared Decision Making: A Review*. National Centre for Health Outcomes Development. Available at: http://phi.uhce.ox.ac.uk.

McIver, S. (1993) *Obtaining the Views of Health Service Users about Quality of Information*. London: The King's Fund.

McIver, S. (1998) *Healthy Debate? An Independent Evaluation of Citizens' Juries in Health Settings*. London: King's Fund.

McIver, S. (2005) Listening to 'quiet' voices. In J. Burr and P. Nicolson (eds) *Researching Health Care Consumers: Critical Approaches*. Basingstoke: Palgrave Macmillan.

Mechanic, D. (1998) Public trust and initiatives for new health care partnerships. *Milbank Quarterly*, 76(2): 281–302.

Mullen, P. and Spurgeon, P. (2000) *Priority Setting and the Public*. Oxford: Radcliffe.

NICE (2008) *Community Engagement to Improve Health*. NICE public health guidance 9. London: NICE.

O'Connor, A. (2001) Using patient decision aids to promote evidence-based decision making. *Evidence Based Medicine*, 6: 100–2.

O'Connor, A. et al. (2003) Decision aids for people facing health treatment or screening decisions. *Cochrane Database Systematic Review*, CD001431(2).

Pollitt, C. (1996) Business approaches to quality improvement: why are they hard for the NHS to swallow? *Quality and Safety in Health Care*, 5: 104–10.

Potter, C. and Whittaker, C. (2001) *Enabling Communication in Children with Autism*. London: Jessica Kingsley Publishers.

Rakow, T. (2001) Differences in belief about likely outcomes account for differences in doctors' treatment preferences: but what accounts for differences in belief? *Quality in Health Care*, 10(suppl.): 144–49.

Rose, D., Fleischmann, P., Tonkiss, F., Campbell, P. and Wykes, T. (2002) *User and Carer Involvement in Change Management in a Mental Health Context: Review of the Literature*. London: Natural Co-ordinating Centre for NHS Service Delivery and Organisation Research and Development.

Saltman, R.B. (1994) Patient choice and patient empowerment in Northern European health systems: a conceptual framework. *International Journal of Health Services*, 24(2): 201–29.

Serrano-Aguilar, P. et al. (2009) Patient involvement in health research: a contribution to a systematic review on the effectiveness of treatments for degenerative ataxias. *Social Science and Medicine*, 69(6): 920–5.

Stevenson, F.A., Barry, C.A., Britten, N., Barber, N. and Bradley, C.P. (2000) Doctor–patient communication about drugs: the evidence for shared decision making. *Social Science and Medicine*, 50: 829–40.

Stewart, J., Kendall, E. and Coote, A. (eds) (1994) *Citizens' Juries*. London: Institute for Public Policy Research.

Taylor, D. and Bury, M. (2007) Chronic illness, expert patients and care transition, *Sociology of Health and Illness*, 29(1): 27–45.

Telford, R., Boote, J.D. and Cooper, C.L. (2004) What does it mean to involve consumers successfully in NHS research? A consensus study. *Health Expectations*, 7: 209–20.

Towsley, R. (2000) Archive – *Avon calling*. 5 June. Available at: www.communitycare.co.uk.

Van Wersch, A. and Eccles, M. (2001) Involvement of consumers in the development of evidence based clinical guidelines: practical experiences from the North of England evidence based guideline development programme. *Quality in Health Care*, 10: 10–16.

Wensing, M. and Elwyn, G. (2002) Research on patients' views in the evaluation and improvement of quality of care. *Quality and Safety in Health Care*, 11: 153–7.

Wensing, M., Grol, R., van Montfort, P. and Smits, A. (1996) Indicators of the quality of general practice care of patients with chronic illness: a step towards the real involvement of patients in the assessment of the quality of care. *Quality in Health Care*, 5: 73–80.

Williams, B. (1994) Patient satisfaction: a valid concept? *Social Science and Medicine*, 38(4): 509–16.

Williamson, C. (2001) What does involving consumers in research mean? *Quarterly Journal of Medicine*, 94: 661–4.

World Health Organization Europe (2006a) *Report of the Ninth Futures Forum on health systems governance and public participation.* Geneva: World Health Organization. Available at: www.euro.who.int/pubrequest.

World Health Organization Europe (2006b) *What is the Evidence on Effectiveness of Empowerment to Improve Health?* Available at: www.euro.who.int.

Wullink, M. et al. (2009) Doctor–patient communication with people with intellectual disability: a qualitative study, *BMC Family Practice*, 10: 82.

Zakus, J.D. and Lysack, C.L. (1998) Revisiting community participation. *Health Policy and Planning*, 13(1): 1–12.

Websites and resources

Consumers Health Forum of Australia: www.chf.org.au.

INVOLVE. A national advisory group, funded by the Department of Health, which aims to promote and support active public involvement in NHS, public health and social care research: www.invo.org.uk.

King's Fund. An independent charitable institution which researches and evaluates health and social care policy: www.kingsfund.org.uk.

Patient Information Forum. An independent not-for-profit organization that supports people involved in the production and use of consumer health information: www.pifonline.org.uk.

Picker Europe. Patient survey advice and information:
www.pickereurope.org.

US Institute for Healthcare Improvement: www.ihi.org.

World Health Organization Europe: www.who.int.

Healthcare management and leadership

CHAPTER

19

Leadership and governance

Naomi Chambers

Introduction

To the manager, practitioner or student who is new to the field, leadership and governance might appear nebulous or slippery concepts. To get us started, it is helpful to see them as two sides of a coin: leadership as the human aspect and governance as the technical systems aspect of steering and controlling organizations. The argument runs that they are interdependent and need to work in tandem. There are a number of recent texts that highlight this, whether the authors focus on organization failures (for example, Gandossy and Sonnenfeld 2004) or on how to improve organization performance (for example, Chait et al. 2005). For our purposes, however, to gain an initial understanding, it is worth examining each concept separately.

There are as many definitions of leadership as there are theories: a useful one is given by Northouse, which emphasizes processual and relational themes: 'Leadership is a process whereby an individual influences a group of individuals to achieve a common goal' (Northouse 2007: 3). This hints that the provision of direction and the maintenance of control alluded to above are necessary, but not sufficient, for the enactment of leadership. The concept of leadership is quite culturally specific: the word 'leadership' itself is common in English-speaking countries but many other languages do not have their own equivalent, the nearest being a word which means 'direction' (for example, in French). There is greater consensus on the other hand about definitions of governance, particularly at the organization level (that is corporate governance) which are discussed on p. 000. The OECD definition is widely used: '[Governance is] ... the structure through which the objectives of the company are set, and the means of attaining those objectives and monitoring performance are determined' (OECD 2004: 11). These are the panoply of rules, policies, procedures and processes that all organizations beyond a certain size require to have in place to operate effectively and legally.

The chapter begins by framing health systems through the lens of leadership and governance challenges. There follows an analysis of the main leadership theories which are particularly relevant in the healthcare setting. The debate about management and leadership and its utility in the healthcare arena is also referred to here. We then proceed to a discussion of governance arrangements, particularly at the level of the healthcare organization, and the role of boards in organization governance. We conclude that the leadership and governance dynamic in relation to efficiency and effectiveness of healthcare delivery is not well understood and would benefit from a fresh look from the perspective of systems thinking.

Leadership and governance challenges facing healthcare systems

There is a raft of enduring leadership and governance challenges facing all healthcare systems, which have been well rehearsed by a number of authors, (for example, WHO (2008), Blank and Burau (2004), Saltman et al. (2000) and Goodwin (2006). These challenges have much in common with those in other public sector or social welfare programmes (education, housing, and so on) but it can be argued that there is a greater number and greater complexity of strands coming together in health which makes the leadership endeavour here at the same time more intractable and more compelling. Six strands are identified here (see Box 19.1) which have to be handled by leaders contemporaneously. These add up to the wicked and critical problems identified by Grint (2010) and the need for 'clumsy' rather than elegant solutions as posited by the same author.

Box 19.1: *Six system and leadership/governance challenges in healthcare*

- Financial pressures: need for comprehensive controls
- Quality and safety of care: need for good systems and implementation
- National and local politics: need for astuteness over competing forces
- Consumer demands: need for prioritization tools and patient focus
- Power of the professions: need for negotiation and influencing skills rather than command-and-control approaches
- Complexity of the health system: need for inter-organizational governance and collaborative leadership

---

Since the global economic downturn in 2008, and given the rate of technological advances in healthcare, top of the list of challenges has to be the affordability of care. Fiscal stress has been identified as one of five policy drivers by the OECD in its review of common pressures faced by governments (OECD 2005). Governance which includes comprehensive controls and prioritization tools to avoid overspending is therefore essential. Second is the question of quality and safety in patient care. This demands good measures and data, excellent systems of monitoring and sophisticated influencing abilities over highly qualified professionals. Even in countries such as the UK, which boasts a national health service stretching back to 1948 and an elaborate professional regulation infrastructure, inquiries into failures of care, which first started in the 1960s, continue today, without, apparently, the basic lessons being learnt and applied. These governance failures are replicated worldwide (Walshe and Shortell 2004). Third is the confounding factor of politics in healthcare which nationally drives successive top-down reorganizations and restructurings (Klein 1998), and which locally 'interferes with' evidence-based reconfigurations of services. Political astuteness in manoeuvring around this is called for. Fourth is increasing consumer demands and steadily increasing dissatisfaction with services (Ham 2004: 249), requiring a response which is both economic, for example, through the construction and implementation of technical prioritization tools, and socio-emotional, for example, through ensuring the design and delivery of services which are 'patient-centred'. Fifth is the power of the professionals, particularly doctors, who deliver the services and who can sabotage attempts to make changes if the changes make no sense to them (Goodwin 2006). The only realistic way forward is through co-ownership, management by influence and distributed forms of leadership. And finally, although it increases complexity, there is a growing acknowledgement that health services are managed more effectively in health systems which cross institutional boundaries than they are within single organizations (Pratt et al. 1999) which requires consideration of multi-form and multi-level governance and collaborative forms of leadership.

There are also some enduring themes in health governance in all types of health systems (for example, whether social health insurance is operated or tax funded and privately provided or government run). These include the place of doctors and other clinicians in organizations run as professional bureaucracies (Mintzberg 1981) that have had to evolve to meet the needs of the era of New Public Management and its aftermath. The roles of other actors are also germane: the complementary or conflicting roles of politicians, civil servants, professional managers and 'lay' people in health governance contribute to a crowded scene.

Leadership theories and frameworks for healthcare settings

There is a voluminous literature on leadership and some excellent summaries with a practical emphasis underpinning the theories (for example, Storey 2004; Northouse 2007; Bass and Bass 2008). One of the characteristics of this literature is the extent to which evidence relating to each of theories is contested and 'old' theories are rejected in favour of 'new'. This translates for managers into frames of reference around leadership and leadership which are constantly changing. Looking closely at the different concepts, it is in fact possible to identify overlaps and connections between them. The main theories and debates are summarized in Table 19.1 and then discussed with some examples of how they relate to the healthcare management and leadership challenges outlined earlier.

Trait theory

This is the oldest theory, alternatively called 'great man' theory, and indicates, briefly, that great leaders possess a particular set of personality characteristics which they are born with. In simplistic terms, this theory argues that leaders are *born* not *made*. Even

TABLE 19.1 Competing theories of leadership

Theory	Key points	Critique
Trait	Leaders are born not made, and key personality traits of successful leaders include intelligence, self-confidence, determination, integrity and sociability	'Great man' school takes no account of context or process, and over-emphasizes the importance of the individual. Little empirical evidence. Rooted in a US/British cultural model of leadership
Skills	Leaders are made not born, and key skills can be developed – effective leaders need technical skills, human skills and conceptual skills	Again takes too little account of context and process, and may seem over-functional in its focus on competencies and leadership development. Again little empirical evidence
Style	Leadership styles are identified such as authoritarian vs democratic, task vs people, and particular styles are thought to be more effective for types of situation or organization	Also not well related to context and process (though some discussion of what style fits what situation). Again, not much evidence, and some suspicion that the styles are really cultural stereotypes
Situational	Matches leadership styles explicitly to characteristics such as organizational setting/context, subordinate behaviours, task or purpose, etc. These produce different combinations of leadership behaviours like directing, coaching, supporting and delegating	Raises useful idea of the leadership repertoire, but little real evidence to link particular leadership behaviours to specific contexts. Can seem to simply suggest that everything is contingent on context
Transactional or transformational	Dichotomy between transactional leadership (task, stability, process and delivery focus) versus transformational leadership (empowering, visionary, collaborative)	Seen by some as a false dichotomy which implicitly privileges transformational leadership on the basis of little or no empirical evidence
New public leadership	Ideas of individual leadership are outmoded – focus is on collective and collaborative leadership within and across organizations	Could seem like a return to management by consensus with effective veto by some interests. Long history of focus on partnership working between organizations but poor evidence of effectiveness

leadership trait theorists would argue that these characteristics, although necessary, are not sufficient. There is a growing body of data that points to the important role of various personality traits. Although lists vary between writers, they tend to include intelligence, self-confidence, determination, integrity and sociability (Northouse 2007). Although these are deemed traits, there is no doubt that they can also be developed (akin to the skills approach) and also self-consciously 'performed'. In the healthcare setting, for example, tackling service quality and patient safety issues in an organization requires leaders to draw upon determination, intelligence and self-confidence to overcome sometimes endemic, ingrained and enduring professional and system barriers to change.

The trait approach has great intuitive appeal: it relates to our need for heroic or charismatic leadership and the authority that is derived from charisma (Weber et al.

1947). There is some evidence that certain personality traits are associated with effective leadership. And the theory does guide personal development. The drawbacks with this approach is that is open to subjective interpretation, there is no consensus about the list of attributes deemed essential and there are only weak links between traits and outcomes (Northouse 2007). Most tellingly, it does not focus on leadership as a process or take different situations and circumstances into account.

Skills theory

Put simply, skills theory argues that leaders are *made* not *born* and focuses on abilities that can be learned rather than characteristics that are fixed. Adair (2009) argues that leadership skills can be developed so that individuals can appear to be 'natural' leaders when in fact they have progressively honed their skills. These skills need to be directed at the task, the needs of the team and the needs of the individual (Adair 2009).

There is a line of argument that the emphasis on leadership skills shifts with increasing seniority. This is outlined in the three skills model (Katz 1955). The first is the technical suite of skills which includes task competence, specialized knowledge, tools and techniques and is particularly important at the supervisory level and declines in importance with increasing seniority. The second suite is human skills, the ability to work with people which is uniformly important at all levels. The third is the group of conceptual skills, which includes the application of intelligence and judgement, which becomes more critical the greater the strategic component of the leadership role (Katz 1955). In the healthcare setting, the example of the medical profession is instructive. In the operating theatre, we would like the surgeon to be technically proficient but if he or she is not capable of successfully leading a team, the patient will also suffer. If or she does not fully grasp the strategic context in which the hospital operates, this is not material. As a clinical leader, the technical skills become less important but knowledge and scrutiny of the medical strengths and weaknesses of colleagues are critical to ensure patient safety. Tackling clinical failures also requires human relations skills. As a CEO, the doctor will put technical skills largely to one side as he or she tackles the strategic challenges faced by the hospital.

The attraction of the skills approach is that it focuses on individual potential to improve through the acquisition and honing of leadership expertise. It provides a structure for personal competency and leadership development, and is used to populate leadership development frameworks such as the one widely used in the UK NHS, the leadership qualities framework, which utilizes cumulative levels of leadership qualities (NHS Institute for Innovation and Improvement 2006).

The limitations of the skills-based approach include the fact that the evidence suggests that it is weak in predictive value (Northouse 2007) and that *prima facie* it does not take into account different contexts and situations.

Style theory

There is a growing interest in the role of style in leadership. This is predicated on the notion of choices that leaders make about how they behave, which, clustered together, become a dominant style. Lewin (Lewin et al. 1939) identified three key leadership styles: authoritarian, democratic and *laissez-faire*. He drew the conclusion from his research that the first and second had merit in different circumstances, for example, the first is preferred during times of crisis and the second when creativity was called for, but the third was unproductive unless the followers were highly skilled and experienced. The evidence adduced by Lewin goes some way to counter the argument that leadership is an ephemeral or romantic notion. Other classic authors in this field are Blake and Mouton (1964), who argued that leaders essentially had a preference for people or for the task and, depending on how they enacted that preference, the resulting predominating style was strong on performance management (high on task and low preoccupation with people), indulgent with people (vice versa), a clear team focus (high on task and on people), neglectful or coasting (low on both), or middle of the road (medium in both areas).

Reflecting on their prevailing leadership styles can assist individuals to understand the impact they are having on followers or peers, and, conversely, can help staff to understand why they find some styles in their colleagues or leaders more conducive than others. The charge, however, that these ideas do not take account of different contexts and circumstances can still be made.

Situational leadership theory

Unlike the other theories touched on so far, situational leadership takes organizational context into account. This body of theory identifies varying leadership styles for different circumstances. Hersey and Blanchard (1977) derived four main styles depending on the maturity, intelligence and commitment of followers or subordinates. According to these authors, the level of supportive or directive behaviour should match the characteristics of staff or 'followers': *directing* is appropriate where there are low levels of trust and expertise; *coaching* where high support and direction are required; *support* where direction is less important but encouragement is still required; and *delegating* is appropriate where there are high levels of commitment, experience and expertise among subordinates.

In a variant of the styles approach advocated by Blake and Mouton described above, Fiedler (1967) proposed that a particular leadership orientation (that is a focus on the goal or on the team) fits particular circumstances, for example, how clearly defined the task structure is, the position power of the leader, and the degree of trust and confidence in leader–follower relations (which relates also to the Blanchard frame). Fiedler argued that leaders who are task oriented do well in very favourable or very adverse situations, and leaders who are relationship focused do better in moderately favourable situations where there is a degree of goal ambiguity, and there exist only medium levels of trust and confidence in the leader.

These situational and contingency theories intuitively have much appeal. They suggest the need for leaders to develop a leadership repertoire which can be adapted to meet the circumstances. They also suggest that it is important to choose leadership roles which match the preferences of individuals. For example, a leadership role which requires managing strategic change (for example, a reconfiguration of services in a local health economy) requires a different orientation from one in which major incident management is a feature.

Transactional and transformational leadership

One of the most popular dichotomies proposed in recent years which the healthcare sector has found attractive is the distinction between transactional and transformational leadership. The former is considered by some authors (for example, Alimo-Metcalfe 1999) as less effective than the latter. Transactional leadership works 'above the surface' and offers reward for measurable performance, manages by exception, and does not particularly focus on the needs or personal development of subordinates. With echoes of trait theory (see above), transformational leadership focuses on a charismatic, motivating and empowering style of leadership and includes creating a clear vision, being a strong role model, promoting collaboration and making people feel good about themselves (Alimo-Metcalfe 1999). It has also been identified as an appropriate response to the complex challenges for leaders grappling with and operating within changing and multiple modes of governance for example in partnerships (Newman 2005).

But transactional leadership also relates to the formal or proper administration of systems and processes, with the leadership element of that relating to the value that is placed on this and the behaviours that are modelled that emphasize the importance of getting the day-to-day routines right. It has been argued elsewhere that some of the failings in governance in healthcare can be attributed to the absence of transactional leadership (Walshe and Chambers 2010). One of the recurring themes from studies into inquiries in failings of care in England over 30 years (Walshe and Higgins 2002) is that the organizations concerned were characterized by chaotic administrative systems including missing medical records, poor human resource management systems and unsatisfactory processes for handling complaints, all the stuff of day-to-day administrative routines in large organizations. Recent research (Boyd and Nelson 2011) into cultures for improvement in the local government sector have identified the concept of 'intelligent application' as an important characteristic and this seems to combine elements of transactional and transformational leadership, combining as it does intelligence (or technical expertise) with application (the discipline and energy to see things through), suggesting that the two do not have to be mutually exclusive.

New public leadership

A recent body of theory which is gaining momentum in the public sector is predicated on the notion that the study of leadership based on the individual may be outmoded. There are two main reasons for this. First, in organizations, there is a growing need for *distributed* leadership – exercised by the many rather than by a few – to tackle challenges, manage change and drive improvement in today's speeded-up times, and in acknowledgement that solo heroic leadership may have had its day (Badaracco 2001). Second, with the growth of system management and network governance, there is a need for inter-organizational collaboration, or leadership which is *shared* across organizations (Brookes and Grint 2010). Collective leadership, a combination of distributed and shared approaches, is argued by these authors to be the foundation block of

New Public Leadership (NPL). This builds on some of the concepts of New Public Management (NPM), such as continuous improvement and performance management, but with a shift in emphasis away from measuring targets to incorporate the idea of public value from Moore's work (Moore 1995) and the notion of collaborative advantage, as well as the complex process and practice of leadership in the public sphere (Brookes 2010b). Discussions on public leadership are not confined to Anglo-Saxon world: although somewhat dependent on the western academic literature, countries as diverse, for example, as China and Bulgaria are investigating these concepts (Pittinsky and Zhu 2005).

How do notions of public leadership apply in the healthcare sector? The language of networks, collaborations, partnerships and integrated care organizations to commission, purchase and deliver health services now abounds. These 'chains of care' extend across health service institutions (for examples, hospitals and primary healthcare), across professions (for example, clinical networks) and across sectors (for example, joint commissioning units for health and social care). Different forms of chains of care can be found in government-operated health systems such as the UK, in countries with social health insurance such as the Netherlands and in pro-market outliers such as the USA. Operating in such systems, Goodwin (2006) has proposed four main interconnected variables from his research with chief executives in the UK NHS that resonate strongly with the public leadership discourse. These include the quality of the CEO's team as perceived by others (this would be an example of distributed leadership), the history and current strength of inter-organizational relations, the development of alliances and the extent of power sharing across organizations (these last three being examples of shared leadership).

Given the increasing prominence in later iterations of theories of new public management that are given to networked governance and to performance management of programmes rather than institutions (see, for example Pollitt, 1999), this emerging public leadership discourse has a distinctive attraction. There is, however, as yet little empirical evidence to underpin the theory of public leadership (Brookes 2010b).

Social construction of leadership

For a different perspective, Grint (2005) and others posit that the concept of leadership exists only in the eye of the beholder. The argument runs that leadership does not exist without followership. Thus, in order for it to be realized, leadership has to be enacted, performed and witnessed. This gives it somewhat of an ephemeral quality. This has also been described as the 'romance of leadership': a series of studies found that leadership was used as an explanatory concept for organization outcomes, laying the foundation for later debates about the attributional perspective on leadership (Meindl et al. 1985). Further studies have emphasized the importance of rhetoric, small talk, the 'halo' effect and institutional dynamics (Sjostrand 2001) and below the surface dynamics (Huffington et al. 2004).

The relationship between leadership and power is also relevant here: the power that is vested in leaders by others and the power that is taken up by them. French and Raven (1959) identified five types of power which increase the leader's ability to influence the attitudes and behaviours of staff. These include powers of reward (which transactional leadership draws from), the power of coercion (the power to make someone do something they would not otherwise volunteer to do), the power of position, and referent power which emanates from others wanting to be associated with you (attraction as a role model), and expert power that comes from having a suite of expert skills that are in demand.

Within the healthcare sector, the social construction of leadership can be seen in how the managerial and professional (particularly medical) elites are formed and sustained. In the case of the latter, they draw on sources of reward, position, referent and expert power and, through the medium of the consultation, continuously re-enact this power and reinforce followership in patients and junior colleagues and other professions ancillary to medicine.

Leadership and management

One area that has courted a good deal of controversy is the difference between leadership and management. Kotter (1990) argues that they are different but complementary systems of action, both of which are required for organizational success. Management is about dealing effectively with certainty although in the context of sometimes complex systems and processes, and handling also 'tame' but resolvable problems (cf. Grint 2010). Leadership, on the other hand, deals with uncertainty and with wicked or critical problems. The three complementary practices highlighted are planning and budgeting versus direction setting, organizing and staffing versus aligning people, and controlling and problem solving versus motivating and inspiring (Kotter 1990). Grint offers a third system of action, to handle critical problems, which, in contrast to management (for 'tame' problems) and leadership (for 'wicked' problems) is command. Grint argues that of the three (command, management and leadership), leadership is required when there is maximum uncertainty about what the solution to the problem is and where there is a high level of requirement for collaborative resolution, and argues that the dominant mode behaviour has to be inquiring (rather than telling or instructing) and to deploy emotional as well as rational intelligence to the problem (Grint 2010).

There is a tendency in some of the language used to privilege leadership over management, particularly when the latter is described as transactional, itself considered 'second class' to transformational. The emerging discussions about the discipline of 'intelligent application' in the management of change (Boyd and Nelson 2011) may offer support for a rebalancing here. It is also arguable that management lays the foundations without which leadership cannot flourish, for example, in healthcare, without the smooth running of a hospital or in the absence of the efficient administration of a funding system, leaders cannot embed innovation and improvement or facilitate transformational change.

Middle management is also arguably a meeting point between management and leadership. Authors provide a variety of definitions of 'middle manager', mainly focusing on where they are located within an organizational hierarchy. Livian (Livian and Burgoyne 1997) suggests an expansion to this by suggesting that they are also in the 'middle' in terms of time-scale and in the scope of decision-making between strategic and routine supervision, and 'middle' in terms of organizational impact between fundamental and inconsequential. On this last point, others would argue the reverse: that middle managers are critical for the effective management of change (Pettigrew et al. 1992) and for the delivery of high performance (Mannion et al. 2003).

In a review of changes across Europe (Livian and Burgoyne 1997) detects progressively less tightly specified roles for middle managers, a reduction in numbers, job security, and career prospects, the need for the development of new attitudes and competencies, and the need for new 'people' skills in coaching and facilitation. Middle managers will require a better and deeper understanding of the organization's strategy, which they have rarely contributed to, in order to implement it with less close supervision. They have to build a legitimacy which lies between technical expertise and managerial talent. They need to move from performance enforcer to performance facilitator which is, arguably, where management meets leadership.

Leadership in different healthcare settings

If we apply the belief that leadership is situational, it would follow that different styles and characteristics are appropriate in different parts of healthcare systems (for example, in primary care, mental health, hospital care, planning and provision) and in different countries. Chambers and Colin-Thome (2009) have argued that, because of the organization environment, doctors managing in primary care in general should be people who prefer working in networks rather than hierarchies, show clinical and managerial entrepreneurial spirit, are tolerant of ambiguity and uncertainty, are inherently optimistic, are personally resilient and can see both the 'big picture' and be concerned with detail. It would not be difficult, by extension, to argue that hospital work may suit leaders with different preferences, since the 'command' element is likely to be relatively strong and system and strategic leadership, except in the top echelons, less in demand.

Organization performance is central to governance and the role of leaders is to some extent prescribed by the organization governance arrangements that are in place. These change over time. Since the Second World War, the Netherlands, which operates a compulsory social health insurance funded system, has had three reorganizations, and is currently operating in a quasi-marketized system in which the competition is among purchasers as well as providers. In England, by contrast, which has endured reorganization more than most countries, there have been at least six major reorganizations affecting governance since 1948 (1972, 1984, 1990, 2001, 2006, and forthcoming in 2012). Mirroring the rise of new public management, the cultural context for leadership in England has shifted three times in that period from traditional bureaucracy (leaders were administrators or hospital secretaries), to managerialism (leaders were chief executives in a unified system) to a quasi-marketized system (leaders are chief executives of either purchasing or competing providing healthcare organizations) with the prospect by 2013 of a new cultural context for leadership which will be medically led, at least on the purchasing side (Department of Health 2010). Management control in these different cultures is the business of governance. Attention will therefore now turn to a consideration of healthcare governance and in particular the part played by organization governance.

Governance: an introduction

The term 'governance' has only relatively recently gained currency as a distinct entity within the study of the management of organizations. The development of the debate around governance can be largely traced to incidents relating to the high profile organization failures of the early 1990s (Maxwell, Polly Peck, Barings Bank), the US corporate scandals (Enron, WorldCom) a few years later and which have continued on into this century with Equity Life, Parmalat, and the banking failures that heralded the global economic recession of 2008–9. These examples demonstrate that the problem is international. The responses to these events have provided much of the impetus for clarifying concepts of 'good' governance and have also framed the discussions around the management of corporate risk.

A number of different elucidations of the term governance exist and it is worth examining these in order to arrive at a working definition for the purposes of this discussion. Within a political science paradigm, Pierre and Peters (2000) argue that at a state level, governance revolves around the capacity of government to make and implement policy – in other words, to steer society. An OECD review identified six levers in modernizing governance at state level, including open government, performance management, restructuring, marketization and new forms of employment (OECD 2005).

Within healthcare, Davies and colleagues examine markets, hierarchies and networks as the main contrasting forms of governance, relating these to different incentives and hence to different outcomes (Davies et al. 2005). Newman notes that each mode of governance has its own form of leader, for example, an administrative leader in a bureaucracy and a competitive leader in a market, and putatively transformational one in a network (Newman 2005).

At an institution level, the Cadbury Report describes corporate governance as a system by which an organization is directed and controlled (Cadbury 1992). This is amplified by a subsequent OECD definition of corporate governance as 'the structure through which the objectives of the company are set, and the means of attaining those objectives and monitoring performance are determined' (OECD 2004: 11). The Langlands Review of governance for public services in the UK outlines the following as the function of governance: 'to ensure that an organization or partnership fulfils its overall purpose, achieves its intended outcomes for citizens and service users, and operates in an effective, efficient and ethical manner' (Independent Commission for Good Governance in Public Services 2004: 7).

Beyond the notion of governance as steering, four clear generic strands, which are all non-country or sector-specific, emerge from these statements: the need for direction, the importance of control, the relevance of an underpinning set of values and the requirement to demonstrate accountability. These strands are also, as we shall see, embedded within the health sector. It is interesting to note that governance discussions are dominated more by terms relating to control and accountability than by those relating to renewal and entrepreneurship. This has implications for priorities in the management of health services: one of the consequences is that lapses of control are more likely to be deemed governance failures rather than lack of attention to innovation. We can track this in the development of and the focus of attention paid to governance arrangements in the English NHS over the past 20 years.

Case study of healthcare governance: developments in the English NHS

Having adopted a private sector business model in place of the stakeholder model for its local bodies in 1990, the NHS in England, via guidance from HM Treasury, moved quickly to embrace lessons from the corporate failures of the 1990s. A number of reports emanating from these failures were used to strengthen corporate governance in the NHS. Despite the plethora of guidance (Cadbury Report 1992; Nolan Report 1994; Turnbull Report 1999), challenges remain. These documents imply that the existence of frameworks and audit trails will suffice. The evidence from financial and wider organizational failings in the NHS and beyond (see Box 19.2) suggests that this is somewhat wishful thinking.

On the clinical and reputational side, organizational failures in the NHS over the past 20 years, referred to in more detail elsewhere in this book, have, arguably, matched or surpassed those in the commercial sector in the UK. The question has to be asked about who is responsible for this apparent unevenness of quality and

---

Box 19.2: *Governance failings in healthcare*

- **North Bristol NHS Trust (UK)**: £44 million overspend in 2003; independent review found relationship breakdowns and failings within the finance directorate, internal audit, the executive team and the board who had all failed to spot and track the growing deficit.

- **Grantham Hospital (UK)**: Beverley Allitt, a nurse, murdered a number of babies in her care. The inquiry (1994) found *inter alia* that the approved HR recruitment policy had not been followed in the appointment process to her post at the hospital.

- **HealthSouth (USA)**: Following a raid by the FBI on the company headquarters, the CEO was accused in 2003 of instructing senior managers to falsify the company accounts to mislead investors to the tune of $1.4 billion about the income and value of the company; he was found not guilty but was later convicted of separate bribery charges.

- **Walter Reed Army Medical Center (USA)**: In 2007, the *Washington Post* exposed neglect, dirty and rundown facilities and labyrinthine bureaucratic processes for soldiers attempting to access care and treatment. This resulted in a series of dismissals of ever more senior service officials responsible for the Center and for the wider healthcare system providing for serving soldiers and veterans.

assurance within a dense architecture of corporate governance arrangements, and within a 'national' health service: it is not unreasonable to suggest that local boards which have ultimate control for what goes on in their organizations, bear at least some of that responsibility.

Structures of health boards

Boards, as Pointer has pointed out, are late nineteenth-century inventions. They were developed as a result of the Industrial Revolution and the growing commercial complexity of business. Boards, as agents of the owners, represented absent shareholders' interests, and management became the agents of the board. The function of the board in the commercial and the non-profit and state sectors today is essentially the same – the main difference being that shareholders are replaced by 'stakeholders' (Pointer 1999). The term 'board' itself is not universal. In different parts of the public sector in the UK, for example, in school education, the equivalent is the governing body; within the voluntary sector, it might be the trustees; in local government, it is the council. The term council is used in different countries to denote the body that oversees the management or procurement of local health services.

Local boards in the NHS in England since 1990 are derived in structure from the Anglo-Saxon private sector unitary board model which predominates in UK and US business (Ferlie et al. 1996; Garratt 1997). The unitary board typically comprises a chair, chief executive, executive directors and a majority of appointed independent (or non-executive) directors. All members of the board bear collective responsibility for the performance of the enterprise. First established in 2004, NHS Foundation Trusts, on the other hand, are independent public benefit corporations modelled on cooperative and mutual traditions, which by 2010 encompassed more than half the acute hospital and specialist mental care providers in England (Monitor 2010: 51). The governance structure of Foundation Trusts comprises are two boards – a board of governors (up to about 50 people) made up of people elected from the local community membership, and a board of directors (around 11 people) made up of a chair and non-executive directors appointed by the governors, and a chief executive and executive directors, appointed by the chair and approved by the governors. This whole structure resembles the Anglo-Saxon unitary board model we have seen adopted by the NHS in England but nested within a two-tier European or Senate model, commonly found in the Netherlands, France and Germany.

The Senate model comprises a lower-tier operational board which deals with management and strategic issues and an upper-tier supervisory board which ratifies certain decisions taken by the operational board, sets the direction and represents the different interests in the company, particularly those of shareholders and employees (Johnson et al. 2005). This model can be seen, for example, in public hospitals in the Belgian system which have a four-part governance structure comprising a constituent authority, hospital board, executive committee, and medical council (Eeckloo et al. 2004).

In a variant of the NHS structures in England, and an example of a wholly non-executive board, New Zealand has 21 District Health Boards tasked with strategic oversight of local health services, but in this case all 11 people on the board are non-executive directors: seven are elected at the time of local government elections and four are appointed by the Ministry of Health; the chief executive is appointed by and accountable to the board but is not a board member (www.moh.govt.nz/districthealthboards). This mirrors the governance arrangements typically found in the voluntary sector where there are boards of trustees, and employed staff such as administrators or directors are invited only 'in attendance' to boards.

From the US perspective, Pointer outlines four types of boards commonly found within US healthcare. Parent boards govern free-standing independently owned institutions; subsidiary boards are local boards of large enterprises; advisory boards provide steering and guidance without a formal corporate governance role; and affiliate organization boards serve their members' interests. There are 7,500 hospital and health system boards in the USA – part of an economic and social system which supports 5.5 million boards altogether or one for every 45 citizens (Pointer 1999).

Within the four home countries of the UK itself, with the advent of devolution, there have been deepening policy differences (for example, in the role of the market) and an increasing divergence in the structures for managing health services. The Welsh board model is stakeholder-based with up to 25 members on each board, resembling the NHS in England pre-1990. Scotland has an integrated health model and a unified board structure with strong local authority representation and is experimenting with democratic elections on to boards.

The above illustrates the broad range of board structures and models in use in health services and demonstrates the highly contextual nature of the board form chosen. There are non-executive boards, executive boards, two-tier boards and unitary boards; there are models for different health service purposes: for insurers, commissioners, providers and for partnerships (a cross between public sector and public/private). Board membership is achieved through different processes of nomination, appointment and election, and can be paid or unpaid.

Governance and performance

What is the evidence on the relative effectiveness of these different board models? In his review of public sector boards, Cornforth (2003) argues that searching for an idealized board model and membership is ultimately futile, but that boards can work on enhancing their legitimacy and their effectiveness. (Cornforth 2003). Carver argues that key governance principles can work with whatever structural arrangements have come about as a result of a board's composition, history, and particular circumstances (Carver and Carver 2001).

There is more evidence available about the conditions under which boards preside over organization failures. Inquiries and reviews have repeatedly pointed to a lack of challenge by the board at critical junctures. In his examination of US corporate failures, Makosz points out the importance of members of the board to ask the tough questions and to review the effectiveness of internal controls (www.csa-pdk.com). The Francis Report (2010) into the failings at mid-Staffordshire NHS Foundation Trust found that the board lacked focus on the job of a hospital, had poor insight and a confused system of governance. The literature suggests that the challenge for health service boards is not to embark upon a quest for the perfect structure or model but to acknowledge the need for clarity of purpose in order to steer high performing organizations towards providing or securing safe and high quality healthcare for patients.

There are some clues from the literature about what boards do need to pay attention to (Chambers and Cornforth 2010). Smaller boards with well-functioning sub-committees are associated with better performance. A board focus on strategy, use of resources and talent management is important. Board dynamics is emerging as a crucial element, particularly a culture of high trust, high challenge and high engagement in and out of board meetings. The energy and expertise of non-executive directors are crucial in partnering with managers to shape strategy and in tracking performance (Chambers and Cornforth 2010). Cornforth (2003) has identified that, whatever the structure of boards, competing theories about boards do drive different kinds of board behaviours, for example, a belief in agency theory engenders a compliance model of behaviour (typified by high challenge and low trust in the management) in contrast with a belief in joint stewardship, which facilitates partnership behaviours (typified by moderate challenge and high trust in management) or a third model which is managerial hegemony (typified by a 'rubber stamping' board). Until these differences are surfaced, there is a potential for board conflict, disengagement and dysfunction.

What do boards do?

The Langlands Review produced six core principles for good governance to guide the work of public service boards (see Figure 19.1). This 'good governance standard' indicates both core style and key content for board work in the public sector, and comes closest to the iterative and cyclical framework that authors working in the commercial sector advocate.

Turning now to some of these authors who work within the private sector, Garratt (1997) has developed Tricker's (1984) model of four principal board roles into a board tasks model reproduced in a simplified form in Figure 19.2. Garratt argues that boards have to pay attention to both the conformance (accountability and supervision of management) and to the performance (policy formulation and strategic thinking) aspects of their role, and, in turn, to the iterative cycle of policy development, strategic formulation, supervision/monitoring and accounting to key stakeholders. Within these cycles, boards need to be sensitive to the well-being of their own organization and be attuned to the external environment, and to take into account both short-term pressures and longer-term trends in making their decisions.

The conclusion appears to be that there is a need to pay appropriate attention to activities in all four quadrants, to face inwards and outwards and to find a balance between short and long-term thinking, but how easy is this to achieve?

High-profile corporate failures in the UK and the USA have, as we have seen, prompted stricter rules on conformance through tighter corporate governance arrangements and clearer controls assurance frameworks. As organizations are subjected to ever more rigorous risk management, is 'performance' being subjugated to 'conformance'? Power (1999) warns against the growing influence of the audit society,

1 **Good governance means focusing on the organization's purpose and on outcomes for citizens and service users**
   ● What is this organization for?
   ● What is being done to improve services?
   ● Can I easily find out about the organization's funding and how it spends its money?

2 **Good governance means performing effectively in clearly defined functions and roles**
   ● Who is in charge of the organization?
   ● How are they elected or appointed?
   ● At the top of the organization, who is responsible for what?

3 **Good governance means promoting values for the whole organization and demonstrating the values of good governance through behaviour**
   ● According to the organization, what values guide its work?
   ● What standards of behaviour should I expect from the organization?
   ● Do the senior people put into practice the 'Nolan' principles for people in public life (selflessness, integrity, objectivity, accountability, openness, honesty, and leadership)?

4 **Good governance means taking informed transparent decisions and managing risk**
   ● Who is responsible for what kinds of decisions?
   ● Can I easily find out what decisions have been taken and the reasons for them?
   ● Does the organization publish a clear annual statement on the effectiveness of its risk management system?

5 **Good governance means developing the capacity and capability of the governing body to be effective**
   ● How does the organization encourage people to get involved in running it?
   ● What support does it provide for people to get involved?
   ● How does the organization make sure that all those running the organization are doing a good job?

6 **Good governance means engaging stakeholders and making accountability real**
   ● Are there opportunities for me and other people to make our views known?
   ● How can I go about asking the people in charge about their plans and decisions?
   ● Can I easily find out how to complain and who to contact with suggestions for changes?

FIGURE 19.1 How far does the board of your organization meet the tests of the Good Governance Standard?
Source: Adapted with kind permission from *Good Governance Standard for Public Services*, the report of the Independent Commission on Good Governance in Public Services (CIPFA/OPM 2004).

CONFORMANCE   PERFORMANCE

EXTERNAL FOCUS

Accountability	Policy formulation
Supervision of management	Strategic thinking

INTERNAL FOCUS

SHORT TERM   LONG TERM

FIGURE 19.2 Board tasks model
Source: After Garratt (1997).

reward systems which pay checkers more than doers, and the rituals of verification: 'Does the rustle of paper systems . . . provide only slogans of accountability and quality which perpetuate rather than alleviate organisational rigidity?' (1999: 123).

In another framing of the conformance/performance dichotomy, Hodgkinson and Sparrow argue that organizations depend for their survival on developing strategic competence. This is defined as an ability to acquire, store, recall, interpret and act upon information of relevance to the longer-term survival and well-being of the organization (Hodgkinson and Sparrow 2002: xiv–xv). Strategic competence comes from organizational memory, learning, knowledge management, creativity, intuition and use of knowledge elicitation techniques. The authors warn against the competency trap ethos where there is no place for devil's advocates or court jesters and where organizations always favour exploitation (of existing expertise and knowledge base) over exploration (search for new knowledge).

How can we place the work of health service boards within these discussions? The unitary learning board model described by Garratt has clear resonances with the NHS in England where board structures and *modus operandi* are heavily drawn from the private sector business model. NHS boards are expected to operate along all four of Garratt's quadrants from developing a clear vision, to clarifying strategic direction, and also to monitoring performance and accounting to local communities and to government. The key challenges for NHS boards can therefore be segmented into these four quadrants and guidance reinforces this. *The Healthy NHS Board* (2010), published by the National Leadership Council, for example, focuses on three main roles of the board: formulating strategy, shaping culture and ensuring accountability with the three building blocks of context, intelligence and engagement. It also emphasizes health system governance across organizations (National Leadership Council 2010).

Developing effective boards in healthcare

There is indeed no shortage of steer for boards. The NHS Confederation has identified four key characteristics of effective boards: a focus on strategic decision-making, trust and corporate working, constructive challenge and effective chairs. In their examination of boards at work, however, the authors found that 'the daily grind' often obscured strategic decision-making and, while there was often a good deal of trust between board members, there was too little constructive challenge, and therefore some missed opportunities (NHS Confederation 2005). Peck argues, on the other hand, that even as a mainly ratifying body, the board ritual has some value in itself as a way of according significance to important decisions (Peck et al. 2004).

In recent years there has been a particular focus on the role of the non-executive director. The Higgs Report (2003) into this role within the UK commercial sector called for greater clarity on responsibilities, induction, development and performance. In the USA, there is a focus on developing governance tools for boards, for example, by the Center for Healthcare Governance (www.americangovernance.com). Extensive guidance about the work of board committees is also available, for example, from the Audit Commission in the UK. As we have seen from the liturgy of past failures and the complexity of present challenges facing health service governance across the world, there still remains a way to go.

An exploratory study to determine the utility of a model for board development adapted from Garratt's four board tasks (see Figure 19.2) revealed that, with refinements, the model had both resonance and relevance (Chambers and Higgins 2005). In the first main refinement, the study found that the board development cycle needs a further iteration to reflect different levels of maturity, depending on the newness of whole boards and individual new appointments to boards. Second, as it stands, the framework omits to sufficiently acknowledge the need for boards to do work around the identification, articulation, espousal and demonstration of a set of core values for the organization. These values inherently imbue all parts of the board cycle of work, for example, from the principles agreed which underpin policy development, the range of legitimate strategic choices and tactics employed, the monitoring of organization behaviours and the style of accounting to stakeholders. There is a final lesson for boards in this study about the intelligent commissioning of external facilitators with a grounding in governance and the health sector as well as versatility in style to support their development (Chambers and Higgins 2005).

Conclusion: the leadership and governance dynamic

How much does all this matter? A key challenge in debates about leadership and governance at the state and the institutional level is how to engage a wider audience beyond those immediately engaged in, affected by or intellectually interested in the topic. One way of doing this is to demonstrate how leadership and governance issues can directly affect people's lives. We have pointed to the complex challenges facing healthcare.

The main leadership theories have been analysed for their relevance to this sector. The importance, in particular, of situational leadership styles, collaborative leadership and seeking a balance between transformational and transactional leadership approaches have been highlighted. We have traced the evolution of market and network forms of governance, and the development of the 'audit society' and demonstrated how the impact of failures across the world have influenced how health service organizations are governed. Issues of control are arguably accorded more weight than those of renewal. Put simply, we might be in danger of continuing to do the same thing better at times when we should be trying out new things. In organizations, leaders and their boards are responsible for making these kinds of choices. This means that within health services, deep-seated beliefs and values which leaders and boards espouse, will guide decisions affecting staff performance and behaviours, and the kinds of care and treatments provided to patients.

One way forward would be to build on the work discussed earlier on collective or new public leadership (Brookes 2010a, 2010b) and to make more use of what some have called systems thinking (Seddon 2008). It certainly seems likely that the command-and-control and targets-driven culture in healthcare organizations which engenders particular leadership styles and governance structures is shifting towards one in which there is a greater focus on designing against demand led by customers, users or patients. The core principles for such organizations include understanding and managing variability and uncertainty, training against demand, making the worker also the inspector, choosing measures which control and improve, and designing governance around the system (Seddon 2008). The kind of leadership required in the future may therefore be an amalgam of a number of approaches described earlier in this chapter, but with a particular emphasis on aspects of transformational leadership and new public leadership.

Summary box

- There are a large number of leadership theories but closer scrutiny reveals overlaps and a degree of commonality between them.
- Differences between management and leadership can be found but it is important not to privilege one activity over the other.
- There is a need to contextualize leadership in healthcare settings.
- Ideas on governance in public sector are evolving and are particularly affected by high-profile organization failures across the world.
- There are many different board models; the perfect model may not be attainable and is less important than certain behaviours and clarity of purpose.
- Boards and board members need structured development in order to be more effective.
- There is a need for better evidence and articulation about the value and purpose of leadership and governance.

Self-test exercises

1 Think of a leader that you respect and another whom you are critical of. What are their predominant styles? What might your judgements say about you as a leader? Relate the answers to the trait, skill, style and situational leadership theories described in this chapter.

2 What are the main challenges facing your organization? Thinking about management and leadership as two different activities, what would you consider are the most appropriate management and leadership tasks and approaches to tackling these challenges?

3 How far does the board of your organization meet the tests of the Good Governance Standard (see Figure 19.1)?

4 Ask to attend a board meeting (many are held in public anyway), reflect on content and behaviours and examine how much attention is paid to the four areas of board focus in the four quadrants in Figure 19.2.

References and further reading

Adair, J. (2009) *Effective Leadership*. London: Pan Macmillan.

Alimo-Metcalfe, B. (1999) Leadership in the NHS: what are the competencies and qualities needed and how can they be developed? In A. Mark and S. Dopson (eds) *Organisational Behaviour in Health Care*. Basingstoke: Palgrave Macmillan

Avon, Gloucestershire and Wiltshire NHS Strategic Health Authority (2003) *North Bristol NHS Trust: Financial and Governance Review*. London: Deloitte and Touche.

Badaracco, J. (2001) We don't need another hero. *Harvard Business Review*, September: 111–16.

Bass, B. and Bass, R. (2008) *The Bass Handbook of Leadership: Theory, Research, and Managerial Applications*. New York: Free Press.

Blake, R. and Mouton, J. (1964) *The Managerial Grid: The Key to Leadership Excellence*. Houston, TX: Gulf Publishing Co.

Blank, R. and Burau, V. (2004) *Comparative Health Policy*. Basingstoke: Palgrave Macmillan.

Boyd, A. and Nelson, N. (2011) Knowing and doing: the value of 'intelligent application in local government improvement. *Public Money and Management*, 31(4): 249–56.

Brookes, S. (2010a) Telling the story of place: the role of community leadership. In S. Brookes and K. Grint (eds) *A New Public Leadership Challenge?* Basingstoke: Palgrave Macmillan.

Brookes, S. (2010b) Reform, realisation and restoration: public leadership and innovation in government. In S. Brookes and K. Grint (eds) *A New Public Leadership Challenge?* Basingstoke: Palgrave Macmillan.

Brookes, S. and Grint, K. (eds) (2010) *A New Public Leadership Challenge?* Basingstoke: Palgrave Macmillan.

Cadbury, A. (1992) *Report of the Committee on the Financial Aspects of Corporate Governance*. London: Gee.

Carver, J. and Carver, M. (2001) *Carver's Policy Governance Model in Non Profit Organisations*. Available at: www.carvergovernance.com.

Chait, R., Ryan, W. and Taylor, B. (2005) *Governance as Leadership: Reframing the Work of Nonprofit Boards*. New York: John Wiley & Sons.

Chambers, N. and Colin-Thome, P. (2009) Doctors managing in primary care: an international focus. *Journal of Management and Marketing in Health Care*, 2(1): 28–43.

Chambers, N. and Cornforth, C. (2010) The role of corporate governance and boards in organisation performance. In K. Walshe and G. Harvey (eds) *From Knowing to Doing: Connecting Knowledge and Performance in Public Services*. Cambridge: Cambridge University Press.

Chambers, N. and Higgins, J. (2005) *Building a Framework for Developing Effective NHS boards*. Manchester: University of Manchester Press.

Cornforth, C. (2003) *The Governance of Public and NonProfit Organisations*. London: Routledge.

Davies, C. et al. (2005) *Links between Governance, Incentives and Outcomes: A Review of the Literature*. London: National Co-ordinating Centre for NHS Service Delivery and Organisation R & D.

Department of Health (2010) *Equity and Excellence: Liberating the NHS*. London: HMSO.

Eeckloo, K., Van Herck, G., Van Hulle, C. and Vleugels, A. (2004) From corporate governance to hospital governance: authority, transparency and accountability of Belgian non-profit hospitals boards and management. *Health Policy*, 68: 1–15.

Ferlie, E., Ashburner, L., Fitzgerald, L. and Pettigrew, A. (1996) *The New Public Management in Action*. Oxford: Oxford University Press.

Fiedler, F. (1967). *A Theory of Leadership Effectiveness*. New York: Harper and Row Publishers Inc.

Francis Report (2010) *Independent Inquiry into Care Provided by Mid Staffordshire NHS Foundation Trust*. London: The Stationery Office.

French, J. and Raven, B. (1959) The bases of social power. In D. Cartwright and A. Zander (eds.) *Group Dynamics*. New York: Harper & Row.

Gandossy, R. and Sonnenfeld, J. (2004) *Leadership and Governance from the Inside Out*. New York: Wiley.

Garratt, B. (1997) *The Fish Rots from the Head*. London: HarperCollins.

Goodwin, N. (2006) *Leadership in Health Care: A European Perspective*. London: Routledge.

Grint, K. (2005) *Leadership: The Heterarchy Principle*. London: Palgrave Macmillan.

Grint, K. (2010) *Wicked Problems and Clumsy Solutions: The Role of Leadership in the New Public Leadership Challenge*. Basingstoke: Palgrave Macmillan.

Ham, C. (2004) *Health Policy in Britain*. Basingstoke: Palgrave Macmillan.

Hersey, P. and Blanchard, K.H. (1977) *Management of Organizational Behavior: Utilizing Human Resources*, 3rd edn. Englewood Cliffs, NJ: Prentice Hall.

Higgins, J. (2001) Adverse events or patterns of failure? *British Journal of Health Care Management*, 7(4): 145–7.

Higgs, D. (2003) *Review of the Role and Effectiveness of Non-Executive Directors*. London: Stationery Office.

Hodgkinson, G. and Sparrow, P. (2002) *The Competent Organisation*. Buckingham: Open University Press.

Huffington, C. et al. (eds) (2004) *Working Below the Surface: The Emotional Life of Contemporary Organisations*. London: Karnac.

Independent Commission for Good Governance in Public Services (2004) *The Good Governance Standard for Public Services* (The Langlands Review). London: OPM and CIPFA.

Johnson, G., Scholes, K. and Whittington, R. (2005) *Exploring Corporate Strategy*. Harlow: Pearson Education.

Kanter, R. (1982) The middle manager as innovator. *Harvard Business Review*, July–August, 60(4): 95–105.

Katz, R. (1955) Skills of an effective administrator. *Harvard Business Review*, January–February, 33(1): 33–42.

Klein, R. (1998) Why Britain is reorganizing its National Health Service – yet again. *Health Affairs*, 17(4): 111–25.

Kotter, J. (1990) What leaders really do. *Harvard Business Review*, May/June: 103–11.

Lewin, K., Llippit, R. and White, R.K. (1939) Patterns of aggressive behaviour in experimentally created climates. *Journal of Social Psychology*, 10: 271–301.

Livian, Y.-F. and Burgoyne, J. (1997) *Middle Managers in Europe*. London: Routledge.

Mannion, R., Davies, H.T.O. and Marshall, M. (2003) *Cultures for Performance in Health Care*. York: Centre for Health Economics, University of York.

Mannion, R. et al. (2010) *Changing Management Cultures and Organisational Performance in the NHS*. Research Report. London: Department of Health National Institute for Health Research Service Delivery and Organisation Programme.

Meindl, J., Ehrlich, S. and Dukerich, J. (1985) The romance of leadership. *Administrative Science Quarterly*, 30: 68–102.

Mintzberg, H. (1981) Organization design: fashion or fit? *Harvard Business Review*, 59(1): 108–116.

Monitor (2010) *Annual Report and Accounts 2009–2010*. London: The Stationery Office.

Moore, M. (1995) *Creating Public Value: Strategic Management in Government*. Cambridge, MA: Harvard University Press.

National Leadership Council (2010) *The Healthy NHS Board: Principles for Good Governance*. London: Department of Health.

Newman, J. (2005) Enter the transformational leader: network governance and the micro-politics of modernization. *Sociology*, 39(4): 735–53.

NHS Appointments Commission (2004) *Code of Conduct/Code of Accountability*. London: Department of Health.

NHS Confederation (2005) *Effective Boards in the NHS?* London: NHS Confederation.

NHS Institute for Innovation and Improvement (2006) *NHS Leadership Qualities Framework*. Warwick: NHS Institute.

Nolan Report (1994) *Nolan Committee Report on Standards in Public Life*. London: HMSO.

Northouse, P. (2007) *Leadership: Theory and Practice*. Thousand Oaks, CA: Sage.

OECD (2004) *Principles of Corporate Governance*. Available at: www.oecd.org.

OECD (2005) *Modernising Government: The Way Forward*. Paris: OECD.

Peck, E., Perri, B., Gulliver, P. and Towell, D. (2004) Why do we keep on meeting like this? The board as ritual in health and social care. *Health Services Management Research*, 17: 100–9.

Pettigrew, A. et al. (1992) *Shaping Strategic Change*. London: Sage.

Pierre, J. and Peters, B.G. (2000) *Governance, Politics and the State*. Basingstoke: Macmillan.

Pittinsky, T. and Zhu, C. (2005) Contemporary public leadership in China: a research review. *Leadership Quarterly*, 16(6): 921–939.

Plumridge, N. (2005) Opinion. *Health Service Journal*, 3 November: 17.

Pointer, D. (1999) *Board Work: Governing Health Care Organizations*. San Francisco, CA: Jossey-Bass.

Pollitt, C. (1999) *Performance or Compliance?* Oxford: Oxford University Press.

Power, M. (1999) *The Audit Society*. Oxford: Oxford University Press.

Pratt, J., Gordon, P. and Plamping, D. (1999) *Working Whole Systems*. London: Kings Fund.

Saltman, R., Figueras, J. and Sakellarides, C. (2000) *Critical Challenges for Health Care Reform in Europe*. Buckingham: Open University Press.

Seddon, J. (2008) *Systems Thinking in the Public Sector*. Axminster: Triarchy Press.

Sjostrand, S.-E. (2001) *Invisible Management: The Social Construction of Leadership*. London: Thomson Learning.

Storey, J. (2004) *Leadership in Organisations: Current Issues and Key Trends*. London: Routledge.

Tricker, R.I. (1984) *Corporate Governance*. Aldershot: Gower.

Turnbull Report (1999) *Internal Control Guidance for Directors on the Combined Code*. London: Institute of Chartered Certified Accountants in England and Wales.

Walshe, K. and Chambers, N. (2010) Healthcare reform and leadership. In S. Brookes and K. Grint (eds) *The New Public Leadership Challenge*. Basingstoke: Palgrave Macmillan.

Walshe, K., Harvey, G., Hyde, P. and Pandit, N. (2004) Organisational failure and turnaround: lessons for public services from the for-profit sector. *Public Money and Management* August: 201–8.

Walshe, K. and Higgins, J. (2002) The use and impact of inquiries in the NHS. *British Medical Journal*, 325: 895–900.

Walshe, K. and Shortell, S.M. (2004) When things go wrong: how health care organisations deal with major failures. *Health Affairs*, May–June 23(3).

Weber, M., Henderson, A. and Parsons, T. (1947) *Theory of Social and Economic Organisation*. Oxford: Oxford University Press.

WHO (2008) *The World Health Report 2008: Primary Health Care: Now More Than Ever*. Geneva: World Health Ogranization.

Websites and resources

Some of these websites provide additional information for subscribers only but all provide some useful information to non-subscribers.

Center for Healthcare Governance in the USA which is a membership organization with aims to promote innovation and accountability in healthcare governance: www.americangovernance.com.

NHS Appointments Commission website providing details of vacancies, information about the work of local NHS Boards, and guidance on the roles of boards, chairs and non-executives. This body is being abolished in 2012: www.appointments.org.uk.

Canadian website with practical information about corporate governance tools, workshop presentations, references and a control self-assessment process for companies to use: www.csa-pdk.com.

Department of Health information and guidance including information for NHS Boards: www.dh.gov.uk.

Monthly newsletter on issues of corporate governance and boardroom performance and useful links: www.governance.co.uk.

Institute of Directors' website with factsheets, policy papers, information about corporate governance initiatives and views on the economic outlook: www.iod.com.

NHS Alliance represents NHS primary care organisations and issues reports and policy briefings: www.nhsalliance.org.

NHS employers organization representing PCTs and Trusts with a focus on influencing health policy and providing information and support to NHS organizations: www.nhsconfed.org.

New Zealand District Health Boards, which were established in 2001: www.moh .govt.nz/districthealthboards.

Organisation for Economic Development and Co-operation website which includes full-text documents relating to corporate governance initiatives: www.oecd.org.

CHAPTER 20

Personal and organizational development in healthcare

Elaine Clark[1]

Introduction

Transforming and enhancing the quality of care delivered to patients is widely acknowledged to be contingent on the development of effective personnel, equipped to function effectively within organizational systems which are increasingly complex by virtue of their size, the number and diversity of their internal and external stakeholders, and the uncertainty of the political, social and economic environments within which they operate. Revans (1982) famously claimed that organizations would survive where learning was greater than the rate of change, and in a context where the only certainty is the ever increasing pervasiveness of change, the need to learn and to develop is at an all time high.

It is no surprise therefore that there is currently a growing, international emphasis on both personal and organizational development within healthcare. The plethora of training courses over recent years, focused on developing the organizational members and potential leaders of health services, bear witness to this claim and to the assumption that developed individuals will result in developed organizations. In the professional journals, publications about personal and organizational development (Bhatti and Viney 2010), show a growing awareness of the importance of developing healthcare personnel and an increasing focus on their personal development as a means of achieving this.

In this chapter we will explore the meaning of personal and organizational development within a healthcare setting. The chapter will introduce some of the key processes utilized in these spheres of development and will consider why the link between personal and organizational development is often sub-optimal.

This is a short chapter on a subject of great breadth and depth, and the processes and methods discussed draw on our experience of teaching and using them – we make no special claim to their supremacy as developmental tools, and would acknowledge that there are many other approaches to personal and organizational development available.

Personal development in healthcare

Definitions of personal development

The introduction of this chapter referred to the growing emphasis on personal development within healthcare, but what does personal development mean, and more aptly, what does it mean for the health services of today? In an attempt to explore this question, this chapter will now look at some early definitions and related dictionary definitions and will propose a definition applicable to healthcare.

Aristotle provides what may be one of the earliest definitions of personal development, defining it as a category of *phronesis* or practical wisdom, where the practice of virtues, *arête,* leads to *eudaimonia,* commonly translated as 'happiness' but more accurately understood as 'human flourishing' or 'living well'. For Aristotle, 'happiness is the supreme good' and is the 'activity of soul in accordance with virtue' (Thomson 1976: 12–13). The positive psychologist Martin Seligman develops this in a way which has particular relevance to health services, asserting that happiness comes not from power, status or possessions, but from 'using your signature strengths and virtues in the service of something greater than you are' (Seligman 2002: 263). Seligman's description identifies two necessary components of personal development; a heightened self-awareness and an awareness of an ultimate goal or 'calling'. This is particularly relevant to the realm of healthcare, where collectively, even if not individually, healthcare managers have the potential to exercise considerable influence, with the power to impact upon the lives and livelihoods of both health service employees and the patients and carers whom they serve.

There is no formal dictionary definition of 'personal development', although definitions are available of the separate terms. *Webster's New Illustrated Dictionary* defines 'develop', 'development' and 'personal' as follows (emphasis author's own):

> **Develop:** to expand or *bring out the potentialities or capabilities*; to cause to come to completeness or perfection.
>
> **Development:** *gradual evolution* or completion; the result of gradual evolution or completion.
>
> **Personal:** pertaining to, or *characteristic of, a particular person*.
>
> **Person:** a human being including *body and mind*.

Combining aspects of these definitions with Aristotle's teleological, or purposeful, view of human nature, I would offer the following definition of personal development:

> Personal development in healthcare is the development of sensitivity, the development of an enhanced awareness of one's own feelings, attitudes, behaviours and cognition and the utilization of this awareness to enhance the realization of practical goals in order to support the development of interpersonal relationships and to enable the fulfilment of one's potential in service, becoming a more conscious, whole and healthy human being, who is able to live in accordance with personal values and virtues.

If personal development is defined in this way, the role of personal development within healthcare, becomes one of

> enabling health service professionals to develop and become aware of, both their personal strengths and areas for development, in order to support the identification of means of improving personal capability and capacity, of managing change (to include the building and maintaining of new relationships) and of enhancing sustainability.

Personal development in healthcare is therefore a process of learning about oneself, learning about the context and about others and using that learning to achieve personal excellence as a healthcare professional. It is also therefore a process of *learning to listen*; to oneself, to others and to the emergent learning.

Processes in personal development

Proceeding from the definition above, the key processes within personal development in healthcare, can be identified as follows:

- recognition of strengths and weaknesses;
- identification of requisite means of increasing capability and capacity;
- building new relationships, both internal and external;
- management of, and amidst, change;
- sustainability – of self and of learning.

Central to all of the processes of personal development described above is a process of reflective analysis, linked to practice in the field.

Reflective practice

Healthcare professionals today are increasingly required to demonstrate reflective practice, both in their initial training and in their ongoing professional development. This chapter will describe some of the more popular models and theories of reflection, including Kolb's learning cycle (1984) and Argyris and Schön's 'double-loop learning' (1984) and will make a link with Honey and Mumford's (1986) work on learning styles.

Kolb's learning cycle

The seeds of reflective practice can be traced back to the educational philosopher John Dewey (1933, 1938) who argued that the ability of an individual to reflect is initiated when they are not only able to identify a problem, but also to recognize the uncertainty that this recognition generates. Dewey claimed that reflection requires a continual evaluation of beliefs, assumptions and hypotheses, requiring not only reflection on the problem of practice, but also on the inner world of the individual practitioner.

Perhaps one of the most popular models for reflection is that provided by Kolb (1984). Kolb described learning as 'the process whereby knowledge is created through the transformation of experience' (1984: 38) and for Kolb, as for other authors such as

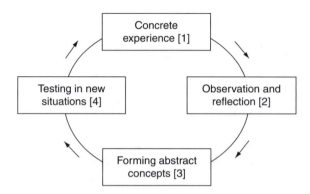

FIGURE 20.1 Kolb's learning cycle

Schön (1983) and Schein (2001), reflection and reflective analysis linked to practice, are pivotal to this process.

Kolb's theory of experiential learning (Kolb 1984) can provide a useful model with which to consider reflection and its link to practice, in a healthcare setting. Core to Kolb's theory is Kolb's learning cycle, a cycle comprising four stages of learning from experience. While these stages can be entered at any point, Kolb (1984) suggests that the stages should be followed in sequence for successful learning to take place.

Kolb's learning cycle suggests that for practice-based learning, or development, to occur, it is necessary to reflect on the experience of practice, then to use that reflection to form abstractions and generalizations and, in turn, to use these to formulate concepts which can be applied to new situations. This learning must then be tested out in new situations. The learner must make the link between the theory and action by planning, acting out, reflecting and relating it back to the theory.

Learning styles

At the beginning of this chapter, the need for healthcare managers to develop holistically, both in terms of their cognition and their emotions, was mentioned as part of the definition of personal development. This developmental need has been supported by Honey and Mumford's (1986) work into learning styles. They described four learning styles, corresponding to the various stages of Kolb's learning cycle:

- **Activists:** gregarious, live in the 'here and now', bored with implementation. Corresponds to concrete experience stage.
- **Reflectors:** thoughtful, gather data, analytical. Corresponds to reflective observation.
- **Theorists:** rationally objective, assimilate facts into theories. Corresponds to abstract conceptualization.
- **Pragmatists:** practical, down-to-earth, enjoy problem solving. Corresponds to active experimentation stage.

For optimal personal development and in order to maximize our potential learning, it is suggested that we need to develop our potential to engage with all four learning styles, (Reynolds 1999) and to engage with all stages of the learning cycle.

Schön: reflection in, and on, action

While Kolb's learnings cycle suggests that experience must take place prior to reflection, Donald Schön made explicit reference to the link between reflection and practice with his term the 'reflective practitioner' (Schön 1983) and in his distinction between 'reflection *in* action' and 'reflection *on* action'. While Kolb's learning cycle separates the processes of action and reflection, Schön defined 'reflection in action' as the ability of professionals to 'think about doing something while doing it' (Schön 1983: 54). This process of 'reflection in action' is a process which Schön described as instigated by an unexpected experience, by a discrepancy between expectation and reality (Schön 1983). Schön's concept of 'reflection on action' refers to conscious reflection *after* the event. Hence in Box 20.1 we see an example of both types of reflection taking place.

Box 20.1: *Example of reflection in, and on, action*

Dr A is a GP registrar who is training to become a GP. During one of her morning surgeries, she encounters a patient with a new presentation of hypothyroidism. The patient complains of weight gain and tiredness. Dr A has not encountered this before and wonders if the patient may be suffering from depression. Dr A questions the patient further to explore this initial diagnosis and discovers that the patient has recently suffered a bereavement. Dr A arranges for some further tests to collect additional evidence and makes an appointment to review the patient in a week's time.

Following the consultation, Dr A meets with her supervisor and discusses the case. Her supervisor raises some questions to make Dr A reflect on how the consultation progressed, the supervisor asks what feelings led Dr A to question her initial diagnosis of depression and asks if there is anything which, in hindsight, Dr A would have done differently.

During the consultation, Dr A was forced, by the new experience, to '*reflect in action*' drawing on her existing and tacit knowledge. In discussion with her supervisor, Dr A *reflects on action*, drawing out more of the learning from the experience, identifying knowledge gaps which could then be addressed and identifying learning which will be applicable to situations wider than treatment of patients with hypothyroidism. In the reflection on action, Dr A is hence able to begin a process of abstract conceptualization (cf. Kolb's learning cycle above), concepts which will be tested out in practice in future consultations. The questioning by Dr A's supervisor supported Dr A in linking her reflection in action to her existing frames of reference at the time of her action and in identifying gaps in knowledge.

Argyris and Schön: theories of action and double-loop learning

With his colleague, Chris Argyris, Donald Schön extended his consideration of reflection as a mechanism for development and change, through the introduction of the concepts of theories of action (1974) and double-loop learning (1978). Argyris and Schön (1974) claim that individuals have mental maps, guiding how to act in any situation. From this, Argyris and Schön make a distinction between what they claim are two contrasting theories of action. The distinction is between those theories that are implicit in what we do as practitioners and managers, and those which we use to speak about our actions to others. The former are described by Argyris and Schön (1974) as *theories-in-use*. They govern actual behaviour and tend to be tacit structures, which contain assumptions about self, others and environment – these assumptions constitute 'a microcosm of science in everyday life' (Argyris and Schön 1974: 30). Somewhat in contrast to these theories in use, Argyris and Schön offer the term *espoused theory* to describe the theory we espouse, a theory which conveys what we do, what we think we should do, or what we would like others to think we do. As an example of these theories of action, if someone is asked how he would behave in a certain situation, the answer he would usually give is his espoused theory of action. This is the theory of action to which he gives allegiance, and which, upon request, he communicates to others. However, according to Argyris and Schön, the theory that actually governs his actions is his theory-in-use (Argyris and Schön 1974: 6–7), and this provides his existing framework for action.

Making this distinction between the two theories of action, provides opportunities for asking questions about the congruence, or otherwise, between behaviour claimed, and behavior exhibited in practice. In other words, is there congruence between the two theories of action?

Argyris (Argyris and Schön 1978) claims that effectiveness, both in terms of the individual and the organization, results from developing congruence between theory-in-use and espoused theory. Reflection and constructive discussion, therefore have the potential to serve a useful purpose in exposing incongruence between the two theories of action and taking action to produce congruence between these two theories.

Argyris and Schön (1978) introduced a two-level model of learning to accommodate learning about, and taking action to change, the theory in use. This theory is termed double-loop learning.

In what Argyris and Schön term single-loop learning, individuals, groups, or organizations modify their actions according to the difference between expected and obtained outcomes. In double-loop learning, the learner, be it the individual, group or organization, questions the values, assumptions and frameworks that led to the actions in the first place: the theories in action. When the learner is able to view and modify these assumptions and frameworks, double-loop learning occurs.

Critical reflection

The emphasis on changing assumptions and behaviours, which is inherent in double-loop learning, goes some way towards countering the criticisms sometimes levelled at Kolb's learning cycle, of neglecting the social, institutional and/or cultural aspects of which experience is comprised (Reynolds 1999). Healthcare management, perhaps more than any other area, has the potential to impact deeply on the lives of individuals and society, not only because of the influence of managers on healthcare for patients and the potential impact which this has on informal carers, but also because of the vast size of the healthcare workforce and its continued absorption of more than 10 percent of the gross domestic product of most developed nations. For this reason reflection which ignores the social and political context within which it is taking place, is reflection which could be accused of omitting important and influential dynamics. Critical reflection aims to redress this imbalance by deliberately extending reflection to include the social and political forces at play and possibly impacting on reflection.

Critical reflection (Alvesson and Wilmott 1992; French and Grey 1996; Burgoyne and Reynolds 1997, Prasad and Caproni 1997; among others) operates through:

- a commitment to questioning assumptions and taken-for-granteds, embodied in both theory and professional practice, and to raising questions that are moral as well as technical in nature and concerned with ends at least as much as means; (Reynolds 1999);
- a committed focus on the processes of power and ideology subsumed within the existent culture of the organization;
- a perspective which encompasses the social and sees the experience of the individual as socially constructed;
- the underlying aim of a society based on fairness and democracy (Freire 1972; Reynolds 1999).

Critical reflection owes much of its origins to the work of Jürgen Habermas (1972) and differs both from the traditional concept of reflection, as outlined above and also from critical thinking, in the sense of adopting a critique of literature and/or ideas. A consideration of critical reflection can be useful to the healthcare manager or student of healthcare management, in promoting an awareness of the power dynamics and social forces acting within the context of healthcare, forces which can have an impact on the reflective capacity of both individuals and organizations. Chapter 6 in this volume is a useful reference for more on the social context of healthcare.

Supporting reflection in practice

The following section describes some tools and processes used to support reflection in practice.

Action learning

Action learning is an approach to problem solving and learning, designed to assist with the development of learning in, and for practice, for individuals, teams, organizations and systems. Central to this learning, or development, is action or experience, since action learning holds that there can be no learning without action and no knowing without the effort to practise and implement what is claimed as knowledge (Revans 1982).

The process of action learning involves the identification and utilization of programmed knowledge, p (learning from books, 'experts', external sources) and q, questioning insight (questioning oneself and others). Hence learning (L) can be represented by the equation below:

$$L = p + q$$

With its emphasis on questioning of assumptions, q, action learning can be seen to link to double-loop learning and critical reflection.

Action learning as a framework was pioneered by Reg Revans, who developed the approach as a means of developing managers during the 1940s and who utilized its value in the Coal Board, Health Service and Education. Revans claimed that organizations and the individuals working in them, cannot flourish unless the rate of learning (L) is equal to, or greater than, the rate of change being experienced (C):

$$L > C$$

Revans distinguished between puzzles (challenges which have one answer) and problems (challenges which have many different possible solutions). Action learning is for solving problems; ones which are of importance to the person involved and for which the presenting individual has a degree of management responsibility.

Action learning is a dynamic process that involves a small group of people solving real problems, while at the same time reflecting upon what they are learning and how their learning can benefit not only themselves as individual managers, but also their team and the organization as a whole. This multi-dimensional impact enables action learning to be a vehicle ideally suited to the demands of both personal and organizational development within today's health services. Action learning is a process which can therefore have impact on the personal, team and organizational/wider systems level ('I, We and They'; Pedler 2004; Clark 2007).

As a process for personal development, action learning assists in facilitating reflection on action, facilitates reflection on the learning process itself; assists in enabling an awareness of assumptions, resources and challenges and enables knowledge sharing among peers. As a means of team development, action learning, through the auspices of the action learning set, a group of six to eight individuals, who come together at regular interviews to discuss their problems in practice, can assist in the development of skills of conflict management and collaborative working. As a means of organizational development, action learning provides a process for linking theory and evidence with practice and as a means of facilitating 'new solutions to tough and complex organizational problems' (Burke and Noumair, cited in Boshyk and Dilworth 2010).

TABLE 20.1 The three systems of action learning

System alpha	System of diagnosis of the problem facing the manager in the workplace. System alpha consists of three questions ● What needs to be done? ● What stands in the way? ● What resources, inner (personal) and outer, exist to meet this challenge?
System beta	System beta: described by Revans as a 'cycle of negotiation' (Revans 1982: 334), system beta also has resonance with the Kolb's learning cycle and comprises: ● Survey stage: in which data for system alpha is identified ● Trial decision stage in which a first design for action is selected ● Action stage in which the trial decision is implemented ● Audit stage, during which the observed outcome of the action is compared with the expected outcome when the design was selected ● Control stage, during which action is taken on the conclusions drawn from the audit. This action might include to confirm, modify or reject the first design or to repeat the cycle of negotiation in the light of experience
System gamma	This system comprises the interaction between the problem system and the manager himself. This system is comprised of the manager's value system, frame of reference and assumptions. It is a system which may be the cause of a gap between a manager's 'theory in use' and 'espoused theory' (Argyris and Schön double-loop learing).

In working to assist practitioners to take action on these problems, Action learning draws on three systems: alpha, beta and gamma (Table 20.1). Through these systems, action learning aims to facilitate learning on three levels:

● learning about the problem which is presenting;
● learning about oneself;
● learning about the process of learning, i.e. 'learning to learn'.

Key to the learning for, and from, action, is the development of questioning insight within the environment of the action learning set. The role of the set members is not to provide advice, but to raise questions which will encourage the individual to reflect on the problem facing them and their own role within that problem. Sets are often facilitated by a *learning advisor*, whose role is to help set members identify and acquire the skills of action and learning. However, Revans himself advocated self facilitation of the set by its members, keen to locate power within the set and the members themselves.

Personal development planning

Reflection plays a key role in personal development planning, providing a structured reflective process which requires the individual to identify their personal developmental needs and to take action to meet those needs. The Quality Assurance Agency for Higher Education describes personal development planning as: 'Structured and supported processes to develop the capacity of individuals to reflect upon their learning and achievement and to plan for their own personal education and career development' (Quality Assurance Agency for Higher Education 2000).

Personal development planning is a cyclical process which requires the identification of personal development needs, the sourcing of resources to meet those needs, taking action to utilize those resources, reflection on and evaluation of impact of both action and resources, and the identification of continuing developmental needs.

The keeping of a reflective journal is often a core component of personal development planning, designed to facilitate the process of reflection on action and theory, and to support a process of sense-making through reflection on experience.

Time management

> Things which matter most, must never be at the mercy of things which matter least.
>
> (Goethe, quoted in Koch 1998: 164)

In times of increasing expectations, risk, confusion and uncertainty, today's healthcare managers and students of healthcare management, can frequently find themselves juggling competing demands and expectations, amidst an ever decreasing time for reflection. In this context an effective mode for identifying priorities and managing time in order to ensure that priorities can be met, becomes an operational imperative. Indeed many systems and techniques for time management centre upon the identification of priorities.

One such system of time management is that provided by Stephen R. Covey (Covey 1989). Covey's system of time management stems from his description of what he claims to be the seven habits of highly effective people. Effective people, claims Covey (1989, 2005: 13–14) do the following:

1 Are proactive – acting as agents of change and taking responsibility for their own choices.

2 Begin with the end in mind – creating their own future by identifying and committing to the principles and purposes which are important to them.

3 Put first things first – organizing their time and activities around their most important priorities.

4 Think win-win – maintaining a positive outlook.

5 Seek first to understand, then to be understood.

6 Synergize – working with others to solve problems, seize opportunities and resolve differences.

7 Sharpen the saw – care for themselves physically, socially, mentally and spiritually.

From these principles, or habits, Covey (1989) introduced four quadrants of activities/demands, categorized on the basis of urgency and importance. Urgent activities require immediate attention, while important activities relate to values, mission, the desired end result. By identifying the importance and urgency of tasks, it becomes possible to identify priorities and thereby to reduce the number of competing demands at

	Urgent	Not urgent
Important	**Quadrant I** Crises Pressing problems	**Quadrant II** Preventative measures Relationship building Planning
Not important	**Quadrant III** Interruptions Some mail Some meetings	**Quadrant IV** Trivia Time wasters Gossip Some email

FIGURE 20.2 Time management matrix
Source: Covey (1989).

any one time. These can be represented within a time management matrix, as shown in Figure 20.2.

Covey claims that effective time management will result in being proactive, freeing time by pre-empting crises and utilizing time to ensure that more time is spent on important activities at a non-urgent stage, quadrant II in the matrix. Through effective planning and time management, quadrant I, the urgent and important, is shrunk in size, to allow more time to be spent in quadrant II, an area which will be productive in terms of facilitating the fulfilment of ultimate goals.

Relating time management to our initial definition of personal development, any system of effective time management will also entail a reflective awareness of how time is currently utilized and its relationship to ultimate goals of development and practice. It is often said that 'time flies' and it is easy for time to pass without an awareness of where our energy is placed in terms of using this time. One way of countering this, and of achieving reflective awareness, is to make a note of how time is spent, how the activities engaged with relate to ultimate goals and how future activities may be prioritized in order to enable more time to be spent on the important activities/tasks.

Another way of identifying priorities may be through a consideration of Maslow's hierarchy of needs. Maslow (1943) claimed that an individual, or society, has a hierarchy of needs, all of which need to be addressed. First proposed in 1943, the hierarchy represents various needs that motivate human behaviour. Maslow's hierarchy of needs is most often displayed as a pyramid, with the lowest levels of the pyramid made up of the most basic needs while the more complex needs can be found at the top of the pyramid. Maslow claims that only when the basic needs such as the physiological needs of hunger, thirst, etc., the need for safety, the need to belong and be accepted, and the need for recognition are met, can the higher needs of needing to know and understand, the aesthetic needs for beauty and symmetry and the need for self-actualization and to serve a higher cause be addressed. While this provides a perspective to identify where an individual may be in terms of having the full gamit of their needs actualized, it is interesting to view this in terms of our initial definition of personal development, in which self-actualization and fulfilment of a higher calling are placed as priorities, suggesting that needs are less hierarchical than suggested by Maslow.

The Myers-Briggs Inventory (MBTI)

Central to all of the approaches to time management is the recognition of the need to know oneself and to utilize this knowledge to communicate with others and to fulfil demands. Healthcare management today demands that its managers have the capacity and capability to motivate, to communicate and to build relationships across, both internal and external, boundaries. This demand can become easier to meet with the help of a process for understanding self and others. One such process which claims to help in this way, is the Myers-Briggs Inventory, one of a number of psychometric personality tests, tests which measure mental traits, capacities and processes.

The Myers-Briggs Inventory is a questionnaire, designed to measure psychological preferences for how people view the world and make decisions. It is based on the work of Carl Jung and his theory of psychological types. Jung proposed that 'It is one's psychological type which from the outset determines and limits a person's judgment' (Jung, 1961, 207) and Myers-Briggs was developed by a mother and daughter, Katherine Cook Briggs (1875–1968) and Isabel Briggs-Myers (1897–1980), as a means of developing aspects of Jung's ideas, sorting personality preferences into a structure of four dichotomies, based on ways of perceiving the world. According to CPP, the main licensor of MBTI, these four dichotomies are:

- **Where the individual gets their energy from.** Extraversion (E) and Introversion (I): This differentiates people who have a preference for drawing energy from the world around them through people and doing (extraverts) from those who are energized primarily from their internal world through reflection, time alone and thinking (introverts).

- **What type of information the individual pays attention to.** Sensing (S) and Intuition (N): differentiating people who have a preference for specific facts and who like to focus on what is happening (sensing) from those who have a preference for connections, the big picture and the art of the possible (intuition).

- **How the individual makes decisions.** Thinking (T) and Feeling (F): differentiating people who make decisions primarily based on logic and objectivity from people who make decisions primarily based on personal values and the effects their decisions will have on others

- **How the individual prefers to live their life.** Judging (J) and Perceiving (P): differentiating people who prefer structure, plans, and achieving closure quickly from those who prefer flexibility, spontaneity, and keeping their options open

(adapted from Cameron and Green 2004: 44)

These dichotomies give rise to 16 personality types, described as 'dynamic energy systems with interacting processes'.

The Myers-Briggs Inventory can offer ways of appreciating difference and diversity. However, there are a number of possible criticisms. For example, the inventory does not appear to make allowance for a bias in people's responses in relation to how individuals may think they 'should' respond. This can be a response to an individual's conditioning either from childhood, from peer pressure or from the organization.

In addition the impact of the context in which the questionnaire is completed may perhaps have an impact, which is not accounted for in the Myers-Briggs Inventory and while Myers-Briggs claims that all preferences are equal, within a caring setting, is it possible that some would be considered 'more equal than others' (Orwell 1945) and therefore more desirable, again placing pressure on the individual respondent to respond in a particular way. Furthermore, does the Myers-Briggs Inventory perhaps represent an over-simplification, can it really be valid to claim that there are only 16 types of person?

Despite possible critiques, the licensee of the questionnaire, CPP, reports that this system for identifying preferences has now been used by millions of people in more than 25 different countries and it remains a popular tool for appreciating and reflecting on, difference.

The Johari Window

While tools such as Myers-Briggs can assist in enabling us to recognize traits in ourselves and others, having a perception of how we appear to others can be elusive. The Johari Window is a tool aimed at providing insights into how we are perceived by self and others and was devised by American psychologists Joseph Luft and Harry Ingham in 1955, while researching group dynamics within a university setting. The model provides a framework for identifying self-perception and perception of self by others. In order to do this, the model requests that an individual, or group, identify what they view as their key traits; the model then goes on to require that others give their perceptions of the individual's/group's key traits. The model uses this information to identify four main areas of information or 'regions'. These regions are as follows:

1 **Open area** (open self, free area, free self): what is known by the person about him/herself and also known by others.
2 **Blind area** (blindspot, blind self): what is unknown by the individual but known by others.
3 **Hidden area** (avoided area, hidden self): what is known by the individual about himself but not known by others.
4 **Unknown area:** unknown by both the individual and others.

The Johari Window model views it as desirable to have a large 'open area' and a small 'blind area' and the model is a means of facilitating feedback from others about oneself, information which can then be utilized to improve self-awareness and awareness of how one is perceived by others. Relating back to the earlier models of reflection, the Johari Window can be viewed as a potential means of exposing unconscious theories in use, through sharing knowledge of self as perceived by others and exposing blind spots. Viewed in this way, the Johari Window model can be a useful aid to personal development through providing additional sources of evidence, evidence which can be used to stimulate reflection on, and awareness of, an individual's self-assumptions and beliefs.

Organizational development

In this section we will widen our gaze to consider the development of the organization. Beginning with a description of the origins and definition of organizational development, the chapter will then progress to consider a number of processes which are used for organizational development (OD).

When it comes to defining organizational development, a plethora of descriptors can be found, reflecting both the historical origins of the term and changing definitions of the organization. Organizational development, as a field, is one which is constantly evolving and one which can be elusive when seeking to identify a definitive essence.

Although OD practitioners have been thinking, writing and debating about the underlying nature of the field for decades (Friedlander 1976; Greiner 1980; Weisbord 1982; Goodstein 1984; Church et al. 1992; Sanzgiri and Gottlieb 1992; Cummings and Worley 2005), the field itself has yet to reach agreement.

The field has a number of different origins, which may to some extent explain the divergence of opinion on what defines organizational development. The most frequently quoted origins are listed in the Table 20.2.

TABLE 20.2 Origins of organizational development

Origin	Key figures	Focus
T-group (laboratory training)	Lewin et al. 1940s	Focus on the processes within groups. Looks at impact of individual behaviours on the group and of group processes and their impact on the organization. Feeds back observations to group members.
Action Research	Lewin et al. 1940s Likert	Focus on linking research to action. Systematic collection of survey data and feedback to participants as evidence for action. Three processes to change: unfreezing (creating motivation for change), movement (making change, engaging new behaviours), refreezing (establishing means of embedding new behaviours).
Socio-technical	Trist 1950s	Interdependency of social and structural/technical elements of organizations. Examples include structural reconfigurations, total quality management initiatives.
Strategic change	Beckhard et al. 1960s	Improving alignment between organization's environment, strategy and organizational design. Description and analysis of organizations environment and strategy. Introduced formula for change D = Dissatisfaction with how things are now S = Vision of what is possible; F = First, concrete steps that can be taken towards the vision. Claimed that change is possible where the product of these three factors is greater than R = resistance.
Normative	Friedlander 1976; Burke 1982; Margulies and Raia, 1990	Human relations approach with focus on improving planning and communication to facilitate better work life. Also aimed at improving human dignity, democracy, empowerment in organizations.

TABLE 20.3 Definitions of organizational development

Beckhard (1969)	Organization development is an effort (1) planned, (2) organization wide and (3) managed from the top, to (4) increase organization effectiveness and health through (5) planned interventions in the organization's 'processes', using behavioural science knowledge.
French (1969)	Refers to a long-range effort to improve an organization's problem-solving capabilities and it's ability to cope with changes in its external environment with the help of external or internal behavioural-scientist consultants, or change agents, as they are sometimes called.
Beer (1980)	A systemwide process of data collection, diagnosis, action planning, intervention and evaluation aimed at (1) enhancing congruence among organizational structure, process, strategy, people and culture: (2) developing new and creative organizational solutions; and (3) developing the organization's self-renewing capacity. It occurs through the collaboration of organizational members working with a change agent using behavioural science theory, research and technology.
Warner Burke (1982)	A planned process of change in an organization's culture through the utilization of behavioural science technology, research and theory.
Neilsen (1984)	Organization Development is the attempt to influence the members of an organization to expand their candidness with each other about their views of the organization and their experience in it, and to take greater responsibility for their own actions as organization members. The assumption behind OD is that when people pursue both of these objectives simultaneously, they are likely to discover new ways of working together that they experience as more effective for achieving their own and their shared (organizational) goals. And that when this does not happen, such activity helps them to understand why and to make meaningful choices about what to do in light of this understanding.
Worley and Feyerherm (2003)	Organizational development (1) focuses on, or results in, the change of some aspect of the organizational system; (2) involves learning, or the transfer of knowledge or skill to the client system; and (3) has evidence or intention to improve the effectiveness of the client system.
McLean (2006)	A process based on behavioural sciences that has the potential to develop desired outcomes in an organizational setting

Definitions of organizational development reflect changing views of the organization. Some definitions, reflecting contemporaneous understandings of the nature of the organization are listed in Table 20.3.

Each of the definitions in Table 20.3 has a slightly different emphasis: while Beckhard (1969) places the responsibility for change in hierarchical structures of authority, Beer (1980) and Burke (1982) focus attention on the culture of the organization as a goal of change, and on the *process* of change. Neilsen (1984) emphasizes team working and the responsibility of all members of the organization as change agents and Worley and Feyerherm (2003) focus on learning and the production of evidence of, and for, change.

Processes of organizational development

This section of the chapter will explore some of the models and processes advocated as means of facilitating organizational development. In particular, the chapter will explore Lewin's change model, the Action Research model and the Positive model.

Lewin's change model

Lewin (1951) is one of the early researchers in organizational development and is mentioned in Table 20.2. Lewin conceived of change as a manipulation of the forces keeping a system's behaviour stable and maintained that at any moment in time, an organization's behaviour is the result of two sets of forces: those striving to maintain the status quo and those seeking change.

Lewin advocated that modifying the forces maintaining the status quo would produce less resistance than increasing forces for change and that this is therefore a more effective change strategy. Lewin viewed the change process as comprising three steps:

1 **Unfreezing** – reducing the forces maintaining the organization's current behaviour. This may be achieved by introducing information which demonstrates a discrepancy between desired and actual behaviour.

2 **Moving** – This step involves intervening to change the behaviour of the organization, department or individual. The step requires the development of new behaviours, values and/or attitudes through changes in organizational structures and processes.

3 **Refreezing** – This step involves reinforcing the new organizational state and is often accomplished through the use of policies, structures or other supporting mechanisms intended to embed the new culture/system/norms.

A stakeholder analysis, listing stakeholders and whether their energy is focused on maintaining status quo or supporting change can be one way of using Lewin's ideas to support the developmental process. This analysis can then be utilized to identify areas for attention when seeking to implement change.

Action Research

Action Research is an orientation to inquiry which is described as

> a participatory, democratic process concerned with developing practical knowing in the pursuit of worthwhile human purposes, grounded in a participatory worldview ... It seeks to bring together action and reflection, theory and practice, in participation with others in the pursuit of practical solutions to issues of pressing concern to people.
>
> (Reason and Bradbury 2001: 1)

Action Research is aimed at helping organizations to implement planned change, while also developing knowledge which can be applied to other contexts.

An Action Research process, when applied to organizational development, is a cyclical process, beginning with a series of planning steps, conducted by the consultant and client working together to diagnose the nature of the problem, gather evidence of the need for, and nature of the change and commence joint action planning. During this stage, to relate back to Argyris and Schön's work on 'reflection on action' and espoused theory (Argyris and Schön 1974) the client becomes aware of problems which they may not have previously been conscious of.

During the next, action, or 'moving' stage, action, in the form of learning processes or to facilitate behavioural/attitudinal change within the organization takes place. This represents the 'moving' stage of Lewin's three-stage model. Because Action Research is a collaborative, participatory method, results of this stage will be fed back to the client, usually in a group or work-team meeting.

The third stage of the Action Research process is the results stage, corresponding to the refreezing stage of Lewin's model. In this stage, data about the change implemented is collected and measurement of change may take place. This stage continues the feedback process and may include the implementation of policies and structures designed to maintain the desired change.

The positive model

The third model of change to be considered in this chapter is the positive model, a model which significantly departs from the other two models discussed, through its focus upon areas of achievement and opportunity. While Lewin's change model and the action research model are deficit based, starting with the problems facing the organization and how these problems might be tackled to improve organizational effectiveness, the positive model begins with an appreciation of what is good about the organization and uses this appreciation to build on those capabilities and develop the organization further.

The approach to positive organizational development which is most prevalent is a process known as appreciative inquiry. This concept and approach were developed by David Cooperrider for his PhD, in collaboration with his supervisor, Suresh Srivasta and completed in 1986 as *Appreciative Inquiry: Towards a Methodology for Understanding and Enhancing Organisational Innovation*.

Srivasta and Cooperrider describe the Appreciative Inquiry cycle as one of 'discover, dream, destiny and design' (Cooperrider and Whitney 2005) and this is shown in Figure 20.3.

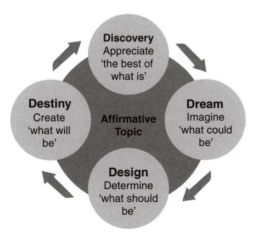

FIGURE 20.3 The Appreciative Inquiry cycle

Box 20.2: *Appreciative Inquiry process*

Select an area of your work place (past or present) that you are familiar with, e.g. a ward, department or classroom.

DISCOVER

1 Identify the stakeholders, i.e. make a list of all of the people who have an interest in this ward/department. (This should include service users as well as employees.)

2 What is really good about the ward/department/area?

3 What is good from the perspective of the employees? Give an example.

4 What is good from the perspective of the service users? Give an example.

5 What else might you want to say?

DREAM

6 What would you like more of?

7 If resources were not a consideration, what three things would really make a difference from the employee perspective?

8 What three things would really make a difference from the service user perspective?

9 Imagine your organization 10 years from now, when everything is just as you wished it to be. What is different?

10 How will you have contributed to this dream organization?

Now consider this in action by looking at Box 20.2 which sets out the appreciative inquiry process. The questions in Box 20.2 are questions typical of the discover and dream stages of the Appreciative Inquiry cycle and would be used to devise an action plan for realizing the vision described in the dream stage. A synergy can be seen between Appreciative Inquiry and our definition of personal development, through the focus on reflective questioning, identification of goals and priorities and realization of goals through action.

While Appreciative Inquiry was greeted with initial cynicism, today it is a highly sought after and regarded process for organizational development. As an example of its growing status, in 1999, David Cooperrider was requested to bring Appreciative Inquiry into a programme started by His Holiness the Dalai Lama in an effort to facilitate new levels of cooperation and peace across the world's great religions. In 2000, the journal, *Organizational Practitioner* dedicated its millennium edition to Appreciative Inquiry and the editor, Peter Sorenson, described Appreciative Inquiry as 'more than a method; it is a paradigm change uniquely created for the opportunities of the 21st Century while at the same time extending the deepest and most important early values of the field' (Sorenson et al. 2000).

Personal and organizational development: a natural progression?

In the Introduction I described the assumption that personal development would have an impact on the organization: the processes of organizational development outlined above extend this assumption and are underpinned by the belief that through a rational process of diagnosis, intervention, evaluation and review, organizational members may act as change agents. It could be claimed therefore that the 'theory in use' of organizational learning put forward within this chapter occurs as a consequence of the result of the sum of individuals learning within the organization.

However, in reality, the learning of individuals does not always facilitate a learning, or developed, organization, with evaluations of personal and organizational learning showing a balance towards individual, as opposed to organizational, outcomes (Clark et al. 2009).

One way of making sense of this inertia stems from viewing the organization as a dynamic created from the interaction of politics (power relations) and emotion. These politics and emotions, including those produced by expectations (both self-imposed and passed down through organizational structures), such as health service targets and patient demands, play a mediative role in supporting (or otherwise) learning within an organization (Coopey 1995; Vince 2001). Viewed in this way, emotions, in particular, anxiety, can provide a key to an understanding of how development both occurs and is prevented (Schein 1993; Vince 1996, 2001) and the organization may be viewed as learning when the emotions and politics at play are surfaced to conscious reflection.

Of course, health services are rife with emotion and were described by Revans, following his Hospital Internal Communication Project of the 1960s as 'institutions cradled in anxiety' (Revans 1982: 263). Healthcare professionals encounter emotions every working day; not only their own emotions at the process of change and of confrontation with death and illness, but also the powerful emotions of patients and carers, faced with change in their own life and sense of identity, as a result of illness and trauma. Healthcare professionals' roles often involve making decisions which can affect lives, and the process of change, ever accelerating in healthcare, is itself a process which elicits emotions (Kelly 2001); indeed, it can be perceived that 'Emotion is our experience of, or resistance to change' (Bannister and Fransella 1986: 21).

In the midst of this context and anxiety, personal and organizational development demands a process of reflection, yet reflection and learning are not only cognitive processes, but emotional ones too. These multitudinous emotions can be absent from consideration in traditional models of reflection, yet their impact on organizing can be significant, inhibiting processes of organizational development and contributing what Easterby-Smith (1997: 1090) considers to be the main 'problems' with organizational learning; these are the problems of extending learning from the individual to the organization, defensive reactions among individuals and groups, and under-developed processes of communication within organizations.

One approach which seeks to focus on the impact of emotions on processes of development, and in particular, the impact of emotions on the process of reflection, on both the personal and organizational level, is a psychodynamic approach to learning.

Isabel Menzies-Lyth is one of a number of key figures including W. Bion (1961); Fineman (1993) and M. Klein (1932, 1975) writing in the field of the impact of emotions within healthcare systems and interested in the relationship between the individual, the group and the wider system. In her study of the nursing service of a general hospital, Menzies-Lyth in her 1959 paper, 'The functions of social systems as a defence against anxiety,' described empirical evidence which demonstrated the impact of the stresses of nursing and the emotions produced had on organizing within healthcare, demonstrating an inhibitory effect upon positive organizational change.

A psychodynamic approach to personal and organizational development will use processes of reflection but will draw attention to the emotions and politics at play within the organization and manifesting at a group and individual level. This psychodynamic approach is becoming increasingly popular in action learning, where the set can offer a means of exposing politics and emotions at play within the organization and where it is often combined with critical reflection as a means of surfacing barriers to action and reflection.

Conclusion

The subject of personal and organizational development in healthcare is a complex one and one with a multitude of definitions and processes. The overarching aim of improving the performance of healthcare organizations and their personnel, through creating a continually reflexive and developing/learning organization; one which is able to listen to itself and to its patients, carers and staff, in order to improve patient care, emerges as the unifying and salient thread.

As we enter a new epoch of growing scarcity and diminishing resources, it is vital that the space for reflection and for development is protected, in order to enable individuals and organizations to learn and to improve patient care in response to patient needs and feedback. Through protecting this space, individual, group and organizational processes of learning to listen and to learn, in order to take action in order to improve patient care have a chance to be facilitated, enabling organizations to seize opportunities and to flourish within uncertainty.

Summary box

- Organizations can only survive when their rate of learning is at least as great as the rate of change in their environment. Personal and organizational development are essential ways to promote and support learning at both the individual and the collective level.

- Personal development involves recognizing one's own strengths and weaknesses, identifying ways to increase capacity and capability, building and maintaining relationships, managing the self amidst and through change, and creating a sustainable form of learning.

- There are a number of tools and frameworks aimed at supporting personal development, but whichever tool is used, emphasis is placed on becoming a 'reflective practitioner' with the ability to question assumptions and taken-for-granteds, to raise questions, and to be aware of the social and organizational constructions which underpin the visible manifestations and behaviours of people and organizations.

- Organizational development (OD) is a planned and organization-wide effort to increase organizational effectiveness and health through interventions in organizational processes which draw on the behavioural sciences. Different models of OD accentuate organizational authority, culture, teamworking, change processes and learning.

- Approaches to organizational development such as Lewin's change model, Revan's Action learning or Cooperrider's Appreciative Inquiry have much in common with the ideas of critical reflection at a personal level. They provide a framework for people to work collectively in identifying characteristics or features of the organization which are capable of improvement, for generating and implementing change, and for testing or evaluating the results and their impact on organizational effectiveness.

Self-test exercises

1 Thinking back to the earlier definitions of personal development, what does the term 'personal development' mean to you? What do you see as your own personal development needs? What resources do you have available to help you fulfil these needs?

2 How would you describe your own learning style? How good a match have your various learning experiences to date been with this learning style?

3 Take note of how you spend time for a whole day. Write down all activities which take your time and how long you spend on each one. How does the activity rate in terms of urgency and importance? How did you feel while engaged in the activity? What can you learn from this?

4 Recall a change programme which you have been involved with.
  - Who were the various stakeholders influencing the programme?
  - What processes/models of change did you utilize?
  - What were the most memorable moments for you and why?
  - What would you do differently, knowing what you know today, and why?
  - Moving on to consider your role as a change agent today, or in the future, what can you do to help to facilitate transformational change?

Note

1 The inspiration for this chapter came from teaching on personal and organizational development at Manchester Business School which was initiated and directed by Dr Amanda Shephard. Her work in creating an innovative, student-centred programme, with a positive impact on student's lives and futures, is appreciated and acknowledged.

References and further reading

Alvesson, M. and Wilmott, H. (1992) *Critical Management Studies*. London: Sage.

Argyris, C. and Schön, D. (1978) *Organizational Learning: A Theory of Action Perspective*. Reading, MA: Addison-Wesley.

Argryris, C. (1991) Teaching smart people how to learn. *Harvard Business Review*, May–June: 99–109.

Argyris, M. and Schön, D. (1974) *Theory in Practice. Increasing Professional Effectiveness*. San Francisco, CA: Jossey-Bass.

Aristotle (2010) *Nichomachean Ethics*, trans. W.D.Ross. In *Basic Works of Aristotle*, section 1142. Online in 'The Internet Classics Archive of MIT'. Available at: http://classics.mit.edu//Aristotle/nicomachaen.html (accessed 23 July 2010).

Armenakis, A.A. and Bedeian, A.G. (1999) Organizational change: a review of theory and research in the 1990s. *Journal of Management*, 25(3): 293–315.

Bannister, D. and Fransella, F. (1986) *Inquiring Man: The Psychology of Personal Constructs*. London: Croom Helm.

Beckhard, R. (1969) *Organization Development: Strategies and Models*. Reading, MA: Addison-Wesley.

Beckhard, R. and Harris, R.T. (1987) *Organizational Transitions: Managing Complex Change*, 2nd edn. Reading, MA: Addison-Wesley.

Beer, M. (1980) *Organization Change and Development: A Systems View*. Santa Monica, CA: Goodyear.

Bhatti, N and Viney, R. (2010) Coaching and mentoring. *BMJ* Available at: http://careers.bmj.com/careers/advice/view-article.html?id=20001206# (accessed 24 July 2010).

Bion, W. (1961) *Experiences in Groups and Other Papers*. New York: Tavistock Publications.

Brophy, S. (2006) 'Personal Excellence' as a value for health professionals: a patient's perspective. *International Journal of Health Care Quality Assurance*, 19(5): 373–83.

Buchanan, D., Abbott, S., Bentley, J. et al. (2005) Let's be PALS: user-driven organizational change in healthcare *British Journal of Management*, 16(4): 315–28.

Burgoyne, J.G. and Reynolds, M. (eds) (1997) *Management Learning: Integrating Perspectives in Theory and Practice*. London: Sage.

Boshyk, Y. Dilworth, R.L. (2010) *Action Learning History and Evolution*. Basingstoke: Palgrave Macmillan.

Burke, W. and Noumair, D.A. (2010) Action learning and organization development. In R. Dilworth and Y. Boshyk (eds) *Action Learning and its Applications*. Basingstoke: Palgrave Macmillan.

Burke, W.W. (1982) *Organization Development: Principles and Practices*. Glenview, IL: Scott, Foresman.

Burke, W.W. (1994) *Organization Development: A Process of Learning and Changing*, 2nd edn. Reading, MA: Addison-Wesley.

Burke, W.W. and Litwin, G.H. (1992) A causal model of organizational performance and change. *Journal of Management*, 18: 523–45.

Cameron, E. and Green, M. (2004) *Making Sense of Change Management: A Complete Guide to the Models, Tools and Techniques of Organizational Change*. London: Kogan Page.

Church, A.H., Hurley, R.F. and Burke, W.W. (1992) Evolution or revolution in the values of organization development? Commentary on the state of the field. *Journal of Organizational Change Management*, 5(4): 6–23.

Clark, E. (2007) Learning to act, learning to listen, listening to the learning: (using action learning to 'shift the balance of power' in an acute NHS Trust). Unpublished PhD thesis, Manchester Business School, University of Manchester.

Clark, E., Smith, L. and Harvey, G. (2009) Evaluation of Action Learning for improvement programme for senior managers within the NHS. Unpublished.

Coile, Jr, R.C. (2001) Magnet hospitals use culture, not wages, to solve nursing shortage. *Journal of Healthcare Management*, 46(4): 224–7.

Conlon, M. (2003) Appraisal: the catalyst of personal development. *British Medical Journal*, 327: 389–91.

Cooperrider, D.L. and Whitney, D.K. (2005) *Appreciative Inquiry: A Positive Revolution in Change*. San Francisco, CA: Berrett-Koehler Publishers Inc.

Coopey, J. (1995) Managerial culture and the stillbirth of organizational commitment. *Human Resource Management Journal*, 5(3): 56–9.

Cottrell, S. (2003) *Skills for Success: The Personal Development Planning Handbook*. Basingstoke: Palgrave Macmillan.

Covey, S.R. (1989) *The Seven Habits of Highly Effective People*. London: Simon and Schuster.

Covey, S.R. (2005) *The Seven Habits of Highly Effective People: Personal Workbook*. London: Simon and Schuster.

Cummings, T.G. and Worley, C.G. (2005) *Organization Development and Change*. 8th edn., Ohio: Thomson South Western.

Dewey, J. (1933) *How We Think. A Restatement of the Relation of Reflective Thinking to the Educative Process* (revised edn). Boston: D.C. Heath.

Dewey, J. (1938) *Experience and Education*. New York: Collier Books.

Easterby-Smith, M. (1997) Disciplines of organizational learning: contributions and critiques. *Human Relations*, 50(9): 1085–113.

Fineman, S. (1993) *Emotion in Organizations*. London: Sage.

Freire, P. (1972) *Pedagogy of the Oppressed*. Harmondsworth: Penguin.

French, R. and Grey, C.J. (1996) *Rethinking Management Education*. London: Sage.

French, W. (1969) Organization development: objectives, assumptions, and strategies. *California Management Review*, 12(2): 23–34.

Friedlander, F. (1976) OD reaches adolescence: an exploration of its underlying values. *Journal of Applied Behavioral Science*, 12: 7–21.

Goleman, D. (1995) *Emotional Intelligence*. London: Bloomsbury.

Goodstein, L.D. (1984) Values, truth, and organization development. In D.D. Warrick (ed.) *Contemporary Organization Development: Current Thinking and Applications*. Glenview, IL: Scott Foresman, pp. 42–7.

Greiner, L. (1980) OD values and the 'bottom line'. In W.W. Burke and L.D. Goodstein (eds) *Trends and Issues in Organization Development*. San Diego, CA: University Associates, pp. 319–32.

Habermas, J. (1972) *Knowledge and Human Interests*. Boston MA: Beacon Press.

Honey, P. and Mumford, A. (1986) *Manual of Learning Styles*. Maidenhead: Peter Honey Publications.

Jarvis, P. (1992) Reflective practice and nursing. *Nurse Education Today*, 19: 452–63.

Jung, C.G. (1961) *Memories, Dreams, Reflections*. New York: Vantage Books.

Kelly, G. (2001) *The Psychology of Personal Constructs: Theory and Personality*, Vol. 1. London: Routledge.

Klein, M. (1932) *The Psychoanalysis of Children*. London: Hogarth Press.

Klein, M. (1975) *Envy and Gratitude and Other Works 1946–1963*. Ed. M. Masud and R. Khan. *The International Psycho-Analytical Library*, 104: 1–346. London: The Hogarth Press and the Institute of Psycho-Analysis.

Koch, R. (1998) *The 80/20 Principle: The Secret to Success by Achieving More with Less*. New York: Doubleday.

Kolb, D.A. (1984) *Experiential Learning*. Englewood Cliffs, NJ: Prentice Hall.

Lewin, K. (1946) Action research and minority problems. *Journal of Social Issues*, 2: 34–46.

Lewin, K. (1951) *Field Theory in Social Science*. New York: Harper & Row.

Margulies, N. and Raia, A. (1972) *Organization Development: Values, Process, and Technology*. New York: McGraw-Hill.

Margulies, N. and Raia, A. (1990) The significance of core values on the theory and practice of organization development. In F. Massarik (ed.) *Advances in Organization Development*, vol. 1. Norwood, NJ: Ablex, pp. 27–41.

Maslow, A. (1943) A theory of human motivation. *Psychological Review*, 50: 370–96.

Maslow, A. (1971) *The Farther Reaches of Human Nature*. New York: The Viking Press.

Maslow, A., and Lowery, R. (eds) (1998) *Toward a Psychology of Being* (3rd edn). New York: Wiley & Sons.

McLean, G.N. (2006) *Organizational Development: Principles, Processes, Performance*. San Francisco, CA: Berrett-Koehler Publishers, Inc.

Menzies-Lyth, I. (1959) The functions of social systems as a defence against anxiety: a report on a study of the nursing service of a general hospital. *Human Relations*, 13: 95–121.

Morgan, G. (1986) *Images of Organization*. London: Sage.

Myers-Briggs, I. with Myers, B.P. (1980) *Gifts Differing: Understanding Personality Type*. Mountain View, CA: Davies-Black Publishing.

Neilsen, E.H. (1984) *Becoming an OD Practitioner*. Englewood Cliffs, NJ: Prentice Hall.

Orwell, G. (1945) *Animal Farm*. Harmondsworth: Penguin.

Peck, E. (ed.) (2005) *Organisational Development in Health Care: Approaches, Innovations, Achievements*. Oxford: Radcliffe.

Pedler, M. (2004) Editorial. *Journal of Action Learning: Research and Practice*, 1(1): 3–7.

Pettigrew, A.M., Woodman, R.W. and Cameron, K.S. (2001) Studying organizational change and development: challenges for future research. *Academy of Management Journal*, 44(4): 697–713.

Prasad, P. and Caproni, P.J. (1997) Critical theory in the management classroom: engaging power, ideology and praxis. *Journal of Management Education*, 21(3): 284–91.

Quality Assurance Agency for Higher Education (2000) cited in S. Cottrell (2003) *Skills for Success: The Personal Development Planning Handbook*. Basingstoke: Palgrave Macmillan.

Reason, P. and Bradbury, H. (eds.) (2001) *The SAGE Handbook of Action Research. Participative Inquiry and Practice*. London: Sage.

Revans, R.W. (1982) *Origins and Growth of Action Learning*. Bromley: Chartwell-Bratt.

Reynolds, M. (1999) Critical reflection and management education: rehabilitating less hierarchical approaches. *Journal of Management Education*, 23(5): 537–53.

Sanzgiri, J. and Gottlieb, J.Z. (1992) Philosophic and pragmatic influences on the practice of organization development, 1950–2000. *Organization Dynamics*, 21(2): 57–69.

Schein, E.H. (1993) How can organizations learn faster? The challenge of entering the green room. *Sloan Management Review*, Winter: 3–16.

Schein, E.H. (2001) Clinical inquiry/research. In P. Reason and H. Bradbury (eds) *Handbook of Action Research*. London: Sage, pp. 228–37.

Schön, D. (1983) *The Reflective Practitioner*. New York: Basic Books.

Seligman, M.E.P. (2002) *Authentic Happiness: Using the New Positive Psychology to Realise Your Potential for Lasting Fulfilment*. New York, NY: Free Press.

Senge, P. (1990) *The Fifth Discipline: The Art and Practice of the Learning Organization*. London: Century Business.

Sorenson, P.F., Yaeger, T. and Nicholl, D. (2000) Appreciative Inquiry 2000: Fad or important new focus for OD? *OD Practitioner*, 32(1): 3–5.

Taylor, R. and Humphrey, J. (2002) *Fast Track to the Top: Skills for Career Success*. London Kogan Page.

Thomson, J.A.K. (1976) *Aristotle – Ethics*. London: Penguin.

Vince, R. (1996) *Managing change: Reflections on Equality and Management Learning*. Bristol: The Policy Press.

Vince, R. (2001) Power and emotion in organizational learning. *Human Relations*, 54(10): 1325–51.

Warner Burke, W. (1982) *Organization Development: Principles and Practices*. Boston: Little Brown & Co.

Weick, K. (1995) *Sensemaking in Organisations*. London: Sage.

Weisbord, M.R. (1982) The cat in the hat breaks through: reflections on OD's past, present, and future. In D.D. Warrick (ed.) *Contemporary Organization Development: Current Thinking and Applications*. Glenview, IL: Scott Foresman, pp. 2–11.

Worley, C.G. and Feyerherm, A.E. (2003) Reflections on the future of organizational development. *Journal of Applied Behavioural Science*, 39: 97–115.

Web links and resources

Action Learning: Research and Practice Journal Website of the prime Action Learning journal. The journal is quarterly and features articles on both the theory and practice of Action Learning: www.tandf.co.uk/journals/titles/14767333.asp.

Appreciative Inquiry Commons: Provides Appreciative Inquiry timeline and brief explanation of events. Also provides bibliography, access to Appreciative Inquiry community and number of events: http://appreciativeinquiry.case.edu/intro/timeline.cfm.

Business Balls: free website with material, tools and articles relating to both personal and organizational development: www.businessballs.co.uk.

CPP – supplier of Myers-Briggs test. Information about the Myers-Briggs Inventory and its use: www.cpp.com/products/mbti/mbti_info.aspx.

NHS Institute for Innovation and Improvement Provides access to resources relating to personal and organizational development in healthcare, including a section on application of NHS tools/techniques across the globe: www.institute.nhs.uk.

Revans Academy for Action Learning and Research: webpage for the Revans academy of action learning at Manchester Business School. Provide a number of free seminars on the subject of Action Learning and has information about the subject: www.mbs.ac.uk/research/revans_academy/revans-academy.aspx.

CHAPTER 21

Managing change

Jeffrey Braithwaite and
Russell Mannion

Introduction

This chapter deals with the way change is actually managed, which we label 're-alized change management', and the way it ought to be managed, which we call 'idealized change management', in healthcare environments. Much literature on the topic is normative, and deals with the second of these. It concentrates on providing frameworks, ideas, tools, strategies and approaches for leaders who seek to manage change in accomplished and sophisticated ways. We contribute an assessment of this literature.

But it is also necessary to come to grips with, and provide an appreciation of, the messy, political, deceptive, multi-faceted and unpredictable nature of the real world of healthcare, in which change is actually managed. This is less like the static world described in a textbook, and more like the dynamic world portrayed by part political thriller, part dense sociological treatise, part anthropological review and part critical theorist's account. According to this view, change may be realized, but not always in the way hoped, or intended by, the managers seeking to lead and accomplish it. And sometimes initiatives will fail.

To achieve the goal of apprehending both realized and idealized management of change, the chapter is structured into nine parts. A brief background on *What managers do* comes after this *Introduction*, and this in turn is followed by a section on *Contextualizing change in healthcare organizations*. Then, we present *Popular tools and techniques for change management* and offer advice on *Developing and implementing project plans* using software support, after which a section on *Appreciating your own and others' perspectives on change* is provided. We then move to a key topic in the management of change: *Culture and cultural change in healthcare organizations*. Penultimately, we draw our analysis to a close by presenting two case reports on change in *Bringing it together: two case studies in healthcare change*, and offer some experts' comments in addressing the cases. Finally, we end the chapter, providing a brief discussion of the main learning points. An appendix with five different specific models and tools for culture change is also given.

What managers do

One way to appreciate the difference between idealized and realized change management is to review seminal papers dating from 60 years ago to the present which assessed what managers actually do when they manage, in contrast to what scholars have traditionally, and idealistically, said about managers and their work. Classically, managerial scholars hypothesized that managerial work could be reduced to functional components. Managers plan, lead, organize, control, motivate, delegate, staff the organization, decision-make, and the like, according to the theorists (e.g., Urwick 1938; Fayol 1949). Even today, management textbooks are often broken down into chapters with these kinds of headings. However, starting with research by Carlson (1951) and Mintzberg (1971) and via a range of observational work or case studies by researchers such as Stewart (1967), Kotter (1986) and Stewart (1998), scholars have transformed both our knowledge of management work and our perspective on managerial activities, and helped us clarify how managers process change.

Managers do not conduct their work by executing functions in orderly ways, but grapple with many issues simultaneously, facing various organizational complexities, politics, competing agendas and resource allocation decisions. Managerial work is busy, reactive, multi-faceted, fragmented, discontinuous and to a large extent unpredictable. Managers' days are subjected to demanding schedules including many meetings, unscheduled encounters, telephone and email communications, and political jostling among each other in sociologically convoluted settings. Mintzberg (1973) evocatively categorized these behaviours into ten roles in three groups: interpersonal (the manager as figurehead, leader, liaison); informational (the manager as monitor, disseminator, spokesperson); and decisional (the manager as entrepreneur, disturbance handler, resource allocator and negotiator).

Healthcare management has additional stresses, including the drama of life and death decisions, ethical dilemmas, many vocal stakeholder groups, jealously guarded professional autonomy and clinical complexities, making for a heady mix of responsibilities and accountabilities. Braithwaite led a series of studies to derive a grounded model from observational, questionnaire, focus group and interview data of healthcare managers and clinician-managers of their real-world activities, which he called their managerial behavioural routines (Figure 21.1), specifying their key modes of operating and pursuits (Braithwaite 2004).

The model shows the range of tasks of managers who are sensemaking (Weick 1995), that is, apprehending, creating meaning and working within the multiple complexities of their political milieu, striving to discharge various managerial responsibilities under challenging time pressures. Their key pursuits – the activities on which they spend most of their time – are the management of finances, staff, organizational/institutional matters and customers. They are also engaged in the management of data, quality, processes, strategy and planning, and external relations, but these are secondary to their major pursuits. The key modes of operating – the methods by which they undertake their work, and attempt to meet their objectives – are by adopting an achievement orientation, through the structure and hierarchy, and by managing change, in making decisions and

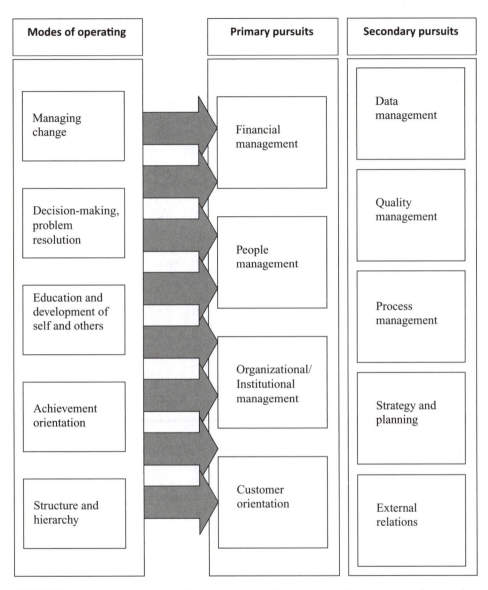

FIGURE 21.1 Managerial behavioural routines: major modes of operating and primary and secondary pursuits
Source: Braithwaite (2004) © Emerald Group Publishing Limited, all rights.

solving problems, and educating and developing self and others. Germane to all of this activity is striving for change and improvement – this is the *raison d'être* of managerial work. This might take the form of trying to deliver improved productivity, implement a new information technology (IT) system, allocate resources to a new project, manage a budget over-run or deal with a difficult staff member. Managers, despite the multi-variant nature of their endeavours, are somehow striving to make sense of, and make progress in improving, complicated socio-professional environments where many people and stakeholder groups are pulling sometimes together, sometimes apart.

Contextualizing change in healthcare organizations

The context of healthcare, in which managers are attempting to execute their responsibilities, engendering more effective relations and enhancing productivity, is complicated, multi-faceted and fast-paced. In the public sectors of healthcare, governments and bureaucrats are forever seeking to reform the sector, and introduce new policies, information systems, funding mechanisms, structures, technologies, strategies and enhancements. In private healthcare, owners and boards are keen to compete with others, widen the range of services, and win market share. This means both sectors are constantly aiming to improve things. Change therefore is ubiquitous, and the burden of coordinating and implementing change initiatives rests predominantly with management staff.

In a seminal paper, Ferlie and Shortell (2001) conceptualized four levels of change: (1) the whole health system; (2) institutional/organizational levels; (3) groups and teams; and (4) at the level of the individual. They pointed out that taking a multi-level approach was not only useful, but might enable comparisons between health systems as they make progress on improving the quality of their care. For our purposes, change management is recursively happening at all four levels.

A related aspect of the context for change management is in terms of localized health systems hierarchies (for discussions, see Braithwaite and Westbrook 2005; Braithwaite et al. 2006; Lega 2007; Walshe 2010). There are multiple hierarchical domains in healthcare settings. Formally, there are the layers depicted by the organizational chart, from the chief executive officer to the staff on-the-ground who deliver direct care to patients. Less formally, within and across the professions there are various clinical pecking orders in which clinical staff are arranged in political and professional rankings according to status, reputation, power or importance, or a combination of these. In power terms, medicine often outranks nursing which mostly outranks allied health. Within each profession there are various layerings. Medicine, for instance, has levels based on years of experience until one reaches the exalted status of specialist or consultant, but within the various 'ologists' groupings there are differentiable socio-professional structures. The relative status of surgeons, imaging specialists, anaesthetists, internal medicine specialists and general practitioners, for example, differs in complicated ways within the clinical pecking order. Against these often hard-to-read social, professional and political structures, managers must navigate and negotiate the socio-political landscape, and influence and shape behaviours and attitudes, in order to implement change, adapt and adopt new ideas, equipment, strategies and policies, and meet targets and milestones.

Another way to conceptualize the context for change is in terms of timeframes for change initiatives. Immediate or short-term endeavours are typically uni-dimensional and do-able (e.g., fix the leaking tiles on the roof; have a quick meeting to make a small but perhaps important decision, say, about someone going on extended leave; or conduct interviews for a vacant position). Medium to long-term problems require more thought and time, and usually the allocation of more resources (e.g., refurbish a series of wards; make concerted efforts to implement a new clinical information technology system; or establish and later evaluate a breakthrough collaboration to address central line infections in intensive care). Longer-term challenges can be thought of in terms of extended organizational or clinical journeys. The ideas of Van de Ven and colleagues (1989, 1999), on the stochastic complexity of innovation journeys lasting decades as organizations and ideas traverse long sweeps of time, point to the importance of persistence, willingness to navigate across extended periods and the capacity of change agents to manoeuvre across lengthy and often interrupted timescales.

Popular tools and techniques for change management

In order to realize change in such challenging environments, managers need tools and techniques. One popular framework for managing change, and one of the most widely used and cited, is Kotter's model (Figure 21.2) (Kotter 1996; Kotter and Cohen 2002). It specifies an eight-point action plan for effective leadership of change. In Figure 21.2, we provide a summary. Transformative action moves from creating the setting for change (steps 1–4), initiating and enacting the change (steps 5–7) and striving for sustainability of the initiatives (step 8).

There are many other tools for conceptualizing and managing change. A selection of some of the most useful is presented in Table 21.1. The ones we have summarized, borrowing from Kassirer (2009) and other sources, are generally personal in nature. They are centred not so much on organizational or institutional change, but what individuals can do to encourage, discourage, motivate, seek support from or involve people – colleagues, superordinates or subordinates – in change.

As Table 21.1 illustrates, the change agent – the person designated with responsibility for initiating, shaping or sponsoring the change – can, for example, build motivation, provide feedback, create financial incentives or disincentives, appeal to standards and customs, secure commitment, overcome obstacles, provide prompts, communicate with people the change proposals, establish guiding principles, engage or involve people in initiatives, pilot the change, or provide research results about the change to convince people along the way. Such strategies are designed to increase the likelihood that others will embrace the change and that it will stick.

There are various other tools and techniques available to change managers. These include brainstorming (generating multiple ideas and candidate solutions) (Osborn 1963), business process reengineering (revamping clinical and organizational processes) (Hammer and Champy 1993), soft systems methodology (embracing political, social and cultural as well as technical systems solutions) (Braithwaite et al. 2002) and project management (developing and documenting formal plans) (Nokes and Greenwood 2003). There are also specific models and tools for cultural change, which we will deal with later.

Another important technique for change agents is to consider their approach to change. What style will be adopted? Will they be demanding, even coercive, or democratic and consultative? To some extent this depends on the change manager's personality, but most experts and experienced change agents will suggest that such choices

EIGHT STEPS TO TRANSFORMING
YOUR ORGANIZATION

1 Establishing a Sense of Urgency
- Examining market and competitive realities
- Identifying and discussing crises, potential crises, or major opportunities

2 Forming a Powerful Guiding Coalition
- Assembling a group with enough power to lead the change effort
- Encouraging the group to work together as a team

3 Creating a Vision
- Creating a vision to help direct the change effort
- Developing strategies for achieving that vision

4 Communicating the Vision
- Using every vehicle possible to communicate the new vision and strategies
- Teaching new behaviors by the example of the guiding coalition

5 Empowering Others to Act on the Vision
- Getting rid of obstacles to change
- Changing systems or structures that seriously undermine the vision
- Encouraging risk taking and nontraditional ideas, activities, and actions

6 Planning for and Creating Short-Term Wins
- Planning for visible performance improvements
- Creating those improvements
- Recognizing and rewarding employees involved in the improvements

7 Consolidating Improvements and Producing Still More Change
- Using increased credibility to change systems, structures, and policies that don't fit the vision
- Hiring, promoting, and developing employees who can implement the vision
- Reinvigorating the process with new projects, themes, and change agents

8 Institutionalizing New Approaches
- Articulating the connections between the new behaviors and corporate success
- Developing the means to ensure leadership development and succession

FIGURE 21.2 Kotter's eight-step model

TABLE 21.1 A selection of tools for change, and their attributes

Tool	Attributes
Building motivation over time	To increase the likelihood people will support the ideas for change
Feedback, evaluation	Helps individuals learn from their actions to make improvements Highlights progress and the difference people are making
Financial incentives, disincentives	Powerful for encouraging or discouraging specific behaviours
Norm appeals	People are more likely to accept/replicate behaviour from observing others
Obtaining a commitment, contracting	People who commit to a task are more likely to do it
Overcoming specific barriers	Barriers that discourage people from performing a task should be removed to make it easier for the person to complete the task
Prompts	Cues that remind people to perform a task are important as many tasks are not completed for the simple reason that people forget about them
Communication	Compelling and personalized communication is more likely to be remembered and acted on
Guiding principles	Have a plan for the implementation of the project but be prepared to adapt this plan
Engaging support	Having a plan for change is important, but it is gaining the commitment and support of the people that is fundamental to the success of any change
Using a pilot	Starting with a small trial of the proposed change, using people who are supportive of the change will increase the chance of success and pave the way for broad implementation of the plan. Pilots can highlight barriers to change, so plans can be adapted as necessary and are useful in assessing the best method of implementation
Formative research	Learn about all aspects of what you want to change to help guide the design of the project

Sources: Modified from Kassirer (2009); Victorian Quality Council (2006); Salem et al. (2008).

depend on the circumstances, and the change agent's responsibilities and role in the change initiative. There are other pertinent questions. What scale of change will be embraced? Is it the whole of the organization, or does it affect a division or section of the organization, or a local service, group or individual? What pace of change will be engendered? Does the change agent want to promote a rapid accomplishment strategy, before any opposing forces can mobilize, or a slower, consensus-building approach? Will the change mostly involve individuals, or groups? Does the change manager intend to deal with or work through the formal structures or informal opinion leaders, or both? In what ways can champions, or those already supportive or predisposed toward the change, be reached and mobilized? How, and to what extent, will the change agent build in measures of sustainability to the initiatives? Each of these questions generates options for change agents on the type of approach they will take, their style and the scope of change. They will also help determine the associated tools and techniques that will be mobilized in support of the changes sought.

Developing and implementing project plans

One important strategy for change agents is to develop, design, document and then implement a formal plan. Often these are conducted via computer-supported means.

Methods and tools include the use of Gantt charts, formalized scheduling processes and critical path analysis such as those contained in Microsoft Office Project or other similar software-supported systems. Other computer-aided conceptualization and mind-mapping tools include Visual Mind, BCisive and iMindMap. These enable users to conceptualize key issues and related topics in change strategies.

Other tools enable people to work remotely, and contribute virtually to projects. These help dispersed groups to collaborate effectively at a distance. Table 21.2 provides a summary of some of those that we have found useful.

Appreciating your own and others' perspectives on change

The manager's own perspective on change is dependent on many factors including his or her training, interests, political ideology, personality, capacities, idiosyncrasies and individual variables. One way to think about change agents' contributions to change is to consider where they are coming from, what are their perspectives, what their style and approach to managing change are, and their role on an issue. Another way is to be reflexive – that is, for change agents to mull over how their own predilections, assumptions and actions affect the thing they are trying to change, and to be aware of the effects they have had or are having as the change unfolds. A third is to use a framing device through which to view the dimensions of change that are being led. A commonly used framework is that provided Bolman and Deal (2008). They suggested, in a popular text used in many MBA-type courses, that there are four dimensions to change, and that an accomplished leader will have regard to the structural, cultural, human and political aspects of any particular change initiative. Bolman and Deal made the case that it is possible to reframe the change process. If, for example, there is too much emphasis on structural change, and hence recourse to the organizational chart and hierarchy is excessive, then more attention to the other dimensions – say, the cultural aspects – might be needed.

What about others' perspective on change? These, too, vary with the individual or group experiencing the change, and shift from issue to issue, and over time. While it is virtually universal to think of those above to be sponsoring and supporting change, subordinates as resistant to change in various ways, and colleagues at the same level as having differing agendas depending on their needs and stake in the change, this is overly simplistic both in theory and practice. It is the case that some subordinates, depending on their interests, needs and views will be resistant to change, or to aspects of the proposal, plan or implementation of it. Yet other subordinates can be expected to support it, others to be passionate champions of it, and still others to be neutral or disengaged. Senior executives or others above the change initiator in the hierarchy may not uniformly support the initiatives. They may be locked in political battles among themselves, for example, and too deeply involved in boardroom conflict to notice the change agent's efforts, or be unconvinced about their plan, strategy or approach. They may or may not have resources to allocate to the change endeavours, or may be worried about the change agent's competence for the task, or simply be too busy with their own work. Fellow managers at the same level as the change agent might well process information about the change initiative, and support or resist it or aspects of

TABLE 21.2 Computer-supported methods and tools

Tool/Method	Attributes
Visual Mind	Software based on the mind mapping technique. Allows people to easily and quickly see and organize their work
Microsoft Project	Enables change agents to effectively create manage a range of projects. It allows them to easily manage deadlines, select necessary resources and communicate with internal and external stakeholders
	It helps reduce costs and drive efficiencies
	It features: demand management, portfolio selection and analytics, resource management, schedule management, financial management, time and task management, team collaboration, business intelligence and reporting, administration scalability and extensibility
BCisive	Visual thinking software for thinking, planning and presenting. It assists with decision-making and planning, team problem-solving and collaboration. It features argument maps, concept maps, decision diagrams and logic trees
iMindMap	A project management system with features including: Microsoft Office integration (including Microsoft Project), e-learning course builder, in-built presentation mode, audio notes, template system and creative resources
Innovation Portal	A collaborative platform for internal and external stakeholders' knowledge sharing
Aviz Thought Mapper, BrainMine, Cayra Maps, Concept Draw Mindmap Professional Creative Thinker, Eminec MYmap, FreeMind, HeadCase for Windows, Inspiration Software, JCVGantt, Map It! MindMap Software, Mayomi.net Online Mind Mapping, Mind Mapping, Mind Mapping Software Shop, Mind Pad, Mind2Chart, Mind42, MindCad Pyramid, MindChart, MindManager, MindManuals, mindMapp, MindMapPaper, MindMapper 2008, MindView, MindVisualizer, MyThoughts for Mac NovaMind, PersonalBrain, PiCoMap, Pocket Mindmap, Smart Ideas Concept Mapping Software, SoftNeuron, Spinscape, Spinscape.com, Strategic Transitions – Business templates for Inspiration mind-mapping software, theRealizer, ThinkGraph, TPAssist, VisiMap, Visual Concept, Visual Mind, Visual Strategist, WiseMapping, XMIND	These are various kinds of mind mapping software with various features and facilities. In general, these tools allow users to create visual diagrams to map ideas, typically centred on a core idea, topic or issue. Essentially this is a brainstorming technique. Many of these programs allow people to share their mind maps virtually so people can collaborate at a distance
Rationale: argument visualization software	Designed to help improve reasoning abilities, develop stronger arguments, communicate complex cases, produce better documents and make better decisions.
	It features grouping maps, reasoning maps and multi-premise argument maps
Gantt chart	Helps plan and schedule complex projects
Critical Path Analysis	Assists with the scheduling and management of complex projects
	It helps monitor achievements and shows actions to get back on target if needed

Sources: Mind Technologies (2010); Microsoft (2010); van Gelder (2008); Buzan et al. (2010); Cognistreamer; Frey (2010); Gantt (1974); Manktelow (2010).

it, depending on their personal and organizational goals. Not everyone at the change agent's level and above will ubiquitously want him or her to succeed, as in doing so the change agent might shine, thereby taking the gloss off others, or even reducing their career prospects. Rivals are everywhere in the management ranks, often emerging unexpectedly.

The lessons are that change agents might need to work hard not only to tackle resistance to change among subordinates, by applying tools and approaches discussed earlier (see Figure 21.2 and Table 21.1), but also consider who among the other organizational players are their supporters, who will help champion the cause and what do others perceive is in this for them, their group and their profession? How are people around the change agent processing the question: 'will this serve my interests?' The old saying you can't make an omelette without breaking eggs is perennially true in the management of change, but so is this aphorism: detractors might be everywhere, yet supporters can often come from unsuspecting quarters.

Culture and cultural change in healthcare organizations

We turn to a key matter in the management of change: organizational culture. Organizational culture and change are intimately entwined. Culture is often identified as a key influence on the relative success or failure of both planned and opportunistic programmes of organizational change (Braithwaite 1995). Indeed, the rhetoric supporting healthcare reform frequently invokes notions of 'cultural change' as a means of achieving performance improvement and good quality healthcare (Braithwaite et al. 2010; Mannion et al. 2010). Questions then arise as to what organizational culture is and whether framing of healthcare organizations in cultural terms offers a useful means of understanding and managing change, with the potential for beneficial improvements in both the processes and outcomes of care.

Academic analysts generally agree that culture signifies something which is *shared* between an organization's members, for example, the prevailing beliefs, values, assumptions and attitudes, and from these the local norms of behaviour. These shared ways of thinking and behaving help to define what is legitimate and acceptable within an organization. They are the social and normative 'glue' that bind people in collective enterprise; or 'the way things are done around here'. They guide the discretionary behaviour of professionals and underpin management strategy and practice.

A diverse range of conceptual frameworks and models for understanding organizational culture and culture change have emerged (see Appendix). This diversity reflects a lack of theoretical consensus surrounding both definitions of organizational culture and the processes of organizational change (Alvesson and Sveningsson 2008). Perhaps the most critical cleavage in contemporary definitions is that identified by Smircich (1983): in brief, culture may be treated as a property of an organization (something it 'has') or something about its fundamental nature, i.e. that the organization 'is'. The former approach defines culture as the values and beliefs in an organization that organizational members have in common. Thus, this approach treats culture as a variable or attribute, alongside organizational structure and business strategy that can be managed or manipulated to improve organizational performance. In contrast, the latter approach implies the existence of fewer levers by which management might secure change, since the entire organization is seen as a cultural system in itself with analytic interest focused primarily on how it is accomplished and reproduced.

A wide range of models of culture change are available in the literature (Brown 1995; Mannion et al. 2005; Callen et al. 2007). Despite some manifest differences in the models, they almost all share some common foci:

- **Crisis:** as a trigger for significant organizational change.
- **Leadership:** in detecting the need for change and in shaping that change.
- **Success:** to consolidate the new order and to counter natural resistance to change (as one of the features of culture is to establish and stabilize a way of living, resistance is inherent to any culture change effort).
- **Re-learning and re-education:** as a means of embedding and helping explain the assimilation of new cultures.

Instruments and tools for assessing and managing organizational culture in healthcare organizations

The language of culture change that is central to discussions of healthcare improvement has prompted a practical need to assess and measure culture and culture change in healthcare contexts (Braithwaite 2006a, b). A recent review of culture assessment instruments in the English NHS found that around a third of healthcare organizations were using a culture assessment instrument or tool to guide organizational change and almost all the instruments utilized focused on the assessment of safety cultures rather than broader aspects of quality and organizational performance (Mannion et al. 2009). The three most commonly used tools in this domain are summarized in Box 21.1 (Mannion et al. 2009). We might consider the practical application of cultural assessment methods. These may be classified broadly as serving formative, summative or diagnostic purposes.

Formative assessment provides organizations with feedback on the cultural elements of performance and change, and can be used to inform organizational development and learning. Formative cultural assessments might be used, for example, to do the following:

- help staff (and other stakeholders) to understand and engage with the concept of organizational culture as one aspect of organizational performance and change;
- highlight the multidimensionality of organizational culture, and the complex and contingent relationships between different types of culture and performance;
- bring to the fore the cultural characteristics of an organization and the potential strengths and weaknesses of these characteristics (for example, with respect to key organizational objectives), and help staff to explore the dynamics of culture change.

Box 21.1: *Three major culture assessment instruments used in the NHS*

- The **Manchester Patient Safety Framework** (MaPSaF), developed at the University of Manchester, is a facilitative educational tool. It aims at providing insight into an organization's safety culture and how it can be improved among teams. It uses nine dimensions of patient safety and describes what an organization would look like at different levels of patient safety.

- The **Safety Attitude Questionnaire** (SAQ) is the main safety climate questionnaire package developed in the USA by Bryan Sexton and colleagues at the Center of Excellence for Patient Safety Research and Practice, University of Texas. The instrument is available at the University of Texas Centre of Excellence for Patient Safety Research and Practice site. The SAQ is a refinement of the Intensive Care Unit Management Attitudes Questionnaire which was derived from the Flight Management Attitudes Questionnaire, widely used in the aviation industry. The various versions of the SAQ, together, comprise 60 survey items, designed in the form of five-point Likert scales to help organizations assess their safety culture and track changes over time. The instrument is used to measure provider attitude about six patient safety-related domains: safety climate, team work climate, stress recognition, perceptions of management, working conditions and job satisfaction. Individual scores are aggregated to give an indication of the strength of the organization's extant safety culture.

- The **Safety Climate Survey** (SCS) is a version of the SAQ. The application of the SCS, in particular, has been promoted by the Institute for Healthcare Improvement (IHI) and is being piloted among a small number of hospitals in the UK National Health Service as part of the Health Foundation's Safer Patients Initiative.

Source: Mannion et al. (2009).

Summative assessment can provide a cross-sectional or longitudinal measure of culture and its relationship to other organizational variables. This approach can be used to make a judgement about the 'type' of culture, or the nature of several different dimensions of culture within an organization; the strength of that culture or those cultural dimensions; the congruence of cultural perceptions between individuals, across staff groups or management hierarchies, or between organizations; and the relationship(s) between culture and other organizational variables, including organizational performance.

Practical applications of summative and formative assessments also involve a substantive *diagnostic* element. *Diagnostic assessment* can provide an appreciation of the existing cultural traits within an organization and their functionality *vis-à-vis* promoting desirable organizational processes and outcomes. Diagnostic cultural assessments might be used to: identify areas of strengths and weakness in an organization; assess capacity, receptiveness and readiness for (culture) change at an organization, division or team level; target and prioritize external interventions; or serve as a benchmark or baseline to gauge the impact of culture change policies over time.

Some options for managing organizational culture

What does this mean for managing organizational culture? We argue, and much experience and evidence support our claim, that it requires time, concerted effort and a multi-pronged approach to change culture. In many respects an organization's culture is not amenable to simplistic change strategies. Yet it clearly can be subject to, and it can respond to, attempts to influence, shape, or affect it over time. This can happen quickly in response to a crisis, but these do not come along every day. The essential task is to shift the shared attitudes and values, that is, the collective cognition of organizational groups, and their behaviours and practices, that is, the way people work, relate and interact, longitudinally. We can think of culture as an iceberg (Braithwaite 2011), with the observable aspects, i.e. the organization's collective behaviours and practices, above the waterline, and the unobservable, but no less important, collective attitudes and values below the waterline (Figure 21.3).

Collective behaviours and practices: 'the way we do things'

Collective attitudes and values: 'the way we think about things around here'

FIGURE 21.3 The iceberg model of culture

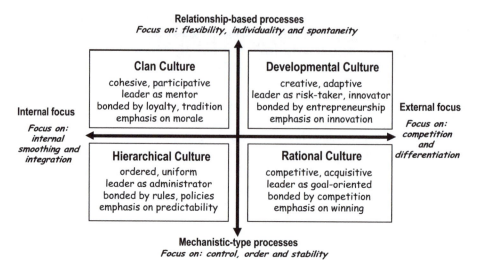

FIGURE 21.4 The competing values framework
Source: Quinn and Rohrbaugh (1983) and Cameron and Quinn (2005).

The model suggests that successfully changing culture requires a shift both above and below the waterline – in terms both of the collective attitudes and values, and behaviours and practices. Common ways of effecting culture change include measuring the extant culture; deciding the cultural features to be adopted; modelling the attitudes and behaviours expected of others; narrating organizational stories that explain and account for the preferred culture; understanding the current unwritten rules that reflect attitudes and drive behaviour, and trying to change them; applying some of the better practices in more productive, effective or inclusive sub-cultures to other poorer-performing sub-cultures in the organization; and allocating resources to, and encouraging, team-building and inter-professionalism.

One way to determine the kind of culture to pursue is via the competing values framework (Quinn and Rohrbaugh 1983; Cameron and Quinn 2005) (Figure 21.4). This model suggests that all organizational cultures will be a mix of four quadrants (clan, developmental, hierarchical and rational cultures), but the organization can be diagnosed to discern the most dominant cultural type. Then plans can be developed to move to the preferred type or mix, implementing strategies to move in a direction toward the preferred cultural characteristics.

Bringing it all together: two case studies in healthcare change

As a way of drawing our work together and illustrating some of the points we have been making, we provide two case studies of interest (Boxes 21.2 and 21.3). We also provide a brief commentary on the case studies by way of appreciating some of

Box 21.2: *Case study 1: The Royal Saint Everywhere NHS Trust under a microscope*

The situation

Within two years of each other, the Royal Saint Everywhere NHS Trust experienced two incidents of widespread media interest. The first was the case of three deaths in quick succession in the accident and emergency department's waiting area. The second was a series of adverse events involving the orthopaedic surgeons, who appeared to have much higher than average infection rates. The department was characterized by many battles and fights within operating theatres, e.g. between the surgeons and anaesthetists, and within the surgeons' own ranks, but also between the surgeons and other wards, units and departments. An inquiry into the Trust revealed that (a) the staff in emergency department seemed uncaring, and unwilling to make improvements, but the series of deaths did not seem to be anyone's fault and reflected merely an unexplained cluster; (b) the orthopaedic surgeons did seem to have some practices which were inappropriate for the modern era including constant inability to work effectively together and with others, poor handwashing compliance and little in the way of handover or other communication within orthopaedics and between these staff and others.

Your responses

Consider the facts above. What is going on here? What are your initial impressions? What do you think you will do about these issues in the short, medium and long term?

Change management tasks

1 You are the newly appointed general manager of Royal Saint Everywhere NHS Trust. You are the ninth GM in eleven years. You have been asked to present to a Department of Health inquiry on (a) your analysis of the situation at Royal Saint Everywhere NHS Trust leading up to the events; (b) how you in your new role plan to take the organization forward; (c) as a senior, respected health professional, what you suggest is needed to improve these matters; (d) what tools, frameworks, strategies and approaches would likely be useful for you.

2 Prepare your strategy for managing change effectively.

3 Discuss the likelihood that you will succeed, and why.

Box 21.3: *Case study 2: Using guidelines*

The situation

One solution advocated by many experts is the use of guidelines to enable best practice. The idea is that in an environment of constant, rapid change, the guideline becomes the centre of gravity – the core tool to focus attention on what is best local practice for particular units. Practice that is based on best evidence and which takes into account local conditions can be agreed by all participating clinicians for common conditions. Examples are guidelines for cardiac rehabilitation, head injury, stroke, or discharge.

Your responses

Consider whether you accept these propositions on guidelines. Why or why not?

Change management tasks

1. Discuss the processes that go on in your organization, or one you have encountered. What is the extent of guideline use?
2. What are the barriers to guideline use?
3. How can you overcome these?
4. What could you be doing to improve practice and ensure high standards?
5. What are your next steps in a workplace, assuming you were a change agent with responsibility for implementing increased guideline use, after doing this case?

---

their notable ingredients, and how our analysis in this chapter might help in tackling them. Four experts (an intensive care specialist with experience in managing critical care divisions and intensive care units; a sociologist with expertise managing academic and service units, and teaching in healthcare policy and management; a health services researcher who has managed both government programmes and academic research projects; and a health informatics academic with an engineering background, with expertise in managing and researching IT projects of differing kinds) examined the cases and offered responses. We summarize their comments in Boxes 21.4 and 21.5.

Conclusion

We have attempted in this chapter to provide not so much a theoretical treatise but a practical guide, albeit with reference to theory-oriented and empirical literature, to

Box 21.4: *Case 1: Synthesis of experts' comments*

Although Royal Saint Everywhere NHS Trust might have problems, they may not be any different from other health services except in degree. The issues highlighted may be symptomatic of broader cultural dysfunctionalities across the organization. The local behaviours of participants are the product of their training and long-standing cultural features in the environment in which they work. The problems hint at a common root: management and leadership failure, disregard or incompetence. There appears to be no quick fix. Changes will be needed over a medium- to longer-term time frame.

Taking the organization forward, developing an implementation plan, and proposing a strategy for change would involve securing support from the Department of Health and the internal governance structures. Starting to address the issues may exacerbate the political and cultural problems, because doing so makes them more explicit, but it would not be tenable to wallpaper over the cracks. Diligently checking out the troublesome departments, and discussing the issues with their heads, is a key step. Attempting to tackle the problem while trying to enrol departmental staff supporting improvements would be important.

On a wider front, conducting hospital-wide management by walking around, fact-finding, getting to know other departments, wards and units, and discerning whether there were other deep-seated problems were key initiatives. Team building and using related mechanisms to build relationships were also considered to be central activities. Also important in addressing the problems specified were strategies to identify examples of best practice, and harnessing opinion leaders who were supportive of improvement. One expert advocated setting up a change council, suitably resourced and staffed, similar to Kotter's (1996) guiding coalition (see Box 21.1). Another argued for a long-term approach to involve as wide a body of participants as possible across the organization to focus on quality of care and embrace clinical and organizational improvement strategies. It would be crucial to model appropriate behaviours from the top, work with people to engage them, and insist on compliance and best practice where standards called for this.

Box 21.5: *Case 2: Synthesis of experts' comments*

In most organizations the experts knew, had worked in or researched, guidelines were readily available or at least accessible, but were used sporadically. There were three types of problem with guidelines: the evidence on which they were based, the way they were produced, and the way they were used. If clinicians did not agree with the evidence contained in the guidelines, or the way it was being argued they should be used, for example, take-up was unlikely. In most health systems, doctors have traditionally had considerable autonomy, which makes the implementation of initiatives promoting standardized practice difficult.

One key problem with guidelines, however, rested with an over-arching issue. They are able to be supported in the abstract but denied in practice. Guidelines are normative[1] documents, which can be readily supported publicly or in principle, but they may be seen by some clinicians as not really applying to their particular situation, or their patient groups, or be seen as unwieldy.

If guidelines are inflicted on an institution or clinical group, according to one of the experts, they are more likely to be resisted than would be the case if the organization encouraged departments to develop or adapt their own. Another difficulty is the workload increase association with guideline adoption, often with no additional resources.

The overall aim is to have guidelines in place which reflect contemporary, evidence-based practice. To achieve this it is necessary to decentralize the adaptation or development of guidelines, and allocate resources to this. Securing agreement for compliance, and measuring agreed patient outcomes, were other strategies. It is important to have short-term and longer-term plans to improve take-up. Leaders setting examples in guideline use, i.e. modelling behaviours expected of others, involving clinicians, making guidelines relevant and useable, and importantly differentiating guidelines for differing populations (e.g. based on gender, and modifying guidelines for disabled populations, and minority groups) were considered very important for equity.

[1] So like apple pie, motherhood and the national anthem, guidelines are supported virtuously universally. Almost everyone categorizes them as tools that *ought* to be used.

assist potential and practising managers. We also designed the chapter to provide other stakeholders – policy-makers, clinicians and researchers – with some frameworks, concepts and language for appreciating change, and how it can be and in fact is managed. This is a major message for change managers and others interested in this topic. Tools, techniques and strategies in the literature and helpful websites often portray change management in positive terms, offering optimistic advice. But changing healthcare structures and cultures, implementing the latest systems, adopting new policies and improving productivity, the quality of care and levels of patient safety are mostly harder than anticipated and take longer to achieve than planned. The objective and subjective rewards for making progress and enhancing healthcare institutions, organizations and clinical services, however, are considerable.

Acknowledgements

We thank Ms Danielle Marks, who sourced many of the references and websites, formatted the chapter, and obtained permissions for use of the models we cite from other scholars. We express our appreciation to the members of the expert panel for reviewing the cases and sharing their knowledge with us: Dr David Greenfield, Professor Ken Hillman, Dr Farah Magrabi and Dr Joanne Travaglia. Professor George Rubin provided case 2, which we modified for the chapter.

Summary box

- An important distinction for change managers and other stakeholders interested in change is between the way change is actually managed and the way textbooks and models portray the way it ought to be managed.

- Managers of all types, and particularly those involved with considerable change, often spend substantial effort and time figuring out what is going on around them, and striving to create meaning out of their experiences – known as sensemaking.

- Similarly, change agents typically find it useful to appreciate, reflexively, their own perspectives and frames on change. Understanding where others are coming from is usually time well spent, too.

- A key attribute of any organizational setting is its culture – the sets of cognitions and experiences shared collectively by organizational members and groups. This is hard to change, and striving to influence, shape or modify it is usually a medium- to longer-term endeavour.

- There are many tools and techniques to help the change manager, a range of which are documented in this chapter.

Self-test exercises

1 Of the popular tools and techniques for change management discussed in the text and documented in Tables 21.1 and 21.2, which have you used to good effect, or do you believe would be most useful for your work? Why?

2 Consider Braithwaite's model of managerial behavioural routines (Figure 21.1). Are there any other primary or secondary pursuits, and modes of operating, that you have observed managers enacting? Which of these activities is most crucial in your current work? How will you develop your skills across a range of these activities?

3 Review the cases provided and write down your answers to the questions posed. How closely do you agree with some of the key points of the experts?

Appendix

The follwing are specific models and tools for culture change (Figures 21.5–21.9).

FIGURE 21.5 Lundberg's model of oganizational change
Source: Lundberg (1985). Copyright 1985 by SAGE Publications Inc Books. Reproduced with permission of SAGE Publications Inc Books in the format Textbook via Copyright Clearance Centre.

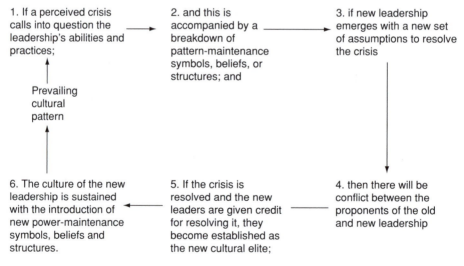

FIGURE 21.6 Dyer's cycle of cultural evolution
Source: Dyer (1985). Reprinted with permission of John Wiley & Sons, Inc.

Schein's Life Cycle Model

Growth stage	Function of culture	Mechanism of change
I. Birth and early growth Founder domination, Possibly family Domination *Succession phase:*	• Culture is a distinctive competence and source of identity • Culture is the 'glue' that holds Organisation together • **Organisation strives towards more Integration and clarity** • Heavy emphasis on socialisation as evidence of commitment • Culture becomes battleground between conservatives and liberals • Potential successors are judged on whether they will preserve or change cultural elements	1. Natural evolution 2. Self-guided evolution through therapy 3. Managed evolution through hybrids 4. Managed 'revolution' through outsiders
II. Organisational midlife • New product development • Vertical integration • Geographic expansion • Acquisitions, mergers	• Cultural integration declines as new subcultures are spawned • Crisis of identity, loss of key goals, values, and assumptions • Opportunity to manage direction of cultural change	5. Planned change and organisational development 6. Technological seduction 7. Change through scandal, explosion of myth 8. Incrementalism
III. Organisational maturity • Maturity of markets • Internal stability or stagnation • Lack of motivation to change *Transformation option* *Destruction option* • Bankruptcy and reorganisation • Takeover and reorganisation • Merger and assimilation	• Culture becomes a constraint on innovation • Culture preserves the glories of the past, hence is values as a source of self-esteem, defence • Culture change necessary and inevitable, but not all elements of culture can or must change • Essential elements of culture must be identified, preserved • Culture change can be managed or simply be allowed to evolve • Culture changes at basic levels • Culture changes through massive replacement of key people	9. Coercive persuasion 10. Turnaround 11. Reorganisation, destruction and rebirth

FIGURE 21.7 Schein's life-cycle model

Source: Schein (1985). Reprinted by permission of John Wiley & Sons, Inc.

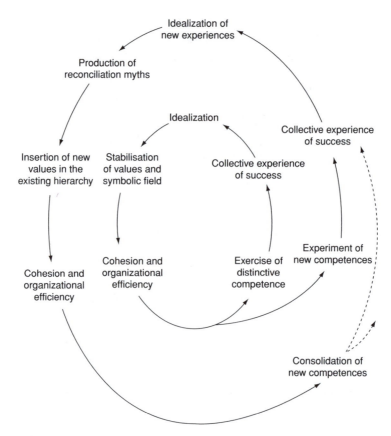

FIGURE 21.8 Gagliardi's model of organizational culture
Source: Gagliardi (1986). Copyright © 1986. Reprinted by permission of SAGE.

Contextual	Social	Cognitive
Unfreezing mechanisms	Rites of questioning and destruction	Anticipation
	Rites of rationalisation and legitimation	
Experimentation	Rites of degradation and conflict	Confirmation
	Rites of passage and enhancement	Culmination
Refreezing mechanisms	Rites of integration and conflict reduction	Aftermath

FIGURE 21.9 Brown's compilation model of organizational change
Source: Brown (1995). Copyright © Pearson Education Australia.

References and further reading

Alvesson, M. and Sveningsson, S. (2008) *Changing Organizational Culture: Cultural Change Work in Progress*. New York: Routledge.

Bolman, L.G. and Deal, T.E. (2008) *Reframing Organizations: Artistry, Choice and Leadership*, 4th edn. San Francisco, CA: Jossey-Bass.

Braithwaite, J. (1995) Organizational change, patient-focused care: an Australian perspective. *Health Services Management Research*, 8(3): 172–85.

Braithwaite, J. (2004) An empirically-based model for clinician-managers' behavioural routines. *Journal of Health Organization and Management*, 18(4): 240–61.

Braithwaite, J. (2006a) Analysing structural and cultural change in acute settings using a Giddens-Weick paradigmatic approach. *Health Care Analysis*, 14: 91–102.

Braithwaite, J. (2006b) An empirical assessment of social structural and cultural change in clinical directorates. *Health Care Analysis*, 14(4): 185–93.

Braithwate, J. (2011) A lasting legacy from Tony Blair? NHS culture change. *Journal of the Royal Society of Medicine*, 104(2): 87–9.

Braithwaite, J., Hindle, D., Iedema, R. and Westbrook, J.I. (2002) Introducing soft systems methodology plus (SSM+): why we need it and what it can contribute. *Australian Health Review*, 25(2): 191–8.

Braithwaite, J., Hyde, P. and Pope, C. (eds) (2010) *Culture and Climate in Health Care Organizations*. Basingstoke: Palgrave Macmillan.

Braithwaite, J. and Westbrook, M. (2005) Rethinking clinical organisational structures: an attitude survey of doctors, nurses and allied health staff in clinical directorates. *Journal of Health Services Research and Policy*, 10(1): 10–7.

Braithwaite, J., Westbrook, M., Hindle, D., Iedema, R. and Black, D. (2006) Does restructuring hospitals result in greater efficiency? An empirical test using diachronic data. *Health Services Management Research*, 19(1): 1–12.

Brown, A. (1995) *Organisational Culture*. London: Pitman.

Buzan, T., Griffiths, C. and Lee, B. (2010) iMindMap. Available at: http://www .thinkbuzan.com/intl/products/imindmap/ultimate/features (accessed 28 July 2010).

Callen, J., Westbrook, J. and Braithwaite, J. (2007) Cultures in hospitals and their influence on and attitudes to, and satisfaction with, the use of clinical information systems. *Social Science and Medicine*, 65(3): 635–9.

Cameron, K. and Quinn, R. (2005) *Diagnosing and Changing Organizational Culture: Based on the Competing Values Framework*. San Francisco, CA: Jossey-Bass.

Carlson, S. (1951) *Executive Behaviour*. Stockholm: Strombergs.

Cognistreamer *Innovation Portal*. Available at: http://www.innovationportal.eu/ (accessed 28 July 2010).

Dyer, W. (1985) The cycle of cultural evolution in organizations. In R. Kilmann, M. Saxton and R. Serpa (eds) *Gaining Control of the Corporate Culture*. San Francisco, CA: Jossey-Bass.

Fayol, H. (1949) *General and Industrial Management*. London: Pitman.

Ferlie, E. and Shortell, S. (2001) Improving the quality of care in the United Kingdom and the United States: a framework for change. *The Milbank Quarterly*, 79(2): 281–315.

Frey, C. (2010) *Mind Mapping Resource Centre*. Available at: http://www.innova tiontools.com/resources/mindmapping.asp (accessed 28 July 2010).

Gagliardi, P. (1986) The creation and change of organizational cultures: a conceptual framework. *Organizational Studies*, 7: 117–34.

Gantt, H. (1974) *Work, Wages and Profits*. Easton, PA: Hive Publishing Company.

Hammer, M. and Champy, J. (1993) *Reengineering the Corporation*. New York: Harper-Collins.

Kassirer, J. (2009) *Tools of Change*. Available at: http://www.toolsofchange.com/en/tools-of-change/ (accessed 20 July 2010).

Kotter, J.P. (1986) *The General Manager*. New York: Free Press.

Kotter, J.P. (1995) Why transformation efforts fail. *Harvard Business Review*, May–June, pp. 59–67.

Kotter, J.P. (1996) *Leading Change*. Boston: Harvard Business School Press.

Kotter, J.P. and Cohen, D.S. (2002) *The Heart of Change: Real-Life Stories of How People Change Their Organizations*. Boston: Harvard Business School Press.

Lega, F. (2007) Organisational design for health integrated delivery systems: theory and practice, *Health Policy*, 81(2): 258–79.

Lundberg, C. (1985) On the feasibility of cultural intervention. In P. Frost, L. Moore, M. Louis, C. Lundberg and J. Martin (eds) *Reframing Organizational Culture*. Newbury Park, CA: Sage.

Manktelow, J. (2010) *Critical Path Analysis*. Available at: http://www.mindtools.com/critpath.html (accessed 28 July 2010).

Mannion, R., Davies, H.T.O., Harrison, S. et al. (2010) *Changing Management Cultures and Organisational Performance in the NHS*. London: National Institute for Health Research Service Delivery and Organisation Programme.

Mannion, R., Davies, H.T.O. and Marshall, M.N. (2005) *Cultures for Performance in Health Care*. Maidenhead: Open University Press.

Mannion, R., Konteh, F. and Davies, H.T.O. (2009) Assessing organisational culture for quality and safety improvement: a national survey of tools and tool use. *Quality and Safety in Health Care*, 18: 153–6.

Microsoft (2010) *Microsoft Project 2010*. Available at: http://www.microsoft.com/project/en/us/project-professional-2010.aspx (accessed 28 July 2010).

Mind Technologies (2010) *Visual Mind*. Available at: http://www.visual-mind.com/about.html (accessed 28 July 2010).

Mintzberg, H. (1971) Managerial work: analysis from observation. *Management Science*, 18(2): B97–B110.

Mintzberg, H. (1973) *The Nature of Managerial Work*. New York: HarperCollins.

Nokes, S. and Greenwood, A. (2003) *The Definitive Guide to Project Management*, 5th edn. London: FT Prentice Hall.

Osborn, A. (1963) *Applied Imagination: Principles and Procedures of Creative Problem Solving*, 3rd edn. New York: Charles Scribner's Son.

Quinn, R. and Rohrbaugh, J. (1983) A spatial model of effectiveness criteria: towards a competing values approach to organizational analysis. *Management Science*, 29: 363–77.

Salem, R., Bernstein, J. and Sullivan, T. (2008) *Tools for Behaviour Change Communication*. Baltimore, MD: Johns Hopkins Bloomberg School of Public Health.

Schein, E. (1985) *Organizational Culture and Leadership*. San Francisco, CA: Jossey-Bass.

Smircich, L. (1983) Concepts of culture and organizational analysis. *Administrative Science Quarterly*, 28(3): 339–58.

Stewart, R. (1967) *Managers and their Jobs: A Study of the Similarities and Differences in the Way Managers Spend their Time*. London: Macmillan.

Stewart, R. (1998) *Managerial Work*. Aldershot: Ashgate.

Urwick, L.F. (1938) *Scientific Principles and Organization*. New York: American Management Association.

Van de Ven, A., Angle, H. and Poole, M.S. (eds) (1989) *Research on the Management of Innovation: The Minnesota Studies*. New York: Ballinger Publishing/Harper and Row.

Van de Ven, A., Polley, D., Garud, R. and Venkataraman, S. (1999) *The Innovation Journey*. New York: Oxford University Press.

van Gelder, T. (2008) Austhink software. Available at: http://bcisive.austhink.com/ (accessed 28 July 2010).

Victorian Quality Council (2006) Successfully Implementing Change. Department of Human Services, Victoria, Australia.

Walshe, K. (2010) Reorganisation of the NHS in England. *British Medical Journal*, 341: c3843.

Weick, K. (1995) *Sensemaking in Organisations*. London: Sage.

Websites and resources

For a good selection of computer-supported methods and tools, see Table 21.2.

Managing resources

Anne Tofts and Kieran Walshe

Introduction

If there is one characteristic that is ubiquitous across healthcare systems in both the developed and developing world, it is that resources are constrained, and pressure on resources grows each year as the ability of the healthcare system to produce outstrips the capacity of society to pay for it. Two particular characteristics of the healthcare sector serve to magnify the problem of resource constraint. One is the demographic and technological dynamic, which means that an increasingly elderly and unwell population is combined with an ever growing range of costly treatments for diseases. That creates major cost pressures. The other characteristic is the so-called Baumol effect – the observation that unlike many other industries where order of magnitude productivity improvements have produced massive price decreases, in the healthcare sector, productivity has been largely static or even declining (Jacobs and Dawson 2003). As a result, healthcare systems have not been able to fund all or even part of the growing demand for healthcare through greater efficiency and productivity.

In this environment, it is critical that health managers are equipped with skills in managing resources – in areas such as business planning, cost control, budget management and productivity improvement. Resource management is also a key area for health clinicians and professionals who play a role in managing a service or team. Anybody who has a responsibility for resources including people, equipment and buildings as well as money, should work in partnership with managers and finance professionals to contribute to the planning and shaping of the resources required for the future delivery of healthcare services.

This chapter covers three main areas which are central to resource management. First, it explores the business planning process, and maps out how business plans are developed from a strategic assessment of the environment and the organization's objectives, transformed into meaningful objectives, plans and targets, and then monitored and reviewed in implementation. Then it turns to discuss budgets and financial management, and explains how healthcare costs are categorized, and how budgets are set and managed. Finally, it sets out a detailed framework for developing a business case for new investments or service developments, including the processes for option appraisal, risk assessment and cost and benefit analysis. The chapter concludes by arguing that in a resource-constrained healthcare system, managers and clinicians need to be financially aware and astute, and have a detailed understanding of the financial consequences and implications of their decisions. Equally, it argues, finance professionals need more than their accounting skills to make an effective contribution to managing resources – increasingly, they need a full understanding of the clinical and organizational realities which lie behind their budget statements and spreadsheets.

Business planning and performance management

Business planning is the process by which healthcare professionals and managers plan how best to use available resources to meet the organization's strategic objectives. The three main categories of resources that the business plan will address in a health context are people, finance and facilities. 'Business planning' is a term that sometimes seems foreign to healthcare professionals who do not necessarily regard the healthcare organizations in which they work as businesses, and are not overly concerned with issues of profit and loss or return on investment. However, a business plan is as relevant in all parts of a health service as it is in the world of business. It is a tool that helps health professionals and managers to plan and communicate future intentions and developments. It is sometimes perceived as not fitting with public sector values and ethos, and instead managers talk about service or development plans. In effect, these are all part of the business planning process. A business plan can be defined as follows:

> A list of actions so ordered as to attain, over a particular time period, certain desired objectives derived from a careful analysis of internal and external factors likely to affect the organisation, which will move the organisation from where it is now to where it wants to be.
>
> (Puffit 1993: 9)

The attributes of a good plan business plan should be:

- to set out the objectives of the department or unit in relation to the overall organizational goals;
- to provide a structured analysis of the current strengths, weaknesses, opportunities and threats in relation to its goals;
- to develop a detailed action plan to build on the strengths, address the weaknesses, optimize the opportunities and respond to the threats to achieve the objectives;
- to include a budget for the level of financial resource needed to achieve the objectives;
- to include a workforce development plan to enable the staff to achieve the objectives.

Where many organizations fail is in the integration of all business or service plans developed by constituent departments or service areas into a single organization-wide planning framework: a framework that has a cohesive set of broader strategic objectives owned not only by all health professionals and managers within that organization but also by partner agencies and stakeholders such as patient groups, commissioners and local government.

This section explores how we analyse and define the wider organizational environment and objectives, provides a framework for business planning, outlines how stakeholders should be involved in the process, discusses the setting of objectives and targets, examines resource planning, and turns finally to measuring implementation.

Analysing the organization and the environment

A good starting point for business planning is to undertake an analysis of the internal and external issues that will impact on the organization's or department's ability to achieve its objectives. A common and simple model to aid this analysis is SWOT (Strengths, Weaknesses, Opportunities, Threats). What can seem at first glance to be a simple, straightforward analysis can be used as an inclusive process involving staff and other key stakeholders. Some people may perceive strengths as weaknesses, and opportunities as threats, and vice versa, and hence the dialogue that the manager engages in will help staff and stakeholders to share their hopes and concerns. A common understanding of objectives and the current situation can also be built through such a dialogue. During the SWOT analysis, all resources should be analysed: staff; financial; equipment; facilities; estates; transport; systems, etc. The SWOT analysis is undertaken in relation to its purpose and objectives and a resource is only a strength if it is 'fit for purpose' to achieve the stated objectives, taking advantage of opportunities and overcoming threats. For example, a health unit that has stated its purpose as specializing in orthopaedic care might perceive staff with appropriate clinical skills as a strength but staff highly skilled in other areas as a weakness. Many business plans include a SWOT analysis but few contain a detailed action plan that addresses this analysis. The action plan should demonstrate how the organization or department plans to do following:

- build on its strengths;
- overcome its weaknesses;
- take advantage of opportunities;
- minimize the risk from threats.

The process of scanning the external environment can be further strengthened using the PEST environmental analysis tool (sometimes known as STEP). PEST stands for: **P**olitical; **E**conomic; **S**ociological; **T**echnological.

- **Political:** e.g. national and local government initiatives that may advance or hinder the service/organizational objectives; or patient lobby groups that may have an influence on service developments.
- **Economic:** e.g. budgetary or funding issues at national, local or organizational level that might impact positively or negatively.
- **Sociological:** e.g. demographic trends that may impact on service needs; the organization's ability to attract the workforce needed to achieve its objectives; or local population growth trends.

- **Technological:** e.g. technological advances in clinical equipment that may assist in the organization's ability to achieve its service objectives; or advances in information technology.

PEST can help the manager to assess external pressures and influences on their service area or department that may be perceived as opportunities or threats within the SWOT analysis. Short-term objectives can be agreed with staff and other stakeholders which they feel are achievable, address the issues raised within the SWOT analysis and take the organization or department in the direction of travel required to achieve the long-term goal.

Business planning framework

The simple but effective framework for a business plan set out in Figure 22.1 is often used by health professionals and managers with their teams and stakeholders as a means of fully engaging them from the start. Weak business planning processes can result in faulty assumptions and costly errors in the development of new services and approaches to healthcare.

Stakeholder involvement

Every service or department involves a group of individual clinicians and managers contributing to its running and success. Each will have a specific view of the direction that the service or department should be moving in and the best way of doing it. The process of producing a business plan enables everybody to contribute their experience and ideas, providing a common agreement on where the service is going and how to get there. An effective and inclusive business planning process can therefore prove to be a very effective tool for team building, providing a common view of the future and commitment to achieving it. It goes without saying that it is important for all health organizations to engage their stakeholders in the process of service and business planning, stakeholders being those people likely to have an interest in, be affected by, or be able to influence the outcome of the proposed service improvement or business development.

Professionals and managers should be planning a service that meets the needs of their patients, service users and carers. The commissioners or purchasers of the service will also have expectations and views, as will the organization's own board or senior management team. These are all stakeholders. No single department or service within a health organization can work in isolation. There is always some level of interdependence. For instance, clinical services rely on non-clinical departments to be able to function effectively. All departments rely on the personnel or human resources department to recruit and retain their staff. Wards are dependent on an efficient service from the hospital porters, patient information and records departments. The list is endless, but the principle is the same – to be effective, planning must involve and be owned by all stakeholders who have expectations of that service and will either performance manage it or be in a position to express views on its effectiveness. Planning within one department or service must involve and be owned by the departments that it serves, or upon which it is reliant.

Where we have been and where we are now

A full analysis of the current services, organization and its environment identifying:

• Service and patient needs
• Strengths and weaknesses of the organization, current service and resources
• Opportunities for and threats to the service
• Drivers and barriers to change

Where we want to be

Determining the future direction and goals with key stakeholders including patients and staff, and identifying:

• Tangible and specific service objectives
• Financial targets
• The workforce and ways of working that will be needed to deliver the service objectives
• Infrastructure needed, e.g. information and communication systems, buildings and equipment

How we are going to get there

A detailed resource and action plan to achieve the vision and goals including a gap analysis (what is needed to move from the current position to the desired future position):

• Service improvements or redesign
• Changes in ways of working and practice
• Staff education and training
• Patient education
• Change management plan
• Equipment requirements
• Building requirements
• Systems changes
• Financial planning

How will we know how we are doing and when we have got there?

Regular monitoring of progress against agreed timescales and milestones

Ongoing review and refinement of the plan to reflect progress and changing circumstances

FIGURE 22.1 A simple framework for business planning

Tangible and achievable objectives

The objectives framed in business planning should be SMART – **S**pecific, **M**easurable, **A**chievable (i.e. challenging but not unobtainable), **R**ealistic (explicit about constraints) and **T**ime-related (identifying target dates and milestones along the way). For example, a business plan that says we want 'to improve access to daycare services for older people' expresses an aspiration, but the objective is not couched in terms which make it useful for planning and service delivery. It needs to be specific about the services and access targets, to express them in measurable terms, to be realistic about what can be achieved, and to be related to a specific timescale for delivery. The objective would be more useful if it said, for example, that we want to 'improve access to daycare services for older people by building an extension to the existing daycentre enabling the provision of 20 additional places per day from September 2011'. Of course the 'how we are going to do get there' part of the business planning framework in Figure 22.1 is still needed. What will be the impact on staffing requirements? How much will the extension cost? What new equipment and services will be needed? What will be the impact on other services for older people?

A long-term business plan should include both long-term and shorter-term SMART objectives. The short-term objectives or milestones should take the service or department in the direction needed to achieve the long-term objective. Regular monitoring and review against short-term objectives allow the manager to review progress towards the long-term objective, adjusting plans accordingly. Short-term objectives should be achievable within the given resources, thus providing staff with a sense of achievement motivating them to continue to strive to achieve the long-term goal.

Resource planning

Most of us do not have the luxury of planning from scratch or working from a 'clean sheet of paper'. We are normally working with an 'envelope' of resources that has been built up over a period of time. These resources may, for example, be existing buildings, equipment and people with specific sets of skills, knowledge and attitudes. Our ability to change these will be limited by the availability of money and time for investment. Possibly the most important factor to consider is the time period within which a service development must be achieved, balanced against the complexity and scale of change required and the existing resource envelope. Can the development realistically be achieved while maintaining the existing service? Resource factors must be considered at all stages of the planning process if planning is to be an exercise based in reality and not just the production of a 'wish list' of what it would be nice to do given unlimited resources. It is easy to demotivate staff and service users by setting expectations during the planning process that cannot be met within available timescales or financial resources. An essential part of the planning process is to assess the ability:

- of current resources to be used in new and different ways to meet changing needs;
- to increase the productivity of existing resources;
- to acquire new resources.

It should always be remembered that within the resource package are included staff (clinical and non-clinical), equipment and buildings as well as finance.

Measuring performance

A business plan should not be a static document – written and then filed or forgotten. It should be constantly reviewed and updated, and progress against the objectives should be monitored. So every business plan needs to include some mechanisms for monitoring and measuring implementation. One useful way to organize the targets, measures and indicators within a business plan is to use a measurement framework like Moullin's (2002) public sector scorecard, which is illustrated in Figure 22.2.

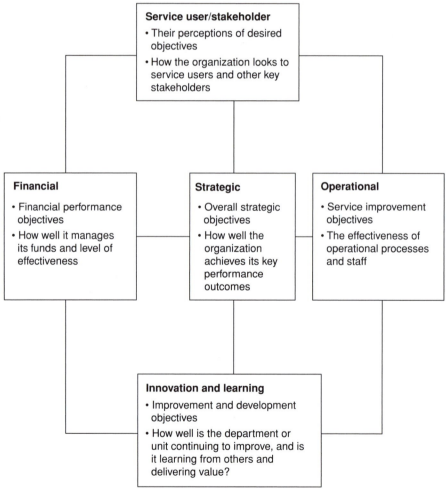

Service user/stakeholder
- Their perceptions of desired objectives
- How the organization looks to service users and other key stakeholders

Financial
- Financial performance objectives
- How well it manages its funds and level of effectiveness

Strategic
- Overall strategic objectives
- How well the organization achieves its key performance outcomes

Operational
- Service improvement objectives
- The effectiveness of operational processes and staff

Innovation and learning
- Improvement and development objectives
- How well is the department or unit continuing to improve, and is it learning from others and delivering value?

FIGURE 22.2 The balanced scorecard for performance measurement
Source: Adapted from Moullin (2002).

This framework is based on the ideas of Kaplan and Norton's (1992) balanced scorecard. It splits the measures or indicators into three main categories – financial, strategic and operational – and separately identifies two other areas for measurement – service user perspectives, and organizational learning and development. The use of a scorecard approach can assist managers to work together with professionals to develop multiple objectives that reflect internal organizational and external stakeholder expectations, balancing the need for both quality and financial performance. The scorecard is often used both in the context of performance development and performance measurement. For performance development, it provides a framework for a focused review of how well the organization or department is doing, along with an organizational development plan needed to achieve the agreed objectives. The framework likewise enables tangible objectives to be set and measured in the context of performance management.

If the interests of service users and patients are not met, then it is unlikely that the organization will be able to meet the needs of other stakeholders. In many healthcare systems where patients can exercise choice between providers or insurers, it is increasingly important for business planning processes to recognize the importance of service users', carers' and patients' perceptions, and their impact on financial, operational and strategic objectives. For instance, a hospital that fails to satisfy patients' expectations of the quality of service is unlikely to meet its financial targets as patients will choose an alternative service provider.

The balanced scorecard is a useful framework to help teams analyse how well they are doing against a range of expectations and objectives. It can also be used to shape discussion with stakeholders in determining future objectives. The scorecard approach can likewise be used to determine the purpose of the organization or department. How closely the service or business purpose is defined will determine how effective the business planning process is and there can be advantage in leaving the purpose very open or flexible, although it is then difficult to plan effectively.

Use of the balanced scorecard enables the organization to develop and communicate a clear purpose and establish objectives that are aligned with its need to respond to the health needs and expectations of the local population, to meet clinical and service quality standards and to work within financial constraints.

Budgets and financial management

For many clinicians and managers, taking responsibility for holding a budget for the first time can be a challenging experience. The arrival of monthly spreadsheets outlining spending against budget, often with historical data for the same period for the previous year, spending in the current year to date, and details of variances can provoke more questions and anxieties than they resolve. It is important for budget holders to have a clear understanding of the costs and revenue sources shown in their budget and how they have been calculated, to be involved in and understand the budget setting process, and to know what questions to ask when they monitor their budget and how to deal with problems or concerns.

Costs and how they are calculated

The costs of resources that a service uses can be split into three main groups: fixed, variable, and semi-variable. These are straightforward categories to understand:

- **Fixed costs.** These do not vary within a given period of time with the level of use or service activity. They would still have to be paid if a service or department was closed for a short period of time – examples include equipment hire costs and rent for premises.
- **Variable costs.** These vary in direct relation to the level of use or service activity. They do not have to be paid if the level of activity stops – examples include the cost of food consumed by patients, theatre consumables like dressings or surgical supplies, or the costs of drugs prescribed and dispensed.
- **Semi-variable costs.** It is difficult to classify some costs as either fixed or variable – and so we use the term 'semi-variable' to describe them. For example, the cost of staff wages on a ward is neither strictly fixed nor wholly variable. If the ward closed then it may be possible to move some staff to other wards, though some staff may still have to be paid over a period of time before they could be redeployed. But if the ward remains open, even with very few patients, it still has to be staffed. So the staff costs are not wholly variable, nor wholly fixed.

Additionally, costs can be categorized as direct or indirect: *direct costs* are those directly related to the department or service, while *indirect costs or overheads* are incurred in running the organization within which the service or department is located. Using a ward as an example, direct costs would include: ward staff costs; bed linen costs; catering costs for the ward's patients. Indirect costs would include: the costs of the hospital having a personnel and finance department to support the ward manager; the sterile supplies department that services the ward. Both direct and indirect costs can be fixed or variable.

The way that indirect costs are allocated to service areas and departments will vary within each organization. It is important for the service manager to understand how these costs have been allocated as they can have a major impact on unit costs and affect the manager's ability to manage costs and budgets within their area of responsibility. For example, the costs of running the sterile supplies department could be apportioned to ward budgets according to how many patient episodes they have, or how many beds they have, or could be directly calculated on the number of units of sterile supply packs they use. In general, it is better for indirect costs to be calculated according to use rather than apportioned according to some proxy for use.

The concepts of *stepped costs* and *opportunity costs* are also important for a manager to understand. Stepped costs occur when an additional unit of service results in an additional fixed cost. An example of stepped cost would be within an occupational therapy unit where it has been decided that one therapist can safely work with ten patients. At present, the unit is only servicing eight patients and there are two spare places – if these two places are filled, then there is no increase in the fixed staff cost, although there may be increases in variable costs such as catering. However, if the unit is instead asked to take three additional patients to fill the vacancies then this would require the appointment of an additional member of staff as it would take the unit above the safe ratio of ten patients to one staff. There is a significant increase in the fixed cost; this would be classed as a stepped cost.

Resources are always limited. Therefore, using resources in one way is always at the expense of another option. This is the concept of opportunity cost. If a manager has limited development money and has two or more development proposals to consider, then the opportunity cost of funding one proposal is that the resources cannot be used to develop the other proposals.

Most of the discussion of costs above relates to revenue costs – spending that recurs from year to year. Capital expenditure relates to expenditure that has an ongoing value to the business such as fixed assets including land, buildings, furniture and equipment. To be categorized as capital, items usually have to have a life of more than a year and organizations will typically determine a minimum level of expenditure that is required per item for an asset to be determined as capital. Revenue is expenditure on items that continually recur, or the ongoing costs of running a service or department. Revenue will include employee costs, rent, rates, utilities, consumables and training. This is an important distinction as sources of revenue and capital funding in healthcare organizations are often different, and budget setting processes usually deal mainly with revenue spending.

Budget setting

A key element of any business planning process is to estimate the level of income and expenditure that will be needed to achieve the objectives and allocate this to specific activities. This is the process of budget setting. A budget is a financial plan that details:

- **income:** funding available for a service or department.
- **expenditure:** how it is planned to allocate funding.

The process of setting and monitoring budgets should be an important part of both the planning and performance management cycle. Involvement by managers and health professionals at an early stage encourages them to take ownership of a budget that reflects the real needs of their service area. The process of negotiating a budget at the beginning of the financial year is often rushed, resulting in cost-cutting decisions that do not reflect service priorities. Equally, a flawed budget setting and monitoring process at the beginning of the year can lead to unplanned service cuts towards the end of the financial year to quickly reduce expenditure to be able to 'balance the books'. In a well-planned process that fully involves health professionals at all stages, department and service heads would work together to identify areas where cost-effectiveness improvements can be made that will have least effect on the quality of services and patient care. Equally, more effective use will be made of surpluses identified late in the financial year.

There are three main techniques of budget setting used in health organizations:

- zero-based budgeting;
- incremental budgeting;
- activity-based budgeting.

The *zero-based* approach to budgeting is most frequently associated with the business planning process. A zero-based budget assumes that the budget is calculated from scratch for each activity needed to achieve the business plan objectives. It starts from zero and re-evaluates all resource assumptions to create a plan for the future.

The *incremental* approach is the most commonly used in many health organizations. It builds on the historical budget, the budget that was in place the previous year. This forms the baseline for the following period, usually being raised by an agreed percentage for inflation and adjusted for other known factors such as planned savings or growth.

Activity-based budgeting provides a detailed budget for each specific activity involved in delivering a service or within a department or organization. It is only feasible where clear separation between the costs of different activities can be identified and costs can be accurately attributed. Activity-based budgeting has been used in many healthcare systems to develop 'standard' costs for each unit of activity, for example, an inpatient stay or outpatient attendance, and to then monitor actual spending against those costs, down to the ward, clinician or even individual patient level.

Some of the advantages and disadvantages of each approach are summarized in Table 22.1.

Budget monitoring

Managers and health professionals are usually responsible for the monitoring and control of revenue budgets for their service area or department. Effective budget

TABLE 22.1 Advantages and disadvantages of approaches to budgeting

Budget approach	Advantages	Disadvantages
Zero-based	<ul><li>A realistic achievable budget is set</li><li>It is proactive and forward-looking</li><li>Links to business plans</li><li>Transparency about the relationship between cost and activity</li></ul>	<ul><li>Very time-consuming to prepare</li><li>Requires clear objectives</li><li>Can be difficult to implement</li></ul>
Incremental	<ul><li>A quick process to complete</li><li>Accurate if there is little change in activity</li><li>Simple to calculate</li><li>Builds from a known and proven base</li></ul>	<ul><li>Use of historical information can lead to inaccuracies</li><li>Inefficiencies can be hidden</li><li>No relationship between funding, cost and actual activity</li></ul>
Activity-based	<ul><li>Links finance to specific activity</li><li>Allows a budget that can flex</li><li>Simple to adjust to reflect changing activity levels</li></ul>	<ul><li>Income may not flex with the budget</li><li>Difficult to allocate resources shared by different activities</li><li>Changes to standard costs may not be recognized</li></ul>

management is dependent on the effectiveness of the initial budget setting process and the service/department manager and senior health professional should have worked in collaboration with the management accountant at the beginning of the financial year to ensure that a realistic budget was set. To be realistic, a budget should reflect the resources and activity needed to meet the agreed business plan objectives. The manager's monitoring role is then to investigate budget variances during the year, identifying why the variance occurred and taking management action to bring the budget back in line. A budget variance is the difference between planned and actual expenditure. There can be many reasons for variance to occur; it is not always an indication of poor management performance. In time, unforeseen circumstances may mean that the budget no longer reflects reality and should be adjusted for new and changing circumstances – for example, changed levels of service activity, new price discounts negotiated with suppliers, and staff absence resulting in increased use of agency staff.

The designated budget holder should be given responsibility and accountability to be able to control spending in terms of the major expenditure items. They may also be given authority to vire between budgets. Virement is the process by which funds can be moved from one budget heading to another – for example, changes in service activity in a day centre for older people may mean that catering costs are going to be higher than planned, while the usage of transport was overestimated and will not cost as much as originally planned. A proportion of the funds allocated to transport can be moved or vired to the catering budget to meet the additional costs. Virement is a way of managing budgets more efficiently when changes in activity or circumstances result in overspends in some areas and underspends in others. In practice, it makes the budget setting and monitoring process more meaningful. When the budget is being renegotiated at the beginning of the following year, any virement should be analysed and the proposed budget adjusted to better reflect planned activity and expected costs.

Developing a business case

A business case is a management tool that supports planning and decision-making. Its purpose is to demonstrate how a preferred course of action best meets service needs and provides key decision-makers with sufficient information on costs, benefits and risks to be able to assess proposals for service or business developments. A well-prepared business case should provide decision-makers with the evidence needed when making choices between different health treatments or approaches. For example:

- Is it worth investing in providing a new physiotherapist-led service for back pain, to divert some patients from seeing an orthopaedic consultant?
- What are the costs and benefits of putting a GP-led primary care service co-located with the accident and emergency service at the hospital, to see and triage patients and aim to reduce unnecessary or avoidable admissions to hospital?
- Would it be feasible and cost-effective to discharge patients undergoing joint replacement surgery earlier, and provide community-based nursing and telephone access for advice to a specialist orthopaedic nurse instead?

Every healthcare organization will have similar examples where a systematic approach to developing a business case is needed to support decisions about both new developments and existing services. The aim of a good business case is not to recommend the proposal under consideration, but to provide a balanced, dispassionate and objective analysis of costs, benefits and options so that the best decision can be made.

Framework for a business case

There is much common ground between the business planning process discussed earlier and the development and presentation of a business case, though the latter is more usually focused on informing a major decision about service development, reconfiguration or change. A business case should provide a structured analysis of the service need and objectives, a detailed description of the available options and an appraisal of each against some common and agreed criteria, and for the preferred option an implementation plan and a detailed approach to identifying and realizing the intended benefits.

Scoping the need

The business case should start by setting out the service or development need and the context, and may include a strategic assessment of the internal and external environment that impact on the proposed service development using appropriate tools such as SWOT and PEST. It should explore the implications for maintaining existing services and the anticipated outcomes and benefits of the proposed development. It should set out the objectives in SMART terms – specific, measurable, achievable, realistic and timely.

Option appraisal

This section of the business case identifies a number of different options to achieve the SMART objectives. The options usually include a status quo or 'do nothing' option as a benchmark. The following should be included for *each* option:

- analysis of costs and benefits (both financial and non-financial);
- analysis of the feasibility of achieving the SMART objectives;
- risk assessment of feasible options.

The identification and assessment of a range of options should involve a wide range of stakeholders. An inclusive process provides an opportunity to be creative and innovative, to challenge the status quo and constraints, and to ensure that stakeholders understand and are committed to the process of change.

This section will end with the identification of a *preferred* option after assessing each against a set of agreed criteria A scoring system agreed with stakeholders should be used to ensure an objective evaluation of options and identification of the preferred option. Each option is assessed against each of the agreed benefit criteria. Benefit criteria that might be used to appraise options for introducing a new system of admitting patients for elective surgery might include:

- reduction of waiting times for admission
- improved waiting list management
- patient comfort and safety
- improved utilization of theatre space
- improved productivity of theatre staff
- improved working environment.

Implementation plan for the preferred option

This section provides a detailed analysis and implementation plan for the *preferred* option which includes the following:

- project implementation plan including key milestones and timelines
- benefits realization plan
- funding strategy – with a detailed cost appraisal (including opportunity costs) and identification of sources of funding
- staff and equipment plan
- change management strategy
- risk management plan
- communication plan
- monitoring and evaluation plan.

Identification and realization of benefits

The definition of SMART objectives to meet the specific service need at the beginning of the process will ensure that options can be evaluated against explicit criteria that are agreed by all stakeholders. Objectives should focus on the desired outcome of the service development; the 'what', and not on the process of achieving that outcome; the 'how'. In the private sector the identification of return on investment (ROI) is a key part of the business case. This is translated in the public sector into identification of quantifiable benefits for the investment made. Benefits may include:

- clinical outcomes
- improvement to the patient experience
- improved quality of life for the patient
- increased capacity to meet demand
- improvements for the workforce
- economic benefits such as efficiency in service delivery, cost savings, increased productivity
- economic benefits gained by returning the patient to work early.

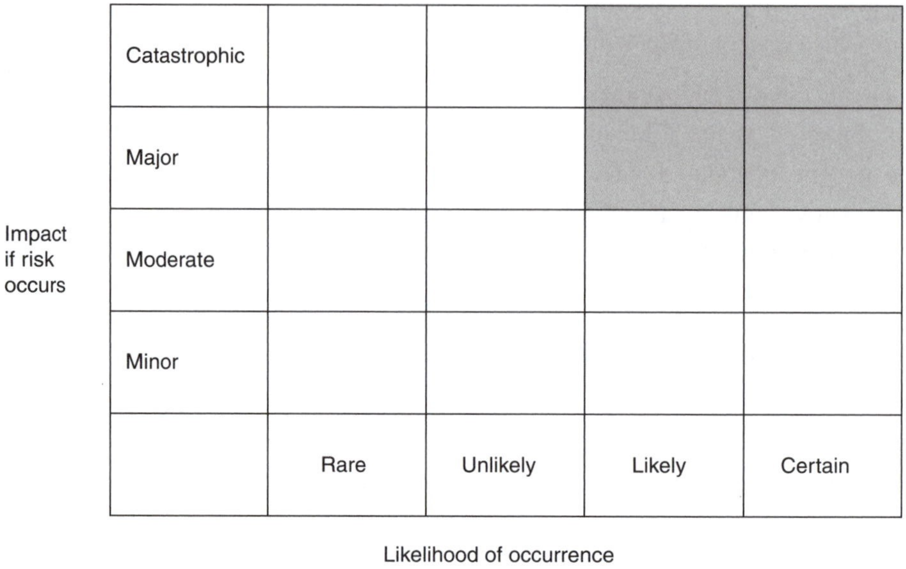

Impact if risk occurs				
Catastrophic				
Major				
Moderate				
Minor				
	Rare	Unlikely	Likely	Certain

Likelihood of occurrence

FIGURE 22.3 Risk assessment framework

A benefits realization plan which expands on each of the anticipated benefits identified in the option appraisal is needed, setting out how they will be achieved, who is responsible, the timescale for realizing benefits, and a process for review.

Risk assessment in business cases

An important part of the business case is the identification and assessment of risks associated with the implementation of the preferred option. Once again, it is useful to involve stakeholders in this process. Figure 22.3 provides a simple matrix that can be used to list and score or rate risks both according to how likely they are and how serious their implications would be. All potential risks, however small or unlikely, are listed and these are then plotted on the matrix according to the likelihood of their occurrence – from rare to certain, along with the impact they will have on the project, from minor to catastrophic.

A risk management strategy must be developed for all risks that fall into the shaded quadrant. A decision will need to be taken on how other risks are to be addressed. It may be decided to ignore those that fall into the 'rare to unlikely' and 'minor to moderate' quadrant. The cost of managing these less likely risks will need to be weighed up against the cost and likelihood of their occurrence.

Conclusion

This chapter has emphasized the need for all healthcare managers and professionals to develop an understanding and competence in planning the effective use of resources.

At the start of this chapter we referred to the rather dismal record of the healthcare sector in securing productivity improvements, at least when compared to other manufacturing and service sectors – the so-called Baumol effect. But research shows that when we give control of resources to clinicians and managers working together, with appropriate support and information systems, they can often make major performance improvements in quality, efficiency and productivity. Perhaps the key problem is not that healthcare processes themselves are not capable of dramatic productivity improvement, but that healthcare organizations are not designed, structured or managed in ways that will deliver that improvement (Berwick 1996). Creating structures which bring finance professionals, managers and clinicians together to plan and manage health services, and combine the clinicians' understanding of clinical processes and standards with managerial and financial expertise seems essential if resource-constrained healthcare systems are to find ways of doing more with less in the future.

Summary box

- Healthcare systems are increasingly resource constrained, and the management of resources is important both for managers and clinicians. The healthcare sector has a track record of static or even declining productivity, in contrast to many other sectors.

- Business planning is the process by which healthcare professionals and managers plan how best to use available resources to meet the organization's strategic objectives. A good business plan should follow a recognized framework or structure, be very clear about objectives, targets and actions required, and contain suitable indicators and processes for monitoring and review.

- Managing budgets requires a good understanding of costing systems and methods, budget setting processes, and the way that financial information is analysed and presented. Budget holders need to be able to control or influence the behaviours and activities which result in expenditure, and to understand mechanisms for analysing and dealing with variance and overspend.

- Business cases are essential tools in making major decisions about service developments, reconfigurations or changes. A business case should provide a structured analysis of the service need and objectives, a detailed description of the available options and an appraisal of each against some common and agreed criteria, and for the preferred option an implementation plan and a detailed approach to identifying and realizing the intended benefits.

- Managing resources and improving efficiency and productivity requires a combination of the clinical expertise and insight of healthcare professionals such as doctors, nurses and therapists and the managerial and financial expertise of managers and finance professionals.

Self-test exercises

1 Take a recent business plan from your own organization for a service and department, and analyse it against the framework in Figure 22.1. Identify areas of strength
and weakness and list the major revisions or improvements you think are needed
in that business plan.

2 Using the concepts of cost categories and types, analyse the costs of your service
or department, identifying those that you can control and those that are out of your
control. Are you effectively managing the direct and variable costs within your
control? Make some recommendations to improve management of those costs.

3 Write an outline business case for a new service development in your department
or organization, using the structure and format set out above. Your outline should
contain as much information as is readily available about two or three potential
options (including the status quo). Evaluate the options using a common set of
criteria and identify your preferred option.

References and further reading

Bailey, D. (2002) *The NHS Budget Holder's Survival Guide*. London: Royal Society of
Medicine Press.

Bean, J. and Hussey, L. (1997a) *Business Planning in the Public Sector*. London: HB
Publications.

Bean, J. and Hussey, L. (1997b) *Finance for Non Financial Public Sector Managers*.
London: HB Publications.

Berwick, D. (1996) A primer on leading the improvement of systems. *British Medical
Journal*, 312: 619.

Brambleby, P. (1995) A survivor's guide to programme budgeting. *Health Policy*, 33(2):
127–45.

Calpin-Davies, P. (1998) A comprehensive business planning approach applied to
healthcare. *Nursing Standard*, 12(46): 35–41.

Currie, G. (1999) The influence of middle managers in the business planning process:
a case study in the UK NHS. *British Journal of Management*, 10(2): 141.

Dye, J. (2002) Business planning: a template for success. *Clinical Leadership and Management Review*, 16(1): 39–43.

Eagar, K., Grant, P. and Lin, V. (2002) *Health Planning: Australian Perspectives*. London:
Allen and Unwin.

Finkler, S. (2005) Cost containment. In A. Kovner and J. Knickman (eds) *Health Care
Delivery in the United States*, 8th edn. New York: Springer.

Finkler, S.A. and Kovner, C.T. (2000). *Financial Management for Nurse Managers and
Executives*, 2nd edn. Philadelphia, PA: W.B. Saunders.

Finkler, S. and Ward, D. (1999) *Cost Accounting for Health Care Organisations: Concepts and Applications*, 2nd edn. New York: Aspen.

Harrison, J., Thompson, D., Flanagan, H. and Tonks, P. (1994) Beyond the business plan. *Journal of Health, Organisation and Management*, 8(1): 38–45.

Jacobs, K. (1998) Costing healthcare: a study of the introduction of cost and budget reports into a GP association. *Management Accounting Research*, 9(1): 55–70.

Jacobs, R. and Dawson, D. (2003) Hospital efficiency targets. *Health Economics*, 12: 669–84.

Kaplan, R. and Norton, D. (1992) The balanced scorecard: measures that drive performance. *Harvard Business Review on Measuring Corporate Performance*, 70(1): 71–9.

Mitton, C. and Donaldson, C. (2004) Health care priority setting: principles, practice and challenges. *Cost Effectiveness and Resource Allocation*, 2(3). doi:10.1186/1478-7547-2-3.

Moullin, M. (2002) *Delivering Excellence in Health and Social Care: Quality Excellence and Performance Measurement*. Maidenhead: Open University Press.

Piggot, C.S. (1996) *Business Planning for NHS Management*. London: Kogan Page.

Puffit, R. (1993) *Business Planning and Marketing: A Guide for the Local Government Cost Centre Manager*. London: Longman.

Ratcliffe, J., Donaldson, C. and Macphee, S. (1996) Programme budgeting and marginal analysis: a case study of maternity services. *Journal of Public Health Medicine*, 18(2): 175–82.

Thompson, D. (1996) Business planning in Hong Kong hospitals: the emergence of a seamless health care management process. *Health Services Management Research*, 9(3): 192–207.

Twaddle, S. and Walker, A. (1995) Programme budgeting and marginal analysis – application within programmes to assist purchasing in Greater Glasgow Health Board. *Health Policy*, 33(2): 91–105.

Worthern, J.C. (1992) Business planning: who, what, when, where, why and how. *Top Health Care Finance*, 18(3): 1–8.

Websites and resources

Health Care Financial Management Association: http://www.hfma.org.uk/.
World Bank health, population and nutrition: http://www.worldbank.org/hnp.
World Health Organization healthcare financing:
    http://www.who.int/health_financing/en/.

Managing people

Valerie Iles

Introduction

M anaging people is where healthcare management goes right or wrong. Whatever the nature of the healthcare system, and however much one applies the concepts described in the other chapters, if a manager is not able to work with and through other people, they will not be successful in delivering the kind of healthcare to which they aspire.

Managing people is a very personally engaging matter. It is not something a manager can do from behind a closed office door, it involves getting to know the people you are managing and finding ways of helping them to flourish in their healthcare role. At heart, it is about helping people to use their talents in pursuit of things both you and they, and the organization in which you are working, believe are valuable. In general, for people to choose to use their talent and energy in this way they have to *want* to (or at least see the need to), and they also need to feel *able* to do this.

More than this, they need to keep refreshing and renewing their sense of purpose, so that they can continue to be creative, reflective, enthusiastic and ambitious in pursuit of that purpose, and do not become complacent in their thinking and practice.

Managing people is not therefore a science, it is more of an art, and it requires judgement as much as evidence, and practical wisdom as much as theory. The style of this chapter reflects that difference, for it too is active, personal, and based on experience and observation as much as theory and evidence. It will give you ideas and encouragement and leave the rest to you. The practical ideas presented in this chapter are the result of nearly 30 years of development work carried out by the author with individuals and organizations in healthcare, and drawing on theory from a broad range of sources.

Helping people to flourish involves enabling and challenging

As humans, we are a complex mix of complacency and striving, of altruism and self-interest. So if we are to flourish, we all need to be supported and enabled in our altruistic creativity and endeavour, while also being challenged out of our self-interested behaviours and complacent attitudes. So when we are managing others we need to support and enable them and also to challenge them. This is a point worth stressing: with few exceptions, if you are not supporting, enabling and challenging, then you are not managing. Similarly if you are not being supported, enabled and challenged, you are not realizing your potential. So this chapter is about supporting, enabling and challenging the people you are likely to be managing in healthcare.

Three basic rules for managing people

Whenever you are managing people, or indeed whenever you are relying on them, whether you manage them or not, there are three rules to keep in mind:

1 Agree with them what it is they are expected to achieve.
2 Ensure you are both confident they have the skills and resources to be able to do it.
3 Give them ongoing feedback about whether they are achieving it.

Simple to articulate, these rules are nevertheless hard to implement. In part, this is because they must be tailored to the individual and the setting. Thus when dealing with someone who likes a lot of detail and is perhaps in a well-defined role, you could implement the first rule in the course of several rich and detailed conversations and probably reach agreement on a number of specific outcomes. Where the field is new and the individual involved is a 'big picture' thinker, the conversations you would have would again be rich but they would be exploratory and the outcomes you agree might include a degree of fuzziness that would be inappropriate elsewhere. Similarly you would observe the three rules differently with someone carrying out a job as a cleaner or gardener than with a chief executive of a large organization. The time horizons, the degree of detail, and the ways in which you ascertained how well they were performing – all would be different, although the principles would be the same.

Ensuring that people have the skills and resources to achieve what is expected of them is not as easy as asking them or looking at their references. You will need to observe them in action and observe the results of their work. Where they themselves are managing people as part of their role, those results will include how much their staff are being supported, enabled and challenged, and how they are flourishing. This is not the sort of thing that can be ascertained by sitting behind a desk, it requires active engagement with people and processes and practices in ways that have to be devised according to the setting.

The third rule, giving feedback, is again something that needs to be done face to face and on an ongoing basis. The feedback must be genuine (i.e. you must mean it) and include enough detail for the other person to believe it is genuine. So, for example, it would not be enough to say something like 'you seem to be settling in well' or 'you are a good member of the team'. To be credible, it needs to give examples of specific incidents: 'the report you wrote on . . . was very helpful', 'I particularly liked the point you made about . . .'; or 'I thought you handled Mrs J's concerns very sensitively.'

When you have criticisms of your colleague's work and you want them to make changes to the way they are doing something,[1] it is often helpful to give some positive feedback along with the negative, and at the same level of detail – preferably with about twice as much positive as negative content to the conversation. There are many reasons for this, for not only does it help you keep things in perspective, but it also makes it much easier for the recipient to hear the criticisms you are raising or exploring. Giving negative feedback needs careful preparation on your part if it is to be effective. You will want to prepare what it is you are going to say, and it will also be important to prepare yourself emotionally for the conversation. It is often helpful to remember that what you are aiming for is that the other person leaves the conversation feeling that they *want* to make changes and that they feel confident in their *ability* to do so.

Here is an example of giving feedback:

> I thought what you said at the team meeting on Monday was very helpful. The points you made about X, Y and Z helped us all to see the situation rather differently and we made a better decision as a result of them. Thank you.
>
> When Jane gave you some feedback from the patient experience surveys at the Clinical Governance meeting yesterday I felt you brushed it away rather than listening to it and taking it on board. I was disappointed because I thought it was important and I know you care very much about your service. Could you have another look at it? And perhaps think about whether you were a bit off-hand in the meeting?
>
> You've demonstrated many times, not least in the meeting on Monday, that you really want to ensure the patients feel warmly welcomed so I'm sure you will want to.

Simple purposeful conversations

Observing the three rules set out above is an ongoing process that can start at any time. They are very valuable when someone is new in post, and are equally appropriate if you have been working together for some time. Using the rules is most effective when it takes the form of frequent conversations in a variety of settings: in the corridor, the coffee room, informally at a work station or more formally at a pre-arranged time and place. While appraisal systems are important, they are not a substitute for this day-to-day exchange of information and regard.

Over time, the conversations should include three viewpoints: the enthusiasms, concerns, interests and ambitions of both of you, and the needs and constraints of the organization in which you are working. As the manager, you will have ambitions for the service and you have the right to express those ambitions. The person you manage will also have interests, enthusiasms and ambitions for the service or for parts of it, and a discussion between you that encompasses both sets of views will be motivating and creative. The organizational setting in which you are working may present constraints or additional requirements and it is important that these receive enough attention, yet do not become the *focus* of every discussion, merely a context.

Here is an example of a three-viewpoint conversation:

'Sharon, I noticed when I was on the ward yesterday that it took a long time for the patient alarm bell to be switched off – are you and your team having any problems responding to these?'

'Yesterday! We were so busy yesterday morning, everyone was completely involved in something else: drug round, stripping and changing the beds (it's really important we get that done by mid-morning or we're trying to catch up with ourselves all day), we just can't be everywhere at once. We did get to them as quickly as we could.'

'I can see all those things are important and it's good to know you are really on top of things like changing the beds, and I know how important that is for you. What's most important for me is that patients have confidence in us and in their care here, and the orderliness of the ward certainly contributes to that. If they ring the call bell and no-one comes, it jeopardizes that so badly, so that's the reason I think it's so important to answer those very promptly – whatever else is going on. How can we meet both of our agendas do you think? After all we both care about both of them, they are both important.'

'Another healthcare assistant in the mornings would make all the difference.'

'If that isn't in the budget, then that just isn't possible. And actually when I last looked at the figures the staffing levels here were pretty compatible with those of similar wards in other hospitals. Don't you find that when you talk to your colleagues? Ward G have found that it works well if they nominate one of the team to respond to all the call buttons, leaving the others to carry on with what they were doing and helping out when they aren't needed by patients. How about trying that out here?'

'Well, Ward G is very different from ours but I suppose we could try it out. Or I heard someone talking about a system called something like 'hourly rounding' where every patient on the ward is visited by a nurse every hour. They said it worked really well (I'm not sure I believe it but we could try it out). Apparently it led to much calmer wards and almost no use of the call buttons.'

'Well, either of those sound like a good way forward, how will you get started? If it helps, I could do a web search of this hourly rounding and email you some links – perhaps in time for your team meeting on Thursday? Can we agree that you'll make this a priority and that we'll talk about it again in a couple of weeks when you've had a chance to try out the nominated person idea, and to find out more about the other?'

The person with whom you are conversing will, naturally, have a different personality from your own and you will find the dialogue more productive if you choose your words and arguments so they are most likely to be able to hear them and not reject them. There are a number of ways of clustering personalities into different types and of describing the kinds of arguments and of behaviours the different types prefer, and

---

Box 23.1: *Using a Belbin team roles analysis with a team*

For example, if you used a Belbin team roles analysis with your own team, once the members know who has preferences for taking on the roles of shaper, implementer, monitor/evaluator, etc., then when they behave to that type, you can reflect this back to them: 'That's the shaper in you again, pushing for a solution before we've considered how people are going to feel about this! Shall we ask our "team worker" to comment on that?'

Or 'Don't worry Sam, that's just Mo being a Monitor Evaluator again – subjecting the idea to criticism before he commits. You know he'll support you all the way once he's convinced.'

It needs to be handled lightly and with care, but can be very valuable in preventing things said in meetings from being taken personally.

---

many of these are useful. Some of the most common ones are the Myers-Briggs Type Indicator, 16 PF, or simpler ones such as Belbin's team roles (see Box 23.1), or Honey and Mumford's Learning Styles. Whichever you choose, it is worth using the personality analysis tool to think ahead about how you yourself are going to behave and talk and what you are going to say. You can use the tool and its explanatory notes again once the meeting is over to reflect on how effective your approach was and what you might do differently another time.

Simple hard versus complicated easy

We have considered three rules and three perspectives and the need to use these frequently and in a range of settings, taking into account the personality of the people involved. That sounds simple, and indeed it is simple – simple but hard. Hard because it will require you to be: thoughtful in your discussion of what it is they are to achieve; perceptive and empathetic in your observation of how they are approaching things; and courageous when you have to give them feedback they may not enjoy hearing. We are all easily tempted to move from these 'simple hard' ways of managing into the 'complicated easy'.

The 'complicated easy' are activities that require us to use our brains but not much else. They include things like writing plans or strategies, and undertaking analyses. For people who are intellectually able, the lure of the 'complicated easy' is very great. On the other hand, the 'simple hard' will sound dull (no intellectually satisfying 'aha' moments) and will call upon other aspects such as our integrity, wisdom and courage. So it will feel hard and can also feel unsatisfying for we will not really feel we are getting it 'right', only that we are doing it better than we used to. However, keeping focused on the 'simple hard' will keep energy within a system, whereas the 'complicated easy' often drains it away.

Imagine, for a moment, that you were banned from using the words communication, communicating, communicate, and yet you wanted to discuss how you would implement a particular new policy. You would have to think about things such as:

- Who needs to hear what, from whom?
- Who needs to say what to whom?
- Who needs to ask what, of whom?
- Who needs to discuss what, with whom?

These are all 'simple hard' activities. The actions themselves and the energy around them feel quite different from that of 'developing and implementing a communication strategy', which is the complicated easy way of approaching it. You will probably want to jot down these 'simple hard' actions (who you are going to ask what, what you need to find out from whom, who you need to tell that something is happening, etc.). You can then call this your communication strategy, but it will look and feel different from the paper you would have produced if you had tackled the task the other way round.

What do we mean by care?

When we are managing people involved in healthcare, it is helpful to be clear about what we mean by, and it is not discussed in management courses as often as might be expected.

In the *Road Less Travelled*, M. Scott Peck (1990) defined love as 'the will to extend one's self for the purpose of nurturing one's own or another's [personal] growth'.[2] Furthermore, he suggested that 'If an act is not one of work or of courage then it is not an act of love. There are no exceptions.' One way of thinking about care is as a 'thinner', or a more widely disseminated form of love, and in that case we could use a similar definition for care: care is the will to engage in acts of work and/or courage in order to nurture personal growth.

David Seedhouse, a philosopher who has observed and considered issues of health and healthcare for many years, suggests, in his book *Liberating Medicine* that

> any genuine theory of health will be concerned to identify one or more human potentials which might develop, but which are presently or likely to be blocked. Health work, however it is defined, will seek first to discover and then prevent or remove obstacles to the achievement of human potential.
>
> (1991: 48)

This suggests that we could see 'personal growth' and 'health' in the same terms – progress towards the achievement of potentials, and thus that care is about the overcoming obstacles to the achievement of those potentials.

Thus, combining these definitions, we could say that healthcare involves acts of work and/or courage undertaken with the intention of enabling the potential of patients. Using an Aristotelian concept, we could also frame this as acts of work and courage that enable or promote flourishing.

These definitions are valuable when you want to enquire of yourself or of the people you are managing: 'Are we caring?' or 'Are we caring enough?' You can think of particular patients and ask yourself or others 'were we courageous enough?', 'Did we put in enough work?', 'Were we focused on helping them to flourish?'

In just the same way that the three rules for managing people apply everywhere but need to be tailored to the setting, so these definitions of care need to be discussed, interpreted and articulated differently depending on the care setting. Occasions to do so include the simple purposeful conversations described above.

If our healthcare professionals are to be able to engage in acts of courage on behalf of patients, then they themselves need to feel they are cared about and encouraged to flourish. One of the most important aspects of managing people is therefore caring about them – engaging in acts of work and courage that enable them to flourish in the service of others. Just as we can ask questions about whether we cared enough for a particular patient, so we can ask whether we cared enough for a particular member of staff. We can ask ourselves: 'Was I courageous enough to challenge them about that area where they really need to develop?' and 'Did I put enough work into observing how they … to form a view about how what help they may need or what opportunity they might value?'

Managing teams

In healthcare, many of the people we manage work in teams. Sometimes we manage the team as a whole, sometimes not. What is it that makes a group of people a team? Usually, when people are asked this question, they will answer 'a shared goal' or 'shared values', but in many healthcare teams it is difficult to define a goal that is genuinely important to all the members – unless we resort to such a high level of abstraction (e.g. 'good patient care' or 'putting the patient at the centre of care') that it is akin to what we often refer to as 'motherhood and apple pie'. Similarly, values that are shared can often only be described at such a generic level that they do not drive behaviour on a day-to-day basis.

Teams we work with and manage in healthcare tend to be characterized by interdependency – I can only achieve my goals if you achieve yours, and the way I achieve my goals must not conflict with the way in which you achieve yours. Thus when you are working with teams, and want to improve their performance, it is often more productive to discuss what these interdependencies are than to try and articulate team vision and values – at least to start with. Once you have got people discussing with each other what each truly cares about, you may find that they volunteer views on values and vision. If, however, you start with values and vision, you can easily end up with a list of platitudes and a feeling that time has been wasted.

Since you are relying on the team and the members are relying on each other, the three rules need to be observed here too:

1 Agree with the team (as a whole) what it is they are expected to achieve.
2 Ensure that both you and they (as a team) are confident they have the skills and resources to be able to achieve it
3 Be sure that they receive feedback (as a team) on whether they are doing so. You will also need to ensure that team members are relying on each other do the same.

The different personalities you find within any team are almost bound to cause friction from time to time, so another of your roles when managing a team may be to defuse or avoid tensions by educating team members on personality types and the kind of behaviours and preferences associated with them, in the same way as discussed above. This can give a team a vocabulary for dealing with points of tension and helps individuals to take disputes less personally.

Designing roles and teams

It was Frederick Herzberg who said, 'If you want people motivated to do a good job, give them a good job to do' (Herzberg 1959) and this is an important point to bear in mind when we are designing the roles we ask people to undertake. It is just as important when we are designing the teams within which people work.

There are a lot of unhealthy (less than whole) roles and teams around. The symptoms of this lack of wholeness include:

- people not getting a sense of meaning and purpose from their work;
- people having to change their sense of who they are when they come to work;
- people not believing in the organization's goals;
- people feeling that their physical health is affected by work.

This kind of 'un-whole' work is detrimental for everyone involved: the patients, staff, management, and others. Finding ways of making work whole and healthy in large organizations that have significant amounts of complexity and specialization is far from easy, especially given the need to account for performance.

If that is 'un-whole' work, what is its opposite? It is called whole work.[3] Whole work can be described as 'people working together in a multi-skilled, human-scale teams, responsible for something significant and purposeful, owning the whole set of tasks related to achieving that and empowered to plan that work, deliver it, and to "evaluate" how they are performing it.' This is a rich description and each of its terms deserves more attention than can be given here. Let us, however, illuminate the term 'evaluating'. This can be defined as 'bringing to full value that which was conceived', so in this context it includes an element of reviewing where we are now in relation to the idea or plan we started with, and what needs to be done to remedy any gap. We might also think of this as 'learning to do it better next time'.

The principles of whole work organization design involve:[4]

- mapping the primary work flow, which might be a flow that is informational, physical, mental, social or emotional – or, in reality, a mixture of all of these. In health organizations this is often a whole person view of the patient pathway;
- identifying the purposeful, transformational, significant events on which to base the different teams. These events usually involves a transformation in the patient's (perceived) state. For example, in healthcare, these might be based on prevention, diagnosis, treatment or recovery;

- for each team in turn, identifying all the tasks that are closely associated with achieving their transformational significant event, and ensure they have the skills and support they need to these;
- making sure each team is of a 'human scale' so that team members can identify and relate to each other;
- empowering the team to plan its work, deliver it and 'evaluate' it;
- ensuring that the team has appropriate leadership, pulling it together and linking it with the wider organization;
- setting them appropriate, simple performance measures that relate closely to achieving the significant event.

It has been found within healthcare organizations, with now numerous case studies (see Box 23.2), that by following these simple principles, whole work can be designed for

---

Box 23.2: *Case studies*

- **Maternity services:** A whole system review of maternity services in a district in New Zealand began with the simple (but hard!) questioning of what were the relevant significant events. This led local clinical leaders to realize that they had insufficiently recognized the importance of post-natal care – the core transformational significant event is from 'new mother [and father] with a new baby' to 'coping parent(s)' – and to value the key role healthcare assistants were actually playing in supporting new mothers. They also realized that creating a true 'whole work team' for elective and emergency caesarean sections gave an opportunity for the much more productive deployment of theatre staff.

- **Older people's health and social care services:** On a much larger scale, the application of thinking around significant events has been used to develop a person-centred health and social care pathway model for older people's care in England. This has been used to map current resources across councils and NHS services in Essex and, supported by a best practice review, has enabled a coordinated and aligned improvement programme to be developed across councils and health commissioners and to be embedded in local NHS efficiency plans.

- **Urology ward:** A series of apparently very competent ward managers struggled to manage a busy 35-bedded urology ward – things always felt chaotic and patient experiences were sometimes compromised while the budget was not controlled. The decision was taken to change the ward manager (again) but this time triggered by some minor building work, the ward was split into two smaller wards, each with their own leader and team. Much to the surprise of the local management, the two new mini-wards were both much calmer and more effective, and costs even fell overall. Serendipitously, the changes created two whole work teams of a much more appropriate human scale to the large and effectively unmanageable 35-bedded single ward team.

teams that is motivating, empowering and healthy. This is good for everyone concerned. If a large, complex organization can be built up from a network of these whole work teams, the organization is found to have a clear and purposeful structure that makes sense to people, delivers better outcomes for patients and in which people enjoy their work more.

Managing high status professionals

We established at the beginning of this chapter that managing people involves support-ing, enabling and challenging them. In healthcare we run into a specific difficulty: the status in which different groups of healthcare professionals are held by society. Support-ing, enabling and challenging high status individuals and groups can be problematic. We next consider how status is awarded, and how one can ensure it is used wisely and well.

The nature of status

Status is valuable, for otherwise it would not have evolved and persisted. It is accorded by society and allows people with status to be able, in the interests of society, to withstand pressure from people of lower status to do things in ways they deem not to benefit society. In other words, it confers a degree of professional autonomy. We can see it in action whenever newspapers support views of doctors over those of managers, or lawyers over those of administrators. When used wisely, status can be an important safeguard, enabling us to draw on professional wisdom and expertise. It can, however, be misused and then it may skew decisions so that they are not taken in the interests of all but only those of a few.

Status used wisely has two characteristics: it draws on the experience, expertise, and specialist knowledge base that is the reason the status has been awarded; and it is used in the service of society or its members. So when a consultant surgeon argues for a particular practice in theatre, having thought clearly and deeply about alternatives, consulted others involved and decided that this is the way the best outcomes will be achieved for patients, then we are wise to listen to her or him carefully, and perhaps defer to their judgement. When the same surgeon argues for a particular car parking scheme and especially if it is a scheme that makes life easier for him or her at the expense of others, then we should make sure that view is heard no more loudly than the views of everyone else involved. When engaging with people of high status (or when engaging *as* a person of high status), being clear about when it is wise to defer and when to insist is important for it not only makes for better decisions but happier professionals and service users.

It is worth knowing which groups are accorded higher status than others, and this is the field of sociologists. There are many theories about status but the one that seems to have most explanatory and predictive value (i.e. you can use it to work out in advance who, in a group of different healthcare professionals in a room will have higher and lower status) is that of Jamous and Pelouille (1970). They suggest that it depends on what they call the 'technicality indeterminacy ratio'. They say that if the knowledge base of your profession or specialty is highly technical and definitive and you can give clear answers to questions (e.g. yes/no/3.95 per cent), then you are likely to hold higher status than a profession or specialty that gives more contingent answers (e.g. it depends, it could be this or that, let's try it and see). However, if your knowledge base is too technical, you could be replaced by a computer protocol or an algorithm, so your status will be protected if your knowledge needs to be interpreted differently in each of the cases you consider.

This is unlikely to be the final word on the nature of status and there will be other ways of thinking about it, but using it should help the manager to think ahead about what the behavioural dynamics are likely to be within a particular group, and hence how they are going to deal with them. For example, what are the kind of issues on which you are likely to defer to professional judgement, and when will you politely reframe a statement made by a high status individual into an indication of preference that will sit alongside other preferences?

Status and productivity

When we are thinking about managing, enabling and challenging others, we have to recognize that it is not enough for them to be working on goals that are agreed between you, but that they are working towards them in ways that do not incur waste – of time or other resources. In other words, we are concerned about their 'productivity', and we are all under pressure to increase the productivity of healthcare, for the benefit of all.

In other industries four ways of increasing productivity are typically brought into play:

1 **Cuts** – unnecessary expenditure is cut and in some cases customers that cannot be served profitably are discarded.

2 **Rationalization** – production from several facilities is rationalized into a single site, realizing all possible synergy. In healthcare this is usually called reconfiguration.

3 **Redesign** – individuals and teams work together to redesign service flows and processes so that they are as efficient and customer-focused as possible.

4 **Reflection** – individuals and teams reflect on their own performance on an ongoing basis to see how it can be improved.

In other industries, all four ways of increasing productivity can be (and are) used because staff can be incentivized and required to engage in all four, in other words, they are part of a *connected* hierarchy. In healthcare, because of the status issues and professional autonomy described above, we face instead what Henry Mintzberg (1996) describes as a *disconnected* hierarchy.

It is a feature of a disconnected hierarchy that staff cannot be *required* to engage in attempts to increase productivity and *incentivizing* them to do so may prove difficult since nearly all of the incentives (the things professionals care enough about to affect their performance) are not in the gift of managers. The regard of professional peers, for example, publications and citations in peer-reviewed journals, and the respect of and gratitude from patients will typically matter more to clinicians than approval from managers. Thus in a disconnected hierarchy, productivity is usually pursued by means of only the first two options (cuts and rationalization). This is a great disadvantage because on their own, these will produce only one-off savings – for ongoing productivity improvements, the other two forms are necessary.

For example, if health service managers respond to the current international financial crisis by imposing cuts and reconfigurations, this will result in a system of inefficient and rationed services. To ensure that health funds are used optimally, managers should, instead, focus on finding ways of engaging clinicians in the redesign of services and in reflecting on the nature of care they themselves and their teams are providing.

Encouraging high status groups to reflect on the wider impact of their individual practice

While it is difficult to require professionals to reflect on their own practice and the shape of the service of which they are a part, they can be encouraged to do so in a number of ways, of which the following are only a few. Indeed, we can imagine that while one or two of these methods are helpful, if they became embedded in 'the way we do things round here', their impact would be very much greater.

Information

Information about how their practice and their service compares with that of others, or with their own practice/service over time, allows practitioners to reach their own decisions about what aspects of their practice they could usefully change. The information needs to be credible (based on robust and relevant data) and presented in a way that is meaningful to those concerned (analysed in terms of activity clusters at the right level of detail/aggregation). It is, however, important not to wait until data are perfect before they are presented – as long as they are 'good enough', the more the data are presented and discussed the better they will get.

Peer example

While *pressure* from peers can be resisted, opportunities to discover that the practice of peers and the design of their services are different and exploring the implications of those differences, can lead to very constructive reflections on both of these. Engaging in this process of discovery is likely, however, to be resisted unless one of the two following features below is present.

Managers who are genuinely concerned about the care that is being offered and who want to help clinicians improve that care

When managers are concerned first and foremost about care and only second about their organizations (as the best means of offering good care), and demonstrate that commitment by their interest in and creative and timely response to suggestions about service improvements, then their credibility will allow them to draw attention to some of the opportunities described above.

This enthusiasm for care should not deter them from stating clearly financial and other realities, and they must demonstrate their competence at dealing with managerial processes. However, they must be driven first by concern for effective care, and definitely not by a primary concern for balancing books which allows services to suffer in order to achieve it.

Thought leaders who are from a high status group who do not impose their own prescriptions for action but hold high expectations of the performance of others

Similarly the credibility of these individuals allows them to provide the challenges that encourage mature reflection rather than defensive resistance. Imposing a prescription for action is a sign of low expectations of those required to enact it. Expressing a genuine belief that others will choose to behave in a particular (professional) way is very different.

Organizational stewardship

Where high status clinicians are allowed and encouraged to form some kind of 'clinical senate' whose brief is to shape the organization's strategy, ensure the consultant body understands the internal and external pressures that make it the best way forward, and challenge behaviours and practices that are not consistent with that direction, then results can be impressive.

First-hand stories from patients and from other healthcare professionals

While second- or third-hand stories and written complaints can be dismissed and the motives of their authors impugned, first-hand stories are a different matter. These can reflect the experiences of patients or those of other healthcare professionals. It is often one of the most valuable outcomes of discussions about care pathways, as long as the highest status people are in the room to hear the stories, and as long as the discussions are well facilitated so they consist of personal narratives (this is what I experienced) rather than accusation and blame (this is what you did). Methods for eliciting such views and experiences are explored in more detail in Chapter 18 (user and public involvement).

Purposeful conversation

Performance and behaviour are shaped on a day-by-day basis, by the response of others around us to what we do and how we do it. If we want to influence these on the part of our clinicians then we have to shape it on that day-by-day basis by talking with them, by noticing what they are doing and encouraging some actions and discouraging others. This ongoing shaping is called management. It tends to go out of the window when we introduce something called performance management, which requires 'tough' conversations by people who are 'hard' enough to instigate them. Management requires, instead, conversations that are purposeful which can be undertaken by people who possess ordinary levels of niceness.

Another way of thinking about this is that good management aims to increase the capacity of the organization to care, that is, for acts of work and courage. On the other hand, performance management tends to reduce this for it requires acts of work from people, expecting them to look upwards for direction rather than downwards for inspiration and guidance (from the actual experiences of users). Instead of encouraging acts of work and courage focused on patients and frontline staff, performance management requires reports to be written and meetings attended and humiliating 'telling offs' to be endured. The observation of this author is that this leads to the overall capacity for care at the front line being reduced.

TABLE 23.1 Two different ways of envisaging and delivering care

Transactional care	Covenantal care
Healthcare in the market economy – patient as consumer, professional as provider	*Healthcare with elements of the gift economy – patient and professional are in covenantal relationship*
Patient is cared for	Patient is cared about as well as for
Professionals are seen as givers (or suppliers) of services	Professionals recognize that in their encounters with patients they give *and* receive
Focus on calculation and counting – this can be seen as objective	Focus on thoughtful, purposeful judgement – this is necessarily subjective but incorporates objective measures and evidence
Predetermined protocols	Emergent creativity which can include the use of protocols
Discourse and hyperactivity	Wisdom and silence in addition to discourse and action
Explicit knowledge	Tacit knowledge as well as explicit knowledge
Reflection on facts and figures	Reflection on feelings and ethics as well
Focus on efficiency and effectiveness	Focus on the quality of the moment as well
Dealing with the presenting problem	Keeping in mind the meaning of the encounter – for both parties while addressing the presenting problem
Competence is what is called for on the part of the professional	The humanity of the professional is also called upon
Individuals have a relationship with the state and with the market	Individuals have a relationship with the community and with wider society
Good policy ideas MUST degenerate as they are translated at every level of the system into a series of measurable, performance manageable actions and objectives. The focus here is on being able to demonstrate the policy has been implemented.	Policy ideas can stay rich and be added to creatively, so that solutions are responsive, humane, practical, flexible, and adaptable. Here the focus is on solving problems.

Engaging with what matters to people

Whenever we are managing others, we do well to remember the human desire to be contributing to something significant. Thus we need to manage people in a way that speaks to their whole nature (some selfish interests, also altruism, and the desire to make a significant contribution). If we assume healthcare is simply a set of auditable transactions in a market place and manage accordingly, we will get the kind of dynamics listed in the left hand column of the Table 23.1.

If, however, we allow that care often also involves elements of a gift economy where there is a relationship between the giver and recipient of care that could be described as a 'covenant', then we will manage differently. In that case, we will still aim for care that encompasses the transactional (left-hand column) but also for more, namely care that also has the dynamics listed in the right-hand column of Table 23.1.

It is important not to see the care described in the left-hand column as bad and that on the right as good, nor to see the left-hand column as efficient and the right-hand column as wasteful. Rather, we can think of the factors in the left-hand column as the cherries and the care of the right-hand column as the cherry cake. Thus good transactional care will often be all that is needed and covenantal care always encompasses good transactional care but also includes more – a different attitude. It will not (often) require more time or financial resource, but it will call for more professionalism, and for more of the whole person who is offering that care, thus adding more meaning to the encounter.

There are a number of pervasive forces that encourage us all to make choices that lead to the behaviours of the left-hand column. They include:

- the anxiety experienced by patients, professionals, managers and policy-makers;
- the culture of audit now firmly established across the Western world;
- the dominance of a particular kind of management – the technocratic analyst rather than the practical humanist;
- the change in the role of politics from reconciling different interests in society for the good of all, to the rational administration of the market; and
- the digital revolution that has supported and accelerated the last three.

These forces have had many positive outcomes and we are unlikely to be able to challenge their existence. However, if we are aware of them and of the dangers they can pose in respect of pulling us towards the transactional care of the left-hand column instead of ensuring we aim also for the covenantal care of the right-hand column, then we can choose to respond in different ways. We can choose to give proper regard to transactional aspects of care while also engaging in the covenantal aspects when these are wanted or needed.

We have to caution against getting swept up in a culture of audit where we focus only on targets (whether process or outcome) and where there is a great danger that we lose sight of those other aspects of care. The elements in the left-hand column are essential, and we must deliver those (if we care about someone we will also care for them), but we must do so in ways that allow us (managers, professionals, patients) to be whole people.

Conclusion: caring about the people you manage

Managing people engages you as a whole person – it is active and personal. It is also about directing your energy, your thoughtfulness, and your courage towards that which you care about – and because of that you cannot manage well unless you do care. In other words, you need to care about what you are trying to achieve and about the people you are managing.

Care, as we saw above, can be defined as 'acts of work and courage in pursuit of human flourishing'. Since you will care about your service, your staff and yourself, you will be engaging in acts of work and courage to enable all of you to flourish.

Managing people (helping staff and their patients to flourish) is at once simple and hard. That means it will call upon your integrity, your empathy, your courage, and your judgement. In other words, it calls upon YOU. In managing others, you need to bring all of yourself to work, and not put on a mask as you enter the door, or leave parts of you (the softer nicer parts) at home. As you develop your skills in dealing with the 'simple hard' you will find ways of saying hard things in gentle ways, and you will be able to help people to hear the things that will challenge them into realizing their full potential. As you do, you will find that you yourself are expanding your awareness and abilities and coming much closer to realizing your own potential,

In summary, properly managing people in the service of patients and society should enable you to realize your potential. This will be simple, hard, exciting, frustrating and worthwhile. That is why this chapter matters!

Summary box

- Management is a highly personal activity that involves rich interactions with other people. It requires energy and courage as much as intellect. It takes place largely through frequent ongoing conversations. It is simple and hard even though there is pressure to focus on the complicated and easy.
- There are three rules for managing people, three perspectives to take into account, and *defining* care allows us to ensure that both clinicians and managers are able to care.
- Designing work teams on the principles of whole work enables care to be more productive as well as more satisfying.
- Recognizing when status is being used wisely and when inappropriately allows managers to defer or challenge accordingly.
- Ongoing improvements in productivity arise through redesign and reflection. Cuts and mergers yield only one-off savings. There are many effective ways of encouraging clinicians to reflect and redesign.
- Only if managers demonstrate their concern for the covenant of care will clinicians give sufficient attention to improving the transactions of care.
- Managing others involves acts of work and courage with the aim of enabling them to flourish in the service of others.

Self-test exercises

1 When you think of the people you are managing, would you say you are supporting, enabling and challenging them? *How* are you doing so?

2 Are you yourself being supported, enabled and challenged? Where can you find support and challenge if you do not find it from your line manager?

3 Think of one person you manage – or someone you rely on – and think about whether you are observing the 'three rules'. Have you had a face-to-face conversation with them to agree what it is they are expected to achieve? Are you noticing and finding out whether they have the skills and resources to be able to do that? Are you giving them frequent face-to-face feedback on how they are doing?

4 Do you know what their enthusiasms and interests and concerns are? What are their ambitions for the service they are offering? Do they know yours? Are both of you clear about the needs and constraints of your organization?

5 Have you ever used questionnaires to discover the Belbin's team roles or Honey and Mumford's learning styles or Myers-Briggs Type Indicator preferences of yourself and the people you manage? If so, do you use the insights gained from them on a daily basis? If not, who in your organization would be able to help you with those?

6 Notice how often during a day you use or hear the word 'communication'. For a day, whenever you do, try asking yourself (or others) Who needs to know what? Who needs to say what? Who needs to ask what? Notice whether that changes the level of energy that is focused on the problem.

7 If you are managing (or are part of) a team, does everyone in it know who relies on them and their work, and how? Do they use the three rules (agreeing expectations, etc.) with each other so that team members are confident in the value of each other's performance and the team works effectively as a team?

   If you are managing the team do you observe the three rules, and give them feedback as a team?

   Is the team, one in which everyone is contributing to a significant or transformational event? Is it small enough for members to know each other and recognize they are all part of the same team? Are the members taking part in planning, and evaluating the work the team as a whole is undertaking?

8 When you are about to take part in a discussion with individuals or groups who hold high societal status (which is different from organizational status), do you think in advance about how you will challenge them if they try to use their status inappropriately?

   Do you ensure that in meetings that include professionals of different status the views of the lower status groups are properly heard?

9 When you are thinking about how to make care resources go further, do you focus on cuts and mergers or on service redesign and individual reflection?

10 How many of the methods described for encouraging high status groups to reflect on their practice are you using and encouraging?

   How are you encouraging your clinical and managerial professionals to care about *both* good transactional and covenantal care? Do you need to demonstrate your interest in covenantal care for them to take more seriously initiatives to improve the transactions of care?

11 And most importantly of all: how are you caring about those you manage? What acts of work and courage are you engaging in today that will help them to flourish in the service of others? How does their ability to flourish support yours?

Notes

1 Note that the kind of feedback I am discussing here is that undertaken in the course of everyday management. Once there are concerns about performance that require

more specific attention, specialist advice should be sought from a human resources department or other source.

2 He actually used the word 'spiritual' but in a sense that is conveyed well by 'personal' as long as we think of personal in its widest sense – a flourishing sense! See Peck (1990: 81).

3 The idea of whole work stems from 'whole systems' thinking, including the writings and work of Christian Schumacher (1987).

4 For more background on how to apply this approach in health and social care, see www.tricordant.com.

References and further reading

Herzberg, F. (1959) *The Motivation to Work*. New York: John Wiley and Sons.

Iles, V. (2006) *Really Managing Health Care*, 2nd edn. Buckingham: Open University Press.

Iles, V. (2011) Why reforming the NHS doesn't work: the importance of understanding how good people offer bad care. Available at: http://www.reallylearning.com/.

Iles, V. and Cranfield, S. (2004) *Developing Change Management Skills*. Available at: http://www.sdo.nihr.ac.uk/files/adhoc/change-management-developing-skills.pdf.

Iles, V. and Sutherland, K. (2001) *Managing Change in the NHS: A Review of the Evidence*. Available at: http://www.sdo.nihr.ac.uk/files/adhoc/change-management-review.pdf.

Jamous, H. and Pelouille, B. (1970) Professions or self perpetuator systems: changes in the French university hospital system. In J. Jackson (ed.) *Professions and Professionalism*. Cambridge: Cambridge University Press.

Mintzberg, H. (1996) Cited by G. Best, in NHS managers: surfeit or shortage. *Health Director (Journal of the National Association of Health Authorities and Trusts)*, 25: 16, 17.

Peck, M.S. (1990) *The Road Less Travelled*. London: Arrow Books.

Schumacher, C. (1987) *To Live and Work*. New York: Christian Research.

Seedhouse, D. (1991) *Liberating Medicine*. Chichester: John Wiley and Sons.

Websites and resources

Information about the Belbin team analysis method: http://www.belbin.com/.

For information about the Honey and Mumford learning styles questionnaire: http://www.peterhoney.com/.

For an examination of the Myers Briggs approach to analyzing personality type – The Myers-Briggs Foundation: http://www.myersbriggs.org.

For more information about the work of Valerie Iles: http://www.reallylearning.com/.

For an exploration of 'whole work': www.tricordant.com.

For information about the 16 PF questionnaire: http://www.opp.eu.com

CHAPTER

24

Quality improvement in healthcare

Ruth Boaden

Introduction

Quality is a term widely used not only within healthcare but throughout society, with numerous references to the quality of care, commissioning, access to care, quality and payment systems, the regulation of quality of care and service user expectations of quality in this book alone. However, the study and development of quality are often hampered by lack of clarity of definition.

In the healthcare field, the dominance of the medical profession with its own perspective on quality means that 'quality has become a battleground on which professions compete for ownership and definition of quality' (Øvretveit 1997). The medical profession has traditionally 'owned' quality and used its own professional approaches to assuring and regulating it. The rise of quality improvement as something that involves more than the clinical professions has therefore led to 'the quality movement being equated with a change in power or a bid for power by managers within European health care systems' (Øvretveit 1997).

One early pioneer of healthcare quality was Donabedian (1966), whose research and writings were important foundation for other developments, although some would argue that healthcare quality has been an issue since Florence Nightingale's time (Stiles and Mick 1994). Definitions of quality in healthcare abound (Reeves and Bednar 1994), and as the concept has been formalized within the healthcare field, a suite of healthcare-related definitions and 'dimensions of quality' have developed (see Table 24.1).

Quality can be viewed from various perspectives, and while patients may not feel qualified to judge the technical quality of healthcare, 'they assess their healthcare by other dimensions which reflect what they personally value' (Kenagy et al. 1999). The concept of 'quality' outside healthcare was pioneered by Shewhart and his work on statistical process control (SPC) in the 1930s (Shewhart 1931), and the approaches of many of the quality 'gurus' were based on Shewhart's approaches. However, many academic fields of study have contributed to the study of quality, including services marketing, organization studies, human resource management and organizational behaviour. Recent developments into patient safety as one aspect of quality are also multidisciplinary in approach (Walshe and Boaden 2006).

TABLE 24.1 Definitions of healthcare quality

Donabedian (1987)	Maxwell (1984)	Langley et al. (1996)	Institute of Medicine and Committee on Quality Health Care in America (2001)
• Manner in which practitioner manages the personal interaction with the patient • Patient's own contribution to care • Amenities of the settings where care is provided • Facility in access to care • Social distribution of access • Social distribution of health improvements attributable to care	• Access to services • Relevance to need • Effectiveness • Equity • Social acceptability • Efficiency and economy	• Performance • Features • Time • Reliability • Durability • Uniformity • Consistency • Serviceability; • Aesthetics • Personal interaction • Flexibility • Harmlessness • Perceived quality • Usability	• Safety • Effectiveness • Patient-centredness • Timeliness • Efficiency • Equity

The term 'service improvement' appears to be increasingly used in place of 'quality improvement' – possibly because of the contested nature of the term 'quality' but also because of the wide range of approaches that may be used to change or improve services. Perhaps quality improvement is really organizational change (see Chapter 21), performance improvement (see Chapter 25), or change in the dimensions valued by those purchasing healthcare (see Chapter 18)?

There is no doubt that there is an increased focus on quality in all sectors, and particularly in healthcare. However, there is a wide variety of approaches that may be used to improve quality. While these may not be mutually exclusive, there is little guidance on which approaches may be appropriate in differing circumstances although there are two review publications that synthesize the various approaches, how and where they may be used and the supporting evidence (Boaden et al. 2008; Powell et al. 2009).

It has been suggested that a number of approaches may be needed: 'give attention to many different factors and use multiple strategies' (Grol et al. 2004), and these are developed from very differing perspectives on organizational and individual behaviour (summarized by Grol et al. 2004) (see Table 24.2). Table 24.2 could equally well be labelled 'approaches to service improvement' and the term 'quality' replaced by 'performance' since the same principles apply whatever terminology is used. This chapter, however, focuses on aspects of what is often termed 'quality' because of the distinct history and underpinning systematic approaches that characterize the area of quality improvement.

This chapter considers the development of quality improvement, by considering those who established and defined the field and its development in terms of scope to

TABLE 24.2 Approaches to quality improvement

Approaches to quality improvement may have a focus on changing:
- organizations
- professionals
- interactions between participants in the system

Quality may be controlled and improved by:
- self-regulation among professionals (see Chapter 25)
- external control, regulation and incentives (see Chapter 25)
- patient power, which may be exercised through market forces (see Chapter 18)
- reducing variation and waste in organizational processes (see later sections of this chapter)

Quality may be improved from:
- the top down (see later sections of this chapter)
- the bottom up (see later sections of this chapter)
- the outside in (see Chapter 25)

service organizations and healthcare, before outlining the underlying principles of the approaches to improvement, and the tools that support the various approaches. The chapter concludes with the challenges of service and quality improvement.

The development of quality improvement

This section describes the development of the quality improvement 'movement' in general, with reference throughout to where the approaches have been applied to healthcare. These improvement approaches have been targeted at improving organizations and interactions within them although some may also affect the interactions between individuals in the system.

The gurus

There are a number of key figures who have contributed to the development of quality improvement, often referred to as quality 'gurus' (Dale 2003).

- **W. E. Deming** was an American who first went to Japan in 1947 and developed a 14-point approach (Deming 1986) for his management philosophy for improving quality and changing organizational culture. He was also responsible for developing the concept of the Plan–Do–Check–Action (PDCA) cycle. It is argued that his ideas influenced the development of the field of strategic management both directly and indirectly (Vinzant and Vinzant 1999).

- **Joseph Juran** focused on the managerial aspects of implementing quality (Juran 1951). His approach can be summarized as: 'Quality, through a reduction in statistical variation, improves productivity and competitive position.' He promoted a trilogy of quality planning, quality control and quality improvement, and maintained that providing customer satisfaction must be the chief operating goal (Nielsen et al. 2004).

- **Philip Crosby** was an American management consultant whose philosophy is summarized as 'higher quality reduces costs and raises profit', and who defined quality as 'conformance to requirements'. He too had 14 steps to quality and his ideas were very appealing to both manufacturing and service organizations. He is best known for the concepts of 'do it right first time' and 'zero defects' and believed that management had to set the tone for quality within an organization.

- **Armand Feigenbaum** defined quality as a way of managing (rather than a series of technical projects) and the responsibility of everyone (Feigenbaum 1961). His major contribution was the categorization of quality costs into three: appraisal, prevention and failure, and his insistence that management and leadership are essential for quality improvement. His work has been described as relevant to healthcare (Berwick 1989).

There are both similarities and differences between these approaches and there is no clear overarching philosophy of quality improvement, although the key points are as follows (Bendell et al. 1995):

1 Management commitment and employee awareness are essential (Deming).
2 Actions need to be planned and prioritized (Juran).
3 Teamwork plays a vital part (Ishikawa who pioneered the quality circle concept) (Ishikawa 1979).
4 Tools and techniques are needed (e.g. seven quality control tools promoted by Ishikawa).
5 Management tools/approaches will also be needed (Feigenbaum).
6 Customer focus is needed (Deming 1986).

Nielsen et al. (2004) asked the question 'Can the gurus' concepts cure healthcare?' Although their focus was on the overall philosophy rather than the use of individual tools, they concluded:

- Crosby would emphasize the role of leadership in pursuing zero defects.
- Deming would emphasize transformation as he did in the fourteenth of his 14 points (1986) while being disappointed at the reactive behaviour of healthcare organizations and individuals with 'far too little pursuit of constant improvement' (Nielsen et al. 2004).
- Feigenbaum would focus on clearer identification of the customer and the application of evidence-based medicine.
- Juran's emphasis would be on building quality into processes from the start (what he termed 'quality planning').

Total quality management

A commonly used term for an overall organizational approach to quality improvement is 'total quality management' (TQM), whose common themes may be summarized (Berwick et al. 1992; Hackman and Wageman 1995) as follows:

- Organizational success depends on meeting customer needs, including internal customers.

TABLE 24.3 Principles of quality management

---

1 Productive work is accomplished through processes.

2 Sound customer–supplier relationships are absolutely necessary for sound quality management.

3 The main source of quality defects is problems in the process.

4 Poor quality is costly.

5 Understanding the variability of processes is a key to improving quality.

6 Quality control should focus on the most vital processes.

7 The modern approach to quality is thoroughly grounded in scientific and statistical thinking.

8 Total employee involvement is crucial.

9 New organizational structures can help achieve quality improvement.

10 Quality management employs three basic, closely interrelated activities: quality planning, quality control and quality improvement.

- Quality is an effect caused by the processes within the organization which are complex but understandable.
- Most human beings engaged in work are intrinsically motivated to try hard and do well.
- Simple statistical methods linked with careful data collection can yield powerful insights into the causes of problems within processes.

Just as the term 'quality' has a variety of meanings, there is a confusion of terminology in this area, with not only TQM used but also 'continuous quality improvement' (CQI; McLaughlin and Simpson 1999) and 'total quality improvement' (TQI; Iles and Sutherland 2001), although such terms appear to be interchangeable in practice. Another view with a specific healthcare focus is found in Berwick et al. (1990/2002) who describe the principles of 'quality management' (see Table 24.3).

These principles of quality management have been applied in the US healthcare system (see Box 24.1 and Table 24.4).

Widening the scope of quality improvement

Until the 1980s, most of the emphasis on quality improvement was in manufacturing industry, but then the field of 'service quality' developed (Groonroos 1984; Berry et al. 1985), with the widespread use of the SERVQUAL questionnaire (Parasuraman et al. 1988), as well as promotion of the concept of the 'moment of truth' and an emphasis on service recovery. Many of these concepts are applicable to the provision of healthcare as a service, with a recent publication by Leonard Berry (Berry and Seltman 2008) showing how the Mayo Clinic – an 'exceptional service organization' (Berry and Seltman 2008: 2) – have achieved 'sustainable service excellence and what drives it' (Berry and Seltman 2008: 2).

However, a tension between 'hard' (systems) approaches and 'soft' (people/culture) issues (Wilkinson 1992) has also developed, partly in response to the apparent 'failure' of quality improvement (whichever term was used) to achieve sustained improvements

> **Box 24.1:** *Influences on quality in healthcare: Institute for Health Improvement (IHI)*
>
> Established in 1991 as 'a not-for-profit organization driving the improvement of health by advancing the quality and value of health care . . . a reliable source of energy, knowledge, and support for a never-ending campaign to improve health care worldwide. The Institute helps accelerate change in health care by cultivating promising concepts for improving patient care and turning those ideas into action', IHI has had influence not only in the USA but also in the UK. Its work has developed since its establishment to educate, to encourage healthcare staff to work together in collaboratives, to redesign processes and now to promote a quality improvement 'movement'. The story of this 'movement' to pursue quality improvement in healthcare has now been documented (Kenney, 2008) and it is clear that the initial focus for this movement was IHI and its then president, Don Berwick. He has authored a number of books and articles on quality improvement, including *Curing Health Care* (Berwick et al. 1990) which was reissued in 2002 with a Preface reflecting on 'ten things we know now that we wish we had known then' (Table 24.4). These provide an interesting summary of the progress of thinking about quality improvement in healthcare over this period.

in organizational performance. Criticism of the quality improvement literature came from those who described it as 'an evangelical line that excludes traditions and empirical data that fail to confirm its faith' (Kerfoot and Knights 1995); a view that could be justified because of much of the prescriptive research labelled as 'quality' (Wilkinson and Willmott 1995). However, this led to research from the 1990s that offers additional perspectives on quality (Hackman and Wageman 1995; Webb 1995), whose findings are perhaps more applicable to the complex world of healthcare and in particular focus on individuals, their motivation, behaviour and interaction and the way in which this affects quality. The continued success of the Mayo Clinic is attributed to executing its strategy through people: 'the people of Mayo Clinic – the performers of the services – represent the crucial explanatory variable in the Clinic's sustained success' (Berry and Seltman 2008: 255). The same analysis identifies that attracting and retaining people, and having a culture that encourages the best efforts of people and fosters personal growth are the key elements in the quality of service.

Achievements in the area of quality improvement were increasingly the subject of national 'awards'. The Deming Application Prize (Japan) led to the development of the Malcolm Baldrige National Quality Award (the USA) and the European Foundation for Quality Management (EFQM) Award/Excellence Model (Europe), with its associated national and sector-specific derivatives. Quality was increasingly assessed by organizations themselves (self-assessment) as a means of improvement, and these models attempted to integrate the 'hard' and 'soft' factors, with the term 'quality' being replaced by 'excellence'. There is specific guidance for US organizations in healthcare wishing to apply for the Baldrige Award (Baldrige National Quality Program 2009) and the European Excellence award has a 'public sector' category.

TABLE 24.4 If only we had known then what we know now

Ten key lessons for quality improvement (Berwick et al. 1990/2002)	What we know now (Berwick et al. 1990/2002)
Quality improvement tools can work in healthcare	• Spending too much time analysing processes can slow the pace of change • Teams can enter the PDSA cycle in several places • Tools are important in their place, but not a very good entry point for improvement: 'Teams can unconsciously use the tools as a way to delay or avoid the discomfort of taking action'
Cross-functional teams are valuable in improving healthcare processes	• Getting action is more important than getting buy-in • The process owner concept from industry is helpful here
Improvement is a matter of changing the process, not blaming the people	• The shift of blame from individuals to processes is not 100 per cent • There are limits to a blame-free culture, but perhaps not to a process-minded culture
Data useful for quality improvement abound in healthcare	• Measurement is very difficult for healthcare, and healthcare is far behind • Balanced scorecards are helpful • SPC has enormous potential with 'hundreds of as-yet-untapped applications' • Medical records need modernizing to enable better public health data • IT is key
Quality improvement methods are fun to use	• There need to be consequences for not being involved in improvement (not improving should not be an option)
Costs of poor quality are high and savings are within reach	• Waste is pervasive in healthcare; improvement is the best way to save money
Involving doctors is difficult	• Balance is important • Doctors are not well prepared to lead people • Doctors can (and are) learning new skills to supplement their medical training, not to replace it
Training needs arise early	• Healthcare lacks a training infrastructure • The argument here refers to professional boundaries
Non-clinical processes draw early attention	• Clinical outcomes are critical • This is the 'core business' of healthcare and focus on them achieves buy-in from all health professionals
Healthcare organizations may need a broader definition of quality	• Definitions of quality in healthcare must include the whole patient experience – not just clinical outcomes and costs • The Institute of Medicine's six aims for improvement are cited here (2001)
In healthcare, as in industry, the fate of quality improvement is first of all in the hands of leaders	• The executive leader doesn't always have to be the driver of change • This is especially true at the start of improvement, but achieving system-level improvement does require senior commitment

Clinical approaches to improvement

There are some approaches to quality improvement which have been developed specifically within the clinical field. These include clinical governance, clinical guidelines and pathways and a number of approaches to reducing adverse events and focusing on patient safety, although these are not always exclusively clinical (Walshe and Boaden 2006).

Clinical governance can be defined as the 'action, the system or the manner of governing clinical affairs' (Lugon and Secker-Walker 1999) and is a specified statutory duty of all NHS organizations. It was developed as an overall approach as part of policy on quality in the NHS (DH 1998) and it has led to the establishment of formal audit programmes, increased focus on clinical effectiveness and the formal management of risk, among other things. It can be viewed as an overall quality improvement process, but one which focuses specifically on clinical issues while still highlighting the importance of organizational culture, individual behaviour and interaction and may itself use a range of techniques for improvement.

Clinical guidelines/pathways are structured, multidisciplinary plans of care designed to support the implementation of clinical guidelines and protocols, providing guidance about each stage of the management of a patient with a particular condition, including details of both process and outcome. They aim to improve continuity and coordination of care and enable more effective resource planning, as well as providing comparative data on many aspects of quality of care, and are increasingly being used in the UK as patient choice is introduced. They are claimed to reduce variation and improve outcomes (Middleton et al. 2001).

Patient safety is a vast area of study and practice that has developed at least in part from quality improvement (Walshe and Boaden 2006) and was perhaps first brought to light by a US study in the late 1980s (Harvard Medical Practice Study 1990), since replicated in Australia, New Zealand, the United Kingdom and elsewhere, which demonstrated the scale and extent of the problems of patient safety. However, it was not until the late 1990s that an influential report (Institute of Medicine and Committee on Quality Health Care in America 2001) led to the problems of patient safety being taken seriously. Policy-makers across the world have responded with a huge range of initiatives intended to tackle these challenges.

The study of patient safety draws on a range of disciplines, including psychology, sociology, clinical epidemiology, quality management, technology and informatics, and the law, bringing different and complementary theoretical frameworks and conceptual understandings of patient safety problems, leading to a range of methods for improvement. Patient safety cannot be aligned with any one discipline, research design or method of measurement, and nor can quality improvement; understanding and improvement in patient safety require synthesis of a range of perspectives and contributions. Preventing things going wrong is as important as being able to analyze them when they do, although prevention is often given less attention compared to analysis, perhaps because it often raises challenging and complex organizational and system-wide issues that cannot be easily addressed.

Many of the key issues raised in the study of patient safety (Walshe and Boaden 2006) are also applicable to quality improvement:

- Is patient safety considered from the perspective of an individual – doctors, nurses, managers, therapists, and so on – or is it primarily an organizational concern? To what extent are errors or adverse events the result of individual failures, or a property of the system within which the individual works?

- To what extent can healthcare organizations learn from or adopt the safety practices of other industries? This issue is also entirely relevant to quality improvement, as this chapter shows

- The involvement of patients in improving safety, and the importance of safe care for patients, cannot be underestimated and needs continual reinforcement.

The underlying principles of quality improvement

The process view

Many of the quality improvement approaches described in this chapter are focused on organizational change and all are based on the process view of organizations (Slack et al. 2004). Process management is defined as entailing three practices: mapping processes, improving processes and adhering to systems of improved processes (Benner and Tushman 2003). It is argued that taking a process view is one of the key characteristics of organizations that are successful in improvement, along with adopting evidence-based practice, learning collaboratively and being ready and able to change (Plsek 1999).

The process view has also been the basis for the development of systems thinking, which developed into hard systems and soft systems (Checkland 1981), and has been more recently linked with organizational learning (Senge et al. 1994). It can be described as exploration of 'the properties which exist once the parts [of the system] have been combined into a whole' (Iles and Sutherland 2001) and is in some ways simply a combination of processes. Systems thinking has also been proposed as a means of understanding medical systems (Nolan 1998), based on the following principles:

- A system needs a purpose to aid people in managing interdependencies.
- The structure of a system significantly determines the performance of the system.
- Changes in the structure of a system have the potential for generating unintended consequences.
- The structure of a system dictates the benefits that accrue to various people working in the system.
- The size and scope of a system influence the potential for improvement.
- The need for cooperation is a logical extension of interdependencies within systems.
- Systems must be managed.
- Improvements in systems must be led.

This process view is therefore not only about changing organizations but also examining and improving the interaction between elements of the organization, including the individuals who work within them. It can also be seen in the clinical emphasis on pathways and the use of clinical guidelines and the mapping of processes may lead to clinical and resource utilization improvements (Trebble et al. 2010).

Business process redesign

The term 'redesign' covers more than a single technique, although it can be described as 'thinking through from scratch the best process to achieve speedy and effective care from a patient perspective' (Locock 2003) – something which may involve many of the improvement tools described in this chapter. The basic principles of process redesign have been 'packaged' into an approach usually termed 'business process re-engineering', first coined by Hammer and Champy (1993), arguably as a response to the failure of the incremental improvement approach proposed by TQM. This type of approach can be viewed as a 'top-down' approach to improvement. The most publicized and studied application in healthcare was probably that at Leicester (McNulty and Ferlie 2002), although redesigning of healthcare at a whole system as well as at individual organization level is an 'international preoccupation' (Locock 2003).

Flow

Managing the flow of patients through a process is also important and can to some extent draw on approaches widely used in manufacturing (Brideau 2004). Understanding and evaluating flow requires more detailed understanding of demand and capacity than has often been the case in healthcare organizations (Horton 2004). Zimmerman (2004) proposes that studying and improving flow leads to a need to consider alignment within the whole healthcare system and goals within the system, especially between healthcare organizations and clinicians. This should lead to whole systems approaches to improvement.

One quality improvement approach that focuses on flow is theory of constraints (TOC).

Theory of constraints

The basic concepts of the theory of constraints (TOC) are:

- Every system has at least one constraint – anything that limits the system from achieving higher performance.
- The existence of constraints represents opportunities for improvement. Constraints are not viewed as negative, as traditional thinking might do, but as opportunities to improve.

The theory was developed by Elihu Goldratt who believed that the theory of constraints represented 'an overall theory for running an organization' (Goldratt 1988). Although it had evolved from factory-floor concepts, it was applicable to the whole organization; constraints might be managerial policy related rather than related to physical things. It claims to be designed for 'achieving breakthroughs in performance in large complex environments dominated by high uncertainty' (Goldratt Consulting Group 2005), which would seem to make it ideal for healthcare. One of its prerequisites is to establish the goal of the organization, which is often contestable in the complex professionalized environment of healthcare. Its Five Focusing Steps describe how to reduce the impact of the constraint on the system.

A recent review of TOC across all sectors (Mabin and Balderstone 2003) states that over 400 articles and 45 books have been published on the subject since 1993, but without much systematic assessment of its impact. Where research results have been reported, the research is 'anecdotal and fragmented' (Lubitsh et al. 2004) and mainly from the USA. There is some work on the application of TOC in healthcare in the UK (Goldratt Consulting Group 2005), but the results are only reported by those who supported the work.

Variation

Variation within a process is inherent and it is argued that understanding and analysing the variation are keys to success in improvement (Snee 1990). This is especially true in healthcare (Haraden and Resar 2004) and is seen to be the result of clinical (patient) flow and professional variability (Institute for Healthcare Improvement 2003b). Patient variability is 'random' and cannot be eliminated or reduced but must be managed, whereas non-random variability should be eliminated. It is argued (Institute for Healthcare Improvement 2003b) that 'it is variation . . . that causes most of the flow problems in our hospital systems'. The reduction of variation is a key element of the statistical process control (SPC) method and the Six Sigma approach.

Statistical process control (SPC)

The roots of statistical process control (SPC) can be traced to work in the 1920s in Bell Laboratories (Shewhart 1931), where Shewhart sought to identify the difference between 'natural' variation in processes – termed 'common cause' – and that which could be controlled – 'special' or 'assignable' cause variation. Processes that exhibited only common cause variation were said to be in statistical control. One of the many significant features of this work, which is still used in basically the same form today, is that 'the management of quality acquired a scientific and statistical foundation' and in healthcare it is often regarded as a tool for measurement (Plsek 1999).

The statistical approach has been applied in a variety of healthcare areas (Benneyan et al. 2003; Marshall et al. 2004), although it is not promoted centrally within the NHS. The use of control charts (the way in which SPC data is displayed) is viewed as helping to decide how to improve – whether to search for special causes (if the process is out of control) or work on more fundamental process redesign (if the process is under control). Charts can also be used to monitor improvements over time (Benneyan et al. 2003). A study of the effect of presenting data as league tables or control charts for the purposes of decision-making (Marshall et al. 2004) concluded that fewer outliers for further investigation are identified when data is presented in control charts.

There is evidence that discussions about the applications of SPC in healthcare started in the early 1990s (Berwick 1991) and it is certain that there have been a number of applications in US healthcare for some while (Mohammed et al. 2001), as well as some debate (Benneyan and Kaminsky 1995). Mohammed (2004) reports the results of his search on Medline for 'statistical process control' to demonstrate the rapid growth in publications about SPC in healthcare. He was also involved in the widely publicized application of SPC to data about mortality in the light of the Shipman case (Mohammed et al. 2001, 2004), and this raised the profile of SPC among doctors. However, the fact that SPC was first used in manufacturing makes translation difficult: 'there is a reluctance, despite evidence to the contrary, to accept that an approach for improving the quality of "widgets" can be legitimately applied to healthcare' (Mohammed 2004).

Six sigma

Six sigma is an improvement approach which was initially established by Motorola in 1987 and the term represents the amount of variation in a process. The term 'six sigma' refers to a process that has at least six standard deviations (6σ) between the process mean and the nearest specification limit. Six sigma as an approach has a number of fundamental themes:

1 A genuine focus on the customer: six sigma measures start with customer satisfaction, and there is an emphasis on understanding customer expectations and requirements.

2 Data and fact-driven management: decisions based on fact, with the development of an understanding of internal processes.

3 Process focus, management and improvement: understanding the process is the key and controlling the inputs will improve the outputs.

4 Proactive management: developing an understanding of six sigma principles, defining the root causes of problems, challenging 'why' things are done this way.

5 'Boundaryless' collaboration: the approach is teamwork focused.

6 Drive for perfection, tolerance of failure: it is okay to fail during improvement, but the key is to understand why failure occurred and improve it next time.

There are a number of core six sigma methods/tools (many of which are also used in other improvement approaches), but the two key ones are generally agreed to be Define–Measure–Analyse–Improve–Control (DMAIC) and Define–Measure–Analyse–Design–Verify (DMADV; Brassard et al. 2002). DMAIC is the most commonly used methodology and is claimed to be very robust and able to provide a framework and common language, enabling organizations and individuals to 'improve the way they improve' (Brassard et al. 2002).

The academic and theoretical underpinning of six sigma lags rather behind its practical application (Antony 2004). There is a 'paucity of studies that fundamentally critique the phenomena of six sigma in organizations from both people and process perspectives' (Erwin and Douglas 2000). An overview of healthcare applications can be found in Chassin (1998) and Sehwail and DeYong (2003), but it should be noted that 'six sigma has not been widely applied to patient care' (Revere et al. 2004).

The role of the 'customer'

All approaches to quality improvement involve the identification of the customer, which may be internal or external to the organization, and subsequently their needs. The purpose of the process has to be clear before improvement can take place but the role of the customer does vary depending on the approach used (Boaden et al. 2008):

- In six sigma, what is 'critical to quality' as far as the customer is concerned is used to define the measures used to determine the 'defects' to be reduced.
- In lean, the customer's conception of value (which might be thought of as the ratio of benefits to costs) defines which elements of processes are useful (value-adding), the rest being waste (steps or components the customer would not wish to pay for).
- Six sigma and lean are predicated on the principle that the system should seek to provide more quality or benefit to the customer and/or at lower cost, TOC does not automatically assume this is the way to maximize the goal of the organization.

It is in this area that the issue of professionalism and the increasing role of the patient have an impact. while much rhetoric about healthcare systems states that they are patient-driven, this does not appear to be the case in practice. Whether the 'customer' can be defined as the patient is open to question, but it is clear (Walley and Gowland 2004) that, to date, patient involvement in quality improvement has been limited, with lack of attention to the presence of the patient in processes (Shortell et al. 1995) and lack of consumer power also being cited as important (Zbabada et al. 1998). The patient may be seen as the primary customer, but the patient does not pay directly for services where they are publicly funded – other customers may include the patient's family, and society in general, as well as commissioners. 'Depending on the perspective, the definition of value will hence differ. However, because the main mission of healthcare is to treat and cure patients . . . it is argued that the patient should define what creates value in healthcare' (Kollberg et al. 2006: 12). The role of the customer is crucial in the lean approach in defining 'value':

Lean

The term 'lean' has been developed in the context of manufacturing from work carried out at Toyota, and like many other 'approaches', it consists of a number of tools, some of which are also used elsewhere: just-in-time (JIT), the *kanban* method of pull production and mistake proofing (Hines et al. 2004), with an overall focus on the elimination of waste. There are differing descriptions of what Toyota does, with each identifying sets of 'principles' that underpin the lean approach:

'Lean principles' have been described as follows (Womack and Jones 1996):

- identification of customer value;
- management of the value stream;

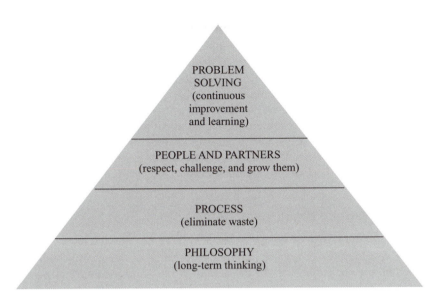

FIGURE 24.1 The Toyota way

- developing the capability to flow production;
- use of 'pull' mechanisms to support material flow;
- pursuit of perfection through reducing all forms of waste in the system.

Alternatively, a series of books by Jeffrey Liker (Liker 2004) describe the way in which Toyota works as the 'Toyota Production System' (TPS). This is summarized in Figure 24.1 where the 'problem solving' approach refers to the use of the PDSA cycle. Many of the lean 'tools' are used in the 'process – eliminate waste' element of the approach, but this is clearly built on an underpinning philosophy of long-term thinking and linked to a specific approach to the people in the organization.

The third description of the Toyota way of working (Spear 2004) has subsequently been distilled into a set of capabilities of 'high velocity' organizations (Spear 2009) with examples of healthcare organizations included. Structurally these organizations design work in a way so that problems become evident when they occur and they are oriented towards processes rather than functional structures. They then continually improve the processes by problem-solving and learning:

> When they see problems, they swarm them very aggressively, and with tremendous discipline, they understand the root cause of the problem, develop a treatment, and then follow up to see if the treatment works. And if it does, they realise they've converted something which they didn't understand – that's why they had the problem – into something which they do understand.
>
> (Spear 2009: 8)

The lean approach is being promoted in healthcare across the work with the implementation of the Toyota production system in a US health centre (Kaplan and Rona

2004) and lean in healthcare (Hill 2001; Bushell and Shelest 2002; Greenwood et al. 2002). There are numerous reports of the application of lean in healthcare (see Boaden et al. 2008, for one list of examples) but in common with other approaches to quality improvement, little rigorous research evidence. Recent research has shown that there is 'relatively little evidence of the complete Lean philosophy being applied in the public sector' (Radnor et al. 2006). There is also evidence to suggest that it is applied in the public sector without a full understanding of the underlying principles, so that it is seen as another policy or set of tools, which leads to Lean being applied to processes that are not suited to it, and considered as a set of tools rather than a fundamental shift in culture and approach (Radnor and Boaden 2008).

The role of people in improvement

The increasing importance of people in improvement has already been described as part of the development of quality improvement. Many of the approaches to quality improvement are not explicit about the role of people and assume that people will automatically be motivated to improve quality. One approach that is based on the role of individuals in small scale improvement is the collaborative approach, itself based on the Plan–Do–Study–Act (PDSA) cycle. Another approach where the involvement of people is explicit is the lean approach.

Plan–Do–Study–Act and the collaborative approach

The Plan–Do–Study–Act (PDSA) model was first formally proposed in healthcare by (Langley et al. 1996) as part of the 'Model for Improvement' to improve processes and therefore outcomes (Deming 1986). This links the PDSA cycle with three key questions and is often referred to as rapid-cycle improvement (Horton 2004), where a number of small PDSA cycles take place one after the other, similar to a learning approach (e.g. Kolb 1984; Schön 1988). The Model for Improvement can be regarded as a philosophy rather than an individual technique and one which can be used as an overarching framework within which other improvement techniques can be utilized. It is, however, a continuous/bottom-up (incremental) improvement approach, rather than a breakthrough/top-down (transformational) approach, and this may be in conflict with management styles or past experience of improvement (Walley and Gowland 2004).

The PDSA cycle is a key part of the collaborative approach which was one of the first large-scale applications of PDSA in healthcare, initiated by IHI as the Breakthrough Series Collaborative approach (Institute for Healthcare Improvement, 2003a, 2003b) and subsequently used worldwide. The approach involves a number of teams with a common interest (e.g. improving cancer services) working together in a structured way with a group of national experts for a period of around 12 to 18 months to plan, implement and monitor improvements in care. Although it is argued that there is insufficient evidence to determine whether collaboratives are more or less cost effective in making and spreading improvements than other approaches (Øvretveit et al. 2002), the approach does have a considerable body of evidence to support it (see Hulscher et al. 2009, for a recent review). The PDSA cycle is an adaptation of the Plan–Do–Check–Act

(PDCA) cycle developed by Deming (Deming 1986) and termed by him the Shewhart cycle (Dale 2003).

Tools to support quality improvement

There are many tools claimed to be useful for quality improvement which can be applied as part of various approaches: a summary and basic description are shown in Table 24.5 (developed from Dale 2003). However, tools on their own will not lead to successful quality improvement – the broader factors discussed in the underlying principles have to be addressed effectively.

Does quality improvement work?

There have been a range of reviews of quality improvement research; although all are challenged by the same issues which make it difficult to decide which approaches 'work'. Most of the papers available are descriptive case studies based on a single site, rather than analytical reviews of the application of improvement approaches. Methodologically, many papers are relatively small-scale, before and after studies, making it difficult to determine whether any reported changes are directly attributable to the quality improvement intervention or not.

A debate about the relevance (or otherwise) of randomized controlled trial methods to investigate the effectiveness of quality improvement approaches is clear. Some authors argued that quality improvement is a complex social intervention, for which methods designed to 'control out' the influence of context on the implementation of the intervention are not relevant. Trials may not be sensitive to the things that influence the success of change: the 'array of influences: leadership, changing environments, details of implementation, organizational history, and much more' (Berwick 2008: 1183).

There are few large-scale, rigorously conducted trials (from a scientific perspective) that provide conclusive evidence to support the assertion that implementing quality improvement programmes and methods leads to improved processes and outcomes of care (Perneger 2006). Very few studies, however, contain any analysis of the economic implications (Øvretveit 2009) or the impact of quality improvement on cost.

In order to address the more complex nature of the intervention, staged approaches such as the Medical Research Council's framework for evaluating complex interventions have been developed (Campbell et al. 2000). This is a phased approach using different research methods in each phase; following a theoretical phase, the components of the intervention are defined, an exploratory trial is carried out, followed by an RCT and then long-term implementation. However, many authors are now arguing for more than one method to be used (Grol et al. 2008).

> The aim is not to find out 'whether it works', as the answer to that question is almost always 'yes, sometimes'. The purpose is to establish when, how and why the intervention works, to unpick the complex relationship between context, content, application and outcomes.
>
> (Walshe 2007: 58)

TABLE 24.5 Quality improvement tools

Tool	Description	Source (where one identifiable)
Benchmarking	Learning from the experience of others by comparing products or processes – can be internal (within a company), competitive (with competitors), functional/generic (comparing processes with 'best in class')	Developed from the work at Rank Xerox in the 1980s, documented by Camp (1989)
Brainstorming	Used with a variety of tools to generate ideas in groups	Term now often replaced by 'thought showering' which is felt to be more politically correct, with some considering the original term to be offensive for those who have epilepsy
Checklists	Lists of key features of a process, equipment, etc. to be checked	Commonly used in a variety of situations
Departmental purpose analysis	Tool used to facilitate internal customer relationships	Originated at IBM in 1984
Design of experiments (DOE)	A series of techniques which identify and control parameters which have a potential impact on performance, aiming to make the performance of the system immune to variation	Dates back to agricultural research by Sir R. A. Fisher in the 1920s, later developed by Taguchi (1986) and adopted in both Japan and the West
Failure mode and effects analysis (FMEA)	A planning tool used to 'build quality in' to a product or service, for either design or process. It looks at the ways in which the product or service might fail, and then modifies the design or process to avoid these or minimize them	Developed in 1962 in the aerospace and defence industry as a means of reliability analysis, risk analysis and management. Termed 'Failure Mode Effect and Criticality Analysis' (FMECA) by Joint Commission on Accreditation of Healthcare Organizations (2005)
Flowcharts	A basis for the application of many other tools. A diagrammatic representation of the steps in a process, often using standard symbols. Many variations available	Developed from industrial engineering methods but no one identifiable source Widely used in systems analysis and business process re-engineering
Housekeeping	Essentially about cleanliness, etc. in the production environment	Based on what the Japanese refer to as the five s: ● *seiri* – organization ● *seiton* – neatness ● *seiso* – cleaning ● *seiketsu* – standardization ● *shitsuke* – discipline
Mistake-proofing	Technique used to prevent errors turning into defects in the final product – based on the assumption that mistakes will occur, however 'careful' individuals are, unless preventative measures are put in place. Statistical methods accept defects as inevitable, but the source of the mistake should be identified and prevented	Developed by Shingo (1986)

Tool	Description	Source (where one identifiable)
Policy deployment	The western tradition of *hoshin kanri* – Japanese 'strategic planning and management process involving setting direction and deploying the means of achieving that direction' (Dale 2003). Used to communicate policy, goals and objectives through the hierarchy of the organization, focusing on the key activities for success	Developed in Japan in early 1960s, concept conceived by Bridgestone Tire Company, and adopted in the USA from the early 1980s, with great popularity in large multinationals with Japanese subsidiaries
Quality costing	Tools used to identify the costs of quality, often using the prevention–appraisal–failure (PAF) categorization	PAF developed by Feigenbaum (1961). Cost of (non)conformance developed by Crosby (1979)
Quality function deployment	Tool to incorporate knowledge about needs of customers into all stages of design and manufacture/delivery process. Initially translates customer needs into design requirements, based on the concept of the voice of the customer. Closely related to FMEA and DOE	Developed in Japan at Kobe shipyard
Total productive maintenance	Can be considered as a method of management, combining principles of productive maintenance (PM) with TQM	Developed by the Japanese from the planned approach to PM
Seven quality control tools		
1 *Cause-and-effect diagram*	Diagram used to determine and break down the main causes of a given problem – sometimes called 'fishbone' diagrams. Used where there is one problem and the causes may be hierarchical in nature. Can be used by teams or individuals	Ishikawa (1979)
2 *Checksheet*	Sheet or form used to collect data	Can be similar to a checklist
3 *Control chart*	The way in which SPC data is displayed, viewed as helping to decide how to improve – whether to search for special causes (if the process is out of control) or work on more fundamental process redesign (if the process is under control). Charts can also be use to monitor improvements over time (Benneyan et al. 2003)	Control charts were used as the basis for SPC development but it is not clear exactly when they were first used
4 *Graphs*	Any form of pictorial representation of data	Basic mathematical technique
5 *Histogram*	Developed from tally charts, basic statistical tool to describe the distribution of a series of data points	Basic mathematical technique

(continued)

TABLE 24.5 (*continued*)

Tool	Description	Source (where one identifiable)
6 *Pareto diagram*	Technique for prioritizing issues – a form of bar chart with a cumulative percentage curve overlaid on it. Sometimes referred to as the 80/20 rule	Named after nineteenth-century Italian economist who observed that a large proportion of a country's wealth is held by a small proportion of the population
7 *Scatter diagram*	Used to examine the possible relationship between two variables	Basic mathematical technique
Seven management tools (M7)	Generally used in design or sales/marketing areas, where quantitative data is less easy to obtain	Developed by the Japanese to collect and analyse qualitative and verbal data. Many have already been used in other TQM applications
1 *Affinity diagrams*	Used to categorize verbal data/language about previously unexplored vague issues	
2 *Arrow diagrams*	Applies systematic thinking to the planning and execution of a set of complex tasks	Used in project management as part of critical path analysis (CPA) and programme evaluation and review technique (PERT)
3 *Decision programme chart*	Used to select the best process to obtain the desired outcome by listing all possible events, contingencies and outcomes	Similar to decision tree for unsafe acts culpability, based on decision trees presented in (Reason 1997)
4 *Matrix data analysis process*	Multivariate mathematical methods used to analyse the data from a matrix diagram	
5 *Matrix diagrams*	Used to clarify the relationship between results and causes or objectives and methods, using codes to illustrate the direction and relative importance of the influence	
6 *Relations diagrams*	Used to identify complex cause-and-effect relationships, where the causes are non-hierarchical and the 'effect' is complex	
7 *Systematic diagrams*	Sometimes called a 'tree' diagram – used to examine the most effective means of planning to accomplish a task or solve a problem	

One attempt to distil common challenges in quality improvement through a review of case studies of healthcare organizations provides a useful overview of the organizing challenges (Bate et al. 2008) (see Table 24.6).

Conclusion

Many believe that 'in matters of quality improvement, healthcare can indeed learn from industry – and perhaps, equally important, industry can also learn from healthcare. The fundamental principles of quality improvement apply to both' (Berwick

TABLE 24.6 Core challenges to organizing for quality (Bate et al. 2008)

Challenge	Lack of this can lead to ...
Structural – organizing, planning and coordinating quality efforts	Fragmentation and a general lack of synergy between the different parts of the organization doing quality improvement
Political – addressing and dealing with the politics of change surrounding any quality improvement effort	Disillusionment and inertia because quality improvement is not happening on the ground, and certain groups or individuals are blocking and resisting change
Cultural – giving quality a shared, collective meaning, value and significance within the organization	Evaporation because the change has not been properly anchored or become rooted in everyday thinking and behavioural routines
Educational – creating a learning process that supports improvement	Amnesia and frustration as lessons and knowledge are forgotten or fail to accumulate, and improvement capabilities and skills fail to keep abreast of growing aspirations
Emotional – engaging and motivating people by linking quality improvement efforts to inner sentiments and deeper commitments and beliefs	Loss of interest and fade-out as the change effort runs out of momentum due to a failure to engage front-line staff
Physical and technological – the designing of physical systems and technological infrastructure that supports and sustains quality efforts	Exhaustion as people try to make change happen informally, without a system or standardized set of routines to take the weight of necessary everyday activities

Source: Bate et al. (2008).

et al. 1990/2002). However, given the variety of perspectives on quality improvement, especially those from an organization/process perspective and those developed by professionals, there are challenges for all:

- Quality improvement needs to be demystified: 'much of it is common sense, accessible to all and not the preserve of a few. The tendency for each new quality improvement theory to generate its own jargon and esoteric knowledge must be resisted' (Locock 2003).
- Healthcare professionals need to recognise their role and responsibility to the wider system: 'the need to balance clinical autonomy with transparent accountability, to support the systematization of clinical work' (Degeling et al. 2003).
- Managers need to recognise the limits of their authority in improvement: 'there was no evidence that managers alone could produce . . . clinical buy-in' (Dopson and Fitzgerald 2005).

In the continually changing world of healthcare, quality is always going to be important and the differing perspectives and multidisciplinary approaches must be taken into account.

Summary box

- Quality is a widely used term with a variety of meanings attributed to it.
- Approaches to quality improvement may have a focus on changing organizations, professionals and interactions between participants in the system.
- Quality improvement developed from the ideas of a series of gurus in manufacturing, with these concepts later translating to service organizations and to a more 'total' (i.e. organization-wide) approach to improvement.
- The principles common to all approaches to quality improvement are a focus on processes, consideration of flow and variation, an explicit role for the 'customer' and guidance on how people are involved in quality improvement.
- The different approaches – which include the plan–do–study–act model, collaboratives, statistical process control, six sigma, lean, theory of constraints and process redesign – vary in their focus on each principle.
- Clinically developed approaches to improvement include clinical governance, clinical pathways and some approaches to patient safety.
- Healthcare is different from other sectors in terms of quality improvement primarily because of the professional autonomy of many of its staff, but improvement is a challenge for all parties who need to simplify concepts, recognize their responsibilities and the limits of their authority.

Self-test exercises

1 What were the influences on the development of the quality movement from its origins in both manufacturing and professional practice?

2 There are many quality improvement techniques available but which ones do you think would be most useful in improving quality:
   - in a hospital emergency department?
   - in a large organization where multiple performance measures are used?
   - in a pathology laboratory?
   - in a primary care centre where there are often queues of patients waiting to see health professionals?

3 What are the challenges of getting clinicians to accept methods of improvement other than those developed as 'clinical governance'?

4 What needs to be in place if quality improvement in healthcare is to continue to develop?

References and further reading

Antony, J. (2004) Some pros and cons of six sigma: an academic perspective. *TQM Magazine*, 16(4): 303–6.

Baldrige National Quality Program (2009) Health care criteria for performance excellence. Available at: http://www.nist.gov/baldrige/publications/upload/2009_2010_HealthCare_Criteria.pdf (accessed 1 September 2010).

Bate, P., Mendel, P. and Robert, G. (2008) *Organizing for Quality*. Oxford: Radcliffe.

Bendell, T., Penson, R. and Carr, S. (1995) The quality gurus – their approaches described and considered. *Managing Service Quality*, 5(6): 44–8.

Benner, M.J. and Tushman, M.L. (2003) Exploitation, exploration and process management: the productivity dilemma revisited. *Academy of Management Review*, 26(2): 238–56.

Benneyan, J.C. and Kaminsky, F.C. (1995) Another view on how to measure health care quality. *Quality Progress*, 28(2): 120–5.

Benneyan, J.C., Lloyd, R.C. and Plsek, P.E. (2003) Statistical process control as a tool for research and healthcare improvement. *Quality Safety Health Care*, 12(6): 458–64.

Berry, L.L. and Seltman, K.D. (2008) *Management Lessons from Mayo Clinic*. New York: McGraw-Hill.

Berry, L.L., Zeithaml, V.A. and Parasuraman, A. (1985) Quality counts in services too. *Business Horizons*, 28(3): 44–52.

Berwick, D. (1989) Continuous improvement as an ideal in healthcare. *New England Journal of Medicine*, 320: 53–6.

Berwick, D. (1991) Controlling variation in healthcare: a consultation from Walter Shewhart. *Medical Care*, 29: 1212–25.

Berwick, D. (2008) The science of improvement. *JAMA*, 299(10): 1182–4.

Berwick, D., Endhoven, A. and Bunker, J.P. (1992) Quality management in the NHS: the doctor's role. *British Medical Journal*, 304: 235–9, 304–8.

Berwick, D., Godfrey, A.B. and Roessner, J. (1990/2002) *Curing Health Care*. San Francisco, CA: Jossey-Bass.

Boaden, R.J., Harvey, G., Moxham, C. and Proudlove, N. (2008) *Quality Improvement: Theory and Practice in Healthcare*. Coventry: NHS Institute for Innovation and Improvement.

Bowns, I.R. and McNulty, T. (1999) *Re-engineering Leicester Royal Infirmary: An Independent Evaluation of Implementation and Impact*. Sheffield: University of Sheffield.

Brassard, M., Finn, L., Ginn, D. and Ritter, D. (2002) *The Six Sigma Memory Jogger*. Salem: GOAL/QPC.

Brideau, L.P. (2004) Flow: why does it matter? *Frontiers of Health Services Management*, 20(4): 47–50.

Bushell, S. and Shelest, B. (2002) Discovering lean thinking at progressive healthcare. *Journal for Quality and Participation*, 25(2): 20.

Camp, R.C. (1989) *Benchmarking: The Search for Industry Best Practice that Leads to Superior Performance*. Milwaukee: ASQC Quality Press.

Campbell, M., Fitzpatrick, R., Haines, A. et al. (2000) Framework for design and evaluation of complex interventions to improve health. *BMJ*, 321(7262): 649–96.

Chassin, M. (1998) Is health care ready for six sigma quality? *Milbank Quarterly*, 76(4): 565–91.

Checkland, P. (1981) *Systems Thinking, Systems Practice*. New York: Wiley.

Crosby, P. (1979) *Quality is Free*. New York: McGraw-Hill.

Dale, B.G. (ed.) (2003) *Managing Quality*. Oxford: Blackwell.

Degeling, P., Maxwell, S., Kennedy, J. and Coyle, B. (2003) Medicine, management, and modernisation: a 'danse macabre'? *British Medical Journal*, 326(7390): 649–52.

Deming, W.E. (1986) *Out of the Crisis*. Cambridge, MA: MIT, Center of Advanced Engineering Study.

Department of Health (1998) *A First Class Service: Quality in the New NHS*. London: Department of Health.

Donabedian, A. (1966) Evaluating the quality of medical care. *Milbank Memorial Fund Quarterly*, 44(3): 166–206.

Donabedian, A. (1987) Commentary on some studies of the quality of care. *Health Care Financing Review*, annual supplement: 75–86.

Dopson, S. and Fitzgerald, L. (eds) (2005) *Knowledge to Action?* Oxford: Oxford University Press.

Erwin, J. and Douglas, P. (2000) Six sigma's focus on total customer satisfaction. *Journal for Quality and Participation*, 23(2): 45–9.

Feigenbaum, A. (1961) *Total Quality Control*. New York: McGraw-Hill.

Gershon, P. (2004) *Releasing Resources to the Front Line: Independent Review of Public Sector Efficiency*. London: The Stationery Office.

Goldratt Consulting Group (2005) Healthcare the TOC way. Available at: http://www.healthcare-toc.com/TOCFORHEALTH.htm (accessed 12 December 2005).

Goldratt, E.M. (1988) Computerised shop floor scheduling. *International Journal of Production Research*, 26(3): 453.

Golembiewski, R., Proehl, C. and Sink, D. (1982) Estimating success of OD applications. *Training and Development Journal*, 72: 86–95.

Greenwood, T., Bradford, M. and Greene, B. (2002) Becoming a lean enterprise: a tale of two firms: both an aircraft manufacturer and an oral surgeon are reaping efficiencies from following the principles of lean transformation. *Strategic Finance*, 84(5): 32–40.

Grol, R., Baker, R. and Moss, F. (eds) (2004) *Quality Improvement Research: Understanding the Science of Change in Health Care*. London: British Medical Journal Books.

Grol, R., Berwick, D.M. and Wensing, M. (2008) On the trail of quality and safety in health care. *BMJ*, 336(7635): 74–6.

Groonroos, C. (1984) *Strategic Management and Marketing in the Service Sector*. London: Chartwell-Bratt.

Hackman, J.R. and Wageman, R. (1995) Total quality management: empirical, conceptual and practical issues. *Administrative Science Quarterly*, 40(2): 309–42.

Hammer, M. and Champy, J. (1993) *Reengineering the Corporation: A Manifesto for Business Revolution*. New York: HarperCollins.

Haraden, C. and Resar, R. (2004) Patient flow in hospitals: understanding and controlling it better. *Frontiers of Health Services Management*, 20(4): 3–15.

Harvard Medical Practice Study (1990) *Patients, Doctors and Lawyers: Medical Injury, Malpractice Litigation and Patient Compensation in New York*. Harvard, New York: Harvard College.

Hill, D. (2001) Physician strives to create lean, clean health care machine. *Physician Executive*, 27: 5.

Hines, P., Holweg, M. and Rich, N. (2004) Learning to evolve: a review of contemporary lean thinking. *International Journal of Operations and Production Management*, 24(10): 994–1011.

Horton, S. (2004) Increasing capacity while improving the bottom line. *Frontiers of Health Services Management*, 20(4): 17–23.

Hulscher, M., Schouten, L.M.T. and Grol, R. (2009) *Collaboratives*. London: The Health Foundation.

Iles, V. and Sutherland, K. (2001) *Organisational Change: A Review for Health Care Managers, Professionals and Researchers*. London: National Co-ordinating Centre for NHS Service Delivery and organisation.

Institute for Healthcare Improvement (2003a) *The Breakthrough Series: IHI's Collaborative Model for Achieving Breakthrough Improvement*. IHI Innovation Series White Paper. Boston: Institute for Healthcare Improvement. Available at: www.IHI.org.

Institute for Healthcare Improvement (2003b) *Optimizing Patient Flow: Moving Patients Smoothly through Acute Care Settings*. Boston: Institute for Healthcare Improvement.

Institute of Medicine and Committee on Quality Health Care in America (2001) *Crossing the Quality Chasm*. Washington, DC: Institute of Medicine.

Ishikawa, K. (1979) *Guide to Total Quality Control*. Tokyo: Asian Productivity organisation.

Joint Commission on Accreditation of Healthcare organisations (2005) Failure mode effect and criticality analysis. Available at: http://www.jcaho.org/accredited+organizations/patient+safety/fmeca/index.htm (accessed 11 March 2005).

Juran, J. (ed.) (1951) *The Quality Control Handbook*. New York: McGraw-Hill.

Kaplan, G.S. and Rona, J.M. (2004) Seeking zero defects: Applying the Toyota production system to health care. Presented at: 16th National Forum on Quality Improvement in Healthcare, Orlando, Florida.

Kenagy, J.W., Berwick, D.M. and Shore, M.F. (1999) Service quality in health care. *JAMA*, 281(7): 661–5.

Kenney, C. (2008) *The Best Practice: How the New Quality Movement is Transforming Medicine*. New York: PublicAffairs.

Kerfoot, D. and Knights, D. (1995) Empowering the 'quality worker'? The seduction and contradiction of the total quality phenomenon. In A. Wilkinson and H. Willmott (eds) *Making Quality Critical*. London: Routledge.

Kerr, D., Bevan, H., Gowland, B., Penny, J. and Berwick, D. (2002) Redesigning cancer care. *British Medical Journal*, 324(7330): 164–7.

Kolb, D.A. (1984) *Experiential Learning: Experience as the Source of Learning and Development*. New York: Prentice-Hall.

Kollberg, B., Dahlgaard, J.J. and Brehmer, P. (2006) Measuring lean initiatives in health care services: issues and findings. *International Journal of Productivity and Performance Management*, 56(1): 7–24.

Langley, G.J., Nolan, K.M., Nolan, T.W., Norman, C.L. and Provost, L.P. (1996) *The Improvement Guide*. San Francisco, CA: Jossey-Bass.

Liker, J. (2004). *The Toyota Way: 14 Management Principles from the World's Greatest Manufacturer*. New York: McGraw-Hill.

Locock, L. (2003) Healthcare redesign: meaning, origins and application. *Quality and Safety in Health Care*, 12(1): 53–8.

Lubitsh, G., Doyle, C. and Valentine, J. (2004) The impact of theory of constraints (TOC) in an NHS trust. *Journal of Management Development*, 24(2).

Lugon, M. and Secker-Walker, J. (eds) (1999) *Clinical Governance: Making it Happen*. London: Royal Society of Medicine Press.

McLaughlin, C.P. and Simpson, K.N. (1999) Does TQM/CQI work in healthcare? In C.P. McLaughlin, and A.D. Kaluzny (eds) *Continuous Quality Improvement in Health Care: Theory, Implementation and Applications*. Gaithersburg: Aspen.

McNulty, T. and Ferlie, E. (2002) *Reengineering Health Care: The Complexities of Organisational Transformation*. Oxford: Oxford University Press.

Mabin, V.J. and Balderstone, S.J. (2003) The performance of the theory of constraints methodology: analysis and discussion of successful TOC applications. *International Journal of Operations and Production Management*, 23(6): 568–95.

Marshall, T., Mohammed, M.A. and Rouse, A. (2004) A randomized controlled trial of league tables and control charts as aids to health service decision-making. *International Journal of Quality Health Care*, 16(4): 309–15.

Maxwell, R.J. (1984) Quality assessment in health. *British Medical Journal*, 288: 1470–2.

Middleton, S., Barnett, J. and Reeves, D. (2001) What is an integrated care pathway? *What is?* 3(3): 1–8.

Mohammed, M.A. (2004) Using statistical process control to improve the quality of health care. *Quality and Safety in Health Care*, 13(4): 243–5.

Mohammed, M.A., Cheng, K.K., Rouse, A. and Marshall, T. (2001) Bristol, Shipman, and clinical governance: Shewhart's forgotten lessons. *The Lancet*, 357(9254): 463–7.

Mohammed, M.A., Rathbone, A., Myers, P. et al. (2004) An investigation into general practitioners associated with high patient mortality flagged up through the Shipman inquiry: retrospective analysis of routine data. *British Medical Journal*, 328(7454): 1474–7.

NHS Modernisation Agency (2005) NHS Institute for Innovation and Improvement supersedes the Modernisation Agency. Available at: http://www.wise.nhs .uk/cmsWISE/aboutUs/AboutMA.htm (accessed 12 December 2005).

Nielsen, D.M., Merry, M.D., Schyve, P.M. and Bisognano, M. (2004) Can the gurus' concepts cure healthcare? *Quality Progress*, 37(9): 25–6.

Nolan, T.W. (1998) Understanding medical systems. *Annals of Internal Medicine*, 128(4): 293–8.

Øvretveit, J. (1997) A comparison of hospital quality programmes: lessons for other services. *International Journal of Service Industry Management*, 8(3): 220–35.

Øvretveit, J. (2009) *Does Improving Quality Save Money?* London: Health Foundation.

Øvretveit, J., Bate, P. and Cleary, P. (2002) Quality collaboratives: lessons from research. *Quality and Safety in Health Care*, 11: 345–51.

Parasuraman, A., Zeithaml, V.A. and Berry, L.L. (1988) SERVQUAL: a multiple item scale for measuring consumer perceptions of service quality. *Journal of Retailing*, 64(1): 14–40.

Perneger, T. (2006) Ten reasons to conduct a randomized study in quality improvement. *International Journal for Quality in Health Care*, 18(6): 395–6.

Plsek, P. (1999) Quality improvement methods in clinical medicine. *Pediatrics*, 103(1): 203–14.

Pollitt, C. (1993) The struggle for quality: the case of the NHS. *Policy and Politics*, 21(3): 161–70.

Powell, A.E., Rushmer, R.K. and Davies, H.T.O. (2009). *A Systematic Narrative Review of Quality Improvement Models in Health Care*. Edinburgh: NHS Quality Improvement Scotland.

Radnor, Z. and Boaden, R. (2008) 'Editorial: lean in public services: panacea or paradox? *Public Money and Management*, 28(1): 3–7.

Radnor, Z., Walley, P., Stephens, A. and Bucci, G. (2006) *Evaluation of the Lean Approach to Business Management and its Use in the Public Sector*. Edinburgh: Scottish Executive, Office of Chief Researcher.

Reason, J. (1997) *Managing the Risk of Organisational Accidents*. Aldershot: Ashgate.

Reeves, C.A. and Bednar, D.A. (1994) Defining quality: alternatives and implications. *Academy of Management Review*, 19(3): 419–56.

Revere, L., Black, K. and Huq, A. (2004) Integrating six sigma and CQI for improving patient care. *TQM Magazine*, 16(2): 105–13.

Robertson, P.J. and Seneviratne, S.J. (1995) Outcomes of planned organisational change in the public sector: a meta analytic comparison to the private sector. *Public Administration Review*, 55(6): 547–58.

Schön, D.A. (1988) *Educating the Reflective Practitioner. Toward a New Design for Teaching and Learning in the Professions*. San Francisco, CA: Jossey-Bass.

Sehwail, L. and DeYong, C. (2003) Six sigma in health care. *International Journal of Health Care Quality Assurance*, 16(6): 1.

Senge, K.A., Roberts C., Ross R.B. and Smith B.J. (1994) *The Fifth Discipline Fieldbook*. London: Nicholas Brearley.

Shewhart, W.A. (1931) *Economic Control of Quality of Manufactured Product*. New York: Van Nostrand.

Shingo, S. (1986) *Zero Quality Control: Source Inspection and the Poka-Yoke System*. Cambridge, MA: Productivity Press.

Shortell, S., Levin, D., O'Brien, J. and Hughes, E. (1995) Assessing the evidence on CQI: is the glass half empty or half full? *Journal of the Foundation of the American College of Healthcare Executives*, 40: 4–24.

Slack, N., Chambers, S. and Johnston, R. (2004) *Operations Management*. Harlow: FT/Prentice Hall.

Snee, R.D. (1990) Statistical thinking and its contribution to total quality. *American Statistician*, 44(2): 116–21.

Spear, S.J. (2004) Learning to lead at Toyota. *Harvard Business Review*, 82: 78–86.

Spear, S.J. (2005) Fixing healthcare from the inside, today. *Harvard Business Review*, 83(9): 78–91.

Spear, S.J. (2009) *Chasing the Rabbit*. New York: McGraw-Hill.

Stiles, R.A. and Mick, S.S. (1994) Classifying quality initiatives: a conceptual paradigm for literature review and policy analysis. *Hospital and Health Services Administration*, 39(3): 309.

Taguchi, G. (1986) *Introduction to Quality Engineering*. New York: Asian Productivity Organisation.

Trebble, T.M., Hansi, N., Hydes, T., Smith, M.A. and Baker, M. (2010) Process mapping the patient journey: an introduction. *BMJ*, 341.10.1136/bmj.c4078.

Vinzant, J.C. and Vinzant, D.H. (1999) Strategic management spin-offs of the Deming approach. *Journal of Management History*, 5(8): 516–31.

Walley, P. (2003) Designing the accident and emergency system: lessons from manufacturing. *Emergency Medical Journal*, 20(2): 126–30.

Walley, P. and Gowland, B. (2004) Completing the circle: from PD to PDSA. *International Journal of Health Care Quality Assurance*, 17(6): 349–58.

Walshe, K. (2007) Understanding what works – and why – in quality improvement: the need for theory-driven evaluation. *International Journal for Quality in Health Care*, 19(2): 57–9.

Walshe, K. and Boaden, R. (eds) (2006) *Patient Safety: Research into Practice*. Maidenhead: Open University Press.

Webb, J. (1995) Quality management and the management of quality. In A. Wilkinson and H. Willmott (eds) *Making Quality Critical*. London: Routledge.

Wilkinson, A. (1992) The other side of quality: soft issues and the human resource dimension. *Total Quality Management*, 3(3): 323–9.

Wilkinson, A. and Willmott, H. (eds) (1995) *Making Quality Critical*. London: Routledge.

Womack, J.P. and Jones, D.T. (1996) *Lean Thinking*. London: Simon and Schuster.

Zbabada, C., Rivers, P.A. and Munchus, G. (1998) Obstacles to the application of TQM in healthcare organisations. *Total Quality Management* 9(1): 57–67.

Zimmerman, R.S. (2004) Hospital capacity, productivity and patient safety – it all flows together. *Frontiers of Health Services Management*, 20(4): 33–8.

Websites and resources

Accreditation Canada: http://www.accreditation.ca/.
Agency for Healthcare Research and Quality: http://www.ahrq.gov/.
Care Quality Commission: http://www.cqc.org.uk/.
European Society for Quality in Healthcare: http://www.esqh.net.
Institute for Healthcare Improvement: www.ihi.org.
International Society for Quality in Healthcare: http://www.isqua.org/.
The Joint Commission: http://www.jointcommission.org/.
National Institute for Health and Clinical Excellence (NICE): http://www.nice.org.uk/.
NHS Institute for Innovation and Improvement: http://www.institute.nhs.uk/.
NHS Quality Improvement Scotland: http://www.nhshealthquality.org/.

Managing performance

Kieran Walshe

Introduction

For many healthcare managers today, it can seem as if their – and their organization's – performance is under constant scrutiny, from all directions. They face the publication of performance data and its use by the media and the public; a constant stream of directives and guidance from government, national agencies, professional associations and others telling them what they should or should not be doing; visits, inspections and surveys from regulators and other agencies with a variety of statutory powers to investigate and intervene; and, of course, oversight from their own governance arrangements including but not limited to their board and the internal system of committees or groups tasked with reviewing and monitoring performance. We live in what Michael Power (1997) termed the 'audit society' in which, he argued, we have progressively withdrawn our trust from institutions (hospitals, universities, the church, the government) and professions (doctors, teachers, lawyers and the clergy) and instead now place our faith in systems of measurement, information, audit and control designed by auditors, in the widest sense of the term.

Why has this happened? It is not unreasonable to depict the healthcare system in the past as a place where users were passive, grateful and submissive; healthcare professionals were authoritative, unchallengeable and dominant; and institutions were conservative, complacent, closed and largely unaccountable. Indeed, this model probably still largely persists in the healthcare sector in many countries, much more so than it persists in other areas or domains (such as schools, local government, or higher education). The traditional model has perhaps been most in retreat in the Anglophone world, where the performance 'movement' originated and from which many of the ideas, methods and approaches described in this chapter have emerged (Radin 2006; Moynihan 2008).

There are several reasons why the management of performance in healthcare – and in other areas of both the public and private sector – has received more attention in the past two decades than in before, and we have seen a massive growth in what might be termed the infrastructure for performance management – the creation of information systems and organizations designed, in short, to hold healthcare organizations and those who work in them to account. First, and perhaps most important, we have seen a societal shift in people's views and expectations – the zeitgeist has changed. Social attitudes to power and authority, ideas about the balance between the rights and needs of the collective and the individual, and behaviours across a wide range of domains of social and economic life have altered in ways that longitudinal studies graphically demonstrate (Putnam 2000). Second, we have seen a technological transformation in our ability to gather, store, process and apply information of all kinds. The technical component of performance management should not be underestimated – we do things sometimes simply because we can, and we can now gather a huge volume of patient level data from surveys, routine data sources, and increasingly from wholly digitally held clinical records; we have massively increased processing capacity to manipulate that data; and the science of performance measurement, and our ability to use statistical and econometric techniques to make sense of large and heterogeneous data sets has also advanced (Buchan 2011). Moreover the internet has totally transformed the accessibility and usability of this tidal wave of information – meaning that for the first time the huge information asymmetry between healthcare professionals and organizations, on the one hand, and users and the public, on the other, has been reduced. Third, all this information has shown, time and again, that large and unexplainable variations in performance exist, and it has focused attention on some high profile examples of healthcare services and organizations where performance has been unacceptably poor and many patients have been harmed as a result (Cutler and Sheiner 1998; Walshe and Shortell 2004).

This chapter first explores some theories of performance and sets out a conceptual framework for understanding and analysing performance management with the intention of bringing some clarity and definitional precision to what can sometimes seem to be a confused and confusing topic. It then uses that conceptual framework to structure what follows around three main themes: performance measurement, and the science of designing and using measures or indicators of organizational performance; performance management, and the structures, systems and institutions which can be used as mechanisms for bringing about change in organizational performance; and a critical evaluation of performance measurement and management and how it works (or doesn't). The chapter concludes by looking forward, at the future development of systems for managing performance in healthcare systems and key likely trends and coming changes.

Theories of performance

What do we mean by performance? Conceptually, ideas about organizational performance are rooted in a positivist, rationalist and mechanistic model of organizations (Morgan 1988) which tends to conceive of them as entities whose structures and workings can be objectively analysed and described, and whose functioning is a rational process in which everything is or can be made clear – the organizational purpose or goal, what needs to be done to achieve the goal, what actually gets done, what resources the organization consumes, what outputs the organization produces, what outcomes result and how those outcomes relate to the original goals. This 'clockwork' model of organizations is wholly contestable, and we return to these fundamentals

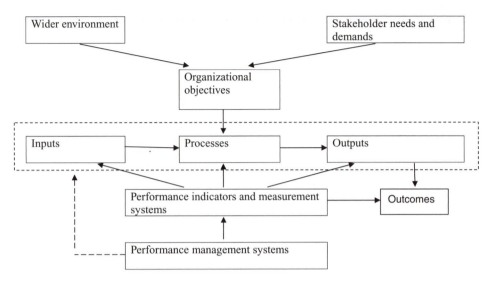

FIGURE 25.1 An analytic framework for performance management
Source: Drawing on Bouckaert and Halligan (2008), Moynihan (2008), and Talbot (2010).

towards the end of this chapter in a critical evaluation of the development and impact of performance management (Radin 2006). For now, we need to live with some of those presuppositions because they are fundamental to the performance movement.

At the heart of most thinking about performance lies a model or framework which relates the organizational goals or purposes, to resources, processes and outputs. Figure 25.1 provides an example, based on the work of Bouckaert and Halligan (2008) but also drawing on theorists like Moynihan (2008) and Talbot (2010).

- **Organizational objectives** – are shaped and framed both by the organization's stakeholders and their needs and demands (such as shareholders, funders, government, users, or professionals) and by the wider environment in which the organization exists (characteristics like societal values and norms, financial and economic drivers, political values and beliefs, and so on). For example, a health insurance fund's mission is set by its members and their interests, and by government through its regulation and oversight over the health insurance industry.

- **Organizational functioning** – this is what goes on in the organization itself, shown in the dotted box in Figure 25.1, and it consists of inputs (resources such as finance, human capital, knowledge and information, facilities, and so on), processes (such as care pathways and packages through which health services are delivered), and outputs (such as numbers of patients treated, the volume of patient contacts or episodes of care, and so on).

- **Outcomes** – these are the changes in people's lives which result from healthcare interventions or services – such as improvements in health status and functioning, reductions in morbidity and mortality, or changes in other important domains which are attributable to the healthcare processes and outputs described above.

Attribution – knowing that healthcare processes and outputs actually produced the health outcomes that are seen – is often problematic.

- **Performance indicators and measurement systems** – the systems for performance measurement draw together data as shown in Figure 25.1 on organizational resources, processes, outputs and outcomes to relate performance to organizational objectives. Individual indicators may measure one of these domains or link data to show relationships between domains – such as organizational productivity (process and output per unit of resource).

- **Performance management systems** – these are the mechanisms put in place to use performance indicators and measurement systems to influence the organization to change and improve. Some performance management systems are essentially internal to the organization, but many are external. They usually involve the publication and dissemination of performance data and its application by actors such as healthcare funders/commissioners, patients/users, regulators and government.

The architecture for performance management is often complex, and deserves rather more exploration. All organizations are subject to some kind of governance structure which usually consists of multiple stakeholders, institutions and interest groups, all with varying forms and levels of power or influence over the organization and all seeking directly or indirectly to steer or shape the organization's performance. This is what Talbot and Johnson (2005) have termed the 'performance regime' and they argue that understanding organizational performance first requires an understanding of the structure and form of the performance regime. This model suggests that an organization such as a hospital might have a performance regime consisting of central government departments and the legislature; local government authorities; regulatory agencies; professional associations; healthcare funders or commissioners; patient or user groups; trades unions; the courts; the media, and so on. For example, a poorly performing hospital might come under pressure to improve from several of these components in the performance regime – high profile coverage in the press, patients suing the hospital in the courts for negligence, professional associations threatening to withdraw it is recognition as a place for training doctors and nurses, regulators mounting unannounced inspections and warning that its licence to operate could be restricted or withdrawn, and government stepping in to order changes if it is publicly owned.

Figure 25.2 shows the typical performance regime for a public hospital in the English NHS, as described in a government publication on public services reform and it neatly illustrates both some of the strengths and weaknesses of thinking about performance management. It suggests that there are four main elements to the system for performance management – top down direction; markets, competition and contestability; user choice and voice; and capability and capacity building.

There is a plausible but perhaps somewhat superficial sense of coherence about Figure 25.2. It suggests that the performance regime axiomatically produces 'better public services for all' and it implies that the many different performance management initiatives shown in the figure work together, in a way that is mutually reinforcing, to achieve this goal. Both these assumptions are open to question, and we return to these issues later in the chapter. But it provides a useful conceptual framework with which

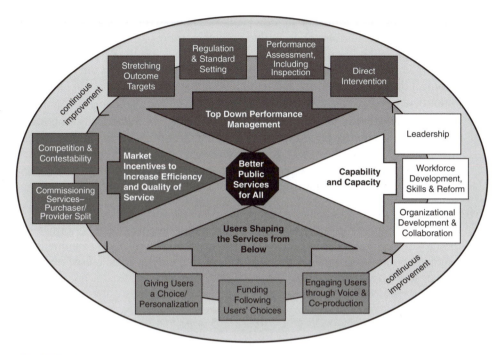

FIGURE 25.2 Public services performance regime in England: a conceptual framework
Source: Cabinet Office (2006).

to organize our analysis of performance management systems into four categories or types:

- **Top down performance management** – is seen most obviously in integrated and publicly owned healthcare systems, where there is a direct line of hierarchical control between a ministry of health or other government agency and healthcare provider organizations, though it is also a feature of more or less any large integrated healthcare system regardless of its ownership, such as for profit hospital chains or large nursing home providers. But as Figure 25.2 suggests, regulation is also a form of top down performance management, though the regulator's authority is based on legislation rather than ownership, and regulators have no direct responsibility for managing the health services they oversee.

- **Markets, competition and contestability** – are mechanisms in which healthcare funders or commissioners seek to influence performance by the way they purchase health services – either directly, through contracts, competitive tendering processes and the like or indirectly through shaping individual consumer decisions about which providers to use.

- **User choice and voice** – are mechanisms in which the users of health services, either as individuals or collectively, are empowered and informed in ways that enable them to use performance information to shape organizational performance.

User choice is predominantly an individual mechanism, relying on the individual decisions of large numbers of users about whether or not to use a particular health service or provider to drive change, while user voice is mostly a collective mechanism, giving users some form of representation and influence in the healthcare organization through its governance structures and thus allowing them to influence performance.

- **Capability and capacity** – are perhaps the less tangible but equally important mechanisms to improve organizational performance through organizational development. Here, interventions may involve efforts to promote continuing professional development and training, improve skills and capacity in the healthcare workforce, and especially to build leadership capacity in healthcare organizations.

We now turn first to a discussion of performance measurement and how data is turned into indicators which tell us something meaningful about organizational performance, and then to an exploration of performance management, in which we examine how those indicators are used through the four main categories of mechanism outlined above to try to shape or change organizational performance.

Performance measurement: indicators and standards

In order to manage performance, you first have to be able to measure it, and this section focuses on the way that performance measures or indicators are constructed. At its simplest, a performance indicator is constructed from one or more items of data about a healthcare organization – often linking the four domains described in Figure 25.1 as inputs, processes, outputs and outcomes. They should be connected in some way of course to organizational objectives and based on robust evidence that they are meaningful measures of organizational performance – in other words, that the primary determinant of variation in the indicator is within the locus of control of the organization (Audit Commission 2000). Behind each indicator therefore lies some kind of explicit or implicit standard – at the least, an implied expectation of what constitutes 'good' or 'poor' performance for that indicator, but often a more explicit definition of performance expectations and the required standards of care. Perhaps the most robust and rigorously derived performance indicators are those that are based firmly on established methodologies for developing evidence-based guidelines and standards (Cluzeau et al. 1999).

But indicators rarely come singly – in most health systems we find a suite of indicators, organized around some kind of framework or set of domains of performance such as:

- **Economy** – measuring levels of spending, often across particular disease or service areas or major spending categories. For example, what do we spend on stroke care, and how does it compare with other places? What is the level of spending on pharmaceuticals per head of population and how does it vary across patient groups?

- **Efficiency** – measuring levels of spending or amounts of resources used per unit of production, often couched in terms of productivity. For example, what is the average length of stay in acute care? What is the mean cost of each episode of fractured neck of femur?

- **Effectiveness** – measuring the outputs or outcomes of the healthcare organization or system. For example, what is the survival rate at 5 years post diagnosis for a range of common cancers? What are the failure or revision rates for joint replacement surgery? What are the rates of blindness and peripheral neuropathy among diabetics?

- **Equity** – measuring the distribution of healthcare needs, health services and resources and health outputs and outcomes across the served population and examining differences by age, gender, social class, income, geography, and so on. For example, how do rates of the incidence of heart disease vary geographically or by social class and gender? How then do rates of intervention (such as angioplasty or surgery) vary, and how do health outcomes such as survival vary?

- **Acceptability** – measuring what patients, users and the public think about all aspects of health services and measuring dimensions of those services through their reported experiences. For example, what proportion of patients attending an outpatient clinic felt that all their questions were answered during the consultation, or reported that they were usually seen by the same doctor?

- **Access** – measuring whether those who need health services are able to access them in a timely and appropriate fashion. For example, how long do patients wait on average after referral from primary care for a needed outpatient appointment or operation? What proportion of patients are not insured and so do not have access to health services? How often do patients fail to access needed health services because of cost?

For example, the Organisation for Economic Co-operation and Development (OECD) has for many years been developing and publishing an annual set of indicators and statistics designed to allow comparisons in health system performance to be made across its 34 member countries. This data set now contains around 600 separate indicators, organized across 11 major domains in areas like expenditure, utilization, health status, and so on. The indicators in one domain (health status) are shown in Figure 25.3 and it can be seen that they focus mainly on issues of mortality and morbidity – one problem with health status is that there is relatively little routine data available on which to draw. For the OECD data set, a further challenge is that different countries define and collect this data in different ways, and some data is available in some countries but not in others. There is a laborious process of mapping and national data sets to the OECD definitions, and often it is necessary to place caveats on the use of the data because of problems with its comparability.

To take another example, the Department of Health in England has for some time set a national target for all healthcare organizations in the NHS that no patient should

Health status	**Mortality**	Life expectancy for a range of age/gender groups Causes of mortality Maternal and infant mortality Potential years of life lost
	Morbidity	Perceived health status Infant health Dental health Communicable diseases Cancer Injuries in RTAs Absence from work through illness

FIGURE 25.3 A selection of indicators from the OECD Health Data Set for one domain: health status
Note: The other major domains in the OECD Health Data Set are: healthcare resources; healthcare utilization; long-term care resources and utilization; expenditure; healthcare financing; social protection; pharmaceutical market; non-medical determinants of health; demographics; and macroeconomics.

wait for longer than 18 weeks from referral by their general practitioner to treatment – which is clearly an access measure in the typology above. It has collected a very detailed data set from healthcare providers to enable it to measure performance against this national target, which requires around fifty pages of guidance notes, definitions and numerous case studies to make it work. For example, to define when a waiting period begins it says:

> A waiting time clock starts when any care professional or service permitted by an English NHS commissioner to make such referrals, refers to:
>
> **a)** a consultant-led service, regardless of setting, with the intention that the patient will be assessed and, if appropriate, treated before responsibility is transferred back to the referring health professional or general practitioner.
>
> **b)** an interface or referral management or assessment service, which may result in an onward referral to a consultant-led service before responsibility is transferred back to the referring health professional or general practitioner.
>
> A waiting time clock also starts upon a self-referral by a patient on-to a consultant-led treatment pathway, where these pathways have been agreed locally by commissioners and providers and once the referral is ratified by a care professional permitted to do so.
>
> Department of Health 2010

Figure 25.4 shows time series data for the percentage of admitted patients treated within 18 weeks from 2007, when the target was introduced, to 2011. It can be seen that relatively good compliance with the target was secured within a year, but it is worth

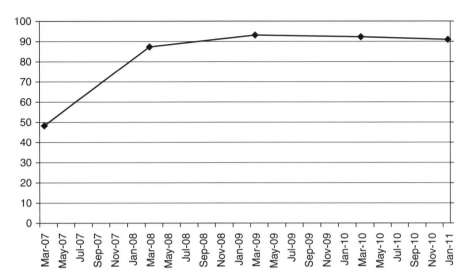

FIGURE 25.4 Percentage of admitted patients with RTT (referral to treatment) time of 18 weeks or less March 2007 – January 2011 in the NHS in England
Source: Department of Health

noting that since the national target was abolished in mid-2010 by the new government, performance has declined.

There are many problems – practical and conceptual – which face those who develop performance indicators, but they can be grouped into four main areas or themes (Carter et al. 1992; Smith 1995; Freeman 2002):

- **Validity** – is the indicator actually measuring what it purports to measure, and is that a valid marker of organizational performance? Here the complexities and uncertainties of healthcare delivery are often a problem – indicators tend to treat organizations, services and patients as if they are homogeneous when in practice there is great heterogeneity of context. For example, the rates or proportions of delayed discharges from hospital might be seen as measuring the hospital's performance in effective bed management and discharge planning, but it could equally be affected by poor quality and availability in community health services post-discharge, or by patient characteristics such as the availability of family and carer support.

- **Reliability** – is the indicator accurate, and what problems might affect its accuracy? For example, is the data complete or are there problems with missing data?; is the data collected consistently and accurately across organizations?; does the indicator make use of proxy data items (where we measure one thing because data on another is not available and assume the two to be related)?; are there statistical issues of uncertainty because the data is based on relatively small numbers of cases, and so on?

- **Comparability** – almost all indicators are used for the purposes of comparison, and those comparisons may be made with an externally set target, over time, with other similar organizations, or with other different organizations. In each case, the question has to be whether the comparison is appropriate and meaningful. So, for example, when making comparisons over time (how a healthcare organization's performance has changed since last year), it is important to consider what has changed in the wider context or environment and what other plausible explanations might exist for any temporal trend. When comparing one organization with another, one has to consider whether the two organizations differ in important respects which may affect performance. For example, a large specialist hospital and a small district general hospital will have very different case-mixes of patients and acuity burdens, which will affect their use of resources such as length of stay, diagnostics and pharmaceutical costs, and so on.

- **Attribution or causation** – perhaps the most fundamental and continuing question about any performance indicator is whether it can be fairly attributed to organizational performance, or whether other factors outside the organization or beyond its control are actually the causal drivers. For example, does a rising trend in the numbers of complaints against a healthcare organization show problems with the quality of care, or does it show that the organization is getting better at recording and responding to patients' concerns, or does it show that people in general are becoming more assertive and discerning consumers who are readier to voice dissatisfaction?

The health status measures from the OECD health data set listed in Figure 25.3 illustrate these problems of validity, reliability, comparability and attribution very well. One topical example is the mortality rate and morbidity rate or incidence for common cancers such as lung cancer, breast cancer, cervical cancer, prostate cancer, gastrointestinal cancer and skin cancer. The validity of these measures as indicators of health system performance is open to question because important environmental and social determinants shape cancer rates; their reliability is questionable because practice from country to country in recording cancer diagnoses and deaths varies; the comparability of countries with and without certain key health systems (for example, free and comprehensive screening programmes for breast cancer) is dubious; and because we really don't understand the causes of strong temporal trends in skin and prostate cancer (both of which have become more common) we should be cautious about attributing change to health system behaviours. In short, performance indicators often raise questions but do not answer them, and caution should be exercised in using them to draw definitive conclusions.

The developers of performance indicators often seem more interested in the data than in how it will be used, and concerned more with the technicalities of indicator design than with the application of indicators in pursuit of improvement. But without well-established and effective mechanisms for performance management, performance measurement can become little more than an academic exercise, and so now we turn to an exploration of performance management.

Performance management: mechanisms and approaches

We illustrated in Figure 25.2 a performance regime which structured the approaches to performance management into four main areas – top down performance management; markets, competition and contestability; user choice and voice; and capability and capacity building. We now examine each of these four areas in turn to understand how performance information is used to shape and influence organizational performance, and which mechanisms for performance management exist.

Top down performance management

Perhaps the most traditional way to get things done is to tell people to do them. In many large and hierarchical organizations, whether in the public or private sector, what is sometimes termed bureaucratic direction is the order of the day. The longevity of the traditional bureaucracy is a testament to its effectiveness and resilience (du Gay 2000). Of course, central control and top down direction are known to have their problems and limitations – it presumes that the centre knows what to do, it applies homogeneous and one-size-fits-all prescriptive instructions when in fact local contextual variations may be not just legitimate but necessary, and most of all it may be profoundly disempowering and disabling for leaders at the frontline, who are neither encouraged nor rewarded for creativity, initiative and enterprise. But Bevan and Hood's (2006) insightful account of the use of 'targets and terror' in the English NHS, Berwick's (2008) comparisons of quality improvement efforts in the UK and the USA and Kizer et al.'s (2000) experience in reforming the US Veterans Administration healthcare system all demonstrate that, though it has its limitations and unhelpful side effects, central control and direction in a large integrated healthcare system can produce rapid and widespread performance improvement when there is a clear and relatively simple central vision and a strong central will backed by measurements, incentives and sanctions.

Of course there are relatively few countries these days where the whole health-care system is structured and organized as if it were a single organization, and in most places the healthcare sector is a complex and confusing landscape of funders like insurers and sickness funds, and healthcare providers of all sorts (state, not-for-profit or for-profit entities), and regulators provide some or even most of the top down performance management to be seen. Healthcare regulation is used widely in many countries, with regulators tasked with overseeing or scrutinizing healthcare organizations, licensing and inspecting them, and taking enforcement action when they perform poorly (Walshe 2003). Some have argued that regulatory oversight of this kind has increasingly supplanted or replaced government ownership, direction or intervention in public services such as healthcare systems (Majone 1994).

Regulatory agencies generally have a statutory responsibility for the oversight of healthcare organizations, and the regulatory architecture and focus are determined by its legislative foundations, but in most cases regulators are tasked with three main responsibilities: (1) setting out their expectations of performance in standards or directions; (2) monitoring compliance with those expectations through data collection, surveys or visits, investigations and the like; and (3) acting to deal with organizations which do not comply through some kind of enforcement (Hood et al. 1999). Performance measurement is therefore a core concern for most regulators, and many invest substantial effort in both defining and collating a range of performance information for the organizations they regulate. Many regulators also use this information in regulatory enforcement – they publish performance data and use the effects of public and peer pressure on healthcare organizations to drive improved performance. One important difference – which we return to at the end of this chapter – is that regulators usually work with a wide range of both quantitative and qualitative performance data – and a spectrum from what is sometimes termed 'hard' to 'soft' intelligence (Goodwin et al. 2006). For example, the regulator overseeing a large hospital may have quantitative comparative data on performance in areas like mortality and morbidity, qualitative and quantitative data from patient surveys, and other data such as information about complaints, reports and views from stakeholders such as local physicians, local authorities and patient groups, and so on. It faces the difficult task of deciding how to integrate and weight this information in shaping its actions on regulatory enforcement. But top-down performance management through regulation is very different in scale, scope and reach from direct bureaucratic direction of the kind described earlier. Regulatory agencies often have a huge scope, overseeing thousands of clinics, nursing homes and hospitals, and very limited regulatory resources. While they can design their regulatory regime to be intelligent, responsive and proportionate (Ayres and Braithwaite 1992), it is inevitable that they deal mostly with the worst performing organizations, and are usually concerned with setting minimum standards rather than driving improvement across all organizations.

Markets, competition and contestability

Markets for public services, and particularly for health services, are very different from the idealized form of the market beloved of some economists. Without rehearsing all the important differences, key ones include the information asymmetries which exist between healthcare providers, on the one hand, and consumers and funders, on the other; the fact that service users are usually not paying directly for the services they consume and so do not have the normal behavioural incentives of buyers in a market; the natural monopolies and near monopolies which often exist in healthcare provision; and the co-produced and differentiated nature of health services where standardized products are rare and services are a product of provider–patient interaction. Given our interest is in performance management, a particular concern may be whether providing performance information redresses the information asymmetries referred to above, and makes consumers and funders more informed and discerning in their purchasing decisions.

There is good evidence from the USA and more limited evidence elsewhere that competition among healthcare providers produces two kinds of performance improvement – reduced prices, and improved quality (Kessler and McClellan 2000; Propper et al. 2008). It is generally easier to measure the former than the latter, because data on costs and prices is more robust and more routinely available. But it is not unusual for prices in healthcare markets to be fixed, through a system of set tariffs and prospectively determined payments for particular services. Healthcare funders or governments set those prices, and then competition between providers on price is essentially eliminated and competition on other dimensions of performance such as responsiveness, access, clinical quality and environment come to the fore, but the quality and availability of information in these areas are often limited.

User choice and voice

In healthcare systems where users have the opportunity to choose which healthcare provider they turn to for healthcare, substantial effort has often been invested in providing performance information in ways and formats that users and the public may be able to use in their decision-making. The publication of performance information and ratings for healthcare organizations and sometimes even for individual clinicians has become relatively common, and some healthcare organizations have themselves taken to publishing such data for themselves. For example, someone choosing a nursing home in the United States can through the government-funded NH-Compare website access virtually all the performance data collected by regulators about the nursing homes in their area, including information about complaints, inspections, staffing levels, facilities, and so on (Harrington et al. 2003). But research on the public disclosure of performance information suggests that it is often not well used by patients or the public, who may distrust the sources, not understand its meaning, and place greater store by other information such as shared personal experience (Marshall 2000; Marshall et al. 2007). Even so, public disclosure does seem to drive healthcare professionals and healthcare organizations to respond in a variety of ways – some of which improve performance though there can be perverse behaviours and effects as well (Berwick and Wald 1990).

There is probably a stronger evidence base for using patients and the public collectively rather than individually as a mechanism for performance management, by institutionalizing arrangements for patient 'voice' either internally (through patient or user groups, councils, patient representatives on boards or governing bodies, and so on) or externally (through patient and public engagement in regulatory or other oversight arrangements, democratic accountability through local government, and other forums). Well-organized patient groups, particularly those focused on a particular disease area where there is a motivated and articulate patient population, can be powerful advocates for change and improvement, as examples like mental health, maternity services, and services for the elderly all demonstrate (Barnes and Newman 2007).

Capability and capacity building

The final area of performance management shown in Figure 25.2 is described as capability and capacity building, and might alternatively be described as organizational development (the subject of Chapter 20 in this book). In short, it encompasses the support for performance improvement which may be provided by a range of external agencies – including management consultancies, professional associations, universities and other education and training organizations, and so on. Such support may be sought by an organization which recognizes its need for organizational development or may be offered or even pressed on poorly performing organizations by agencies such as regulators or government.

One area where capability and capacity building has been particularly prominent in the past decade in many healthcare systems is leadership, and leadership development. Policy-makers and national agencies have invested substantial resources in creating national leadership programmes aimed at senior clinicians (doctors, nurses and other professionals) and at both current and future senior managers, with a founding assumption that improving organizational leadership will improve organizational performance (Hartley 2010). In fact, empirical evidence for a connection between leadership and performance is not easy to come by (Boyne and Dahya 2002). Nevertheless, across Europe, the perceived need for better leadership has led to the development of leadership academies, development programmes, coaching and mentoring support for top leaders, talent management programmes, and the like (Goodwin 2006). In the UK, national policy has focused particularly on widening clinical participation in leadership, and growing a future generation of clinicians (particularly doctors) who are more competent, adaptable, effective and emotionally intelligent leaders. The professional associations – the medical Royal Colleges, the Academy of Medical Sciences, the General Medical Council and the British Medical Association – have been involved in developing both competency frameworks for medical leadership and programmes of education and training in this area (Clark et al. 2008).

A second area of substantial investment in capability and capacity building related particularly to poorly performing, troubled or failing healthcare organizations, where external advisors and support for organizational 'turnaround' is increasingly used. In some cases, organizations in difficulties seek this kind of intervention, and bring in consultancies or other agencies with the specific skills they need, but in other cases turnaround interventions are prescribed and administered at the command of shareholders, regulators, government departments and others, with the reluctant assent of the targeted organization. This kind of turnaround work has been described as consisting of three basic stages – replacement, retrenchment and renewal (Walshe et al. 2004). In the first phase, key senior leaders are often removed from the organization and a new or revised top team is put in place. In the second, rapid and often radical changes to services are planned and implemented to stem losses, deal with the major short-term problems, and stabilize the organization. In the final phase, a new future strategic direction for the organization is developed, and the transition of control back to a competent internal leadership and normal governance arrangements is effected.

Critiques of performance management: control or chimera?

So far, we have largely taken performance management on face value, but this section sets out to explore some common critiques which, at the very least, deserve to be heard. We examine four main arguments. The first concerns what might be seen as the clash of ideologies or paradigms between performance management and the healthcare sector. The second relates to the functional purpose and effectiveness of performance management – does it work? The third concerns the robustness, rigour and utility of performance measures themselves and the perverse behaviours and unintended or unexpected consequences of their application. The fourth and last relates to the way that performance management has grown and spread across countries and sectors, and the self-fulfilling nature of its internal logic.

First, performance management is certainly not value-free – in fact, it is strongly ideologically driven and is founded on a fairly neo-liberal 'new public management' view of healthcare organizations (Clarke and Newman 1997). It was noted on p. 518 that the underlying theoretical framework is essentially positivist, rationalist and reductionist, and the organizational metaphor which fits most readily with the performance movement ideology is that of the organization as a machine. Yet this sits uneasily with the lived experience of performance management and improvement in healthcare, which often places particular emphasis on the unique professional culture and the shared sets of social norms it creates, the sense of social mission and purpose in healthcare organizations and its capacity to unite diverse groups around a common aim, the collective nature of leadership in healthcare organizations, and the place of science and evidence in decision-making (Walburg et al. 2006). There is a discordance between the rhetoric of managerialism and control beloved of the performance management movement and the reality of both clinical and managerial processes in healthcare organizations and healthcare systems which are more politically shaped, more negotiated, and simply rather more messy and muddled than the rhetoric acknowledges (Klein 2010).

Second, we should ask a question which might be thought to matter greatly to the advocates of performance management – quite simply, does it work? After all, in the positivist, rational model, the functional effectiveness of performance management must be the main or even only measure of its success. The evidence is somewhat equivocal, as a number of researchers have noted over the years (Carter et al. 1992; Hood 1998; Pollitt et al. 2010), and reviews largely conclude that performance management is an imperfect tool, with rather weak and mixed effects, which should be deployed with intelligence, caution and care (Freeman 2002). But we can identify particular areas of patient care where performance measurement and management seem, on the face of it, to have worked rather well. For example, the publication of performance data has become widely accepted in cardiothoracic surgery – across Europe, surgeons from 23 countries now contribute data to the European cardiothoracic surgery database. That initiative has been in place for about four years, but in England surgeons have been collecting and sharing similar performance data for eight years, and the results show that over that time both crude and case-mix adjusted mortality rates have fallen, while case complexity has risen (Bridgewater et al. 2007). The European comparisons show that the UK has the lowest mortality rates for cardiac surgery in Europe, and manages to have low lengths of stay as well – something that UK surgeons attribute to the long tradition of gathering and using performance data in this specialty, ever since a high profile scandal over poor quality paediatric cardiac surgery at the Bristol Royal Infirmary in the 1990s led to the establishment of systems for comparative performance measurement (Walshe and Offen 2001).

Third, as we have already noted, there are constant debates about the validity, reliability, rigour and robustness of performance indicators and their suitability for some of the purposes to which they are put. A particular concern which we have not yet examined is that their use is essentially distorting and damaging – leading to unintended and unwanted consequences and what some have labelled perverse behaviours, often directly subverting or undermining the intentions of performance measurement (Smith 1995). There are many ways in which this can happen, but we examine five of the most significant: the neglect of the unmeasured; goal displacement; adaptation to the performance cycle; floor, ceiling and other threshold effects; data manipulation and data falsification.

Performance measurement cannot be all encompassing, and there will always be important areas of performance which are not measured. There is therefore a risk that the unmeasured aspects of performance are neglected by organizations, and all attention and resources are focused on those issues which are the subject of perfor-mance measurement. Equally, there is a risk that valid and important local goals for the organization are displaced by the national targets and standards embedded in performance measurement systems. The performance cycle is often annual, quarterly or even monthly – and the shorter the cycle of measurement, the more it may drive organizations to adopt short-term measures and methods for improvement which are focused on the timeline set by performance measurement rather than on other more natural or useful timelines. When indicators and standards are cast in terms of thresh-olds such as a minimum or maximum value that must be achieved, organizations may respond to such thresholds either by treating them as limits on effort (there is no point in 'overperforming' the target) or by making only token efforts at improvement if they perceive little realistic prospect of them meeting the target. Finally, the data used in performance measurement is mostly collected by healthcare organizations and they therefore have the opportunity to change data collection in ways that would en-hance their apparent performance. At its most benign, this may mean ensuring that data is as complete and accurate as possible; more significantly, it might mean ensur-ing that cases are coded by diagnosis in ways that maximize apparent case intensity and case-mix so that income is increased; ultimately it may involve deliberate data falsification, such as the omission of some cases from the data, or the alteration of key dates and other data items to make the organizations appear compliant when it is not.

Fourth, it can be argued that performance management has a life of its own – and, once established, tends to grow and spread because of what Pollitt et al. (2010) have called the 'logic of escalation'. For example, the number of performance indicators tends to grow, the areas of coverage extend, and the statistical complexity of measures increases. Formative approaches to performance tend to become summative, and the levers for changed performance are ramped up with the growing use of both incen-tives and sanctions. A performance 'industry' of regulators, government departments, professional organizations, consultancies, academic units and others grows up, all of whom have self-interested reasons to want the continuing existence and further growth of performance management. All in all, performance measurement and management are much easier to introduce and extend than they are to remove or reduce, and they are very rarely abolished – though successive policy-makers, dissatisfied with the results of performance management, often reform them again and again.

Conclusion

Performance management has both its advocates and its detractors. Some see it as bringing a necessary rigour and accountability to complacent and mediocre healthcare organizations. Others regard it as subverting the human values of professionalism and caring and the sense of social mission which are so important in the healthcare sector, and setting aside the skills and judgements of healthcare professionals in favour of the dessicated calculations of accountants and auditors. The truth is probably somewhere in between. Healthcare organizations have neither wholly knightly nor knavish motivations (Le Grand 2006) and perhaps the greatest contribution of performance management can be to bring rigour and clarity to bear in reinforcing rather than attenuating the noble values and aspirations of healthcare organizations.

Looking to the future, what differences might we see in healthcare performance management over the next decade? Making predictions can be perilous, but we can identify some clear trends in current thinking which are likely to be important in coming years. First, and most obviously, our technical capacity to gather, process and report on data continues to grow rapidly, and to enable ever more detailed and comprehensive performance measurement systems. The internet allows us to make this data available, in all kinds of ways, in near real time, to anyone who wants to use it. Of course, as was noted earlier, the capacity of patients and the public to use such information may lag well behind the healthcare system's capacity to produce it, but the pervasive influence of informatics on everything from how we choose consumer products to how democratic process work will not pass by the healthcare system. Second, while the measurement of performance has been cast largely in terms of the professional and managerial perspective on health services and organizations to date, there is a growing interest in and influence for patient perspectives. Regular and ongoing patient surveys can now provide a hugely detailed data set on patients' experiences and reports and on their expectations and views of those experiences. Moreover, when patients are asked to report on their health status and functioning, we can now map and measure the changes in health status and function which result from significant healthcare interventions. In the future, we will have patient-reported outcome measures for people with chronic conditions like diabetes and rheumatoid arthritis, and for people undergoing costly surgery such as joint replacement or cardiac artery bypass grafting. This data is likely to reveal big variations in clinical practice which until now have been largely hidden from view. Third, the performance measurement and management systems have been largely focused on quantitative data up to now, even though we know that more qualitative data often has greater value and credibility in making judgements about performance. One reason for that is, quite simply, that quantitative data is easier to collect, manage, process and report on – but as technology makes it cheaper and more feasible to gather and use qualitative data, we may see the more widespread use of aggregated qualitative data in performance management.

Summary box

- Performance measurement and management systems have grown and spread across healthcare systems in many countries over the past two decades, because of increased societal expectations of accountability and oversight, greater technical capacity for measurement, and extensive evidence of performance variations.

- Performance management is founded on a positivist, mechanistic and rationalist paradigm which does not fit well with the political dynamics and lived experience of healthcare systems and organizations.

- Performance measurement uses data on organizational inputs, processes and outputs and on healthcare outcomes to build indicators which are intended to be meaningful measures of organizational performance – in other words, the primary determinant of variation in the indicator is within the locus of control of the organization.

- Performance indicators cover many domains, such as economy, efficiency, effectiveness, equity, acceptability and access. Key problems in forming indicators relate to their validity, reliability, comparability, and attribution or causation.

- Performance management mechanisms draw on performance measures and use that data to bring about improved performance. Four key mechanisms exist: top-down performance management; markets, competition and contestability; user choice and voice; and capability and capacity building.

- Critiques of performance management include the clash of ideologies or paradigms between performance management and the healthcare sector; the functional purpose and effectiveness of performance management; the robustness, rigour and utility of performance measures themselves and the perverse behaviours and unintended or unexpected consequences of their application; and the way that performance management has grown and spread across countries and sectors, and the self-fulfilling nature of its internal logic.

Self-test exercises

1 Map the performance regime for your own healthcare organization, showing all the external agencies and institutions which have some interest in steering or influencing your organization's performance. For each agency/institution, write a short account of what data it uses for performance measurement, and what mechanisms it has in place for performance management.

2 Take one of the main domains of measurement contained in the OECD health data set and chose four or five countries including your own and others that are similar in terms of level of economic development but different in the arrangements for healthcare funding and provision. Produce a structured comparison of the countries' performance on each indicator and overall across the domain, and identify plausible explanations for the variations in performance you find.

References and further reading

Audit Commission (2000) *On Target: The Practice of Performance Indicators*. London: Audit Commission.

Ayres, I. and Braithwaite, J. (1992) *Responsive Regulation: Transcending the Deregulation Debate*. Oxford: Oxford University Press.

Barber, M. (2007) *Instruction to Deliver: Tony Blair, Public Services and the Challenge of Achieving Targets*. London: Politicos.

Barnes, M. and Newman, J. (2007) *Power, Participation and Political Renewal: Case Studies in Public Participation*. Bristol: Policy Press.

Berwick, D. (2008) A transatlantic review of the NHS at 60. *BMJ*, 2008; 337: a838.

Berwick, D.M. and Wald, D.L. (1990) Hospital leaders' opinions of the HCFA mortality data. *JAMA*, 263(2): 247–9.

Bevan, G. and Hood, C. (2006) What's measured is what matters: targets and gaming in the English public health system. *Public Administration*, 84(3): 517–38.

Bouckaert, G. and Halligan, J. (2008) *Managing Performance: International Comparisons*. London: Routledge.

Boyne, G.A. and Dahya, J. (2002) Executive succession and the performance of public organizations. *Public Administration*, 80(1): 179–200.

Bridgewater, B., Grayson A.D., Brooks, N. et al. (2007) Has the publication of cardiac surgery outcome data been associated with changes in practice in northwest England?: an analysis of 25730 patients undergoing CABG surgery under 30 surgeons over eight years. *Heart*, 93: 744–8.

Buchan, I. (2011) Health informatics. In K. Walshe and J. Smith (eds) *Healthcare Management*, 2nd edn. Maidenhead: Open University Press.

Cabinet Office (2006) *The UK Government's Approach to Public Services Reform*. London: Cabinet Office.

Carter, N., Klein, R. and Day, P. (1992) *How Organisations Measure Success: The Use of Performance Indicators in Government*. London: Routledge.

Clark, J., Spurgeon, P. and Hamilton, P. (2008) Medical professionalism: leadership competency – an essential ingredient. *The International Journal of Clinical Leadership*, 16(1): 3–9.

Clarke, J. and Newman, J. (1997) *The Managerial State*. London: Sage.

Cluzeau, F., Littlejohns, P., Grimshaw, J.M., Feder, G. and Moran, S.E. (1999) Development and application of a generic methodology to assess the quality of clinical guidelines. *International Journal of Quality Health Care*, 11(1): 21–8.

Cutler, D.M. and Sheiner, L. (1998) The geography of Medicare. *American Economic Review* 89(2): 228–33.

Department of Health (2010) *Referral to Treatment Consultant-led Waiting Time Rules: A 'How to' Guide to Applying National Waiting Time Rules Locally*. London: Department Health.

Du Gay, P. (2000) *In Praise of Bureaucracy*. London: Sage.

Freeman, T. (2002) Using performance indicators to improve health care quality in the public sector: a review of the literature. *Health Services Management Research*, 15: 126–37.

Goodwin, N. (2006) *Leadership in Healthcare: A European Perspective*. Abingdon: Routledge.

Goodwin, N., Harvey, G., Hyde, P. et al. (2006) *Recognising, Understanding and Addressing Performance Problems in Healthcare Organisations Providing Care to NHS Patients: A Developmental Resource*. London: Department of Health.

Harrington, C., O'Meara, J., Kitchener, M., Simon, L.P. and Schnelle, J.F. (2003) Designing a report card for nursing facilities: what information is needed and why. *The Gerontologist* 43(suppl 2): 47–57.

Hartley, J. (2010) *Leadership for Healthcare*. Bristol: Policy Press.

Hood, C. (1998) *The Art of the State: Culture, Rhetoric and Public Management*. Oxford: Clarendon Press.

Hood, C., Scott, C., James, O. et al. (1999) *Regulation Inside Government*. Oxford: Oxford University Press.

Kessler, D. and McClellan, M. (2000) Is hospital competition socially wasteful? *Quarterly Journal of Economics*, 115(2): 577–616.

Kizer, K.W., Demakis, J.G. and Feussner, J.R. (2000) Reinventing VA Health Care: systematizing quality improvement and quality innovation. *Medical Care* 38(6): 17–116.

Klein, R. (2010) *The New Politics of the NHS: From Creation to Reinvention*. Oxford: Radcliffe.

Le Grand, J. (2006) *Motivation, Agency and Public Policy: Of Knights and Knaves and Pawns and Queens*. Oxford: Oxford University Press.

Majone, G. (1994) The rise of the regulatory state in Europe. *West European Politics*, 17(3): 77–101.

Marshall, M. (2000) The public release of performance data: what do we expect to gain? A review of the evidence. *Journal of the American Medical Association*, 283: 1866–74.

Marshall, M., Noble, J., Davies, H. et al. (2007) Development of an information source for patients and the public about general practice services: an action research study. *Health Expectations*, 9: 265–74.

Morgan, G. (1988) *Images of Organisations*. Beverly Hills, CA: Sage.

Moynihan, D.P. (2008) *The Dynamics of Performance Management: Constructing Information and Reform*. Washington, DC: Georgetown University Press.

O'Neill, O. (2002) *A Question of Trust*. Cambridge: Cambridge University Press.

Pollitt, C., Harrison, S., Dowswell, G., Jerak-Zuiderent, S. and Bal, R. (2010) Performance regimes in health care: institutions, critical junctures and the logic of escalation in England and the Netherlands. *Evaluation* 16: 13.

Power, M. (1997) *The Audit Society: Rituals of Verification*. Oxford: Oxford University Press.

Propper, C., Burgess, S. and Gossage, D. (2008) Competition and quality: evidence from the NHS internal market 1991–99. *Economic Journal*, 118: 138–70.

Putnam, D. (2000) *Bowling Alone: The Collapse and Revival of American Community*. New York: Simon & Schuster.

Radin, B. (2006) *Challenging the Performance Movement: Accountability, Complexity and Democratic Values*. Washington, DC: Georgetown University Press.

Smith, P. (1995) The unintended consequences of publishing performance data in the public sector. *International Journal of Public Administration*, 18(2): 277–310.

Talbot, C. (2010) *Theories of Performance: Organizational and Service Improvement in the Public Domain*. Oxford: Oxford University Press.

Talbot, C. and Johnson, C. (2005) *Exploring Performance Regimes: A Report for the National Audit Office*. Manchester: Manchester Business School.

Walburg, J., Bevan, H., Wilderspin, J. and Lemmens, K. (eds) (2006) *Performance Management in Health Care*. London: Routledge.

Walshe, K. (2003) *Regulating Healthcare: A Prescription for Improvement?* Buckingham: Open University Press.

Walshe, K., Harvey, G., Hyde, P. and Pandit, N. (2004) Organisational failure and turnaround: lessons for public services from the for-profit sector. *Public Money and Management*, 24(4): 201–8.

Walshe, K., Harvey, G. and Jas, P. (eds) (2010) *From Knowing to Doing: Connecting Knowledge and Performance in Public Services*. Cambridge: Cambridge University Press.

Walshe, K. and Offen, N. (2001) A very public failure: lessons for quality improvement in healthcare organizations from the Bristol Royal Infirmary. *Quality in Health Care*, 10: 250–6.

Walshe, K. and Shortell, S.M. (2004) What happens when things go wrong: how healthcare organizations deal with major failures. *Health Affairs*, 23(3): 103–11.

Websites and resources

Commonwealth Fund international comparisons of health system performance: http://www.commonwealthfund.org/Topics/International-Health-Policy.aspx.

Department of Health performance and statistics: http://www.dh.gov.uk/en/Publicationsandstatistics/Statistics/Performancedataandstatistics/index.htm.

Medicare Nursing Home Compare: www.medicare.gov/nhcompare/.

NHS Information centre: www.ic.nhs.uk/.

OECD Health Data Set: www.oecd.org/health/healthdata.

World Health organization regional office for Europe health data: http://www.euro.who.int/en/what-we-do/data-and-evidence.

CHAPTER 26

Managing strategic collaboration

Helen Dickinson and Helen Sullivan

Introduction

Boundaries are an inevitable part of organization. Analyse any health system in any part of the world and you will find boundaries. These boundaries might be structural, but they may also be procedural, professional, cultural, disciplinary, institutional or a combination of these and others. While boundaries between different parts of healthcare services (e.g. primary/secondary care, nurse/allied health professional, nephrology/endocrinology) are important, the types of boundaries that exist between healthcare organizations and wider welfare services have in recent years received much attention. Working across sectoral boundaries through different forms of collaboration is regarded as a crucial activity in providing high quality welfare services to a population. Many countries have developed initiatives that have attempted to bring together health organizations with those from social care, education, leisure, housing, etc., often encompassing not just statutory bodies, but also non-governmental, commercial and voluntary sector organizations. Collaboration may take place between an extensive array of potential partners and at many different levels.

This chapter uses the term collaboration specifically to refer to those joint or shared activities that take place primarily at a strategic level. We focus on interactions that address high-level and long-ranging objectives and activities for welfare services within a specific area, be this geographical or service. We argue that the need for these types of arrangements has intensified due to wider changes in how public services are organized and delivered in different country contexts. The combined impact of the introduction of market principles into the public sector, specialization and user involvement has led to increasing 'congestion' in welfare services as more and more different bodies have become involved in the service design, delivery and regulation. In many countries, collaboration has been used as a mechanism for steering the actions of this diverse range of partners. Clearly this is just one form of collaborative activity and other forms of healthcare collaboration and coordination are covered in different chapters of this volume (e.g. Chapter 10 on chronic disease and integrated care).

The case for collaboration is made most frequently on the basis that working together should improve outcomes for service users, carers and the wider population. However, despite considerable investment in research and evaluation of collaborative action, the available evidence does not seem to entirely support this case. One reason that has been offered for this partial evidential picture is the difficulty of evaluating collaborative action in general and outcomes in particular.

In this chapter, we argue that these difficulties and complexities are not insurmountable, although the costs may not be considered worthwhile in practice. More problematic is the lack of clarity among policy-makers and practitioners about what strategic collaboration is aiming to achieve beyond a broad sense that it is something that is innately 'good'. Ambitious claims to improve services and outcomes for individuals and populations are rarely supported by detail of what successful strategic collaboration would look like and how it could be recognized. This chapter examines literature from a range of different national settings to examine what strategic collaboration might be able to deliver and how partners might seek to work together effectively in collaboration.

The first section of the chapter sets out a short account of why it is that strategic collaboration has come to be seen as an important activity in the field of welfare services. A consideration is then made of what the evidence says about the impact of strategic collaboration, identifying both the limitations of available evidence and the potential negative impacts of collaboration that can fail to be recognized. The chapter then considers the key issues for the future of strategic collaboration, before offering some conclusions on the material covered in this chapter.

A brief history of strategic collaboration

Since the mid-1990s there has been a significant interest in collaborative activities in many different areas of the world. Collaboration is not a 'new' issue by any means; aspirations for health organizations to work with other bodies and sectors have been around for some time. For example, in the UK context, Glasby (2007) argues that by establishing the welfare state on a series of functionalized organizational silos (health, education, social security, etc.), policy-makers institutionalized a set of organizational boundaries. Overcoming these boundaries in order to provide more 'seamless' support and care for individuals has been a key feature of successive administrations in the post-war period.

Similarly, in many other developed countries, public health organizations have long experience of working together with town planning, environmental health, education, transport, law enforcement and others in an attempt to help reduce and eradicate epidemic infectious diseases. In many areas these types of diseases have been brought under control, but this has been counterbalanced by a rise in chronic illnesses which are non-communicable. These kinds of shifts in disease aetiology and changes in demographic compositions, along with the rise of so-called 'wicked issues' (Rittel and Webber 1973) are argued to have driven the need for more effective collaboration between health agencies and others.

But it is not simply just changes in disease patterns and social challenges that have driven this interest in strategic collaboration. This has also been driven by wider factors surrounding a perceived move from 'government' to 'governance'.

In the late nineteenth and early part of the twentieth century, many developed countries expanded the role of government in social and public life. The development of welfare states in countries including Germany, the Netherlands, New Zealand, Denmark, Sweden and Uruguay reflected the view that government should accept greater responsibility for the health and welfare of their populations. Over time these government functions expanded to take on a range of different welfare responsibilities as well as deciding what kinds of services should be delivered to their populations and how these would be provided. However, from the late 1970s, following a series of international economic crises, a management paradigm known as New Public Management (NPM) emerged.

New Public Management (NPM)

Essentially, NPM is founded on a critique of bureaucracy as the organizing principle of public administration (Dunleavy 1991). The NPM view of bureaucracy is that it is inflexible and overly hierarchical. The top-down decision-making processes associated with this model were suggested to be increasingly distant from the expectations of citizens. NPM theorists drew on the commercial sector for lessons, arguing that because of the large-scale international competition private sector organizations had been exposed to from the 1980s onwards, those successful had become increasingly efficient, while also offering consumers products which they wanted. The commercial sector had undergone radical change but it was argued that the public sector remained 'rigid and bureaucratic, expensive, and inefficient' (Pierre and Peters 2000: 5).

Although it is never described as such by the authors, one text that illustrates facets of an NPM approach is Osborne and Gaebler's (1993) *Reinventing Government*. One of this text's key principles is that governments should 'steer, not row'. The implication here is that if governments concentrate more on *what* should be delivered (and performance managing this), instead of *how* it should be delivered, they will be more effective. As big bureaucracy had 'failed to deliver', the solution was to disaggregate these large governments via the creation of 'arm's length agencies', separate 'purchasers' and 'providers' of services, and non-state providers. In many countries 'in-house' provision was replaced by provision from a multiplicity of public, private and voluntary organizations.

In many areas of the world, commentators have become concerned about the impact of markets on welfare services. They have questioned the degree to which a 'pure' market might work in health and have pointed to the risks associated with the operation of markets, including the increasing fragmentation and 'congestion' of the public sector which presented significant challenges to the state's steering capacity. Fragmentation refers to the separation of functions within welfare services, e.g. the split between commissioners and providers of services, while congestion refers to the increasing number of commissioners and providers engaged in service design and delivery. This is discussed by Sullivan and Skelcher (2002: 15–20) in terms of 'the hollowed out state', where government continued to be responsible for identifying what services were needed, but much less involved in actually delivering them.

Networks

Paradoxically at the very time that governments in many countries were starting to focus on more complex, cross-cutting social problems, their capacity to respond to them using the traditional 'command and control' mechanisms of *government* had been dissipated. Alternative mechanisms were needed that were able to coordinate the multiplicity of providers involved in the 'patchwork' of service delivery. Attention shifted to the potential of networks to respond to this coordination challenge. Networks appear inherently 'desirable in that they are more flexible and responsive than hierarchies, and capable of avoiding the 'anarchic' disbenefits of markets' (Newman 2001: 17).

The changing role of the state and the increasing involvement of non-state actors involved in providing services have been characterized as representing a shift from *government* to *governance*. These patterns in governance have been described by Osborne (2006) in his account of New Public Governance and the characteristics of this are set out in Table 26.1. This table is helpful in setting out the types of characteristics and values associated with these different modes of governance. It is a short-hand way of looking at international patterns of governance, but this does not mean in all areas that there was a simple linear progression from hierarchy through markets to networks in terms of welfare delivery. Yet, this perspective is an over-simplification in the sense that these types of discussions of governance tend to suggest that markets, hierarchies and networks are mutually distinct forms of organizing which are identifiably different from one another. Indeed, this is the position held by a number of prominent theorists (for example, Powell 1990). However, as empirical research has demonstrated, networks can take a number of different forms; some of which are 'hierarchical networks' (e.g. Hennart 1993) and others 'market networks' (e.g. Macneil 1980; Williamson 1985). The concept of the quasi-market denotes the presence of some broadly market-based relationships but within a predominantly hierarchical setting (Le Grand and Bartlett 1993).

In recent years there has been a tendency to equate collaboration, or partnership efforts, with networks (e.g. Hudson 2004). Indeed, there is a significant literature associated with the international study of health and welfare networks and the benefits that these ways of organizing have over other governance forms such as hierarchies and markets. However, in practice, what has emerged in most countries are not forms of 'networked governance' in a pure sense, but forms of hybrids between these ways of organizing. Rummery (2002: 230) succinctly makes this point, stating:

> While the British welfare state probably never exhibited 'pure' forms of either bureaucratic or marketised methods of governing, and is probably also unlikely to ever exhibit 'pure' forms of networked governance, in theory partnerships are to networked governance what contracts are to markets and command-and-control mechanisms are to bureaucracies: an essential element of that particular method of government.

Implications of governance for healthcare managers

This does not mean that we can say that these movements are not important though. There are a number of significant implications of these developments for the management of health and welfare services. There is a much wider range of bodies

TABLE 26.1 Elements of the NPG, in contrast to PA and the NPM

Paradigm/key elements	Theoretical roots	Nature of the state	Focus	Emphasis	Relationship to external (non-public) organizational partners	Governance mechanism	Value base
Public Administration	Political science and public policy	Unitary	The policy system	Policy implementation	Potential elements of the policy system	Hierarchy	Public sector ethos
New Public Management	Rational/public choice theory and management studies	Disaggregated	Intra-organizational management	Service inputs and outputs	Independent contractors within a competitive market-place	The market and classical or neo-classical contracts	Efficacy of competition and the market-place
New Public Governance	Organizational sociology and network theory	Plural and pluralist	Inter-organizational governance	Service processes and outcomes	Preferred suppliers, and often inter-dependent agents within ongoing relationships	Trust or relational contracts	Neo-corporatist

Source: Osborne (2006: 383).

involved in the design and delivery of welfare services. Therefore healthcare managers need to interact with an array of different actors, who might come from statutory or commercial bodies, and the voluntary and community sector. These different agencies and organizations might have very diverse perspectives on what should be delivered in terms of health services and how. In addition, health organizations might not have any form of direct control over these bodies, so health managers may find that they have to develop alternative means of interacting with them to get what they want. Strategic collaboration has become understood as the way that health organizations work to influence others in the delivery of health and welfare services.

One of the implications of managers having less direct control over those involved in designing and delivering services is the need to rethink how responsibility and accountability for services and outcomes are manifest. In practice, network arrangements for service delivery – linked by horizontal and relational rules and processes (e.g. some clinical networks, informational networks, service user networks) – have co-existed with the continuation of hierarchical arrangements for accountability, with health managers responsible for the services in an area and the outcomes of service users accessing these.

One response to this tension is for managers and their organizations to attempt to strengthen control within network relationships either through tightening up contractual arrangements over pooled budgets or re-introducing different types of authority relationships through structural forms (an example of this is provided below). As McGuire notes, writing from a US perspective: '[I]t is important to recognise that bureaucracy is not going away; collaboration still complements, rather than supplants, single organization and management' (2006: 40). Even where markets and networks have become more prominent in recent years, they are typically new ways of handling relationships between hierarchies.

A primary example of this is found in the UK in relation to community mental health teams. These teams began in some areas of the country as rather organic relationships between mental health professionals and community-based workers, general practitioners, nurses and social workers. With growing numbers of people with mental health conditions being cared for in the community, rather than institutional settings, this changed the types of roles for mental health professionals and the settings that they worked within. The success of informal, voluntary community mental health arrangements led the UK government to mandate that they should be established in all localities. The function and responsibility of community mental health teams were set out, but guidance suggests that teams might take whatever form was most appropriate in that local area (Department of Health 2002).

In practice, most community mental health teams have emerged as a form of tightly integrated health and social care team with a clear accountability structure akin to that of a traditional hierarchy. Community mental health teams are responsible for the well-being of mental health service users in the community who often have quite high levels of need and may also have additional substance misuse or forensic needs. A number of high profile cases of homicide by mental health service users have led to these teams being directed to pay much more attention to the protection of the general public, often following official reviews of these events (for example, the death of Tina Stevenson and her unborn twins in Hull in 2005 and Ivy Torrie who was killed in 2003 by her son). These types of events are not simply confined to the UK and other countries such as Sweden (Fazel and Grann 2004), Barbados (Evans and Malesu 2001) and the USA (James and Glaze 2006) have experienced homicides by individuals with mental health issues and in these countries there have been debates about how these individuals and others with mental health issues should be treated and who should be responsible for their actions (Large et al. 2008).

Where the responsibility for the well-being of individuals and populations falls on a particular professional group, a common response seems to be to turn any less formal arrangements into structures akin to hierarchical arrangements where the routes for the discharge of responsibility are apparent (Peck and Dickinson 2008). Clearly these types of hierarchical relationships do not guarantee that these events do not occur; homicides by the mentally ill go back centuries and the level committed has remained relatively constant at around 50 per year since the 1950s, even though homicides overall have roughly tripled over the same period (BBC 2009). These types of integrated structures might not prevent these sorts of events, then, but what they do achieve is they make it clear who is responsible in the event of such an issue – and who to blame. Thus, a number of the manifestations of collaborative working have been rather structural in practice, with rather fewer of the types of organic and relational ties which we have come to associate with networks.

Having set out an account of why it is that collaboration is a crucial consideration in healthcare and some of the characteristics of this in practice, the following section considers what the evidence says about the impact of collaboration in practice.

What does the evidence say about the impact of collaboration?

Despite the fact that collaboration has been vigorously pursued in many countries around the world, there is limited evidence from the literature about its positive impact on services or outcomes (Dowling et al. 2004; Glasby and Lester 2004; Leathard 2005; Dickinson 2008; Glasby and Dickinson 2008). In addition, evidence also suggests some negative impacts of collaboration – although this tends to be much less reported in practice. From their review of the literature, Dowling et al. (2004) observe that most research into collaboration tends to focus on process (how bodies work together), rather than outcomes (what impact this has on service users). This is an interesting observation and one that others have made elsewhere (e.g. Dickinson 2008). This section investigates three possible reasons for this trend:

- the difficulties involved in evaluating the outcomes of collaboration;
- the failure to identify what outcomes collaboration should achieve;
- an assumption that collaboration is a public good.

Difficulties with evaluation

Various researchers have noted at length the difficulties involved in making a link between collaborative activities and service user outcomes (e.g. Glendinning et al. 2005) and suggest that a lack of evidence of this link might relate to the fact that collaboration is difficult to research. Indeed, the complexities of researching collaborative activities are well established (see Box 26.1 for an overview of these complexities). However, many of the difficulties that are associated with evaluating collaboration are equally applicable to other types of complex policy initiatives. Therefore these difficulties might not be insurmountable – although the costs may be for some. The reason for interest in processes over outcomes may run beyond the technicalities of designing appropriate research frames to a much wider issue of what it is that collaboration is fundamentally supposed to achieve.

Box 26.1: *Some of the complexities in researching strategic collaboration*

- Collaboration takes many different forms, can you be sure you are comparing like with like?
- Collaboration brings together diverse groups – what do different stakeholders consider to be measures of the success of collaboration or what does success look like according to these different perspectives?
- How do the aims of collaboration differ to previous arrangements and from other improvement programmes?
- Where do the agendas of partners overlap and form joint work and what falls outside this collaborative endeavour?
- Which outcome measures are most appropriate to the aims and objectives of collaboration?
- What aspects of the context have helped/hindered formation and functioning of collaboration?
- What are the chains of causality/theories underpinning the impact that collaboration is intended to have?
- How can we measure unintended consequences?
- Over what timescales would you expect to see outcomes occur?
- How can you be certain that any changes in outcomes are due to collaboration and not other influences/policies in the local area?
- Is your local population broadly similar to that at the start of the project? Are you measuring effects on individuals who have received collaborative services?
- How can you prove you have prevented something?
- What would have happened if you had collaborated and had continued to deliver services in their previous form?

Source: Based on Dickinson (2008: 30).

What outcomes should collaboration achieve?

In their analysis, Dowling and colleagues observe that:

> [O]utcome measures tend to be as widely applicable to other modes of coordination as to partnerships. Improving the accessibility, efficiency, effectiveness and quality of services, and making their distribution more equitable, are not exclusive to partnerships or dependent on partnerships for their accomplishment (although it might be argued that partnerships are more likely to realise them). After, all, much social policy during the 1980s and 1990s in the UK sought to achieve precisely these objectives by introducing markets into both health and social care. Equally, enhanced experiences for staff, users and carers are outcomes sought in many social welfare systems, whether these utilise partnerships or not.
>
> (2004: 314)

Dowling et al. are expressing a fundamental concern that it is not clear precisely what ends collaboration should achieve and how this differs from other modes of improvement. A concern with which outcomes – or which aspects of performance to consider when researching collaboration – is also a concern of the wider inter-organizational relations (IOR) literature:

> 'Performance is something of the Holy Grail of IOR research. Most efforts to evaluate IORs either explicitly or implicitly discuss some aspect of organisational performance. While performance can be measured, there are two basic problems. First, which measures of performance should be considered? Second, to what extent is an organisation's performance attributable to its involvement with other organisations?
>
> (Provan and Sydow 2008: 702)

Provan and Sydow argue that it is unclear in the IOR literature what kinds of performance should be measured and then there are further technicalities with assessing the contribution that each partner makes to that outcome. These issues and others are considered by Schmitt (2001) who draws on 25 years of experience of collaboration in a US setting. She suggests that what is often missing from evaluations of collaborative efforts is an explanation of *why* certain outcome indicators were selected. Schmitt laments the absence of a rationale linking what it is that collaboration should achieve and the selection of outcome indicators to measure this and argues that it is often unclear why collaborative efforts are held to account against particular outcomes or why some measures are valued over others.

What is implicit in the arguments of Dowling and colleagues and that of Provan and Sydow is a sense that collaboration is a clear means for bringing about specified ends. In making the case about why health organizations should collaborate, government documents tend to make fairly vague and abstract allusions to the idea that this will be broadly better for service users and carers, but with little more specificity than this. For example, in New Zealand, the Healthy Homes initiative argues that:

> [P]artnering is essential for solving complex problems . . . Healthy Homes initiatives, which focus on making homes warmer, drier and healthier, have the potential to achieve multiple benefits across multiple sectors. Outcomes are dependent upon many different agencies and sectors continuing to work together at national, regional and local levels.
>
> (Department of Internal Affairs 2006: 5)

A further example comes from England where the 2005 social care Green Paper *Independence, Well-Being and Choice* (Department of Health 2005) stated that in order 'to turn the vision for social care into a reality', 'clear outcomes for social care' were needed, 'against which the experience of individuals can be measured and tested' (2005: 25–6). This document went on to develop the outcomes set out in *Every Child Matters* (HM Treasury 2003) for adult social care services. These outcomes were then given further emphasis in the following year when they were included in the joint health and social care White Paper *Our Health, Our Care, Our Say* (Secretary of State for Health 2006). The outcomes set out in these documents are illustrated in Box 26.2 and arguably represent the main attempt within English policy to articulate the outcomes that health and social care agencies should be aiming to achieve together.

A striking feature of these outcomes is their aspirational nature. These are large and encompassing measures. Beyond simply the technical difficulties in measuring these and making attributions to public sector actions, if services were really held to account against these measures, they would inevitably fail. How could the interventions of health and social care services really secure the improved health of the entire population, let alone the economic well-being, personal dignity and freedom from discrimination? However, they do possess a degree of power in their vagueness and abstraction. The same set of outcomes can be made applicable to a whole range of different types of services, despite the fact that they may not be interpreted in quite the same way by all stakeholders. In this sense they could be considered well-suited outcomes for

---

Box 26.2: *Children and adult service outcomes in policy*

Children's services outcomes
- Being healthy
- Staying safe
- Enjoying and achieving
- Making a positive contribution
- Economic well-being

Adult service outcomes
- Improved health
- Improved quality of life
- Making a positive contribution
- Exercise of choice and control
- Freedom from discrimination or harassment
- Economic well-being
- Personal dignity

collaboration. They provide an overarching vision which multiple partners can sign up to, without actually meaning very much at the same time. Given their lack of further explanation and exploration, it is unclear what their ultimate purpose is beyond offering some rather vague and abstract vision for services – although this itself may be significant.

In terms of what evidence there is of the impacts of collaboration, we have briefly summarized these in Table 26.2. We have separated these into the categories of efficiency, effectiveness and efficacy (after McKenzie 2001). Efficiency is considered as a means to utilize the minimum inputs possible to obtain a required quantity and quality of outputs. Efficiency therefore might be represented as '*doing the thing right*'. Effectiveness refers to the extent to which an organization has a programme of activities that will deliver its established goals or intended aims; effectiveness, therefore, is about '*doing the right thing*' to deliver the outcomes it has determined (or has been set). Efficacy, on the other hand, relates to the extent to which an organization is perceived to be achieving outcomes that are valued by its main stakeholders. Efficacy, then, is about '*according with conceptions of rightness*' in the eyes of service users, their carers, members of the public and their democratic representatives. Efficacy therefore clearly incorporates consideration of the types of institutions which are influential in terms of particular stakeholder groups and settings. Although efficacy is less familiar within healthcare, this is arguably a crucial factor given that collaborative activities often involve attempting to influence a range of stakeholders that one might not have any direct or hard power over.

What Table 26.2 illustrates is that the evidence about the positive impacts of collaboration is far from compelling. Although some areas have reported positive impacts in terms of functional indicators and there are some suggestions of improved access times and referral processes, there is little information about whether these were directly linked to the acts of collaboration or simply due to increased attention on the activities of that area. One thing that does seem to be clear though is that structural change alone rarely achieves its stated objectives (Glasby and Dickinson 2008). The economic benefits are modest at best, and may be outweighed by unanticipated direct costs and unintended negative consequences (such as a decline in productivity and morale). Senior management time is often focused on the process of merger and this can stall positive service development for at least 18 months, if not longer. The after-effects of structural change can continue for many years after the changes have taken place (Peck et al. 2006).

Assumption that collaboration is a public good

Returning again to the theme of why collaboration evaluations have tended to focus on process over outcomes, we can suggest a more fundamental explanation for this trend. This is that the assumption that collaboration will lead to better outcomes is so ingrained within the public sector (and researchers' beliefs) that it mitigates the need for an examination of its impact. In other words, if the efficacy of collaboration is such that it is fundamentally assumed to be a public good, then it is much cheaper, easier and takes considerably less time to undertake a process evaluation and use this as a proxy indicator of effectiveness.

TABLE 26.2 Summary of evidence of collaborative performance

Type of performance	Evidence
Efficiency	• Collaboration 'costs before it pays' and it is difficult to give an accurate figure due to all the 'invisibles' that need to be quantified (Leutz 1999)
	• In structurally integrated teams (e.g. PRISMA, Darlington experiment), some evidence of cost savings where downward substitution takes place, although only effective where financial incentive (Johri et al. 2003), is present
	• Some early evidence of efficiency savings through wider collaborative programmes, e.g. Total Place although questions regarding sustainability
	• What proves to be efficiency savings for collaboration might have knock-on effect on other areas of public sector, e.g. referral threshold criteria
	• More effective joint work might actually reveal more need which is potentially more costly in the short term.
Effectiveness	• Some evidence of impact on functional indicators (On Lok PRISMA), but little of clinical indicators – although series of questions pertaining to methodological reliability
	• Some evidence of individuals supported in community setting longer before being institutionalized (e.g. On Lok, Vittorio Veneto and Rovereto)
	• However, some projects show increased institutional care (Social HMO, Wiltshire) suggesting greater sharing of information and some possible lowering of risk thresholds
	• Some evidence of improved service user satisfaction (e.g. PACE), although not across all service user groups
	• Easier self-referral processes and quicker referral processes (e.g. Wiltshire)
Efficacy	• Collaboration as a key term with a high degree of cultural salience
	• Value of new collaborative arrangements is in their innovativeness, which attracts quality leadership. Symbolic value of arrangements
	• Collaboration starting to experience perceived loss of faith through negative media reporting, scandals (e.g. Cornwall), etc. although the problems which are being linked to partnership are not expressly 'partnership' issues but long-term endemic problems within health and social care communities

Given the proliferation of process-based research, there is an extensive literature which sets out the main features necessary for the processes of collaboration to be 'effective', but without ever defining what effective collaboration actually is (see for example, Wildridge et al. 2004). Yet, this is hardly a new observation, with Yuchtman and Seashore commenting in 1967 on the nature of network performance that 'little attention … has been given to the concept of effectiveness itself. The latter remains conceptually a vague construct' (Yuchtman and Seashore 1967: 891). The more descriptive contributions to the literature often set out what they consider to be 'effective' processes and then prescribe these, stating that these factors must be implemented in *all* collaboration that seeks to be effective (e.g. Stein and Rieder 2009). In being prescriptive it appears that there is a correct or ideal way to 'do collaboration', yet without ever being clear about for what ends. Collaboration is essentially assumed to be a positive mechanism for the wider good without ever really being clear about what this might entail.

An example of the assumed good of collaboration may be found in Rummery's (2002) critique of partnership 'health assessment' tools such as the *Partnership*

Assessment Tool (Hardy et al. 2003) and the *Working Partnership* (Markwell et al. 2003). These tools are generally seen as cheap, relatively quick and cost-effective means through which a snapshot of the processes of partnership working might be viewed. Rummery is not the first to criticize these types of approaches. Asthana et al. (2002) express concern that they do not provide a comprehensive framework and explicitly fail to distinguish between inputs, processes and outcomes. Rummery (2002) goes further than this and states that these types of tools sidestep the issue of what partnerships might ultimately reasonably be expected to achieve: improved outcomes for welfare users. In this argument, she is warning against assuming that partnerships *do* lead to better outcomes for service users, but simultaneously asserting that partnerships *should* be about achieving better outcomes for welfare users. While helpful in the sense that she points out the untested assumption about collaboration and its assumed positive impact on service user outcomes that is implicit in these types of tools, Rummery is reproducing the assumption that what health and social care collaboration is ultimately aiming to do is improve service user outcomes.

Key issues for the future of collaboration

Balance between structure and agency

Collaborations comprise rules, relationships and resources. Rules are devised to govern how the collaboration works and how individuals will conduct themselves. Where necessary, collaborations will have legal underpinning. They will also take a structural form – which kind will vary depending on the purpose and activities the collaboration is engaged with. Collaborations draw on a range of resources – physical, financial and human. The ways in which collaborations make use of financial resources, in the form of additional targeted monies or financial flexibilities, has been a core interest of government for some time, and has been evident in health and social care innovations. However, in collaborations, actors most often refer to the importance of human resources and relationships as key enablers of or blockages to collaborative action.

The balance between structure and agency in collaboration is as contested as it is in other aspects of public governance and management. We have indicated above the limited impact of structural changes intended to promote collaborative action. Here we focus on the role of actors in collaboration and explore how important they are in overcoming structural problems or acting as blockages to collaborative action. The human dimension of collaboration features prominently in actors' own accounts of why collaborations do or do not work and it has been receiving increased attention in recent years as researchers acknowledge the limits of structural explanations.

Williams and Sullivan (2009) argue that the conceptual ambiguity that surrounds the term collaboration and other terms associated with working across boundaries creates opportunities for agents to shape what is meant by collaboration in any particular context, giving them considerable power over potential agendas and actions. Meanings may be constructed in different ways and individual actors will be influenced in their framing of collaboration by a range of factors including 'disciplinary backgrounds, organizational roles, past histories, interests, and political/economic perspectives' (Schön 1987: 4). There is a close relationship between frames and interests, and they can be traced to sponsoring institutions and groups of actors (Schön and Rein 1994). Williams and Sullivan focus on a specific groups of actors sometimes referred to as 'boundary spanners' (Williams 2002) who help to 'surface different meanings, and through effective inter-personal skills, networking, communication and negotiation' influence the design and implementation of collaboration.

Leadership is also identified as a key source of agency in collaboration by a number of commentators. Evidence suggests that leaders may be found in different roles and spaces in collaborative arrangements, that is, they may not necessarily be the formal leaders of organizations. Expressions of leadership will also vary depending on the circumstances of the collaboration. So in Williams and Sullivan's (2009) study of integration in health and social care in Wales, leadership was recorded in different case studies as being: strong leadership from key individuals at the top of the partner organizations over a sustained period of time; as multi-level and connective involving the development of linkages by a nurse director into mainstream programmes; as leadership for governance from the chair of a steering committee; as leadership for day-to-day management from the project manager and clinical team lead; and as leadership in the context of diverse interests and contested power relationships.

Professional identities and interests are also influential in shaping what may or may not be achieved in collaborative relationships, particularly in relation to the extent to which professional actors are prepared to share power and work with others. Often structural and physical realignment such as shared management and co-location belie the fact that actors remain professionally attached to a particular set of codes and practices that define their role and status as culturally distinct from those of others in the collaboration. Should collaborative action threaten to challenge these, for example, by promoting a particular model of working or new lines of accountability, then professionals can draw on their cultural allegiances to resist 'unprofessional' interventions. The extent to which they are able to block collaboration will depend on how powerful their professional status is; in general, medical doctors have far greater agency than health professionals.

Efficiency

Another major theme within healthcare and within this text is that of efficiency. How we might make our healthcare systems more efficient and how we can make decisions and spend money in healthcare in a more effective manner are key preoccupations of many in this field. The current and future impacts of global recession mean that these are becoming more pressing issues than ever and health systems around the world are looking to make increased efficiency savings. As the previous section illustrated, collaboration has been seen as a way in which we might secure increased efficiency. Through the reduction of duplication and by producing more streamlined welfare services, it is assumed that we might be able to save money by agencies working together. A review of the existing literature concerning the efficiency of integrated care concludes that:

> Meeting people's needs with a preventative and integrated approach to health and social care can create efficiencies and savings. However, future studies do need to consider the long-term financial benefits. Many of the studies that concluded that integrated care was not cost effective were

conducted over short time periods, and many of the benefits will accrue as individuals remain independent well into the future. In particular, those integrated services that have a focus on early intervention are designed to prevent needs escalating in years to come, and therefore, the real benefits will be realised over time.

(Turning Point 2010: iii)

This is potentially a helpful aspiration for a number of health managers as they seek to make efficiency savings in austere times. However, this should not simply be taken at face value. Not all collaboration saves money. Collaborative activities often need significant investment to make them a reality. Further, considering the efficiency of whole systems means that questions are inevitably asked about measures of need. From a series of Australian studies, Esterman and Ben-Tovim (2002) concluded that a lack of coordination may hide a lack of resources. What this implies is that more effective collaboration might actually reveal needs that are not met. If public services have a responsibility to meet these needs, this will increase costs at least in the short term. In the long term, this might increase the prevalence of upstream interventions and reduce overall costs, but as the Turning Point (2010) review indicates, at present, we do not have the evidence to make these judgements.

Being clear about outcomes of collaboration

These findings have significant implications for the role and design of strategic collaborations and organizations' enthusiasm for them. What this means is that actors and agencies need to be clearer than ever in terms of what they are aiming to achieve by their collaborative activities. From the outset it becomes important to have discussions concerning what outcomes agencies and organizations are aiming to achieve through working together, how they each will contribute to the production of these impacts and what are the underpinning logics about how these activities might be achieved. Without this type of underpinning arrangement, there is a danger that partners might enter into collaboration with little sense of what success might look like for their joint efforts. Further there is a danger that without this prior agreement that any relationship might turn out not to be the innate public good that agencies had assumed and instead be concerned with other fundamentally different issues that may not necessarily be in that agency's best interest.

So what does this all mean in terms of how health managers might best approach strategic collaboration? Williams and Sullivan's (2007) review identified a number of practical implications for managers which complement the discussion in this chapter. They emphasise that collaboration is not a panacea. Managers should be clear from the outset about the type of collaborative activities they are entering into in terms of its nature, its purpose and intended impacts. Once these have been determined, there are a range of other issues that managers will also need to attend to including: determining who does what in the collaboration to avoid duplication or gaps in service delivery, investing in relationship building and management to ensure that the requisite levels of trust are present to sustain the collaboration; identifying the appropriate leadership and other relevant skills and resources – human, financial and physical; paying sufficient attention to 'delivery' which is usually more difficult than partners expect; developing effective accountability arrangements to funders, users and partners, and monitoring collaborative activity in relation to intended impacts and linking this to broader learning about the potential and limits of collaboration.

There are no easy answers to these questions and all involve intensive communication within and between partners in order to give collaborative efforts their best chance of thriving.

Conclusion

As this chapter has illustrated, collaboration may take a range of different forms but it is seen internationally as way of delivering more efficient and effective health and welfare services. But we need to be careful with this concept. Collaboration is not always easy and it is not a panacea. It will not solve all that is wrong with our health and welfare systems. Organizations need to think carefully about where they put their efforts into joint working and be clear that this will deliver what individuals and populations require from their local services. What is clear is that structural change is not the solution. Being clear about outcomes with partners, however, might help to facilitate joint working.

Summary box

- Strategic collaboration is likely to remain a key element of health and welfare systems where steering and coordination of complex services and multiple actors are needed.

- Collaborations will rarely reflect 'pure' models of markets, networks or hierarchies, rather, they will be hybrids combining features of different models.

- Evidence of the impact of collaboration on improving outcomes for services users is both limited and mixed. This is partly because outcomes are poorly defined and articulated.

- Practitioners' commitment to collaboration may be an expression of efficacy, rather than efficiency or effectiveness, influencing their focus on process rather than impact in evaluation.

- Structures and agency interact to shape and constrain what it is possible for collaborations to accomplish. An emphasis on structures has latterly been balanced by an interest in agency, particularly the role of 'boundary spanners', leadership and health and welfare professionals.

- In constrained economic circumstances considerations of cost will reshape how decisions about collaboration are made and what kinds of collaboration will be considered efficacious.

Self-test exercises

1 List all the different collaborative activities that you are involved with and think about: the types of links between partners (loose/tight); what binds these partners together (finance/professional values/legal mandate, etc.); and what this collaboration is trying to achieve in terms of outcomes. Is it clear what these outcomes are and is this most effective way of 'doing' collaboration for these ends?

2 What interpersonal and management skills do you posses? How might these be useful in supporting collaborative working? What other skills might be required to promote effective collaborative working? Where might you access these? What organizational or contextual factors might inhibit effective collaboration? To what extent can you influence these?

3 With a mixed group of staff, ask each professional group to list the attributes of their professional/organization in terms of what they admire and what frustrates them. Then ask them to repeat this for another profession/organization. Bring the group back together to share these perceptions and facilitate a discussion about what can be done about these perceptions, whether these reflect the situation locally and what might be done to build on the positive commonalities and tackle potential barriers.

4 What do service users in your local area value in terms of outcomes? Do you have a good idea of this? How might the needs and desires of service users be more effectively harnessed in planning of local services?

References and further reading

Asthana, S., Richardson, S. and Halliday, J. (2002) Partnership working in Public Policy provision: a framework for evaluation. *Social Policy and Administration*, 36: 780–95.

BBC (2009) 'No rise' in mental health murders, 5th May.

Department of Health (2002) *Mental Health Policy Implementation Guide: Community Mental Health Teams*. London: Department of Health.

Department of Health (2005) *Independence, Well-Being and Choice: Our Vision for the Future of Social Care for Adults in England*. London: HSMO.

Department of Internal Affairs (2006) Putting partnering into practice: collaboration on complex issues – Healthy Homes. Available at: www.communityoutcomes.govt.nz (accessed 29 November 2010).

Dickinson, H. (2008) *Evaluating Outcomes in Health and Social Care*. Bristol: Policy Press.

Dowling, B., Powell, M. and Glendinning, C. (2004) Conceptualising successful partnerships. *Health and Social Care in the Community*, 12: 309–17.

Dunleavy P. (1991) *Democracy, Bureaucracy and Public Choice*. New York: Harvester Wheatsheaf.

Esterman, A.J. and Ben-Tovim, D.I. (2002) The Australian coordinated care trials: success or failure? *Medical Journal of Australia*, 177: 469–70.

Evans, C. and Malesu, R.R. (2001) Homicide in Barbados: an 18 year review. *Journal of Forensic Psychiatry*, 12(1).

Fazel, S. and Grann, M. (2004) Psychiatric morbidity among homicide offenders: a Swedish population study. *American Journal of Psychiatry* 161: 2129–31.

Glasby, J. (2007) *Understanding Health and Social Care*. Bristol: The Policy Press.

Glasby J. and Dickinson H. (2008) *Partnership Working in Health and Social Care*. Bristol: The Policy Press.

Glasby, J. and Lester, H. (2004) Cases for change in mental health: partnership working in mental health services. *Journal of Interprofessional Care*, 18: 7–16.

Glendinning, C., Dowling, B. and Powell, M. (2005) Partnerships between health and social care under 'New Labour': smoke without fire? A review of policy and evidence. *Evidence and Policy*, 1: 365–81.

Hardy, B., Hudson, B. and Waddington, E. (2003) *Assessing Strategic Partnership: The Partnership Assessment Tool*. London: ODPM.

Hennart, J.F. (1993) Explaining the 'swollen middle': why most transactions are a mix of 'market' and 'hierarchy'. *Organization Science*, 4: 529–47.

HM Treasury (2003) *Every Child Matters*. London: The Stationery Office.

Hudson, B. (2004) Analysing network partnerships: Benson re-visited. *Public Management Review*, 6: 75–94.

James D.J. and Glaze L.E. (2006) Mental health problems of prison and jail inmates. US Department of Justice, Office of Justice Program, http://www.ojp.gov/bjs/pub/pdf/mhppji.pdf.

Johri, M. and Beland, F. and Bergman, H. (2003) International experiments in integrated care for the elderly: a synthesis of the evidence. *International Journal of Geriatric Psychiatry*, 18: 222–35.

Large, M., Smith, G., Swinson, N., and Nielssen, O. (2008) Homicide due to mental disorder in England and Wales over 50 years. *The British Journal of Psychiatry* 193: 130–3.

Leathard, A. (2005) Evaluating interagency working in health and social care: politics, policies and outcomes for service users. In D. Taylor and S. Balloch (eds) *The Politics of Evaluation: Participation and Policy Implementation*. Bristol: The Policy Press.

Le Grand, J. and Bartlett, W. (1993) *Quasi-Markets and Social Policy*. Basingstoke: Macmillan.

Leutz, W. (1999) Five laws for integrating Medical and Social Services: lessons from the United States and the United Kingdom. *The Milbank Quarterly*, 77: 77–110.

Macneil, I. (1980) *The New Social Contract: An Inquiry into Modern Contractual Relations*. New Haven, CT: Yale University Press.

Markwell, S., Watson, J., Speller, V., Platt, S. and Younger, T. (2003) *The Working Partnership*. London: Health Development Agency.

McGuire, M. (2006) Collaborative public management: assessing what we know and how we know it. *Public Administration Review*, 66: 33–43.

McKenzie, J. (2001) *Perform or Else: From Discipline to Performance*. London: Routledge.

Newman, J. (2001) *Modernising Governance: New Labout, Policy and Society*. London: Sage.

O'Leary, R. and Blomgren Bingham, L. (eds) (2009) *The Collaborative Public Manager. New Ideas for the 21st Century*. Washington, DC: Georgetown University Press.

Osborne, D. and Gaebler, T. (1993) *Reinventing Government: How the Entrepreneurial Spirit is Transforming the Public Sector*. London: Penguin Books.

Osborne, S.P. (2006) The new public governance? *Public Management Review*, 8: 377–87.

Peck, E. and Dickinson, H. (2008) *Managing and Leading in Inter-Agency Settings*. Bristol: The Policy Press.

Peck, E., Dickinson, H. and Smith, J. (2006) Transforming or transacting? The role of leaders in organizational transition. *British Journal of Leadership in Public Services*, 2: 4–14.

Pierre, J. and Peters, B.G. (2000) *Governance, Politics and the State*. New York: St Martin's Press.

Powell, W.W. (1990) Neither market nor hierarchy: network forms of organisation. In B. Bacharach (ed.) *Research in Organisational Behaviour*, Vol. 12. Greenwich, CT: JAI Press.

Provan, K.G. and Sydow, J. (2008) Evaluating inter-organizational relationships. In S. Cropper, M. Ebers, C. Huxham, and P. Smith Ring (eds) *The Oxford Handbook of Inter-Organizational Relations*. Oxford: Oxford University Press.

Rittel, H. and Webber, M. (1973) Dilemmas in a general theory of planning. *Policy Sciences*, 4: 155–69.

Rummery K. (2002) Towards a theory of welfare partnerships. In C. Glendinning, M. Powell and K. Rummery (eds) *Partnerships, New Labour and the Governance of Welfare*. Bristol: The Policy Press.

Schmitt, M.H. (2001) Collaboration improves the quality of care: methodological challenges and evidence from US health care research. *Journal of Interprofessional Care*, 15: 47–66.

Schön, D.A. (1987) *Educating the Reflective Practitioner*. San Francisco, CA: Jossey-Bass.

Schön, D.A. and Rein, M. (1994) *Frame Reflection: Toward the Resolution of Intractable Policy Controversies*. New York: Basic Books.

Secretary of State for Health (2006) *Our Health, Our Care, Our Say: A New Direction for Community Services*. London: The Stationery Office.

Stein, K.V. and Rieder, A. (2009) Integrated care at the crossroads: defining the way forward. *International Journal of Integrated Care*, 9.

Sullivan, H. and Skelcher, C. (2002) *Working across Boundaries: Collaboration in Public Services*. Basingstoke: Palgrave Macmillan.

Turning Point (2010) *Benefits Realisation: Assessing the Evidence for the Cost Benefit and Cost Effectiveness of Integrated Health and Social Care*. London: Turning Point.

Wildridge, V., Childs, S., Cawthra, L. and Madge, B. (2004) How to create successful partnerships: a review of the literature. *Health Information and Libraries and Journal*, 21, 3–19.

Williams, P.M. (2002) The competent boundary spanner. *Public Administration*, 80: 103–24.

Williams, P. and Sullivan, H. (2007) *Learning to Collaborate: Lessons in Effective Partnership Working in Health and Social Care*, Cardiff: NLIAH.

Williams, P. and Sullivan, H. (2009) Faces of integration. *International Journal of Integrated Care*, 9: 1–13.

Williamson, O. (1985) *The Economic Institutions of Capitalism.* New York: Free Press.

Yuchtman, E. and Seashore, S. (1967) A system resource approach to organizational effectiveness. *American Sociological Review*, 52: 891–903.

Websites and resources

The Canadian government's managing for results self-assessment tool is available at: http://www.tbs-sct.gc.ca/rma/account/transmod/tm_e.asp.

CARMEN – network of organizations and countries focusing on the care and management of services for older people across the European Union. Supported by the European Health Management Association, the CARMEN website contains links to a range of reports, good practice guides and resources for managers: http://www.vilans.nl/EHMA/is_00.html.

Centre for the Advancement of Interprofessional Education (CAIPE) – UK national body dedicated to supporting education and training that helps workers from different backgrounds to come together to learn from and with each other: www.caipe.org.ul.

European Centre for Social Welfare Policy and Research – provides expertise in the fields of welfare and social policy development, particularly in areas that call for multi-or interdisciplinary approaches, integrated policies and inter-sectoral action: http://www.euro.centre.org/.

International Journal of Integrated Care – a free online journal with articles from a range of different countries: www.ijic.org.

Journal of Integrated Care – practice-focused UK publication devoted to exploring inter-agency collaboration. With contributions from managers, practitioners and academics, it contains a range of accessible discussion pieces, summaries and new research studies in relation to collaboration: www.pavpub.com.

The New Zealand government's managing for outcomes programme includes a tool specifically designed to help organizations consider their progress in results-based management and identify objectives:
http://www.ssc.gov.nz/managing-for-outcomes.

CHAPTER 27

Evidence-based decision-making for managers

Kieran Walshe

Introduction

This chapter is about how healthcare managers and policy-makers find and use knowledge when they make decisions, and it argues that by making more effective use of evidence, managers and policy-makers could make much better decisions. It is in short a call to arms for what some have called 'evidence-based management' (Pfeffer and Sutton 2006; Reay et al. 2009).

We know that it is not difficult to find examples of bad decisions, which not only look like mistakes in retrospect, but which flew in the face of evidence available at the time. For example, mergers between healthcare organizations have often been justified on the grounds that the new, larger organization would be more efficient, with lower administrative costs and savings from the rationalization of clinical services, buildings and facilities. In the UK, there has been an epidemic of acute hospital mergers and reconfiguration based on little or no real evidence (Edwards and Harrison 1999; Fulop et al. 2002, 2005) and similar waves of merger have been seen in many other countries. In fact, the research evidence suggests that such mergers rarely achieve their explicit objectives, that there are often as many diseconomies as economies of scale and that after merger it takes years for the new organization to become properly integrated and begin to realize any of the potential advantages of its scale (Weil 2010). There are even a number of well-documented examples of frankly disastrous mergers that have come close to destroying the unfortunate organizations which have been pressed into merging (Kitchener 2002). So why, faced with all this evidence, do managers and policy-makers continue to have such faith that organizational mergers 'work'? The unpalatable truth may be that managers and their organizations do not know about the evidence around them; do not understand, trust or believe it if they do know it exists; and allow other factors such as ideology, fashion and political convenience to predominate in the decision-making processes in their organizations (Abrahamson 1996; Marmor 2001; Smith et al. 2001; Pfeffer and Sutton 2006).

This chapter first explores the growth of the evidence-based healthcare movement in the 1990s and the increasing role played by research evidence in clinical decision-making. It then argues that while managerial and clinical decision-making are very different processes, decision-making by managers and policy-makers can and should be more directly and systematically informed by evidence, but achieving that requires a new approach to managing knowledge. Next, the chapter explores how knowledge is used in organizations and what we understand about the processes of knowledge production, mobilization and utilization. It then sets out some practical approaches that healthcare managers and organizations can use to find, appraise and apply relevant evidence in their decision-making. It concludes by suggesting that the technical challenges of providing the right evidence, at the right time, in the right format for managers to use are not negligible but are also not insuperable. However, making better use of evidence requires a real cultural shift among managers – towards a more scientifically informed, intellectually rigorous way of thinking and behaving – and among researchers, towards a more engaged and practically relevant model of research which integrates with and supports knowledge mobilization and use.

The rise of evidence-based healthcare

In the 1990s, there was a widespread international change in the way that healthcare professionals, researchers, and health systems thought about and used evidence about research in clinical decision-making, which has been labelled as the rise of the 'evidence-based healthcare movement' (Davidoff et al. 1995; Sackett and Rosenberg 1995). It was driven in part by a growing realization of what is sometimes termed the 'research–practice gap' – that healthcare interventions which we knew to be effective took a long time to enter common clinical practice, while other interventions which we knew did not work also took a long time to be discarded by clinicians (Antman et al. 1992). The Institute of Medicine (1999) described these as problems of underuse, overuse and misuse, and there was no shortage of practical and high-profile examples. Thrombolytic therapy for myocardial infarction – a drug treatment for people with heart attacks which, if given promptly reduces the likelihood of the person having another heart attack in the future and significantly reduces mortality – became the 'poster child' for the EBM movement because there was good evidence that it had taken a decade or more for physicians to adopt it after the research evidence for its effectiveness was incontrovertible (Birkhead 1999). But just as high-profile examples of overuse, underuse and misuse can be identified in the clinical domain, we can also find cases in the managerial arena as Table 27.1 shows.

In retrospect, we saw a real shift in the 1990s in the paradigm that dominated our thinking about how health services research was conducted; how research findings were disseminated or communicated to healthcare professionals and organizations; and how those findings were implemented and used to change clinical practice (Lemieux-Charles and Champagne 2004). This shift is mapped out in Table 27.2 and can be summarized as a move away from seeing all these matters as issues primarily for individuals – researchers and practitioners – to seeing them as issues which organizations and healthcare systems needed to grapple with; and a shift from allowing these issues to be treated passively and reactively, leaving them almost wholly unmanaged and un-controlled, to being much more proactive and strategic in setting direction, managing implementation and monitoring progress.

TABLE 27.1 The research–practice gap

	Clinical domain	Management and policy domain
Overuse	• Prophylactic extractions of asymptomatic impacted third molars (wisdom teeth) • The widespread/general use of screening for prostate cancer	• Organizational mergers as a response to problems of service quality, capacity or financial viability in healthcare organizations
Underuse	• Smoking cessation through nicotine replacement therapy • Compression therapy for venous leg ulcers	• Skillmix changes in the healthcare workforce which often involve the replacement of physicians with other healthcare professionals at lower cost but with similar or better outcomes
Misuse	• Pressure-relieving equipment in the prevention of pressure sores • Selection of hip prostheses in hip replacement surgery	• The adoption and implementation of total quality management, continuous quality improvement or lean thinking/management initiatives

Source: Adapted from Walshe and Rundall (2001).

The idea that evidence should play a bigger part in decision-making has an intuitive appeal and it quickly began to appear in a much wider literature, in public policy fields such as housing, social care, criminal justice and education (Davies et al. 2000; Pawson 2006) and in other areas of management (Tranfield et al. 2003; Pfeffer and Sutton 2006; Rousseau 2006; Reay et al. 2009).

Health policy and management have been on the front line of this developing movement (Kovner and Rundall 2006; Shortell et al. 2007). Clinicians challenged to justify the adoption of a new surgical technique or new pharmaceutical have often responded by arguing that the same evidentiary standard should be applied to management decisions – like proposals to change or reconfigure services, to introduce new organizational structures, or to change payment or incentive systems (Hewison 1997; Kovner et al. 2000). It is a difficult argument to resist. While some commentators have asserted that policy and management decisions are different in some important and fundamental ways which mean they are not simply amenable to technocratic, rationalist analysis (Klein 2000), and while others have cautioned about the unthinking transfer of methods and techniques for research synthesis and application from the biomedical to the managerial arena, few would argue that there is not scope to improve the quality of managerial decisions and policy choices by bringing robust evidence to bear (Lomas et al. 2005).

Developments in evidence-based management

So what can managers learn from the experience of their clinical colleagues in using evidence to make decisions? Table 27.3 summarizes and compares the clinical and managerial domains. In broad terms, they have very different cultures and the clinical culture places much greater value on empiricism and science, while the managerial culture gives priority to personal experience and experiential learning. They draw on quite different literatures. The clinical literature is better organized and

TABLE 27.2 The paradigm shift of evidence-based healthcare

	From	To
Research strategy	No national leadership of healthcare research, funding fragmented across many research funders with poor communication and coordination	Growing strategic lead at a national level, coordination of research activity and funders leading to a more coherent overall research agenda
Research direction	Researcher-led, tied to academic agendas, little coordination	Needs-led, tied to health service priorities, focused on major service areas/needs, well coordinated
Research quality	Much ad hoc, piecemeal, small-scale, poor quality research, sometimes repetitive, not well managed or reviewed	Coherent research programmes made up of well-planned, larger research projects of high quality
Research methods	Inflexibility about methods, with frequent mismatches between research questions and methods used	More appropriate use of research methods, from experimental methods to qualitative approaches, depending on the research questions
Research outputs	Publications in peer-reviewed academic journals seen as researchers' primary goal	Changes in clinical practice seen as primary aim of research, with publication as one step towards that goal
Dissemination of research findings	Journals, textbooks, expert opinions, and narrative reviews	Online databases, summaries of evidence, clinical guidelines, secondary journals, systematic reviews
Mode of access to research findings	'Pull' access, reliant on clinicians seeking information by accessing libraries, journals, databases, etc.	'Push' access, with relevant research findings delivered to clinicians proactively, as close to the relevant point of care as possible
Practitioner understanding of research findings	Focused on reports of individual research studies	Focused on meta-analyses and systematic reviews of relevant, appraised research
Practitioner attitudes to research	Uninformed, suspicious of methods and motives, lacking skills in research appraisal and interpretation	Informed, accustomed to using and participating in research, skilled in appraising and applying research to own clinical practice
Major influences on clinical practice	Personal clinical experience, precedent, tradition, expert opinion	Clinical epidemiology, empirical evidence, research
Responsibility for implementing research findings	Left to individual clinical professionals and clinical teams, with little corporate interest or involvement in decision-making	Seen as a key organizational function, supported by investments in information resources, etc., with corporate involvement and oversight alongside clinical team in decision-making

Source: Adapted from Walshe and Rundall (2001).

TABLE 27.3 The clinical and managerial domains compared

	Clinical practice	Healthcare management
Culture	• Highly professionalized, with a strong formal body of knowledge and control of entry to the profession resulting in coherence of knowledge, attitudes and beliefs • High value placed on scientific knowledge and research, with many researchers who are also practitioners (and vice versa)	• Much less professionalized, with much less formal body of knowledge, no control of entry, and great diversity among practitioners • Personal experience and self-generated knowledge highly valued, intensely pragmatic • Less understanding of research, some suspicion of value, and of motives of researchers • Divide between researchers and practitioners, with little interchange between the two worlds
Research and evidence	• Strong biomedical, empirical paradigm, with focus on experimental methods and quantitative data • Belief in generalizability and objectivity of research findings • Well organized and indexed literature, concentrated in certain journals with clear boundaries, amenable to systematic review and synthesis	• Weak social sciences paradigm, with more use of qualitative methods and less empiricism • Tendency to see research findings as more subjective, contingent, and less generalizable • Poorly organized and indexed research literature, spread across journals and other literature sources (including grey literature), with unclear boundaries, heterogeneous and not easy to review systematically or synthesize
Decision-making	• Many clinical decisions taken every day, mostly by individual clinicians with few constraints on their decisions • Decisions often homogeneous, involving the application of general body of knowledge to specific circumstances • Long tradition of using decision support systems (handbooks, guidelines, etc.) • Results of decision often relatively clear, and some immediate feedback	• Fewer, larger decisions taken, usually by or in groups, with many organizational constraints, often requiring negotiation or compromise • Decisions heterogeneous, and less based on applying a general body of knowledge to specific circumstances • No tradition of using any form of decision support • Results of decision and causal relationship between decision and subsequent events often very hard to determine

Source: Adapted from Walshe and Rundall (2001).

structured, easier to search and more positivist and oriented toward generalizing research findings, while the management literature is less coherently defined and organized, less amenable to searching and synthesis and makes fewer claims to generalizability. The decision-making process is different too. Clinicians make many homogeneous decisions to which it is sensible and simple to apply algorithmic approaches (guidelines, protocols and procedures) to define and standardize the process and to embed the use of evidence. In contrast, managers' decision are more heterogeneous and less clearly bounded and are often made in combination with others (Walshe and Rundall 2001).

In short, while the principles of evidence-based decision-making should clearly apply in the managerial arena, their practical application is likely to be rather different. The challenges are less concerned with the technical and logistic problems of delivering the right evidence in the right place at the right time to support the decision-making process, and more about changing attitudes and beliefs among both researchers and managers, promoting linkage and exchange between the two communities and creating an organizational culture and capacity which supports the use of evidence in decision making (Lomas 2000). Increasingly, the terms knowledge mobilization or knowledge utilization have come to be used to describe these challenges, and over the past decade much has been learned about how to use evidence in healthcare management from the wider study of areas such as innovation, learning and change in organizations and the connection between knowledge and performance (Walshe et al. 2010). From this perspective, the challenges of evidence-based decision-making are a particular example of a more general issue – how organizations manage knowledge and use it to produce improved performance. The term 'absorptive capacity' has been coined to describe the mechanisms that organizations have in place to acquire, assimilate and apply knowledge to improve organizational performance (Lane et al. 2006).

Over the past decade, considerable progress has been made both in understanding knowledge mobilization in healthcare organizations and in putting practical systems and processes in place to help managers use evidence in their decision-making (Kovner and Rundall 2006). In this field, the Canadian Health Services Research Foundation (CHSRF) has been a pioneer and international exemplar. It defines its purpose as to 'support the evidence-based decision making in the organization, management and delivery of health services through funding research, building capacity and transferring knowledge' and aims to 'establish and foster linkages between decision makers (managers and policymakers) and researchers' (CHSRF 2004). CHSRF has tackled this ambitious mission on several fronts. They fund programmes of research which have to have co-funding from healthcare organizations, a requirement which is designed to ensure that researchers have managerial commitment and support for their work and have to engage with the practice community. They also support training for managers in research appraisal and research application and training for researchers aimed at developing research capacity and researcher skills in knowledge translation and utilization. They invest directly in the process of linkage and exchange through events, workshops and forums in which researchers, policy-makers and practitioners are brought together to discuss issues of common concern, and through publications like their evidence briefings and 'mythbuster' series, designed to provide clear, credible and comprehensible summaries of the evidence on a topic for a practitioner audience.

The work of CHSRF provides an eloquent proof of principle, showing that it is possible to bring evidence to bear on the worlds of managers and policy-makers, and that research can make a real and important contribution to decision-making. More importantly, its experience supports the contention that action at a health system level is needed to promote linkage and exchange between the research and practice communities, to change cultures and attitudes, and to build capacity on both sides in knowledge translation and utilization. For other countries, the work of CHSRF has been held up as a model to follow or learn from (NAO 2003).

In the UK, the NHS Confederation, which is the membership organization for healthcare providers and funders, has played an increasing role in getting evidence into practice, both through its briefings and report and more specifically by hosting two dedicated networks on health services research aimed at healthcare managers. The Medical Research Council and the National Institute of Health Research, which are the main government funders for health sciences and services research, have begun to recognize the importance of research impact and implementation (Walshe and Davies 2010) and NIHR has invested in an ambitious programme of healthcare organization-based collaborations for research designed to bring researchers, clinicians and managers together to implement research evidence (Baker et al. 2009).

A practical approach to evidence-based management

Some management questions may really need new primary research, involving empirical fieldwork that gathers data to try to answer the questions, but many others may be better answered by seeking and summarizing the findings from existing research through a process of searching, appraisal and synthesis (Pawson 2002, 2006; Lavis et al. 2005). Moreover, the timescale for doing new research is often much longer than the timescale by which decision-makers need to take decisions – and however good that new research might be, if it delivers results months or years after it is needed, it is not much use. So in this section, we focus on how managers can take a practical approach to using the existing research evidence in their decision-making by looking first at the types of evidence managers might use, and then at how they can find, appraise and apply evidence effectively. Perhaps the main purpose here is to demystify these processes, and to illustrate that evidence-based management does not require heroic dedication or intellectual genius – it is simply good managerial practice.

What is evidence?: a useful conceptual framework

In the field of evidence-based medicine there is an established 'hierarchy of evidence' which regards quantitative evidence from experimental studies (such as randomized controlled trials) as the 'gold standard', and places less faith in evidence of other kinds, such as observational studies, case studies and the like. Some have argued that this approach simply does not work in the social sciences, and that a broader and more pluralistic conception of evidence is needed (Davies et al. 2000; Glasby et al. 2007).

One useful approach is the typology shown in Table 27.4, which categorizes evidence not by its strength but by the contribution to knowledge it makes. First, there is a fundamental role for 'theoretical evidence' which makes explicit the underlying programme theory behind an initiative, helps us to understand how it is meant to work, and is essential if we are to then design sensible ways to evaluate or research the initiative because it guides us on what to measure. Second, we need 'empirical evidence' which is likely to be the results of such research evaluations, often testing out the initiative

TABLE 27.4 A typology of evidence for management decision-making

Type of evidence	Description	How it contributes to knowledge	Problems if evidence not available or used
Theoretical evidence	Ideas, concepts and models used to describe the intervention, to explain how and why it works, and to connect it to a wider knowledge base and framework	Helps to understand the programme theories which lie behind the intervention, and to use theories of human or organizational behaviour to outline and explore its intended working in ways that can then be used to construct and test meaningful hypotheses and transfer learning about the intervention to other settings	We don't understand how and why an intervention worked (or didn't) and we are therefore unable to replicate it in other organizations, or to change it in ways that we know will improve its effectiveness
Empirical evidence	Information about the actual use of the intervention, and about its effectiveness and outcomes in use	Helps to understand how the intervention plays out in practice, and to establish and measure its real effects and the causality of relationships between the intervention and desired outcomes	We don't really know whether it works or not, and we risk rolling out the intervention and using it elsewhere when in fact it is not very effective – or abandoning it because we think it hasn't worked, when in fact it has
Experiential evidence	Information about people's experiences of the service or intervention, and the interaction between them	Helps to understand how people (users, practitioners and other stakeholders) experience, view and respond to the intervention, and how this contributes to our understanding of the intervention and shapes its use	We don't know enough about the 'human side' of the intervention, and how it affects things like culture, behaviour, attitudes, motivation and interpersonal relations

Source: Adapted from Glasby et al. (2007).

in comparative or longitudinal studies designed to find out whether it works, and how effective it is. Third, we need 'experiential evidence' which is not another word for anecdote or personal experience, but is rigorous and scientifically valid information about the way people and organizations experience and interact with the initiative, and their responses to it. It can be argued that for any issue, we should aim to have a synthesis of theoretical, empirical and experiential evidence to hand.

Finding the evidence: what do we know?

Most policy-makers and managers are not in a position to commission research when they face a decision – and do not have the time to wait for research findings anyway.

TABLE 27.5 Research findings: some key sources

Databases	NHS Evidence and the National Electronic Library for Health
	Cochrane Library
	WHO Health Evidence Network
	European Observatory on Health Systems and Policies
Bibliographic databases	Medline
	ABI-INFORM/Proquest
	Health Management Information Consortium (HMIC)
Key research agencies	Canadian Health Services Research Foundation
	National Institute for Health Research
	US Agency for Healthcare Research and Quality
	European Union Framework 7 research programme – health systems
Key journals	*Health Affairs*
	Health Services Research
	Health Services Management Research
	Journal of Health Services Research and Policy
	Milbank Quarterly
	Frontiers of Health Services Management

Therefore, what matters most is their ability to access, appraise and apply the findings from existing research to the situations or decisions they face. The first step is finding that research.

Unfortunately, while a huge investment has been made in organizing the clinical evidence base, particularly through the worldwide Cochrane Collaboration and its associated library of systematic reviews, randomized controlled trials and other evidence, the literature on management and policy issues remains fragmented, heterogeneous, distributed and difficult to access. There is no single portal or gateway to use and so it is very important to work out a clear search strategy. Ideally, that search strategy would achieve three things: (1) it would be sensitive (which means it finds all the relevant research and does not miss anything out); (2) it would be specific (which means it does not find any irrelevant or unrelated research); and (3) it would be realistic (which means it can be done in the time and with the resources available). In reality, there is an inevitable trade-off to be made between sensitivity, specificity and realism, depending in part on the circumstances and context for the decision. If resources and time are short, then 'quick and dirty' searching is needed, while if there is more space for reflection and analysis, a more sophisticated and comprehensive search can be undertaken. Obviously, the more important and significant the decision, the more should be invested in the search for evidence.

Table 27.5 sets out four main sources of evidence to which managers might turn, broadly in the order in which they could or should be searched: evidence databases; bibliographic databases; key research agencies; key journals.

The place to start is the evidence databases, though as has already been observed, no one source can be relied on as a portal to the evidence on healthcare management and policy-making. Table 27.5 suggests four sources. First, the NHS Evidence website produced and maintained by the National Institute for Health and Clinical Excellence (NICE) in England provides a wide and very usable range of resources which their researchers have checked and deemed to be sufficiently high quality for inclusion. They also provide a series of 'specialist collections' which were formally part of the NHS National Electronic Library for Health (NeLH) and give very useful topic-based entry points to areas like health management or particular conditions and service areas. Although there is a UK-centric focus to some of the material, most of it is of great international relevance and indeed much of the evidence is drawn from the international literature. Second, the Cochrane Library, although mainly focused on clinical interventions, contains some reviews and other data relevant to organizational issues (Lavis et al. 2006). For example, it holds evidence on the impact of stroke units on the management of stroke, and reviews of interventions to change professional practice like the use of financial incentives and educational programmes. Third, and with a more international orientation, the World Health organization's Health Evidence Network provides an integrated, searchable interface to the evidence and information from a wide range of agencies in many countries, as well as undertaking its own syntheses on questions raised by members of the network. Fourth, the European Observatory on Health Systems and Policies produces a range of evidence-based reports and briefings, some of them in collaboration with the WHO Health Evidence Network.

The next step – and one that many practitioners will find more difficult – is to access the relevant bibliographic databases which index the contents of academic and practitioner journals, and also provide some coverage of books, official reports and other materials. Here, recommendations are much more difficult to make as there are dozens of such databases with overlapping and complementary coverage, but three particular examples are cited. The first port of call for many people will be Medline – the database of medical and health-related literature created and maintained by the US National Library of Medicine. While it is somewhat Americocentric, it has by far the best overall international coverage both of clinical and policy/management materials in the health sector and it is freely available through the NLM's PubMed service. However, much of the relevant literature on management issues is not health-sector specific and will have been published in more generic business and management journals. To access the literature on issues like leadership, organizational design and development, quality improvement and many other topics it is very important not to confine the search to the health-related literature covered by Medline. The most useful database in this area is ABI Inform (also known as Proquest) which gives comprehensive coverage of the business and management literature. However, neither ABI Inform nor Medline cover what some people call the 'grey literature' – publications from healthcare organizations, health ministries and agencies, think tanks, government departments, and others. In this area, for the UK, the Health Management Information Consortium database (HMIC) provides by far the best coverage. It combines the catalogues of collection at the UK Department of Health's library services and the King's Fund and is particularly useful because it indexes and abstracts UK practitioner journals like the *Health Service Journal* and official reports and publications, though its coverage is very UK focused.

For most purposes, the search strategy is likely to stop after accessing evidence and bibliographic databases, but some may find it useful to search the information resources provided by key research agencies like those listed in Table 27.5. Searching these sites for research on a specific issue is likely to be a frustrating and unproductive experience, but browsing them to get a better sense of the research resources, themes and issues they have covered is certainly worthwhile. Similarly, few managers will have the time to undertake hand searches of key journals like those listed in Table 27.5, but it can be very useful to scan the contents pages of past issues to understand their coverage, or to subscribe to the contents page services most journals now offer, so that summary details of each new journal issue are received by email as it is published.

Searching some or all of these sources is made much easier with some informed and trained support from a knowledge officer, information scientist or librarian who understands the search structures and terminology used. It is common for untrained searchers either to cast their search too broadly – using terms which return hundreds or even thousands of 'hits' – or too narrowly, so that they get little or nothing and miss relevant materials. But finding the evidence is only one step in the process – the next challenge is knowing whether to trust it and what it means.

Appraising the evidence: can we rely on it?

Just because research is published in a prestigious journal or produced by a government agency does not mean it should be taken on trust. Many agencies have a political or organizational agenda, covert or overt, and the authors of the research may have been influenced by their own beliefs and values. However stringent the quality control and peer review process, badly designed, poorly conducted research studies still get published even in the best journals. Moreover, the findings from research are not always clear and unambiguous – they can be open to interpretation or difficult to understand. Even if the findings are clear, it is important to consider how generalizable or transferable they are – in other words, to what extent they can be applied to a particular organization or context, and whether there are important differences between the setting for the research and the setting in which it is to be applied. The ability to appraise research evidence critically and carefully is essential (Coomarasamy and Khan 2004). There are three key questions to be asked in appraisal:

1 Can I trust this research? Has it been conducted properly, using the right research methods, to tackle a meaningful set of research questions?

2 What does this research mean? What are the findings, and how much confidence can I place in them?

3 How can this research be applied to our local situation? Is it appropriate to generalize or transfer from the setting in which the research was conducted, and what implications are there from any differences in setting?

Of course, the way these questions might be asked would be different for different sorts of research. Appraising a qualitative study involving interviews with health professionals may require different criteria from those used to appraise a quantitative experimental study such as a randomized controlled trial. But the three issues remain the same – trust, meaning and application. Table 27.6 sets out a critical appraisal framework which could be used to analyse a randomized controlled trial (RCT) or a qualitative study. Similar sets of questions can be produced to appraise other kinds of study – case

TABLE 27.6 Appraising research evidence: key questions to ask

	Randomized controlled trial	**Qualitative study**
Can you trust this research?	Did the trial address a clearly focused issue? (Are the population, intervention and outcome studied clear?)	Was there a clear statement of the aims of the research? (what were they trying to find out, and was it relevant and important?)
	Was the assignment of patients to treatments randomized?	Is a qualitative methodology appropriate?
	Were all patients entered into the trial properly accounted for at its conclusion?	(Does research seek to understand/illuminate experiences or views?)
	(Look at completion of follow-up and whether groups analysed by intention to treat).	Was the sampling strategy appropriate to address the aims of the research?
		(Consider where sample selected from, who and why, how and why, sample size, non-participation.)
	Were patients, health workers and study staff blind to the treatment?	Was the data collection appropriate to address the aims of the research?
		(Consider where and how collected, how recorded, whether methods modified during study.)
	Were the groups similar at the start of the trial?	Was the data analysis appropriate to address the aims of the research? (Consider whether method is clearly explained, how it was done, how categories/themes were derived from data, if credibility of findings tested, whether all data taken into account.)
	Aside from the experimental intervention, were the groups treated equally?	How well were research partnership relations handled? (Did researchers critically examine their own role, bias and influence? How was research explained to participants? How and where was data collected?)
What does it mean?	How large was the treatment effect? How precise was the estimate of the treatment effect?	Is there a clear statement of the findings? (Are they explicit and easy to understand?)
	Were all the important outcomes of the intervention considered?	Is there justification for data interpretation? (Sufficient data to support the findings, selection of data for paper explained.)
How can it be applied locally?	Can the results of this study be applied to your local population? (Consider what differences might exist and how significant they might be.)	How transferable are the findings to a wider population? (Consider context of study, sufficient details to compare to other settings, whether all relevant outcomes considered.)
	Are the benefits of this intervention worth the costs and/or harms, for your local population?	How relevant and useful is the research?
		(Address the research aim, add new understanding, suggest further research, relevance to your setting.)

Source: Adapted from the CASP, JAMA and EBM tools, all available from the SCHaRR Netting the Evidence Website (see web resources).

study designs or economic evaluations, for example – and to appraise secondary research such as systematic reviews.

Synthesizing the evidence: what does it all mean?

The next step, having acquired a range of evidence, is to synthesize it – bringing
the evidence together in a systematic and coherent way that both identifies areas of
convergence and divergence. This is far from a straightforward task, and while there are
some established methodologies for synthesizing some very specific types of evidence
(such as the use of meta-analysis to combine the results from randomized controlled
trials), there is less consensus about how to combine diverse sources of evidence. One
promising development in recent years has been the rise of realist synthesis (Pawson
2002, 2006) which essentially argues for a theory-driven model of research synthesis.
It sees synthesis as theory-building in action, and argues that it is about explanation
(how, why and when does something work) rather than quantification (does it work
and if so how much?). The realist synthesis approach begins by mapping the territory of
the review, and identifying and building a theoretical model for the intervention. Only
then does the reviewer search for primary studies, and they are used to test, confirm,
disconfirm or understand parts of the theoretical model which gets modified along
the way. The process is iterative and selective. The literature now contains a growing
number of research reviews which have adopted this methodology (Greenhalgh et al.
2007; Walshe 2010).

Applying the evidence: informed decision-making?

The final step – and perhaps the most difficult one – is to use the evidence in a local
context as part of the decision-making process (Lavis et al. 2005). Experience and
research both suggest that it is unrealistic to expect this to be a simple or linear process
in which the evidence – packaged or presented as a product by researchers – directly
shapes an individual decision. It is more likely that evidence plays a more indirect and
longer-term part, shaping the context in which decisions are made and contributing
to an iterative local debate in which evidence, values, politics, resources and other
priorities all play a part. It is unlikely that for most health management or policy issues
the research evidence will offer unambiguous or universal prescriptions for action.
Rather, it is more probable that any recommendations will be contingent and will offer
a range of possible courses of action with different potential benefits and costs.

Researchers may find their engagement in the decision-making process exciting
and rewarding, as they see their endeavours having a real-world impact on health
services and organizations. However, they may equally find the process alien and
uncomfortable, and be disappointed by the way their carefully created and presented
research findings are dealt with rather sceptically or abruptly, and other considerations
accorded greater value. Researchers also need to consider how they are viewed by other
stakeholders in the decision-making process – as honest brokers, offering information as
a currency in the debate to all parties, or as yet another vested interest, allied to one side
or another and using evidence as ammunition. The challenge for researchers is to engage

closely with policy-makers and practitioners while at the same time maintaining some distance. The researcher should not lose the disinterested and objective perspective on issues which they bring to the debate and for which they will be valued.

Conclusion

The quality of management and leadership in healthcare organizations is a fundamental determinant of the quality of service they provide to patients. Well-managed and effectively led organizations provide an environment in which high quality clinical care is both clearly valued and more capable of being delivered consistently. The decisions made by managers in organizations and, at a health system level, by policy-makers inevitably influence organizational capacity, capability and behaviour.

There is no doubt that the more effective use of research evidence in the decision-making process could make for better decisions, less prone to fashion, ideology or personal conviction and more likely to be considered, rational and, in the longer term, more beneficial. But we are a long way from that position now. We have at the moment separate and divided research and practice communities, with different and conflicting notions of what constitutes evidence, and how to use it in decision-making. Managers and researchers need to learn to speak each other's languages, to understand and respect each other's expertise, and to trust and value the contribution each can make to improving healthcare organizations and health systems. Healthcare organizations need to give explicit attention to the systems and processes they have for acquiring, assimilating and applying knowledge and to invest in building capacity for evidence-based management.

Summary box

- By making more effective use of evidence from research in decision-making, managers and policy-makers in healthcare organizations and health systems could improve the quality of decision-making which would have direct benefits for the quality of health services.

- The rise of the evidence-based healthcare movement has led to a shift in paradigm for knowledge creation, translation and utilization in many sectors, to place greater emphasis on the use of evidence in decision-making.

- There are important differences between the clinical and managerial or policy-making domains which mean that the way evidence is collated and used may be very different. There is a real need to change attitudes and beliefs among researchers and managers, and to promote linkage and exchange between the two communities.

- Some research funders, such as the Canadian Health Services Research Foundation and the National Institute for Health Research in the UK are showing that research can make a more significant contribution to health management and policy development.

- Managers can make some immediate progress in their own organizations searching for, appraising and applying evidence in their own decision-making. There are a growing number of sources of evidence available intended to support a more evidence-informed approach to management.

- Managers and researchers need to learn to speak each other's languages, understand and respect each other's expertise, and to trust and value the contribution each can make to improving healthcare organizations and health systems.

Self-test exercises

1 Undertake an audit of the evidence resources available in your organization to support managers. Visit your postgraduate centre, library, information services department and other potential resources. Explore what training is available in searching, critical appraisal and other areas. Find out whether information scientists/librarians are available to support you in accessing evidence. Consider whether there are important gaps in provision and, if appropriate, draw up a short report to discuss with colleagues.

2 Choose an issue or topic of current relevance to your organization – something on which important decisions are being made in the near future. Search some of the sources of evidence described in the chapter and listed in the website and resources section. Appraise the evidence you find using the framework set out in Table 27.5. Consider how the information from this process could be used by decision-makers in your organization.

References and further reading

Abrahamson, E. (1996) Management fashion. *Academy of Management Review*, 21(1): 254–85.

Antman, E., Lau, J., Kupelnick, B., Mosteller, F. and Chalmers, I. (1992) A comparison of the result of meta-analysis of randomised controlled trials and recommendations of clinical experts. *Journal of the American Medical Association*, 268: 240–8.

Baker, R., Robertson, N., Rogers, S. et al. (2009) The National Institute of Health Research (NIHR) Collaboration for Leadership in Applied Health Research and Care (CLAHRC) for Leicestershire, Northamptonshire and Rutland (LNR): a programme protocol. *Implementation Science*, 4: 72.

Birkhead, J.S. (1999) Trends in the provision of thrombolytic treatment 1993–1997. *Heart*, 82: 438–42.

Canadian Health Services Research Foundation (2004) *Annual Report*. Ottowa: CHSRF .

Coomarasamy, A. and Khan, K.S. (2004) What is the evidence that postgraduate teaching in evidence based medicine changes anything? A systematic review. *British Medical Journal*, 329: 1017–22.

Davidoff, F., Haynes, B., Sackett, D. and Smith, R. (1995) Evidence-based medicine. *British Medical Journal*, 310(6987): 1085–6.

Davies, H.T.O., Nutley, S.M. and Smith, P.C. (eds) (2000) *What Works? Evidence-based Policy and Practice in Public Services*. Bristol: The Policy Press.

Edwards, N. and Harrison, A. (1999) The hospital of the future: planning hospitals with limited evidence: a research and policy problem. *British Medical Journal*, 319: 1361–3.

Fulop, N., Protopsaltis, G., Hutchings, A. et al. (2002) Process and impact of mergers of NHS trusts: multicentre case study and management cost analysis. *British Medical Journal*, 325: 246–52.

Fulop, N., Protopsaltis, G., King, A. et al. (2005) Changing organisations: a study of the context and processes of mergers of health care providers in England. *Social Science and Medicine*, 60: 119–30.

Glasby, J., Walshe, K. and Harvey, G. (2007) Making evidence fit for purpose in decision making: a case study of the hospital discharge of older people. *Evidence and Policy*, 3(3): 425–437.

Greenhalgh, T., Kristjansson, E and Robinson, V. (2007) Realist review to understand the efficacy of school feeding programmes. *BMJ*, 335: 858.

Hewison, A. (1997) Evidence-based medicine: what about evidence-based management? *Journal of Nursing Management*, 5: 195–8.

Institute of Medicine (1999) *The National Round-Table on Health Care Quality: Measuring the Quality of Care*. Washington, DC: Institute of Medicine.

Kitchener, M. (2002) Mobilizing the logic of managerialism in professional fields: the case of academic health center mergers. *Organization Studies*, 23(3): 391–420.

Klein, R. (2000) From evidence-based medicine to evidence-based policy? *Journal of Health Services Research and Policy*, 5(2): 65–6.

Kovner, A.R., Elton, J.J. and Billings, J. (2000) Evidence-based management. *Frontiers of Health Services Management*, 16(4): 3–46.

Kovner, A.R. and Rundall, T.G. (2006) Evidence based management reconsidered. *Frontiers of Health Services Management*, 22: 3–22.

Lane, P.J., Koka, B.R. and Pathak, S. (2006) The reification of absorptive capacity: critical review and rejuvenation of the construct. *Academy of Management Review*, 31(4): 833–63.

Lavis, J., Davies, H.O., Oxman, A. et al. (2005) Towards systematic reviews that inform health care management and policy-making. *Journal of Health Services Research and Policy*, 10(3): S35–S48.

Lavis, J., Gruen, R., Davies, H. and Walshe, K. (2006) Working within and beyond the Cochrane Collaboration to make systematic reviews more useful to healthcare managers and policymakers. *Healthcare Policy*, 1(2): 21–33.

Lemieux-Charles, L. and Champagne, F. (2004) *Using Knowledge and Evidence in Healthcare: Multidisciplinary Perspectives*. Toronto: University of Toronto Press.

Lomas, J. (2000) Using linkage and exchange to move research into policy at a Canadian foundation. *Health Affairs*, 19(3): 236–40.

Lomas, J., Culyer, T., McCutcheon, C. et al. (2005) *Conceptualising and Combining Evidence for Health System Guidance*. Ottowa: CHSRF.

Marmor, T. (2001) *Fads in Medical Care Policy and Politics: The Rhetoric and Reality of Managerialism*. London: Nuffield Trust.

National Audit Office (2003) *Getting the Evidence: Using Research in Policy Making*. London: NAO.

Pawson, R. (2002) Evidence based policy: the promise of realist synthesis. *Evaluation*, 8(3): 340–58.

Pawson, R. (2006) *Evidence-based Policy: A Realist Perspective*. London: Sage.

Pfeffer, J. and Sutton, R.I. (2006) *Hard Facts, Dangerous Half Truths and Total Nonsense: Profiting from evidence-based management*. Boston: Harvard Business Press.

Reay, T., Whitney, B. and Kohn, M.K. (2009) What's the evidence on evidence-based management? *Academy of Management Perspectives*, Nov.: 5–18.

Rousseau, D.M. (2006) Is there such a thing as 'evidence based management'? *Academy of Management Review*, 31: 256–9.

Sackett, D.L. and Rosenberg, W.M. (1995) The need for evidence-based medicine. *Journal of the Royal Society of Medicine*, 88(11): 620–4.

Shortell, S.M., Rundall T.G. and Hsu, J. (2007) Improving patient care by linking evidence-based medicine and evidence-based management. *Journal of the American Medical Association* 298: 673–6.

Smith, J., Walshe, K. and Hunter, D.J. (2001) The redisorganisation of the NHS. *British Medical Journal*, 323: 1262–3.

Tranfield, D., Denyer, D. and Smart, P. (2003) Towards a methodology for developing evidence informed management knowledge by means of systematic review. *British Journal of Management*, 14: 207–22.

Walshe, C. (2010) District nurses' role in palliative care provision: a realist review. *International Journal of Nursing Studies*, 47(9): 1167–83.

Walshe, K. and Davies, H. (2010) Research, influence and impact: deconstructing the norms of health services research commissioning. *Policy and Society*, 29: 103–11.

Walshe, K., Harvey, G. and Jas, P. (eds) (2010) *From Knowing to Doing: Connecting Knowledge and Performance in Public Services*. Cambridge: Cambridge University Press.

Walshe, K. and Rundall, T. (2001) Evidence based management: from theory to practice in healthcare. *Milbank Quarterly*, 79(3): 429–57.

Weil, T. (2010) Hospital mergers: a panacea? *Journal of Health Services Research and Policy*, 15(4): 251–3.

Websites and resources

Cabinet Office: Policy hub website providing resources on evidence-based policymaking: http://www.policyhub.gov.uk/.

Canadian Health Services Research Foundation: http://www.chsrf.ca/.

Critical Appraisal Skills Programme. http://www.phru.nhs.uk/casp/casp.htm.
ESRC Centre for Evidence-Based Policy and Practice: http://www.evidencenetwork.org/.
European Observatory on Health Policies and Systems: EU and WHO-supported international research centre on health policy:
http://www.euro.who.int/en/home/projects/observatory.
National Electronic Library for Health. Pages on evidence-based decision making and many other topics: http://www.library.nhs.uk.
NHS Evidence: Portal to a wide range of evidence on healthcare services managed by the National Institute for Health and Clinical Excellence:
http://www.evidence.nhs.uk.
NHS Centre for Reviews and Dissemination. http://www.york.ac.uk/inst/crd/.
SCHaRR Netting the Evidence: http://www.shef.ac.uk/scharr/ir/netting/.
US Agency for Healthcare Research and Quality: http://www.ahrq.gov/.
World Health Organization's Health Evidence Network: http://www.euro.who.int/HEN.

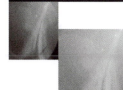

Index

A READER IN HEALTH POLICY AND MANAGEMENT

Ann Mahon, Kieran Walshe and Naomi Chambers

9780335233687 (Paperback)
2009

eBook also available

This reader offers instant access to fifty classic and original readings in health policy and management. Compiled by experts, the editors introduce a framework setting out the key policy drivers and policy levers, giving a conceptual framework that provides context for each piece.

The book reflects the dominant and enduring themes in health policy and management and has a selection of internationally renowned readings. Brought together with insightful commentaries, the text looks to the future of health policy and management as well as considering the contribution of the past. This key text is a must-have reader that both students and practitioners will return to again and again.

COACHING AND MENTORING AT WORK
Developing Effective Practice
Second Edition

Mary Connor and Julia Pokora

9780335243853 (Paperback)
January 2012

eBook also available

The focus of *Coaching and Mentoring At Work, 2e* is that of developing effective practice. The book offers 9 principles for effective practice and, using interactive case examples, each chapter answers a key question asked by coaches, mentors and clients.

Key features:

- Two new chapters on frequently asked questions
- Presents a greater focus on critical evaluation
- This book is practical, logical, accessible and broad-ranging

www.openup.co.uk